THE INTERNATIONAL CRIMINAL RESPONSIBILITY OF WAR'S FUNDERS AND PROFITEERS

This book is concerned with the commercial exploitation of armed conflict; it is about money, war, atrocities and economic actors, about the connections between them, and about responsibility. It aims to clarify the legal framework that defines these connections and gives rise to criminal or, in some instances, civil responsibility, referring both to mechanisms for international criminal justice, such as the International Criminal Court, and domestic systems. It considers which economic actors among individuals, businesses, governments and States should be held accountable and before which forum. Additionally, it addresses the question of how to recover illegally acquired profits and redirect them to benefit the victims of war. The chapters shine a critical light on the options provided by a network of laws to ensure that the 'great industrialists' of our time, who find economic opportunities in the war-ravaged lives of others, are unable to pursue those opportunities with impunity.

NINA H. B. JØRGENSEN is Professor of Public International Law and Deputy Head of School (Research) in the School of Law at the University of Southampton. She was previously Professor of Law at the Chinese University of Hong Kong. From 2001 to 2010, she worked in various capacities at the Special Court for Sierra Leone in Freetown (including as Senior Appeals Counsel and Senior Legal Adviser for the Office of the Prosecutor), the Extraordinary Chambers in the Courts of Cambodia in Phnom Penh (Senior Judicial Coordinator for the Pre-Trial Chamber), and the International Criminal Tribunals for the Former Yugoslavia and Rwanda. She has a D.Phil. from the University of Oxford and was called to the Bar of England and Wales (Gray's Inn) in 1999. She is the author of *The Responsibility of States for International Crimes* (2000) and *The Elgar Companion to the Extraordinary Chambers in the Courts of Cambodia* (2018).

T0382166

THE INTERNATIONAL CRIMINAL RESPONSIBILITY OF WAR'S FUNDERS AND PROFITEERS

Edited by

NINA H. B. JØRGENSEN

University of Southampton

CAMBRIDGE
UNIVERSITY PRESS

University Printing House, Cambridge CB2 8BS, United Kingdom

One Liberty Plaza, 20th Floor, New York, NY 10006, USA

477 Williamstown Road, Port Melbourne, VIC 3207, Australia

314-321, 3rd Floor, Plot 3, Splendor Forum, Jasola District Centre, New Delhi - 110025, India

103 Penang Road, #05-06/07, Visioncrest Commercial, Singapore 238467

Cambridge University Press is part of the University of Cambridge.

It furthers the University's mission by disseminating knowledge in the pursuit of education, learning and research at the highest international levels of excellence.

www.cambridge.org
Information on this title: www.cambridge.org/9781009257824
DOI: 10.1017/9781108692991

First published 2020
First paperback edition 2022

A catalogue record for this publication is available from the British Library

ISBN 978-1-108-48361-2 Hardback
ISBN 978-1-009-25782-4 Paperback

CONTENTS

      Fines, Forfeiture and Reparations   423**

16 Catching War's Funders and Profiteers: The Disjointed
    Web of Corporate Criminal Liability in England and
    Wales   425
    RUSSELL HOPKINS

17 Asset Recovery at International(ised) Criminal Tribunals:
    Fines, Forfeiture and Orders for Reparations   455
    DALEY J. BIRKETT

18 Reparation Mechanisms for Victims of Armed Conflict:
    Common and Basic Principles   481
    SHUICHI FURUYA

    Conclusion: The Relationship between Economic
    and Atrocity Crimes: Challenges and Opportunities   506
    STEPHEN J. RAPP

    Index   524

ILLUSTRATIONS

CONTRIBUTORS

DALEY J. BIRKETT is Vice Chancellor's Senior Fellow in Law at Northumbria University and a research fellow in the Amsterdam Center for International Law's War Reparations Centre at the University of Amsterdam, where he is completing his PhD. His research has been published in the *Leiden Journal of International Law*, the *Chinese Journal of International Law* and the *Journal of Conflict and Security Law*, among other leading journals. Daley holds an LLM (*cum laude*) from Leiden University and an LLB from Durham University. He formerly worked for the United Nations Assistance to the Khmer Rouge Trials as Legal Consultant to the Supreme Court Chamber of the Extraordinary Chambers of the Courts of Cambodia, as a research associate at the University of Nottingham Human Rights Law Centre and as an intern in the Appeals Division of the International Criminal Court.

LIU DAQUN was Vice-President of the International Criminal Tribunal for the Former Yugoslavia (ICTY) from 2015 to 2017 and Judge of the ICTY from 2000 to 2017. He is currently a judge of the United Nations Residual Mechanism for International Tribunals. Prior to being elected to the ICTY, he held a variety of positions in the Chinese Foreign Ministry, culminating in his appointment in 1999 as Chinese Ambassador to Jamaica and as China's Permanent Representative to the International Seabed Authority. He was also Deputy Head and Chief Negotiator of the Chinese Delegation to the Rome Conference on the establishment of the International Criminal Court. He is a member of the International Court of Arbitration and of the Institute de Droit International and a council member of the International Institute of Humanitarian Law, San Remo. He has been a professor of international law at China's University of Political Science and Law and a professor at the Centre of Cooperative Innovation and Judicial Civilization of that university.

HANS OTTO FRØLAND is Professor in Contemporary European History at the Department of Historical Studies, Norwegian University of Science and Technology in Trondheim. He has twice served as head of department in this institution. He achieved his Dr.Philos. degree in 1993 on Scandinavian wage bargaining and incomes policy in the decades after the Second World War. He has published widely on Norway's relation to European integration, Nordic cooperation and globalization. Between 2012 and 2016 he led a research project on Nazi Germany's use of foreign forced labour in Norway during the Second World War, for which he co-edited *Industrial Collaboration in Nazi Occupied Europe: Norway in Context* (Palgrave Macmillan, 2016). Since 2016, he has been leading the international research project 'Fate of Nations: Natural Resources and Historical Development, 1880–2015'. His latest publication is 'Europe Cannot Engage in Autarchical Policies: European Raw Materials Strategy from 1945 to the Present', in A. R. D. Sanders et al. (eds.), *The Political Economy of Resource Regulation: An International and Comparative History*, 1850–2015 (University of British Columbia Press, 2018).

SHUICHI FURUYA is Professor of Law at Waseda Law School, a member of the UN Human Rights Committee (since 2019), a member of the International Humanitarian Fact-Finding Commission (since 2012; Vice-President 2015–2016), Co-Rapporteur of the Committee on Reparation for Victims of Armed Conflict, International Law Association (ILA) (2004–2014) and a member of the Committee on Complementarity in International Criminal Law (since 2014). He is the editor-in-chief of the *Journal of International Law and Diplomacy* (2014–2016) and a member of the editorial boards of the *Netherlands Quarterly of Human Rights* (since 2003) and the *Japanese Yearbook of International Law* (since 2006).

KATHERINE GALLAGHER is Senior Staff Attorney at the Center for Constitutional Rights. She works on universal jurisdiction and international criminal law cases involving US and foreign officials and torture and other war crimes, and cases involving private military corporations and torture at Abu Ghraib. She has been a vice-president on the international board of the International Federation for Human Rights (FIDH), is a member of the editorial committee of the *Journal for International Criminal Justice* and is an adjunct professor of law at the City University of New York (CUNY) School of Law. In addition to her court admissions in the United States, Katherine is admitted to the list of counsel at the International Criminal Court. Prior to coming to the Center for Constitutional Rights, she worked at the United Nations International Criminal Tribunal for the former Yugoslavia from 2001 to 2006, as a legal adviser for the Organization for Security and Cooperation in Europe in Kosovo, with the Special Court for Sierra Leone in Freetown and as a member of the Women's Caucus for Gender Justice in the International Criminal Court during the negotiations to establish the ICC. She graduated from New York University with a joint MA in journalism and Middle East studies and from the CUNY School of Law, where she served as editor-in-chief of the *New York City Law Review*.

TOMAS HAMILTON is a senior legal consultant for the United Nations Assistance to the Khmer Rouge Trials (UNAKRT) at the Extraordinary Chambers in the Courts of Cambodia (ECCC). He has worked as an associate legal officer in the Chambers of the International Criminal Court (ICC), in a leading firm of London solicitors, in academic research positions and in advisory roles for human rights NGOs. His PhD research at King's College London concerns secondary liability under international law and focuses on the role of arms transfers in genocide, war crimes and crimes against humanity. He was called to the Bar of England and Wales in 2011 and studied at the University of Cambridge and the University of Oxford.

RUSSELL HOPKINS is a practising barrister at Bright Line Law in London. His practice focuses on the liability of corporate actors for international human rights violations. He spent several years as an expert legal adviser to the Cambodian trial judges of the Khmer Rouge tribunal in Phnom Penh, Cambodia. Previously, he practised as a solicitor and a solicitor advocate at international law firm Herbert Smith Freehills and clerked for Lord Collins and Lord Wilson at the Supreme Court of the United Kingdom. He holds an LLM (Distinction) from the University of Strathclyde.

NINA H. B. JØRGENSEN is Professor of Public International Law, Deputy Head of School and Director of Research in the School of Law at the University of Southampton. She was previously Professor of Law at the Chinese University of Hong Kong. From 2001 to 2010, she worked in various capacities at the Special Court for Sierra Leone in Freetown (including as Senior Appeals Counsel and Senior Legal Adviser for the

Office of the Prosecutor), the Extraordinary Chambers in the Courts of Cambodia in Phnom Penh (Senior Judicial Coordinator for the Pre-Trial Chamber) and the International Criminal Tribunals for the former Yugoslavia and Rwanda. She has a DPhil from the University of Oxford and was called to the Bar of England and Wales (Gray's Inn) in 1999.

MARK D. KIELSGARD is an associate professor of law at City University of Hong Kong where he teaches criminal law, human rights law and international law. At City University, Dr Kielsgard serves as Director of the JD Programme, Director of Research and Associate Director and co-founder of the Centre for Public Law and Human Rights. He researches in the areas of domestic, comparative and international criminal law and human rights, particularly focusing on international criminal tribunals, counter-terrorism and the crime of genocide. Prior to becoming an academic, Dr Kielsgard was a trial attorney in the United States practising mostly in the field of criminal law and appeals.

EVE LA HAYE is a senior legal adviser in the Legal Division of the International Committee of the Red Cross (ICRC), in charge of issues related to the status of the ICRC, its immunities and privileges as well as issues of confidentiality. She joined the ICRC in 2007 as a legal adviser in the Arms Unit of the ICRC Legal Division before working from 2011 as a member of the ICRC project to update the Commentaries on the Geneva Conventions of 1949 and their Additional Protocols of 1977. From 2001 to 2005, she worked as an associate legal officer in the Appeals Chamber of the International Criminal Tribunal for the former Yugoslavia and Rwanda. Eve holds a doctorate in law from the London School of Economics and a Master's in international relations and international law from the Graduate Institute of International Studies in Geneva. She has taught in several universities and has published several articles on international humanitarian law and international criminal law as well as a monograph entitled 'War Crimes in Internal Armed Conflicts' (Cambridge University Press, 2008) which was awarded the Lieber Prize of the American Society of International Law.

MARINA LOSTAL is a senior lecturer at Essex Law School and a consultant for the Trust Fund for Victims of the International Criminal Court. In 2017, she was appointed as an expert by the Trial Chamber in the reparations phase of the *Al Mahdi* case, which concerned the destruction of world heritage sites. She holds a PhD from the

European University Institute and an LLM from the University of Cambridge. Her publications in the field of cultural property include a book entitled *International Cultural Heritage Law in Armed Conflict* (Cambridge University Press, 2017) and a co-authored report with Geneva Call on the relationship between armed non-state actors and the protection of cultural heritage.

JUAN P. CALDERON-MEZA is an associate legal officer at the Appeals Division of the International Criminal Court. A Colombian advocate interested in corporate accountability, he has worked at the Harvard Law School's International Human Rights Clinic, received the Eleanor Roosevelt Fellowship at the Harvard Law School's Human Rights Program and also worked for EarthRights International. He has clerked at the Extraordinary Chambers in the Courts of Cambodia and advised pro bono the Colombian Campaign to Ban Landmines, which is part of the International Campaign to Ban Landmines. He has also worked in accountability projects with the Northwestern Law Center for International Human Rights.

MICHAEL RAMSDEN is an associate professor in the Faculty of Law at the Chinese University of Hong Kong. He was educated at Berkeley, Cambridge and King's College London. He is a barrister of Lincoln's Inn and a door tenant at 25 Bedford Row, London. He has published extensively in the fields of comparative and international public law, international criminal law and international institutional law. He has also served as a visiting professional in the Appeals Division of the International Criminal Court.

STEPHEN J. RAPP is a distinguished fellow at the United States Holocaust Memorial Museum's Center for Prevention of Genocide. He also serves as Chair of the Commission for International Justice and Accountability (CIJA). From 2009 to 2015, he was Ambassador-at-Large heading the Office of Global Criminal Justice in the US State Department. Rapp was Prosecutor of the Special Court for Sierra Leone from 2007 to 2009 where he led the prosecution of former Liberian President Charles Taylor. From 2001 to 2007, he served as Senior Trial Attorney and Chief of Prosecutions at the International Criminal Tribunal for Rwanda, where he headed the trial team that achieved the first convictions in history of mass media leaders for the crime of direct and public incitement to commit genocide. Before becoming an international prosecutor, he was United States Attorney for the N. District of Iowa from 1993 to 2001.

KIRSTEN SELLARS is currently Visiting Fellow at the Coral Bell School of Asia Pacific Affairs, Australian National University. Dr Sellars' research focuses on public international law – specifically, international criminal law, the laws governing uses of force, and law of the sea – with particular emphasis on South and East Asian perspectives. Her latest books, *'Crimes against Peace' and International Law* (2013), the edited volume *Trials for International Crimes in Asia* (2016) and her next book, *The Making and Remaking of the Law of the Sea* (due out in 2021), are published by Cambridge University Press.

GÖRAN SLUITER is Professor of International Criminal Law at the University of Amsterdam. He is also Professor of Criminal Law and Procedure at the Open University in the Netherlands and a lawyer and partner at Prakken D'Oliveira Human Rights Lawyers. He studied law at the University of Maastricht (1996) and obtained his PhD in international criminal law at Utrecht University (2002). He joined the University of Amsterdam as a senior lecturer in (international) criminal law in 2004 and became a professor in international criminal law in 2006. Göran is the principal investigator in the Vici funded research project 'Rethinking the Outer Limits of Secondary Liability for International Crimes and Serious Human Rights Violations', which runs from September 2018 until September 2023.

JAMES G. STEWART has spent the past twenty years working in international criminal justice, as either a practitioner or a scholar. He joined the University of British Columbia Law Faculty in August 2009, after spending two years as an Associate-in-Law at Columbia Law School in New York. Before then, he was an appeals counsel with the Prosecution of the United Nations International Criminal Tribunal for the former Yugoslavia. He also worked for the Legal Division of the International Committee of the Red Cross, the Prosecution of the International Criminal Tribunal for Rwanda and as a senior legal adviser (part-time) to judges of the Appeals Chamber of the Extraordinary Chambers in the Courts of Cambodia. He holds degrees from Victoria University of Wellington, New Zealand, in both law and philosophy, a Diplôme d'études approfondies in international humanitarian law from the Université de Genève and a JSD from

Columbia Law School. He has received the Cassese Prize in International Criminal Justice, an Open Society Fellowship, and was a Global Hauser Fellow at NYU Law School for his research on the relationship between atrocity commerce and international criminal law. This research, together with a blog on associated issues, is available online at www .jamesgstewart.com.

HENDRIK VANDEKERCKHOVE studied law at KU Leuven, majoring in international and European law, and obtained his Master's degree in 2014. During the second year of his Master's, he did a two-month internship at the Office of the Registrar at the International Court of Justice. After concluding his Master's studies, Hendrik started an LLM in public international law at Utrecht University. The same year, Hendrik participated in the Philip C. Jessup moot court as a member of the team representing Utrecht University. In the summer of 2015, Hendrik was also accepted to attend the Public International Law session at the Hague Academy of International Law. Hendrik is currently working at the Leuven Centre for Global Governance Studies. He is writing his PhD within the framework of a project called 'JusinBellgium'. His PhD deals with questions on the contribution of national – in particular Belgian – courts to international criminal justice. Additionally, he is an assistant editor of the *International Encyclopaedia of Laws*.

WILLIAM H. WILEY is founder and director of the non-profit Commission for International Justice and Accountability (CIJA), a criminal-investigative body with the principal mission of preparing dossiers to a criminal law standard of evidence in response to allegations of war crimes and crimes against humanity perpetrated by the belligerent parties to the Syrian and other conflicts. Dr (Bill) Wiley is a Canadian citizen with twenty years' experience as a practitioner in the field of international criminal and humanitarian law (ICHL) secured in the Middle East (e.g., Iraq, Syria), Central Africa (e.g., Rwanda) and Eastern Europe (e.g., the former Yugoslavia). He previously served with the Crimes Against Humanity and War Crimes Section of the Department of Justice of Canada as well as the Offices of the Prosecutor of the International Criminal Tribunal for the former Yugoslavia, the International Criminal Tribunal for Rwanda and the International Criminal Court. He was additionally a legal adviser at the Iraqi High Tribunal during the trials of Saddam Hussein and other senior Baathist leaders and, in an earlier life, served as an infantry officer in the Canadian Army.

SEAN SHUN MING YAU is presently pursuing a career in legal practice in Hong Kong. From September 2018 until September 2019 he worked as a PhD researcher at the University of Amsterdam on secondary liability for international crimes. Sean studied at Leiden University (LLM in public international law), the University of Hong Kong (LLB) and Hebrew University of Jerusalem (Diploma in international law). He was a legal researcher at the UN International Law Commission (*jus cogens*) and Human Rights Institute, Columbia Law School. In 2018, Sean was Legal Assistant to the African Union before the International Criminal Court, where he previously served as Judicial Intern (Appeals Chamber) for the judges.

JAN WOUTERS is Full Professor of International Law and International Organizations, Jean Monnet Chair ad personam European Union and Global Governance, Director of the Institute for International Law and of the Leuven Centre for Global Governance Studies (both a Jean Monnet Centre of Excellence and a University Centre of Excellence) at KU Leuven and President of the University's Board for International Policy. He is Adjunct Professor at Columbia University (New York) and Visiting Professor at Sciences Po (Paris), LUISS (Rome) and the College of Europe (Bruges). A member of the Belgian Royal Academy and of counsel at Linklaters, he has published widely on international and EU law, international organizations and global governance. He is the coordinator of a large Horizon 2020 Project, RECONNECT (Reconnecting Europe with Its Citizens through Democracy and Rule of Law). He advises and trains regularly international organizations and governments and is often asked to comment on international events in the media. In 2020–21 he is Visiting Professor at Université Paris2 Panthéon-Assas (Paris), Queen Mary University (London) and the World Trade Institute (Bern).

ACKNOWLEDGEMENTS

I wish to express my gratitude first and foremost to the authors for their contribution to this project and their commitment to justice in respect of 'war's funders and profiteers' reflected in the book's pages.

The idea for the book project originated in a symposium held in the Law Faculty at the Chinese University of Hong Kong (CUHK) on 23–24 June 2017. I would like to take the opportunity to thank the speakers in the symposium (Daley Birkett, Hans Otto Frøland, Reinhold Gallmetzer, Matthew Gillett, Tomas Hamilton, Mark Kielsgard, Jennifer Kreder, Joanna Kyriakakis, Liu Daqun, Marina Lostal, Larry Maybee, Stephen Rapp, Kirsten Sellars, Göran Sluiter, James Stewart, Hendrik Vandekerckhove and William Wiley) and the chairs (Kevin Cheng, Steven Gallagher and Stephen Hall). My thanks also go to Jeannie Kow and her team for the superb practical organization of the event. Additionally, I am very grateful to the Faculty of Law at CUHK for the funding and academic facilities that made both the symposium and the book project possible.

The idea for the symposium emerged from my consultancy work with the Commission for International Justice and Accountability (CIJA) in 2016 and I would like to thank CIJA's directors for such a unique opportunity and for their continued support of this scholarly venture.

Many of the symposium participants are also contributors to the book, but I wish to extend special thanks to those contributors who were invited but unable to attend the symposium or who joined the book project at a later stage. My thanks also go to those contributors who took time to review and comment on other chapters, which generated productive dialogue.

I am grateful to the School of Law at the University of Southampton for providing a welcoming and conducive academic environment in which to complete this project especially through its Centre for Law,

Policy and Society, and to Southampton PhD candidate Jiufeng Chang for helping to edit one of the chapters.

Finally, I wish to extend my thanks to Joe Ng at Cambridge University Press for his patient guidance and belief in the project and to the team at CUP for all their work in taking it forward.

ABBREVIATIONS

ATCA	American Alien Tort Claims Act
ALFNOR	Allied Land Forces Norway
ATS	Alien Tort Statute
AWCIN	Allied War Crimes Investigation Branch Norway
AUC	Autodefensas Unidas de Colombia
CCDS	Compensation Commission for Darfur, Sudan
CHF	Swiss francs
CUHK	Chinese University of Hong Kong
CIJA	Commission for International Justice and Accountability
CPB	Cyprus Property Board
CRPC	Commission for Real Property Claims of Displaced Persons and Refugees
CRT-I	Claims Resolution Tribunal for Dormant Accounts in Switzerland
CVF	Crime Victims Fund
DFID	Department for International Development
DNA	deoxyribonucleic acid
DPC	Dutch Penal Code
DRC	Democratic Republic of Congo
DSO	Defence & Security Organisation
EAC	Extraordinary African Chambers
EECC	Eritrea-Ethiopia Claims Commission
ECCC	Extraordinary Chambers in the Courts of Cambodia
ECOMOG	Economic Community of West African States Cease-Fire Monitoring Group
EU	European Union
FATF	Financial Action Task Force
FCPA	Federal Corrupt Practices Act
FIDH	International Federation for Human Rights
FTCA	Federal Tort Claims Act
GDP	gross domestic product
GFLCP	German Forced Labour Compensation Programme
HPCC	Housing and Property Claims Commission
HVAP	Holocaust Victim Assets Programme

IACHR	Inter-American Commission on Human Rights
ICC	International Criminal Court
ICHEIC	International Commission on Holocaust Era Insurance Claims
ICJ	International Court of Justice
ICL	international criminal law
ICHL	international criminal and humanitarian law
ICOM	International Council of Museums
ICT	international(ised) criminal tribunal
ICTR	International Criminal Tribunal for Rwanda
ICTY	International Criminal Tribunal for the former Yugoslavia
IHL	international humanitarian law
IHT	Iraqi High Tribunal
IMT	International Military Tribunal
IMTFE	International Military Tribunal for the Far East
INTERPOL	International Criminal Police Organisation
IPCC	Iraq Property Claims Commission
ISIL	Islamic State of Iraq and the Levant
JCE	joint criminal enterprise
KPCC	Kosovo Property Claims Commission
KSC	Kosovo Specialist Chambers
LRA	Lord's Resistance Army
LURD	Liberians United for Reconciliation and Democracy
MICT	International Residual Mechanism for Criminal Tribunals
NATO	North Atlantic Treaty Organisation
NPFL	National Patriotic Front of Liberia
OAS	Organisation of American States
OECD	Organisation for Economic Co-operation and Development
OT	Organisation Todt
OTP	Office of the Prosecutor
POCA	Proceeds of Crime Act
POW	prisoner of war
PTC	Pre-Trial Chamber
RFA	requests for assistance
RUF	Revolutionary United Front
SCSL	Special Court for Sierra Leone
SD	Sicherheitsdienst
SLORC	State Law and Order Restoration Council
SPSC	Special Panels for Serious Crimes
SS	Schutzstaffel
STL	Special Tribunal for Lebanon
SYP	Syrian pounds
TDG	thiodiglycol

TFV	Trust Fund for Victims
TVPA	Torture Victims Protection Act
ULIMO	United Liberation Forces of Liberia
UMHK	United Mines of Upper Katanga
UN	United Nations
UNCC	United Nations Compensation Commission
UNGA	United Nations General Assembly
UNMIK	United Nations Interim Administration Mission in Kosovo
UNSC	United Nations Security Council
UNSG	United Nations Secretary-General
UNWCC	United Nations War Crimes Commission
UNESCO	United Nations Educational, Scientific and Cultural Organisation
UNIDROIT	International Institute for the Unification of Private Law
UNITAD	United Nations Investigative Team to Promote Accountability for Crimes Committed by Da'esh/Islamic State in Iraq and the Levant
UNTAET	United Nations Transitional Administration in East Timor
US	United States
USSR	Union of Soviet Socialist Republics
UWO	Unexplained Wealth Order
VOCA	Victims of Crimes Act
WWII	World War II
XAF	Central African francs

~

Introduction

NINA H. B. JØRGENSEN

Origins and Objectives

This book is concerned with the commercial exploitation of armed conflict. It is about money, war, atrocities and economic actors, about the connections between them, and about responsibility. The key words are 'connections' and 'responsibility'. What sort of legal framework defines these connections and gives rise to criminal responsibility? Which economic actors among individuals, businesses, governments and states are accountable? What is the appropriate forum for accountability? How can the profits of war be recovered and redirected to benefit the victims of war?

The idea for the book was conceived at a conference on 'The International Criminal Responsibility of War's Funders and Profiteers' held at the Chinese University of Hong Kong on 23–24 June 2017 where the above questions were discussed and explored. While it was acknowledged that there was already a growing body of literature covering distinct themes within this broad topic,[1] a comprehensive volume

---

[1] See, for example, Special Issue on 'Transnational Business and International Criminal Law' (2010) 8 *Journal of International Criminal Justice*; J. Kryriakakis, 'Corporations and the International Criminal Court: The Complementarity Objection Stripped Bare' (2008) 19 *Criminal Law Forum* 115; J. Kryriakakis, 'Corporate Criminal Liability and the ICC Statute: The Comparative Law Challenge' (2009) 56 *Netherlands International Law Review* 333; J. Kryriakakis, 'Justice after War: Economic Actors, Economic Crimes, and the Moral Imperative for Accountability after War' in L. May and A. T. Forcehimes (eds.) *Morality, Jus Post Bellum, and International Law* (Cambridge University Press, 2012), p. 113; J. Kyriakakis, 'Corporations Before International Criminal Courts: Implications for the International Criminal Justice Project' (2017) 30 *Leiden Journal of International Law* 221; J. G. Stewart, 'The Turn to Corporate Criminal Liability for International Crimes: Transcending the Alien Tort Statute' (2010) 47 *NYU Journal of International Law and Politics* 121; J. G. Stewart, 'Corporate War Crimes: Prosecuting the Pillage of Natural

connecting these themes appeared to be lacking. Writing on Mark Kersten's *Justice in Conflict* blog in 2015, Barrie Sander provided an overview of the state of the literature concerning international criminal law and the economic dimension of mass atrocities.[2] He noted that the economic perspective had long been a 'blind spot' of international criminal law but that this situation was rapidly changing. At the Nuremberg Forum 2017 on 'The Fight against Impunity at a Crossroad', organised by the International Nuremberg Principles Academy, there were calls from participants to further address the responsibility of businesses and financial actors who help to sustain conflict and profit from criminal activity under the cover of war.[3] The book is therefore intended to serve as a timely contribution to the literature.

The book's title is not perfectly descriptive, although it captures the essence of the material set out in the nineteen chapters. The use of the word 'international' does not mean that domestic procedures are excluded but rather that the emphasis falls upon responsibility for international crimes and on what participants in international justice might learn from or contribute to domestic systems. Similarly, as the book focuses on the most egregious violations of international norms, it seemed appropriate to include the word 'criminal' in the title even though alternatives to criminal prosecutions are also considered. The

Resources', Open Society Justice Initiative (2011); L. van den Herik, 'Corporations As Future Subjects of the International Criminal Court: An Exploration of the Counterarguments and Consequences', in C. Stahn and L. van den Herik (eds.), *Future Perspectives on International Criminal Justice* (TMC Asser Press, 2010), p. 350; H. van der Wilt, 'Corporate Criminal Responsibility for International Crimes: Exploring the Possibilities' (2013) 12 *Chinese Journal of International Law* 43; K. Roberts, 'Corporate Liability and Complicity in International Crimes', in S. Jodoin and M. Cordonier Segger (eds.), *Sustainable Development, International Criminal Justice, and Treaty Implementation* (Cambridge University Press, 2013), pp. 190–211; M. J. Kelly, *Prosecuting Corporations for Genocide* (Oxford University Press, 2016); L. Bilsky, *The Holocaust, Corporations, and the Law: Unfinished Business* (University of Michigan Press, 2017); International Commission of Jurists, 'Corporate Complicity and Legal Accountability' (2008) www.icj.org/wp-content/uploads/2012/06/Vol.2-Corporate-legal-accountability-thematic-report-2008.pdf; Amnesty International, 'Commerce, Crime and Human Rights: Closing the Prosecution Gaps' (Project, ongoing since 2014) www.commercecrimehumanrights.org/about/the-project/.

2 B. Sander, 'Addressing the Economic Dimensions of Mass Atrocities: International Criminal Law's Business or Blind Spot?', *Justice in Conflict* blog (8 June 2015) https://justiceinconflict.org/2015/06/08/addressing-the-economic-dimensions-of-mass-atrocities-international-criminal-laws-business-or-blind-spot/.

3 Information about the conference is available at: www.nurembergacademy.org/events/nuremberg-forum-2017/.

crimes under consideration are not limited to those defined as war crimes under international humanitarian law but include the range of atrocities typically associated with armed conflicts, such as crimes against humanity and genocide and the underlying acts that may constitute those crimes. The reference to 'war' deliberately harks back to the idea expressed at Nuremberg that aggression is the 'supreme international crime differing only from other war crimes in that it contains within itself the accumulated evil of the whole'.[4] While this may now be regarded as an outdated notion, there is little doubt that a situation of armed conflict creates the conditions for unchecked exploitative economic activity that may contribute towards war crimes, crimes against humanity and genocide. Indeed, the United Nations Secretary-General observed in 2002 that the 'commercial exploitation of conflict' was having an increasing detrimental impact on the protection of civilians.[5] This trend has continued despite the UN's efforts to bring more attention to the problem. The expression 'war's funders' covers the full gamut of economic actors who help to finance the activities of warring factions, from bankers to businesspersons to crowd-funders to donors. The term 'profiteer' potentially has a very broad scope; during World War I, even profiting from the demand for war poetry attracted criticism.[6] However, in the current context the term is restricted to economic actors who derive a financial benefit from their contribution to conduct that is, or becomes, associated with international crimes, and who stand correspondingly to have their illegally acquired assets confiscated, whether or not they themselves are prosecuted.

War's Funders and Profiteers

At both a governmental and a private business level, the trade in arms, natural resources and sometimes art and cultural heritage, coupled with pure economic gifts, sponsorship and loans, helps to provide the financial fuel to sustain conflict. In war's economic substructure, politicians, financiers and industrialists authorise and profit from forced and slave labour, while commanders direct troops to engage in rampant looting of villages and cities often on behalf of superiors. Women and children who

[4] Trial of the Major War Criminals Before the International Military Tribunal, Nuremberg, 14 November 1945–1 October 1946, Vol. 1, 1947, p. 186.
[5] Report of the Secretary-General to the Security Council on the protection of civilians in armed conflict, S/2002/1300, 26 November 2002, para. 58.
[6] S. Featherstone, *War Poetry: An Introductory Reader* (Routledge, 1995), p. 38.

are rendered homeless and vulnerable become the victims of trafficking into sexual slavery by opportunists or increasingly by terrorist groups. Meanwhile, banks and legitimate businesses collapse and black markets flourish.

Despite this classic depiction of the consequences of warfare, accountability for economic participation in international crimes remains underdeveloped. At the time of the post-World War II trials, the Allies considered it to be important to prosecute the economic and financial leaders of Germany and Japan for their involvement in military aggression and, at least in respect of the European theatre, to hold the so-called 'great industrialists' responsible for crimes such as forced labour, looting and spoliation to the same degree as politicians, diplomats and uniformed personnel.[7] However, more recent prosecutions at the international level have almost entirely overlooked the economic aspect. A possible exception is the case of the former Liberian president Charles Taylor. Taylor was convicted by the Special Court for Sierra Leone (SCSL) for aiding and abetting international crimes committed during the conflict in Sierra Leone through the provision of arms and ammunition, military personnel, operational support and monetary donations.[8] These forms of support were all found to have been connected to Taylor's personal involvement in the illicit diamond trade.

The International Criminal Court (ICC) Office of the Prosecutor (OTP) produced a policy paper in 2003 in which it indicated that an important area of investigation would involve 'financial links with crimes', such as the purchase of arms used in the commission of atrocities, and called on national investigative authorities to share information on financial transactions which might be essential to the ICC's investigations.[9] By the same token, the policy paper envisioned that prosecutions by national courts, with evidential assistance from the ICC, would 'be a key deterrent to the commission of future crimes, if

---

[7] See e.g. J. A. Bush, 'The Prehistory of Corporations and Conspiracy in International Criminal Law: What Nuremberg Really Said' (2009) 109 *Columbia Law Review* 1094, 1104–1112.

[8] *Prosecutor* v. *Taylor*, SCSL-03–01-T, Judgment, Trial Chamber, 18 May 2012.

[9] ICC Office of the Prosecutor, 'Paper on some policy issues before the Office of the Prosecutor', September 2003, pp. 2–3, www.icc-cpi.int/NR/rdonlyres/1FA7C4C6-DE5F-42B7-8B25-60AA962ED8B6/143594/030905_Policy_Paper.pdf. See further R. Gallmetzer, 'Prosecuting Persons Doing Business with Armed Groups in Conflict Areas: The Strategy of the Office of the Prosecutor of the International Criminal Court' (2010) 8 *Journal of International Criminal Justice* 947, describing the ICC-OTP's network of national law enforcement agencies and other specialized organizations and institutions (LEN).

they can curb the source of funding'.[10] The approach of the ICC-OTP reflected the idea that those who provide the finance for the commission of international crimes, and thereby the means and incentives, should be tried either alongside the direct perpetrators or by national courts. The deterrent aspect may be viewed as particularly compelling in respect of business actors who are perceived as 'rational' and risk-conscious, ostensibly driven not by politics or ideology but purely by profit, the pursuit of which may not be worthwhile if there is the prospect of a criminal penalty.

There has been little indication since 2003 that the ICC is following through on this policy, except to a limited extent in the *Bemba* case, which included the charge of pillage of civilian property.[11] In its 2016 policy paper on 'case selection and prioritisation', the OTP adjusted the emphasis somewhat as it concerned the link between economic factors and international crimes and referred to the economic *impact* of such crimes on 'affected communities'.[12] In this context the OTP stated that it 'will give particular consideration to prosecuting Rome Statute crimes that are committed by means of, or that result in, *inter alia*, the

---

[10] ICC Office of the Prosecutor, 'Paper on some policy issues before the Office of the Prosecutor', September 2003, p. 3, www.icc-cpi.int/NR/rdonlyres/1FA7C4C6-DE5F -42B7-8B25-60AA962ED8B6/143594/030905_Policy_Paper.pdf.

[11] ICC-01/05–01/08A, *Situation in the Central African Republic, Prosecutor v Jean-Pierre Bemba Gombo*, Decision Pursuant to Article 61(7)(a) and (b) of the Rome Statute on the Charges of the Prosecutor Against Jean-Pierre Bemba Gombo, 15 June 2009, paras. 314–340, confirming the charge of pillaging villages and towns as a war crime under article 8(2)(e)(v) of the ICC Statute. Bemba was acquitted of all charges on appeal: ICC-01/05–01/08A, Judgment on the appeal of Mr Jean-Pierre Bemba Gombo against Trial Chamber III's 'Judgment pursuant to Article 74 of the Statute', 8 June 2018. The ICC has also commenced proceedings relating to the Kivu provinces in the Democratic Republic of the Congo where UN reports suggest that the conflict has been fuelled by the illegal trade in natural resources, but the charges in these cases have similarly included pillage of civilian property. See e.g. ICC-01/04–01/12, *Prosecutor v. Sylvestre Mudacumura*, Decision on the Prosecutor's Application under Article 58, 13 July 2012. See also UN Security Council, S/2008/773, Final Report of the Group of Experts on the Democratic Republic of the Congo, 12 December 2008, alleging that the *Forces démocratiques de libération du Rwanda* (FDLR) raised funds principally through the illegal trade of mineral resources such as cassiterite, gold, coltan and wolframite; UN Security Council, S/2003/ 1027, Final Report of the Panel of Experts on the Illegal Exploitation of Natural Resources and Other Forms of Wealth of DR Congo, 23 October 2003, stating at para. 68 that the 'international community now has a deeper understanding of the illicit exploitation of natural resources in the Democratic Republic of the Congo, including the role of companies and business people involved'.

[12] ICC Office of the Prosecutor, 'Policy paper on case selection and prioritisation', 15 September 2016, para. 41, www.icc-cpi.int/itemsDocuments/20160915_OTP- Policy_Case-Selection_Eng.pdf.

destruction of the environment, the illegal exploitation of natural resources or the illegal dispossession of land'.[13] This is different from a distinct policy to pursue economic actors but suggests that the ICC will place emphasis on the role of corporations in acts such as 'landgrabbing'. Landgrabbing involves the illegal taking of land from its inhabitants, usually by a government, and often 'through violence and intimidation, to make way for mining, timber or agricultural plantations' and in certain circumstances may amount to a crime against humanity.[14]

In its most recent 'Strategic Plan', issued in 2019, the ICC-OTP indicated that it would review its investigative strategies and methods in collaboration with national partners, focusing especially on the area of financial investigations.[15] In the event, notwithstanding the ICC-OTP's expressed interest in working with national authorities to encourage the latter to take up the baton of addressing the economic aspects of international crimes, to date prosecutions at the domestic level have been infrequent. Indeed, due to investigative challenges and capacity, domestic systems may opt to focus in this context on, for example, financial crimes, tax evasion, corruption, terrorist financing and the violation of national legislation implementing arms embargoes rather than war crimes and crimes against humanity.[16]

Important domestic precedents were nonetheless set by the Dutch cases against Frans van Anraat, a businessman found guilty of complicity in war crimes through his role in the delivery of thousands of tonnes of a chemical precursor used in the production of mustard gas to Saddam Hussein's regime in Iraq, and Guus Kouwenhoven, a timber-merchant

---

[13] Ibid.

[14] A. Simms, 'Unprecedented Case Filed at International Criminal Court Proposes Land Grabbing in Cambodia as a Crime Against Humanity', *Huffington Post, The Blog* (7 October 2014) www.huffingtonpost.co.uk/andrew-simms/land-grabbing_b_5938500 .html?guccounter=1. See further on a communication brought before the ICC-OTP concerning alleged land grabbing in Cambodia: Global Diligence, Communication Under Article 15 of the Rome Statute of the International Criminal Court, 'The Commission of Crimes Against Humanity in Cambodia, July 2002–present' (summary), 7 October 2014, www.fidh.org/IMG/pdf/executive_summary-2.pdf. For further documentation see Global Diligence, 'ICC Cambodian Case Study', at www.globaldiligence.com/about-us/icc-cambodian-case-study/.

[15] ICC Office of the Prosecutor, Strategic Plan 2019–2021, 17 July 2019, para. 16.

[16] In 2004, Samih Ossaily and Aziz Nassour were convicted of money-laundering, arms trafficking, dealing in conflict diamonds and belonging to a criminal organization by the Belgian courts, applying the Belgian Criminal Code, in respect of allegations of trading in diamonds and weapons in Sierra Leone and Liberia. See Gallmetzer (n. 9 above), footnote 6.

similarly convicted of complicity in war crimes by providing financial assistance to Charles Taylor's regime during the Liberian civil war.[17] Prior to his death in custody, Michel Desaedeleer was accused before the Belgian courts of pillage and enslavement by virtue of his participation in the illicit diamond trade in Sierra Leone.[18] The proceedings in France against LafargeHolcim constitute the most notable recent development. The Lafarge case concerns the activities of a multinational cement firm accused of paying millions of euros to terrorist groups such as the Islamic State through intermediaries in order to keep its factory open in Syria.[19] In an unprecedented development, the company itself has been charged with both complicity in crimes against humanity and financing terrorism.[20] The case is conceptually significant in that it not only combines charges of international crimes and terrorism offences but also suggests that a company may become an accomplice to crimes against humanity by financing terrorism and failing to ensure the security of its employees.

Overview of Chapters

Part I of the book is entitled 'Financiers and Profiteers after World War II: Legal and Political Perspectives'. The Nuremberg trials of industrialists and

---

[17] *Public Prosecutor* v. *Frans Cornelis Adrianus van Anraat*, BA4676, Court of Appeal of The Hague, The Netherlands, Judgment dated 9 May 2007, www.internationalcrimesdatabase.org /Case/168; *The Public Prosecutor* v. *Guus Kouwenhoven*, 's-Hertogenbosch Court of Appeal, The Netherlands, Ruling of the three judge panel at the Court of Appeal in 's-Hertogenbosch, 21 April 2017, L.2, www.internationalcrimesdatabase.org/Case/3308.

[18] See Civitas Maxima Press Release, 'Michel Desaedeleer Dies in Custody in Belgium', 29 September 2016, claiming 'it would have been the first trial in history to deal with international crimes allegedly committed in furtherance of natural resource trade', www .civitas-maxima.org/sites/default/files/docs/2017-01/Civitas_Maxima_Press_Release_2016 _09_29.pdf.

[19] 'Lafarge Charged with Complicity in Syria Crimes Against Humanity', *The Guardian* (28 June 2018) www.theguardian.com/world/2018/jun/28/lafarge-charged-with-complicity-in-syria-crimes-against-humanity.

[20] Alexandru Tofan, 'The Lafarge Affair: A First Step towards Corporate Criminal Liability for Complicity in Crimes against Humanity', *Doing Business Right Blog*, Asser Institute (2 October 2018) www.asser.nl/DoingBusinessRight/Blog/post/the-lafarge-affair-a-first-step-towards-corporate-criminal-liability-for-complicity-in-crimes-against-humanity-by-alexandru-tofan; 'Lafarge in Syria: Accusations of Complicity in War Crimes and Crimes Against Humanity', European Center for Constitutional and Human Rights (ECCHR), Case Report (November 2016); 'Landmark Decision: Company Lafarge Indicted – Complicity in Crimes Against Humanity Included', ECCHR Press Release (28 June 2018).

other economic actors have retained their importance as precedents and there is a wealth of historical material in this area that is still being studied and interpreted.[21] The first two chapters take national perspectives as a starting point – Soviet and Norwegian – and analyse the extent to which the respective approaches influenced or were influenced by ideas then under discussion amongst the victorious Allied powers. For its part, the third chapter introduces an economic framing of the landscape of international criminal justice as it has emerged, offering what might be termed a political economy of international criminal courts and tribunals. More specifically, in Chapter 1, **Kirsten Sellars** uncovers the origins of the concept of 'economic crimes against peace' in Soviet political and legal thought as the basis for prosecuting both the leading Axis 'instigators' of the war (the politicians and generals) and the 'aiders and abettors' (the financiers and industrialists) who were eventually charged with crimes against humanity. In Chapter 2, **Hans Otto Frøland** considers the reasons for the neglect of the evidence of exploitation of foreign forced labour in the Norwegian legal settlement and trials after World War II in the face of the international legal developments at Nuremberg. In Chapter 3, **Mark Kielsgard** examines the economic factors that influence the selection of situations for investigation and prosecution in modern-day international courts and tribunals. He suggests that economic interests are key to understanding the political motivations in this area of international decision-making while arguing, in addition, that these interests are more in evidence in relation to UN-established tribunals than the ICC.

Part II is entitled 'Arms Fairs and "Flying Money": The Circulation of Weapons, Art and Cash in Conflict Zones'; this part seeks to establish the practical context for the book. The concept of 'flying money' can be traced to ninth-century China, where the tea traders performed a function not dissimilar to that of modern-day central bankers. As trade flourished, the inconvenience of transferring bags full of copper coins over large distances became apparent. The coins were replaced by paper bills of credit known as 'flying money' because of their tendency to

---

[21] On the Pacific Theatre, see e.g. Z. D. Kaufman, 'Transitional Justice for Tōjō's Japan: The United States Role in the Establishment of the International Military Tribunal for the Far East and other Transitional Justice Mechanisms for Japan after World War II', (2013) 27 *Emory International Law Review* 755, discussing the Allied desire to prosecute 'economic officials' and the Russian dissatisfaction with the neglect of the Japanese *zaibatsu*. Several trials held in Singapore dealt with the ill-treatment and deaths of prisoners of war and civilians who worked as labourers on projects such as the infamous Burma–Siam Railway. See information at: www.singaporewarcrimestrials.com/case-summaries#forced-labour.

blow away. This metaphor provides a helpful visual image of the movement of sources of finance in and out of conflict zones, often across international borders; it likewise points to the challenge of gathering evidence insofar as the proceeds of the trade in arms, cultural property and other commodities are often untraceable. This evidence must in turn be sufficient to meet the high legal standard for connecting economic actors to international crimes through modes of liability such as aiding and abetting.

The chapters in Part II delve into the relevant practical, legal and evidentiary issues against the background of specific country or thematic contexts. In Chapter 4, **William Wiley** and **Nina Jørgensen** provide an overview of investigations of economic actors in the Syrian conflict conducted by the Commission for International Justice and Accountability (CIJA). Additionally, this chapter considers some of the legal and investigative challenges arising, especially in terms of establishing the linkage between financial transactions and international crimes within the legal framework for aiding and abetting liability adopted at Nuremberg, which has been developed further in more recent proceedings. **Marina Lostal** addresses the topical issue of the trafficking of cultural property in Chapter 5. She explains how this illicit trade has become a threat to international security with the emergence of terrorist groups such as the Islamic State (IS), calling into question the effectiveness of the current regulatory framework. In Chapter 6, **Tomas Hamilton** addresses the role of the ICC as a potential frontrunner in developing the elements of criminal accountability in respect of arms traders – a uniquely important category of persons who contribute the physical means for the commission of crimes but who often do not share the criminal intentions of the perpetrators. In this context, he offers an interpretation of the phrase 'knowingly contributing to the commission or attempted commission of a crime by a group acting with a common purpose' pursuant to Article 25(3)(d)(ii) of the Rome Statute.

Part III is entitled 'Developing the Available Law: Economic War Crimes and Crimes against Humanity'. The phrase 'economic war crimes' was in current usage around the time of the Nuremberg proceedings, but it lacks a distinctive definition and has not become a term of art. For example, the case against members of the Roechling Enterprises heard by the General Tribunal of the Military Government of the French Zone of Occupation in Germany pursuant to Control Council Law No.10 was described as involving 'war crimes of an economic nature'.[22] The Tribunal found that in his various roles, especially as Plenipotentiary General and Reich Commissioner for the iron industry of the Departments Moselle and Meurthe-et-Moselle in France, Hermann Roechling was effectively 'dictator for iron and steel in Germany and the occupied countries'.[23] The Superior Court overturned Roechling's conviction for crimes against peace but upheld the verdict in respect of the 'economic war crimes' including systematic looting, forced labour and spoliation.[24] In addition to these established categories, candidates for inclusion in the list of acts that may be construed as 'economic war crimes' are the illegal exploitation of natural resources and human trafficking. In Chapter 7, **Eve La Haye** provides a concise introduction to pillage in international humanitarian law, explaining the customary nature of pillage as a war crime and comparing pillage with the related concepts of 'plunder', 'exploitation', 'spoliation', 'looting' and 'sacking'. She goes on to examine the scope and essential elements of the crime of pillage in armed conflict. In Chapter 8, **James Stewart** takes up a theme from the ICC's Policy Paper of 2016, framing the practice of landgrabbing as a displacement crime to be interpreted with reference to the International Criminal Tribunal for the Former Yugoslavia's extensive jurisprudence on deportation and forced transfer. In Chapter 9, **Michael Ramsden** considers the developing international legal framework through which human traffickers might be held criminally responsible, noting the relationship with transnational organised crime but focusing in particular on the explicit inclusion of human trafficking as a form of enslavement under the ICC Statute.

Part IV is entitled 'Where Should the Buck Stop? The Legal Framework for Economic Aiders and Abettors'; it is concerned with modes of liability, especially aiding and abetting as applied in both international and domestic prosecutions. The SCSL is to date the only international tribunal since Nuremberg to try an 'economic actor' (although Charles Taylor was much more than that). Chapter 10 by **Nina Jørgensen** considers the lessons that may be learned from the SCSL's handling of modes of liability in the *Taylor* case and touches on the findings and recommendations of the Liberian Truth and Reconciliation Commission concerning the role of economic actors and economic activities in

---

[22] *Commissioner* v. *Roechling et al.*, Trials of War Criminals before the Nuremberg Military Tribunals under Control Council Law No. 10, October 1946–April 1949, Vol. XIV, Appendix B, p. 1066.
[23] Ibid., p. 1079.
[24] Ibid., p. 1098.

contributing to and benefiting from the armed conflict in Liberia. In Chapter 11, **Jan Wouters** and **Hendrik Vandekerckhove** uncover the meaning of the notion of aiding and abetting as it concerns war's funders. They link their discussion to the complex issue of corporate criminal liability, highlighting the fact that although companies can be direct funders of wars, they cannot currently be held criminally accountable at the international level. In Chapter 12, **Göran Sluiter** and **Sean Shun Ming Yau** analyse the cases of van Anraat and Kouwenhoven, presenting in the course of their chapter a fresh interpretation of the standard of causation for aiding and abetting in the context of companies and businessmen who contribute to international crimes.

Part V is entitled 'Criminal Accountability and Beyond: Future Directions for Individual and Corporate Responsibility'. This part of the book remains concerned with the question of how to shape liability both internationally and domestically, though it moves beyond aiding and abetting in criminal law to address the three related areas of terrorist financing, corporate criminal liability and civil liability under the law of tort. The case concerning LafargeHolcim signifies a potential shift from the prioritisation of the offence of financing terrorism as defined under domestic law over the prosecution of core international crimes on the grounds that terrorism offences may be easier to prove.[25] In Chapter 13, **Liu Daqun** studies the international instruments on terrorism. He offers in the process an interpretative analysis of the modes of participation contained in the International Convention for the Suppression of the Financing of Terrorism, drawing on the jurisprudence of the ad hoc international tribunals and the ICC. In Chapter 14, **Juan Calderon**

---

[25] Under Section 17 of the UK Terrorism Act 2000, for example, a person commits an offence if he or she enters into an arrangement to make money available to another and 'knows or has reasonable cause to suspect that it will or may be used for the purposes of terrorism'. The question of the correct interpretation of 'reasonable cause to suspect' came before the UK Supreme Court, which found that an objective assessment was appropriate, with the result that 'an accused can commit this offence without knowledge or actual suspicion that the money might be used for terrorist purposes'. This did not mean that the accused's state of mind was irrelevant, however, since the emphasis was on 'what information the accused had'. *R* v. *Sally Lane and John Letts* (AB and CD), Judgment of 11 July 2018, [2018] UKSC 36, para. 24. This interpretation has led to convictions in the UK under anti-terrorism laws in respect of relatively small financial contributions when a case based on similar facts might not have succeeded if framed as aiding and abetting war crimes or crimes against humanity. See e.g. L. Dearden, 'Jihadi Jack: Parents of British Isis Fighter Spared Jail for Funding Terrorism', *The Independent* (21 June 2019) www.independent.co.uk/news/uk/crime/jihadi-jack-parents-trial-sally-lane-john-letts-syria-terror-funding-a8969141.html.

Meza provides an account of the litigation movement which has sought to bring corporate actors to justice, using the legal tools available under both criminal law and civil law. In Chapter 15, **Katherine Gallagher** analyses the current state of play as it concerns litigation under the US Alien Tort Statute specifically in relation to private military contractors. She examines the defences that are typically raised and notes that the doctrines relied upon by courts to block adjudication are more often grounded in prudential concerns related to domestic enforcement of international law rather than a normative bar to corporate liability.

Part VI is entitled 'Discovering and Recovering the Profits of War: Fines, Forfeiture and Reparations' and explores the options to prevent the 'flying money' and looted goods such as artefacts from disappearing by means of strengthening forfeiture procedures and reparations mechanisms for the benefit of victims. Notably, the UN Security Council has highlighted its potential role 'in authorizing the use of assets frozen under sanctions regimes for reparations payments and for supporting national reparations programmes'.[26] The Security Council has also indicated that it should consider directing coercive measures at 'companies and individuals involved in plundering of resources in conflict situations', finding that these actors often have no incentive to behave differently.[27] The final section of the book introduces the angle of restorative justice when considering the responsibility of financial actors for funding (or profiting from) conflict.

In Chapter 16, **Russell Hopkins** provides a critical overview of the different options available to prosecutors or claimants when seeking remedies against war's funders and profiteers before the courts of England and Wales. He focuses primarily on the criminal law and the web of UK corporate liability, which he concludes is not tightly spun, shifting the emphasis to alternative methods for redress. In Chapter 17, **Daley Birkett** outlines the history of asset recovery at international and mixed international and domestic ('internationalised') criminal tribunals and analyses the fines and forfeiture regime in the ICC Statute as the mechanism enabling the enforcement of future reparation awards. In Chapter 18, **Shuichi Furuya** provides a detailed catalogue and assessment of the basic principles derived from fifteen reparations mechanisms, relating to eligibility, type of harm suffered and appropriate form of

---

[26] Report of the Secretary-General on the protection of civilians in armed conflict, S/2012/376, 22 May 2012, para. 70.
[27] Report of the Secretary-General to the Security Council on the protection of civilians in armed conflict, S/2002/1300, 26 November 2002, paras. 59–60.

remedy. He highlights the fact that victims of armed conflict have a right to reparation from the responsible parties under international law but notes that political obstacles may stand in the way of a successful claims process.

Finally, in the Conclusion, **Stephen Rapp** tightens the strands linking a wide spectrum of international and domestic legal instruments and offers original insights on the book's central theme. He highlights the relationship between international and domestic responses to economic crimes and suggests the importance of coordination, cooperation and political will.

There is scope for further research on all the topics represented in this book and it is hoped that, by bringing various themes together in one volume, the connections between them become more apparent. As a starting point in this journey, the chapters shine a critical light on the options provided by a network of laws to ensure that the 'great indus-trialists' of our time who find economic opportunities in the war-ravaged lives of others are unable to pursue those opportunities with impunity.

PART I

Financiers and Profiteers after World War II

Legal and Political Perspectives

Economic Aggression

A Soviet Concept

KIRSTEN SELLARS[*]

1.1 Introduction

On 8 May 1943, Sumner Welles, the American Under-Secretary of State, delivered a speech in Toledo, Ohio, entitled 'Freedom from Economic Aggression'. His aim was to show that Germany's wartime economic policies were more predatory than those of the United States, but the more he said, the less certain his arguments became.

Economic aggression, he stated, could take two forms. The *selfish* form arose out of 'short-sighted and unintelligent' policies that, while motivated by narrow self-interest, were not driven by the wish to dominate or injure other people.[1] By contrast, the *vicious* form was conceived as part of 'the same cruel design to conquer and to dominate and to exploit as that which inspires military aggression'.[2] While the United States was guilty of selfishness, Germany was guilty of viciousness because it had 'with malice aforethought chosen guns instead of butter'.[3] In other words, the difference between the two was not the infliction of injury, as such, but the *intent* to injure others – one being negligent, the other purposeful.

Turning to specifics, Welles admitted that during the interwar decades the United States, Britain and almost every other nation had engaged in some form of economic warfare: protective tariffs were,

---

[*] This chapter expands on the ideas first presented in 'Treasonable Conspiracies at Paris, Moscow and Delhi: The Legal Hinterland of the Tokyo Tribunal' in K. Sellars (ed.), *Trials for International Crimes in Asia* (Cambridge University Press, 2016).
[1] S. Welles, 'Freedom from Economic Aggression', *Department of State Bulletin* (8 May 1943), p. 405.
[2] Ibid., p. 405.
[3] Ibid., p. 406.

after all, designed to 'injure the country against which protection is desired'.[4] By this measure, the history of British imperial preferences was 'a history of economic aggression in the sense of which I am now using the term'.[5] Unlike Germany, though, these powers had inflicted only 'heedless rather than calculated' injuries on other peoples; they had not engaged in economic aggression as 'an adjunct of conquest'.[6] Indeed, once they had recognised the damaging effect of protectionism, they had tried to inaugurate a global system based on cooperation and free trade,[7] while Germany, bent on conquest, had gone the other way.[8]

When referring to the merely 'selfish' powers, Welles' arguments seemed a trifle disingenuous. How had Britain acquired the Empire that gave rise to imperial preferences if not by conquest? Was not the United States' embrace of the free market every bit as self-interested as its protectionism? But the most striking feature of his speech was his admission that almost all states had been implicated one way or another in economic aggression. In this dog-eat-dog world, the only distinction that he could point to between the Anglo-American and the German forms of economic warfare was that the former was less calculatedly predatory. As a recommendation of capitalist enterprise, this was far from a ringing endorsement.

At the end of the war in Europe, the problem that Welles had grappled with – of where to draw the line between Germany's economic aggression and everyone else's – arose once again. At the Nuremberg tribunal, the Allies wished to prosecute, alongside the German ministers, generals and gauleiters, some of the financiers and industrialists who had re-armed Germany and bankrolled the Nazi regime. But how could the actions of the German magnates be distinguished from those of their Allied equivalents? And at what point did legitimate profit-making, the object of every capitalist, turn into criminal profiteering, the subject of criminal proceedings? This question was never properly answered, but it is not surprising that the most active proponents of the idea of trying individuals for economic aggression hailed not from the capitalist world but from the USSR.

[4] Ibid., p. 407.
[5] Ibid.
[6] Ibid., p. 408.
[7] Ibid.
[8] Ibid.

1.2   Lenin's Critique of Imperialism

To address the problem of economic aggression from the Soviet perspective, one must start with Vladimir Ilyich Lenin's writings on imperialism. In his pamphlet 'Imperialism, the Highest Stage of Capitalism', published on the eve of the 1917 revolution, he argued that capitalism in its final moribund stage would inevitably give rise to conflicts between the major capitalist powers. Or, put even more simply, imperialism entailed aggression. As Lenin wrote, 'imperialist wars are absolutely inevitable under *such* an economic system, *as long as* private property in the means of production exists'.[9] World War I, driven by economic imperatives, was an archetypical war among imperialist powers; World War II (which he predicted but did not live to see[10]) would be another.

What, then, is imperialism? It is the special and most developed form of capitalism that emerged at a particular historical juncture – the start of the twentieth century[11] – and is characterised, Lenin wrote, by its over-ripeness,[12] its tendency to decay.[13] This new stage of capitalism, he explained, was marked out by novel features that had emerged out of, and then displaced, free-market capitalism.[14] The shift to imperialism had begun in the advanced capitalist economies, which had seen the merger of production and capital to form ever larger conglomerates and the fusion of industrial capital with banking capital to create 'finance capital'.[15] In other words, capital was being concentrated into the hands of fewer and fewer enterprises and industrial monopolies were linking up with bank monopolies to exploit their market dominance – notably, Krupp in Germany, Schneider in France and Armstrong in Britain.[16] 'The supplanting of free competition by

---

[9] V. I. Lenin, 'Imperialism, the Highest Stage of Capitalism: A Popular Outline' (1917) in *Collected Works*, 45 vols (Moscow: Foreign Languages Publishing House, 1960–1970) [hereafter *LCW*], vol. 22, p. 190. Original emphases.

[10] For example, 'Japan and America are on the verge of war, and there is absolutely no possibility of preventing that war, in which another ten million will be killed and twenty million crippled' (V. I. Lenin, 'First All-Russia Congress of Working Cossacks' (1 March 1920) in *LCW*, vol. 30, p. 393).

[11] V.I. Lenin, 'Revision of the Party programme' (6–8 (19–21) October 1917) in LCW, vol. 26, p. 167.

[12] V. I. Lenin, 'Imperialism, the Highest Stage of Capitalism: A Popular Outline' (1917) in *LCW*, vol. 22, p. 242.

[13] Ibid., p. 276.

[14] Ibid., p. 298.

[15] Ibid., pp. 266, 298–9.

[16] Ibid., p. 244.

monopoly,' Lenin wrote, 'is the fundamental economic feature, the *quintessence* of imperialism.'[17]

The trouble was that monopoly capitalism could not sustain itself on the domestic market alone; it had to expand internationally in search of new sources of raw materials and new opportunities for investment. In contrast with free-market capitalism, which was distinguished by the export of goods, the newer monopoly capitalism was thus distinguished by export of *capital*.[18] So capital went global, as vast internationalised monopolies partitioned the world's market sectors among them.[19] And the flag followed capital, as the advanced states, seeking new sources of raw materials, completed the colonial project, laying claim to the last 'unclaimed' territories on earth.[20]

At this point, imperialism, driven by these economic forces, turned deadly. How could it continue to expand if the world was already divided up? After all, 'there are *no* more "free" lands that can be grabbed without war against a rival nation'.[21] The only solution was to go to war to redistribute the assets. World War I was therefore essentially 'the clash of the two most powerful groups of multimillionaires, Anglo-French and German, for the *redivision* of the world'.[22] This, Lenin noted, had a devastating effect on all those caught up in the conflict:

> The imperialist war lasted over four years, tens of millions were killed and crippled. What for? For the division of the capitalists' spoils, for markets, profits, colonies and the power of the banks. ... The Anglo-French imperialist predators defeated the German imperialist predators. With every passing day they are exposing themselves for what they are – robbers and plunderers ... who batten on the misery of the people and tyrannise weak nations.[23]

So Lenin's message could not have been more different from Welles'; in his view, it was impossible to distinguish among the imperialist powers because all of them were compelled to go to war. Without a revolution,

---

[17] V. I. Lenin, 'Imperialism and the Split in Socialism' (December 1916) in *LCW*, vol. 23, p. 105 (original emphasis).

[18] V. I. Lenin, 'Imperialism, the Highest Stage of Capitalism: A Popular Outline' (1917) in *LCW*, vol. 22, p. 240.

[19] Ibid., pp. 266–7, 298–9.

[20] Ibid., pp. 266, 299–300.

[21] V. I. Lenin, 'Revision of the Party Programme' (6–8 (19–21) October 1917) in *LCW*, vol. 26, p. 166. Original emphasis.

[22] V. I. Lenin, 'Letters from Afar: Fourth Letter' (12 (25) March 1917) in *LCW*, vol. 23, p. 335. Original emphasis.

[23] V. I. Lenin, 'Two Years of Soviet Power' (7 November 1919) in *LCW*, vol. 30, p. 126.

this lethal cycle was destined to continue: 'It cannot be prevented, not because the capitalists, taken individually, are vicious – individually they are just like other people – but because they cannot free themselves of the financial meshes in any other way.'[24] In short, war between the imperialist powers was not a choice; it was an imperative.

The months following the publication of *Imperialism* saw Lenin's return to Russia and the October 1917 revolution. This immediately plunged the fledgling state into a civil war, which pitted the Red Army, under Leon Trotsky's command, against the counter-revolutionary White armies, under Generals Denikin, Kolchak, Yudenich, Wrangel and others. At the same time, the entente powers, led by Britain, France, Japan and the United States, mounted bellicose 'interventions' against the Bolsheviks: imposing economic sanctions, supplying the White armies with *materiel* and money, and sending troops to Archangel, the Caucasus, Petrograd, Siberia and South Russia.[25] In the years after Lenin's death in 1924, the regime that took shape under Josef Stalin's leadership often invoked the 'interventions' as grounds for vigilance against new threats: imperialist agents, foreign spies and Russian traitors. Meanwhile, Lenin's ideas, while formally lauded, were selectively filleted and bent to new ends – including his concept of imperialism. The latter was drained of most of its economic content and repurposed first as rigid doctrine (Stalin's 'Concerning Questions of Leninism'[26]) then as caricature (the imperialist octopus, with legs labelled 'Britain', 'France', 'America', etc.) and finally as mere epithet ('imperialist aggressor').

1.3   Stalin's Turn to the Law

By the beginning of the 1930s, the party leadership, agitated by the growing threat posed by Germany and Japan, and recalling the experience of the 'interventions', began to consider the protections that the law might afford to the USSR against external threats. This line of thought would eventually produce the 'crimes against peace' charges deployed at the post-war international military tribunals, but the path from Moscow to Nuremberg was not an entirely smooth one. One impediment along the way was the Soviet revolution-era 'negationist' approach to the law – espoused, to a greater or

---

[24] V. I. Lenin, 'First All-Russia Congress of Working Cossacks' (1 March 1920) in *LCW*, vol. 30, p. 393.

[25] V. I. Lenin, 'Two Years of Soviet Power' (7 November 1919) in *LCW*, vol. 30, p. 124.

[26] J. V. Stalin, 'Concerning Questions of Leninism' (25 January 1926) in J. V. Stalin, *Works*, 13 vols (Moscow: Foreign Languages Publishing House, 1952–1955), vol. 8, p. 13.

lesser degree, by jurists including Pyotr Stuchka and Evgeny Pashukanis, as well as by Lenin himself (another lawyer)[27] – which saw laws and courts as residues of bourgeois society that would eventually wither away along with the state itself.

It was not until the 1930s that the opponents of the 'negationist' view, led by Procurator General Andrei Vishinsky, were able to steer the party towards a different view of the law – instead of laws and courts eventually being swept away along with the state, as the 'negationists' proposed, they should instead be retained to *consolidate* state power. The first shift in Vishinsky's direction took place in 1932–1933, when Stalin, keen to silence the many prominent critics of his collectivisation policies and to rein in the excesses that had occurred in the countryside, started to look to the law as an instrument of systematic social control. Having laid the groundwork in 1933–1934 with the introduction of policies designed to professionalise the procuracy and the judiciary and with exhortations to officials to stick to the letter of the law, Stalin and Vishinsky turned to the courts to manage the fallout from collectivisation and deal with the political opposition.[28]

Both were acutely aware of the criticisms being levelled at the party leadership by senior members of the Bolshevik old guard, who accused it of having sloughed off Leninism with its dalliances with the imperialist League of Nations, abandonment of the bread-card system, acceptance of post-Stakhanov wage differentials, campaigns against abortion and divorce, and criminalisation of young offenders. (Lenin had dismissed the last idea with the telling words, 'Courts and prisons are *corrupting*.'[29]) As well as Lenin's legacy, there was also Leon Trotsky's to contend with. Although Trotsky had been deported from the USSR in 1929, his internationalist rebuttal of Stalin's 'socialism in one country' still had to be reckoned with. What the leadership required, then, was a pretext for destroying the remaining members of the opposition. This pretext was provided by the murder of Sergei Kirov, the party leader in Leningrad, on 1 December 1934. That same month, Stalin issued two decrees on terrorism, one depriving defendants of the right of appeal and the other

---

[27] V. I. Lenin, 'The State and Revolution: The Marxist Theory of the State and the Tasks of the Proletariat in the Revolution' (1917) in *LCW*, vol. 25, pp. 472–4, 476.

[28] P. H. Solomon, *Soviet Criminal Justice under Stalin* (New York: Cambridge University Press, 1996), pp. 162–3, 164–5.

[29] V. I. Lenin, 'The Prosecution of Minors: Notes and Amendments to the Draft Decree' (4 March 1920) in *LCW*, vol. 42, p. 182. Original emphasis.

mandating execution immediately after conviction. The stage was set for dramatic new developments in the field of law.

1.4   Conspiracies and the Moscow Trials

The three 'purge' Moscow trials, conducted in 1936, 1937 and 1938, held all of the accused guilty of treason and terrorism under Article 58 of the Russian (RSFSR) Criminal Code dealing with counter-revolutionary offences.[30] While these trials were by no means the first to convict people for political crimes against the Soviet state, they were distinctive in targeting people who were, or who had once been, at the very pinnacle of the party hierarchy – in other words, *national leaders*.

The first trial, of the 'Trotskyite-Zinovievite Terrorist Centre', opened on 19 August 1936 to try sixteen oppositionists. The two most prominent defendants, Grigory Zinoviev and Lev Kamenev, had with Stalin formed the USSR's *troika* government in 1923, but Stalin had soon rid himself of them both, assuming sole leadership two years later. They had then formed the 'New Opposition', which had led to their expulsion from the party in 1927. Apparently inspired by Trotsky, they and the other defendants were accused of conspiring to commit treason and terrorism – namely, plotting to assassinate Stalin and his ministers (Kirov purportedly being the first) in order to seize power for themselves.[31]

The second and more ambitious trial, of the 'Anti-Soviet Trotsky Centre', opened on 23 January 1937 to try seventeen recanted oppositionists from the various economic sectors, including Y. L. Pyatakov, Commissar of Heavy Industry, and Y. A. Livshitz, Deputy Commissar of the Railways. As well as being charged with conspiring to commit treason and terrorism, they were also accused of espionage, wrecking and diversion, with the aim of restoring capitalism in the Soviet Union.[32]

---

[30] 'Russian Criminal Code, as Amended with Notes' (24 November 1933), pp. 31–7: Roll 19, 861.04, T1249; RG 59, Records of the Department of State Relating to Internal Affairs of the Soviet Union, 1930–1939, US National Archives and Records Administration [hereafter NARA].

[31] Report of Court Proceedings: The Case of the Trotskyite-Zinovievite Terrorist Centre Heard before the Military Collegium of the Supreme Court of the USSR, Moscow, August 19–24, 1936 (Moscow: People's Commissariat of Justice of the USSR, 1936), p. 10.

[32] Report of Court Proceedings in the Case of the Anti-Soviet Trotskyite Centre Heard before the Military Collegium of the Supreme Court of the USSR, Moscow, January 23–30, 1937 (Moscow: People's Commissariat of Justice of the USSR, 1937) [hereafter 1937 trial records], pp. 4, 6.

The final and most expansive trial of all, of the 'anti-Soviet bloc of Rights and Trotskyites', opened on 2 March 1938 to try twenty-one defendants, including surviving critics from the 'Right Opposition', such as Lenin's deputy Aleksei Rykov and *Pravda* editor Nikolai Bukharin. At this last trial, all were tried for conspiring to commit treason, terrorism, espionage, wrecking and diversion, as well as for undermining the Soviet Union's military power and for prompting foreign states – Germany, Japan, Britain and Poland – to attack it with the aim of restoring capitalism in the USSR.[33]

According to the official transcripts of these proceedings, translated into a number of foreign languages, the defendants confessed to extraordinary and outrageous crimes, denounced former colleagues and fellow defendants, and begged for hard labour instead of the bullet. But behind these stormy spectacles, methodical, even pedantic, didactic forces were at work. The instructive function of the trial was never in doubt: as the jurist Max Radin pointed out at the time, almost all of the defendants had admitted their guilt at the outset so there was really no need to go through a trial process simply to establish their guilt all over again.[34]

At each successive trial, the regime made ever bolder claims about the targets, scope and nature of the alleged offences. It is notable, for example, how the number of victims piled up: at the first trial, the victim was Sergei Kirov; at the second trial, it was the Soviet state and its people; at the third trial, it was the global proletariat. The defendants were accused of consorting with foreign powers with the aim of encouraging their attacks on the USSR, which would culminate in the nation's dismemberment: the republics would be turned into 'colonies of the imperialists' and the rule of landlords and capitalists would be restored[35] – the very epitome of economic aggression. The defendants were also held responsible for the structural faults within the Soviet economic system; precisely the sorts of fault that struck a raw nerve with Soviet citizens. At the second and third trials, for example, Knyazev, Turok and Rataichak were accused of plotting to cause train disasters and industrial explosions;[36] Chernov of infecting cattle and horses with plague and

---

[33] Report of Court Proceedings in the Case of the Anti-Soviet 'Bloc of Rights and Trotskyites' Heard before the Military Collegium of the Supreme Court of the USSR, Moscow, March 2–13, 1938 (Moscow: People's Commissariat of Justice of the USSR, 1938) [hereafter 1938 trial records], pp. 5–7.

[34] M. Radin, 'The Moscow Trials: A Legal View', *Foreign Affairs* (October 1937), 66.

[35] 1938 trial records, p. 631.

[36] 1937 trial records, pp. 11, 12.

epizootic diseases;[37] Grinko of stirring up public discontent about wage delays and the savings banks;[38] and Zelensky of holding up the distribution of eggs, sugar and makhorka (as well as spiking butter supplies with glass and nails).[39]

As the trials progressed, the prosecution, each time led by Vishinsky, alleged ever-widening circles of *conspiracy* directed against the USSR. This is not to say that conspiracies did not exist – the Germans and the Japanese were indeed conspiring against the Soviets – but the suspicion of their existence was refracted through the prism of trials designed to eviscerate Stalin's domestic opponents.

As a consequence, the doctrine of complicity played a central role throughout the proceedings. At the first two trials, the prosecution relied on Article 17 of the Russian Criminal Code, which outlined the basic concept of complicity and identified three types of participant: 'instigators', 'accomplices' and 'perpetrators'.[40] Yet, in the prosecution's view, this did not quite capture the magnitude of the alleged crimes: surely the absent Trotsky was more than a mere 'instigator'; he was the arch-conspirator! So, after the end of the second trial, in March 1937, the journal *Sotsialisticheskaia Zakonnost'* (*Socialist Legality*) reported the drafting of a new criminal code which showed the altered line of thinking about complicity.[41] A fourth category of conspirator would be added to the list – 'organiser' – who would be punished more harshly than a 'perpetrator', even if the crime was not carried out.[42] This was a refinement of the premise, apparent throughout the trials, that planning a crime was just as serious as perpetrating one.

At the 1938 trial, Vishinsky expounded more fully on the issue of complicity. He began by asking to what extent the accused would be held answerable for the crimes committed by the conspiracy and answered: 'Fully. Why? Each of the accused must be held answerable for the sum total of the crimes as a member of a conspiratorial organization whose criminal objects and aims, and whose criminal methods of carrying out these aims, were known to, approved of and accepted by each of the

[37] 1938 trial records, p. 793.
[38] Ibid., pp. 672, 673.
[39] Ibid., p. 18.
[40] 'Russian Criminal Code, as Amended with Notes', pp. 8–9.
[41] For a summary of this article, see 'Recent Tendencies in Soviet Law' (14 September 1937), p. 27: Roll 19, 861.04, T1249; RG 59, Records of the Department of State Relating to Internal Affairs of the Soviet Union, 1930–1939, NARA.
[42] Ibid.

accused.'[43] He then addressed the problem of intent. Although the aforementioned draft code of 1937 had specified that intent or negligence was a necessary component of a crime, thereby readmitting the concept of fault into Russian jurisprudence, Vishinsky was having none of it. He wrote: 'This viewpoint is wrong. . . . Life knows of examples when the results of joint criminal activity are brought about through the independent participation in such activity by individual accomplices, who are united only by a single criminal object common to all of them.'[44] To prove complicity, then, one was not required to prove a person's intent, only a common purpose – a united will to commit a crime – among the conspirators.

> To establish complicity, we must establish that there is a common line uniting the accomplices in a given crime, that there is a common criminal design. . . . If, say, a gang of robbers . . . set fire to houses, violate women, murder and so on, in one place, while another part of the gang will do the same in another place, then even if neither the one nor the other knew of the crimes committed separately by any section of the common gang, they will be held answerable to the full for the sum total of the crimes, if only it is proved that they had agreed to participate in this gang for the purpose of committing the various crimes.[45]

1.5 'Socialist Legality'

While the Moscow trials were in progress, the purge claimed yet another victim, Evgeny Pashukanis, who was scapegoated for his earlier espousal of 'negationist' views on the law. After his arrest in April 1937, Loy Henderson, the American Ambassador in Moscow, reported:

> It looks as though the Soviet legal theories which have prevailed from the time of the Revolution up to the present are being ripped wide open. The idea that laws were a sort of disgraceful and necessary heritage of bourgeois regimes . . . is apparently being abandoned. . . . It is my understanding that the arrest of Pashukanis has been followed by the arrest of a number of other professors of Soviet law and the instructors of the law schools are not quite certain what they should teach since many of the text books which they have been using have been condemned.[46]

---

[43] 1938 trial records, p. 694.
[44] Ibid., pp. 694–5.
[45] Ibid., p. 695.
[46] L. Henderson to R. F. Kelley (29 April 1937), p. 3: Roll 2, 681.00/11652–11710, T1249; RG 59, Records of the Department of State Relating to Internal Affairs of the Soviet Union, 1930–1939, NARA.

In July 1938, after Pashukanis's execution, Vishinsky, one of the architects of his downfall, triumphantly laid out his own vision for the future of Soviet legal doctrine in a *Pravda* article entitled 'About Tasks of the Soviet Socialist Law Science'.[47] He stated that his aim was to eliminate 'the consequences of the wrecking activities that were carried out by the despicable Trotskyite-Bukharin gang' in the field of Soviet legal science.[48] This gang, Vishinsky wrote, included Pashukanis (now deceased) and Nikolai Krylenko (a Stalinist rival), whose efforts 'were directed to prove that Soviet theory of law cannot and should not exist' and who were therefore responsible for 'the most shameless falsification of Marxism'.[49] He continued: 'Wreckers ranted that our law is not only moribund but also bourgeois. They implanted an idea of bourgeois law as the culminating point in the development of law.'[50]

This, he maintained, was wholly wrong. Whereas bourgeois legality brought stagnation and conservatism, socialist legality was 'a creative force promoting social development, helping toilers in their advance forward'.[51] So law not only continued to play an essential role in Soviet society but also assumed its most developed form within it: '[The] law gets its solid ground and its genuine development not in the heyday of bourgeois-capitalist relations but in the heyday of socialist relations. The era of socialism is the time of the greatest development of law and the greatest development of the rule of law; it is the triumph of law and legality.'[52]

Turning to the problem of external threats to the Soviet Union, Vishinsky encouraged the development of a Soviet doctrine of international law, which should proceed from the 'leading role of the Leninist-Stalinist foreign policy in the struggle for peace, for collective security . . . against the forces of reactionism, fascism and war'.[53] He argued that particular attention should be paid to the problem of international aggression.[54] He also called for the formation of institutions to further the global struggle 'against terrorism, against international provocations,

---

[47] A. I. Vishinsky, 'O zadachakh nauki sovetskogo sotsialisticheskogo prava', *Pravda* (26 July 1938), p. 3. Thanks to Valentyna Polunina for her translation of these excerpts from Vishinsky's *Pravda* article and Trainin's book on complicity.

[48] Ibid.

[49] Ibid.

[50] Ibid.

[51] A. I. Vishinsky, quoted in S. Kucherov, *The Organs of Soviet Administration of Justice: Their History and Operation* (Leiden: E.J. Brill, 1970), p. 661.

[52] A. I. Vishinsky, 'O zadachakh nauki sovetskogo sotsialisticheskogo prava', 3.

[53] Ibid.

[54] Ibid.

and against attempts to adapt international law to the needs and interests of fascist aggressors'.[55]

It was this international framing of the idea that would be taken up by the Soviet criminologist Aron N. Trainin and transmitted to the Nuremberg and Tokyo trials. Inspired directly by Vishinsky's *Pravda* article, Trainin began work on the first book on the Soviet theory of complicity, *Uchenie o souchastii (Doctrine of Complicity)*, published in 1941.[56] Like Vishinsky, Trainin focused on the role that the complicity doctrine might play in the management of domestic threats. He defined complicity as 'a joint participation of several persons in committing the same crime, provided each has both guilt and connection to the criminal result'.[57] It exists, he explained, only when two conditions are met: first, that two or more people are involved in the commission of a crime; and second, that these people have entered into a subjective relationship with each other in order to carry it out. '[C]omplicity is not an isolated criminal activity of several individuals,' he wrote; 'liability for complicity requires a certain subjective link between conspirators.'[58] This subjective link was that conspirators were 'serving one goal'.[59]

No sooner had Trainin's *Doctrine of Complicity* been published than the Germans invaded the Soviet Union, and he began to consider the potential for deploying the doctrine against those posing external threats to the regime. On 26 August 1943, the Soviets broadcast a radio piece entitled 'The Responsibility for Nazi crimes', based on an article Trainin had written for the journal *War and the Working Class*; and the following day, the Soviet foreign press agency Tass distributed an English-language transcript through its Soviet embassies abroad.[60] The Soviets were clearly testing the waters with the other Allies about the legal instruments that might be used when settling accounts with the German leadership at the end of the war.

In his piece, Trainin made little reference to 'imperialism' – unlike Lenin, he trod a careful line between one set of imperialist powers, the

---

[55] Ibid.
[56] A. N. Trainin, 'Uchenie o souchastii' in N. F. Kuznetsova (comp.), *Trainin, Izbrannye proizvedeniia* (St Petersburg: Iuridicheskii Tsentr Press, 2004).
[57] Ibid., p. 265.
[58] Ibid., p. 364.
[59] Ibid., p. 286.
[60] A. Farrin [Trainin], 'The Responsibility for Nazi Crimes', *Soviet Monitor* (27 August 1943): FO 371/34377, UK National Archives [hereafter TNA]. (For an earlier discussion of this report, see K. Sellars, *'Crimes against Peace' and International Law* (Cambridge University Press, 2013), pp. 48–52.)

USSR's allies, and another set, the USSR's enemies. His point was that it was the German leadership, not imperialism as such, that was responsible for the war. He argued that although material and political responsibility for waging aggressive wars resided with the state, criminal responsibility must necessarily rest with the individuals vested with its authority. Thus, it was Hitler, his cabinet and the heads of the German government who were the 'most dangerous and most vicious body of international offenders'[61] because they 'took the lead in preparing, organising and perpetrating the most heinous crime in the history of the human race, the perfidious attack on the Soviet Union'.[62] Solipsistic though this statement was, Trainin immediately grasped the essential point about aggression: that if it were to be designated a crime, it would be a crime of *leadership*, because only national leaders, with their hands on the levers of power, could operate the machinery of war.

As for the economic underpinning of German aggression, Trainin proposed to hold to account not just ministers, diplomats and military figures, but also the financiers and industrialists who had used their financial clout to underwrite the Nazi regime, which had unleashed Operation Barbarossa against the USSR in June 1941. He wrote:

> Hermann Buecher, owner of a German electrical concern, or Ernst Pengen, a steel king, do not, of course, physically help the Hitlerite soldiers and officers who have streamed over Europe to rob the peaceful population or to burn collective farm property. But these financial magnates, giving every possible support to the Hitlerite clique with their resources, factories and guns, do afford real aid to the Fascist criminals and reinforce the system of Hitlerite State banditry. Consequently the German financial and industrial heads must also be sent to trial as criminals.[63]

In order to tie the economic figures in with the political and military figures, he turned to the doctrine of complicity. Using the same formula that had been advanced at the Moscow trials, he argued that irrespective of whether such-and-such banker or captain of industry had direct personal connections with Hitler and his ministers, the 'individual members of a gang or group may not be known to one another and may yet be responsible for all the crimes the gang or group commit'.[64] The following year, in July 1944, with the publication of his book *Ugolovnaia*

[61] Farrin [Trainin], 'The Responsibility for Nazi Crimes', pp. 2–3.
[62] Ibid., p. 3.
[63] A. N. Trainin and A. Y. Vishinski (eds.), *Hitlerite Responsibility under Criminal Law*, A. Rothstein (trans.) (London: Hutchinson, 1945), p. 85.
[64] Farrin [Trainin], 'The Responsibility for Nazi Crimes', p. 3.

otvetstvennost' gitlerovtsev (released in English the following year as *Hitlerite Responsibility under Criminal Law*), Trainin was much more explicit about the doctrine's use at the third Moscow trial, and even approvingly quoted Vishinsky's courtroom comments about complicity being 'a common line uniting the accomplices in a given crime'.[65] What he was proposing, then, was that the doctrine of complicity that had first been used against those accused of committing treason against the Soviet state could now be used against the German leaders accused of committing *internationalised* treason against the society of states.

Trainin's focus on the German leadership's conspiracy to commit aggression was highly significant. By fusing the novel charge of aggression with a new internationalised mode of liability, he laid the groundwork for the prosecution of groups of national leaders – political, military and economic – for embarking on aggressive wars.

With the end of the war in sight, Western officials were also beginning to consider the problem of how to deal with the German leaders, and started to focus on Trainin's work, paying particular attention to what he called 'crimes of the Hitlerites against peace'.[66] It was precisely his approach that would be taken up at the Nuremberg and Tokyo tribunals, where the linked charges of 'crimes against peace' and 'common plan or conspiracy' were used to sweep ministers, police chiefs, bankers, diplomats, generals and ideologues into the prosecution's net.

1.6   Nuremberg and Economic 'Crimes against Peace'

In the months following the end of the European war, the discussion about how to handle the German leaders shifted to London. At the month-long London Conference, which opened on 26 June 1945, the 'big four' Allies – Britain, France, the United States and the USSR – planned the trial of the German leaders before a tribunal to be convened in Nuremberg. The Soviets fielded an experienced delegation at the conference, led by Iona T. Nikitchenko, a member of the Supreme Court of the USSR who had been one of the five judges who had heard the case of Zinoviev, Kamenev and others in August 1936; and his deputy, Aron N. Trainin, who would play an especially important role in the conference committee responsible for drafting the 'crimes against peace' charge.

---

[65] Trainin and Vishinski, *Hitlerite Responsibility under Criminal Law*, p. 84.
[66] Ibid., p. 42.

The Soviets insisted that the trial should address economic crimes as a component of the 'crimes against peace' charges: Operation Barbarossa had wreaked utter devastation across the western marches of the USSR, and those who had created the war machine and profited from the exploitation of occupied Europe should be brought to book. As Trainin argued, 'the penalty for crime must fall not only on those guilty of carrying out aggression, but also on those who try to fan the flame of war, who prepare aggression'.[67] Perhaps to their surprise, the Soviets found that they were not alone in this: two of the other Allies were also keen to indict German industrialists and financiers. One was France, which had suffered plunder, spoliation and exploitation at Germany's hands under the occupation,[68] and the other was the United States, which was keen to break up the German cartels that had excluded American firms from European markets since the 1930s.[69] (This was one of the reasons why Sumner Welles and other Washington officials lauded the free market, and why Treasury Secretary Henry Morgenthau aimed to dismantle the German economy with his 'pastoralization' plan.)

At the London Conference, the delegates of France and the United States (as well as the USSR) followed Trainin's lead by relying on both the new substantive charge of 'crimes against peace' and the internationalised mode of liability, 'common plan or conspiracy', to capture those who had bankrolled the German regime's war economy. These international legal instruments were essential because without them, a British official noted, there would be no other way of holding certain German individuals to account, 'since they have not committed specific atrocities'.[70] With this problem in mind, Robert Jackson, the American delegation leader, observed that it was only the Nuremberg tribunal 'agreement' that was capable of trapping someone like Hjalmar Schacht, the former head of the Reichsbank, and plenipotentiary of the war economy: 'If you take him out from under this agreement, you have nothing to try him on at all. Nothing except the common-plan or conspiracy theory will reach that type of man.'[71] The Soviet delegate

---

[67] Ibid., p. 37.

[68] D. Scott-Fox (18 August 1945): FO 371/50984, TNA.

[69] On the Americans' decartelisation policies in Germany after the war, see T. Bower, *Blind Eye to Murder: Britain, America and the Purging of Nazi Germany: A Pledge Betrayed* (London: Andre Deutsch, 1981), pp. 343, 347, 349, 352–5.

[70] D. Scott-Fox (18 August 1945): FO 371/50984, TNA.

[71] London Conference, Report of Robert H. Jackson, United States Representative, to the International Conference on Military Trials (Washington, DC: Department of State, 1949), p. 254.

Nikitchenko agreed, arguing that international proceedings were necessary to deal with those like Schacht 'who were the instigators of the wars of aggression, and who are, in fact, much greater criminals than the minor people who carried out murders, ill-treatment of prisoners, et cetera'.[72]

For the Western powers, however, the old problem of how to distinguish between lawful and criminal capitalist activities had not been resolved. At one of the first meetings convened to draft the indictment, Jackson observed that 'one important and troublesome problem is what we are going to do with the economic or financial side of the case'.[73] The problem was that 'we can't denounce aggressive war and in the same breath denounce trade methods and financial manipulations in international trade which, after all, are essentially peaceful means rather than war-like means'.[74]

One solution was simply to ignore economic aggression, but, of the four Allies, only the British proposed doing so. Their motives for taking this position were mixed: they observed, along with the others, that it was hard to distinguish the Germans' commercial and financial activities from the general run of capitalist enterprise; they also acknowledged, at least among themselves, that British bankers had previously done business with some of the German figures now being slated for prosecution.

On the eve of the London Conference, three Foreign Office officials who would later be closely associated with the 'crimes against peace' case at Nuremberg (for which the British prosecution team would be responsible) discussed the economic problem. Patrick Dean predicted that although the British line was to 'omit charging any economic or commercial leader', it was likely the Americans would insist on pursuing this course nevertheless.[75] David Scott-Fox agreed, but pointed out that if the other Allies were bent on highlighting the criminality of Germany's economic activities, they would find it difficult to make a good case 'unless there was an actual representative of these activities before the court'.[76] Basil Newton sounded a warning about their pursuing this line: the Germans, he said, should not be tried retroactively for economic activities that were not crimes when carried out, as this would 'shake

---

[72] Ibid.
[73] S. Alderman, 'Meeting, Friday Morning' (10 August 1945), p. 2: Box 107, Jackson Papers, Library of Congress.
[74] Ibid.
[75] P. Dean (29 June 1945): FO 371/50981, TNA.
[76] D. Scott-Fox (19 July 1945): FO 371/50983, TNA.

public confidence in the new International Court and create a precedent for grave injustices in the future'.[77]

In the event, the majority overrode the British objections, and by the end of the London Conference the question was not *whether* industrialists and financiers would be indicted for economic 'crimes against peace' but *who* would be indicted. Two names came up more than any others: those of the arms manufacturer Gustav Krupp and the banker Hjalmar Schacht.

1.7   The 'Merchants of Human Blood'

While the Allies were drafting the indictment, James Passant of the Foreign Office's Research Department weighed the likelihood of the Tribunal convicting Gustav Krupp of economic aggression. 'Unless evidence that he played a political role can be produced,' he wrote, 'the whole case against Krupp must rest on the financial support rendered by him and his fellow manufacturers to the Nazi party.'[78] The trouble with this approach was that it might invite the question: 'How much did Vickers and Baldwins (or others) contribute to the Conservative Party funds, or Dupont (and other firms in America) to the Republican and/or Democratic Party funds? Why are not the Directors of these firms, "merchants of human blood" here in the Dock beside Krupp?'[79]

As it turned out, Krupp *was* indicted but never tried. A fortnight before the start of the trial, a medical panel reported him to be senile and thus unfit to stand trial. Two days later, at a meeting of Allied prosecutors, Robert Jackson proposed that they indict Gustav's son Alfried instead.[80] The British prosecutor David Maxwell Fyfe resisted this idea: it would convey the impression that the son was inheriting the charges laid against the father.[81] Jackson protested: the Krupp firm was 'the very symbol of aggressive warfare' because 'it was their weapons which had made Europe a battleground' and, furthermore, 'Krupp typified the sinister forces which he, Mr. Justice Jackson, was sent to punish.'[82] The other prosecutors, who were unwilling to summon up a substitute for the Krupp family at that late

---

[77] B. Newton (20 July 1945): FO 371/50983, TNA.
[78] J. Passant, 'Keitel, Dönitz, Schacht and Krupp as War Criminals' (15 August 1945), p. 3: FO271/50984, TNA.
[79] Ibid.
[80] 'Minutes of Meeting of Chief Prosecutors' (9 November 1945), p. 1: FO 371/50999, TNA.
[81] D. Maxwell Fyfe, 'The Situation Arising [from] the Medical Report on Gustave Krupp' (10 November 1945): FO 371/59999, TNA.
[82] 'Minutes of Meeting of Chief Prosecutors', p. 1.

stage, voted three to one against indicting any other industrialists.[83]
Jackson delivered a parting shot: without Krupp as a representative of
German industry, '[i]t would always be said by the Left Wing that we had
deliberately failed to include any industrialists'.[84]

That left Hjalmar Schacht. James Passant, again appraising the likelihood of the Tribunal convicting him, thought the case against him was
weak.[85] 'It is well known that Schacht's economic policy . . ., in particular
his manipulation of the exchanges, was of vital assistance to the Nazis in
building up their economic system and in bringing the States of south-
eastern Europe under German economic influence,' he wrote.[86] 'But i[t]
is evident that a policy of economic penetration and control does not
necessarily imply military conquest, and may, indeed, be ruined by it.'[87]
He warned against indicting him: although he was 'an unpleasant and
unreliable character', he was 'not a war criminal in this sense of the
prosecution', and could well be acquitted.[88]

Schacht was indeed acquitted. The judges split over his guilt, and this
became public knowledge when someone in the retinue of American
judge Francis Biddle (or perhaps Biddle himself) leaked the story to the
journalist Drew Pearson.[89] Pearson duly published an account of the
judges' discussion in his syndicated column, 'Washington Merry-Go-
Round': 'At first the vote was divided – the United States and the Russian
judge voting for conviction, the French judge voting for a sentence of five
years and the British judge, Sir Geoffrey Lawrence, voting for acquittal.
(British bankers cooperated closely with Schacht for some time before the
war.)'[90] Two decades later, Biddle himself took up the story:

> [Schacht's] position was that he never wan[t]ed Germany to plunge Europe
> into war, but sought re-armament to give her a place at the conference table.

---

[83] So Alfried Krupp escaped trial for 'crimes against peace' at the international military tribunal.
Like his father, he had run the various Krupp enterprises on slave labour during the war
years, albeit on a much larger scale. Eventually, the British, who were holding him, handed
him over to the Americans, who, after trying him in 1947–1948, convicted him for war
crimes and crimes against humanity and sentenced him to twelve years' imprisonment.
Then, three years later, they pardoned him, as well as rescinding the order for the confiscation
of his property – which even the British thought was going too far (Cabinet Minutes, CM(51),
12th Conclusion, Minute 5 (8 December 1951): PREM 8/1570, TNA).

[84] 'Minutes of Meeting of Chief Prosecutors', p. 2.

[85] Ibid.

[86] J. Passant, 'Keitel, Dönitz, Schacht and Krupp as War Criminals', p. 2.

[87] Ibid.

[88] Ibid., p. 3.

[89] D. Pearson, 'Washington Merry-Go-Round', *Washington Post* (13 July 1947).

[90] Ibid.

Re-armament was not in itself a crime under the Charter. ... The case against him depended on whether he did in fact know of the Nazi plans to wage aggressive war. I voted him guilty, and that afternoon all but Lawrence agreed. The French wavered; and by the next morning Lawrence had persuaded Donnedieu De Vabres, the French member, to change his vote to 'not guilty'. This made an even vote which meant under the Charter that he was declared innocent. My younger associates wanted me to file a dissent – but to what end? It was, I believed more important that we should speak as a unit ... than that I should express my view that a banker could be as guilty as a general, even though acting with cleaner hands.[91]

Nikitchenko, aghast, *did* dissent. Citing documents produced in court, he asked: had Schacht not organised the financing of the Nazi Party's election campaign in 1933, demanding three million marks from fellow industrialists?[92] Had he not 'used swindler's tactics and coercion' to acquire raw material and foreign currency for armaments?[93] Had he not declared that the Reichsbank under him was 'none other than a National Socialist institution'?[94] Had he not admitted to saying that colonies had to be acquired if not by negotiation then by seizure?[95] Was he not kept constantly informed about the financing required for the development of the German armed forces?[96] And did he not boast that the Reichsbank's credit policy had created an 'unsurpassed ... war machine'?[97]

In the Judgment, the Tribunal tried to paper over the rift. It acknowledged that Schacht was a pivotal figure in Germany's re-armament programme, but also noted that, under the Nuremberg Charter, re-armament was not a crime: 'To be a Crime against Peace under Article 6 of the Charter it must be shown that Schacht carried out this rearmament as part of the Nazi plans to wage aggressive wars.'[98] It accepted his defence that he had tried to slow down the pace of re-armament after discovering the regime's plans to pursue aggressive war, and then, finding him not guilty, ordered his release.

---

[91] F. Biddle, 'The Sentences at Nurnberg' (1966), pp. 2–3: Box 7, Folder 53, Biddle Papers, Georgetown University Library.

[92] 'Dissenting Opinion of the Soviet Member', in International Military Tribunal, Trial of the Major War Criminals before the International Military Tribunal, 'The Blue Series', 42 vols (Nuremberg: IMT, 1947–1949), vol. 1, p. 342.

[93] Ibid., p. 343.

[94] Ibid.

[95] Ibid., p. 346.

[96] Ibid., p. 345.

[97] Ibid.

[98] Judgment, ibid., p. 307.

1.8   Conclusion

Schacht's acquittal at Nuremberg signalled the winding down of the Allied powers' attempts to criminalise aggression in both its economic and its military forms. At the subsequent *IG Farben* and *Krupp* cases mounted by the Americans at Nuremberg in late 1947, all thirty-six industrialists were acquitted of 'crimes against peace' and associated conspiracy counts (although a number were convicted of war crimes and crimes against humanity). At another tribunal convened by the French at Rastatt in early 1948, industrialist Hermann Röchling was convicted of waging aggressive war (and crimes against humanity), but, months later, the aggression finding was reversed on appeal.[99] Meanwhile, at the 1946–1948 International Military Tribunal for the Far East in Tokyo, none of those responsible for bankrolling Japan's war or running the *zaibatsu* were brought to trial for their economic activities during the Asia-Pacific War.

By the early 1950s, the Soviets, having earlier turned to legal means to settle the bill with their wartime enemies, resorted to more traditional political mechanisms for dealing with their new Cold War foes, including denouncing them as 'imperialist aggressors'. This shift was bound up with the suspicion of any form of international criminal law with potential application to themselves: it was one thing for Moscow to support ad hoc tribunals dealing exclusively with the Germans and the Japanese at Nuremberg and Tokyo, but quite another to accept the jurisdiction of an international criminal court over the 'crime of aggression' – a stance which the Russian Federation still maintains today.

As a consequence, the Soviets' decisive contribution to the articulation of the substantive charge of 'crimes against peace', their identification of the attendant mode of liability of complicity, and their insistence on prosecuting economic as well as military aggression, have rarely been properly acknowledged. This is not surprising because it draws attention to an unpalatable truth: that the lineage of the modern concepts of 'aggression' and 'complicity' in international criminal law can be traced straight back to the Moscow trials of 1936–1938.

---

[99] T. Taylor, 'The Nuremberg War Crimes Trial', *International Conciliation* 450 (1949), 339.

Forced Labour and Norwegian War Profiteers in the Legal Purges after World War II

HANS OTTO FRØLAND

After being found guilty in November 1948 of national treason due to commercial collaboration with Germany during its occupation of Norway, the businessman Ditlef Lexow was given one of the harshest sentences among the 3,355 Norwegians found guilty before the Norwegian courts of criminal commercial collaboration with the enemy. According to the sentencing judgment: 'The accused has been one of our country's largest war profiteers, who immediately after the invasion entered into commercial relations to the benefit of the enemy and who continued to proactively serve the Germans. His appetite on German contracts was apparently insatiable. He seems to have been devoid of national sentiment in this respect.'[1] Operating as a shipbroker before the invasion, he had entered into contracts with the enemy only a few days after the German attack on 9 April 1940, and he contributed to German naval logistics long before the campaign ended. Responding subsequently to German demands from various sources, he established several new companies to provide services and commodities which the court in 1948 regarded as important for the enemy's war effort. The sentencing decision confiscated a large proportion of his profits, imposed a fine, suspended some of his democratic rights as a citizen, and imposed upon him eight years of forced labour.

The Lexow case confirms that the notion of improper war profits was the pivotal point when the courts addressed the massive commercial involvement of Norwegian business with the enemy during the occupation. Yet the court ignored the fact that some of Mr Lexow's companies had from 1943 employed around 700 civilian forced labourers from the Soviet Union. The Lexow case was not an exception in this respect.

---

[1] Riksarkivet (National Archives), Oslo (henceforth RA), Landssvikarkivet, L-sak, 4303–4304, Ditlef Lexow, box 3, folder 12b.

Possible exploitation of foreign forced labour by Norwegian firms was largely ignored during police investigations, in the indictments, and during court proceedings. During the purges, no nexus was ever established between Norwegian war profits and possible ill-treatment of forced labourers working for the firms. Neither were possible war crimes by the Norwegian firms against these foreign workers investigated.

This consistent neglect stands in contrast to what happened in the Nuremberg trials, where the 'slave labour program' – a term introduced in the trials – was a count in the indictment against several members of the Nazi elite.[2] In the prosecution of Nazi industrialists during the subsequent Nuremberg trials between 1946 and 1949, abuse and ill-treatment of slave labourers was again a core count. Historian Kim Priemel maintains: 'Indeed, forced labour would become the center of the industrialist trials, due to the massive amount of available evidence which rendered outright denial impossible but also on account of the manifest moral implications.'[3] Most of the leaders and owners of the IG Farben, Flick, and Krupp concerns had a penalty imposed on them, while other industrialists were acquitted.

The comparison is relevant because the Nuremberg trials largely focused on foreign forced labour brought to the *Reich,* and Norway was a large net receiver as well (whereas most other occupied countries were net suppliers). Therefore, the overall question guiding this chapter is why the nexus between excessive war profits and exploitation of forced labour was so weak during the Norwegian legal settlement. The answer takes account of the fact that the focus on exploitation of forced labour at Nuremberg and subsequent tribunals corresponded to norms inherent in international law (war crimes, crimes against humanity) whereas the Norwegian neglect followed from a strict framing of national law. Cases related to criminal commercial collaboration were pursued from the perspective of national treason. Because the Allies had agreed that each country should prosecute war crimes against its nationals, Norwegian jurisprudence was allowed to sustain its bias towards national treason. This meant that Norwegian businesses which had in various ways been involved in the Nazi slave

---

[2] R. E. Conot, *Justice at Nuremberg* (New York: Harper & Row, 1983), pp. 429–44; K. C. Priemel, Arbeitsverwaltung vor Gericht. Das Reichsarbeitsministerium und die Nürnberger Prozesse 1945-1949, in A. Nützenadel (ed.), *Das Reichsarbeitsministerium im Nationalsozialismus: Verwaltung, Politik, Verfahren* (Göttingen: Wallstein Verlag, 2017), pp. 461–93.

[3] K. C. Priemel, *The Betrayal: The Nuremberg Trials and the German Divergence* (Oxford: Oxford University Press, 2016), p. 209.

labour programme were never properly investigated for possible exploitation of foreign forced labour. Consequently, whereas German historiography has elaborated on the nexus between forced labour and war profits, the Norwegian counterpart has not.[4]

The first section of this chapter explains the massive economic collaboration and the extensive use of forced labour that followed from the German construction schemes. The second section elaborates on how the notion of improper war profits influenced the legal purge of business collaborators and the third section goes on to analyse the reasons why the exploitation of forced labour was neglected.

2.1 The German Economic Expansion in Occupied Norway

Nazi Germany occupied Norway for military-strategic reasons, to serve as a naval bridgehead that would allow the German navy access beyond the anticipated British blockade in the Skagerak waters. The geo-strategic significance increased in 1941 as Germany attacked northern Soviet Union from northern Norway through northern Finland and the Anglo-American convoys heading towards Murmansk started operating. Further, Hitler himself feared an Allied landing in Norway. In sum, Norway's strategic significance led Germany to maintain a large garrison in the country, making up between 10 per cent and 20 per cent of the indigenous population.

Military and civilian infrastructure was generally poor in the occupied country. Consequently, Norway was soon made into a large construction site where various German builders established airfields, harbours, naval docks, submarine shelters, artillery fortifications, as well as roads, railway lines, power stations, and various industrial infrastructures. In 1941, the Reich Commissariat, the dictatorial civilian government established by Hitler, counted 1,600 construction projects and admitted that German builders controlled 90 per cent of construction activity in the country.[5] The German agencies offered generous contracts and pay, and therefore

---

[4] Regarding compensation for forced labour, see in particular the four-volume series by C. Goschler et al., *Die Entschädigung von NS-Zwangsarbeit am Anfang des 21. Jahrhunderts. Die Stiftung "Erinnerung, Verantwortung und Zukunft" und ihre Partnerorganisationen* (Göttingen: Wallsten Verlag, 2014). On the precedent setting court decision, see J. R. Rumpf, *Der Fall Wollheim gegen die I.G. Farbenindustrie AG in Liquidation* (Frankfurt: Pieter Lang, 2016). On industry's handling of its forced labour legacy, see S. Brünger, *Geschichte und Gewinn. Der Umgang deutscher Konzerne mit ihrer NS-Vergangenheit* (Göttingen: Wallstein Verlag, 2016).
[5] H. O. Frøland, 'Organisasjon Todt som byggherre i Norge' [Organisation Todt as builder in Norway] (2018) 97(3) *Historisk Tidsskrift* (Norwegian) 168–89.

demand caused a bonanza in the economy which drained resources to the German sector and soon removed domestic unemployment. German ambitions had exceeded Norwegian resources by spring 1942 and Hitler ordered Albert Speer to accelerate the war-related building schemes. Hitler ordered an increase in the resources to be taken from Germany and brought to Norway. Since the Norwegian business and labour force was already fully exploited, Speer mustered firms from the German *Reich* and forced labour from occupied countries for a massive *Norwegeneinsatz*. Estimates indicate that possibly 500 foreign companies were mobilised. Many Norwegian firms or companies combined operations as sub-contractors with the German firms, but many continued to work directly for German agencies as well. Unfortunately, the records do not reveal the exact number of Norwegian companies involved. Neither do we know the exact number of Norwegian workers on the German schemes. Estimates vary between 150,000 and 300,000.[6] If we assume that a population of 3 million had a workforce of slightly below 1 million persons, a considerable share worked on the German account during the occupation. Some of these workers were allocated through the Norwegian Labour Offices, which were given increasing powers to allocate labour.[7] A rough estimate indicates that between 50,000 and 60,000 Norwegians were forced labourers.[8] When preparing the official Norwegian demand for German war reparations in the autumn of 1945, the government estimated that 540,000 Norwegian annual full-time equivalents had been performed on the German account.[9]

Already by spring 1941, the Norwegian labour shortage was a bottleneck that constrained the German construction schemes. As indicated above, labour supply had to originate from abroad. Nazi

---

[6] H. Espeli, 'De gjorde landet større' [They enlarged the country] (2006) 106(1) *Historisk Tidsskrift* (Danish), 382–99.

[7] H. O. Frøland, G. D. Hatlehol and M. Ingulstad, 'Regimenting Labour in Norway during Nazi Germany's Occupation', Working Paper Series A, No. 12, Working Papers of the Independent Commission of Historians Investigating the History of the Reich Ministry of Labour (*Reichsarbeitsministerium*) in the National Socialist Period, www.historikerkommission-reich sarbeitsministerium.de/sites/default/files/inline-files/Working%20Paper%20UHK% 20A12_Fr%C3%B8land%2BHatlehol%2BIngulstad_0.pdf.

[8] G. Hatlehol, 'Tvangsstyringen av arbeidslivet under hakekorset 1940–1945: Diktat og kollaborasjon' [Governing labour under the swastika: force and collaboration] (2018) 22 *Arbeiderhistorie* 49–71.

[9] *Stortingstidende* 8 November 1948, in Kongeriket Norges niogåttiende ordentlige Stortings fortsatte forhandlinger 1945. Forhandlinger i Stortinget [parliamentary papers] (Oslo: Centraltrykkeriet, 1945), p. 185.

Germany had from 1939 employed foreign forced labour within its borders. The number peaked in September 1944 when it reached around 7.5 million persons, which then made up 21 per cent of the total labour force.[10] The number of foreign citizens who for shorter or longer periods were forced to work in the *Reich* during World War II reached almost 15 million, of which around 10 million were civilians and 4.6 million prisoners of war (POWs).[11] As the number of German citizens conscripted to military service increased from 1.4 million to 12.4 million between 1939 and 1944, the massive supply of foreign forced labour allowed the Nazis to largely sustain its labour force, which only sank from 39 million to 36 million in this period.[12]

Immediately after the attack on Poland, the German Army supplied Polish POWs to German agriculture and industry. Although the number of Polish POWs was relatively low, it passed a million after the French defeat in the summer of 1940. Whereas Germany retained about 80,000 Polish POWs as Poland ceased to exist, a share of the French was returned as the Vichy government negotiated a release programme. Belgium, the Netherlands, and Norway negotiated release as well. The number of POWs in Germany nevertheless increased massively from 1942, as Hitler in October 1941 decided to exploit Soviet POWs rather than let them deliberately die of starvation.[13] Soviets and French made up the bulk of POWs but about half a million Italians were included after the Italian armistice in 1943. Nationals of the Balkan states were also represented. In January 1945, the employment of POWs peaked at 2.2 million.[14]

The Nazis generally treated Western POWs in accordance with the Geneva Convention, though with some exceptions for French and Belgian Waloons.[15] However, in general they did not comply with the Geneva Convention for POWs from Eastern Europe.[16] According to the

---

[10] H. Pfahlmann, *Fremdarbeiter und Kriegsgefangenen in der deutschen Kriegswirtschaft* (Darmstadt: Wehr und Wissen Verlagsgesellschaft, 1968), p. 228.

[11] M. Spoerer, *Zwangsarbeit unter dem Hakenkreuz* (Stuttgart: DVA, 2001), p. 223.

[12] D. Petzina, 'Die Mobilisierung deutscher Arbeitskräfte vor und während des Zweiten Weltkriegs' (1970) 18(4) *Vierteljahrshefte für Zeitgeschichte* S. 445–55, 450.

[13] C. Streit, *Keine Kameraden. Die Wehrmacht und die sovjetischen Kriegsgefangenen, 1941–45* (Stuttgart: DVA, 1978), p. 201.

[14] Ibid., p. 70.

[15] S. P. MacKenzie, 'The Treatment of Prisoners of War in World War II' (1994) 66(3) *The Journal of Modern History* 487–520.

[16] On the Geneva Convention, see T. Meron, 'The Geneva Conventions as Customary Law' (1987) 81(2) *American Journal of International Law* 348–70. On prisoners of war, see A. Rosa, *The Legal Status of Prisoners of War in International Humanitarian Law Applicable in Armed Conflicts* (Helsinki: Academic Bookstore, 1976).

historian Mark Spoerer, for some of these nationalities the Nazis completely ignored the protections laid down in international law.[17] There is general agreement among historians that the Soviet POWs suffered the hardest conditions, continuously receiving insufficient provisions. Among the 3.3 million Soviet POWs, 57 per cent died in German captivity. Nazi Germany legitimised the harsh treatment of Soviet citizens by relying on the fact that the Soviet Union, in contrast to Germany, had not ratified the Geneva Convention of 1929.[18]

The German Ministry of Labour had started recruiting foreign civilians as well in 1939. Initially, the Nazis targeted workers from the Protectorate before moving to occupied countries, where they set up recruitment agencies. In Eastern Europe, the agencies soon applied means of compulsion, whereas in Western Europe, allured by generous pay, citizens enlisted for work in Germany. A balance between supply and demand nevertheless took a long time to be achieved, leading the Nazi authorities in spring 1942 to appoint Fritz Sauckel as plenipotentiary for work recruitment.[19] He immediately started targeting complete birth-year cohorts in the Soviet Union. The havoc he wreaked in Eastern Europe, where individuals and groups were often arbitrarily captured, soon became infamous. Sauckel implemented equivalent programmes in Western Europe from 1943, first in France and Belgium, and later in the Netherlands. Although less brutal than in the East, recruitment in the West was now by force.[20] Having initially entered into contracts voluntarily, foreign labourers could no longer leave their contracts freely. The largest groups of civilian forced labour consisted of Soviet, Polish, and French citizens. Yet workers from the Netherlands, Belgium, and the Protectorate made up less than half a million each. Conforming with the Nazi racial hierarchy, living and working conditions varied greatly among the different nationalities. Soviet and Polish workers faced the harshest conditions.

Neither POWs nor civilians from Norway were taken to Germany to perform forced labour. On the contrary, the Reich Commissariat in Oslo had already by March 1941 started elaborating on the plan to procure

---

[17] Spoerer, 2001 (*supra* n. 11), p. 99.
[18] Geneva Convention of 27 July 1929 relative to the treatment of prisoners of war.
[19] S. Grewe, Der Generalbevollmächtigte für den Arbeitseinsatz und das Reichsarbeitsministerium, in A. Nützenadel (ed.), *Das Reichsarbeitsministerium im Nationalsozialismus: Verwaltung, Politik, Verfahren* (Göttingen: Wallstein Verlag, 2017), pp. 387–442.
[20] H. Klemann and S. Kudryashov, *Occupied Economies: An Economic History of Nazi-Occupied Europe, 1939–1945* (London and New York: Berg, 2012), pp. 119–71.

foreign forced labour for Norway and in August the first Soviet POWs arrived. However, it was only in 1942 that Soviet POWs started arriving in large numbers, after Hitler himself in August ordered 33,000 new Soviet POWs to work for *Organisation Todt* (OT) in Norway.[21] This building organisation, which originated in the state agency responsible for erecting Hitler's *Autobahn* network, had in 1938 been commissioned by Hitler to build the Westwall (Siegfriedline), the defence line against France. Since the attack on Poland, the OT had been part of the Wehrmacht's auxiliary forces (*Wehrmachtgefolge*) in occupied territories ('front zones') and was covered internally by the German military penal code (Militärstrafgesetzbuch) and externally by the laws and customs of war.[22] The Army established a Commander of POWs in Norway (*Kriegsgefangenen-Bezirkskommandant Norwegen*) to coordinate the allocation of the POWs to various Norwegian building sites.[23] The number of Soviet POWs forced to work in Norway reached more than 90,000.[24] Having by early 1942 called for 225 Soviet POW camps in Norway, in May 1945 the number was approaching 500. As evidence of the harsh conditions, after the war a British investigation found that calories for Soviet POWs, which had been low to begin with, went down progressively during the last year of occupation. Due to exhaustion, malnutrition, and disease, at least half of the POWs were unfit for work.[25] An estimate maintains that around 13,700 died, of which 10,700 died on land and 3,000 under transport at sea. In addition to the Soviet POWs, about 1,600 Polish POWs were procured.[26] Their conditions were considerably better. Although they were not accepted as

---

[21] G. Hatlehol, 'Norwegeneinsatz' 1940–1945. Organisasjon Todts arbeidere og graden av tvang (OT's workers in Norway and their subjection to force), unpublished doctoral dissertation (Trondheim: Norwegian University of Science and Technology, 2015), pp. 209–10.

[22] S. Gogl, Laying the Foundations of Occupation. Organisation Todt and the German Construction Industry in Occupied Norway, unpublished doctoral dissertation (Trondheim: Norwegian University of Science and Technology, 2019), pp. 164–6.

[23] Hatlehol, 2015 (*supra* n. 21), pp. 214–15.

[24] M. N. Soleim, *Sovjetiske krigsfanger i Norge 1941–1945. Antall, organisering og repatriering* (Soviet POWs in Norway: Number, organisation and repatriation) (Oslo: Spartacus Forlag, 2009), p. 44.

[25] National Archives, Kew, London (henceforth NA), FO 371/57653, War Crimes Investigation Branch, Norway: War Crimes in Norway, 21 March 1946.

[26] Soleim, 2009 (*supra* n. 24), p. 43; Hatlehol, 2015 (*supra* n. 21), p. 213; E. Denkiewicz-Szczepaniak, 'Polske OT-tvangsarbeidere og krigsfanger i Norge under annen verdenskrig' [Polish forced labour under OT in Norway] (1997) 76(2) *Historisk Tidsskrift* (Norwegian) 268–81.

POWs *de jure* as Poland was no longer a legal entity, they were de facto acknowledged as POWs in accordance with the Geneva Convention, and received visits and provisions by the International Red Cross. Whereas about 10 per cent of the Soviet POWs died on Norwegian soil, the Polish share was only 1 per cent.[27]

A national group that was treated even worse than the Soviet POWs was the about 4,500 ethnic Serbs (many of whom were of Croatian nationality). Consistently referred to as partisan prisoners, these were regarded as criminals and not recognised as POWs. The SS took care of security and surveillance, for which it established an SS guard battalion of around 360 Norwegians (*SS Vaktbataljon Norge*) which tended to be as brutal as German SS staff.[28] Lack of adequate camp facilities led to very poor hygienic conditions and caused diseases to spread, but deliberate killings, including mass killings, occurred as well. The first year, in the five Yugoslav camps in northern Norway, the survival rate was only 27 per cent. The poor humanitarian conditions became known in international media, whereas the Wehrmacht and OT voiced concerns about annihilating scarce labour. Therefore, the Wehrmacht took over surveillance and guarding of the camps and, as a consequence, the working and living conditions improved considerably. The Yugoslavs were from that moment onwards treated as POWs and allowed to receive support from the International Red Cross. When Norway was liberated in May 1945, the Yugoslavs were generally in much better health than the Soviet POWs.[29]

To summarise, having initially employed Norwegian (and Danish) voluntary workers, the German agencies would rely locally on possibly 60,000 Norwegian forced labourers as well. Gunnar Hatlehol has estimated the number of civilians brought to Norway through Fritz Sauckel's trans-European operations from 1942 to be around 15,000, possibly more. Twenty-one nationalities were represented, but the largest group originated in the Soviet Union, the so-called *Ostarbeiter* from Russia, Belarus and Ukraine. In Norway, as in Germany, the civilian workforce from Eastern European faced less generous conditions than their

[27] Soleim, 2009 (*supra* n. 24), pp. 96–8; Hatlehol, 2015 (*supra* n. 21), pp. 248–50.
[28] N. Christie, *Fangevoktere i konsentrasjonsleire. En sosiologisk undersøkelse av norske fangevoktere i 'serberleirene' i Nord-Norge 1942–43* [A sociological inquiry into the Yugoslav camps in Northern Norway] (Oslo: Pax Forlag, 1972).
[29] M. Stokke, Jugoslaviske fanger i Norge 1942–1945. Fra SS-regime til Wehrmacht regime, [Yugoslav captives in Norway from SS to Wehrmacht regime], unpublished doctoral dissertation manuscript.

counterparts from Western Europe.[30] In addition to the civilians came the POWs, 90,000 Soviets and 1,600 Poles, and a further 4,500 Yugoslav prisoners. By working for German agencies or companies, Norwegian workers and companies were more or less integrated into the Nazi slave labour programme.

2.2   Legal Purges of War Profiteers and Confiscation of War Profits

The Norwegian government authorised through its criminal law the investigation of around 16,500 legal subjects, companies and individuals, for their commercial relations with German agencies, during the legal settlement. Around 20 per cent of those investigated were convicted. Among the 3,355 convictions, about 1,900 – 42 per cent – were exclusively for war profiteering, while the remaining convictions included political-ideological treason.[31] For most of the 3,355 convictions, the courts imposed rather mild penalties.[32] Only 777 persons were sentenced to prison or detention and 105 among these, including Ditlef Lexow, were sentenced to hard labour as well.[33] The large majority of convicted persons received fines in addition to being forced to return profits to the state.

The purpose of this section is to explain why so few were convicted in light of the extent of collaboration by Norwegian business and industry with German agencies. This is a significant question because the penal law stated that war profits would be confiscated only from legal subjects convicted of national treason.[34] However, it remains unknown how much of the confiscated 290 million kroner that originated in war profiteering was applied in respect of other forms of treason as well.

To understand this, we shall return to the *Lexow* case. The court concluded that Mr Lexow's business collaboration was an obvious case of national treason, but the fact that in autumn 1940 he had also joined the Quisling Party (*Nasjonal Samling*) made the sentence harsher, although he had been a passive member. This suggests that political-ideological

---

[30] Hatlehol, 2015 (*supra* n. 21), pp. 416, 355–60.
[31] H. F. Dahl, *En kort historie om rettsoppgjøret* (Short history of the post-war legal purge) (Oslo: Pax Forlag, 2018), pp. 94–5.
[32] Norges Offisielle Statistikk XI.179, Statistikk over landssvik 1940–1945 (Official statistics on national treason) (Oslo: Statistisk Sentralbyrå, 1954), p. 30.
[33] Ibid., p. 31.
[34] E. Solem, *Landssvikanordningen (Prov. Anordn. Av 15. desbr. med tillegg) med kommentarer* [The Treason Ordinance with comments] (Oslo: Johan Grundt Tanum, 1945).

collaboration was the prime target during the purges. Of the about 46,000 convictions during the legal settlement, more than 43,000 fell under political-ideological collaboration.[35] It is telling in regard to priorities that the government-in-exile, based in London, adopted the ordinance covering treason for political-ideological relations with the enemy in January 1942 and the equivalent for commercial relations in December 1944. The former ordinance was given retroactive effect, being valid in law from the day of the German invasion. Furthermore, for membership of the Quisling Party, the ordinance imposed joint and several liability.[36] Scholars have concluded that, in terms of norms of justice, this part of the purges was deficient, and it has even been characterised as 'class justice'.[37]

What appeared as a moderate confiscation of war profits in contrast to the strict jurisprudence of political treason turned into a pertinent question for the newborn Norwegian democracy. The Court of Appeal acquitted several citizens who had received a sentence for commercial treason in the lower courts. Therefore, critics soon called in the public media for a general confiscation of war profits and stated that the soft treatment of commercial collaboration must catch up with the jurisprudence concerning political-ideological treason.[38] The Ministry of Justice appointed a committee in 1946 to elaborate on whether Parliament should enact a provision that allowed the government to confiscate war profits on civil grounds, which in practice would allow for the targeting of citizens who were not criminalized. This was rejected by the committee as well as the ministry.[39] The aim of the Labour government was to 'confiscate' non-criminal profits through fiscal policy, but the monetary reform was less profound than initially envisaged.[40]

---

[35] B. H. Borge and L.-E. Vaale, *Grunnlovens største prøve. Rettsoppgjøret etter 1945* [A major test of the Constitution. The post-war legal purge] (Oslo: Scandinavian Academic Press, 2018), p. 12.

[36] Ibid., p. 66.

[37] H. Espeli, 'Det økonomiske forholdet mellom Tyskland og Norge 1940-1945' [The economic relationship between Norway and Denmark], in H. F. Dahl et al. (eds.), *Danske tilstander-norske tilstander 1940–1945* (Oslo: Forlaget Press, 2010), p. 158; H. P. Graver, 'Rettsoppgjøret i Norge etter krigen-tid for nytt juridisk blikk?' [The post-war legal purge – time for revisionism?] (2015) 54(2) *Lov og Rett* 65–86.

[38] E.g. *Adresseavisen* (Norwegian newspaper) 10.9.1946 and 7.10.1946.

[39] Ot. meld.nr.2 (1945–46) Om inndragning av tyskerfortjeneste utenfor landssvikforhold [On confiscation of war profits beyond national treason], in *Stortingsforhandlinger* (Parliamentary papers) 3b, 1945–46.

[40] E. Lie, 'Pengesanering og reguleringsøkonomi' [Monetary reform and regulation economy] (1994) 73 *Historisk Tidsskrift* (Norwegian) 54–71.

Hence, only war profits from convicted collaborators would be confiscated. The legal basis for the courts when judging whether commercial collaboration fell under national treason was the Criminal Law of 1902 and the Treason Ordinance enacted in 1944. Indeed, existing criminal law included provisions to convict Norwegian citizens for aiding an enemy state through commercial relations, but the parliament had passed this legislation in 1902 with a short war in mind. Admittedly, a potential war against Sweden lingered as the political elite pursued independence from Sweden (the Swedish Norwegian Union was dissolved in 1905), but the argument was general. The notion of total war was far away from the legislators' imagination and the legislation anticipated neither a long occupation nor the rights of an occupying power laid down in the Convention Respecting the Laws and Customs of War on Land (Hague IV, 1907). The 1902 Law, which prescribed a minimum sentence of three years' imprisonment for aiding the enemy, also failed to account for the fact that economic collaboration was an imperative during a long occupation, or that Hague IV authorised Nazi Germany to draw supplies from the occupied country to maintain the occupation. Therefore, the government-in-exile enacted the 1944 Treason Ordinance to account for legitimate commercial collaboration with the enemy by legally drawing up the boundary as to when commercial collaboration would be subsumed under national treason. Further, the ordinance diversified legal sanctions against treason.

Business collaboration with German agencies had not been much of a concern when the government-in-exile enacted the ordinance covering political-ideological collaboration in early 1942. On the contrary, civilian Norwegian authorities in Oslo and London had since the invasion encouraged business collaboration to avoid the social crisis of an economic collapse.[41] A highly import-dependent Norway had supplies from the UK and the United States cut off and would have to collaborate. This policy changed incrementally in 1941–1942, implying that London increasingly encouraged 'good Norwegians' to work slowly and sabotage silently. Negative connotations attached to war profits and war profiteers had lingered in the public since the invasion in 1940, as commercial collaboration expanded. The term 'barracks baron' had surfaced in 1940, meaning a Norwegian who made excessive war profits by supplying the

---

[41] N. D. Kroglund, *Hitlers norske hjelpere: Nordmenns samarbeid med Tyskland 1940–45* [Hitler's Norwegian helpers: Norwegians' collaboration with Germany] (Oslo: Forlaget Historie & Kultur, 2010), pp. 65–122.

Wehrmacht garrison with barracks. The term 'Judas money' surfaced after the Nazi surrender, meaning war profits derived from national betrayal. The government's changed policy towards collaboration reinforced the negative sentiment towards war profiting. In retrospect, the Norwegian historian Magne Skodvin provided a convincing interpretation for why this occurred: 'good Norwegians' ought not to earn excessive war profits because these were 'inversely related to fellow citizens' misery'.[42] By 1942, the German civilian security agencies turned more repressive towards the civilian society. In effect, excessive war profits were from 1942 more clearly regarded as being inconsistent with general norms of 'national behaviour'.

Legal experts in the leadership of the Resistance Movement in Oslo worked out the revision of the Treason Ordinance, which was accepted by the government-in-exile in London. The preparatory works disclosed its motivation: 'Financial punishment of traitors has emerged as a people's demand during the occupation. . . . Those who have betrayed their country and inflicted misery and damage upon fellow citizens and our community must not retain their wealth after the purge.'[43] The ordinance would therefore allow for fines and confiscation of war profits. The Resistance wanted to sharpen the legislation on commercial treason as well but acknowledged that it would be impossible for the government to treat the bulk of its citizens as traitors: 'One has to de-criminalise many relations which under a short war would have led to penalties.'[44] To take account of this overall dilemma, they introduced the legal notion of 'improper' commercial relations with the enemy to distinguish between legitimate collaboration and national treason. The Treason Ordinance explicitly maintained that 'improper' meant operating proactively in pursuit of profits, for example by initiating a commercial relation with

---

[42] M. Skodvin, 'Historisk innleiing' [Historical introduction], in *Om landssvikoppgjøret. Innstilling fra et utvalg nedsatt for å skaffe til veie materiale til en innberetning fra Justisdepartementet til Stortinget* [About the post-war legal purge. Report by commission appointed to submit a report to the parliament] (Gjøvik: Mariendals boktrykkeri, 1962), p. 33.

[43] Innst.S.nr. 160 (1963–64) Innstilling fra justiskomiteen om landssvikoppgjøret [Position by the parliament's Justice Committee on the report mentioned in footnote 42], in *Stortingsforhandlinger* (Parliamentary papers) 6a, 1962–63, 333.

[44] J. Andenæs, *Det vanskelige oppgjøret: rettsoppgjøret etter okkupasjonen* [Difficult jurisprudence: the post-war legal purge] (Oslo: Tano Aschehaug, 1998), p. 157; E. Løchen, 'Om behandling av norske økonomiske forbrytere under landssvikoppgjøret' [On the treatment of economic crimes during the post-war legal purge] (1991) 2 *Lov og Rett* 105–13.

the enemy without being forced, expanding or accelerating the business, or seeking other collusive benefits from the German partner. The jurist Erik Solem, who took part in working out the Ordinance in 1944 and authored its published commentaries before the legal settlement started in the summer of 1945, maintained that a company established during the occupation would more easily be regarded as 'improper' whereas a company established before the occupation would more easily be regarded as 'proper'.[45] Although Solem added that the term was not exhaustively defined in the Ordinance and that subsequent jurisprudence must take account of all relevant circumstances, the core element of commercial treason was the notion that opportunistic pursuit of war profits violated the solidarity of the nation. War profiting was 'nationally blameworthy'.

The rather ambiguous notion of 'improper' made the legal settlement regarding commercial collaboration quite ambiguous as well.[46] Its practical implication would be decided in the jurisprudence. Therefore, in a speech to the national association of judges in September 1946, the Director of Public Prosecutions (*Riksadvokaten*) provided a set of guiding criteria and called for the courts, implicitly the Supreme Court, to set a precedent.[47] A commission appointed by the parliament maintained in retrospect that the change of legal norms regarding commercial collaboration during the war necessarily confused legal enforcement.[48] Many of the 3,355 cases were appealed and around 250 ended up in the Supreme Court. Johs. Andenæs, a professor in criminal law who worked for the Director of Public Prosecutions during the legal settlement, maintained in retrospect that the jurisprudence was not consistent.[49] The legislators nevertheless reached their objective, namely to target Norwegian war profiteers without criminalising a large part of the population. This interpretation is supported by the fact that, already before the settlement started, ordinary workers and functionaries were in fact excluded unless their cases were obvious acts of commercial treason.

---

[45] Solem, 1945 (*supra* n. 34), pp. 51–9.

[46] E. Corneliussen, *Det økonomiske landssvikoppgjøret* [The economic treason purge] (Oslo: E. Corneliussen, 1947).

[47] S. Arntzen, 'De økonomiske landssviksaker' [The cases on economic treason], *Riksadvokatens Meddelelsesblad* [Journal of the Director of Public Prosecutions], September 1946, 1–17.

[48] St. meld. nr. 17 (1962–63) *Om landssvikoppgjøret. Innstilling fra et utvalg nedsatt for å skaffe til veie materiale til en innberetning fra Justisdepartementet til Stortinget* (*supra* n. 42), in *Stortingsforhandlinger 3b, 1962–63.*

[49] Andenæs, 1998 (*supra* n. 44), pp. 156–65.

The Treason Ordinance prescribed milder fines for subordinate employees although their work fell within the borders of treason, and the Director of Public Prosecutions instructed the regional prosecution agencies not to take any action against Norwegian workers employed by Norwegian firms until the firms themselves had been sentenced. Admittedly, this decision was justified by capacity constraints, and rightly so, but the decision fits neatly into the overall dilemma as well.

How was the Ordinance enforced? A close reading of the records from selected cases covering commercial treason suggests that, during the investigations, the prosecutions, and in the court proceedings, the primary focus was on identifying and providing evidence of opportunistic war profiteering. Records disclose that Ditlef Lexow was not a unique case, although most foreign forced labourers were working for German companies. Several Norwegian companies accepted the inclusion of forced labour in their contracts with German agencies or companies, yet an aggregate quantitative estimate is missing. Nevertheless, this element was largely neglected by the legal machinery enforcing the Treason Ordinance. Investigators recorded the occurrence of forced labour for many firms but did not make much effort to investigate. It was often mentioned in indictments and prosecutions but served as contextual information, as in the case against Lexow.[50] This applied in the Supreme Court as well, for example in the case against Willy Andrew Rudjord, whom the court acquitted after the lower court imposed a fine for proactive ('improper') collaboration. The argument of the Supreme Court was that his pursuit was not profits but work out of necessity to pay for his expenses. It is important in this context that Rudjord, when working for the German company Fix Söhn, had been responsible for surveilling the work of a group of Russian POWs. Allegations of ill-treatment (beating and kicking) existed, but what appears to have been a shallow investigation did not lead to proof of those allegations. The District Court as well as the Supreme Court appeared completely indifferent towards the allegations and the evidence when making their judgements.[51] The building contractor Frank H. Torgersen's actions were regarded as criminal and the Prosecution Agency imposed on him a fine of 500 NOK and confiscated 75,000 NOK of profits from his contract with the German company *Nordag* (though it was registered in Norway) between 1941 and 1944. The company had been set up to

---

[50] RA, Landssvikarkivet, L-sak 4303–4304 – Ditlef Lexow, box 1.
[51] *Riksadvokatens Meddelelsesblad*, nr. 28 (1947), 151–160.

massively expand Norwegian capacity to produce aluminium for the German airforce. The fact that *Nordag* supplied the company with between about 80 and 150 forced labourers every month during 1943, the bulk of which came from the Soviet Union and some from France, seems to have had no impact whatsoever.[52] Norwegian 'barrack barons' who had supplied parts of or whole barracks for accommodation of forced labourers were not investigated and therefore not judged for their actions, an example being the case of Leif Normann.[53]

The consistent neglect of possible illegal exploitation of foreign forced labour by Norwegian businesses followed from the strict framing of national law, as will be further elaborated on in the next section. However, it is reasonable to speculate why the exploitation of Norwegian forced labour which was supplied through the Norwegian Labour Offices to Norwegian companies failed to attract attention as well. Indications in the records of this conduct being addressed are marginal. The case against the building contractor Alfred Faber Swensson, who had earned large profits from several business contracts and was sentenced to three and a half years of hard labour, is telling. The fact that Swensson had accepted to receive Norwegian forced labour seems to have been of no significance, although this obviously lay within Norwegian jurisdiction.[54] On the other hand, several government officials who had worked out and implemented the labour requisition schemes for Norwegian citizens were sentenced pursuant to the criminal law. For Eilif Guldberg, a committed Nazi who from 1942 served as the leading official in the Norwegian forced labour scheme, the sentence was eight years of forced labour.[55] However, their involvement in the forced labour scheme was not a weighty count as compared with their political affiliation with the Nazi regime. This is another indication that political-ideological collaboration was treated differently from commercial collaboration.

There is considerable evidence that German agencies and individuals in Norway committed war crimes through ill-treatment of foreign POWs and foreign civilian forced labour.[56] Because Norwegian firms' involvement with forced labour was neglected or registered only superficially

[52] RA, Landssvikarkivet, L-sak 7977 – Frank H. Torgersen, box 1.
[53] RA, Landssvikarkivet, S-3138 – Leif Normann, box 1.
[54] RA, Landssvikarkivet, L-sak 3410 – Alfred Faber Swensson, box 1.
[55] RA, Landssvikarkivet, L-sak 4047 – Eilif Guldberg, box 1.
[56] NA, FO 371/57653, War Crimes Investigation Branch, Norway: War Crimes in Norway, 21 March 1946.

during the investigations for commercial treason, the possibility that such firms were involved in equivalent ill-treatment cannot be excluded. However, no evidence has so far suggested that Norwegian firms committed war crimes against POWs or civilian forced labourers. Consequently, the possibility that the involvement of Norwegian firms had a constraining effect and contributed to the reduction of ill-treatment cannot be excluded, although there is no empirical evidence underpinning this suggestion.

2.3   The Legal Exclusion of Norwegian War Crimes

The last provisional ordinance enacted by the government-in-exile in London, on 4 May 1945, covered war crimes committed by foreign citizens against Norwegians.[57] This War Crimes Ordinance, which originated in the joint work of the Allies to target Nazi war crimes, strengthened the Norwegian tendency to neglect the potential nexus between war profits and forced labour. This neglect was solidified by the Supreme Court in a precedent-setting ruling in February 1946. This section elaborates on the course of this development.

By criminalising bondage, the Criminal Law of 1902 rendered authority to the War Crimes Ordinance, which diversified the range of sanctions. Further, the War Crimes Ordinance extended the availability of the death penalty, a sanction that had disappeared from the Criminal Law of 1902 but was reintroduced by the government-in-exile in 1941. However, the context from which the Ordinance developed was the international law regarding war crimes, such as the Convention IV respecting the Laws and Customs of War on Land (Hague IV, 1907) and the Convention relative to the Treatment of Prisoners of War (Geneva Convention, 1929). The criminal acts listed in the War Crimes Ordinance were copied from a list that had been worked out before the international settlements after World War I, and included deportation of civilians, civilian forced labour, internment under harsh conditions, POW forced labour related to military operations, and ill-treatment of various kinds, including maltreatment of the sick and wounded. The combination of Nazi racial ideology and the large number of foreign and Norwegian forced labourers in the building schemes implied that Norwegian workers and

---

[57] Provisorisk anordning av 4. mai 1945 om straff for utenlandske krigsforbrytere og Justisdepartementets innstilling til anordningen [Provisional Ordinance regarding punishment of foreign war criminals and the position taken by the Ministry of Justice] (Oslo: J.Chr. Gundersen Boktrykkeri, 1945).

companies might directly or indirectly be involved in atrocities covered by these conventions.

The point of departure for enacting the War Crimes Ordinance was various agreements among the Allied powers on the approach to war crimes which maintained that prosecutions should occur in the home country of the victims.[58] The result was that the prosecution of war crimes against the massive bulk of foreign forced labour in Norway would take place abroad. There is no evidence in the records that the Norwegian government-in-exile was against this. On the contrary, it was aware that it did not have the capacity to enforce the legislation in the interests of such a large group of victims of forced labour.

As an allied state occupied by Germany but still taking part in the war from London, Norway signed the Declaration of St. James in January 1942, in which the Allies confirmed their intention to prosecute Nazi war crimes. Norway additionally took part in various deliberations among exiled legal experts on the boundary between national and international jurisdiction related to war crimes.[59] Consequently, Norway participated in the UN War Crimes Commission (UNWCC), which started operating in October 1943 and was dissolved in March 1948.[60] The UNWCC was primarily a fact-finding body with advisory functions that never operated within the jurisdiction of the member countries. The UNWCC filed lists of suspected war criminals and, after the Nazi surrender, it pursued equal treatment of war criminals by distributing Law and Trial Reports among the member countries. The Charter of the August 1945 London Conference, which laid the foundations for the subsequent Nuremberg tribunals, was infused by the UNWCC discourse. Allied deliberations and the workings of the UNWCC certainly affected Norwegian positions as well, as they

---

[58] Norsk Hjemmefrontmuseums okkupasjonshistoriske samlinger [Achive of the Norwegian Resistance Museum], Oslo, FO II 7.1, box 0004, War Criminals and Security Suspects, 16 January 1945 (SHAEF ECLIPSE Memorandum No. 18); B. Nøkleby, *Krigsforbrytelser. Brudd på krigens lov i Norge 1940–45* [War Crimes. Breaches of the laws of war in Norway] (Oslo: Pax Forlag, 2004), p. 16.

[59] K. von Lingen, 'Setting the Path for the UNWCC: The Representation of European Exile Governments on the London International Assembly and the Commission for Penal Reconstruction and Development, 1941–1944' (2014) 25 *Criminal Law Forum* 45–76.

[60] A. J. Kochavi, *Prelude to Nuremberg: Allied War Crimes and the Question of Punishment* (Chapel Hill: University of North Carolina Press, 1998); D. Plesch and S. Sattler, 'Changing the Paradigm of International Criminal Law: Considering the Work of the United Nations War Crimes Commission of 1943–1948' (2013) 15(2) *International Community Law Review* 203–23; D. Plesch, *Human Rights after Hitler: The Lost History of Prosecuting Axis War Criminals* (Washington: Georgetown University Press, 2017).

contributed to anchoring government political discourse in the vocabulary of international law.[61] This is evident not only from the enactment of the War Crimes Ordinance in May 1945 but also from the Norwegian memorandum prepared for the Nuremberg trials.[62]

Soon after liberation, the Norwegian government appointed a Prosecutor for War Crimes who would start preparing for the legal settlement authorised by the War Crimes Ordinance. Although governed by Norwegian law, he was expected to coordinate his operations with equivalent settlements in allied countries.[63] He kept contact with Allied Land Forces Norway (ALFNOR), in practical terms British forces who ran the Allied War Crimes Investigation Branch Norway (AWCIN) as well. The Norwegian Prosecutor soon made an agreement with the AWCIN to the effect that he would handle allegations of war crimes against Norwegians while AWCIN investigated German war crimes against non-Norwegians on Norwegian territory.[64] Concerned about the low capacity of his office, the Prosecutor continuously signalled that AWCIN must not leave cases for the weak Norwegian machinery that formally belonged to foreign states.[65] AWCIN established 153 case files but completed investigations in only 124. Some of them covered thousands of victims and hundreds of perpetrators. Ninety-seven victims were classified as Soviet, eleven as Yugoslav and five as Polish, which testifies to the victimisation of Eastern Europeans in terms of forced labour. Further, 264 suspects were transferred to the Soviet Union, 35 to Yugoslavia and 8 to Poland.[66] In accordance with the division of labour agreed during the war, ALFNOR implemented the repatriation of foreign POWs and forced labourers from Norway to their country of domicile for the

---

[61] R. N. Torgersen, 'Den folkerettslige side av rettsoppgjøret med landssvikerne' [Aspects of international law pertaining to the treason purge], *Tidsskrift for rettsvitenskap*, 1945, 17–48; R. N. Torgersen, 'Nürnbergprosessen. Noen spredte bemerkninger før dommen faller' [Comments on the Nuremberg trial before the court decision], *Tidsskrift for rettsvitenskap* 1946, 344–57.

[62] *Preliminary Report on Germany's Crimes against Norway. Prepared by the Royal Norwegian Government for use at The International Military Tribunal in trials against the major war criminals of the European Axis* (Oslo: Grøndahl & Søn, 1945).

[63] H. Sund, 'Krigsforbryterne i Norge og oppgjøret med dem' [The legal purge against war criminals in Norway], *Tidsskrift for rettsvitenskap*, 1946, 1–29.

[64] Ibid., 13.

[65] Nøkleby, 2004 (*supra* n. 58), pp. 57–8.

[66] NA, FO 371/57653, War Crimes Investigation Branch, Norway: War Crimes in Norway, 21 March 1946.

large majority before the end of 1945.[67] This swift move complicated investigations as many witnesses had left the country.[68]

The Norwegian legal machinery produced ninety-five court cases alleging war crimes of which eighty-nine resulted in convictions. However, far more cases were investigated.[69] Although Norway had ratified Hague IV and the Geneva Convention, the prevailing legal doctrine maintained that international law would not be incorporated into national law.[70] Consequently, although norms of international law and agreements would be taken into account as far as possible, jurisprudence would be constrained by domestic law. This bias in favour of domestic law had succinctly been maintained in the preparatory works for the War Crimes Ordinance by the Ministry of Justice of the government-in-exile, which explicitly maintained that crimes falling under the laws and customs of war committed in Norway or against Norwegians must be punished in accordance with Norwegian domestic law and that public sentiment would not accept otherwise. Courts must not be allowed to use international law arbitrarily as it was not an integrated part of domestic law, it concluded.[71] For several German citizens whose domicile had been Norway for a long period of time, and who committed crimes in the service of the enemy, charges were brought under the Treason Ordinance.[72] This followed from the demarcation between nationals, for whom criminal treason constituted the underlying discourse, and foreigners, for whom the underlying discourse was war crimes. Germans who were domiciled in Norway were treated as nationals for the purposes of these ordinances.

The two ordinances reflected the demarcation line, but both were subordinate to the existing Criminal Law. However, the norms and references surrounding the War Crimes Ordinance were permeated by international law on war crimes. Jurisprudence set by the Supreme

---

[67] RA, Flyktnings- og fangedirektoratet, Sentralt arkiv, E, box 81, Allied Land Forces Norway Prisoners of War Executive Headquarters, Final report (Period 11 May–15 Dec 45), 14 December 1945; Soleim, 2009 (*supra* n. 24), pp. 240–313.

[68] Nøkleby, 2004 (*supra* n. 58), p. 23.

[69] Nøkleby, 2004 (*supra* n. 58), pp. 69, 165.

[70] F. Castberg, *Folkerett* [International Law] (Oslo: Christiansen Boktrykkeri, 1937), pp. 40–46.

[71] *Provisorisk anordning av 4. mai 1945 om straff for utenlandske krigsforbrytere og Justisdepartementets innstilling til anordningen* (*supra* n. 57); Ot.prp. nr. 96, 1945–46 Om lov om straff for utenlandske krigsforbrytere [Bill on punishment of foreign war criminals], in *Stortingsforhandlinger* [Parliamentary papers] 3a, 1945–46.

[72] Nøkleby, 2004 (*supra* n. 58), pp. 71–4.

Court soon reinforced the legal distinction between Norwegian and foreign citizens with regard to criminal law enforcement. Legal scholars have convincingly argued that the *ratio decidendi* for the Supreme Court's decision in February 1946 to uphold a death sentence for a German citizen referred to international law.[73] The German citizen Karl-Hans Hermann Klinge had worked for the Gestapo and was prosecuted for the ill-treatment and torture of several Norwegian citizens, among which one died. Pursuant to the War Crimes Ordinance of May 1945, the lower court unanimously sentenced him to death in December that year. Klinge appealed with reference to the prohibition against giving laws retroactive effect laid down in the Norwegian Constitution (§§ 96 and 97), but the Supreme Court in plenary rejected the appeal. A majority of nine out of eleven judges argued that the sentence was derived from international legal norms as opposed to national law and therefore the Constitution did not apply. Whereas the Norwegian government in London had entered into international agreements and enacted the War Crimes Ordinance lawfully, German invaders were not covered by the Constitution, it concluded. The United Nations War Crimes Commissioner subsequently stated that 'no shadow of an objection could be raised to the sentence on the ground that it constituted an unjust use of the discretion thus permitted by International Law, since it was shown that a death had resulted from the ill-treatment meted out by the accused'.[74] Obviously, the majority vote found international legitimacy.

By this majority vote, the Supreme Court sanctioned the principle that equal acts of war crimes committed by country residents and foreign residents would fall under different legal sources. In practical terms, this meant that Norwegian citizens would be prosecuted from the angle of the Criminal Law and the Treason Ordinance, whereas foreign citizens would be prosecuted under international law. Judge Paal Berg, who had been Chief Justice in 1940 and in the autumn laid down the operative functions of the Supreme Court to avoid its abuse by the Germans, and who subsequently became a leading member of the civilian resistance movement, put it this way: 'We have no other legal duties to them [the invading Germans, HOF] than those acquired through international

---

[73] Sund 1946, (*supra* n. 63), 18–29; H. P. Graver, 'Okkupasjon, folkerett og dødsdommen mot Klinge' [Occupation, international law and the death sentence against Klinge] (2013) 52(4) *Lov og Rett* 275–94; Borge and Vaale, 2018 (*supra* n. 35), pp. 237–48.

[74] *Law Reports of Trials of War Criminals*, Vol. III (London: United Nations War Crimes Commission, 1948), p. 13, quoted in Graver, 2013 (*supra* n. 73), 277.

law.'[75] His judgment was part of the majority vote, which included no discussion whatsoever of whether Norwegian citizens might be covered by the same international law. According to Graver, the judges ought to have done so because the ruling excluded Norwegian citizens from war crimes law enforcement authorised in international law within Norwegian jurisdiction: 'Punishment of war crimes and crimes against humanity must be a result of equal treatment whether the indicted is Norwegian or German.'[76] The majority vote of the Supreme Court has since been heavily criticized by legal scholars, who argue that it violated the principle of the rule of law.[77]

The Norwegian majority government in 1951, when Norway became bound by the UN Declaration of Human Rights, stated that statutory provisions given by international bodies that were authorised by treaties Norway had ratified were not valid in Norway if they contradicted Norwegian material law.[78] However, the dual tenet saying that Norwegian law and international law are two separate legal systems has been modified since the Supreme Court upheld Klinge's death sentence in 1946, although there is broad consensus that it still applies.[79] One example is the Human Rights Law, which came into force in May 1999.[80] This incorporated in Norwegian law the European Convention of Human Rights, the UN Convention on Civil and Political Rights, the UN Convention on Economic, Social and Cultural Rights, the UN Convention on the Rights of the Child, and the UN Convention on the Elimination of all Forms of Discrimination against Women. Another expression of this is the amendment of the Criminal Law in 2005 (see chapter 16[81]), in force from 2008, which introduced penal provisions for genocide, crimes against humanity, and war crimes.[82] The Rome Statute

---

[75] *Norsk Retstidende* 1946, 198–224, quote at 201.

[76] Graver, 2013 (*supra* n. 73), 289.

[77] The critics and their arguments are listed in Borge and Vaale, 2018 (*supra* n. 35), pp. 230–48.

[78] Borge and Vaale, 2018 (*supra* n. 35), p. 242.

[79] M. Ruud and G. Ulfstein, *Innføring i folkerett* [Introduction to international law] (Oslo: Universitetsforlaget, 2002), p. 56.

[80] *Lov om styrking av menneskerettighetenes stilling i norsk rett (menneskerettsloven)* [Law on the strengthening of human rights in Norwegian jurisprudence].

[81] Chapter 16 of the Norwegian Criminal Law (Penal Code) of 2005: https://lovdata.no/dokument/NLE/lov/2005-05-20-28/KAPITTEL_2#KAPITTEL_2.

[82] *Lov om endringer i straffeloven* 20. november 2005 nr. 28 m.v. [Amendment to the Criminal Law].

of the International Criminal Court, established in 1998, was a source of inspiration.[83]

Hence, the latter law regulated the first war crimes case in Norwegian jurisprudence since the legal purges after World War II, which the Supreme Court handled in 2010. Some years before, the District Court and the Court of Appeal had sentenced a Norwegian-Bosnian citizen who had taken up Norwegian citizenship after some years of asylum after the war in former Yugoslavia to five and four years of imprisonment, respectively, for war crimes against Serb civilians in the Dretelj camp in Bosnia-Herzegovina in 1992. The acts occurred sixteen years before the Criminal Law amendment came into force. Arguing as Karl-Hans Herman Klinge did in 1946, the defendant maintained in the Supreme Court that the Constitution did not authorise the sentence of the lower courts because giving law retroactive effect was illegal. A majority of eleven judges agreed whereas six voted against. In his sentencing judgment, the first voting judge, Judge Møse, who had been president of the International Criminal Tribunal for Rwanda and would soon become a judge at the European Court of Human Rights, maintained that international law did not deprive Norwegian courts of the commitment to judge according to Norwegian law and emphasised that the majority vote's legal reasoning in the case against Klinge in 1946 could not be sustained, with which all eleven majority voting judges agreed.[84] The reasoning of the court in 2010 applied the doctrine that no one can be punished without law (*nulla poena sine lege*). The Criminal Ordinance of 1945 was no longer valid and the war crimes amendment to the Criminal Law of 2005 had not yet been legislated. Because the accused's acts occurred in 1992, the penal sanctions must draw their authority from the Criminal Law as it was in 1992. The Supreme Court sentenced the Norwegian-Bosnian citizen to eight years' imprisonment, much longer than the lower courts had, but the sentencing judgment implied that war crimes committed before 2008 could not be subjected to retroactive sanctions.

The sentencing decision triggered a public reaction, not because of the sentence but because of the choice of source of law. Hanne Sofie Greve, a former judge in the European Court of Human Rights (1998–2004), warned that it would reinforce Norway's reputation as a sanctuary for old

---

[83] Ot.prp. nr. 8 (2007–2008) *Om lov om endringer i straffeloven* 20. mai 2005 nr. 28 m.v. (*skjerpende og formildende omstendigheter, folkemord, rikets selvstendighet, terrorhandlinger, ro, orden, og sikkerhet, og offentlig myndighet*) [Bill on the Amendment of the Criminal Law], 49–52.

[84] *Norsk Retstidende* 2010, 1445; Graver, 2013 (*supra* n. 73), 277.

war criminals.[85] In his 2013 article, Hans Petter Graver elaborated on the legal implications of the 2010 decision. He agreed with Judge Greve that war criminals would try to escape crimes by forum-shopping in countries in which penal provisions in international law were not incorporated in national law. However, his main purpose was to argue that the 1946 majority vote in the case against Klinge should not be set aside so easily. His point of departure was that the Supreme Court's critique in 2010 against the death sentence in 1946 says that it had deviated from the constitutional guarantee of rule of law, namely the constitutional prohibition against retroactive force in jurisprudence. Graver shows that the sentencing judgment in 1946 was based on international law (Hague IV, art. 46 and Geneva Convention, art. 61). It maintained that the state of war itself invoked its penal provisions, that the source of law underpinning the relevant international law included torture, and that war crimes violating 'customs common to civilized nations' made the death penalty applicable. Graver concluded that at least two of the judges behind the majority vote argued that the sentence derived from a direct application of international law. It was not the incorporation that made Klinge's actions criminal in Norway; on the contrary, they were already criminal by virtue of international law, they had argued, according to Graver. The rest of the judges behind the majority vote did not address whether international law applied directly since the War Crimes Ordinance under any circumstance incorporated international law into national law. Consequently, Graver maintained that the sentence against Klinge was not a precedent that allowed courts in extraordinary conditions to depart from the constitutional prohibition against applying retroactive force, as implied by the Supreme Court in 2010. Instead, it demonstrated that Norwegian courts might judge war crimes and crimes against humanity pursuant to international law without a specific Norwegian law that authorises penal provisions at the time of their occurrence.[86]

2.4   Concluding Remarks

Ditlef Lexow was given a harsh sentence because he was a consistent war profiteer. At an early stage he had even started operating as a 'barracks

---

[85] *Aftenposten*, 15 October 2011, www.aftenposten.no/norge/i/Epj8a/-Dommen-fra-Hoyesterett-overrasker-meg.
[86] Graver, 2013 (*supra* n. 73), 289.

baron', the iconic negative term used to encapsulate the national sentiment and to distinguish 'good Norwegians' from the 'unnational' war
profiteering traitors. Yet the purge of war profits and profiteers was
modest and constrained by the legal notion of national treason. In effect,
the potential nexus between war profits and exploitation of forced labour
was completely ignored during the legal purge. The possible investigation
of Norwegian firms and workers committing war crimes against foreign
forced labourers was detached from the legal discourse because the War
Crimes Ordinance established a demarcation line between Norwegians
and foreigners that was confirmed by the Supreme Court. In essence, as
a consequence of deliberate legal framing, Norwegian citizens could not
commit war crimes prohibited under international law against foreign
citizens.

The Supreme Court's decision in the case against Karl-Hans Herman
Klinge solidified this demarcation. The judgments of the majority, irrespective of whether they maintained that international law applied
directly in Norwegian law or was incorporated through the War
Crimes Ordinance, said nothing about whether Norwegian citizens
could be punished for war crimes. Several Norwegians had death penalties imposed on them for crimes that were covered by international law,
but the jurisprudence in these cases was based on the Treason Ordinance.
The Supreme Court's judgment in the Klinge case solidified the notion
that Norwegians could not commit war crimes, only crimes inherent in
domestic law. It seems that the jurisprudence never elaborated on, and
even less challenged, this demarcation issue during the purges. The
Supreme Court's decision in 2010 on the first war crimes case in
Norway after the purges did nothing to remedy the shortcomings of
the post-World War II jurisprudence.

Economic Protectionism

Economic Policy and the Choice of Targets in International Criminal Tribunals

MARK D. KIELSGARD

The politics of target selection at Nuremberg have been well documented. The Allies had different visions of how the court was to proceed, ultimately defaulting to the French model of legitimate tribunals directed at creating a legal precedent for accountability for international crimes.[1] The original selection of targets for prosecution consisted of the military leadership, civil authority representatives, high-ranking Nazi party members and the financial elites who helped build the economics of the German war machine. In one of the early Nuremberg trials, Alfried Krupp and his son were on the original list of potential targets.[2] Alfried Krupp was the owner of ThyssenKrupp, still known today as one of the top steel production companies.[3] I. G. Farben, manufacturer of Beyer Aspirin, was considered a target for its role in the production of Zyklon B gas used in the

---

[1] Prior to the decision made by the United Nations, "the British government supported summary execution of a limited number of arch-criminals without benefit of trial, the Soviets insisted on trials for major war criminals, while Washington was still struggling over a policy towards war criminals"; see A. Kochavi, *Prelude to Nuremberg: Allied War Crimes Policy and the Question of Punishment* (University of North Carolina Press, 1998), p. 110. Only after constant debate did France, the United States and the USSR come to the consensus that a legitimate trial is more preferable; see R. Cryer et al., *An Introduction to International Criminal Law and Procedure* (2nd ed., Cambridge University Press, 2010), p. 111.

[2] J. Kolieb, "Through the Looking-Glass: Nuremberg's Confusing Legacy on Corporate Accountability under International Law" (2016) 32 *American University International Law Review* 569, 580.

[3] "Thyssenkrupp History," www.thyssenkrupp.com/en/company/history.

Holocaust.[4] Neither Krupp nor his son was indicted,[5] and I. G. Farben received no corporate criminal sanctions.[6]

Economic influence on international criminal prosecutions historically played a role in derailing the Constantinople trials after World War I against the 'Young Turks' for atrocities against the Armenians. This influence spurred on the Chester [Oil] concession of 1923 to open new markets and lands as well as natural resources to American corporate interests in oil, minerals and tobacco in post-war Ataturk's Turkey.[7] Ataturk and other high-ranking government officials in the nascent state of Turkey had been targeted for prosecution, but because of pressures brought to bear, including by corporate interests, inter alia, they received impunity for the part they played, while Ataturk assumed the mantle of the father of modern Turkey.[8]

Substantial literature in the field of international human rights law discusses the history of targeting individuals and corporations for the commission of international economic crimes.[9] This chapter employs a different approach by not addressing economic crimes per se; rather, it analyzes the economics of target selection itself. It postulates that, all other political factors aside, prosecutions initiated by the UN Security Council (UNSC) have always been latently screened according to extant trade relations with corporations operating within elite states. By

---

[4] P. R. Dubinsky, "Human Rights Law Meets Private Law Harmonization: The Coming Conflict" (2005) 30 *Yale Journal of International Law* 211, 214.

[5] *The United States of America* v. *Carl Krauch, et al.* [1949] 6 Trials of War Criminals Before the Nuernberg Military Tribunals Under Control Council Law No. 10.

[6] *The United States of America* v. *Krupp* [1948] 9 Trials of War Criminals Before the Nuernberg Military Tribunals Under Control Council Law No. 10.

[7] "A Resolution and Supporting Speech by Senator William H. King: the Lausanne Treaty and Chester Oil" (1974) 27 AR 73, 87–90; R. Trask, *The United States Response to the Turkish Nationalism and Reform 1914–1939* (University of Minnesota Press, 1971), pp. 37–40; V. N. Dadrian, 'The Historical and Legal Interconnection between the Armenian Genocide and the Jewish Holocaust: From Impunity to Retributive Justice' (1998) 23 *Yale Journal of International Law* 503, 512–14.

[8] P. Balakian, *The Burning Tigris: The Armenian Genocide and America's Response* (HarperCollins, 2003), p. 373.

[9] S. Pillay, "And Justice for All? Globalization, Multinational Corporations, and the Need for Legally Enforceable Human Rights Protections" (2004) 81 *University of Detroit Mercy Law Review* 489; D. Aguirre, "Corporate Liability for Economic, Social and Cultural Rights Revisited: The Failure of International Cooperation" (2011) 42 *California Western International Law Journal* 123; N. M. Rubin, 'A Convergence of 1996 and 1997 Global Efforts to Curb Corruption and Bribery in International Business Transactions: The Legal Implications of the OECD Recommendations and Convention for the United States, Germany, and Switzerland' (1998) 14 *American University International Law Review* 257; B. Rider, *Research Handbook on International Financial Crime* (Edward Elgar, 2015).

contrast, though not immune to the political economy of target selection, the International Criminal Court (ICC) carries certain structural safeguards that largely remove economic criteria from the vetting process. This is particularly ironic as many of the initial critiques of the Court were focused on the politicization of the ICC in the choice of situations for prosecution.[10]

To underscore the crucial role the economic vetting process played in the UN-based prosecutions, this chapter will first survey the historic prosecutions during the heyday of the UN international prosecutions of the 1990s and early 2000s. It will review them for the economic ties of the selected states grounded in the significance of trade relations and natural resource production in each situation. It will then compare them to other ongoing situations taking place at the time, where the Security Council failed to initiate criminal prosecutions. Thus, it will consider the economic factors (e.g. significant trade relations) that arguably led to impunity for grievous international crimes. Thereafter, it will compare them to prosecutions undertaken by the ICC to conclude that this institution has notable resilience to economic factors in target selection. While it is acknowledged that there are other unrelated purely geo-political strategic factors in international criminal prosecutions that may otherwise affect target selection in both systems, this study will delimit the focus to economic factors.

3.1 Delimiting the "Economics" of the Political Economy of Target Selection

Target selection for international prosecutions is sensitive to a variety of strategic political and geo-political factors. The character of the UNSC provides an avenue of politicization through the veto power of P5 states precluding prosecutions in situations where there are significant ties or interests at stake. Prosecutions targeting heads of state or senior officers may destabilize existing diplomatic or economic relations between elite states and the targeted leadership. Prosecuting country leaders also has the potential of exposing the complicity of P5 states, or economic organizations operating in P5 states, with the targeted regime. The politicization of prosecutions by the UNSC was a driving factor in the

---

[10] S. C. Roach, *Politicizing the International Criminal Court: The Convergence of Politics, Ethics, and Law* (Rowman & Litttlefields, 2006), p. 94.

development of the ICC,[11] which was designed to put prosecutions on a purely judicial footing.

Another political factor is the necessity of peace-making in conflict zones. Looming criminal prosecutions for competing leaders in conflict zones can significantly impede peace negotiations, which is why the UNSC was accorded the special power in the Rome Statute Article 16, providing for one-year renewable deferral of prosecutions in the ICC.[12] For example, an early barrier to the peace negotiations between LRA leader Joseph Kony and the national Ugandan government was the potential prosecution of Kony by the ICC.[13] Other factors include the strategic location of the territory of the conflict situation as it may be prioritized by powerful states to gain a strategic, high-value foothold in a particular region for geo-political purposes. Moreover, a partial list of other political factors also includes ideologically vulnerable target regimes such as regimes traditionally opposed to free market economics (e.g. the Pol Pot regime in Cambodia); targets whose offending governments have already been removed from power; highly publicized or notorious situations; and prosecutions condoned by status quo governments in the target state.

In some cases, political/economic sensitivity to complicit acts of wealthy elite states was effectively dealt with by imposing temporal or geographic jurisdictional constraints on the tribunals. Examples of this include the brief temporal jurisdiction of the ICTR, which effectively removed alleged French complicity immediately before the Rwandan genocide. The narrow geographic jurisdiction of the Special Panels for Serious Crimes (SPSC) in East Timor excluded Indonesian actors, the chief authors of the atrocities and a state with substantial natural resources with significant trade ties to elite states.

While purely political motivations served as UNSC vetting rationales for some international prosecutions, economic considerations can be

---

[11] B. S. Brown, "The Politicization of International Criminal Law", www.kentlaw.edu/faculty/bbrown/classes/IntlOrgSp07/CourseDocs/IVOnthePoliticizationofInternationalCriminalLaw.pdf; Roach (*supra* n. 10), 63.

[12] The Rome Statute of the International Criminal Court (adopted 17 July 1998, entered into force 1 July 2002) 2187 UNTS 90 (Rome Statute) art 16.

[13] An ICC arrest warrant was issued for Kony on July 8, 2005, also naming Vincent Otti, Raska Lukwiya (subsequently terminated from arrest warrant by pre-trial Chamber II decision ICC-02/04–01/05–248), Okot Odhiambo and Dominic Ongwen. See *Prosecutor v. Joseph Kony and Vincent Otti* (Judgment on the appeal) ICC-02/04–01/05 (September 16, 2009); M. P. Scharf, "From the eXile Files: An Essay on Trading Justice for Peace" (2006) 63 *Washington and Lee Law Review* 339.

bracketed as a separate precondition to the formation of international criminal tribunals. Sensitivity to international trade, embarrassment at international corporate presence and disruption of international trade partnerships, particularly in natural resource collection, served as potent sources of impunity under the historic UNSC system. The reason behind such sensitivity can be traced to the coercive nature of judicial hearings, designed to be transparent, which in effect names and shames those who are under indictment and, significantly, those with whom they are complicit, including corporations operating in elite states. The requirements of making findings beyond a reasonable doubt leaves no room for political deniability and establishes an official stamp on wrongdoing. It also opens the door for guilt by association of those who are not under indictment but, through investigation and the broad-based elicitation of evidence, appear in the official record.

There are three main ways in which the threat of disrupting trade through international criminal prosecutions can be manifested. First, by exposing corporate partnerships with corrupt states and the complicit participation or willful blindness of corporations to the international crimes committed by their partners to increase profitability (e.g. forced labor, abduction of hostages, murder/disappearance of those who resist, destruction of villages, unlawful taking of lands, environmental degradation, inhumane working conditions, etc.). This creates widespread corporate bad faith and negative publicity, and can impact consumer purchasing practices. Second, by creating the risk of the removal of state leaders from power through prosecutions or the stimulation of their removal through domestic backlash, resulting in loss of corporate partners (in highly competitive international markets) or the need for renegotiation of terms with new leaders. Third, by generating the potential for corporate leaders and other associated personnel to become direct targets of prosecution for complicity in international crimes.

In the last ten years, the UNSC has largely abandoned the ad hoc and hybrid models[14] of prosecution and relies on referrals to the ICC. Thus

---

[14] While all UN instigated international criminal tribunals are ad hoc in character, ad hoc here refers to the ICTY and ICTR, funded and organized by the UN, which is of a coercive character authorized under Article 41 of the Charter and based on a threat to international peace and security. These are subsidiary organs of the UN. Hybrid refers to courts established by bilateral agreement with the affected country and the UN such as the SCSL, ECCC, etc. typically using a mix of domestic law and personnel and joint funding. Hybrid courts are of a collaborative character for the purpose of eradicating impunity and not tied to Chapter VII considerations.

far, it has made two referrals, Sudan and Libya, but these referrals also reflect the resiliency of the economic trade vetting process as balanced against other geo-political factors.

3.2   UN Initiated International Criminal Prosecutions

At the conclusion of the Cold War, the Security Council, acting under Article 41 of the Charter, began to initiate prosecutions for international crimes by establishing the International Criminal Tribunal for the Former Yugoslavia (ICTY)[15] and the International Criminal Tribunal for Rwanda (ICTR).[16] The legal groundwork for this type of process was laid at the Nuremberg trials, as well as the ongoing codification and development efforts through the International Law Commission.[17] The political groundwork was laid by the fall of the USSR and the de-bipolarization of international politics. It was also due to the evolution of the concept of "threats to international peace and security" under chapter VII of the UN Charter, which attached not only to threats of international armed conflicts but also to regionally destabilizing massive human rights violations within the territory of a single state that threatened to spill over into other states as seen in the Hutu-Tutsi conflict in Rwanda and the larger Great Lakes region of Africa.[18] The Security Council eventually opted for two forms of international tribunals, ad hoc[19] and hybrid.[20] Though originally contemplated as Article 41 tribunals, the so-called hybrid courts eventually were developed through negotiated agreements between the affected state government and the UN.[21]

---

[15] UNSC Res 827 (May 25, 1993) UN Doc S/RES/827.

[16] UNSC Res 955 (November 8, 1994) UN Doc S/RES/955.

[17] ILC, "Report of the International Law Commission Covering Its Second Session" (5 June–29 June 1950) UN Doc A/1316.

[18] P. Akhavan, "Justice and Reconciliation in the Great Lakes Region of Africa: The Contribution of the International Criminal Tribunal for Rwanda" (1997) 7 *Duke Journal of Comparative and International Law* 325, 325–6.

[19] Examples include ICTR and ICTY; see G.-J. Knoops, *An Introduction to the Law of International Criminal Tribunals: A Comparative Study* (2nd ed., Martinus Nijhoff, 2014), pp. 2–4.

[20] R. Mackenzie et al., *The Manual on International Courts and Tribunals* (2nd ed., Oxford Scholarly Authorities on International Law, 2010); S. Williams, *Hybrid and Internationalised Criminal Tribunals: Selected Jurisdictional Issues* (Hart Publishing, 2012).

[21] See, for example, the ECCC in D. Scheffer, "The Extraordinary Chambers in the Courts of Cambodia," in M. Cherif Bassiouni (ed.), *International Criminal Law* (3rd ed., Martinus Nijhoff, 2008).

3.3   Ad Hoc Prosecutions

3.3.1   ICTY

When the ICTY was first established, Russia was in a state of economic collapse[22] and required rebuilding of its political, economic and social structure. Moreover, the disintegration of the Yugoslav state, a former USSR satellite,[23] was beyond the means of Russia to control or prevent. Though the measure was passed unanimously,[24] a decade earlier Russia would assuredly have vetoed. Economically, the former Yugoslavia was beyond Russian control. The initiation of civil war had destroyed Yugoslavia's economic capabilities, which were modest even prior to the hostilities.

Historically, Yugoslavia had a significant trade history with Western Europe before World War II,[25] but after it came under the sphere of influence of the USSR, trade with the West precipitously declined. Although in the 1960s there were efforts to modernize Yugoslavia's trade to establish international markets, the economy suffered from an extensive trade deficit which considerably worsened owing to the international recession of the 1970s and its dependence on oil imports.[26] Yugoslavia's modest trade with Western states continued to drop sharply in the 1980s.[27] Immediately before the formation of the Tribunal, Yugoslavia's primary industries were insignificant from an international trade perspective and consisted of modest trade to and from other similarly situated states.[28] It depended heavily on assistance from the USSR and primarily traded with economically depressed Soviet satellite states, instead of wealthy states, precluding a lucrative trade basis. With the downturn of the USSR economy and assistance, Yugoslavia could not maintain economic viability. Yugoslavia promised no products or business incentives for trade with Western states, particularly after it had devolved into a state of armed conflict. Its trade allies consisted of other

---

[22] M. McCauley and D. Lieven, "Post-Soviet Russia: The Yeltsin Presidency" (*Encyclopedia Britannica*), www.britannica.com/place/Russia/Post-Soviet-Russia.

[23] V. Vujačić, *Nationalism, Myth, and the State in Russia and Serbia* (Cambridge University Press, 2015).

[24] "Voting Record Search" (*United Nations Bibliographic Information System*), http://unbisnet.un.org:8080/ipac20/ipac.jsp?profile=voting&index=.VM&term=sres827.

[25] "Yugoslavia –Historical Background" (*Country Data*, December 1990), www.country-data.com/cgi-bin/query/r-14864.html.

[26] Ibid.

[27] Ibid.

[28] Ibid.

Russian satellite states within the former Soviet bloc,[29] which similarly had bleak economic prospects and little capital. At the time of the armed conflict, Yugoslavia lacked substantial natural resources or manufacturing capability.

There were no significant economic motives to forestall the creation of the ICTY from the perspective of Security Council P5 states because there was no significant multinational corporate presence to disrupt in the war-torn environment, nor had there been a recent history of significant trade, manufacturing or natural resource production or the local presence of major multinational corporate entities. For decades, Yugoslavia had barely maintained economically. From the European perspective, there were strong political motivations for NATO intervention as the specter of genocide and ethnic cleansing once again loomed on the European continent, recalling the horrors of the Holocaust. Moreover, there were motivations to form the tribunal as part of the intervention as the end of the Cold War provided the opportunity for continuing the tradition of Nuremburg. Economically, the intervention of NATO and the Western presence in former Yugoslavia served the additional purpose of opening the territory to Western markets, particularly Western European markets.

3.3.2   ICTR

In 2017 Rwanda remained one of the poorest countries in the world.[30] In the 2009 Human Development Index, Rwanda ranked 167 of 182 countries,[31] and in 1994 (at the time of the establishment of the ICTR) it was even poorer. The majority of its population is subsistence farmers and, unlike many countries in the region, it contains meager known exploitable natural resources.[32] Rwanda's scanty foreign trade includes agricultural products and modest mining. It primarily trades with Kenya,

---

[29] Ibid.
[30] B. Tasch, "Ranked: The 30 Poorest Countries in the World' (*Business Insider UK*, March 7, 2017), http://uk.businessinsider.com/the-25-poorest-countries-in-the-world-2017-3.
[31] Foreign & Commonwealth Office, "Country Profiles –Rwanda" (*The National Archives*), http://webarchive.nationalarchives.gov.uk/20100306003952/http://www.fco.gov.uk/en/travel-and-living-abroad/travel-advice-by-country/country-profile/sub-saharan-africa/rwanda/?profile=tradeInvestment.
[32] Foreign & Commonwealth Office, "FCO Country Profiles" (*Data.Gov.UK*), https://data.gov.uk/dataset/fco-country-information/resource/d889e1ef-945d-476c-9fab-5f92fc58b954.

Belgium, Germany and the United States. Its principal exports are coffee, (animal) hides and skins, metal ores, pyrethrum and tea.[33] Rwanda's export history to P5 trade partners (the United States) in 1992 came to a paltry 4.8 million USD. In 1993 it was 3.9 million USD and in 1994 it was 1.5 million USD. In 1995 it was 1.8 million USD.[34] The sluggish economy of Rwanda was obviously declining at that time.

Without intervention, Rwanda was at risk of becoming a failed state.[35] France did come under sharp criticism for its alliance with the Hutu government prior to the hostilities and during Operation Turquoise.[36] However, the temporal jurisdictional limitations of the ICTR[37] essentially shielded alleged French complicity from judicial and public exposure. The political factors leading to the formation of the ICTR consisted of the broad-based indisputable evidence and scope of this well-publicized genocide, the timing of the acts during a period of renewal of the principles of Nuremburg with the recent formation of the ICTY, and the prospect of a failed Rwandan state. Significantly, economic preconditions were satisfied because Rwanda lacked significant known natural resources and foreign trade relationships to disrupt or corporate interests to embarrass.

3.4   Hybrid Tribunal Prosecutions

Hybrid tribunals differ from ad hoc tribunals as they are created by treaty between the target state and the United Nations and thus have negotiated jurisdictional structures and unique jurisprudential features usually

---

[33] "Rwanda" (*OEC*), https://atlas.media.mit.edu/en/profile/country/rwa/.

[34] U.S. Census Bureau, "Foreign Trade Statistics: Trade in Goods (Imports, Exports and Trade Balance) with Rwanda" (*Census Gov.*), www.census.gov/foreign-trade/balance/C7690.html.

[35] Though definitions of a "failed state" vary, the first use of the term by Gerald Helman and Steven Ratner describes failed state as "the failed nation state, utterly incapable of sustaining itself as a member of the international community. Civil strife, government breakdown, and economic privation ... imperiling their own citizens and threatening their neighbors through refugee flows, political instability and random warfare"; see S. L. Woodward, *The Ideology of Failed States: Why Intervention Fails* (Cambridge University Press, 2017), p. 28; H. Wollaver, "State Failure Sovereign Equality and Non-intervention: Assessing Claimed Rights to Intervene in Failed States" (2014) *Wisconsin International Law Journal* 595, 599.

[36] A. Wallis, "Silent Accomplice" (*Independent*, December, 13 2006), www.independent.co.uk/arts-entertainment/books/reviews/silent-accomplice-by-andrew-wallis-428277.html.

[37] A. Kantonen, "Rwanda Crisis and Genocide in Case Law of Rwanda Tribunal" (2006) HELDA 15, https://helda.helsinki.fi/bitstream/handle/10138/21548/rwandacr.pdf?sequence=2.

incorporating a hybrid mix of domestic and international criminal law. They also include a mix of national and international judges. As a practical matter, being the product of negotiation, they are formed when the offending leadership or other actors have been displaced by a new government seeking retribution for the offenses of the displaced administration or, if some of the offending actors remain in power, then other negotiated safeguards for those actors as seen in the Cambodian tribunal.[38] Moreover, from the perspective of the UN, the selection of these tribunals was also screened by the economic factors of trade relations. Though eventually these tribunals were not mandated under chapter VII of the Charter as originally contemplated[39] but were largely negotiated by the office of the Secretary General and his delegates, economic protectionism persisted.

In the cases of Kosovo, Cambodia and East Timor, foreign trade was insignificant. In Lebanon, the scope of the prosecution limited to a single political assassination was so narrow that it did not involve significant economic issues. In Sierra Leone, the hostilities did not directly involve corporate interests and the prosecutions were consistent with rebuilding a once significant mining industry that had badly deteriorated during the armed conflict and displaced multinational corporations previously operating there.

3.4.1   Kosovo

Currently, Kosovo has developed as a trade partner based on exploitation of certain mineral resources including lead, zinc and silver.[40] Its chief output is in mining, agriculture and energy.[41] However, in 1999, when the hybrid court was established, Kosovo enjoyed very modest trade, with its chief trade partner being other regions in former Yugoslavia.[42] It had no significant foreign trade. The same economic vetting rationales applicable to the ICTY generally were equally applicable to Kosovo. Since Kosovo's physical and economic infrastructure was decimated,

---

[38] W. W. Burke-White, "A Community of Courts: Toward a System of International Criminal Law Enforcement" (2002) 24 *Michigan Journal of International Law* 1, 30.

[39] Scheffer (*supra* n. 21), pp. 5–8.

[40] "Kosovo Country Brief" (*Australian Government Department of Foreign Affairs and Trade*), http://dfat.gov.au/geo/kosovo/pages/kosovo-country-brief.aspx.

[41] Ibid.

[42] "Comparative Analysis of the Wars in Kosovo and Iraq" (*Economists for Peace and Security*, March 2008), www.epsusa.org/publications/newsletter/2008/march2008/pet kova.pdf.

UN Security Council Resolution 1244 (1999) specifically instituted significant and wide-ranging authority for, inter alia, economic development in Kosovo.[43] The United Nations Interim Administration Mission in Kosovo (UNMIK)[44] was also established for the dual purpose of establishing a hybrid panel consisting of international and local judges[45] and rebuilding Kosovo's economy by "building financial institutions from the ground up to start Kosovo's transition to a market economy. The postwar Kosovo economy was characterized by high unemployment rates, pending reconstruction of roads, houses and industrial plants . . . Kosovo's export potential was limited."[46] This measure met with some success as EU countries became Kosovo's largest trade partners where there were no substantial trade relations prior to UNMIK. Thus, the formation of the tribunal posed no danger of upsetting existing trade or risking exposure to liability for corporate interests and indeed promised to help build new economic alliances consistent with the economic interests of the P5 industrialized states.[47]

3.4.2   East Timor

In 1976, when East Timor ceased to be a colony of Portugal after the death of Salazar,[48] sovereignty was claimed by neighboring Indonesia.[49] This led to nearly thirty years of strife, the destruction of East Timor's infrastructure, the suspension of significant trade, and decimation of its economy despite offshore oil reserves nearby. Indeed, in a move by Australia, Indonesia's claim of sovereignty was acknowledged[50] purportedly for the

---

[43] UNSC Res 1244 (June 10, 1999) UN Doc S/RES/1244.

[44] UNMIK, "Regulation No. 1999/1 on the Authority of the Interim Administration in Kosovo" (July 25, 1999) UNMIK/REG/1999/1.

[45] UNMIK, "Regulation No. 2000/64 on Assignment of International Judges/Prosecutors and/or Change of Venue" (December 15, 2000) UNMIK/REG/2000/64.

[46] *Comparative Analysis of the Wars in Kosovo and Iraq* (*supra* n. 42).

[47] Some suggest that one factor in determining the bombing missions over Kosovo was directed more at a miscreant Milošević for his refusal to comply with economic reforms rather than the plight of the Kosovar Albanians. See J. Norris, *Collision Course: NATO, Russia and Kosovo* (Greenwood, 2005). The Nascent Kosovo Specialist Chambers review cases at every judicial level for violations of international criminal law but are the product of a domestic Kosovo constitutional amendment and thus not formed by the UNSC.

[48] A. W. Ertl, *Toward an Understanding of Europe: A Political Economic Precis of Continental Integration* (Universal, 2008), p. 304.

[49] A. Hopkins, "Australia Let Indonesia Invade East Timor in 1975" (*The Guardian*, September 13, 2000), www.theguardian.com/world/2000/sep/13/indonesia.easttimor.

[50] *East Timor (Portugal v. Australia)* (Judgment) [1995] ICJ Rep 1995.

purpose of exploiting East Timor's oil reserves.[51] Nonetheless, East Timor continued to assert its independence from Indonesia, was one of the last states to come under the jurisdiction of the UN Trustee Council and was eventually officially recognized as an independent state in 2002.[52]

This island state continued to suffer from endemic poverty. By the 2000s its foreign trade partners principally included Australia, the United States, Germany, Indonesia and Portugal.[53] Its economy largely consisted of agriculture,[54] soap manufacturing, handicrafts and textiles, and inshore fishing.[55] By 2005 its exports netted nearly 8 million USD and from off-shore oil production an additional 8 million USD.[56] Though slightly higher than many of the targets selected for ad hoc tribunals, East Timor nonetheless had statistically insignificant trade relations. Years of martial strife precluded the introduction of trade or natural resource extraction and therefore the presence of significant multinational corporate trade in its territory. The establishment of an international criminal tribunal would not be barred by efforts to protect international economic interests. Moreover, the principal author of the hostilities, Indonesia, which has significant natural resources and multinational corporate partnerships, was excluded from the tribunal's jurisdiction,[57] precluding Indonesian authorities from scrutiny.[58]

---

[51] D. Dixon, "Exploiting the Timor Sea: Oil, Gas, Water, and Blood" (2017) 46 *University of New South Wales Faculty of Law Research Series* 2–7, www5.austlii.edu.au/au/journals/UNSWLRS/2017/46.pdf.

[52] "Trust and Non-self-governing Territories (1945–1999)" (*United Nations and Decolonization*), www.un.org/en/decolonization/nonselfgov.shtml.

[53] Republica Democratica De Timor-Leste Ministero Do Plano E Das Fmancas Direccao Nacional De Estatistica, "Timor-Leste Overseas Trade Statistics 2005" (March 2006), www.statistics.gov.tl/wp-content/uploads/2013/12/2005_REPORT.pdf.

[54] East Timor's main agricultural products are coffee, rice, maize, cassava, sweet potatoes, soybeans, cabbage, mangoes, bananas and vanilla. See ibid.

[55] Ibid.

[56] Ibid.

[57] UNTAET, "Regulation No. 2000/15 on the Establishment of Panels with Exclusive Jurisdiction over Serious Criminal Offences" (June 6, 2000) UNTAET/REG/2000/15.

[58] The hybrid Court of East Timor (Timor Leste) was established under the Serious Crimes Unit (SCU) and originally set to expire in 2005, as part of pervasive UN Security Council initiatives (Security Council Res. 1272 (1999) establishing the United Nations Transitional Administration in East Timor (UNTAET) and Security Council Res. 1410 (2002) establishing the United Nations Mission of Support in East Timor (UNMISET). See UNSC Res 1272 (October 25, 1999) UN Doc S/RES/1272; UNSC Res 1410 (May 20, 2002) UN Doc S/RES/1410, which included social and economic rebuilding efforts as well as the creation of a Truth and Reconciliation Commission; see "Truth Commission: Timor-Leste (East Timor)" (*United States Institute of Peace*, February 7, 2002), www.usip.org/publications/2002/02/truth-commission-timor-leste-east-timor. According to the Feb. 4, 2004 report issued by the Office of the Deputy General Prosecutor for

3.4.3   Cambodia

Cambodia trades in timber, garments, rubber, rice and fish.[59] Key industries include agriculture, cement, cigarette production, fishing, forestry, rubber production, textiles and wood products.[60] Trade partners include former European communist states, the former USSR and Vietnam.[61] Cambodia has never been a significant trade partner with P5 states and at the time of the conflict in the 1970s it had evolved into an isolationist state, with the Khmer Rouge discriminative policy against Cham Muslims and an economy grounded in subsistence farming and Marxist ideology. It had no significant multinational corporate interests, nor did it develop significant economic trade during the thirty years of conflict that ended in 1997.[62] Accordingly, the formation of the hybrid tribunal satisfied the economic precondition set out in the latent vetting process.

Moreover, other political conditions were satisfied as the court reserved prosecution for only the most culpable actors,[63] effectively shielding contemporary Cambodian leaders from scrutiny. The targets of prosecution were active from 1975 to 1979 and have played no significant economic or political role since that time. The targets were also steeped in anti-capitalist ideology such that their prosecution would not affect domestic economic practices.[64]

Serious Crimes Timor Leste, Serious Crimes Unit, their office had issued 95 indictments against 392 people for charges including crimes against humanity and had won convictions against 74 persons and acquittals or dismissals for 12 cases, but 303 persons had evaded prosecution because they were outside the jurisdiction, the state territory, of the tribunal. Of the 303 who received impunity, 37 were Indonesian military commanders and officers, 60 were Indonesian soldiers, 4 Indonesian Chiefs of Police, the former Indonesian governor and 5 district managers (of East Timor) and the Indonesian Minister of Defense and Commander of the Armed Forces; see "Serious Crimes Unit Update" (Office of the Deputy General Prosecutor for Serious Crimes Timor Leste, February 4, 2004), www.ocf.berkeley.edu/~changmin/Serious%20Crimes%20Unit%20Files/all_documents/SCU%20Updates/SCU%20Update-English%20February%202005.pdf.

[59] "Trade Summary for Cambodia 2016" (*World Integrated Trade Solution*, February 26, 2018), https://wits.worldbank.org/countrysnapshot/en/KHM.

[60] Ibid.

[61] Ibid.

[62] "Cambodia Trade, Exports and Imports" (*Economy Watch*, March 11, 2010), www.economywatch.com/world_economy/cambodia/export-import.html.

[63] T. Fawthrop, "Facing History in Cambodia" (*New Internationalist*, March 2, 2009), https://newint.org/columns/essays/2009/03/01/facing-history-cambodia.

[64] Article 2 of the Law on the Establishment of the Extraordinary Chambers states: "The Extraordinary Chambers shall be established ... to bring to trial senior leaders of Democratic Kampuchea and those who are most responsible for the crimes and serious

At the time of the establishment of hybrid tribunals, the three target states (Kosovo, East Timor and Cambodia) had a history of largely agriculture-based economies, some relying on subsistence farming, little known natural resources and insignificant trade histories. Their lack of natural resources made them low-impact potential trade partners. Furthermore, Kosovo's and Cambodia's Marxist ideological roots (that emphasize societal structure and class struggle) were further distanced from neo-liberal economic policy and judicial intervention posed no threat to contemporary economic elites. All three states during the relevant time had experienced long-term conflict (lasting up to thirty years), further minimizing their potential trade impact as suitable places to do business. There was no important multinational corporate presence in their territory and no corporate collaborations to upset or economic interests to embarrass by becoming the subject of criminal investigation. In East Timor and Cambodia, the substantive offenses were decades old and new regimes had assumed power. In Kosovo, the UN intervention was designed, inter alia, to rebuild its economy and ultimately improve trade relations. Additionally, the absence of known significant natural resources in these countries precluded them as likely venues for trade with the most powerful extraction industries.

3.4.4 Sierra Leone

The Special Court for Sierra Leone (SCSL) differed from the other tribunals because, at the time of its formation, Sierra Leone possessed significant known natural resources, especially diamonds and rutile. It also had a history of important trade partners, though this had suffered a long decline. Trade almost completely fell apart during the civil war. The 2008 U.S. State Department Report described Sierra Leone as rich in minerals, especially diamonds.[65] However, the 1970s and 80s saw a slow-down in trade, which seriously degraded in the 1990s.[66] The conflict essentially halted trade. Export figures during and shortly thereafter

---

violations ... that were committed during the period from 17 April 1975 to 6 January 1979"; see Law on the Establishment of Extraordinary Chambers in the Courts of Cambodia for the Prosecution of Crimes Committed During the Period of Democratic Kampuchea, with inclusion of the amendments as promulgated on October 27, 2004 (NS/RKM/1004/006) [2001] (unofficial translation).

[65] U.S. Department of State, "Background Note: Sierra Leone: Profile" (*Bureau of African Affairs*, June 2008) 3–4, as cited in M. D. Kielsgard, *Reluctant Engagement: US Policy and the International Criminal Court* (Martinus Nijhoff, 2010), p. 290.

[66] Ibid.

reflect a total of 1.2 million USD in 1999.[67] In the post-conflict economic recovery these figures rose more than a hundred-fold to 142 million USD in 2005. The U.S. State Department observed:

> Sierra Leone has one of the world's largest deposits of rutile, a titanium ore used as paint pigment and welding rod coatings. Sierra Rutile Limited, owned by a consortium of U.S. and European investors, began commercial mining operations near Bonthe in early 1979. Sierra Rutile was then the largest nonpetroleum U.S. investment in West Africa. The export of 88,000 tons realized $75 million in export earnings in 1990. The company and the Government of Sierra Leone concluded a new agreement on the terms of the company's concession in Sierra Leone in 1990. Rutile and bauxite mining operations were suspended when rebels invaded the mining sites in 1995, but exports resumed in 2005.[68]

As trade had largely ceased immediately before and during the conflict, intervention was essential to re-establish this trade partner of economic potential. The best-known individual target of prosecution was Charles Taylor,[69] leader of Liberia, who financed the rebels through illegal timber and diamond smuggling.[70] Any exposure of the great diamond merchants in Europe doing business with Taylor was minimal as they were removed from the conflict zone and Taylor had already abdicated from office before the relevant time (and sought refuge in Nigeria).[71] Taylor was not arrested until years later[72] after he had ceased to be economically important or in a position to impact the diamond trade. Moreover, the illegal diamond trade and all "conflict stones" were already under considerable scrutiny with UN Resolution 1306 prohibiting all imports of

---

[67] Ibid.
[68] Ibid., p. 4.
[69] "The Prosecutor vs. Charles Ghankay Taylor" (*Residual Special Court for Sierra Leone*), www.rscsl.org/Taylor.html.
[70] According to USAID reports, "[s]ustaining a fighting force requires a steady flow of money. Diamonds directly financed the UNIT A rebels in Angola in the 1990s, while in Liberia, Charles Taylor first used timber, then diamonds, as the lucrative source of funds. Likewise, governments and other groups (including militaries) have used minerals to sustain wars against secessionist groups and rebels. An expert panel reported to the UN Security Council in 2002 that the DRC conflict had become a war for access, control, and trade of five key mineral resources. In the DRC and elsewhere, governments and/or insurgents have sold mineral rights to private interests to generate funds for buying arms and hiring mercenaries"; see USAID, "Minerals & Conflict, A Toolkit for Intervention" (2005) USAID 4, http://pdf.usaid.gov/pdf_docs/Pnadb307.pdf.
[71] SCSL (*supra* n. 69).
[72] Ibid.

rough diamonds.[73] Illegal diamond smuggling declined during the relevant period and the UN-based export certificate system "led to a dramatic increase in legal export."[74] After the conflict and Taylor's removal, Liberia also experienced substantial economic growth largely from foreign investment in industries including mining. The corporation, Arcelor Milia Steel, invested over 1.5 billion USD in the mining sector.[75]

Therefore, similar to Kosovo, international intervention played a role in rebuilding the economies of both Sierra Leone and Liberia. Domestic strife had disrupted trade, particularly with Sierra Leone, and served as a motivation for intervening to a greater extent than Kosovo as it had vast natural resources prized by major corporations. Sierra Leone differs from Cambodia and East Timor as economic interests were indifferent to the latter two. The quantum of atrocities committed in all situations, during the era of international criminal accountability, fueled judicial scrutiny but only so long as it was compatible with trade interests.

3.5   UNSC Referrals to the ICC

3.5.1   Sudan

The first UNSC referral to the ICC was Sudan in the Darfur situation.[76] In this referral the United States and China abstained.[77] The massacres in this region were at the hands of the Janjaweed militias acting with the tacit approval of the government in Khartoum.[78] This ignited widespread international attention and became the cause célèbre of many famous film stars among others.[79] The conflict in Darfur also resulted in massive migration of populations to neighboring Chad, resulting in huge refugee

---

[73] UNGA Res 1306 (July 5, 2000) UN Doc S/Res/1306; UNSC "Security Council Decides to Impose Prohibition on Imports of Rough Diamonds from Sierra Leone" (July 5, 2000) Press Release SC/6886.

[74] B. K. Taylor, *Sierra Leone: The Land, Its People and History* (New Africa Press, 2014), p. 82.

[75] "Background Note: Liberia Profile" (*supra* n. 65).

[76] V. Verna, "The United Nations Security Council Referrals of Situations to the International Criminal Court" (*HELDA*, 2013), https://helda.helsinki.fi/handle/10138/39373.

[77] UNSC, "Security Council Refers Situation in Darfur, Sudan, to Prosecutor of International Criminal Court" (March 31, 2005) Press Release SC/8351.

[78] "Sudan's Darfur Conflict" (*BBC News*, February 23, 2010), http://news.bbc.co.uk/2/hi/africa/3496731.stm.

[79] S. Inskeep, "'Not on Our Watch': A Mission to End Genocide" (*NPR BOOKS*, May 1, 2007), www.npr.org/templates/story/story.php?storyId=9928999.

camps.[80] In its comments on the referral, the United States articulated that an ad hoc tribunal would have been a better solution.[81] It nonetheless abstained in the referral reflecting the United States' lukewarm position on the ICC but, significantly, did not veto. This may have shown a new willingness on the part of the United States to engage with the ICC, though reluctantly. On the other hand, it also reflects the economic vetting process as the United States had no significant trade relationship with Sudan. In any event, the creation of an ad hoc tribunal would have been structurally and strategically untenable as the principal perpetrators, and therefore targets for prosecution, were high-ranking government officials who would never have agreed to partnering with the UN to prosecute themselves in a hybrid tribunal acting in good faith.

More instructive in the nuance of economic vetting was the role played by China. China had a trade relationship with Sudan.[82] It was one of Sudan's more important trade partners but, relative to China's burgeoning economic growth during the 2000s, Sudan was substantially less important to China. Moreover, while China was developing its trade partners during this time, it was particularly sensitive to international complaints concerning its own human rights record. Given the high-profile nature of the Darfur situation, the perceived backlash from a veto of the referral by China would have had a deleterious effect on the growth of its other trade partnerships. The cost–benefit analysis therefore favored an abstention rather than a veto as it precluded China from taking responsibility, by implication, for the crimes of the al Bashir government. This is also particularly relevant as the largest economic sector in China is government-owned business and therefore interceding in the referral would have been considered significant diplomatic bad faith.

3.5.2   Libya

The second UNSC referral to the ICC was to investigate the widespread killings of civilians and crimes against humanity during the Libyan civil

---

[80] "The Impacts of Migration: Refugees" (*BBC*), www.bbc.co.uk/schools/gcsebitesize/geography/migration/types_migration_rev5.shtml.

[81] C. Heyder, "The U.N. Security Council's Referral of the Crimes in Darfur to the International Criminal Court in Light of U.S. Opposition to the Court: Implications for the International Criminal Court's Functions and Status" (2006) 24 *Berkeley Journal of International Law* 650, 652.

[82] J. Hammond, "Sudan: China's Original Foothold in Africa" (*The Diplomat*, June 14, 2017), https://thediplomat.com/2017/06/sudan-chinas-original-foothold-in-africa/.

war.[83] All fifteen UNSC members unanimously voted,[84] and, shortly after, the NATO intervention called for an order to ceasefire immediately in Libya.[85] The situation was critical considering the human rights violations, while the political drives for a regime change[86] after Gaddafi nationalized Libya's natural resources and proved himself a dictator were in line with the perceived economical benefits of other states. Nonetheless, the underlying political struggles behind the second referral were so strong that the economic vetting process was of little weight comparatively, as NATO had already intervened.

Originally, having the richest oil reserve in Africa, Libya had the highest GDP per capita in Africa throughout the 1990s to the early 2000s.[87] Libya's economy drastically declined after the NATO intervention, with its GDP dropping by half from 74.77 billion USD in 2010 to 34. 7 billion USD in 2011.[88] Its relations with the P5 states also deteriorated. Exports to the UK decreased by two-thirds[89] and exports to the United States dropped by 70 percent[90] from 2010 to 2011. EU imports from Libya between 2012 and 2016 also dropped significantly by 85 percent.[91]

3.6   Situations Not Administered by the UN

Equally important in analyzing the economic vetting process of the UNSC are the situations that did not result in international prosecutions. Three particularly relevant representative examples include the situations in Myanmar and Nigeria in the 1990s and especially the Democratic Republic of Congo (DRC) in the late 1990s and early

---

[83]   UNSC Res 1970 (February 26, 2011) UN Doc S/RES/1970.
[84]   B. Aregawi, "The Politicisation of the International Criminal Court by United Nations Security Council Referrals" (*ACCORD*, July 1, 2017), www.accord.org.za/conflict-trends /politicisation-international-criminal-court-united-nations-security-council-referrals/.
[85]   UNSC Res 1973 (17 March 2011) UN Doc S/RES/1973.
[86]   M. Zenko, "The Big Lie about the Libyan War" (*FP*, March 22, 2016), https://foreign policy.com/2016/03/22/libya-and-the-myth-of-humanitarian-intervention/.
[87]   "Libya" (*Washington Post*), www.washingtonpost.com/wp-srv/world/countries/libya .html?noredirect=on.
[88]   "Libya GDP" (*Trading Economics*), https://tradingeconomics.com/libya/gdp.
[89]   "Value of UK Imports of Trade Goods from Libya from 2010 to 2017 (in Million U.S. Dollars)" (*Statista*, 2018), www.statista.com/statistics/477976/united-kingdom-uk-import-value-trade-goods-from-libya/.
[90]   "Trade in Goods with Libya" (*United States Census Bureau*), www.census.gov/foreign-trade/balance/c7250.html#2011.
[91]   European Commission, "Libya", http://ec.europa.eu/trade/policy/countries-and-regions /countries/libya/.

2000s. These situations would have made better venues for international judicial scrutiny than many of the cases undertaken as the offenses either were perpetrated more recently or resulted in greater human losses. However, all three failed to pass the economic litmus test. In these situations, foreign trade was significant and multinational corporations had a presence in the subject state. Though the first two situations (Myanmar and Nigeria) were the subject of American Alien Tort Claims Act (ATCA) cases,[92] the principal actors and those allegedly complicit corporations never faced international criminal prosecutions. Among these situations, the DRC, from 1997 to 2005, reportedly suffered the greatest casualty rate anywhere since the conclusion of World War II.[93]

These examples poignantly illustrate a lack of political will during the relevant time to interfere or disrupt economic ties and the exploitation of natural resources. They also reveal a sensitivity to embarrassing national and/or corporate entities through the exposure of ties between the offending regimes and the transnational corporate interests involved. As already elucidated, there are many other indicia of the phenomenon pertaining to target selection grounded in purely political factors, and the UNSC has taken non-judicial steps in addressing catastrophic international crimes and massive human rights violations, such as the provision of peacekeepers, but these measures fail to address impunity by focusing the glaring lens of judicial scrutiny on those actors, natural or corporate, who are most responsible. Moreover, these three examples, as well as others, lay bare the provocative pattern of target selection historically undertaken by the UNSC.

3.6.1   Myanmar/Nigeria

In the 1990s the government of Myanmar was a military regime, the State Law and Order Restoration Council (SLORC).[94] The SLORC government was known to precipitate widespread human rights violations, inter alia, in connection with the construction and operation of the Yadana gas pipeline.[95] The offenses came to light by a US legal action under the

---

[92] *John Doe* v. *Unocal Corporation et al* [2002] 395 F.3d 932.

[93] Chris McGreal, "War in Congo Kills 45,000 People Each Month" (*The Guardian*, January 23, 2008), www.theguardian.com/world/2008/jan/23/congo.international.

[94] *John Doe* v. *Unocal* (n92) 937–938. SLORC is the abbreviation of the State Law and Order Restoration Council.

[95] Ibid.

ATCA provision representing villagers against the SLORC corporate partner the Unocal Energy Corporation.[96] This complaint alleged atrocities including widespread and systematic "coerced labor, the forced removal of villagers, murder, rape, and torture."[97]

Crimes against humanity were also alleged in the acts against the Ogoni peoples in Nigeria. Extrajudicial executions (including the famous Ken Saro-Wiwa), as well as torture, unlawful detention, murder of peaceful protestors and massive environmental degradation and human rights abuses, were perpetrated against the Ogoniland indigenous peoples.[98] The Nigerian government was in partnership with Royal Dutch/Shell Oil Group to build an oil pipeline in the Ogoniland traditional lands. Ogoni dissent met with violent suppression and the commission of crimes against humanity.

In both cases, these crimes were committed by governments who partnered with wealthy corporate interests for the extraction of natural resources (natural gas and oil). The local governments were in charge of securing unskilled labor, security and access to lands containing the resources. The corporate partner provided the capital, skilled labor, intellectual property and markets – with both partners sharing profits. The provision of slave labor, nationalization of sub-surface resources,[99] extrajudicial takings of land and demolishing of villages in the resource-rich regions (to make way for production facilities) dramatically reduced costs and increased profits for both sets of partners. Thus, these cases reveal the complicit liability of both partners. However, no international judicial scrutiny was undertaken.[100] The allegations consist of significant

[96] Ibid.

[97] Center for Constitutional Rights, "Docket: Doe v. Unocal Synopsis" (January 31, 2005), www.ccr-ny.org/v2/legal/corporate_accountability/corporateArticle.asp? ObjiD=IrRSFKnmmm&Content=45 (as cited in M. D. Kielsgard, "Unocal and the Demise of Corporate Neutrality" (2005) 36 *California Western international Law Journal* 185, 188).

[98] Kielsgard, 2010 (*supra* n. 65), p. 296.

[99] Many countries have nationalized sub-surface resources and, according to the Freeholder Owners Association, '[i]n most modern industrialized democracies, petroleum and natural gas were recognized as strategic commodities and nationalized before any significant deposits which might have presented political barriers to nationalization had been discovered within the jurisdiction. As a result there is no private ownership of subsurface oil and gas in most countries"; see Freehold Owners Association, "About Freehold Mineral Rights," www.fhoa.ca/about-freehold-mineral-rights.html; J. Lowe, *Cases and Materials on Oil and Gas Law* (2nd ed., American Casebook Series, West Academic Publishing, 1993) 17.

[100] Royal Dutch/Shell oil group allegedly conspired to commit the extra-judicial execution of environmental and community leaders Ken Saro-Wiwa and John Kpuinen by

numbers of human casualties and heinous conduct including extrajudicial killings, murder, conscripted labor, induced starvation, the destruction of whole villages and rape. In addition to crimes against humanity, allegations of genocide in the Nigerian delta against the Ogoni ethnic group have been raised.

Beyond Myanmar and Nigeria, numerous other cases during the same time frame involving corporate complicity in international crimes had received notorious publicity but no judicial response from the UN. These cases also involve the crimes of kidnapping, suppression of peaceful protests, torture and cruel and inhumane and degrading treatment and summary execution, among others. A partial list includes partnerships between national governments and Chevron's activities in Parabe, Opia and Ikenyan, Nigeria;[101] Exxon Mobil's activities in Aceh, Indonesia (it subcontracted security to the national government for its corporate natural gas facilities);[102] similar crimes in Guatemala,[103] Ecuador[104] and Columbia;[105] as well as illegal drug testing on children in Kano, Nigeria[106] and human rights violations in Papua New Guinea.[107] This is not an exhaustive list, but it provides a picture of corporate protectionism when taken in tandem with those cases chosen for prosecutions. This is even more significant when considering that these crimes were being committed when international criminal accountability, and UN initiatives, had reached their zenith during the 1990s and early 2000s.

Admittedly, many of these situations may not have resulted in sufficiently massive casualties and failed to meet the gravity threshold (as

hanging, the torture and unlawful detention of other individuals, and the shooting of a woman peacefully protesting the destruction of her crops, in an attempt to suppress the Ogoni peoples' opposition to the long history of the environmental and human rights abuses in the Ogoni region of Nigeria, pursuant to their efforts to build a pipeline. See *Wiwa* v. *Dutch Royal Petroleum Co.*, No. 96 Civ. 8386(KMW), 2002 WL 319887 (S.D.N.Y. Feb. 28, 2002).

[101] *Bowoto* v. *Chevron* 312 F. Supp. 2d 1229 (2004).
[102] Bill Mears, "Exxon Mobil to Face Lawsuit over Alleged Human Rights Violations" (*CNN*, July 8, 2011), http://edition.cnn.com/2011/CRIME/07/08/exxon.mobil.lawsuit/index.html.
[103] *Villeda* v. *Del Monte Produce, Inc.*, 305 F. Supp. 2d 1285 (S.D.Fia. Dec. 12, 2003).
[104] M. Lipman, "Dow, DuPont Sued over Banana Fungicide in Ecuador" (*Law360*, October 23, 2008), www.law360.com/articles/73864/dow-dupont-sued-over-banana-fungicide-in-ecuador.
[105] *Estate of Rodriguez* v. *Drummond Co. Inc.*, 256 F. Supp. 2d 1250 (N.D. Ala. 2003); *Sinaltrainal* v. *Coca-Cola Co.*, 256 F. Supp. 2d 1345 (S.D.Fla. 2003).
[106] *Abdullahi* v. *Pfizer, Inc.*, No. 01 Civ. 8n8(WHP), 2005 WL 1870811 (S.D.N.Y. Aug. 9, 2002).
[107] *Sarei* v. *Rio Tinto*, 221 F. Supp. 2d 1116 (C.D. Cal. 2002).

a threat to international peace and security) for Article 41 action or, alternatively, negotiated bilateral agreements were not feasible. However, for those situations that did meet the gravity threshold, they most certainly involved abhorrent human rights violations that the UNSC failed or refused to take action on. One such case was the Democratic Republic of Congo (DRC).

3.6.2   The DRC

The DRC had suffered perhaps the worst loss of any comparable situation in recent history, with unspeakable atrocities and a constant state of de facto martial strife during the latter 1990s and early 2000s. With a history of several hundred years of foreign aggression and colonialism dating from the early days of the Atlantic slave trade to the so-called Congo Free State to Belgian colonial rule to the modern history of the rapacious rule of Mobutu, few peoples on the globe have suffered such sustained and devastating loss. Though estimates vary, from 1997 (the year Mobutu abdicated office) to 2005 the death toll reached nearly 4 million people, not including those internally displaced or forced to emigrate to foreign countries.[108] The total number of people adversely affected by the wars has been estimated at 50 million.[109] According to historian Adam Hochschild, the situation in the DRC during this time (1997–2005) "has been the largest concentration of war-related fatalities anywhere on earth since the end of World War II."[110] The gap left by Mobutu's departure resulted in competing warlords vying for power and led to the massively destabilizing importation of armed forces of six regional states involved in the conflicts, namely Zimbabwe, Angola, Namibia, Uganda, Rwanda and Burundi.[111] This surely satisfied Article 41 preconditions to threats to international peace and security in accordance with modern definitions.

---

[108] From August 1998 to April 2004 approximately 3.8 million people died in the DRC; see "Congo Civil War" (*Globalsecurity.Org*, June 27, 2017), www.globalsecurity.org/mili tary/world/war/congo.htm. By July 25, 2006 estimates of the DRC casualties had risen to 5.4 million according to the International Rescue Committee (IRC); see "In Pictures: Surviving Congo –Mortality Survey" (*BBCNews*, July 25, 2006), http://news.bbc.co.uk/2/ shared/spl/hi/picture_gallery/08/africa_surviving_congo/html/1.stm.

[109] *Globalsecurity.Org* (*supra* n. 108).

[110] A. Hochschild, *King Leopold's Ghost: A Story of Greed, Terror and Heroism in Colonial Africa* (Pan Macmmilian, 2011), p. 317.

[111] Ibid.

Moreover, the crimes were perhaps the worst taking place in the world at the time and included crimes against humanity, war crimes and genocide. Offenses ranged from recruitment of child soldiers[112] to slavery, torture, decapitation, impalement,[113] sexual slavery, forced incest, gang rape, sexual mutilation and forced cannibalism.[114] UN emergency relief coordinator Jan Egeland observed: "In terms of the human lives lost ... this is the greatest humanitarian crisis in the world today [2005] and it is beyond belief that the world is not paying more attention."[115] Thus, economic factors aside, this situation qualified more for Article 41 international judicial scrutiny than perhaps any other situation taken on during the heyday of UN-initiated international criminal tribunals; horrible crimes, huge numbers of victims and significant threats to international (regional) peace and security. Compared to the Rwandan situation, the DRC suffered over four times the loss of life. The UN was not absent from the DRC – it provided more peacekeeping forces there than any other venue in the world[116] at the time – but it did not address impunity for the perpetrators or accountability measures. By opening a situation in the DRC as one of its first cases, the ICC represented an alternative to the UN in the pursuit of criminal justice,[117] though its intervention was too little and too late.

While all of the preconditions for a UNSC tribunal were clearly established[118] as early as the late 1990s and before the ICC became

---

[112] Ibid.

[113] E. Isango, "Cannibalism Shock as Congo Atrocities Revealed" (*theage.com.au*, March 18, 2005), www.theage.com.au/news/World/Cannibalism-shock-as-Congo-atrocities-revealed/2005/03/17/1110913734387.html.

[114] According to Yalcin Erturk, UN special investigator for violence against women, "[w]omen are brutally gang raped, often in front of their families and communities. In numerous cases, male relatives are forced at gun point to rape their own daughters, mothers or sisters [. . .] Women, who survived months of enslavement, [stated] that their tormentors had forced them to eat excrement or the human flesh of murdered relatives"; see "UN: Congo Women Face Sexual Atrocity" (*NBCNews*, July 30, 2007), www.nbcnews.com/id/20038999/ns/world_news-africa/t/un-congo-women-face-sexual-atrocities/#.WpTmBJNuZE4.

[115] Isango (*supra* n. 113).

[116] K. Allen, "Bleak Future for Congo's Child Soldiers" (*BBCNews*, July 25, 2006), http://news.bbc.co.uk/2/hi/africa/5213996.stm.

[117] In 2004, ICC prosecutor Ocampo announced that the first investigation to be opened would be the situation in the DRC. Press Release, "The Office of the Prosecutor of the International Criminal Court Opens Its First Investigation" (International Criminal Court, June 23, 2004).

[118] In an official letter dated April 1, 2002 from Secretary-General Kofi Annan to the President of the Security Council, Mr. Annan indicated that, despite the Lusaka Ceasefire Agreement, armed forces from Uganda (ADF), Burundi (FDD, FNL),

operationally functional in 2003, no such tribunal was seriously considered.

The DRC provides the best evidence for an economic vetting process in UNSC target selection. Geologically speaking, the DRC is widely considered the wealthiest real estate on earth.[119] It is rich in many ores and stones including diamonds, uranium, zinc, copper, cobalt and tin.[120] It also has the world's largest reserves of coltan, an indispensable ore for the manufacture of computer chips.[121] First exploited by the Portuguese for slaves, then by Leopoldian Belgium for ivory and its rich rubber resources to feed Euro-American needs after the process of vulcanization was invented for bicycle tires and ultimately for automobile tires, the Congo basin's miseries seem to track Western inventions. Natural resources were extracted throughout the colonial period of the DRC, and "it was during this period that transnational networks entrenched themselves in the region to create ... powerful and exploitative conglomerates with tenterhooks in all European and northern American countries."[122] Furthermore, "[t]here was no question that under Belgian rule, Congo had been internationalized, and the race for exploitation of its resources superseded any concerns for the establishment of a viable political unit within its borders."[123] Historically, multinational corporations doing business in the DRC included the United Mines of Upper Katanga (UMHK), Barclays and the Rockefeller Group.[124] Under self-rule and the Mobutu regime, the DRC (then Zaire) developed a major smuggling economy.[125] With Mobutu's departure, in many areas, the government collapsed leaving a collection of warlords financed

---

Rwanda (ALIR), as well as the Congolese FAC and other militias were still actively fighting in the DRC. See UNSC, "Letter dated 1 April 2002 from the Secretary-General addressed to the President of the Security Council" (April 5, 2002) S/2002/341.

[119] D. Julius, "DR Congo: Richest in Resources yet Poorest Country in the World" (*swali Africa*, April 14, 2016), http://blog.swaliafrica.com/dr-congo-richest-in-resources-yet-poorest-country-in-the-world/.

[120] ibid.

[121] M. M. Molango, "From 'Blood Diamond' to 'Blood Coltan': Should International Corporations Pay the Price for the Rape of the Dr Congo?" (2008) 12 *Gonzaga Journal of International Law* 1; "Coltan, Congo & Conflict" (2013) The Hague Centre for Strategic Studies, 42–53, https://hcss.nl/sites/default/files/files/reports/HCSS_21_05_13_Coltan_Congo_Conflict_web.pdf.

[122] L. Juma, "The War in Congo: Transnational Conflict Networks and the Failure of Internationalism" (2006) 10 *Gonzaga Journal of International Law* 97.

[123] Ibid., 124.

[124] G. Nzongola-Ntalaja, *The Congo: From Leopold to Kabila: A People's History* (Zed Books, 2002), p. 227.

[125] Juma (*supra* n. 122) 132.

by smuggling networks.[126] These networks had ready markets from such corporations as America Mineral Fields and Barrick Gold Corporation of Canada.[127] Laurence Juma observed "a linkage of regional dynamics to the international conglomerates of companies, trade patterns and even to the top most political spectrum in the developed nations."[128]

Just as Congo's "rubber terror" was fueled by the then recent development of the vulcanization of rubber in the beginning of the twentieth century, by the century's end the development of computer technology spurred on new miseries as the eastern Congo, Katanga, possesses more than half the known supply of coltan, a mineral used in the manufacture of computer chips and cell phones.[129] Hochschild observed in 2005 that "[t]he rebel militias, Congo's African neighbors, and many of their corporate allies have little interest in ending the country's Balkanization. They prefer a cash-in-suitcases economy to a taxed and regulated one that would give all citizens a real share of the profits from natural resources."[130] Shining the glaring light of international criminal judicial scrutiny into such an environment was politically unthinkable.

3.7 Prosecutions by the International Criminal Court

As a structural distinction, the threshold difference between the ICC and the UN-based criminal prosecutions is that the latter serve political functions as well as judicial ones. While there is a degree of politicization of all courts, the tolerance of political and economic interference is significantly lessened in the ICC. The ICC does include the assembly of states parties but it also differs greatly from the Security Council with one state one vote and no veto powers from economically elite states, which along with targeted states are most likely to observe robust corporate protectionism. Moreover, the triggering mechanism for the initiation of preliminary investigations consists of three sources: state referral

---

[126] Juma (*supra* n. 122) 138.
[127] A. Hochschild, "Congo Back on the Brink II: The Dark Heart of Mineral Exploitation" (2004) *International Herald Tribune* Dec. 24, 1, 6.
[128] Juma (*supra* n. 122) 140–1.
[129] Juma (*supra* n. 122) 316; "Letter dated 16 January 2001 from the Secretary-General addressed to the President of the Security Council" also details the growing trade in conflict minerals in Kenya, DRC, Rwanda, Uganda, Burundi and Zimbabwe including that occupying forces were plundering gold, diamonds and Colombo-tantalite (coltan); see UNSC, "Letter dated 16 January 2001 from the Secretary-General addressed to the President of the Security Council" (January 16, 2001) UN Doc S/2001/49.
[130] Hochschild (*supra* n. 127) 317.

(including self-referral), exercise of proprio motu powers by the office of the prosecutor, or UN referral.[131] Obviously, UN referrals, made by the Security Council, would be subject to the same economic sensitivity according to historic practices, but proprio motu and state referral mechanisms have proven resilient to economic and political factors.

Moreover, Article 42 of the Rome Statute mandates that the Office of the Prosecutor must act independently from external sources[132] and this requirement is also provided in the Code of Conduct for the Office of the Prosecutor.[133] According to the Office of the Prosecutor Policy Paper on Case Selection and Prioritisation: "[I]ndependence goes beyond not seeking or acting on instructions: it means that decisions shall not be influenced or altered by the presumed or known wishes of any external actor."[134] Thus, this process is purely evidence driven, not politically or economically driven.

The ICC has indeed initiated prosecutions and/or investigations in volatile politicized situations with significant foreign corporate presence or for other reasons. The ICC has ongoing preliminary examinations in ten situations that implicate elite states and/or their closest allies. An example of such examinations is the investigation into US activities in Afghanistan since 2017 for alleged war crimes and crimes against humanity.[135] The ICC has also reopened a review of the UK activities stemming from allegations of war crimes in Iraq (reopened in 2017)[136] and initiated preliminary investigations into the politically sensitive situation in the Ukraine[137] and a Palestinian referral of Israeli activities on Palestinian territory.[138] In each of these cases the interests of P5 states or their closest allies are affected. It would hardly be plausible for these prosecutions to be initiated by the UNSC. Other ICC scrutiny situations

---

[131] Rome Statute (supra n. 12) art. 13.
[132] Ibid., art. 42.
[133] ICC-OTP Code of Conduct for the Office of the Prosecutor, 5 September 2013, OTP2013/024322 c2 s2.
[134] ICC-OTP Policy Paper on Case Selection and Prioritisation, September 15, 2016.
[135] Situation in the Islamic Republic of Afghanistan (Pretrial: Request for authorization of an investigation pursuant to article 15) ICC-02/17–7-Red (November 20, 2017).
[136] "Prosecutor of the International Criminal Court, Fatou Bensouda, Re-opens the Preliminary Examination of the Situation in Iraq" (ICC, May 13, 2014), www.icc-cpi.int//Pages/item.aspx?name=otp-statement-iraq-13–05-2014.
[137] "The Prosecutor of the International Criminal Court, Fatou Bensouda, Opens a Preliminary Examination in Ukraine" (ICC, April 25, 2014), www.icc-cpi.int//Pages/item.aspx?name=pr999.
[138] "Referral by the State of Palestine Pursuant to Articles 13(a) and 14 of the Rome Statute" (ICC, May 15, 2018), www.icc-cpi.int/itemsDocuments/2018-05-22_ref-palestine.pdf.

that would have been off limits under the UNSC system are those of Nigeria (though generally for activities of the terrorist group Boko Haram and actions against pro-Biafra groups), oil-rich Venezuela and the DRC.[139] In a Security Council environment, none of these prosecutions could have been politically possible because of their highly politicized character, political stalemate on the UNSC, or corporate protectionism.

The most telling (and advanced) of these situations, under an economic lens, is that of the DRC. Substantial resources have been allocated in the ICC-initiated DRC prosecutions and it was the first of the cases to go to trial. Though no corporate personnel were indicted, Ocampo's statements brought to light the belief of his office in illegal corporate conduct in the DRC and served as a deterrent to future corporate wrongdoing. The ICC has been accused of political prosecutions and more recently of showing a bias against African states, but many of these accusations originally stem from the United States or from other non-party states such as Sudan or other states being investigated. The DRC prosecutions reflect the best evidence of a departure from UN-based corporate protectionist prosecutions.

Another significant issue is whether there should be corporate liability for international crimes. In the ICC, Article 25 of the Rome Statute expressly provides only for the prosecution of natural persons, thus criminal liability for corporations would require an unlikely overhaul of the Court's mandate. Corporate liability was discussed at the Rome Conference, but the topic was dropped. Despite this, in 2003 then-prosecutor Ocampo made intriguing public statements concerning the situation in the DRC and suggested that his office would investigate and pursue corporate officer complicity.[140] While corporations themselves would not face liability, there were fears that corporate personnel might be personally liable. Ultimately, Ocampo did not pursue the liability of corporate officers because he never had sufficient evidence to make a case,[141] but he nonetheless left the door open for future prosecutions.

---

[139] Currently there are ten situations under preliminary examination: Afghanistan, Colombia, Gabon, Guinea, Iraq, Nigeria, Palestine, the Philippines, Ukraine and Venezuela.

[140] A. G. Cabrera Silva and J. Calderón Meza, "International Jurisdiction for Corporate Atrocities: An Interview with Luis Moreno Ocampo," *Harvard International Law Journal*, https://harvardilj.org/2016/07/international-jurisdiction-for-corporate-atrocities-an-interview-with-luis-moreno-ocampo/.

[141] Ibid.

However, it is important not to conflate the distinct issues of corporate criminal liability and target selection in international criminal prosecutions involving the potential of personal liability of corporate officers. Impunity from the latter is a more subtle and ubiquitous form of corporate protectionism. Indeed, this brand of protectionism defeats the goal of eradicating impunity by removing even the slightest possibility of exposure of corporate complicity through surrogate corporate officers. In the historic UN-based sanction system, both forms of protectionism were exercised while the Rome Statute provides for protection only from the threat of criminally charging the corporation but not from personal liability of officers. This is a significant conceptual distinction because while the ICC will not target corporations directly, it will investigate situations where corporate interests are at stake and, as indicated by Ocampo, prosecution of corporate officers is not off the table.[142] Moreover, it can provide an evidentiary record of corporate misconduct whether corporate leaders are targeted or not. In such cases, corporate partnerships with offending state leaders/elites face exposure and the resulting corporate bad faith. Such prosecutions also have the potential of disrupting such corporate partnerships with targets who face removal from office. From the corporate perspective, it is intuitive that bad faith (resulting in loss of profits) or the disruption of lucrative partnerships is a more serious or co-equal sanction then merely a fine, which would be the corporate penalty but for Article 25 of the Rome Statute. Thus, in terms of overall accountability for corporate misconduct, Article 25 of the Rome Statute is, in a practical sense, a paper tiger.

3.8   Conclusion

The ICC has greater limitations than the UNSC in terms of cases it can scrutinize for target selection owing to temporal and territorial jurisdictional constraints. But, of the twenty-one cases it has undertaken for preliminary investigations, full investigations and/or prosecution, it is clear that economic constraints serve little to no bar to its mandate. A cursory review of the cases that have been initiated by the UN and the cases it has refrained from investigating, as compared to those cases undertaken by the ICC, sharply reveal the political bias and corporate protectionism of the UN model in target selection. Consistency of past practices precludes it from being mere coincidence. The ICC does not

[142] Ibid.

practice corporate protectionism on the scale of the UN because of its conceptual application of Article 25 of the Rome Statute, its structural design, which does not default to elite state economic interest, ethical constraints on the Office of the Prosecutor and because of the practical safeguards, including referral mechanisms, built into the Rome Statute.

Currently, we have entered an even more problematic phase of target selection in the UN. Not all target selection is determined solely by economic protectionism. As indicated earlier, economic vetting is only a subset of wider political vetting. This nevertheless creates significant hurdles for any international prosecution initiatives and requires a perfect storm of economic and political factors which must be overcome. Looking ahead, UN corporate and political protectionism in target selection is likely to become more entrenched than during the early post-Cold War era. Given the political trends among the current leadership in the P5 states of Russia, China and the United States, with a marked movement away from internationalism, the further formation of UN criminal tribunals is increasingly unlikely. Moreover, further UN referrals to the ICC are equally unlikely.

In May 2014 Russia and China vetoed a measure to refer the Syrian situation to the ICC.[143] This prompted calls for the development of a UN-based ad hoc prosecution for Syria,[144] but it also failed. Thereafter, in December 2016 the UN General Assembly established "a mechanism to investigate and preserve evidence of international crime in Syria."[145] Though this mechanism can serve to preserve evidence for a subsequent prosecution, the General Assembly is incapable of instigating an ICTY type tribunal under Article 41 as that is solely within the province of the Security Council.[146] In September 2018, a parallel process for Myanmar was initiated with the UN Human Rights Council recommending a mechanism for gathering and collecting evidence with an eye

---

[143] "Russia, China Block Security Council Referral of Syria to the International Criminal Court" (*UN News*, May 22, 2014), https://news.un.org/en/story/2014/05/468962-russia-china-block-security-council-referral-syria-international-criminal-court.

[144] C. de Ponte, former chief prosecutor for the ICTY, called for the development of an ad hoc tribunal for Syria in 2015; see "Call for Special Tribunal to Investigate War Crimes and Mass Atrocities in Syria" (*The Guardian*, March 17, 2015), www.theguardian.com/world/2015/mar/17/call-for-special-tribunal-to-investigate-war-crimes-and-mass-atrocities-in-syria.

[145] A. Whiting, "An Investigation Mechanism for Syria: The General Assembly Steps into the Breach" (2017) 15 *Journal of International Criminal Justice* 231.

[146] D. Jinks, "Does the U.N. General Assembly Have the Authority to Establish an International Criminal Tribunal for Syria?" (*Just Security*, May 22, 2014), www.justsecurity.org/10721/u-n-general-assembly-authority-establish-international-criminal-tribunal-syria/.

toward a referral to the ICC.[147] Whether this measure will succeed in generating an ICC referral is dubious and its creation has been described as being "born out of desperation."[148]

In Sri Lanka, the UN High Commissioner for Human Rights called for the creation of a hybrid criminal court for atrocities committed in that country.[149] However, the establishment of an ad hoc hybrid tribunal was rejected by the Sri Lankan government because, while it would accept foreign assistance in a domestic court, it would not allow the participation of foreign judges[150] or other international personnel or oversight.

Though neither the failed Syrian nor Sri Lankan initiative involved an economic vetting per se, both are indicative of the current hostile environment in the UN toward the creation of international criminal tribunals and/or referrals to the ICC, particularly amongst select elite states. Until this atmosphere changes, international criminal target selection based on evidence rather than corporate protectionism or political bias will largely be left up to the ICC.

---

[147] See "Myanmar: Creation of UN Mechanism a Step toward Accountability" (*International Commission of Jurists*, September 27, 2018), www.icj.org/hrc39-myanmarres/. There are even calls for a permanent mechanism to collect evidence in relevant situations; see also P. L. Mahnad, "An Independent Mechanism for Myanmar: A Turning Point in the Pursuit of Accountability for International Crimes" (*EJIL: Talk!*, October 1, 2018), www.ejiltalk.org/a-turning-point-in-the-pursuit-of-accountability-for-international-crimes/.

[148] Ibid.

[149] UNGA, "Comprehensive Report of the Office of the United Nations High Commissioner for Human Rights on Sri Lanka" (September 28, 2015) UN Doc A/HRC/30/61 Part I; UNHRC "Report of the OHCHR Investigation on Sri Lanka (OISL)" (September 16, 2015) UN Doc A/HRC/30/CPR.2 Part II.

[150] "Sri Lanka Reiterates Not to Allow Foreign Judges in War Probe" (*Xinhua*, June 13, 2016), www.xinhuanet.com/english/2016–06/13/c_135433335.htm.

PART II

Arms Fairs and 'Flying Money'

The Circulation of Weapons, Art and Cash in Conflict Zones

Linking Economic Actors to the Core International Crimes of the Syrian Regime

NINA H. B. JØRGENSEN AND WILLIAM H. WILEY

4.1 Introduction

When the protracted Syrian conflict eventually comes to an end and transitional justice in its many manifestations is properly operationalized, a test case for the prosecution of economic actors under international criminal law may emerge. The evidence of international crimes in Syria has been documented and subjected to scrutiny and analysis since the start of the conflict in 2011, by the United Nations, non-governmental organizations, and domestic investigative bodies. There is no shortage of crime base evidence, in other words the human stories of suffering, victimization, traumatization, loss and injury in multiple geographical locations resulting from state-sponsored, systematic violence. The challenge, especially as it concerns government and business actors who provide the economic fuel for the conflict, is to establish the link between the crime base and the perpetrators, who may hold high office and be geographically remote from the commission of the crimes.

This chapter examines investigative approaches towards uncovering the role of economic actors alleged to have facilitated international crimes attributed to the Syrian regime. The work of the Commission for International Justice and Accountability (CIJA) and the limitations of the CIJA model in investigating international crimes of an economic nature are first explained before outlining the applicable jurisprudential framework with reference to customary international law. The chapter proceeds to examine how economic actors who are engaged in activities in Syria during the conflict might be held to account in law where they are suspected of the perpetration of core international crimes.

4.2   The CIJA and the CIJA Model

The CIJA and its investigative model are increasingly the subject of scholarly inquiry.[1] The CIJA is a non-profit foundation registered in The Hague, The Netherlands, and it undertakes criminal investigations in the midst of ongoing armed conflicts. Formally established in 2012, the CIJA commenced operations informally in Syria in 2011 vis-à-vis the Syrian regime, expanding its efforts in 2014 to encompass Islamic State criminality in Syria and Iraq. Other operations are underway in Asia with new investigations expected to commence in Africa in early 2020. In every conflict in which the CIJA engages, evidence collection in the field is followed by analysis geared towards mapping the command, control and communication arrangements of the target structures with, in turn, the individual criminal responsibility of those most responsible for the perpetration of core international crimes being assessed by CIJA counsel.

The CIJA is not a human rights advocacy organization; it has neither a website nor the capacity to issue press releases, although it does deal with a fair volume of media inquiries. The leadership of the CIJA is primarily drawn from the ranks of investigators, analysts, and lawyers possessed of long practice in public-international institutions seized with questions of international criminal law and international humanitarian law (ICHL); these individuals invariably have like experience secured in domestic contexts. As such, the work of the CIJA is guided by criminal law and focused almost entirely upon the proffering of assistance to international as well as domestic law enforcement and prosecutorial bodies in Western Europe and North America, particularly where the resources of the public sector and its physical risk tolerance are insufficient to operate in conflict zones.

---

[1] For instance, see M. Rankin, 'Investigating Crimes against Humanity in Syria and Iraq: The Commission for International Justice and Accountability' (2017) 9(4) *Global Responsibility to Protect* 395–421; M. Rankin, 'The Future of International Criminal Evidence in New Wars? The Evolution of the Commission for International Justice and Accountability (CIJA)' (2018) 20(3) *Journal of Genocide Research* 392–411; M. Burgis-Kasthala, 'Entrepreneurial Justice: Syria, the Commission for International Justice and Accountability and the Renewal of International Criminal Justice' (2019) 30(4)*European Journal of International Law* 1165–1185; and W. H. Wiley, 'International(ised) Criminal Justice at a Crossroads: The Role of Civil Society in the Investigation of Core International Crimes and the "CIJA Model"', in M. Bergsmo et al. (eds.), *Power in International Criminal Justice* (Torkel Opsahl Academic EPublisher, 2020, forthcoming).

As of mid-2019, the CIJA has prepared sixteen complex case files for international prosecution.[2] Ten files inculpate personnel serving at the highest reaches of the Syrian regime as well as a range of governorate-level security-intelligence and military officers. A further six Islamic State case files have been completed since 2014. As there is no international adjudicative body with jurisdiction over the wars in Syria and Iraq, the CIJA has transmitted these files as well as all CIJA evidentiary holdings – or is otherwise in the processes of so doing – to the Syria IIIM and UNITAD.[3] The relationship of the CIJA with its thirteen domestic partner states in Europe and North America gives rise annually to requests for assistance regarding hundreds of suspected perpetrators of core international crimes known or believed to be present in the West. To date, several arrests in Europe of Syrian regime and Islamic State perpetrators have been executed on the basis of CIJA-collected evidence and, in some cases, the presence of the suspects themselves in the West has been brought to the attention of the partner states by the CIJA, which has its own suspect-tracking capability.

Whilst lying outside of its core mandate, the CIJA nonetheless supports transitional justice efforts, human rights inquiries and civil litigation, where the provision of such support does not impugn the efforts of its partners engaged in the criminal justice realm. For instance, CIJA evidence and expert witness submissions were the key to the recent judgment handed down by a United States Federal Court, which awarded the family of the Anglo-American journalist Marie Colvin, killed in a targeted regime rocket attack in Homs in February 2012, more than 300 million USD to be recovered from Syrian state assets.[4] It is a safe bet that if any of the court-awarded damages are recovered, the assets will in many cases turn out to be hidden under the names of trusted private-sector associates and financial institutions.

In the context of its case-building activities, the CIJA has collected a considerable volume of evidence in the field, ranging from several

---

[2] For reasons of operational security, CIJA investigations will necessarily be described only in broad outline.

[3] The IIIM was established by the United Nations General Assembly (UNGA) through UNGA Resolution 71/248 (December 2016); it is known formally as the International, Impartial and Independent Mechanism to assist in the investigation and prosecution of persons responsible for the most serious crimes under international law committed in the Syrian Arab Republic since March 2011. UNITAD (the United Nations Investigative Team for Accountability of Da'esh/ISIL) was created by the United Nations Security Council (UNSC) through UNSC Resolution 2379 (September 2017).

[4] *Colvin v. Syrian Arab Republic*, 363 F. Supp. 3d 141 (D.D.C. 2019).

thousand witness interviews, including the testimony of a great many regime defectors with insider knowledge, to 800,000 original pages of Syrian regime documentation generated by political, military, and security-intelligence structures. These paper records have been extracted from Syria and digitalized at CIJA headquarters; it is this wealth of information and evidence, concerning both the Syrian regime and Islamic State, which domestic authorities are most especially drawing upon. In support of these authorities, the CIJA additionally assigns analytical as well as field assets to the task of answering bespoke investigative inquiries. Of still further relevance is the well-established CIJA 'cyber' team, which exploits prima facie evidence found online whilst extracting data from captured computers and smart phones, these devices having been acquired in the main from Islamic State sources. Finally, the CIJA retains other specialists who are concerned with, inter alia, the investigation of sexual offences as well as the professional development of CIJA personnel deployed in conflict zones.

4.3   Limitations of the CIJA Model when Applied to Economic Actors

The conceptual interest of the CIJA in the criminal investigation of economic actors has not been disclosed in the public domain to this juncture. The CIJA model – which is applied at the present time only by the CIJA – is highly effective when brought to bear against what might be termed the traditional targets of international criminal investigations, in particular political, military, and security-intelligence leadership personnel. The keys to the success of the CIJA in this respect lie in (i) the high physical-risk tolerance of the CIJA which, unlike public institutions, can deploy large numbers of trained investigators within dangerous operational areas such as Syria and Iraq; and (ii) the ability of the CIJA to operate anywhere within the limits of its physical-risk tolerance, that is, without regard to the sort of political-diplomatic considerations which frequently serve to undermine public-sector investigations (for example, the Syria IIIM cannot send its personnel into Syria without the permission of the government of that state).

These advantages relative to public institutions can be readily employed to facilitate the criminal investigation of economic actors. However, when it comes to the investigation of such actors, the CIJA has something of an Achilles heel. More specifically, as a private body, the CIJA suffers from a significant disadvantage vis-à-vis public-sector institutions arising from the inability of CIJA personnel to secure, on a consistent basis by indisputably lawful means, banking and related records held by financial institutions. Furthermore, requests from the CIJA for investigative assistance to financial institutions would be futile.

Admittedly, the CIJA has within its cyber team the requisite technical capacity to acquire prima facie evidence relating to bank accounts and financial transactions. For several reasons, the CIJA is not prepared to bring this expertise to bear vis-à-vis financial institutions. The most important consideration in this respect is the high probability that the domestic courts with which the CIJA engages would find to be inadmissible any financial data secured by means of subterfuge. It has been the experience of the CIJA to date, in a range of domestic jurisdictions, that the courts would appear to have a limitless tolerance for the admission of physical evidence (most especially, documentation generated by perpetrating structures) collected by the CIJA in the field and moved over international borders into Europe. In particular, the CIJA has seen no indication that the domestic courts of Europe as well as the United States are concerned with the evident fact that the collection of so-called battlefield evidence, where it has been generated by state institutions, presumably contravenes the domestic laws of the states in question (for instance, Syria). At the same time, it is the view of the CIJA that any CIJA effort to secure financial records by electronic means would give rise to not-unjustified allegations, put forward by defence counsel and any other interested observer, that the CIJA had engaged in unlawful searches and seizures from its bases in Europe. The CIJA therefore assesses that the key to the admissibility in Western courts of CIJA-collected information-cum-evidence lies in the physical location of the CIJA personnel responsible for the collection of any given piece of evidence. Where the CIJA is operating physically in conflict zones characterized by the breakdown of law enforcement, Western courts are without doubt prepared to tolerate prima facie violations of the laws of that territory by CIJA personnel. Conversely, where the CIJA is gathering potential evidence by electronic means, from offices based in states that are characterized by the rule of law (for example, in Europe), a different standard of conduct shall assuredly be expected of this private-sector, investigative body by the courts – that is, the same standard that would apply to public-sector authorities.

The foregoing assertions should not lead to the conclusion that the CIJA is in every instance unable to proceed without public-sector assistance when it comes to securing sufficient evidence to facilitate the prosecution of an economic actor. What is required, simply, is that such evidence – documentary evidence, at any rate – should be found in the field. As of mid-2019, the CIJA has prepared one case file that sets out the individual criminal responsibility of a single economic actor of considerable importance to the Syrian regime, whom the CIJA alleges aided and abetted core international crimes perpetrated by the Syrian security-intelligence services.[5] The evidence that underpins this particular case file was found within the large volume of Syrian regime documentation acquired to date by the CIJA and supplemented, where required, by the testimony of insider witnesses.

4.4   The Legal and Conceptual Framework for the Investigation of Economic Actors

4.4.1   The Post-World War II Trials

It is well-known that certain German businesses and financial actors profited from the re-armament programme of the 1930s and the reorganization of the German economy for military purposes which included the establishment of extermination camps and widespread forcible population transfers as slave labour. The post-World War II trials targeted both financiers who contributed to the maintenance of the German war-economy and helped to fund the Nazi regime and industrialists who provided the practical support and materials needed to accomplish the regime's wartime objectives.[6]

One of the defendants before the IMT was the president of the *Reichsbank* (Germany's central bank), Walter Funk. The IMT found that in 1942 Funk had agreed with Himmler that the *Reichsbank* was to receive certain gold, jewels and currency from the SS and that, as a result, the SS sent to the *Reichsbank* the personal belongings taken from victims who had been murdered in extermination camps.[7] While Funk claimed

---

[5] As the suspect in question has been neither apprehended nor charged with any offence, professional ethics and considerations of operational security preclude any further examination in this forum of the case file in question.

[6] The International Military Tribunal for the Far East (IMTFE) at Tokyo convicted three Japanese economic and financial leaders – Naoki Hoshino, General Teiichi Suzuki and Okinori Kaya – for participation in crimes against peace in respect of their contribution towards Japan's military aggression during World War II, but there was found to be no evidence connecting these three accused with war crimes. See further N. Boister and R. Cryer, *The Tokyo International Military Tribunal: A Reappraisal* (Oxford University Press, 2008), pp. 56, 59.

[7] Trial of the Major War Criminals Before the International Military Tribunal, Nuremberg, 14 November 1945–1 October 1946, Vol. 1, 1947, pp. 305–6.

that he did not know that the *Reichsbank* was receiving articles of this kind, the IMT found that he 'either knew what was being received or was deliberately closing his eyes to what was being done'.[8] In his various roles, including as president of Continental Oil Company, Funk was found to have participated in the economic exploitation of occupied territories with knowledge of German occupation policies.[9] By 1943, Funk was a member of the Central Planning Board which determined the total number of labourers needed for German industry and required this labour to be made available, usually by deportation from occupied territories, and he was found to have been aware that this board was effectively importing slave labour.[10] In addition, as president of the *Reichsbank*, Funk was determined to have been indirectly involved in the utilization of concentration camp labour.[11] Funk was convicted of crimes against peace, crimes against humanity, and war crimes, though not of participating in the common plan or conspiracy described in Count 1 of the Nuremberg Indictment.[12]

Hjalmar Schacht was president of the *Reichsbank* from 1923 to 1930 and again from 1937 until his dismissal from the position in 1939.[13] He was also Minister of Economics and Plenipotentiary General for the War Economy in the mid-1930s. He was charged under Counts 1 and 2 of the Nuremberg Indictment with participating in the common plan or conspiracy and crimes against peace on the basis of his active role in organizing the German economy for war, and 'using the facilities of the Reichsbank to the fullest extent in the German rearmament effort'.[14] The IMT acquitted him on both counts. The Tribunal found that 'rearmament of itself is not criminal under the Charter' and that in order to hold Schacht criminally responsible for a crime against peace, it would need to be shown that his conduct formed part of the Nazi plan to wage aggressive wars.[15] Despite being a central figure in Germany's re-armament

---

[8] Ibid., p. 306.

[9] Ibid.

[10] Ibid.

[11] 'Under his direction the Reichsbank set up a revolving fund of 12,000,000 Reichsmarks to the credit of the SS for the construction of factories to use concentration camp laborers.' Ibid.

[12] Ibid., pp. 304–7.

[13] Following a dispute with Göring and after losing favour with Hitler, Schacht was arrested by the Gestapo in 1944 and spent the remainder of the war in a concentration camp. See ibid., p. 308.

[14] Ibid., p. 307.

[15] Ibid., p. 309.

programme who, 'with his intimate knowledge of German finance',[16] understood the purpose of the economic policy that he devised, namely to prepare Germany for war, it was not proved that Schacht 'did in fact know of the Nazi aggressive plans'.[17]

The inclusion of the arms supplier Gustav Krupp in the main trial before the IMT was intended to allow a strong precedent to be set for subsequent proceedings against industrialists.[18] The United States, in particular, adopted the position that 'the great industrialists of Germany were guilty of the crimes charged in the [Nuremberg] Indictment quite as much as its politicians, diplomats, and soldiers'.[19] However, Gustav Krupp was found unfit to stand trial and an American proposal to substitute him with his son, Alfried Krupp, was unsuccessful. The three so-called 'industrialists cases' concerned the managers, directors, and owners of the large German enterprises Krupp, I.G. Farben, and Flick, and formed part of the subsequent proceedings at Nuremberg conducted by the United States pursuant to Control Council Law No. 10.[20]

The Krupp concern was a private company that owned and controlled directly, and through subsidiaries, mines, steel, and armaments plants that provided iron and steel for processing into ships and tanks as part of the Nazi war effort. The basis for Count 2 of the Indictment was that the accused 'exploited, as principals or as accessories in consequence of a deliberate design and policy, territories occupied by German armed forces in a ruthless way, far beyond the needs of the army of occupation and in disregard of the needs of the local economy'.[21] Six defendants, including Alfried Krupp, were convicted under this count of war crimes and crimes against humanity in respect of plunder and spoliation of the property and civilian economies of countries under German occupation. It was found that the 'initiative for the acquisition of properties,

---

[16] Ibid.
[17] Ibid., p. 310.
[18] J. A. Bush, 'The Prehistory of Corporations and Conspiracy in International Criminal Law: What Nuremberg Really Said' (2009) 109 *Columbia Law Review* 1094–262, p. 1112.
[19] Trial of the Major War Criminals (*supra* n. 7), p. 137.
[20] Control Council Law No. 10 on the 'Punishment of Persons Guilty of War Crimes, Crimes against Peace and against Humanity', 20 December 1945, was designed 'to establish a uniform legal basis in Germany for the prosecution of war criminals and other similar offenders, other than those dealt with by the International Military Tribunal' (preamble).
[21] *United States* v. *Alfried Krupp, et al.*, Trials of War Criminals Before the Nuernberg Military Tribunals Under Control Council Law No. 10, October 1946–April 1949, Vol. IX, 'The Krupp Case', p. 1338.

machines, and materials in the occupied countries was that of the Krupp firm and that it utilized the Reich government and Reich agencies whenever necessary to accomplish its purpose'.[22] In relation to Count 3 of the Indictment concerning the slave labour plan and programme of the Third Reich, the argument of the accused that they had scant knowledge of the persecution of Jews by Nazi leaders was dismissed as no more than a gesture. It was found that this fact 'was common knowledge not only in Germany but throughout the civilized world' and that in order to establish the offence it was not necessary to demonstrate knowledge of the persecution in all its 'horrifying and gruesome details'.[23]

The allegations in the case against twenty-four officials of the I.G. Farben firm were similar to those in Krupp, except that membership in the SS was included as a separate charge against certain of the accused. According to the Indictment, by 1939 Farben was immense in terms of its size, technological and financial influence, and in the scope of its interests and affiliations.[24] During World War II, Farben was most active in the fields of synthetic rubber, gasoline, nitrogen, light metals, and, to a lesser extent, explosives. The Indictment viewed Farben as an 'instrumentality' through which the accused acted individually and collectively, the theory being that 'all the defendants were jointly responsible for the acts of the I.G. Farben Konzern because of their related positions and functions as leaders of the Konzern'.[25] The Tribunal made it clear, however, that Farben was not charged with any crime as a corporation.[26]

Several of the accused were convicted of spoliation under Count 2 of the Indictment. However, others were acquitted due to an absence of evidence of their knowledge of or connection to the underlying criminal acts where the evidence of transactions was 'equally consistent with inferences that the acquisitions might have been effected in a legal manner'.[27] The Tribunal stressed that responsibility could only arise in respect of positive conduct on the part of the accused that constitutes 'ordering, approving, authorizing, or joining in the execution of a policy

[22] Ibid., p. 1372.

[23] Ibid., p. 1434.

[24] *United States* v. *Carl Krauch, et al.*, Trials of War Criminals Before the Nuernberg Military Tribunals Under Control Council Law No. 10, October 1946–April 1949, Vol. VII, 'The Farben Case', p. 16.

[25] Ibid., p. 378.

[26] *United States* v. *Carl Krauch, et al.*, Trials of War Criminals Before the Nuernberg Military Tribunals Under Control Council Law No. 10, October 1946–April 1949, Vol. VIII, 'The Farben Case' (continued), p. 1108.

[27] Ibid., p. 1155.

or act which is criminal in character'.[28] It was deemed essential when seeking to attach individual criminal responsibility to acts not personally carried out by the accused that 'the action of a corporate officer in authorizing illegal action be done with adequate knowledge of those essential elements of the authorized act which give it its criminal character'.[29] Further, as it concerned 'transactions apparently legal in form, this means positive knowledge that the owner is being deprived of his property against his will during military occupancy'.[30]

The Farben officials who were found to be implicated in the Nazi enslavement and slave labour programme were convicted of war crimes and crimes against humanity under Count 3 of the Indictment.[31] However, all of the accused were acquitted on the part of Count 3 concerning the chemicals supplied by Farben – in particular, Zyklon B – which were used to murder extermination camp inmates and during unlawful medical experiments. The acquittals pursuant to Count 3 were a function of the court's finding that the defendants' knowledge of the criminal use of the chemicals could not be proved in circumstances in which a non-criminal use was also possible. While Zyklon B had been central to the mass extermination operations, it could also be used as an insecticide.[32]

The 'Flick concern' dominated the German steel and coal industry at the time of World War II. Friedrich Flick, the firm's main proprietor and head, and some of his business associates were charged with participation in the slave labour programme of the Third Reich and the use of prisoners of war in armament production (Count 1); spoliation of public and private property in occupied territories (Count 2); crimes against humanity in compelling by means of anti-Semitic economic pressure the owners of certain industrial properties to part with title thereto (Count 3); and, as members of the Keppler Circle or Friends of Himmler, with knowledge of its criminal activities, contributing large sums to the financing of the SS (Count 4).[33] More specifically, Count 4 charged the accused with war crimes and crimes against humanity, 'in

---

[28] Ibid., p. 1157.
[29] Ibid.
[30] Ibid.
[31] Ibid., p. 1187 (conclusion in relation to Krauch).
[32] Ibid., p. 1169.
[33] *United States* v. *Friedrich Flick et al.*, Trials of War Criminals Before the Nuernberg Military Tribunals Under Control Council Law No. 10, October 1946–April 1949, Vol. VI, 'The Flick Case', p. 1190.

that they were accessories to, abetted, took a consenting part in, were connected with plans and enterprises involving, and were members of organizations or groups connected with: murders, brutalities, cruelties, tortures, atrocities and other inhumane acts committed by the Nazi Party and its organizations, including principally the [SS]'.[34]

Flick and one other accused were convicted under the first count in respect of the procurement of slave labour needed to meet their production quota in a facility producing freight cars that were deemed to constitute military equipment.[35] Flick alone was found guilty under the second count. The third count concerned four transactions by which the Flick interests acquired industrial property formerly owned or controlled by Jews. It was not contended that the accused had 'participated in the Nazi persecution of Jews other than in taking advantage of the so-called Aryanization program by seeking and using State economic pressure to obtain from the owners, not all of whom were Jewish, the four properties in question'.[36] Count 3 was dismissed on the basis of an absence of jurisdiction or that no crime against humanity had been proved. The Tribunal took the view that neither the IMT Judgment nor the law of nations recognized personal guilt under the category of crimes against humanity 'merely by exerting anti-Semitic pressure to procure by purchase or through state expropriation industrial property owned by Jews'.[37] It was also noted that on a proper construction of Control Council Law No. 10, only offences against the person and not offences against property were included.[38]

According to the Tribunal, 'the gist of count four is that as members of the Himmler Circle of Friends, Flick and Steinbrinck with knowledge of the criminal activities of the SS contributed funds and influence to its support'.[39] The Circle consisted of about forty bankers, industrialists, government officials, and SS officers. The Tribunal found that at least half of the members responded to SS requests for funds, raising over one million Reichsmarks annually until 1944. Flick and Steinbrinck contributed a total of 100,000 Reichsmarks each, with Flick's contribution being paid by one of his companies, Mittelstahl, and Steinbrinck's donation being covered by a state-owned corporation with which he was

---

[34] Ibid., p. 23.
[35] Ibid., p. 1202.
[36] Ibid., p. 1212.
[37] Ibid., p. 1215.
[38] Ibid.
[39] Ibid., p. 1216.

connected. It was found that the money was placed in a special fund in the Stein Bank at Cologne and after that into an account in the Dresdner Bank upon which Karl Wolff, Himmler's personal adjutant, drew cheques. Both banks were represented in the Circle. The Tribunal did not find that the accused knew about the second account or the specific purpose of the several cheques drawn on it. Furthermore, in the view of the Tribunal, the prosecution had not shown that any part of the money was used directly for the criminal activities of the SS, and the Tribunal considered it 'reasonably clear' that some of the funds had been used purely for cultural purposes. Nevertheless, the Tribunal viewed 100,000 Reichsmarks as a 'substantial contribution'.[40]

The defence argument was centred on the alleged lack of knowledge by the accused regarding the use of the donated funds for the criminal purposes of the SS. In the event, the Tribunal considered it to be clear from the evidence that the accused 'gave to Himmler, the Reich Leader SS, a blank check' which had helped to maintain the SS, a criminal organization.[41] The Tribunal was satisfied that some of the donated money went towards the maintenance of the SS and it was 'immaterial whether it was spent on salaries or for lethal gas'.[42] Flick and his co-accused were therefore found guilty under Count 4.

The SS and five other organizations had been the subject of proceedings before the IMT pursuant to Article 9 of the Nuremberg Charter which provided that '[a]t the trial of any individual member of any group or organization the Tribunal may declare (in connection with any act of which the individual may be convicted) that the group or organization of which the individual was a member was a criminal organization'.[43] According to Article 10 of the Charter, a declaration of criminality by the IMT against an accused organization was final and could not be challenged in any subsequent proceedings against a member of that organization. The IMT noted that the procedure relating to criminal organizations was 'far reaching and novel' and that sufficient safeguards needed to be in place to avoid 'great injustice'.[44] In particular, it had to be proved that membership of a criminal organization was both voluntary and based on knowledge of the organization's criminal activities.[45] The

[40] Ibid., p. 1220.
[41] Ibid., p. 1221.
[42] Ibid.
[43] See Trial of the Major War Criminals (*supra* n. 7), pp. 255–79.
[44] Ibid., p. 256.
[45] Ibid.

IMT made a declaration of criminality against the Leadership Corps of the Nazi Party, the Gestapo and SD, and the SS. Meanwhile, Control Council Law No. 10 recognized membership in one of the organizations declared criminal by the IMT as a separate crime, potentially punishable by death.[46]

Flick was not charged with membership of the SS as a separate crime. The basis for the conviction under Count 4 appeared to be his provision of support to an organization (i.e. the SS) which had been declared a criminal organization in the IMT proceedings, with knowledge of that organization's criminal activities. Notably, the judgment against Flick considered Count 4 together with a fifth count concerning only Steinbrinck's membership of the SS as a separate crime. Affirming the criminal nature of the SS as an organization, responsible on a large scale for crimes, the Tribunal held that: 'One who knowingly by his influence and money contributes to the support thereof must, under settled legal principles, be deemed to be, if not a principal, certainly an accessory to such crimes.'[47] From the Tribunal's perspective, it was irrelevant that the SS had not formally been labelled a criminal organization at the time of Flick and his co-accused's involvement with the Circle.[48]

The *Zyklon B* case was heard before a British Military Court sitting at Hamburg pursuant to a Royal Warrant dated 14 June 1945 which provided the basis for the exercise of jurisdiction over alleged war criminals. Bruno Tesch, the owner of a firm that produced poison gas, was charged together with his deputy and his technician with supplying gas that was used for the extermination of allied nationals interned in concentration camps, knowing that the gas was to be used for this purpose.[49] Tesch and his deputy were convicted of war crimes and sentenced to death while the technician was acquitted.[50] It is apparent from the verdicts and the summing up of the Judge Advocate that the case turned on proof that the accused knew that the gas, commonly used for the extermination of lice and as a disinfectant, was to be used for the purpose of killing human beings.[51] Although the activities with which the accused were charged were commercial transactions conducted by civilians, the case was

---

[46] Control Council Law No. 10, Articles II(1)(d) and II(3)(a).
[47] 'The Flick Case' (*supra* n. 33), p. 1217.
[48] Ibid.
[49] *The Zyklon B Case, Trial of Bruno Tesch and two others*, United Nations War Crimes Commission, Law Reports of Trials of War Criminals, Vol. I, 1947, p. 93.
[50] Ibid., p.102.
[51] Ibid., p. 101.

regarded as a clear example of the application of the rule that 'the provisions of the laws and customs of war are addressed not only to combatants and to members of state and other public authorities, but to anybody who is in a position to assist in their violation'.[52]

The post-World War II trials are notable for the number of economic actors who were indicted, including bankers, industrialists, and financial planners, and for the tribunals' recognition of various forms of economic participation in war crimes and crimes against humanity as well as in the waging of a war of aggression. Further, it was established that individual criminal responsibility could flow from economic activities even if the motive for the accomplice was pure financial gain. For example, members of the Roechling firm who were tried before a French tribunal pursuant to Control Council Law No.10 were convicted on the basis that they had done everything in their power economically to bring about the triumph of Hitler and support his war aims even though their efforts were primarily directed towards their own enrichment.[53] The principle that 'guilt must be personal' was also emphasised, despite the introduction of the novel concept of criminal organizations.[54] In *Farben*, the Tribunal elaborated upon the 'conception of personal individual guilt' in the context of corporate activity, finding that: 'Responsibility does not automatically attach to an act proved to be criminal merely by virtue of a defendant's membership in the Vorstand. Conversely, one may not utilize the corporate structure to achieve an immunity from criminal responsibility for illegal acts which he directs, counsels, aids, orders, or abets.'[55]

While the cases cited above still represent the most comprehensive treatment to date of the accountability of the funders and profiteers of armed conflict and are frequently invoked to establish the customary international law elements of complicity, they did not fully develop the various modes of liability applied.[56] It emerges from this jurisprudence

---

[52] Ibid., p. 103.
[53] *Commissioner* v. *Roechling et al.*, Trials of War Criminals Before the Nuernberg Military Tribunals Under Control Council Law No. 10, October 1946–April 1949, Vol. XIV, Appendix B, p. 1066.
[54] 'The Krupp Case' (*supra* n. 21), p. 1448.
[55] 'The Farben Case' (continued) (*supra* n. 26), p. 1153.
[56] See also the discussion in International Commission of Jurists (ICJ), Report of the ICJ Expert Legal Panel on Corporate Complicity in International Crimes: Corporate Complicity & Legal Accountability, Vol. 2: Criminal Law and International Crimes, 2008, www.icj.org/report-of-the-international-commission-of-jurists-expert-legal-panel-on-corporate-complicity-in-international-crimes/.

that knowledge of the criminal activities of the principal perpetrator, whether this be an individual or an organization, is an applicable *mens rea* standard for complicity. There is furthermore a suggestion in the *Flick* case that financial contributions must be 'substantial' for liability to ensue, at least in the context of support to a criminal organization. Despite the abandonment of the concept of criminal organizations in modern international law,[57] *Flick* may still serve as a precedent where financial support is provided to a collective, such as a security-intelligence organ, that is proved to be engaged in criminal activities such as torture. The concept of complicity has been further refined in the modern jurisprudence, and the focus has fallen squarely on aiding and abetting as the mode of liability that best captures the involvement of economic actors. While the appropriateness of this focus is open to challenge, and other modes of liability such as joint criminal enterprise may be equally relevant depending on the facts, the focus of the section that follows is on aiding and abetting. It is here that the jurisprudence of the IMT and subsequent proceedings continues to serve as an imperfect, albeit essential guide to the applicable customary international law.

4.4.2 The Modern Jurisprudence

The ad hoc International Criminal Tribunals for the Former Yugoslavia (ICTY) and Rwanda (ICTR) did not single out financial leaders or industrialists in the same way as had the tribunals established after World War II. A considerable amount of evidence, including expert testimony, was adduced during the trial of the former Serbian President Slobodan Milošević to demonstrate how Milošević had financed and conducted the conflicts in Serbia and beyond.[58] The evidence helped to shed light on the financial structures set up to facilitate support for various ethnic Serb enclaves such as the Republika Srpska and the Krajina as well as the sources of the funds used to sustain the

---

[57] On this issue, see N. H. B. Jørgensen, 'The Abandoned Nuremberg Concept of Criminal Organizations in the Context of Justice in Rwanda' (2002) 12 *Criminal Law Forum* 371–406 and 'The Criminality of Organizations under International Law', in A. Nollkaemper and H. van der Wilt (eds.), *System Criminality in International Law* (Cambridge University Press, 2009), pp. 201–21.

[58] Expert reports by a Prosecution 'Financial Investigator', Morten Torkildsen, were admitted in part in the Milošević case; see *Prosecutor* v. *Slobodan Milošević*, IT-02-54, Decision on Admissibility of Morten Torkildsen's Evidence, 27 March 2003. The Expert Witness also testified: Trial Transcript, 10 April 2003, pp. 19006–143.

conflict.[59] Some of this evidence was admitted in other cases, such as *Perišić*, although merely as contextual information.[60]

Perišić, who was chief of the general staff of the Yugoslav Army from 1993 to 1998, was 'alleged to have provided personnel and logistical assistance to the army of the Republika Srpska ("VRS"), contributing substantially and materially to their capacity to commit crimes'.[61] The ICTY Appeals Chamber controversially overturned Perišić's conviction by the Trial Chamber on the basis that 'no conviction for aiding and abetting may be entered if the element of specific direction is not established beyond reasonable doubt, either explicitly or implicitly'.[62] The phrase 'specific direction' originally came from the *Tadić* case where the ICTY Appeals Chamber, in distinguishing joint criminal enterprise from aiding and abetting liability, explained that '[t]he aider and abettor carries out acts specifically directed to assist, encourage or lend moral support to the perpetration of a certain specific crime [. . .]'.[63] While the *Tadić* definition of aiding and abetting was frequently cited in ICTY and ICTR jurisprudence, the notion of 'specific direction' had attracted little sustained attention prior to its reinforcement as a core element of the *actus reus* in *Perišić*.

A differently constituted Appeals Chamber in the *Šainović* case departed from the decision in *Perišić* and concluded that 'specific direction' was not an element of aiding and abetting liability. The *Šainović* Appeals Chamber based its assessment on customary international law and found that the *actus reus* of aiding and abetting 'consists of practical assistance, encouragement, or moral support which has a substantial effect on the perpetration of the crime' while the *mens rea* is 'the knowledge that these acts assist the commission of the offence'.[64] Notably, the Chamber found support for

---

[59] Human Rights Watch, 'Weighing the Evidence, Lessons from the Slobodan Milosevic Trial', vol. 18, no. 10(D), December 2006, p. 19. See also *Prosecutor* v. *Slobodan Milošević*, IT-02-54-T, Amended Indictment (Bosnia and Herzegovina), 22 November 2002.

[60] *Prosecutor* v. *Momčilo Perišić*, IT-04-81-T, Decision on Defence Motion to Exclude the Expert Report of Morten Torkildsen, 30 October 2008, para. 15.

[61] *Prosecutor* v. *Perišić*, IT-04-81-T, Judgment, Trial Chamber, 6 September 2011, para. 6.

[62] *Prosecutor* v. *Perišić*, IT-04-81-A, Judgment, Appeals Chamber, 28 February 2013, para. 36.

[63] *Prosecutor* v. *Tadić*, IT-94-1-A, Judgment, Appeals Chamber, 15 July 1999, paras. 229 (iii) and (iv).

[64] *Prosecutor* v. *Šainović et al.*, IT-05-87-A, Judgment, Appeals Chamber, 23 January 2014 (*Šainović* Appeal Judgment), para. 1649, citing *Prosecutor* v. *Blaškić*, IT-95-14-A, Judgment, Appeals Chamber, 29 July 2004, para. 46, and confirming at para. 1650 that the *Mrkšić and Šljivančanin* and *Lukić and Lukić* Appeal Judgments 'stated the prevailing law in holding that "specific direction" is not an essential ingredient of the actus reus of aiding and abetting'.

its conclusion in the *Zyklon B*, *Roechling*, and *Flick* cases, aside from other post-World War II trials. According to the Chamber, the conclusion to be derived from these cases was that 'they focused on: (i) the degree of each defendant's contribution to a crime, demonstrated through the role he played in, and the impact he exerted on, the commission of the crime; and (ii) whether the defendant knew that his acts contributed to the commission of the crime'.[65] The point was clearly made in relation to *Zyklon B*: 'The analysis [...] focused on whether each defendant had influence over the supply of the gas and knew of the unlawful use of the gas despite the stated lawful purposes, such as disinfecting buildings. Whether the defendants specifically directed the supply of the gas to the extermination was not a basis for the convictions.'[66]

The Appeals Chamber of the Special Court for Sierra Leone (SCSL) had already rejected the *Perišić* interpretation of aiding and abetting in the *Taylor* case, which focused on Taylor's independent support for and trade with rebel groups in Sierra Leone, partly through his abuse of the financial structures of the Liberian state.[67] The SCSL Appeals Chamber presumed that the ICTY Appeals Chamber in *Perišić* had not based its assessment on customary international law but rather on 'internally binding precedent'.[68] The Chamber noted that the post-World War II jurisprudence was 'replete with examples demonstrating the variety of ways in which persons can be found to have culpably assisted the commission of crimes'.[69] Reference was made to the *Flick*, *Farben*, *Zyklon B*, and *Roechling* cases to demonstrate that 'an accused's knowledge of the consequence of his acts or conduct – that is, an accused's "knowing participation" in the crimes – is a culpable *mens rea* standard for individual criminal liability'.[70] Further, it was found that 'the *actus reus* of aiding and abetting liability is established by assistance that has a substantial effect on the crime, not by the particular manner in which such assistance is provided'.[71] Disagreeing with the approach in *Perišić*, the SCSL Appeals Chamber found that 'the requirement that the

---

[65] *Šainović* Appeal Judgment, ibid., para. 1627.
[66] Ibid., para. 1628.
[67] *Prosecutor* v. *Taylor*, SCSL-03–01-A, Judgment, Appeals Chamber, 26 September 2013 (*Taylor* Appeal Judgment), para. 481. The Trial Chamber had previously found that: 'The actus reus of aiding and abetting does not require "specific direction".' *Prosecutor* v. *Taylor*, SCSL-03–01-T, Judgment, Trial Chamber, 18 May 2012, para. 484.
[68] *Taylor* Appeal Judgment, ibid., para. 476.
[69] Ibid., para. 377.
[70] Ibid., para. 436.
[71] Ibid., para. 401.

accused's acts and conduct have a substantial effect on the commission of the crime ensures that there is a sufficient causal link between the accused and the commission of the crime'.[72]

At the domestic level, the Dutch cases of *Frans van Anraat* and *Guus Kouwenhoven* provide the most important precedents. In both these cases, Article 48 of the Dutch Criminal Code provided the framework for accomplice liability. This provision includes both 'intentionally aiding and abetting' and 'intentionally providing the opportunity, means or information' for a serious offence.[73] Frans van Anraat was a Dutch businessman who was accused of selling the chemical thiodiglycol to Saddam Hussein's government in Iraq in the mid-1980s; in turn, this precursor was used in the production of mustard gas employed against Iranian as well as Iraqi-Kurdish targets. Van Anraat was convicted by the Dutch courts of complicity in war crimes by providing the opportunity and means to carry out the relevant attacks with mustard gas. He was sentenced to seventeen years' imprisonment on appeal.[74] The conviction was based on van Anraat's awareness that the thiodiglycol he supplied to a country engaged in a long-standing conflict would be used to produce mustard gas and his knowledge that the gas had already been put to this use.[75] It was not a requirement that the accused's assistance had been indispensable, as long as it had promoted the offence or facilitated its commission.[76]

Guus Kouwenhoven, a Dutch timber merchant, was alleged to have supplied arms to Charles Taylor's regime during the Liberian civil war in the early 2000s. Proceedings against Kouwenhoven before the Dutch courts lasted from 2006 to 2018. In 2017, the Dutch Court of Appeal convicted Kouwenhoven of complicity in war crimes and imposed a sentence of nineteen years' imprisonment. According to the Court of Appeal:

[72] Ibid., para. 480.
[73] Criminal Code of the Kingdom of Netherlands (1881, amended 2012) (English version), *Legislationline*, www.legislationline.org/documents/section/criminal-codes/country/12/Netherlands/show. Section 48(1): 'The following persons shall be criminally liable as accomplices to a criminal offence: 1. any persons who intentionally aid and abet the commission of the serious offence; 2. any persons who intentionally provide opportunity, means or information for the commission of the serious offence.'
[74] *Public Prosecutor v. Frans Cornelis Adrianus van Anraat*, BA4676, Court of Appeal of The Hague, The Netherlands, Judgment dated 9 May 2007, www.internationalcrimesdatabase.org/Case/168.
[75] Ibid., para. 11.16.
[76] Ibid., para. 12.4, commenting that: 'From international criminal law perspective, these requirements for the contribution of the so-called "aider or abettor" are not essentially more severe.'

In order to obtain a conviction with respect to complicity, according to consistent case law it is required that it must not only be proven that the defendant's intention was to promote or facilitate that crime within the meaning of article 48 Dutch Criminal Code, but also that the intent – whether or not in conditional form – was aimed at the commission of the offence by that third party, in this case the commission of war crimes.[77]

The Court went on to reiterate the point made in *van Anraat* that the assistance did not need to be indispensable as long as it promoted or facilitated the crime.[78] Further, the assistance did not need to provide 'an adequate causal contribution to the basic crime'.[79] The Court went on to comment that 'from an international criminal law perspective, the requirements for the contribution of the "aider or abettor" are not significantly heavier or different'.[80] Through his conduct, such as by importing weapons for Charles Taylor's regime and making trucks and drivers available, Kouwenhoven was found to have 'consciously accepted (took into the bargain) the probability that war crimes and/or crimes against humanity would be committed'.[81]

These cases demonstrate that while 'complicity', generally in the form of 'aiding and abetting', is the mode of liability most often invoked in cases concerning economic involvement in international crimes, interpretative issues abound. At the international level, it is possible to identify a definition of aiding and abetting under customary international law, placing reliance on *Šainović* and *Taylor*. However, the issue of 'specific direction' has not been put to rest completely and the elements of aiding and abetting remain a source of extensive litigation. To further complicate the issue, domestic courts, such as the Dutch courts in *van Anraat* and *Kouwenhoven*, apply national law on complicity and serve only as a secondary source of law for international proceedings. While the Dutch courts made reference to international law even as it concerned the mode of liability applied, it is not clear from the *van Anraat* and *Kouwenhoven*

---

[77] *The Public Prosecutor* v. *Guus Kouwenhoven*, 's-Hertogenbosch Court of Appeal, The Netherlands, Ruling of the three judge panel at the Court of Appeal in 's-Hertogenbosch, 21 April 2017, L.2, www.internationalcrimesdatabase.org/Case/3308.
[78] Ibid.
[79] Ibid.
[80] Ibid.
[81] Ibid., L.2.5. In 2018, the Dutch Supreme Court upheld the conviction and sentence imposed by the Court of Appeal. *The Public Prosecutor* v. *Guus Kouwenhoven*, Supreme Court of the Netherlands, The Netherlands, Judgment on the appeal in cassation against a judgment of 's-Hertogenbosch Court of Appeal of 21 April 2017, number 20/001906-10, 18 December 2018, www.internationalcrimesdatabase.org/Case/3309/The-Public-Prosecutor-v-Guus-Kouwenhoven/.

judgments to what extent, if at all, the Dutch Court of Appeal's understanding of aiding and abetting was derived from that of international courts and tribunals.

4.5   Investigating the Economic Aspect of Syrian Regime Crimes

4.5.1   The Syrian Economy since 2011

The accession of Bashar al-Assad to the presidency of Syria in 2000 was followed, from 2005, by a number of steps designed to liberalize the Syrian economy.[82] In the absence of liberal-democratic political institutions, the economic initiatives were bound to fall short and these reforms gave rise to a system that one scholar has characterized correctly as 'a crony capitalist predatory economy' dominated by 'smuggling networks, crony monopolies, illegal capital movements and distorted competition'.[83] Since 2011, the war has served only to exacerbate the economic patterns that became dominant prior to the conflict. In particular, widespread fighting in urban areas has destroyed or otherwise displaced much of the small-to-medium-sized-enterprise sector as it was configured prior to the conflict while concentrating meaningful economic power in the hands of a still-smaller number of families whose material interests rest heavily upon the survival of the Assad regime. Indeed, familial arrangements linking the regime leadership to an economic elite have long been in evidence. The most infamous example of connections of this nature is Rami Makhlouf, a maternal cousin of President al-Assad, who has grown phenomenally wealthy through his dominance of the telecommunications sector as well as by virtue of his allegedly significant holdings in the banking, real estate, and retail industries.[84]

---

[82] For an overview of the pre-war Syrian economy, see B. Haddad, *Business Networks in Syria: The Political Economy of Authoritarian Resilience* (Stanford University Press, 2011).

[83] A. Sottimano, 'The Syrian Business Elite: Patronage Networks and War Economy', *Syria Untold* (24 September 2016), https://syriauntold.com/2016/09/24/the-syrian-business-elite-patronage-networks-and-war-economy/.

[84] The notoriety of Makhlouf and his links to the regime gave rise to his sanctioning by both the European Union and the United States Treasury. Limited, though not insignificant primary source documentation regarding his business interests can be found in the so-called Panama Papers as well as the 'Syria Files' posted by Wikileaks, which, more broadly, offer large volumes of data regarding political-economic relationships at the highest reaches of the government of Syria.

The opening of the Syrian economy prior to 2011 – such as it was – gave rise to something of an import boom that served to undermine the domestic manufacturing base while facilitating the entry of foreign – particularly Lebanese – banks into the financial sector. This latter development was a logical corollary of the physical proximity of Syria and Lebanon, the presence of Syrian forces in Lebanon from 1976 to 2005, and the propensity of Syrian citizens of any financial means to hold Lebanese bank accounts.[85] At any rate, the appearance of foreign banks in Syria served to facilitate foreign direct investment in the country.[86] Investments of this nature, along with foreign remittances received – totalling 1.623 billion USD in 2010, according to the World Bank[87] – additional to exports of oil and gas, provided the regime with foreign currency reserves totalling slightly in excess of 30 per cent of GDP during the three years preceding the war.[88] In the event, exports from Syria declined precipitously to negligible levels at the outset of the conflict, where they remain to this day (i.e. at mid-2019).[89] Whereas no Syrian state institution has published figures for foreign direct investment since 2011, it can safely be assumed that the value of ventures of this nature has fallen to insignificant levels, given the severity of the conflict. In a similar vein, neither the Central Bank of Syria nor any other state institution has published statistics regarding the foreign currency reserves of Syria since 2010. A CIJA enquiry regarding this matter made during the period 2014–2015 concluded that the Syrian state had exhausted all (or most of) its pre-war, foreign currency reserves in or about the second year of the war.

The lack of foreign currency reserves raises the question of how a relatively poor state such as Syria, without a domestic arms industry or indeed any manufacturing sector of which to speak,[90] has prosecuted a high-intensity armed conflict over a prolonged period while concomitantly

---

[85] R. Kattan, 'Mapping the Ailing (but Resilient) Syrian Banking Sector', in *Syria Studies* (2015), http://ojs.st-andrews.ac.uk/index.php/syria/article/view/1175/910.

[86] Foreign direct investment in Syria peaked at 4.751 per cent of GDP in 2009; see www .ceicdata.com/en/indicator/syria/foreign-direct-investment–of-nominal-gdp. By way of comparison, foreign direct investment in Canada during the same period averaged less than 3 per cent of Canadian GDP.

[87] See https://data.worldbank.org/indicator/BX.TRF.PWKR.CD.DT?locations=SY.

[88] See www.ceicdata.com/en/indicator/syria/foreign-exchange-reserves–of-gdp. How the foreign exchange reserves of Syria went from 0.519 per cent of GDP in 2004 to over 61 per cent of GDP in 2005 – the year in which Syrian forces were forced from Lebanon by the UNSC – constitutes a fascinating question, albeit one beyond the scope of this paper.

[89] See www.ceicdata.com/en/indicator/syria/total-exports.

[90] In 2009, the manufacturing sector in Syria constituted 6.9 per cent of GDP – 0.1 per cent higher than the same sector in oil-rich Qatar. See J. Daher, 'Syria's Manufacturing Sector:

mounting a massive security-intelligence operation. Further, how has the state done all this while labouring under the weight of myriad United States Treasury and European Union sanctions imposed upon its government as well as a great many of its senior-most officials and private-sector supporters?

It is a matter of public record that the governments of Iran and Russia, along with Hezbollah, have provided the Syrian regime with extensive support in kind through the deployment of significant numbers of ground troops (in the case of Iran and Hezbollah) as well as ground-attack aircraft (in the case of Russia). Additionally, Russia and Iran can be assumed to have provided Syrian forces with large volumes of military matériel, in particular heavy ordnance, insofar as the Syrian pre-war stocks of munitions would assuredly have, for the most part, been exhausted by pro-regime forces early in the conflict.[91] It is also publicly known that Iran has provided the government of Syria with several billion US dollars in financial credits. However, these credits have evidently been extended to facilitate only the purchase by Syria from Iran of consumer goods as well as oil and gas products. There is no indication of which the CIJA is aware that the loans were extended to facilitate the purchase of military hardware and the like.[92] The CIJA is likewise in receipt of information, which has not been confirmed, that, early in the conflict, regular flights of transport aircraft arriving in Damascus from Moscow contained pallets of US dollars in cash destined for the Central Bank of Syria.[93] In the event, the Russian and, more recently, the Iranian states have found themselves labouring under US Treasury sanctions as well as economic difficulties arising, not least, from the depressed prices of oil and gas products on international markets. It is therefore difficult to see how the Syrian state has been able to cover all of the direct costs of mounting its military and security-intelligence operations, given its foreign currency difficulties. It follows from this that if foreign military aid has not been provided by Russia and Iran at no cost to the government of Syria – at least for the most part – it has assuredly been sent to that country by its allies on the promise of future payment.

The Model of Economic Recovery in Question', *Wartime and Post-Conflict in Syria*, Research Project Report (2019), p. 3.
[91] The Syrian Arab Army and Air Force are equipped with antiquated Soviet systems.
[92] Carnegie Endowment for International Peace, 'Iran's Stakes in Syria's Economy' (2 June 2015), https://carnegieendowment.org/sada/60280.
[93] The information was provided to the CIJA by a sensitive source rather than (in the formal sense of the term) a witness.

Foreign military assistance, military personnel, weapons systems, and munitions are but a fraction of what the Syrian regime has needed to prosecute the war with relative success. The state security-intelligence services have likewise contributed mightily to the favourable – from a regime perspective – political-military outcome. It was not (nor has it been) unlawful per se for the Syrian state to mount security-intelligence operations in answer to the widespread civil disturbances in 2011 which gave rise, in turn, to an armed insurgency. However, the collective conduct of the four security-intelligence organs of the Syrian state[94] have evinced consistently a pervasive criminality that has been much less in evidence where an examination of the conduct of the Syrian Arab Army is concerned. Since 2012, the CIJA has acquired in Syria and, in turn, removed to Europe, collated and analyzed in the context of ICHL several hundred thousand pages of documentation generated by the said security-intelligence services. The criminal case files built by the CIJA upon this and other forms of evidence, including extensive crime base and insider witness testimony, point to a culture within these institutions, at every level of command from Damascus to the governorate branches and their sub-branches, focused upon the indiscriminate sweeping of tens of thousands of suspects into an archipelago of detention facilities. What is more, the exhaustive evidence leaves no doubt that, once taken into security-intelligence custody, detainees could (and can) expect to be abused physically and psychologically as a matter of course, frequently to the point of torture, with many thousands perishing as a result of such mistreatment.

The immense scale of the detention operations of the Syrian state since 2011, which might be said to approximate the abuses of the security services of the Soviet Union under the suzerainty of Joseph Stalin, raises many questions. For instance, how has the state managed to remunerate the thousands upon thousands of rank-and-file members of the security-intelligence services, ensuring their continued loyalty through payments that compensate for the deterioration of the buying power of the Syrian pound (SYP)? Where has the money come from to pay persons not formally on the payroll of the security-intelligence services who are prepared to spy upon their neighbours? How have the lights been kept on in the myriad detention facilities, where the electrical current has not been channelled directly into the bodies of detainees under interrogation?

---

[94] The four security-intelligence agencies of Syria are the Military Intelligence, Air Force Intelligence, State Security and Political Security.

Where has the petrol come from to power the vehicles required to move tens of thousands of detainees between outposts in the archipelago of detention facilities? Where has the communications equipment been acquired in order to enable the vast number of security-intelligence headquarters and offices to communicate effectively as well as securely with one another?[95] By way of a final example, how has the burial of the many thousands who have perished in security-intelligence detention facilities under unlawful circumstances been funded? It is in the search for answers to these and other questions related to the maintaining of Syrian regime security-intelligence operations that those tasked with the investigation of core international crimes might identify economic actors whose conduct warrants prosecution for aiding and abetting the offences of the direct perpetrators.

4.5.2   Identifying Economic Targets

The crony-capitalism model, along with the experience secured prior to 2011 while working around the limited American sanctions imposed upon regime officials and their private sector supporters, left the government of Syria reasonably well placed to respond to the collapse of its foreign currency reserves, amongst the other challenges posed by the transition to a war economy. If only in passing, it will be observed that one of the principal focuses of the Syrian state institutions from the outset of the war, and most especially the Central Bank of Syria, has been to ensure that the SYP retains some semblance of buying power in the domestic market. In the aforementioned examination of the regime response to its foreign currency problems, the CIJA found that the policy of maintaining the buying power of the SYP was at the start predicated, in part, upon the divorce of the formal SYP–USD exchange rate from normal market conditions and the transfer of hard currency into Syria through a complex web of formal as well as informal structures. The CIJA concluded, albeit on the basis of largely inferential evidence, that this policy was designed not least to maintain the buying power of mid- and lower-level regime functionaries paid in SYP and, more broadly, to ensure by similar means the tolerance of the wider population in

---

[95] Syrian Military Intelligence documentation acquired in the field by the CIJA as well as materials found in the Wikileaks Syria Files suggest that the encrypted Tetra communications system used by the said security-intelligence service, including its top leadership, was acquired by two European companies. See CBS News, 'WikiLeaks: Western Firms Boosted Syrian Communications Network' (16 July 2012).

government-controlled areas for continued regime rule. The foreign currency credits which the government of Syria has secured from Iran were evidently solicited for precisely these purposes.[96]

The seriousness with which the government of Syria seeks to maintain as much popular support for the ruling authorities as possible has likewise led to efforts to ensure that sufficient supplies of wheat at below-market prices are available in regime-controlled sectors whilst ensuring the flow of sufficient oil and gas supplies to domestic as well as foreign markets through a range of complex smuggling networks. At the nadir of its military fortunes, maintaining a sufficiency of wheat, oil, and gas supplies on regime territory led to extensive interaction between government of Syria officials and economic actors prepared to broker what were effectively trade agreements between the regime and its (armed) domestic enemies. The ubiquitous arrangements of this nature encompassed an array of belligerent parties, not least Islamic State.[97] The CIJA has identified a number of suspected middlemen engaged in these exchanges, although building credible cases against any of these individuals is unlikely to prove possible in the continuing absence of relevant financial records.

The starting point for any analysis of the evidence of complicity of economic institutions, entities, and actors in the perpetration of core international crimes is the applicable law. As the legal analysis set out in this chapter implies, the body of relevant jurisprudence is sufficiently thin as to constitute a limited guide to the criminal investigation of economic actors in the context of the war in Syria. Clearly, it is unlawful for economic concerns to incorporate thousands of slave labourers into their operations and, as a matter of course, to work them to death. However, the CIJA has seen no evidence that detainees and prisoners held by Syrian state institutions are employed in labour of any kind, at least outside of the facilities in which they are incarcerated. As discussed, the prosecution of Hjalmar Schacht, head of the *Reichsbank* prior to the

---

[96] Carnegie Endowment for International Peace, 'Iran's Stakes in Syria's Economy' (*supra* n. 91).

[97] On the question of wheat supplies to government-held areas, see, by way of example, Carnegie Endowment for International Peace, 'Food Insecurity in War-Torn Syria: From Decades of Self-Sufficiency to Food Dependence' (4 June 2015), https://carnegieendowment .org/2015/06/04/food-insecurity-in-war-torn-syria-from-decades-of-self-sufficiency-to-food -dependence-pub-60320. Where oil and gas supplies are concerned, see, for instance, E. Solomon and A. Mhidi, 'ISIS Inc: Syria's "Mafia Style" Gas Deals with Jihadis', *Financial Times* (15 October 2015). The broad thrust of the *Financial Times* article cited here is supported by information received by the CIJA from a wide range of sensitive sources as well as insider witnesses.

outbreak of World War II, on charges relating to his actions to facilitate the transition of the German economy to a war footing, resulted in an acquittal. Despite holding a fair bit of prima facie evidence generated by (or otherwise relating to) the Central Bank of Syria, the *Schacht* precedent suggests that any effort to criminalize the conduct of those who have sought to keep the SYP afloat as a viable currency would likely come to nought.

More pertinent, perhaps, is the conviction of Flick for having knowingly provided financial support to an organization engaged in criminal activities. In *Flick*, the *mens rea* element was established by the prosecution to the satisfaction of the Tribunal even though the SS had not been declared a criminal organization at the time the financial contributions were made, and consequently the value of the case as a precedent does not depend on continued recognition of the concept of criminal organizations. Additionally, the appellate judgments in *Šainović* and *Taylor* provide important guidance on the customary international law elements of aiding and abetting, though admittedly the appellate judgment in *Perišić* casts something of a shadow of uncertainty over the legal framework, leaving key elements open to conflicting interpretations by judicial benches. Despite being a domestic case, the *van Anraat* saga likewise sets a useful precedent. Whereas next to nothing is known by the CIJA or any other criminal-investigative body regarding the mechanics of the Syrian chemical weapons programme, *van Anraat* and the other cases cited here nonetheless offer criminal investigators wider insights into the proper approach to the investigation of economic actors suspected of aiding and abetting war crimes and crimes against humanity.

Investigators and prosecutors will inevitably need to tailor the preparation and presentation of their cases to the domestic law on aiding and abetting in the jurisdiction in which a case is likely to be heard. Similarly, the applicable law varies between international courts and tribunals according to their constitutional documents. The International Criminal Court, for example, defines aiding and abetting differently from the ICTY, but it has yet to develop fully its jurisprudence on this mode of liability.[98]

---

[98] See Article 25(3)(c) of the Rome Statute which provides for individual criminal responsibility in respect of crimes under the Statute where an accused: 'For the purpose of facilitating the commission of such a crime, aids, abets or otherwise assists in its commission or its attempted commission, including providing the means for its commission.' For a summary of the ICC case law, see M. J. Ventura, 'Aiding and Abetting', in J. de Hemptinne et al. (eds.), *Modes of Liability in International Criminal Law* (Cambridge University Press, 2019), pp. 173–256, paras. 74–83.

Where the CIJA is concerned – a body established to support the widest possible range of domestic as well as international jurisdictions – a conservative interpretation is advisable, to wit, a working definition of aiding and abetting which is based upon the legal characteristics common to the maximum number of jurisdictions. Such a conservative approach would necessarily lead (and has led) CIJA analysts and counsel to prioritize investigations which, from the start, are characterized by prima facie evidence that suspects have provided material support directly to individuals and institutions conducting their operations invariably (and perhaps inevitably) in an indisputably criminal manner, about which those proffering the material support could not reasonably be unaware.

There would appear to be ample scope, given sufficient investigative resources, for the establishment of the individual criminal responsibility of economic actors offering direct, material support to Syrian military operations that have been conducted in a consistently unlawful manner. For instance, pro-regime militia, which have displayed a distinct tendency to murder and forcibly displace ethnic Sunni from villages abutting Shia and Alawite settlements, have in some cases been raised, armed, and otherwise bankrolled by wealthy businessmen with close links to the regime. In this regard, the CIJA holds credible evidence that points to the Central Bank of Syria providing foreign credits to named businessmen in exchange for the latter funding irregular forces. To follow this example further, it is held here that, in principle, evidence of this nature might open the door to a criminal inquiry focused upon the conduct of Central Bank of Syria personnel as well as their relevant private-sector partners engaged in the funding of the aforementioned militia.

Another prospect for the successful prosecution of economic actors engaged indirectly in the waging of the ground war in Syria might arise from an investigation into the manufacture and use of so-called barrel bombs. In this context, one would note by way of a start that the guidance mechanism of this ordnance consists of no more than the feet and hands of the aircrew tasked with rolling the bombs out of regime helicopters, having lit the fuses on these crude devices with their cigarettes. Additionally, there is ample information, in the form of human rights and media reports, that points to the unlawful deployment of these devices. What is more, the casual observer – which those making barrel bombs and the component parts thereof are most certainly not – can find readily on social media video footage made by helicopter aircrews that shows the dropping of barrel bombs over built-up areas. Indeed, the film of this nature corroborates strongly the arguments of human rights observers that the use of these weapons is invariably at odds with the international humanitarian law principles of distinction and proportionality.

By way of a final example, it is arguable that there is significant scope for the establishment of the individual criminal responsibility of economic actors in the Syrian context where they have aided or abetted the security-intelligence organs of the Syrian state. The conduct of these services is so pervasively and uniformly criminal that (i) any and all support to them will arguably be employed in the main or *in toto* in the furtherance of crimes against humanity and (ii) the habitual conduct of the security-intelligence organs is a question of fact that cannot reasonably be unknown to the man on the proverbial omnibus, whether he is riding same in Clapham or in Damascus. As such, there would seem to be ample scope for the linking of economic actors to the crimes of the Syrian security-intelligence services where, for instance, economic actors have knowingly facilitated the payment of meaningful salaries to security-intelligence personnel or otherwise provided material support to the execution of the duties of these particular organs of the Syrian state.

4.6   The Way Forward

At mid-2019, the CIJA is engaged in operational relationships with thirteen domestic war crimes programmes based in Western Europe and North America as well as supra-national bodies such as the IIIM. On an annual basis, these partners submit formal requests for assistance (RFAs) to the CIJA concerning hundreds of named Syrian regime-affiliated suspects. However, RFAs to the CIJA concerning economic actors suspected of supporting the Syrian regime are exceedingly rare, constituting well under 1 per cent of the total number of RFAs received during the period 2014 to mid-2019. It is therefore hardly surprising that, to the best of the knowledge of the CIJA, there is currently only one criminal investigation that is in an advanced state of preparation in a domestic jurisdiction regarding a Syrian regime-affiliated economic actor. There is no indication yet that the IIIM plans to target economic actors.

The relative dearth of public-sector movement against economic actors connected to the Syrian regime or, for that matter, any other armed conflict reflects first and foremost the resource limitations that plague national war crimes programmes. A suite of specialized financial-investigative skills as well as counsel with experience of such prosecutions are almost invariably required for the investigation of private-sector businesspersons. Seen as a whole, national authorities have under their command the necessary expertise, though this is invariably found within transnational (or organized) crime teams. Even though the investigative methodologies informing the investigation of transnational crime and breaches of ICHL are very similar, the two fields of criminal inquiry are nowhere linked under national auspices.

This state of affairs needs to change, not least as a great many conflicts that witness widespread and systematic breaches of ICHL are fuelled by, amongst other things, the illicit trafficking of natural resources and other items, such as weapons and narcotics, the movement of which is invariably governed by restrictive domestic laws. In light of the fact that no domestic authority is showing any sign of bringing together its expertise relating to the investigation of core international crimes and offences of a transnational nature, it logically falls to international investigators – from both the public and the private sector – to bridge the metaphorical gap, that is, to pursue economic actors for complicity in the perpetration of core international crimes. At the present time, the successful investigation of suspected ICHL breaches by economic actors offering support to the Syrian regime lies in melding the Syria expertise, contextual evidence, and high-physical-risk tolerance of the CIJA with the public sector's facilities and know-how in responding to financial crime.

Islamic State and the Illicit Traffic of Cultural Property

MARINA LOSTAL[*]

5.1 Introduction

From its inception, through to its military defeat in Iraq and Syria, Islamic State has enjoyed what could be called an emblematic relationship with cultural heritage.[1] The first documented destruction of cultural heritage in Iraq by Islamic State took place in Mosul in July 2014, when its fighters blew up the shrine of the Prophet Yunus (Jonah), a figure of religious significance for followers of Islam, Christianity, and Judaism alike.[2] However, it was the raid on the Mosul Museum in February 2015 that exposed Islamic State's transnational campaign of cultural annihilation. This was followed by further episodes, including the destruction of the temples of Bel and Baalshamin in the World Heritage Site of Palmyra, as well as the ancient city's tetrapylon and part of its amphitheatre. The last recorded incidence of cultural heritage destruction in Iraq by Islamic State was the detonation of the Great Mosque of al-Nuri (or al-Nuree) in

---

[*] This chapter was written as part of the project 'International Cultural Heritage Governance' in the framework of the Multilevel Regulation Research Group at The Hague University of Applied Sciences. The author is indebted to Ms Alina I. Carrozzini for her research assistance. Author can be contacted at mlostalb@cantab.net.

[1] For the purposes of this chapter, the terms 'cultural heritage' and 'cultural property' are used interchangeably. For debates on the different nuances between the two, see e.g. A. Taşdelen, *The Return of Cultural Artefacts* (Basel: Springer, 2016), pp. 1–7; L. V. Prott and P. J. O'Keefe, 'Cultural Heritage or Cultural Property?' (1992) 1(2) *International Journal of Cultural Property* 308–20.

[2] It is ironic (and somewhat reassuring) that archaeologists found an 'undiscovered palace built before 600 B.C. for the Assyrian ruler King Sennarcherib' underneath the ruins of the shrine. See S. Pruitt, 'In Mosul, Archaeologists Find Hidden Palace under Shrine Destroyed by ISIS', *History* (7 March 2017), www.history.com/news/in-mosul-archaeologists-find-hidden-palace-under-shrine-destroyed-by-isis.

Mosul, and its famous minaret, in June 2017. However, far from being simply another episode in its ongoing programme of destruction, al-Nuri was in fact a reflection of Islamic State's increasing disarray and its awareness of imminent defeat. Instead of immediately claiming responsibility and beaming images of the devastation around the world, it tried (unsuccessfully) to place the blame on US forces. What seems at first glance a surprising change in policy has a simple explanation: the mosque was the spot where the terrorist organization's leader, Abu Bakr al-Baghdadi, chose to declare the birth of a putative Islamic State caliphate, with himself as caliph, in June 2014. When, in 2017, defeat appeared inevitable, al-Baghdadi reportedly fled the city; those fighters who remained seemed to have destroyed this iconic building to prevent the victorious Iraqi forces from announcing the liberation of Mosul from the very place where the aborted caliphate had been proclaimed three years earlier.[3] While episodes of destruction are very well known, this chapter explores the more opaque aspect of the relationship between Islamic State and cultural heritage: their involvement in its illicit excavation and trafficking.

In Islamic State's video celebrating the raid on the Mosul Museum, a representative calls the ancient statues 'false idols', claiming that Allah had ordered their removal. He declares: 'They became worthless to us, even if they are worth billions of dollars.'[4] As it turned out, this was not exactly true. A year later, a US Special Forces operation revealed that Islamic State possessed a highly organized mechanism for the illicit excavation of and trade in antiquities. In order to explore this development, the chapter first takes a brief look at the history of looting and recounts how, after the looting of the National Museum in Baghdad, experts found that the theft of cultural artefacts had taken a more sinister turn and was now associated with the financing of violent armed groups and terrorist organizations. The chapter then turns to consider the US raid targeting an Islamic State official with the *nom de guerre* of Abu Sayyaf; the information retrieved during the raid that led to his killing reveals that the organization possessed a so-called 'Antiquities Division', which used cultural artefacts to generate revenue through taxation, the issuing of

---

[3] M. Chulov and K. Shaheen, 'Destroying Great Mosque of al-Nuri "Is Isis Declaring Defeat"', *The Guardian* (22 June 2017), www.theguardian.com/world/2017/jun/21/mosuls-grand-al-nouri-mosque-blown-up-by-isis-fighters.

[4] G. Beck, *It IS about Islam: Exposing the Truth about ISIS, Al Qaeda, Iran, and the Caliphate* (New York: Mercury Radio Arts, 2015), p. 206.

licenses, and direct theft or looting.[5] It goes on to note some general trends in the black market for such items, while acknowledging that information on the smuggling routes, middlemen, and buyers is still scarce. Lastly, the chapter focuses on international efforts, both legal and non-legal, to combat the illicit traffic in cultural property and bring its perpetrators to justice. It argues that the pervasive looting and trafficking in stolen historic artefacts represents a serious security concern, due to the involvement of terrorist organizations, and that the laws dedicated to the protection of cultural property,[6] including those contained in the ICC Statute, lag behind this increasingly complex phenomenon.

5.2   An Historical Overview of Looting of Cultural Property

The tradition of looting cultural property is as old as war itself. The Romans appear to have been the first society to adopt military plunder as state policy: on the return of its armies to Rome, the fruits of their raids were exhibited in official 'triumphs' or victory parades celebrating the exploits of the victorious military commander. In this way, the people were reminded of the might of Rome and the 'soldiers and politicians [were able to] establish their own collections and libraries'.[7] A later, similarly flagrant example is that of the Crusaders, who pursued a policy of indiscriminate plunder, epitomized by the sack of Constantinople in 1204. During the three days of looting and vandalism, the Crusader army destroyed the city's Great Library, melted down the bronze statue of Hercules, and transported the famous bronze horses from its hippodrome to St Mark's Basilica in Venice. Although they were momentarily looted by Napoleon, the horses were returned to Venice, where they remain to this day.[8]

---

[5] US House of Representatives, Committee on Financial Services, 'Memorandum RE: Task Force to Investigate Terrorism Financing Hearing Titled "Preventing Cultural Genocide: Countering the Plunder and Sale of Priceless Cultural Antiquities by ISIS"' (15 April 2016), 7, http://financialservices.house.gov/uploadedfiles/041916_tf_supplemental_hearing_memo.pdf.

[6] This chapter uses the terms 'cultural property', 'cultural heritage' and 'cultural objects' interchangeably.

[7] A. H. Poulos, 'The 1954 Hague Convention for the Protection of Cultural Property in the Event of Armed Conflict: An Historic Analysis' (2000) 28(1) *International Journal of Legal Information* 1–44, 7.

[8] The horses in the front of St Mark's Basilica are replicas, and the real ones are housed inside.

Napoleon, during the French Revolutionary Wars at the end of the eighteenth century, also acquired a taste for the systematic plunder of the works of art of his defeated enemies.[9] Interestingly, though, his pretext was a little subtler than that of his predecessors, who had used plunder to symbolize their power and domination. Around this time, the idea had begun to take shape that art represented a transnational common good – what we would understand today as the common heritage of humanity. Underlying this concept was the belief that the fine arts comprised a 'republique de lettres'; they belonged to humanity in general and to no one in particular – a belief that was later translated into the legal realm by the 1899 and 1907 Conventions with respect to the Laws and Customs of War on Land.[10] In a questionable attempt to recognize art's intrinsic value, Napoleon appointed himself as the sole possible custodian of European art, since all the other countries in Europe, which in his view were nothing less than tyrannies, were clearly ill-suited for the purpose.[11] However, this self-appointment was met with some disavow. In defence of this emerging vision on art, some contemporaries took a hard stance against Napoleon's plan; such a position was held by, for example, Quatremere de Quincy, who maintained that the best art had a universal quality and therefore could not be possessed but ought to be held in the original context.[12] In the aftermath of Napoleon's final defeat, the representatives of the European heads of state gathered at the Congress of Vienna (1814–1815) and affiliated themselves to Quincy's denunciation of his system of plunder. They characterized it as a violation of the laws of modern warfare, and deemed the return of the looted objects a prerequisite to establishing long-term peace and stability on the continent.[13] Later, the 1899 Hague Convention with respect to the Laws and Customs of War formally prohibited the practice of looting during armed conflict and occupation, and this was reaffirmed in the

---

[9] R. O'Keefe, *The Protection of Cultural Property in Armed Conflict* (Cambridge: Cambridge University Press, 2006), p. 15.

[10] Ibid., pp. 8, 14.

[11] Ibid., p. 15.

[12] Q. de Quincy, *Lettres au general Miranda sur le déplacement des monuments de l'art de l'Italie*, 88–9, cited in J. H. Merryman, 'Cultural Property Internationalism' (2005) 12 *International Journal of Cultural Property* 11, 15

[13] Records show precisely this attitude. Castlereagh is reported to have said 'perhaps there is nothing which would more tend to settle the public mind of Europe at this day, than such an homage on the part of the King of France, to a principle of virtue, conciliation and peace', in J. Otridge et al., *The Annual Register or a View of the History, Politics and Literature for the Year of 1815* (London: Baldwin, Cradock and Joy, 1824), p. 604.

annexed regulations of the 1907 Hague IV Convention on the Laws and Customs of War on Land (1907 Hague IV Regulations), which currently represent customary international law.[14]

Napoleon's belief that he was the true custodian of art was somehow mirrored in the twentieth century by the rhetoric of the Nazi regime. The Nazis established the Einsatzstab Rosenberg, an educational research institute whose mission was to plunder the art of the occupied territories.[15] More than 21,000 artworks were stolen from across Europe under the supervision of the institute's director, Alfred Rosenberg, with the assistance of Wilhelm Keitel, who coordinated the organization of this institutionalized system of plunder by liaising with the military authorities. Rosenberg's staff alone was responsible for the carrying away of '100,000 valuable volumes and 70 cases of ancient periodicals and precious monographs'.[16] However, the Nazis kept only the pieces they considered worthy of admiration; the rest, they labelled 'degenerate art' and it was either destroyed or, if it had market value, sold.[17] This included anything that did not accord with Nazi ideology – for example, abstract compositions were derided, and works by Jewish artists, such as the neo-impressionist Camille Pisarro, were systematically denigrated.[18] Following the war, the Nuremberg Tribunal convicted both Rosenberg and Keitel, inter alia, of the war crime of plunder of public and private property.[19]

5.3   The Link between Armed Non-State Actors and Cultural Property

Because of their economic value, the plunder and sale of antiquities is not limited to periods of war. Illegal excavations and the traffic in historic

---

[14] The customary status of the Hague Regulations has been acknowledged on manifold occasions. See ICTY, *Prosecutor* v. *Kordić and Čerkez*, Case No. IT-95–14/2-T, Judgment, Trial Chamber, 26 February 2001, para. 362. See also UNSC, 'Report of the Secretary-General pursuant to para. 2 of UNSC Res 808' (1993) UN Doc S/25704.

[15] For an excellent account of the fate of artworks during the Holocaust, see J. A. Kreder, 'Analysis of the Holocaust Expropriated Art Recovery Act of 2016' (2017) 20(1) *Chapman Law Review* 1–8. (The original article runs from pp. 1–24.)

[16] IMT, *Judgment of 1 October 1946*, Count 3 (War crimes).

[17] A. F. Vrdoljak, 'The Criminalisation of the Illicit Trade in Cultural Property', in H. Geismar and J. Anderson (eds.), *The Routledge Companion to Cultural Property* (London: Routledge, 2016), p. 4.

[18] See E. Campfens, 'Nazi Looted Art: A Note in Favour of Clear Standards and Neutral Procedures' (2017) XXII(4) *Art, Antiquity and Law* 315–45.

[19] J. Nowlan, 'Cultural Property and the Nuremberg War Crimes Trial' (1993) 6(4) *Humanitaeres Voelkerrecht* 221.

artefacts also occur during peacetime, frequently under the direct sponsorship of the state in which they are located. For example, 'antiquities
smuggling . . . occurred throughout the 1980s and 1990s under the Iraqi
Ba'athist regime of Saddam Hussein, particularly as a means to generate
income amid international sanctions'.[20] However, the country's most
infamous episode of looting occurred in the Iraq War in 2003.
Although many museums and ancient sites were looted during the
conflict and subsequent occupation, the ransacking of the National
Museum of Baghdad remains one of the most emblematic episodes of
cultural heritage destruction of the past few decades. The formal looting
began on 10 April 2003 – that is, one day after coalition forces captured
Baghdad[21] – and two days after the last among the staff fled its premises
fearing for their lives since the building had been caught in between
heavy fighting.[22] Donny George, the museum's former director of antiquities and research, described a situation where '300–400 people gathered at the front of the Museum compound . . . they were all armed with
a variety of hammers, crowbars, sticks, Kalashnikovs, daggers and
bayonets'.[23] Colonel Matthew Bogdanos, at the time head of a counter-
terrorist unit in Iraq, initiated an ad hoc investigation backed by the U.S.
Central Command to assess the extent of the looting and the possible
location of the artefacts.[24] His findings show that there were two different
styles of looting. One was obviously professional: for example, '[t]here
was one exhibit in particular that had 27 cuneiform bricks running from

[20] Financial Services Committee (FSC), 'Task Force to Investigate Terrorism Financing
Hearing Titled "Preventing Cultural Genocide: Countering the Plunder and Sale of
Priceless Cultural Antiquities by ISIS"', *Majority and Minority Staff, Memorandum to
the Members of Committee of Financial Services* (15 April 2016) 5.

[21] B. Isakhan, 'Heritage Destruction and Spikes in Violence: The Case of Iraq', in J. Kila and
J. Zeidler (eds.), *Cultural Heritage in the Crosshairs Protecting Cultural Property during
Conflict* (Leiden: Brill, 2016), pp. 219–47, 229.

[22] S. Al-Radi, 'The Destruction of the Iraq National Museum' (2003) 55(3–4) *Museum
International* 103–107, 105; Isakhan, 2016, ibid. The last ones to leave were 'Jaber
Ibrahim al-Tikriti (the Chairman of Iraq's State Board of Antiquities); Donny George;
a driver; and an elderly archaeologist who lived in the rear of the museum compound';
they left when the level of violence was imminent, but returned as soon as it became
feasible. See M. Bogdanos, 'Thieves of Baghdad: The Global Traffic in Stolen Iraqi
Antiquities', in S. Manacorda and D. Chappell (eds.), *Crime in the Art and Antiquities
World: Illegal Trafficking in Cultural Property* (New York: Springer, 2011), pp.
143–71, 146.

[23] Cited in Isakhan, 2016 (*supra* n. 21), p. 228.

[24] 'Looting Iraq' (*Smithsonian*, 2019), www.smithsonianmag.com/arts-culture/looting-iraq
-16813540/. See also M. Bogdanos, 'The Casualties of War: The Truth about the Iraq
Museum' (2005) 109(3) *American Journal of Archaeology* 477–526.

Sumerian through Akkadian and Old Babylonian to New Babylonian. The nine most exquisite bricks were taken – selected from each time period – and all the others were left behind.'[25] However, there were also spontaneous (amateur) looters who plundered in a more random and unsystematic fashion, dragging away the heavy statues. Bogdanos remarks that 'we could trace every single heavy piece that did leave the museum by following the trail of skid marks left in the floor'.[26] About one-third of the 15,000 pieces stolen from the museum has since been recovered and, on 28 February 2015, days after the Islamic State wreaked havoc in the Mosul Museum, the National Museum of Baghdad formally reopened its doors.[27]

As the inquiry that followed the looting of the National Museum unfolded, the investigative team realized that something more than simple looting had taken place: the recovered artefacts revealed a trail that led back to armed non-state groups. On one occasion, 'US Marines in northwest Iraq arrested five insurgents holed up in underground bunkers filled with automatic weapons, ammunition stockpiles, black uniforms ... [and] night-vision goggles'[28] and also '30 vases, cylinder seals, and statuettes that had been stolen from the Iraq Museum'.[29] Whereas, in the past, looting had been carried out with the purpose of enhancing national or private collections, as a display of might and superiority, or as a way of generating money for the state, it has been documented that, over the past two decades, terrorist organizations have used the theft and illicit trafficking of cultural objects to fund their activities.[30] For instance, according to a 2005 article published in the German newspaper *Der Spiegel*, 'Mohammed Atta, one of the Al Qaeda hijackers of 9/11' sought advice in 1999 from a professor at the University of Gottingen on how to sell Afghani artefacts, in order to raise the money to buy an aeroplane.[31]

---

[25] Bogdanos, 2011 (*supra* n. 22), p. 153.
[26] Ibid.
[27] 'Looted Iraqi Museum in Baghdad Reopens 12 Years On' (*BBC News*, 28 February 2015), www.bbc.com/news/world-middle-east-31672857.
[28] Bogdanos, 2011 (*supra* n. 22), p. 161.
[29] Ibid.
[30] It must be emphasized, however, that it is not the case for the majority of armed non-state actors. A recent empirical study shows how most of them are, to the contrary, interested in protecting cultural heritage from the effects of armed conflict, and some of them have even taken active steps to this end; see M. Lostal, K. Hausler, and P. Bongard, *Culture under Fire: Armed Non-State Actors and Cultural Heritage in Wartime* (Geneva: Geneva Call, 2018), https://genevacall.org/wp-content/uploads/2017/10/Cultural_Heritage_Study_Final.pdf.
[31] Bogdanos, 2011 (*supra* n. 22), p. 162.

Figure 5.1 Cylinder seal and modern impression: Hunting scene, c. 2250–2150 BC (Metropolitan Museum of Art)[32]

Cylinder seals remain one of the most convenient cultural objects to smuggle out of Iraq:

> Cylinder seals were impression stamps, often quite intricate in design, used throughout Mesopotamia ... made from semiprecious stone (such as marble, obsidian, amethyst, lapis lazuli) or metal (gold or silver). These seals were worn by their owners on strings of leather or other material around the neck or wrist or pinned to a garment. Their purpose was to serve as a personal signature on a document or package to guarantee authenticity or legitimize a business deal as one signs a letter or form in the present day. The seal was rolled onto the moist clay of the document as an official, binding signature.[33]

These artefacts are relatively abundant and as small as a piece of chalk, making them easy to carry and hide, yet they can sell for as much as 250,000 USD a piece.[34] As Bogdanos puts it, '[g]iven this almost limitless supply of antiquities, the insurgency appears to have found an income stream sufficiently secure to make any chief financial officer sleep well at night'.[35] This may have been the case for Abu Sayaff, Islamic State's head

[32] Metropolitan Museum of Art (publicly available image at: www.metmuseum.org/art/collection/search/329090).

[33] J. J. Mark, 'Cylinder Seals in Ancient Mesopotamia: Their History and Significance', in *Ancient History Encyclopaedia* (2 December 2015).

[34] Bodganos, 2011 (*supra* n. 22), p. 162.

[35] Ibid.

of finance at the Diwan al-Rikaz (Ministry of Natural Resources),[36] until he was killed in a US raid in Syria on 16 May 2015.

5.4 Illicit Excavations and Sale of Cultural Property under the Islamic State

Sayyaf was only a mid-level official, so the most significant aspect of the raid carried out by US Delta Force was not his death but the retrieval of his laptop, mobile phone and other records and materials[37] which offered a unique insight into Islamic State's financial relationship with cultural objects. It was this special operation that revealed the presence of an Antiquities Division within the Diwan al-Rikaz, which had established a well-oiled mechanism for the illicit trade in cultural artefacts. In his role as the ministry's chief finance officer, while Sayyaf was primarily responsible for overseeing Islamic State's oil and gas operations,[38] he was also appointed head of the Antiquities Division in November 2014, because he was 'very knowledgeable in this field' and 'the people in the Levant who work in this field of antiquities are weak of faith and Abu Sayyaf has experience in dealing with them'.[39]

While oil and gas remained the top income stream for Islamic State (followed by extortion, taxes, and ransoms obtained through kidnapping),[40] coalition air strikes on the oil fields under the organization's control and the subsequent disruption of its lines of communication meant that this source of revenue was compromised. As a result, the Antiquities Division faced an increased level of demand, particularly as cultural objects represented a 'less robust but, nonetheless, difficult to strike stream of revenue'.[41] In fact, the illicit trade in antiquities is a very

[36] United States Government Accountability Office, *Report to Congressional Requesters: Cultural Property – Protection of Iraqi and Syrian Antiquities* (August 2016), p. 7 ('GAO Report'). The operation also captured his wife for interrogation and liberated a young Yazidi woman who was being kept as a slave by the couple.
[37] B. Starr, L. Smith-Park, and R. Sanchez, 'Abu Sayyaf, Key ISIS Figure in Syria, Killed in US Raid' (*CNN News*, 17 May 2015).
[38] The White House, Office of the Press Secretary, 'Statement by NSC Spokesperson Bernadette Meehan on Counter-ISIL Operation in Syria' (16 May 2015).
[39] A. Keller, 'US Department of State: Documenting ISIL's Antiquities Trafficking' (29 September 2015), p. 5, https://2009-2017.state.gov/e/eb/rls/rm/2015/247610.htm.
[40] A. Levallois, 'The Financing of the "Islamic State" in Iraq and Syria (ISIS)', European Parliament Policy Department, Directorate-General for External Policies (September 2017), p. 17.
[41] M. D. Danti, 'The Finance of Global Terrorism through Cultural Property Crime in Syria and Northern Iraq' (Written Statement Submitted for Testimony Before the House

intricate problem to disentangle because, unlike weapons or drugs, the sale of cultural objects is not subject to a similar outright ban.

The pressure to obtain funding was high – unlike Al-Qaida, which also looted and traded in cultural objects,[42] Islamic State had been able to establish a 'state',[43] and conquering and controlling a territory is anything but cheap. In order to accrue more wealth, the group needed to exploit the resources found in its territory, including the approximately 4,500 archaeological sites that were vulnerable to looting and destruction.[44] This area is not called the 'cradle of civilisation' for nothing.

The UN had no doubt that Islamic State was profiteering from the looting and smuggling of cultural heritage and explicitly acknowledged it in Resolution 2199 of 2015 (adopted just a few days before the raid of the Mosul Museum by the Islamic State):

> [The Security Council] *[n]otes with concern* that ISIL, ANF and other individuals, groups, undertakings and entities associated with Al-Qaida, are generating income from engaging directly or indirectly in the looting and smuggling of cultural heritage items from archaeological sites, museums, libraries, archives, and other sites in Iraq and Syria, which is being used to support their recruitment efforts and strengthen their operational capability to organize and carry out terrorist attacks.[45]

However, the Security Council has not indicated the amount of profit the organization was believed to be making. While a definitive figure has yet to emerge, outside the UN there is some agreement that it ranges from tens of millions to a hundred million dollars annually.[46] For example, 'sales receipts indicated that the terrorist group had earned more than $265,000 in taxes on the sale of antiquities over a 4-month period in late 2014 and early 2015'.[47] This figure refers only to revenue obtained through taxes, whereas, as a report from the Center on Sanctions and

Committee on Foreign Affairs – Subcommittee on Terrorism, Nonproliferation, and Trade, 17 November 2015), p. 5.
[42] H. Pringle, 'ISIS Cashing in on Looted Antiquities to Fuel Iraq Insurgency' (*National Geographic*, 27 June 2014).
[43] A. Levallois (*supra* n. 40), p. 4. Levallois explains in her report how, despite the fact that Islamic State is a splinter group of Al-Qaeda, the latter was fundamentally different since it was small and dispersed, mostly funded by the private fortune of Osama Bin Laden and focused on striking 'the enemy' in his homeland (e.g. Kenya, Tanzania, Yemen, and the USA).
[44] FSC (*supra* n. 20), p. 2.
[45] UNSC Resolution 2199, 12 February 2015, para. 16.
[46] GAO Report (*supra* n. 36), p. 9.
[47] Ibid.; FSC (*supra* n. 20), p. 6.

Illicit Finance describes, the records seized in the operation against Sayyaf showed that Islamic State also exploited cultural property through issuing licences and engaging in direct theft and looting. These different financial activities are explained below:

(1) Taxation: *khums* is a type of Islamic tax levied on objects obtained from the ground. Although the word *khums* means one-fifth in Arabic, it was found that Islamic State levied taxes of between 20 per cent and 50 per cent (depending on the region)[48] on the value of the sale of the cultural artefacts to smugglers. To maximize efficiency, it appears that Islamic State gave local residents machinery, such as metal detectors, to excavate the sites.[49]

(2) Licences: Islamic State established a monopoly over the excavation and looting of the archaeological sites and museums in its territory. Its General Governing Committee issued a ban, according to which:

> It is prohibited [for] any brother from the Islamic State to excavate antiquities or give the permit to anyone from the public without receiving a stamped permit issued from the Diwan of Natural Resources and Minerals – Antiquities Division.
> [. . .]
> Anyone proven to be in violation of this order, since its issuing date, is considered disobedient ... and is subject to a penalty in accordance to Sharia courts.[50]

If an individual wished to excavate one of these sites, they were obliged to obtain a licence bearing the official stamp of the Antiquities Division. The existing evidence suggests that licences were awarded in exchange for a percentage (as high as 60 per cent) of the proceeds.[51]

(3) Direct theft, looting and sale: some experts who observed the destruction of statues and other artefacts in the Mosul Museum came to the conclusion that many of the objects that lay smashed on the ground were in fact plaster replicas. According to the report by the Center on

---

[48] A. Al-Azm, S. Al-Kuntar, and B. I. Daniels, '"ISIS" Antiquities Sideline' (*New York Times*, 2 September 2014).

[49] Y. J. Fanusie and A. Joffe, 'Monumental Fight Countering the Islamic State's Antiquities Trafficking' (Center on Sanctions and Illicit Finance, November 2015), p. 10.

[50] A. Keller (*supra* n. 39), p. 12.

[51] APSA2011, 'Al-Rikaz Department of ISIS Licenses Excavation Works in Exchange for Monetary Percentage' (2011).

Sanctions and Illicit Finance, this is a plausible hypothesis – and it may also be applicable to Palmyra. This would suggest that Islamic State had already removed the original objects in order to sell them on the black market.[52] The same report points out that Islamic State looted artefacts from the archaeological site of Nimrud in a professional way, indicating that 'the group's ranks likely include individuals with archaeological expertise who consult with the group willingly or under duress'.[53] This is consistent with the assassination of Khaled al-Asaad, a devoted archaeologist now known as 'Mr Palmyra', who had safeguarded the ruins of Palmyra for forty years, first as the director of the World Heritage Site and then, after his retirement in 2003, as an expert in the Iraqi department of museums and antiquities.[54] When Islamic State captured the site in the summer of 2015, Khaled al-Assad was held hostage and interrogated about the whereabouts of some of its hidden treasures. He consistently refused to disclose this information and was consequently murdered on 18 August 2015.

It is important to note in passing that large-scale looting did not only occur in the territories controlled by Islamic State. For example, a 2015 study carried out by Jesse Casana, based on satellite imagery in Syria, showed that – in aggregate – the number of sites looted in areas controlled by the Kurds, Bashar al-Assad's forces, and rebel groups was greater than the total number of plundered sites controlled by Islamic State. Out of the 565 sites assessed that were under the control of the Kurds, Assad's forces, or rebel groups, 130 had been looted; whereas of the 383 sites assessed that were controlled by Islamic State, the number was 82. However, there was a notable difference in the intensity of the looting – the Islamic State areas recorded a much higher number of severely looted sites. This is consistent with the fact that the Antiquities Division had established a highly organized scheme of excavation and plunder. For example, in the archaeological site of Mari (on Syria's tentative list of world heritage), between March and November 2014, the period when Islamic State consolidated its control over the area, 'approximately 1,286 pits were excavated over 232 days, an average rate of 5.5 pits per day over the seven months'.[55] The areas

---

[52] Fanusie and Joffe (*supra* n. 49), p.10.
[53] Ibid., p. 11.
[54] 'Syrian Archaeologist "Killed in Palmyra" by IS Militants' (*BBC News*, 19 August 2015).
[55] B. I. Daniels and K. Hanson, 'Archaeological Site Looting in Syria and Iraq: A Review of the Evidence', in F. Desmarais (ed.), *Countering Illicit Traffic in Cultural Goods: The Global Challenge of Protecting the World's Heritage* (Paris: ICOM, 2015), pp. 82–95, 88.

controlled by the other armed groups were mainly characterized by moderate or minor episodes of looting.[56]

In terms of the excavations in the areas controlled by the Syrian Army, Kurdish forces, or rebel groups, the lower level of intensity may indicate that the plunder was spontaneous and connected to the general breakdown in law and order. What is of concern, however, is that Casana's study shows there was a dramatic increase in looting in the archaeological sites of Apamea and Ebla (both have been on the Syrian tentative list of world heritage since 1999) at the time of their occupation by the forces of the Syrian regime.[57] It is unknown if the looters were mainly local residents who had turned to this activity out of necessity or soldiers trying to make extra cash.[58] The impact of the loss of unknown quantities of Syrian cultural heritage of inestimable value may be the same whoever carried out the looting, but the distinction has important legal implications. There is a controversy around the meaning of 'any' in the wording of Article 4(3) of the 1954 Hague Convention for the Protection of Cultural Property in the Event of Armed Conflict (1954 Hague Convention) – the applicable instrument which is discussed in detail later in this chapter. According to Article 4(3), parties undertake to put a stop to *any* form of 'theft, pillage or misappropriation'.[59] This could be interpreted either as encompassing any theft, pillage and the like carried out by the members of (state or non-state) armed forces only, or as extending to any form of pillage and misappropriation, including that carried out by the civilian population.[60] If it refers to the former, the

---

[56] J. Casana, 'Satellite Imagery-Based Analysis of Archaeological Looting in Syria' (2015) 78 (3) *Near Eastern Archaeology* 142–52, 151. See also J. Casana and M. Panahipour, 'Satellite-Based Monitoring of Looting and Damage to Archaeological Sites in Syria' (2014) 2(2) *Journal of Eastern Mediterranean Archaeology and Heritage Studies* 128–51.

[57] Casana, 2015 (*supra* n. 56), pp. 148, 150.

[58] One expert claimed that Syrian regime soldiers were actively looting Palmyra when off-duty, but this accusation has not been echoed in art circles since it was made: see 'Syrian Troops Looting Ancient City Palmyra, Says Archaeologist' (*The Guardian*, 1 June 2016).

[59] Article 4(3) of the 1954 Hague Convention for the Protection of Cultural Property in the Event of Armed Conflict reads: 'The High Contracting Parties further undertake to prohibit, prevent and, if necessary, put a stop to any form of theft, pillage or misappropriation of, and any acts of vandalism directed against, cultural property. They shall refrain from requisitioning movable cultural property situated in the territory of another High Contracting Party.'

[60] P. Gerstenblith, 'Protecting Cultural Heritage in Armed Conflict: Looking Back, Looking Forward' (2009) 7 *Cardozo Public Law, Policy & Ethics Journal* 677–708, 693; cf. R. O'Keefe, *The Protection of Cultural Property in Armed Conflict* (Cambridge University Press, 2006), p. 131.

armed forces would not be liable if the extensive looting was carried out by civilians.

5.5   Routes and Buyers

Whatever their origin, it is undeniable that these antiquities find a ready market. However, it is unclear how they are smuggled out and to whom they are sold, as the smuggling routes and networks are still poorly understood. Precisely because of this, the International Council of Museums (ICOM) established an International Observatory on Illicit Traffic in Cultural Goods,[61] aimed at becoming a knowledge hub on illicit trafficking tasked with improving monitoring methods, data gathering and scientific research and with fostering the exchange of good practices. For now, however, a lot of what we know (or think we know) of this activity is based on knowledge of past practices and plausible inferences. This section attempts to summarize the available knowledge on the chain of actors standing in between the looter and the buyer, as a full understanding thereof is vital for the purpose of devising a proper legal strategy against such phenomenon.[62]

It has been asserted that the route to the buyer is divided into four different phases, comprising 'looter, early stage middleman or intermediary, late stage intermediary, and collector'.[63] The differentiation in phases serves the purpose of highlighting the specialized knowledge required by each of the operations that enable the functioning of the trade.[64] During the first phase, the looter analyzes the looting site – which could be a geographical area or an archaeological site, warehouse or museum – for the purpose of locating the antiquities to steal.[65] Then, during the second phase, the stolen artefacts are sold to so-called 'early stage

---

[61] See www.obs-traffic.museum/.

[62] M. V. Vlasic and J. P. DeSousa, 'The Illicit Antiquities Trade and Terrorism Financing: From the Khmer Rouge to Daesh' in C. King, C. Walker, and J. Gurulé (eds.), *The Palgrave Handbook of Criminal and Terrorism Financing Law* (Palgrave Handbooks, 2018), pp. 1167–91, 1171.

[63] P. Campbell, 'The Illicit Antiquities Trade as a Transnational Criminal Network: Characterizing and Anticipating Trafficking of Cultural Heritage' (2013) 20(2) *International Journal of Cultural Property* 113, 116. See also S. Mackenzie and T. Davis, 'Temple Looting in Cambodia: Anatomy of a Statue Trafficking Network' (2014) 54(5) *British Journal of Criminology* 722.

[64] Campbell, 2013 (*supra* n. 63), p. 116.

[65] Further examples of sites can be found in C. Ruiz, 'My Life as a Tombarolo' (March 2000) 112 *The Art Newspaper* 36.

intermediaries', in charge of smuggling the artefacts to the country where they will be sold.[66] These first two stages require the involvement of individuals with a highly specialized degree of knowledge.[67] Indeed, unlike drugs or weapons, antiquities cannot be manufactured; they must be stolen from a cultural site. Further, the identification of their value and their transportation require the individuals involved to possess a level of education sufficient for ensuring that the products that are looted will reach the buyers intact. As such, an individual's participation in either of these stages implies both knowledge of cultural preservation and awareness of the system of looting. The third stage is perhaps the most significant; in its context, 'fences', that is, individuals acting as an intermediary between the illegitimate end of the scale (the looters and smugglers) and the 'legitimate' one (the buyers), carry out a legitimization of the sale.[68] During this process, fences fabricate certificates and licences that accompany the products to be sold.[69] Finally, the fourth stage sees as participants legitimate actors (e.g. collectors, museum curators) who purchase the antiquities.[70]

Previous investigations have indicated that the Western market is more interested in pre-Islamic pieces, whereas buyers in the Gulf have a taste for Islamic art. Looters, however, generally cash in only 1 to 2 per cent of each artefact's value; the profit mainly goes to the middlemen.[71] The team investigating the looting of the National Museum in Baghdad was told that 'professionals had come in just before the war – possibly through Jordan – waiting for the fog of war and the opportunity of a lifetime'[72] – a claim that has been corroborated by evidence of the looters' careful selection of small and especially exquisite pieces. This, in turn, implies that these professional looters had already planned how to move the objects out of the country, and therefore possessed an established, reliable network of underworld connections with access to a final buyer.[73] Given the relative proximity in time and space, present-day looters may well be using the same smuggling routes

---

[66] A. McCalister, 'Organized Crime and the Theft of Iraqi Antiquities' (2005) 9(1) *Trends in Organized Crime* 24, 26.
[67] J. Conklin, *Art Crime* (Praeger, 1994), pp. 158–9.
[68] Campbell, 2013 (*supra* n. 63), p. 116.
[69] J. Pipkins, 'ISIL and the Illicit Antiquities Trade' (2016) 24 *International Affairs Review* 116.
[70] Campbell, 2013 (*supra* n. 63), p. 116.
[71] FSC (*supra* n. 20), pp. 3, 9; Fanusie and Joffe, 2015 (*supra* n. 49), p. 8.
[72] Bogdanos, 2011 (*supra* n. 22), p. 153.
[73] Ibid.

and connections, or may have acquired even greater know-how and a more robust contact list.

In 2016, in compliance with UN Security Council Resolution 2253 (2015), which mandates Member States to inform on the progress on implementation of the cultural property trade embargo, several countries supplied UNESCO with reports concerning cultural objects found in their territory during the smuggled artefacts' illicit journey. Interestingly, Turkey had seized around 50,000 objects of Syrian origin but fewer than 10 from Iraq. A similar pattern was detected in Lebanon.[74] The obvious implication is that smuggled Iraqi artefacts take an alternative route.

The amount of illicitly excavated and looted antiquities is massive. For example, by December 2016, 2,786 objects from Iraq and 1,092 from Syria were registered on the INTERPOL database of stolen art. Nevertheless, there is something else that is troubling observers: despite the appalling level of looting detected by the satellite imagery, there is a relative scarcity of records of sales of Syrian and Iraqi antiquities;[75] these objects do not seem to be appearing in the usual auction houses in London and New York. There may be two explanations for this: first, major auction houses and museums are complying with the ban on the trade in cultural property originating from Iraq and Syria imposed by several Security Council resolutions and/or, second, professional dealers are storing the looted items waiting for the chilling effect produced by such resolutions to dissipate.

Neil Brodie (2011) has conducted a study analyzing the behaviour of the market in Iraqi antiquities after the First Gulf War and the first two Security Council resolutions in 1990 and 2003 banning trade in Iraqi archaeological artefacts after 6 August 1990. Brodie found that, even after Resolution 661 (1990), there continued to be a very dynamic international and most likely illegal sale of Iraqi antiquities, particularly at Christie's auction house in London.[76] However, after Resolution 1483 (2003), which emphasized the trade embargo on cultural property, market behaviour changed and the number of Iraqi antiquities openly

---

[74] Information retrieved at UNODC workshop on illicit traffic of Iraqi cultural property (January 2017). The reports were sent as a requirement of UNSC Resolution 2253 of 2015.

[75] FSC (*supra* n. 20), p. 9.

[76] N. B., 'The Market in Iraqi Antiquities 1980–2009 and Academic Involvement in the Marketing Process', in S. Manacorda and D. Chappell (eds.), *Crime in the Art and Antiquities World: Illegal Trafficking in Cultural Property* (New York: Springer, 2011), pp. 117–33, 117-18.

offered for sale plummeted. Although it cannot be established that the resolution was behind the demise of the trade, the fact is that this happened for both Christie's (in London) and Sotheby's (in New York) at around this time.[77] Given that the Security Council reiterated the cultural property embargo and extended it to Syria in Resolution 2199 (2015), it is not surprising that these objects have failed to appear in the usual markets. However, this begs the question of where they actually are.

The UN Sanctions Monitoring Team has proposed a very plausible hypothesis: local dealers are stockpiling these artefacts, waiting for a time when international attention has waned and the pressure eased.[78] The more professional the dealer, the more patient they are. The items may be stored for years in free ports in Hong Kong or Geneva, time enough to establish a false provenance for the object.[79]

Having said that, it must be noted that a number of cultural objects are circulating for sale online. Brodie reports:

> Between 27 November 2015 and 17 February 2016, seven sellers between them sold 60 figurines for the total sum of £6099. The highest priced figurine sold for £720, the lowest for £12. The average price was £102. Six of the sellers were based in the UK, all in England. One seller, selling only one figurine, was based in the USA.[80]

This is because the difference between the illicit trade of, say, the 1980s and that of today is that now professional dealers may not be focusing only on artefacts of considerable value:

> The Internet market allows the participation of antiquities collectors from a much broader range of socioeconomic backgrounds than was previously the case. It works against traditional merchants who maintain physical galleries in expensive locations such as New York or London and favours a new business model whereby large inventories can be stored in low-cost locations, thus making it financially viable to trade in low-value and potentially high-volume material.[81]

---

[77] Ibid., pp. 118–19.
[78] UN Doc. S/2014/815, 'The Islamic State in Iraq and the Levant and the Al-Nusrah Front for the People of the Levant: Report and Recommendations submitted pursuant to Resolution 2170', para. 73.
[79] FSC (*supra* n. 20), p. 9.
[80] www.marketmassdestruction.com/ebaywatch-1/.
[81] N. Brodie, 'The Internet Market in Antiquities', in F. Desmarais (ed.), *Countering Illicit Traffic in Cultural Goods: The Global Challenge of Protecting the World's Heritage* (Paris: ICOM, 2015), pp. 11–19, 11.

Most of these objects reported by Brodie lacked a certificate of provenance[82] showing when and where the object was found and its chain of sales. Given that these figurines date back to the sixth or seventh centuries BCE, there is no way of knowing whether they have been freshly looted or have been on the market for a hundred years. In other words, we cannot know if they have reached the USA and the UK through the current smuggling routes and networks originating in Syria and Iraq.

What is unquestionable, however, is that looting has become more fierce and extensive since online selling has allowed the demand to morph from one centred on elites interested in rare, expensive items to one targeting the middle-class buyer who happens on a figurine while browsing the Internet for an anniversary gift, probably completely unaware of the illicit origins of their purchase.

5.6   Legal Responses to the Illicit Trade of Artefacts

There are some international instruments that may be advantageous in the fight against illicit trade; this is because the development of the legal framework on the protection of cultural heritage has been mainly reactive. The number of mechanisms devised precisely for the fight against phenomena such as the illicit trade of artefacts has only recently started to rise, thanks mostly to the concern shown by the UN Security Council. This final section surveys some of the international instruments specific to cultural property, as well as the International Criminal Court (ICC) Statute, to assess the extent to which they are able to respond to the illicit excavation of and trade in antiquities. These instruments include the 1907 IV Hague Regulations; the 1970 UNESCO Convention on the means of prohibiting and preventing the illicit import, export, and transfer of ownership of cultural property (1970 UNESCO Convention); the 1995 UNIDROIT Convention on stolen or illegally exported cultural objects (1995 UNIDROIT Convention); the resolutions of the Security Council; and the ICC Statute's list of war crimes.

5.6.1   The 1907 IV Hague Regulations

The 1907 IV Hague Convention of Laws and Customs on Land and Annexed Regulations was adopted in the context of the second Hague

---

[82] In this context, provenance is understood as the history of sales, original ownership and any subsequent changes of title.

Conference, with the aim of building upon the laws and customs of war adopted in 1899. While the Convention's subject-matter does not cover the illicit trade – for evident temporal reasons – its Article 56, which is applicable during occupation, displays an incipient notion of individual criminal responsibility: 'The property of municipalities, that of institutions dedicated to religion, charity and education, the arts and sciences, even when State property, shall be treated as private property. All seizure of, destruction or wilful damage done to institutions of this character, historic monuments, works of art and science, is forbidden, and *should be made the subject of legal proceedings*.'[83]

5.6.2   The 1970 UNESCO Convention

The 1970 UNESCO Convention mandates a system of control according to which the 'source' (or exporting) state parties must issue certificates specifying that the export of the cultural object in question is authorized (Art. 6(a)). For its part, the 'recipient' (or importing) state must check if the cultural object has such a certificate, otherwise it should consider the import illegal (Art. 3). In the past, the 1970 UNESCO Convention was considered weak because most of its parties were 'source' states, as they are naturally the most interested in preventing their cultural heritage from disappearing onto the black market. This is less the case nowadays, although scholars still claim that the Convention's wording has allowed for its obligations to be interpreted very differently by the various domestic legal systems.[84] In the context of Iraq and Syria, the Convention's main limitation is that it applies only to identified and inventoried cultural property, such as the artefacts found in museums and art galleries (Art. 7 (b)(i)); however, most of the illicit traffic concerns antiquities that have been illegally excavated and therefore have no prior record of existence. In addition, even when the items have been stolen from a museum, source countries such as Iraq and Syria correspond to poorer nations in the sense that they have not come close to itemizing all the cultural property they hold in museums or exhibit in galleries. The objectives of the Convention are being supplemented by further international and national efforts. For example, INTERPOL set up both an investigation team and a database

---

[83] Emphasis added.

[84] See, for example, S. Delepierre and M. Schneider, 'Ratification and Implementation of International Conventions to Fight Illicit Trafficking in Cultural Property', in F. Desmarais (ed.), *Countering Illicit Traffic in Cultural Goods: The Global Challenge of Protecting the World's Heritage* (Paris: ICOM, 2015), pp. 129–40.

cataloguing stolen artefacts.[85] Similarly, some countries have created databases or special taskforces to this end. An example is Italy, whose Carabinieri include a special unit called 'The Carabinieri Command for the Protection of Italy's Cultural Heritage', tasked with the protection of Italian cultural property as well as combating the illicit trade.[86]

5.6.3   The 1995 UNIDROIT Convention

The 1995 UNIDROIT Convention, a complementary instrument to the 1970 UNESCO Convention, enhanced the latter convention's scope of application by transposing its precepts into norms to be applied when conflicts between national laws arise.[87] Its most important feature is that it obliges the possessor of a stolen cultural item to either return it (Art. 3(1)) or pay an agreed amount of compensation if they are able to show that they were an innocent party in the transaction and believed that they had acquired ownership of the item (Art. 4(1)). To do this, the buyer has to prove that they conducted due diligence.[88] This procedure consists, for example, of insisting on information about the provenance of the object (in terms of ownership) and double-checking internationally available lists and records of stolen cultural heritage. The advantage of the 1995 UNIDROIT Convention is that it extends its reach to non-inventoried items taken from archaeological excavations, which is particularly significant considering that the Syrian Arab Republic ratified the convention in April 2018, with its commitments entering into force for the country in October 2018.[89] The downsides are that, firstly, at the time

[85] 'Interpol's Stolen Works of Art Database | Www.Icom.Museum' (*Obs-traffic.museum*, 2019), www.obs-traffic.museum/interpols-stolen-works-art-database.
[86] L. Rush and L. Millington, *The Carabinieri Command for the Protection of Cultural Property: Saving the World's Heritage* (Boydell, 2015); see also S. Poggioli, 'For Italy's Art Police, an Ongoing Fight against Pillage of Priceless Works' (*NPR*, 11 January 2017), www.npr.org/sections/parallels/2017/01/11/508031006/for-italys-art-police-anongoing-fight-against-pillage-of-priceless-works.
[87] International Institute for the Unification of Private Law [UNIDROIT] Convention on Stolen or Illegally Exported Cultural Objects (24 June 1995).
[88] In order to understand the due diligence steps required in the purchase of an object of art, the 'Responsible Art Market Initiative' (RAM) may be of assistance. Created to provide practical guidance and a platform for the sharing of best practices to address risks connected with the art market in Switzerland and abroad, RAM features an 'Art Transaction Due Diligence Toolkit'; see http://responsibleartmarket.org/guidelines/art-transaction-due-diligence-toolkit/.
[89] 1995 UNIDROIT Convention on Stolen or Illegally Exported Cultural Objects – Deposit of the 43rd Instrument – Syrian Arab Republic (*Unidroit.org*, 2019), www.unidroit.org

of writing, Iraq is not a party to it. Secondly, it applies only to antiquities looted after 1995, thus excluding from its scope a large part of already-looted artefacts.[90]

Be that as it may, there are two important tools that a would-be buyer should check before purchasing an object if he ever wanted to prove due diligence. One is the INTERPOL database, which contains about 50,000 identifiable objects from 135 countries, including 94 objects taken from the Mosul Museum in 2015.[91] The database is updated every six months, published online and also distributed to key actors such as airport customs. The database is fed by police information (not private communications) and, since 2009, it is accessible to the public. Each one of the missing objects contains a visual and technical description, which makes its identification a lot easier. The downside of the INTERPOL database is that it displays only objects that have been officially reported as stolen by member countries, that is, items for which a prior record existed. The Red Lists of ICOM constitute another important tool to use. Unlike the INTERPOL database, the lists published by ICOM illustrate the *types* of object that are likely to have been excavated and illegally traded. It currently has seventeen Red Lists organized by country,[92] from Afghanistan to Yemen, and it also publishes Emergency Red Lists when there is an urgent need, for example due to the breakout of a conflict.

5.6.4   Engagement by the UN Security Council

The UN Security Council has dedicated a fair amount of attention to the cultural heritage crises in Iraq and Syria. In the context of the First Gulf War, Security Council Resolution 661 (6 August 1990) imposed a prohibition on the import of all commodities (including cultural property) originating in Iraq after the date of the Resolution. Furthermore, it established a committee tasked with monitoring the implementation of the resolution.[93] As a result, states began codifying the prohibition contained

/89-news-and-events/2408-1995-unidroit-convention-on-stolen-or-illegally-exported-cultural-objects-deposit-of-the-43rd-instrument-syrian-arab-republic.

[90] Z. Veres, 'The Fight against Illicit Trafficking of Cultural Property: The 1970 UNESCO Convention and the 1995 UNIDROIT Convention' (2014) 12(2) *Santa Clara Journal of International Law* 6–7.

[91] *Supra* n. 85.

[92] 'Red Lists Database – ICOM' (*Icom.museum*, 2019), http://icom.museum/resources/red-lists-database/.

[93] UNSC Resolution 611 (1988) of 25 April 1988, para. 6.

within the resolution in their legal orders.[94] Security Council Resolution 1483 (2003) expanded the scope of protection by spelling out an obligation in relation to the protection of cultural property – thus remedying the textual vagueness of the previous commitment: it imposed a duty 'to facilitate the safe return to Iraqi institutions of Iraqi cultural property and other items of archaeological, historical, cultural, rare scientific, and religious importance illegally removed from the Iraq National Museum, the National Library, and other locations in Iraq since the adoption of Resolution'.[95]

The Security Council reinforced this prohibition in Resolution 2199 (2015), extending it to items exported from Syria:

> [A]ll Member States shall take appropriate steps to prevent the trade in Iraqi and Syrian cultural property and other items of archaeological, historical, cultural, rare scientific and religious importance illegally removed from Iraq since 6 August 1990 and from Syria since 15 March 2011, including by prohibiting cross-border trade in such items, thereby allowing for their eventual safe return to the Iraqi and Syrian people and calls upon the United Nations Educational, Scientific, and Cultural Organization, Interpol, and other international organizations, as appropriate, to assist in the implementation of this paragraph.[96]

The significance of this passage cannot be understated. The Security Council not only recognized the illicit excavation and trafficking of cultural property but also, by linking it to the maintenance of peace and security, elevated the importance of combating this activity to one of international concern. Since the resolution was passed, the level of attention dedicated to the issue has increased, namely through Resolution 2253 (2015), which tasked the Monitoring Team of the ISIL (Da'esh) and Al-Qaida Sanctions Committee with submitting independent reports every six months on the impact of the resolution's measures, including those related to trade in cultural property.[97] A further ruling, Resolution 2322 (2016), urged UN Member States to introduce national measures and 'broad law enforcement and judicial cooperation in

---

[94] The United Kingdom, for example, adopted in 2003 the Iraq (United Nations Sanctions) Order 2003, which provides that: '[T]he importation or exportation of any item of illegally removed Iraqi cultural property is prohibited.'

[95] However, its wording is short of being effective, as it relies on lesser informative verbs such as 'facilitate'. See P. Gerstenblith, 'Introductory Note to United Nations Security Council Resolution 2347' (2018) 57(1) *American Society of International Law* 155, 156.

[96] UNSC Resolution 2199 (2015) of 12 February 2015, para. 17. This resolution also encompasses the use of language such as 'take appropriate steps'.

[97] UNSC Resolution 2253 (2015) of 17 December 2015, Annex I(a)(iii).

preventing and combating all forms and aspects of trafficking in cultural property and related offences that benefit or may benefit terrorist or terrorist groups'.[98] These obligations have now been reinforced by Resolution 2347 (2017), which has the distinction of being the first Security Council resolution exclusively dedicated to cultural heritage issues.[99] This latter document stresses that the primary responsibility for protecting cultural property in armed conflict lies with the Member States.[100] Continuing what had been started through Resolution 661, Resolution 2347 (2017) stimulated the process of domestic criminalization of conduct attributable to the illicit trade. Indeed, Ecuador, France, Japan, Jordan, Romania, Saudi Arabia, Serbia, Slovakia, Spain, Turkey, Ukraine, and Uruguay all reported that they have already criminalized the illicit trafficking of cultural property, and Italy and Mexico that they are revising their respective legal frameworks.[101]

5.6.5   Council of Europe Efforts

The Council of Europe has also been active in the cultural protection legal field. Its contribution ranges from the adoption of a series of conventions[102] – or attempt thereto, considering that the 1995 European Convention on the Protection of the Archaeological Heritage never entered into force – and soft law instruments such as guidelines,[103] resolutions,[104]

---

[98] UNSC Resolution 2322 (2016) of 12 December 2016, para. 12.
[99] For a commentary on Resolution 2347 (2017), see K. Hausler, 'Cultural Heritage and the Security Council: Why Resolution 2347 Matters' (2018) 48 *Questions of International Law: Zoom-In* 5–19.
[100] UNSC Resolution 2347, 24 March 2017, para. 5
[101] UN Doc. S/2017/969, 'Report of the Secretary-General on the Implementation of Security Council Resolution 2347 (2017)', 17 November 2017, para. 23.
[102] Council of Europe European Convention on Offences relating to Cultural Property, 23 June 1985, ETS 119 and the Nicosia convention, which is discussed later in this section.
[103] Council of Europe, *Guidelines for the Protection of the Archaeological Heritage* (Strasbourg: Council of Europe Publishing, 2000); Council of Europe, *Guidance on the Development of Legislation and Administration System in the Field of Cultural Heritage* (Strasbourg: Council of Europe Publishing, 2000).
[104] See, inter alia, Council of Europe, Resolution no. 1 on the Role of Cultural Heritage and the Challenge of Globalization, adopted at the 5th European Conference of Ministers responsible for the cultural heritage, 5–7 April 2001, http://conservacion.inah.gob.mx/normativa/wp-content/uploads/Documento64.pdf; Council of Europe, Resolution Concerning the Adaptation of Laws and Regulations to the Requirements of Integrated Conservation of the Architectural Heritage, 14 April 1976, Res (76)28E.

recommendations,[105] guiding principles,[106] and declarations.[107] Its most recent and notable achievement is the adoption of the Convention on Offences relating to Cultural Property (the Nicosia Convention, not yet in force) in May 2017. This instrument obliges its parties to criminalize every step of the illicit trafficking business: theft, unlawful excavation and removal, illegal importation and exportation, illegal acquisition and placing on the market of cultural property, as well as the falsification of documents in order to present it as having a licit provenance. It also prohibits its intentional destruction or damage.[108] Further, it represents an important step towards the adoption of a legal framework outlawing conduct related to the illicit trade *internationally*. Indeed, the belief that the protection of cultural heritage was a prerogative of a state's sovereignty had prevented the move towards an international framework prohibiting any such conduct.[109] Its motivation can thus be found both in the need to harmonize states' laws with a view to setting the groundwork for this aim and, fighting the increased security risks adduced by the liberalization of markets, in the context of increased transnational criminal activity.[110] While it is not yet in force, this should not lead to quick assumptions of the Nicosia Convention's success, as it may well have served as a model framework to imitate by domestic jurisdictions.

5.6.6   The International Criminal Court's Efforts

While the ICC Statute prohibits some crimes against cultural property, its reach in relation to the question of looting is more limited. The reason is that the criminalization of the destruction of cultural property found in Article 8(2)(e)(iv), which relates to non-international armed conflicts, does not encompass movable cultural property; it refers only to

---

[105] Council of Europe, Recommendation on Sustained Care of the Cultural Heritage Against Physical Deterioration due to Pollution and Other Similar Factors, 4 February 1997, Rec (97) 2E; Council of Europe, Recommendation on the Integrated Conservation of Cultural Landscape Areas as Part of Landscape Policies, 11 September 1995, Rec (95)9E.

[106] See, for instance, Council of Europe, Third European Conference of Ministers responsible for the cultural heritage, Malta, 16–17 January 1992.

[107] Council of Europe, Helsinki Declaration on the Political Dimension of Cultural Heritage Conservation in Europe, 30–31 May 1996, https://rm.coe.int/16805077fc.

[108] Council of Europe, Convention on Offences relating to Cultural Property, www.coe.int /en/web/culture-and-heritage/convention-on-offences-relating-to-cultural-property.

[109] M. M. Bieczyński, 'The Nicosia Convention 2017: A New International Instrument Regarding Criminal Offences against Cultural Property' (2017) 2(3) *Santander Culture and Art Review* 255, 264.

[110] Ibid.

'buildings dedicated to religion, education, art, science or charitable purposes, historic monuments', and it covers only 'intentionally directing attacks'. The article does not encompass movables such as those artefacts that are easily looted and end up circulating on the black market. In fact, in the context of Mali, it has been reported that thousands of manuscripts dating back to the thirteenth century have been lost and thousands more have been burnt, an issue that was not discussed in the Al Mahdi case.[111] The war crime of pillaging,[112] however, could represent a fall-back option. But for looting to be labelled a war crime, the activity has to satisfy a number of conditions, including whether the perpetrator intended to deprive the owner of the object and to appropriate it for private use, and whether this took place in the context of and in association with an armed conflict.[113] This could encompass acts of looting, but the provision falls short of covering the actions of middlemen and buyers. In addition, the ICC is of limited use when it comes to the crimes of Islamic State, as neither Syria nor Iraq is a party to the ICC Statute. This means that, as things stand, the Court does not have jurisdiction over Iraqi or Syrian nationals who may have carried out acts of looting. Nevertheless, it would have jurisdiction over those members of Islamic State who are nationals of countries that are parties to the Statute (for example, Belgium, the Netherlands, and Spain). A new suspect has been brought to The Hague, Al Hassan Ag Abdoul Aziz Ag Mohamed Ag Mahmoud (Al Hassan), whose warrant of arrest includes the intentional destruction of cultural property.[114]

5.7 Conclusion

Even though looting and illegal trade in antiquities is an old phenomenon, its current links with violent groups, especially Islamic State, has

---

[111] The International Criminal Court (ICC) dedicated an entire case to the prosecution of a perpetrator accused of destroying cultural heritage in Mali. The accused, Ahmad Al Faqi Al Mahdi, was sentenced to nine years' imprisonment for his part in the destruction of nine mausoleums and the door of the fifteenth-century Sidi Yahia mosque, located in the world heritage city of Timbuktu. See *Prosecutor* v. *Ahmad Al Faqi Al Mahdi*, ICC-01/12-01/15, Trial Judgment and Sentence, 27 September 2016.
[112] Articles 8(2)(b)(xvi) and 8(2)(e)(v) concerning international and non-international armed conflicts, respectively.
[113] ICC Elements of Crimes, Article 8(2)(b)(xvi).
[114] See ICC Pre Trial Chamber I, ICC-01/12-01/18-2-tENG, *Warrant of Arrest for Al Hassan Ag Abdoul Aziz Ag Mohamed Ag Mahmoud*, 27 March 2018, p. 9. The charges were confirmed on 30 September 2019.

changed the level of attention paid to this issue. The Abu Sayyaf raid demonstrated that this was not an incidental activity of Islamic State but one where they had put in place a highly systematized mechanism to ensure themselves a humble (when compared to oil and gas) but constant stream of revenue. This, in turn, implies that, to target the most important artefacts, the organization counted on the help of experts and, to make them arrive at a final buyer, on a network of middlemen and routes of which very little is known so far. The other most notable change is that, with the appearance of various venues to sell antiquities online, looting and trafficking has become a wholesale business with devastating effects on the archaeological sites of Iraq and Syria, which are now intensively plundered. There is no one-size-fits-all solution to this problem and, certainly, the international legal framework has major caveats on this front: the 1970 UNESCO Convention does not cover items of which no prior record existed, such as those dug up from Iraqi and Syrian soil; Iraq is not a party to the 1995 UNIDROIT Convention. To date, the looting and illicit sale of cultural property is not considered an international crime at the ICC. Despite the conviction of Al Mahdi at the ICC for the destruction of cultural heritage in Timbuktu (Mali), the ICC Statute has a loophole as it concerns movable cultural property as this category is not covered as such in the war crime against cultural heritage. The war crime of pillage would be a fall-back option, but it would not encompass those who profit the most from this transnational affair, that is, the middlemen and the buyers. As the Security Council has pointed out in Resolutions 2199 and 2253 (2015), 2322 (2016), and 2347 (2017), to stop the illicit trade in cultural property, efforts should focus on strengthening domestic enforcement and laws, as well as international cooperation. The situation will take a while to improve because, while this phenomenon has been going on for decades, the Security Council's interest in the illicit trade in cultural property stems from its newly acquired international security dimension and, as such, the Security Council has arrived quite late to the game. Importantly, this impetus provided by the Security Council should not wane in the upcoming years in order to prevent patient middlemen who may be storing artefacts from fulfilling their business.

6

Arms Transfer Complicity Under the Rome Statute

TOMAS HAMILTON [*]

6.1 Individual Arms Transfer Conduct

From Rwanda to Yemen, Syria to Cambodia, it is often claimed that individuals who provide weapons to the perpetrators of genocide, war crimes and crimes against humanity are to blame for those crimes.[1] An arms supplier who knowingly fuels atrocity may be widely considered morally reprehensible as a 'profiteer of war', yet the scope of their criminal responsibility remains open to discussion.

International and domestic laws are permissive with regard to arms transfers that serve legitimate political, security, economic and commercial interests, while certain transfers are prohibited on the basis that the end-use of the weapons involves serious violations of human rights. The actions and behaviour of an individual involved in such a transfer ('arms transfer conduct') are directly and indirectly regulated by a range of instruments and mechanisms at the international and domestic level: export restrictions in states' municipal laws;[2] international obligations requiring states to prohibit certain transfers;[3] the prohibitions on a state's

[*] I wish to thank Nina Jørgensen, Alejandro Kiss, Russell Hopkins and Juan Pablo Calderón for their enlightening comments on earlier drafts. All views and any mistakes are solely my own.
[1] S. Goose and F. Smyth, 'Arming Genocide in Rwanda' (1994) 73 *Foreign Affairs* 86–96, 91; S. Musa, 'The Saudi-Led Coalition in Yemen, Arms Exports and Human Rights: Prevention Is Better Than Cure' (2017) 22(3) *Journal of Conflict and Security Law* 433–62, 439; J. Ciorciari, 'China and the Pol Pot Regime' (2014) 14(2) *Cold War History* 215–35, 233, 235.
[2] H. Koh, 'A World Drowning in Guns' (2002) 71 *Fordham Law Review* 2333, 2339.
[3] S. Casey-Maslen et al., *The Arms Trade Treaty: A Commentary* (OUP, 2016), p. 166.

complicity in internationally wrongful acts;[4] arms embargoes imposed by, inter alia, the UN Security Council (UNSC);[5] counter-terrorism laws prohibiting material assistance to terrorist-designated organisations;[6] and non-binding commercial standards in the arms trade.[7] There is little research into the collective regulatory effect of this assemblage of global regulation of arms transfers, yet it is clear that many forms of assistive conduct are left unregulated and even where arms transfer conduct that assists an international crime is criminalised, this is often undermined in practice by a lack of effective criminal enforcement and punishment.

A further form of regulation is provided by international criminal law. Since at least the first Nuremberg trial, the principle of individual responsibility under international law has prohibited arms transfer conduct on the basis of complicity in international crimes.[8] The present chapter assesses the criminalisation of arms transfer conduct in the legal framework of the International Criminal Court (ICC) and focuses on three issues of interpretation in the mode of liability in Article 25(3)(d) (ii) of the Rome Statute of 'knowingly contributing to the commission or attempted commission of a crime by a group acting with a common purpose'.[9] This so-called 'residual provision' covers 'any other contribution' not covered elsewhere in Article 25 and its interpretation is likely to determine the 'hard cases' at the outer boundaries of complicit conduct under the Statute.

The first issue concerns the application of Article 25(3)(d)(ii) to individuals who are not members of the 'common purpose group' so-defined.[10] This raises the question of which forms of participation the drafters intended this mode of liability to express. Second, the nature of the Article 25(3)(d) material requirement to contribute to the commission or attempted

---

[4] N. Jørgensen, 'State Responsibility for Aiding or Assisting International Crimes in the Context of the Arms Trade Treaty' (2014) 108(4) *American Journal of International Law* 722–49.

[5] J. Erickson, 'Stopping the Legal Flow of Weapons: Compliance with Arms Embargoes, 1981–2004' (2013) 50(2) *Journal of Peace Research* 159–74.

[6] B. Saul, 'The Legal Relationship between Terrorism and Transnational Crime' (2017) 17 (3) *International Criminal Law Review* 417–52, 433.

[7] J. Stewart, 'Complicity in Business and Human Rights' (2015) 109 *Proceedings of the ASIL Annual Meeting* 4.

[8] C. Burchard, 'Ancillary and Neutral Business Contributions to "Corporate–Political Core Crime": Initial Enquiries Concerning the Rome Statute' (2010) 8(3) *Journal of International Criminal Justice* 919–46.

[9] Rome Statute of the International Criminal Court (adopted 17 July 1998, entered into force 1 July 2002) 2187 UNTS 105.

[10] Section 4.1.

commission of a crime remains ambiguous.[11] There is legal uncertainty as to the existence of a quantitative restriction on 'any other' contribution and there is a need to clarify the causal connection between the contribution and the crime. Third, and flowing from the second issue, what are the *mens rea* requirements of Article 25(3)(d)(ii)? The dual parameters of *degree* and *specificity* of knowledge may be useful tools for judicial discourse.[12]

Inevitably, this chapter's focus on the Rome Statute leaves aside many key issues surrounding arms transfers: the legal person of a corporation and its liability; the ICC's complementarity function and the variability of complicity doctrines in different domestic jurisdictions; the relevance of the status of weapon types such as cluster munitions, landmines and non-conventional weapons that are subject to per se criminal prohibitions on ownership and usage; and jurisdictional issues associated with 'third-state' arms brokering (where export restrictions are evaded by conducting business from a state other than the supplying and recipient states).[13]

A particularly complex issue beyond the scope of this chapter is the attribution of responsibility to individuals for their personal conduct working within large manufacturing and supplier companies.[14] The discussion in this chapter is limited to factual hypotheticals such as small-scale brokers and sole-trading individuals whose 'arms transfer conduct' involves them personally carrying out the arrangements for a shipment of weapons. Although it should go without saying, this chapter is not an attempt to advocate for arms transfer trials at the ICC, nor is the suggestion of such trials a knee-jerk reaction to the difficulties the Court has encountered in recent cases against military and political figures. Instead, the discussion is intended to contribute in some way to the long-term project of interpreting and applying the provisions that determine the outer boundaries of Rome Statute liability, as agreed to by the states parties.

6.2   Global Regulation of Arms Transfer Conduct

The ICC exists in the context of a global assemblage of international and domestic instruments and mechanisms that regulate arms transfer conduct, through both direct prohibitions on arms transfers as well as indirect effects. These regulatory regimes exert varying degrees of

[11]   Section 4.2.
[12]   Section 4.3.
[13]   These issues form part of my doctoral research at King's College London supervised by Nicola Palmer and Philippa Webb.
[14]   See Chapter 16 in this volume.

coercive influence over individual behaviour, through criminal and non-criminal sanctions, as well as non-binding voluntary standards.

6.2.1 Domestic Export Laws

In their national legal systems, states regulate the arms transfer conduct of legal and natural persons by addressing the manufacture, export, import, transportation, insurance, financing, ownership, stockpiling and use of weapons.[15] Harsh criminal penalties for breaching export regulations remain the exception rather than the rule and there are major practical difficulties in ensuring that the true end-user of a shipment of weapons is reflected on the documentation used to satisfy export requirements.[16] There is some evidence of national courts increasingly sanctioning exports on the basis of risks that weapons will be used to commit international crimes, as in the UK Court of Appeal's ruling on the sale or transfer of arms or military equipment to the Kingdom of Saudi Arabia for use in the conflict in Yemen.[17]

6.2.2 International Law Obligations

At the level of states' international commitments, the Arms Trade Treaty was the first multilateral agreement to impose binding obligations to regulate arms transfers.[18] Article 6(3) requires that states parties prohibit transfers where the state has knowledge that the arms would be used to commit an international crime. Article 7 prohibits exports where there is an 'overriding risk' of the arms being used to commit or facilitate an international crime. Despite Article 5(2) requiring states parties to establish 'national control systems' and Article 14 requiring 'appropriate measures to enforce national laws and regulations', the Treaty does not provide that states must enforce individual breaches of the Article 6 and 7 prohibitions with criminal sanctions. Such breaches, as Jørgensen explains, could also render the state responsible under customary international law in accordance with the Articles on State Responsibility for Internationally

---

[15] M. Bothe and T. Marauhn, 'The Arms Trade: Comparative Aspects of Law' (1993) 26(1) *Revue Belge De Droit International* 20–26, 25.

[16] See A. Tan (ed.) *The Global Arms Trade: A Handbook* (Routledge, 2014).

[17] *R (Campaign Against Arms Trade)* v. *The Secretary of State for International Trade* [2019] EWCA Civ 1020.

[18] Arms Trade Treaty (adopted 2 April 2013, opened for signature 3 June 2013, entered into force 24 December 2014) 3012 UNTS.

Wrongful Acts,[19] which would be, indirectly, a further form of regulation of individual behaviour that should come to bear on the arms transfer conduct of state officials, whether senior policy-making members of governments or decision-makers in export licensing authorities.

6.2.2.1   Arms Embargoes

The international system of arms embargoes has a capacity to indirectly regulate individual arms transfer conduct that contributes to an international crime. UNSC embargoes, frequently made in tandem with an EU embargo, may be triggered on the grounds specified in Chapter VII of the UN Charter, including on the basis of the Council's pre-emptive assessment of the risk that arms will be used to commit an international crime. As well as often being temporally and geographically bound, UNSC sanctions have increasingly since the 1990s been targeted at the conduct of particular individuals.[20] Two major limitations of arms embargoes as a regulator of individual conduct are their uneven application across geopolitical scenarios that fail to cover most international crimes and their lack of specified sanctions to follow breach. The UNSC's imposition of targeted Chapter VII arms embargoes thus regulates arms transfer conduct on an ad hoc basis. Even in the relatively rare circumstances when an embargo is imposed, with no member of the UNSC exercising its veto, there is virtually zero criminal law enforcement for 'embargo busters'. While UNSC embargoes are imposed at a supra-national level, consisting in non-permanent international agreements between states, there is no international body dedicated to embargo enforcement. Thus, criminal enforcement is currently possible only at a national level, and, despite the efforts of the Stockholm Process, states have been politically reluctant to advance in this respect.[21]

6.2.3   Counter-Terrorism Laws

Terrorism is not generally characterised as an international crime,[22] yet counter-terrorism laws prohibit conduct as complicity in a crime of

---

[19] Jørgensen (*supra* n. 4) 729–34.
[20] C. Staibano, 'Trends in UN Sanctions' in C. Staibano and P. Wallensteen (eds.) *International Sanctions: Between Wars and Words* (Routledge, 2005), p. 35.
[21] K. Orlovsky, 'International Criminal Law: Towards New Solutions in the Fight against Illegal Arms Brokers' (2006) 29 *Hastings International and Comparative Law Review* 343, 377.
[22] A. Chehtman, 'Terrorism and the Conceptual Divide between International and Transnational Criminal Law', in H. Van Der Wilt and C. Paulussen (eds.) *Legal Responses to Transnational and International Crimes: Towards an Integrative Approach?* (Edward Elgar, 2017), p. 15.

terrorism, which in some contexts may also be legally characterised as complicity in an international crime.[23] The actions of an arms trafficker who supplies a terrorist-designated non-state armed group that is engaged in committing international crimes may be legally characterised as complicity in international or terrorist crimes. It is relevant to consider the extent to which the ongoing and rapid expansion of counter-terrorism treaty law, domestic criminal laws and UNSC terrorism-related sanctions is increasing the breadth of prohibited arms transfer conduct.

The eighteen UN 'sectoral conventions' on terrorism have required states to prohibit and punish an increasingly broad range of complicit conduct.[24] The Financing Terrorism Convention criminalises financiers who know, *ad minimum*, that their funds will be used in terrorist activities.[25] The Terrorism Bombing Convention criminalises those who supply materials used in a terrorist bombing,[26] which is directly relevant to the interpretation of Article 25(3)(d) of the Rome Statute.[27]

Some domestic legal systems are increasingly adopting inchoate terrorism offences to sanction conduct prior to and irrespective of the commission of any harm, thereby expanding the scope of criminal liability in systems that traditionally would not punish mere preparatory acts.[28] The United States is arguably the site of the most dramatic recent expansion of domestic criminal laws in pre-emptive counter-terrorism offences, as seen in *Holder* v. *Humanitarian Law Project*.[29] For those involved in arms transfers, it implies the expansion of criminal liability to cover supplies of arms to a recipient who does not carry out a terrorist attack or even attempt to carry out any terrorist act.

---

[23] M. Drumbl, 'Victimhood in Our Neighborhood: Terrorist Crime, Taliban Guilt, and the Aysmmetries of the International Legal Order' (2002) 81(1) *North Carolina Law Review*.

[24] E. Husabø and I. Bruce, *Fighting Terrorism through Multilevel Criminal Legislation: Security Council Resolution 1373, the EU Framework Decision on Combating Terrorism and Their Implementation in Nordic, Dutch and German Criminal Law* (Brill, 2009).

[25] International Convention for the Suppression of the Financing of Terrorism (adopted 9 December 1999 UNGA Resolution 54/109, entered into force 10 April 2002) 2178 UNTS 229, Articles 2(1), 2(5)(a) and 2(5)(c).

[26] International Convention for the Suppression of Terrorist Bombings (adopted 15 December 1997 UNGA Resolution 52/164, entered into force on 23 May 2001) 2149 UNTS 256, Article 2(3).

[27] Section 4.1.

[28] B. Saul, 'Terrorism in International and Transnational Criminal Law' (2015) Sydney Law School Research Paper No. 15/83, 14.

[29] *Holder* v. *Humanitarian Law Project* 561 U.S. 1 (2010).

6.2.3.1   Arms Embargoes

UNSC sanctions have prohibited all forms of support for specified terrorist organisations, as in Resolution 1267 requiring UN Member States to take measures to ensure that no financial resources are made available to Al-Qaeda or the Taliban.[30] Similarly, EU directives have broadened the criminalisation of arms transfer conduct that is considered to be connected to terrorism, for instance the criminal prohibition on 'receiving instruction on the making or use of explosives, firearms or other weapons or noxious or hazardous substances, or on other specific methods or techniques, for the purpose of committing, or contributing to the commission of terrorist offences'.[31]

6.2.4   Business and Human Rights

Lastly, a steadily evolving set of non-binding business standards deem corporations socially irresponsible if they transfer arms that facilitate atrocity. Compacts such as the *OECD Guidelines for Multinational Enterprises*, the *UN Sub-Commission Norms on Business and Human Rights* and *the Voluntary Principles on Security & Human Rights* are non-criminal in nature, yet they exert a degree of coercive effect on individuals' commercial actions. Though they do not directly criminalise arms transfer conduct, these proclamations of industry standards nonetheless constitute broadly-agreed benchmarks for what is considered acceptable within the 'ordinary course of business' for certain communities. These standards may be relevant for assessing criminal *mens rea*, by providing indicators as to whether an individual knew that a particular transfer of arms was unacceptable by the prevailing acceptable practices of the day.

The assemblage of legal and quasi-legal regulation fails in practice to effectively prevent and punish the conduct of individuals involved in supplying arms for use in international crime. The lacunae in the criminalisation and enforcement should increase interest in the question of whether international criminal tribunals have a legal basis and mandate to investigate and prosecute criminal arms transfers, in particular due to

---

[30] UNSC Resolution 1267 (15 October 1999) UN Doc S/RES/1267. See also UNSC Resolution 1333 (19 December 2000) UN Doc S/RES/1333; UNSC Resolution 1373 (28 September 2001) UN Doc S/RES/1373, para. 2(e).

[31] Directive (EU) 2017/541 of the European Parliament and of the Council of 15 March 2017 on combating terrorism and replacing Council Framework Decision 2002/475/JHA and amending Council Decision 2005/671/JHA, Article 8.

the potential for enforcement against nationals of non-state parties, including those whose arms transfer conduct takes place outside of the Court's jurisdiction yet contributes to a crime within its jurisdiction.

6.3 Complicity Under International Criminal Law for Arms Transfers

The direct criminal responsibility under international law of individuals involved in irresponsible arms production and trade has a long history in legal doctrine, yet only limited instances of enforcement. The case reports of the post-World War II international criminal tribunals, from those of the International Criminal Tribunal for the former Yugoslavia (ICTY), the International Criminal Tribunal for Rwanda (ICTR), the Special Court for Sierra Leone (SCSL), the Extraordinary Chambers in the Courts of Cambodia (ECCC) and the Special Tribunal for Lebanon (STL), to those of the ICC, show that the legal bases for arms transfer liability at these courts were applied in only a small number of cases, of which fact patterns involving commercially-motivated transfers were even less numerous. The cases of *Zyklon B*, *Krupp* and *I.G. Farben* appear to be the only instances of international tribunals trying individuals for the commercial supply of weapons (and poisonous gases) used to commit international crimes, namely, rearming Germany in preparation for aggressive war and providing insecticide used in exterminations.[32] While figures such as Charles Taylor at the SCSL,[33] Momčilo Perišić at the ICTY[34] and Germaine Katanga at the ICC were charged for, inter alia, arms transfer conduct, the defendants' activities were not exclusively commercial in nature.[35] Those defendants thus do not represent the 'hard case' of a disinterested commercial actor. At the national level, there is increasing evidence of a small number of states punishing arms traders for complicity in international crimes in domestic courts, especially the readiness of the Dutch prosecution service to apply international law standards in *Kouwenhoven*[36] and *van Anraat*,[37] as well as US

---

[32] See Chapter 14 in this volume.

[33] *Charles Taylor* (Trial Judgment) SCSL-03–01-T (18 May 2012) ('*Taylor* Trial Judgment') paras. 6909–15.

[34] *Perišić* (Appeals Judgment) IT-04–81-A (28 February 2013) para. 49.

[35] See Chapter 10 in this volume.

[36] H. van der Wilt, 'Genocide v. War Crimes in the van Anraat Appeal' (2008) 6(3) *Journal of International Criminal Justice* 557–67.

[37] See Chapter 12 in this volume.

proceedings against *Chiquita* corporation for transferring weapons to a Columbian paramilitary group.[38]

6.3.1   Liability Under the Rome Statute

The Rome Statute does not at present provide for liability of the legal person of corporations that manufacture and distribute weapons.[39] The Statute does allow for liability of natural persons who work as part of such corporate structures on the basis of their individual decision-making capacity to engage in arms transfer conduct. Of course, any criminal case against an individual member of an organisation is likely to have knock-on deterrent effects on the behaviour of the organisation itself.

Article 25(3)(c) of the Statute is a potential avenue for the liability of an arms trader who '[f]or the purpose of facilitating the commission of [a crime], aids, abets or otherwise assists in its commission or its attempted commission, including providing the means for its commission'. It has often been claimed that a plain reading of the requirement that the assistor must act '[f]or the purpose of facilitating a crime' involves a volitional element of *mens rea* that most disinterested commercial activity will not satisfy.[40] As Cryer, Robinson and Vasiliev note, the purposive requirement in Article 25(3)(c) 'will certainly make prosecuting those who sell arms or other war matériel which is used for international crimes difficult to prosecute'.[41] The *Mbarushimana* Confirmation Decision held as follows:

> The Chamber notes that, unlike the jurisprudence of the *ad hoc* tribunals, article 25(3)(c) of the Statute requires that the person act with the purpose

---

[38]   C. Wheeler, 'Re-examining Corporate Liability at the International Criminal Court through the Lens of the Article 15 Communication against Chiquita Brands International' (2018) 19 *Melbourne Journal of International Law* 369.

[39]   Article 25(1).

[40]   R. Cryer, D. Robinson and S. Vasiliev, *An Introduction to International Criminal Law and Procedure* (2nd ed., Cambridge University Press, 2010), p. 377. The requirement in the Rome Statute that aiding and abetting must offer assistance 'for the purpose of assisting' sets a higher *mens rea* than the knowledge standard for aiding and abetting at the ICTR and ICTY. Nonetheless, much of the commentary on corporate complicity and the ICC has focused on Article 25(3)(c) as of primary relevance, interpreting this Rome Statute text in line with customary definitions of aiding and abetting, often to the exclusion of any discussion of Article 25(3)(d). See L. Bryk and M. Saage-Maaß, 'Individual Criminal Liability for Arms Exports under the ICC Statute: A Case Study of Arms Exports from Europe to Saudi-Led Coalition Members Used in the War in Yemen' (2019) *Journal of International Criminal Justice* 1–21.

[41]   Cryer, Robinson and Vasiliev, 2010, ibid.

to facilitate the crime; *knowledge is not enough for responsibility under this article.* Unless the requisite superior-subordinate relationship exists to charge responsibility under article 28 of the Statute, 25(3)(d) liability is the only other way a person can be held criminally responsible for acting merely with knowledge of the criminal intentions of others.[42]

The Trial Chamber in *Bemba et al* took a different view, holding that the purposive language of Article 25(3)(c) affects only *mens rea* vis-à-vis the aider or abettor's own actions and does not concern the *mens rea* of the principal's crime:

> [for the purpose of facilitating, it] introduces a higher subjective mental element and means that *the accessory must have lent his or her assistance with the aim of facilitating the offence.* It is not sufficient that the accessory merely knows that his or her conduct will assist the principal perpetrator in the commission of the offence. Mindful of the twofold intent of the accessory (i.e., first, the principal offence and, second, the accessory's own conduct), the Chamber clarifies that this elevated subjective standard relates to the accessory's facilitation, *not the principal offence.*[43]

The view of the Trial Chamber in *Bemba et al* thus departed from a literal reading of the Statute, as per the Confirmation of Charges Decision in *Bemba et al*, which had simply stated that the contribution must be 'made with the purpose of facilitating such commission [of the offence]'.[44] The Trial Chamber's view was not endorsed by the Appeals Chamber, which did not take the opportunity to clarify this legal issue, or perhaps saw no need to do so.[45] The Trial Chamber's view is not in agreement with the holding in the Confirmation of Charges Decision in *Blé Goudé* that under Article 25(3)(c) the accused must 'intend . . . to facilitate the commission of the crime',[46] a position that was quoted by the subsequent Confirmation Decisions in *Ongwen* and *Al Mahdi* (both of which also cited the *Bemba et al* Confirmation Decision), thus supporting that the dominant view amongst ICC judges to date has been to reaffirm a literal interpretation of the terms of the Statute.[47]

---

[42] *Mbarushimana* (Confirmation Decision) ICC-01/04–01/10 (16 December 2011), para. 274. Emphasis added.

[43] *Bemba et al* (Trial Judgment) ICC-01/05–01/13–1989 (19 October 2016), para. 97.

[44] *Bemba et al* (Confirmation Decision) ICC-01/05–01/13–749 (15 November 2014) para. 35.

[45] *Bemba et al* (Appeals Judgment) ICC-01/05–01/13–2275 (8 March 2018) para. 21.

[46] *Blé Goudé* (Confirmation Decision) paras. 167 and 170.

[47] *Ongwen* (Confirmation Decision) ICC-02/04–01/15–422 (23 March 2016) fn 24; *Al Mahdi* (Confirmation Decision) ICC-01/12–01/15–84 (24 March 2016) fn 15.

The *mens rea* of Article 25(3)(c) nonetheless remains contested amongst ICC judges.[48] As Van Sliedregt and Popova note, the purposive language cannot be teleologically 'interpreted away, into non-existence'.[49] Without entering further into the active debate surrounding Article 25(3)(c)'s *mens rea*, this chapter notes, as David Scheffer has emphasised in the context of the American courts' interpretation of the Rome Statute, that Article 25(3)(c) was not drafted to reflect customary international law and requires further ICC judicial interpretation before it can be regarded as legally certain.[50] Suffice to say, the *mens rea* of Article 25(3)(c) imposes a 'specific subjective requirement stricter than mere knowledge'.[51]

Due in part to the 'stricter' *mens rea* of Article 25(3)(c), this chapter focuses on the interpretation and application of Article 25(3)(d) of the Rome Statute since it appears to be of greatest relevance to the outer boundaries of arms transfer liability at the ICC. Its *mens rea* is less stringent than 'purpose' (even if the *Bemba et al* Trial Chamber's interpretation of Article 25(3)(c) is accepted) and its *actus reus* extends to 'any other contributions' that are not covered by other modes of liability.[52]

The full text of Article 25(3)(d) provides that a person shall be criminally responsible and liable for punishment for a crime within the jurisdiction of the Court if that person:

(d) In any other way contributes to the commission or attempted commission of such a crime by a group of persons acting with a common purpose. Such contribution shall be intentional and shall either:
  (i) Be made with the aim of furthering the criminal activity or criminal purpose of the group, where such activity or purpose

---

[48] C. Stahn, 'Liberals vs Romantics: Challenges of an Emerging Corporate International Criminal Law' (2018) 50(1) *Case Western Reserve Journal of International Law* 91, 115.

[49] E. van Sliedregt and A. Popova, 'Interpreting "for the Purpose of Facilitating" in Article 25(3)(c)?' (*Blog of James Stewart*, 22 December 2014), http://jamesgstewart.com/interpreting-for-the-purpose-of-facilitating-in-article-253c/.

[50] D. Scheffer, Amicus Curiae Brief in Support of the Issuance of a Writ of Certiorari, Presbyterian Church of Sudan, et al. v. Talisman Energy, Inc., 19 May 2010, Supreme Court of the United States, 5, 7.

[51] K. Ambos, 'Comments on Article 25', in K. Ambos and O. Triffterrer (eds.), *Commentary on the Rome Statute of the International Criminal Court* (CH Beck/Hart/Nomos, 2016), p. 1009.

[52] See K. Ambos, 'The ICC and Common Purpose: What Contribution Is Required under Article 25(3)(d)?' in C. Stahn (ed.), *The Law and Practice of the International Criminal Court* (Oxford University Press, 2015), pp. 595–6; A. Kiss, 'La contribución en la comisión de un crimen por un grupo de personas en la jurisprudencia de la Corte Penal Internacional' (2013) 2 *InDret: Review on the Analysis of Law* 1, 2.

involves the commission of a crime within the jurisdiction of the Court; or

(ii) Be made in the knowledge of the intention of the group to commit the crime.

There is a startling variety of proposed interpretations of Article 25(3)(d), projecting onto the text of the Rome Statute similar-sounding modes of liability from previous tribunals: conspiracy (as per Article 6 of the Nuremberg Charter), membership of a criminal group or organisation (as per Article 10 of the Nuremberg Charter) and conspiracy or joint criminal enterprise as developed in the jurisprudence of the ICTY and the ICTR.[53] Several commentators note that Article 25(3)(d) was a negotiated compromise between states parties that wished to include a conspiracy doctrine of liability in the Statute and those who did not.[54] Some commentators believe that the contradictions in the text of Article 25(3)(d) are so serious that it should be altogether rewritten through statutory amendment.[55]

The Court's jurisprudence thus far has not acquiesced in the face of the admitted interpretive difficulties in the text, Chambers being relatively consistent in pronouncing that Article 25(3)(d) liability requires the following basic elements:[56]

1. A crime within the jurisdiction of the Court was attempted or committed;
2. The crime was committed or attempted by a group of persons acting with a common purpose;
3. The accused contributed to the commission of the crime in 'any other way';
4. The contribution was intentional;[57] and

---

[53] See R. Cryer, *Prosecuting International Crimes: Selectivity and the International Criminal Law Regime* (Cambridge University Press, 2005), p. 315.

[54] G. Werle, 'Individual Criminal Responsibility in Article 25 of the ICC Statute' (2007) 5 *Journal of International Criminal Justice* 970.

[55] J. Ohlin, 'Joint Criminal Confusion' (2009) 12(3) *New Criminal Law Review* 408, 417.

[56] *Mbarushimana* Confirmation Decision (n. 42), paras. 268–89; *Katanga* (Trial Judgment) ICC-01/04–01/07–3436 (7 March 2014) para. 1620; *Gbagbo* (Confirmation Decision) ICC-02/11–01/11–656 (12 June 2014) para. 252; *Ntaganda* (Confirmation Decision) ICC-01/04–02/06–309 (9 June 2014) para. 158; *Ruto* (Confirmation Decision) ICC-01/09–01/11–373 (23 January 2012) para. 351; *Kenyatta* (Summons Decision) ICC-01/09–02/11–1 (8 March 2011) para. 47; *Al Mahdi* Confirmation Decision (*supra* n. 47), para. 27; *Ongwen* Confirmation Decision (*supra* n. 47), para. 44.

[57] The contributor must '(i) mean to engage in the relevant conduct that allegedly contributes to the crime and (ii) be at least aware that his or her conduct contributes to the activities of the group of persons (...)'. *Mbarushimana* Confirmation Decision (*supra*

5. The contribution was made either:
   (i) with the aim of furthering the criminal activity or criminal purpose of the group;[58] or
   (ii) in the knowledge of the intention of the group to commit the crime.

The distinctiveness of the mental states in Article 25(3)(d)(i) and (ii) suggests that they should be construed as reflecting two discrete 'modes' of liability, in the sense that each subsection describes a different state of mind in which the contribution was made. These two forms of criminality correspond to different labels ('intentionally furthering' and 'knowingly contributing' to a group crime). As Jackson emphasises, an accurate distinguishing of a defendant's role ought to be recorded in international tribunal judgments since 'a properly differentiated model of responsibility accurately labels participants in the attribution of responsibility and conveys to the wider public the general nature of their wrongdoing'.[59]

Some scholars have asserted that subsection (i) is unnecessary and redundant since it is subsumed by subsection (ii).[60] However, although it is true that subsection (i) requires a higher *degree* of mental commitment ('intentionally furthering'), subsection (ii) carries a greater *specificity* (the knowledge under this subsection must relate to 'the crime').[61]

---

n. 42), para. 288; *Katanga* Trial Judgment (*supra* n. 56), para. 1639. Arguably, this wording is preferable to a more recent formulation in *Al Mahdi* and *Ongwen* that: 'With respect to the relevant mental element, this form of responsibility requires that the person meant to contribute to the commission of the crimes'. See *Al Mahdi* Confirmation Decision (*supra* n. 47), para. 27; *Ongwen* Confirmation Decision (*supra* n. 47), para. 44. As a non-group contributor under Article 25(3)(d)(ii), meaning to engage in the relevant conduct is not the same as meaning to contribute *to the commission of the crimes.*

[58] This element does not require that the accused satisfy the mental elements of the charged crimes. *Mbarushimana* Confirmation Decision (*supra* n. 42), para. 289. The difference between subsections (i) and (ii) 'seems to be that the second standard requires the prosecution to prove that the person knew the specific crime the group intended to commit, whereas the first standard requires it to prove only that the person intended to further the group's general criminal activity'. K. Heller, 'The Rome Statute in Comparative Perspective', in K. Heller and M. Dubber (eds.), *The Handbook of Comparative Criminal Law* (Stanford Law Books, 2010), p. 26.

[59] M. Jackson, 'The Attribution of Responsibility and Modes of Liability in International Criminal Law' (2016) 29(3) *Leiden Journal of International Law* 879–95, 890. Contra see J. Stewart, 'The Strangely Familiar History of the Unitary Theory of Perpetration', in B. Ackerman et al. (eds.),*Visions of Justice: Essays in Honor of Professor Mirjan Damaška* (Duncker and Humblot, 2016), p. 31.

[60] Ohlin (*supra* n. 55) 417.

[61] Section 4.3.

Accordingly, there are frequently-occurring situations in which an individual supports a group with the aim of furthering its criminal activity or criminal purpose whilst remaining ignorant of a specific crime that the group intends to commit. In such a situation, (i) is not subsumed by (ii). A donor who enthusiastically funds a designated terrorist group with the fervent desire of achieving a long-term political aim may nonetheless be unaware of specific details of the group's plans to carry out a particular terrorist attack. The donor may be liable under (i) even when not liable under (ii).

The differences in *mens rea* nonetheless make subsection (ii) of greater relevance to commercial arms transfers due to the absence of a requirement of volitive *mens rea*.[62] It will rarely be possible to prove that a conventional businessperson harbours an aim to further the criminal activity or criminal purpose of a group that would satisfy the requirement of subsection (i). This is not a question of personal *motive*, which is generally irrelevant to criminal liability. It is rather a practical observation that in commercial cases there will rarely be evidence of anything other than the supplier's pecuniary interest in making a sale.

Before discussing the three issues of interpretation in Article 25(3) (d), it is necessary to say something about what is expected in terms of interpretation and application. As much as it may be desirable to speak of 'settled jurisprudence' at the ICC, it cannot be plausibly claimed to exist at this stage in the Court's history, especially given its limited jurisprudential output. ICC benches are not bound by the common law principle of *stare decisis*[63] and we may still be many years or decades away from being able to talk credibly of a *jurisprudence constante* based on a substantial number of cases, heard by a substantial number of judges from different legal traditions and addressing a substantial range of fact patterns that develop a well-established usage of legal concepts.[64] Only very limited jurisprudence on Article 25(3)(d) has been subjected to Appeals Chamber

---

[62] See S. Finnin, 'Elements of Accessorial Modes of Liability: Article 25(3)(b) and (c) of the Rome Statute of the International Criminal Court' (2012) 61 *International and Comparative Law Quarterly* 325.

[63] Rome Statute, Article 21: '[t]he Court may apply principles and rules of law as interpreted in its previous decisions'.

[64] See R. Henry, '*Jurisprudence Constante* and *Stare Decisis* Contrasted' (1929) 15 *American Bar Association Journal* 11.

scrutiny, and, as Volker Nerlich points out, care must be taken in attributing due weight to isolated judicial decisions.[65]

Beyond the basic elements of Article 25(3)(d), the extent of its liability over arms transfers cannot be considered 'certain' in the legal sense. Increasing legal certainty is desirable, not least since it contributes to the deterrent effects of the Court's work by enhancing and clarifying the social threat of the Court's investigations and prosecutions, including through national prosecutions in accordance with the principle of complementarity.[66] Legal certainty may be particularly significant to the arms trade due to the relatively rational attitude of commercial actors in deciding whether to take actions that may render them liable for international crimes.[67] The prospect that, in addition to moral opprobrium, involvement in an arms transfer will attract criminal responsibility enhances the Court's potential for deterrence in such cases,[68] but a credible threat of investigation and prosecution relies partly on the Court's liability regime being predictable to those involved in arms transfers.

6.4   The 'External' Status of the Contributor

The first issue of interpretation concerns the requirement that 'a person' under Article 25(3)(d) contributes to a crime committed or attempted by 'a group of persons acting with a common purpose'. Some commentators have argued that Article 25(3)(d) was never intended to apply to persons who are also members of the common purpose group and that the contributor must be a non-member.[69] Their position is supported by a good faith reading of Article 25(3)(d) in accordance with the ordinary meaning of its terms,[70] which sees two distinct subjects – the 'person',

---

[65]   V. Nerlich, 'The Status of ICTY and ICTR Precedent in Proceedings before the ICC', in C. Stahn and G. Sluiter (eds.), *The Emerging Practice of the International Criminal Court* (Brill, 2008), p. 314.

[66]   J. Hyeran and B. Simmons. 'Can the International Criminal Court Deter Atrocity?' (2016) 70(3) *International Organization* 443–75 [Corrigendum in (2017) 71(1) *International Organization* 419–21]. Hyeran and Simmons's research focuses on governments and rebel groups rather than commercial accomplices.

[67]   R. Paternoster and S. Simpson, 'Sanction Threats and Appeals to Morality: Testing a Rational Choice Model of Corporate Crime' (1996) 30 *Law and Society Review* 549.

[68]   R. Gallmetzer, 'Prosecuting Persons Doing Business with Armed Groups in Conflict Areas: The Strategy of the Office of the Prosecutor of the International Criminal Court' (2010) 8(3) *Journal of International Criminal Justice* 947–56, 956.

[69]   A. Cassese, *International Criminal Law* (2nd ed., Oxford University Press, 2008), p. 213.

[70]   Vienna Convention on the Law of Treaties (adopted 23 May 1969, entered into force 27 January 1980) 1155 UNTS 331, Article 31(1).

who contributes, and the 'group', whose members share a common purpose.[71] A natural reading would thus suggest that this provision was aimed primarily at encapsulating the conduct of non-group members, such as arms traders, who make an external contribution of assistance to the group. Chambers have nonetheless found the provision applicable to members of the group[72] and most academic commentators concur, sometimes approaching the provision from the opposite direction by asserting that it was primarily intended for group members, the interpretive issue being whether to extend the provision to external individuals.[73] Crucially, however, as Ambos concludes, 'the rationale of the provision [is] to extend punishability to contributions from outside the group since these may otherwise remain exempt from punishment'.[74]

A further indication that the drafters of Article 25(3)(d) did not envisage that the mode of liability would be primarily used for group members is the fact that a distinct mental requirement was stipulated in subsection (i). As a member of the Article 25(3)(d) 'group', the person is amongst those who act with the common purpose and there is no need to assess whether he or she acted 'with the aim of furthering the criminal activity or criminal purpose of the group'. In other words, the mental state in subsection (i) would be subsumed by the individual's shared intentions with the common purpose group specified in the *chapeau* of the provision.

The origins of the text lay in international conventions whose aims and purposes were concentrated on ancillary, non-member contributors to terrorist and organised crime groups. The text of Article 25(3)(d) is nearly identical to Article 2(3)(c) of the International Convention for the Suppression of Terrorist Bombings and many commentators have recognised that it was 'taken directly from' the Convention.[75] Per Saland, a negotiator at Rome, recalled that 'we were helped by the successful negotiation in 1997 of [the Convention], which had been adopted by consensus. . . . [I]t was easy to reach agreement to incorporate, with slight modifications, the text from that Convention which we now find in paragraph 3(d) of Article 25.'[76] Although the academic analysis of

---

[71] See *Katanga* (Defence Filing) ICC-01/04–01/07–3369 (15 April 2013) ('*Katanga* First Defence Observations on Article 25(3)(d)'), para. 115.

[72] *Mbarushimana* Confirmation Decision (*supra* n. 42), para. 275; *Katanga* Trial Judgment (*supra* n. 56), para. 1631.

[73] Ambos (*supra* n. 51), p. 1013. See Chapter 13 in this volume.

[74] Ambos (*supra* n. 51), p. 1013.

[75] Cryer (*supra* n. 53), p. 315; Ambos (*supra* n. 52), pp. 595–6.

[76] P. Saland, 'International Criminal Law Principles' in R. Lee (ed.), *The International Criminal Court: The Making of the Rome Statute* (Martinus Nijhoff, 1999), pp. 189, 199.

Article 25(3)(d) has noted the textual similarities with the Bombing Convention, the importance of the text's origins lie in the specific individuals who were involved in its drafting, namely Ambassador Philippe Kirsch and former ICC Judge and President Silvia Fernández de Gurmendi, both of whom played significant roles in the negotiations preceding not only the Bombing Convention but also the negotiations prior to the Rome Statute, including in contributing to the drafting of the substantive provisions on liability.[77] The existing commentary does not appear to have recognised this feature of the drafting history of Article 25(3)(d), and the weight to be attributed to Judge Fernandez's separate opinion in *Mbarushimana* ought to be considered in this light.[78]

Curiously, neither the jurisprudence nor the existing academic commentary on the ICC appears to have mentioned the fact that Article 25(3) (d) also finds near-identical wording in Article 3(4) of the EU Extradition Convention.[79] The Explanatory Report to the EU Extradition Convention indicates that the wording of the text was originally envisioned as an alternative mode of liability, which could be chosen by Member States by way of treaty reservation, to avoid doctrines of criminal association or conspiracy in relation to terrorist offences, offences related to organised crime including drug-trafficking offences, and violent offences. The Explanatory Report refers to contributions that are 'ancillary in nature (mere material preparation; logistic support to the movement or harbouring of persons and similar conduct)' and it states explicitly that 'the person contributing to the commission of the offence [need not be] a "member" of the group'.[80] The origins of Article 25(3)(d) were likely known to its drafters and cannot be entirely ignored when interpreting their intentions. Similarly, it does not appear to have been noted in the jurisprudence or commentary that near-identical wording to Article 25(3)(d) was adopted in Article 2(4)(c) of the subsequent International Convention for the Suppression of Acts of Nuclear

[77] UNGA, 'Report of the Ad Hoc Committee established by UNGA Resolution 51/210' (17 December 1996) UN Doc Supp No 37, A/52/37 (1997).

[78] *Mbarushimana*, Judgment on the appeal of the Prosecutor against the decision of Pre-Trial Chamber I of 16 December 2011 entitled 'Decision on the confirmation of charges': Separate Opinion of Judge Fernández de Gurmendi, regarding the normative and causal links to assess the *actus reus* of contribution ICC-01/04-01/10-514, 30–34.

[79] Convention Relating to Extradition between the Member States of the European Union (27 September 1996) *Official Journal of the European Communities*, C313.

[80] Council of Europe, 'Explanatory Report on the Convention relating to extradition between the Member States of the European Union' (26 May 1997) *Official Journal of the European Communities*, C191/13.

Terrorism 2005, again with the aim of criminalising external assistive contributions.[81] Thus, Article 25(3)(d) seems to have been most readily envisaged as a form of liability to cover the ancillary contributions of external, non-group individuals who contribute to the commission of a crime by the group.[82] Contrary to this, the practice of the ICC Prosecutor has so far been to deploy Article 25(3)(d) primarily in relation to group members, such as militia leaders, whose contributions might have been more fairly labelled as co-perpetrators.[83] The Prosecutor has also seemed to suggest that Article 25(3)(d) is intended primarily for group members, and only secondarily for external contributors.[84] This is perhaps reflective of a trend in more recent ICC cases to use the 'residual' Article 25(3)(d) to charge (or, arguably, over-charge) individuals who would be phenomenologically considered to be central actors in military or political hierarchical structures. In oral argument in the *Gbagbo and Blé Goudé* half-time hearing, the Prosecutor reasoned that '[t]o confine application of Article 25(3)(d) to outsiders to the group who contribute to the commission of crimes would unduly circumscribe its reach, in contravention of a plain reading of the provision'.[85] Without explaining this 'plain reading', the Prosecutor cited *Mbarushimana* jurisprudence that simply notes that the provision does not specify whether it applies to group members or outsiders.[86]

While there may be no technical barrier to charging a range of modes of liability that fit a suspect's conduct, a lack of specificity in this regard is hardly the mark of a well-developed case theory. This practice poses a real risk to the Court's legitimacy, especially if Article 25(3)(d) becomes a routine 'backdoor' to convict senior high-level perpetrators.[87] Meanwhile, arms suppliers who do not share the common purposes of the group yet knowingly provide assistance are the archetypal 'external contributors' envisaged by the drafters of Article 3(4) of the EU

---

[81] International Convention for the Suppression of Acts of Nuclear Terrorism 2005.

[82] See M. Aksenova, 'The Modes of Liability at the ICC: The Labels that Don't Always Stick' (2015) 15(4) *International Criminal Law Review* 629–64.

[83] E.g. *Katanga* Trial Judgment (*supra* n. 56).

[84] *Gbagbo and Blé Goudé* Prosecution Response to No Case to Answer, para. 1979.

[85] *Gbagbo and Blé Goudé* (Prosecution Filing) ICC-02/11–01/15–1207-Anx1 (8 November 2018) ('*Gbagbo and Blé Goudé* Prosecution Response to No Case to Answer'), para. 1979.

[86] *Mbarushimana* Confirmation Decision (*supra* n. 42), para. 275

[87] See D. Guilfoyle, 'Responsibility for Collective Atrocities: Fair Labelling and Approaches to Commission in International Criminal Law' (2011) 64(1) *Current Legal Problems* 255–86.

Extradition Convention, who also played primary roles in the drafting of Article 25(3)(d) of the Rome Statute.

6.5   The Nature of the Contribution

The second interpretive issue of importance for arms transfers is the nature of the required contribution under Article 25(3)(d). Three aspects of the contribution and its causal relationship to the commission or attempted commission of a crime are addressed below. Given the central importance of causation in criminal law theory, international criminal tribunals (the ICC in particular) have given it surprisingly little attention. Since James Stewart commented in 2012 that 'causation has escaped direct treatment by almost all courts [...] it has received limited attention in the ICC jurisprudence.[88]

6.5.1   Significant Contributions and Causal Remoteness

The *chapeau* of Article 25(3)(d) reads 'in any other way contributes' or '*toutes autres contributions*'. This is clear enough on its face; it covers all arms transfer contributions that are not addressed by Articles 25(3)(a) through (c).[89] Importantly, this renders the material requirement less onerous for the prosecution than, for instance, the SCSL's requirement that 'provision and facilitation of the supply of arms and ammunition [have] a *substantial effect* on the commission of crimes charged'.[90] There appears to be no qualifying criterion to delimit the requirement of '*any* other' contribution. However, the *Mbarushimana* Confirmation Decision imposed a quantitative threshold that the contribution be at least 'significant', out of concerns for the imposition of liability on 'bakers', 'grocers' and other categories of individuals who the Pre-Trial Chamber (PTC) described as making 'infinitesimal' contributions to crimes.[91]

Aside from the plain wording of Article 25(3)(d) and the lack of support in the *travaux préparatoires*, the PTC's concerns were

---

[88] J. Stewart, 'Overdetermined Atrocities' (2012) 10(5) *Journal of International Criminal Justice* 1189–218, 1194, 1217.

[89] *Ruto* Confirmation Decision (*supra* n. 56), para. 354; *Mbarushimana* Confirmation Decision (*supra* n. 42), para. 278.

[90] *Taylor* Trial Judgment (*supra* n. 33), para. 6913; *Prosecutor* v. *Charles Ghankay Taylor*, SCSL-03-01-A, Judgment, Appeals Chamber, 26 September 2013, para. 390 ('*Taylor* Appeal Judgment'), para. 390.

[91] *Mbarushimana* Confirmation Decision (n. 42), para. 283.

unfounded. At a superficial and phenomenological level, the supply of weapons may look very different from the activities of baking bread or selling vegetables (the PTC considered it necessary to protect these so-called 'lawful' activities). However, it is a counterintuitive truth that neither the nature nor the size of a contribution is per se determinative of its unlawfulness. As Keith Smith points out in his singular treatise on criminal complicity, one of the features of accomplice liability is the vast range of conducts and attitudes that it covers.[92] Whereas principal liability is categorically distinguished by the type of crime in question (murder, rape, theft, etc.), secondary liability is not per se defined by a particular category of conduct. Thus, at the level of attribution of responsibility, the lawfulness of a large shipment of missiles is not distinguished from providing a few crates of ammunition, nor from giving food to troops or baking bread for them. These phenomenologically different contributions are not distinguished on the sole basis of intrinsic qualities. The contributions are legally characterised in the same way as 'assistance'. Whether they are criminal depends on the material and mental requirements of the mode of accomplice liability in question.

Put more straightforwardly by Alejandro Kiss, the *Mbarushimana* conception of infinitesimal contributions fails to differentiate between the degree and the nature of a contribution and it overlooks normative considerations that emphasise value judgement, rather than criminal law notions of causation.[93] Article 25(3)(d)(ii) does not render any category of individual conduct prima facie criminal, including arms transfer conduct that may be considered illicit under other international and domestic regulations. Neither is any category of conduct per se innocent, since any form of contributory activity (sale of consumer commodities, provision of financial services, logistical assistance, legal advice, etc.) may be criminalised, provided the necessary elements including causal linkage and *mens rea* exist. A hardware store may innocently sell a thousand pocket knives, yet the sale of a single knife may attract criminal liability when a customer explicitly states that he intends to use it for a murder.

A better resolution to the concerns of the *Mbarushimana* bench over so-called 'infinitesimal' contributions lies in the concept of causal remoteness that has received little articulation in the Court's jurisprudence.

---

[92] K. Smith, *A Modern Treatise on the Law of Criminal Complicity* (Clarendon Press, 1991), p. 142.

[93] Kiss (*supra* n. 52) 19.

Remoteness is the law's recognition that, while there is nothing intrinsically lawful about conduct such as baking bread or selling groceries, such activities are often too remote, causally, to form a basis for liability. In English criminal law, an individual who supplies petrol to the driver of an unroadworthy vehicle is not considered liable for the road traffic offence.[94] The underlying rationale is not that supplying petrol is inherently a non-criminal activity, nor that the contribution of supplying petrol falls below a particular quantitative threshold. Instead, without excluding that the supply of petrol may be causally linked in an absolute sense to the offence (the so-called 'but for' test), the supply of petrol is not deemed sufficiently proximate, in the causal sense, to attribute responsibility.[95]

The more recent Confirmation Decisions, in Al Mahdi and Ongwen, have taken the view that it is unnecessary that the contribution under Article 25(3)(d) be 'significant' or reach a certain minimum degree.[96] Recognising the problems of a quantitative threshold, these views nonetheless retained the 'significance' requirement. Yet, in this context, the term 'significance', taken to mean simply 'more than de minimis' or 'not negligible',[97] adds nothing to the test of 'any other contribution'. As a UK Supreme Court opinion held in a different context: 'this court should avoid attempting to explain the word "significant". It would be a gloss; attention might then turn to the meaning of the gloss and, albeit with the best of intentions, the courts might find in due course that they had travelled far from the word itself.'[98]

Even if Chambers wish to retain the 'significance' standard, perhaps in the spirit of judicial compromise, it can be defined in non-quantitative terms. The Katanga Trial Chamber's interpretation of Article 25(3)(d) came closer to recognising the concept of remoteness by focusing on the causal nexus between the contribution and the commission of the crime. Although the Trial Chamber did not reject the Mbarushimana 'significance' requirement in name, it held that the contribution 'will be considered significant where it had a bearing on the occurrence of the crime and/or the manner of its commission'.[99]

[94] Smith (supra n. 92), pp. 150–1.
[95] Ibid.
[96] Al Mahdi Confirmation Decision (supra n. 47), para. 27; Ongwen Confirmation Decision (supra n. 47), para. 44.
[97] D. Greenberg (ed.), Stroud's Judicial Dictionary (9th ed., Sweet and Maxwell, 2018), 'significant'.
[98] B (a Child) (Care Proceedings: Appeal) Re [2013] UKSC 33, para. 26.
[99] Katanga Trial Judgment (supra n. 56), paras. 1632–3. The Trial Chamber added some ambiguity with the contingent finding: 'the Chamber wishes to lay stress on a contribution which may influence the commission of the crime'. Emphasis added.

A contribution that is too causally remote would thus be one that cannot be said to have 'had a bearing on' the commission of the crime. The reasoning of the *Katanga* trial judgment tended towards the concept of remoteness: 'in international criminal law the prime focus of investigations and prosecutions is those who, whilst physically, structurally or causally remote from the physical perpetrators of the crimes, indirectly committed them or facilitated their commission by virtue of the position they held, however remote'.[100] Yet the Chamber did not elaborate on its view, and, in the absence of reasoning, the Chamber appears to conflate or confuse the factual concepts of physical proximity and organisational hierarchy with the legal concept of causation.

A full exegesis and argumentative defence of the concept of remoteness and its utility is well beyond the scope of this chapter, yet the *Katanga* judgment's recognition that causation may involve an impact on dual parameters, either 'occurrence of the crime' or 'manner of its commission', is significant.[101] In a hypothetical scenario where an individual supplies a state with weapons used by its army to unlawfully relocate a population of a certain ethnic group, for instance, the armed forces may have access to sufficient weaponry such that the supplier's conduct has no bearing on whether the crimes are going to occur. The supply of weapons is thus immaterial to whether the force element of the crime is made out, since the army was able to relocate the population even without the additional supplies. However, the hypothetical scenario might posit that the shipment of weapons is proven to have increased the *degree of force* used in the relocation, or, alternatively, that the type of weapon used means that the *manner in which the force is exercised* is altered. The shipment would now be considered sufficiently proximate, in the causal sense.[102]

James Stewart asserts that it may be desirable to do away entirely with quantitative material requirements for complicity and to recognise that 'those who make imperceptibly small contributions to joint harm are still responsible for that harm when operating in collective constructs'.[103] In

---

[100] *Katanga* Trial Judgment, ibid., para. 1636.

[101] *Katanga* Trial Judgment, ibid., paras. 1632–3.

[102] Likewise, even where there are multiple shipments of arms from different contributors, a mixture of which is used in the commission of a mass atrocity, in many factual scenarios each contributor's shipment of weapons will nonetheless have an independent effect on the factual contours of the manner of commission of crimes by impacting the scale of the violence, the number of victims, the nature of the injuries, etc.

[103] Stewart (*supra* n. 88) 1216.

the terms of Article 25(3)(d), individuals may indeed be responsible for very small contributions to international crimes, yet this is qualified by the criterion of remoteness as a way to delimit the individual's responsibility and avoid an excessive reach or absurd results. The assessment of remoteness would depend on judicial discretion, but if ICC judges were to interpret and apply a causation requirement, the law would benefit from a wealth of case precedent from a variety of jurisdictions as well as scholarly writing on remoteness in criminal law that would enhance the doctrinal coherence of their jurisprudence.[104]

6.5.2   Contributing to 'the Commission or Attempted Commission' of the Crime

A second issue of causation is whether contributing 'to the commission or attempted commission' of the crime under Article 25(3)(d) means something different from contributing to the crime itself. Although some causal nexus is required of the contributor, it is unclear whether it is necessary to show a causal link to each element of the crime. The implications of these questions for those who transfer arms at a physical and hierarchical distance from the direct perpetrators who carry out the crimes are significant, since there will often be little or no evidence that a particular gun or piece of ammunition was used in the perpetration of a specific incident of violence.

According to the Court's current jurisprudence, no direct connection between the arms transfer conduct and the direct perpetrator of the crime is necessary.[105] It appears that Chambers have envisaged some form of 'indirect' connection to the commission of the crime is required, although the jurisprudence has not expounded on the distinction between direct and indirect causal connections in this context.[106] Chambers have sometimes overlooked the distinction between the group's activities in committing the crime and the crime itself, by referring to 'contributing to commission' in their reasoning whilst making their findings with respect to a contribution to the crime itself,[107] or vice versa, thus using the terms interchangeably.[108]

---

[104] See Burchard (*supra* n. 8) 923.
[105] *Katanga* Trial Judgment (*supra* n. 56), para. 1635; *Mbarushimana* Confirmation Decision (*supra* n. 42), paras. 284–5.
[106] See H. L. A. Hart and T. Honoré, *Causation in the Law* (Oxford University Press, 1985), ch. XIV: Causation and the Principles of Punishment.
[107] *Mbarushimana* Confirmation Decision (*supra* n. 42), paras. 283, 285.
[108] *Ruto* Confirmation Decision (*supra* n. 56), paras. 351, 353.

The lack of a direct causal nexus makes sense if we accept that the definition of 'commission' in Article 25(3)(d) must include 'commission' by a group of co-perpetrators as per subsection (a) whose individual responsibility arises from mutual attribution.[109] It stands to reason that a 'common purpose group' in Article 25(3)(d) may commit the crime through the mutual attribution of their respective acts, rather than necessarily from each individual's act being a direct cause of the crime by itself. It follows, as Alejandro Kiss has observed, that the contributor's conduct also cannot be required to be directly causal of the crime.[110]

Important evidentiary implications flow from interpreting Article 25(3)(d)(ii) in this manner. A prosecutor will not need to tender evidence that a defendant's arms transfer conduct caused each element of the crime. This takes on enhanced significance when we consider the fungible nature of weapons and ammunition, whereby it is often difficult to establish that a particular gun, item of weaponry or piece of ammunition was actually used to carry out a particular criminal incident and that, therefore, the individual's conduct was a direct cause of the criminal outcome. Unlike in domestic criminal justice systems where forensic firearm examination and DNA evidence is commonplace in cases of violent crime, international criminal tribunals often deal with unstable conflict environments and frequently lack evidence to identify the use of a particular gun or piece of ammunition, although advances in bullet tracing technologies and associated initiatives are changing this.[111] Even where such evidence exists, an arms supplier may argue the impossibility of establishing that their weapons were used in specific criminal incidents, that another dealer would have stepped in to provide the weapons had they not done so, or that their piece of ammunition was interchangeable with any other available piece of ammunition. As Stewart has pointed out, the criminal complicity of arms transfers is therefore an interesting case for considering whether causal over-determination is problematic, since very often the arms supplier could be immediately substituted for another individual who would act in the same manner.[112]

It is therefore significant that the Court's early jurisprudence on this issue has not required proof of a direct causal nexus made out by

---

[109] *Lubanga* (Trial Judgment) ICC-01/04–01/06–2842 (14 March 2012), para. 994.

[110] Kiss (*supra* n. 52) 9–10.

[111] See Conflict Armament Research, *Weapon Supplies into South Sudan's Civil War: Regional Re-Transfers and International Intermediaries* (November 2018), www.conflictarm.com/reports/weapon-supplies-into-south-sudans-civil-war/.

[112] Stewart (*supra* n. 88) 1189–218, 1209.

evidence of the use of a particular weapon or piece of ammunition in a particular incident, and has instead required a contribution 'to the commission or attempted commission of the crime'.[113] Liability is established on the basis of the assistive nature of the arms transfer in the carrying out of the group's activities in the perpetration of 'the crime' as legally characterised in the charges (e.g. a crime against humanity of murder, rape, pillaging), irrespective of whether it is demonstrated that a particular gun was used to carry out any one particular incident of violence amongst those that comprise the crime. The fungible nature of arms supplies does not therefore appear as a per se ouster of liability under Article 25(3)(d)(ii).

6.5.3   Characterising Arms Transfers as 'Contributions'

Two further features of weapons and arms transfers become apparent when considering causal contributions. First, there is the situation where arms transfer conduct contributes to the commission of crimes whose harm is not a result of victims being shot. The Defence for *Katanga* argued that the accused's arms transfer conduct was relevant only to crimes 'involving bullets':

> Even if the Chamber finds that there is sufficient evidence that Katanga distributed weapons that were used to kill civilians in Bogoro, he can still not be held liable for any of the allegations of rape and sexual slavery. Nor can he be held liable for pillage, destruction or the use of child soldiers. The Prosecutor must prove that he made a direct contribution to the crimes. In the event that the Chamber finds that Katanga's alleged role in the distribution of weapons constituted a direct contribution to the crimes committed by a group of persons acting with a common purpose, this cannot extend to any crimes which did not involve bullets.[114]

Even if, contrary to current ICC jurisprudence, a 'direct contribution to the crime' was required, Katanga's submission that arms cannot assist the commission of crimes of rape, sexual slavery, pillage, destruction or the use of child soldiers is erroneous. The mere presence of weapons may contribute to the commission of crimes, for instance in producing a 'coercive environment' that is taken advantage of to perpetrate

---

[113] *Katanga* Trial Judgment (*supra* n. 56), para. 1635; *Mbarushimana* Confirmation Decision (*supra* n. 42), paras. 284–5; see *Gbagbo and Blé Goudé* (Transcript) ICC-02/11–01/15-T-223-ENG (3 October 2018) 35.

[114] *Katanga* First Defence Observations on Article 25(3)(d), para. 88.

gender-based crimes.[115] Moreover, while a range of crimes other than the crime against humanity of murder or the war crime of murder may occur as a direct result of shooting bullets (extermination, genocide, causing serious injury and so on), there are numerous conventional weapons that do not 'involve bullets', such as explosives and mortars.

A second feature of arms transfers is their legal characterisation as contributions other than physical assistance. It would be a misconception to find that, under Article 25(3)(d), arms transfer contributions cannot impact the commission or attempted commission of the crime through other forms of complicity. The *Katanga* trial bench held: '[the contribution under Article 25(3)(d)] may be connected to either the material elements of the crimes (it may then, for instance, take the form of provision of resources such as weapons) or to their subjective elements (it may involve encouragement)'.[116] The Chamber's choice of illustrative examples should not be understood as restricting the causal impact of arms transfer conduct to the material elements of the crimes. The willingness of a contributor to sell a gun to a perpetrator may embolden and encourage the commission of a crime, for instance where the perpetrator is aware that the seller knows of their intentions.[117] In the situation where most arms suppliers refuse to do business due to the reputational or liability risks associated with supporting international crimes, the individual who exceptionally agrees to supply the weapons may have the effect of encouraging and offering an enhanced degree of approval or support for the recipient's anticipated actions.

Depending on circumstances, a causal connection between the material elements of the arms transfer contribution may be prima facie construed as a contribution to the principal group's *actus reus*, but equally, it may be causally connected as a contribution to the group's *mens rea*. This distinction is highly relevant to the issue of fungibility discussed in Section 6.5.2, in situations where there is no proof of the physical correlation between the supplied weapons and those used in the commission of the crime. Speaking practically, arms transfer conduct can often be construed as both physical assistance and mental encouragement, and, from an evidentiary perspective, the latter may often be easier to prove than the former.

---

[115] See *Bemba* (Trial Judgment) ICC-01/05–01/08–3343 (21 March 2016), para. 102, (iii).

[116] *Katanga* Trial Judgment (*supra* n. 56), para. 1635. See also *Mbarushimana* Confirmation Decision (*supra* n. 42), para. 267.

[117] See *R* v. *Jogee* [2016] UKSC 8 (18 February 2016), para. 10.

6.6   Knowledge of the Group's Intentions

The *mens rea* requirement that the contribution is 'made in the knowledge of the intention of the group to commit the crime' remains open to interpretation. The limited jurisprudence on Article 25(3)(d)(ii) has held that 'the accused must be aware that the intention existed when engaging in the conduct which constituted his or her contribution'.[118] In interpreting what 'knowledge of the crime' entails, it may be useful to consider the dual parameters of *specificity* and *degree*, which Smith argues are a general distinguishing feature of all doctrines of complicity.[119] Compared to Article 25(3)(d)(i), the *mens rea* of subsection (ii) requires a greater *degree* of mental commitment to the group, but a lesser *specificity* with respect to the group's criminality. Likewise, while subsection (i) requires intent ('with the aim of furthering') as to a generalised range of possible criminality described in terms of the group's criminal activity or purpose, subsection (ii) lowers the mental requirement to simple knowledge but requires that knowledge to be related more specifically to knowledge 'of the crime'.

The arms transfer context raises the possibility of unknowing assistance, as in the scenario of a transportation agent who claims to have unwittingly transported a cargo of weapons by air, sea or land without realising that their plane, vessel or vehicle was harbouring weapons. This scenario occurs in drug trafficking cases where captains of ocean-going vessels may be held strictly liable for shipments found on board the vessel in the absence of evidence of the captain's knowledge of the presence of the drugs.[120] Under Article 25(3)(d)(ii), an individual in this scenario would have neither the requisite knowledge of the group's intentions nor the requisite intentionality as to the contribution itself. In this scenario, evidence of larger-scale patterns of distribution may show repeated transfers that make it difficult for the supplier to claim ignorance.

6.6.1   Specificity of Knowledge

The specificity required of the accomplice's knowledge is a significant doctrinal issue for any system of rules of complicity.[121] At one extreme,

---

[118] *Katanga* Trial Judgment (*supra* n. 56), para. 1641.
[119] Smith (*supra* n. 92) 141.
[120] See J. A. C. Cartner, R. P. Fiske and T. L. Leiter, *The International Law of the Shipmaster* (Routledge, 2013), p. 187.
[121] M. Jackson, *Complicity in International Law* (Oxford University Press, 2015), p. 50.

the requirement may be drawn in very general terms, concerning a range of unlawful purposes where the contributor's knowledge need not distinguish a particular offence. Alternatively, a rule of complicity may require an individual to hold more specific awareness of the type of crime (violent, sexual, commercial, etc.) or its legal characterisation (murder, rape, fraud, etc.) or even the attendant circumstances surrounding the crime and the precise manner of its commission (location, timing, identity of intended victims and direct perpetrators, modus operandi, etc.). An individual X might agree to fly a plane loaded with AK-47s to another person Y with the *general* awareness that Y is a broker known to supply non-state armed groups, many of which have dubious records of committing war crimes or crimes against humanity. Alternatively, X might provide Y with explosives in the more *specific* awareness of Y's plan to detonate a motorcycle bomb the following morning to kill a particular named individual. Mere knowledge of a broad category of criminality is unlikely to be sufficient for *mens rea*, as per the reasoning in the English case of *Bullock*: '[I]f an accused lends a man a revolver believing that it may be used to commit *a crime of violence* but with nothing specific in mind, it may not be enough.'[122]

The *Katanga* Trial Chamber affirmed that knowledge of a general criminal intention is insufficient for Article 25(3)(d)(ii) and that knowledge of the intention to commit the crime must be established.[123] The bench held that the contributor must know of the group's intention to commit 'each of the crimes forming part of the common purpose',[124] which should be understood as meaning that it need only be shown that the accused knew of the common purpose of the group to commit 'the charged crime' in question.[125]

The *Katanga* finding does not exclude contributions made in the awareness of a range of potential crimes that are expected to occur based on what is known of the group's intentions at the time of the transfer, even where the group eventually succeeds in attempting or carrying out only one or more of those crimes. It might be thought that expanding specificity to include contemplation of a range of offences is

---

[122] *Bullock* (1955) 38 Criminal Appeal Reports 151, 153. Emphasis added.

[123] *Katanga* Trial Judgment (*supra* n. 56), para. 1642.

[124] '... prouver ... que l'accusé savait que le groupe avait l'intention de commettre chacun des crimes qui faisaient partie du dessein commun'. *Katanga* Trial Judgment, ibid., para. 1642.

[125] See contra *Gbagbo and Blé Goudé* (Defence Filing) ICC-02/11-01/15-1198 (28 September 2018), para. 507.

inconsistent with complicity's fundamental derivative nature.[126] If the contributor's liability is dependent on the commission of the principal's crime, how can it be that he or she is potentially liable for a range of crimes when the principal in fact commits only one of them? As Smith explains, this apparent theoretical difficulty has been accommodated by the English courts on the basis that the contributor's culpability is founded on his or her taking certain actions that he or she knows will expose him or her to being connected to a crime, that is, the assumption of risk, an approach consistent with *Katanga*.[127]

The ICC's jurisprudence has not yet discussed specificity of knowledge in any depth, beyond rehearsing the statutory wording of 'the crime'. Given the lack of provision in the Statute, it may be useful to consider customary standards for specificity of complicit knowledge.[128] The ICC might adopt an 'essential matters' test, similar to the test applied at the ICTY to aiders and abettors, which may be a useful limiting criterion for Chambers to consider for Article 25(3)(d)(ii). The consistent position in ICTY case law is that it is unnecessary for an accomplice to know the 'precise crime' intended or committed by the perpetrator,[129] and instead the applicable standard was an awareness 'that one or a number of crimes would probably be committed'.[130] In *Furundžija*, for example, the ICTY Trial Chamber held:

> [I]t is not necessary that the aider and abettor should know the precise crime that was intended and which in the event was committed. If he is aware that one of a number of crimes will probably be committed, and one of those crimes is in fact committed, he has intended to facilitate the commission of that crime, and is guilty as an aider and abettor.[131]

There is an analogous test of 'essential matters' in modern English case law, recalled in *Johnson v. Youden*: 'Before a person can be convicted of aiding and abetting the commission of an offence he must at least know the essential matters which constitute that offence.'[132] In the context of Article 25(3)(d)(ii), it should be understood that 'essential matters' would refer to the contributor's knowledge of the basic factual contours of the

---

[126] Smith (*supra* n. 92) 194.
[127] Ibid.
[128] Rome Statute, Article 21.
[129] Blaškić (Appeals Judgment) IT-95-14-A (29 July 2014), para. 50.
[130] Strugar (Trial Judgment) IT-01-42-T (31 January 2005), para. 350. See Chapter 10 in this volume.
[131] *Furundžija* (Trial Judgment) IT-95-17/1-T (10 December 1998), para. 246.
[132] *Johnson v. Youden* [1950] 1 KB 544, 546.

crime with which they are charged, rather than necessarily having knowledge of the legal elements of a particular form of criminality.

Applying an 'essential matters' criterion to Article 25(3)(d)(ii) would capture a range of arms transfer conduct. In Burchard's view, it is a fair generalisation to say that commercial suppliers will not usually be aware of a specific impending crime, even if they know of broader criminal purposes.[133] However, the commercial setting in which arms transfers take place is a key variable that limits the generalisability of Burchard's observation. While a bank that provides finance electronically and from a location geographically remote from the commission of crimes may have a greater claim to ignorance of specific crimes, an arms broker who personally flies the plane and hand-delivers the weapons to the perpetrators (as the infamous Victor Bout allegedly did) will often have an immediate awareness of the conflict in which they are doing business. Crucially, although weapons are no different per se from food at the level of attribution of responsibility, factually speaking, the act of supplying armaments carries with it an intrinsic capacity of the weapons to facilitate violence and this will often make it harder to claim ignorance of impending crimes.

In a putative ICC case involving arms transfer conduct, the relevant considerations for the Court's determination as to the legal element of knowledge of 'essential matters' could be elaborated to some extent, in order to provide a form of judicial guidance for this specific type of conduct. For example, the existence of a relevant Chapter VII arms embargo or the publicly-known placement of the arms transfer recipient on a UNSC sanctions list could be taken as factually relevant, in satisfying a supplier's constructive knowledge that the recipient would use the weapons to commit a particular type of crime. In the Dutch case of *Kouwenhoven*, the Court of Appeal held that the defendant must have been aware of the use of the weapons and ammunition due to, inter alia, the fact that his transfers contravened UN resolutions on arms and ammunition.[134] The finding that Kouwenhoven had constructive knowledge of the crimes was based on a range of other information available to him, including his relationship with Charles Taylor, dealings with the Liberian armed forces, his 'use of RTC Camp Bomi Wood as a collection

---

[133] Burchard (*supra* n. 8) 944.
[134] *Kouwenhoven* (Appeal Judgment), 21 April 2017, Netherlands Case Number ECLI:NL: GHSHE:2017:1760 ('*Kouwenhoven* Appeal Judgment') Section L2.1. See Chapter 12 in this volume.

and distribution site for ... arms and ammunition' and his conduct, based primarily on a letter he wrote discussing the deals.[135]

In general, the presence of a UNSC resolution is unlikely on its own to be a sufficient basis from which to extrapolate that a contributor knew that particular crimes would occur, since embargoes are generally imposed on entire states on the basis of broad Chapter VII concerns. However, certain embargoes are imposed due to geographically-, temporally- and thematically-specific human rights violations and with sanctions targeted at certain individuals. In such cases, when combined with an awareness of other publicly-known mechanisms such as a recipient's placement on the US Specially Designated Nationals list, ICC judges might find a sufficient factual basis on which to conclude that an arms trader must have known of the essential matters of the crimes to be committed by the embargoed recipient.

6.6.2   Degree of Knowledge

Alongside the issue of *the specific facts* known to the contributor, the second parameter of *mens rea* under Article 25(3)(d)(ii) is to *what degree of certainty* the contributor must know that the group intends that the facts will materialise. Otherwise put, this is the question of the quanta of knowledge, the extent, the probability, the likelihood or the level of certainty that the contributor is required to be sure of what the group intends to happen in the future. Without such a threshold, 'knowledge' is a shallow concept for practical purposes. As Smith notes, there is greater complexity in doctrines of secondary liability than in those of principal liability, since complicity requires an assessment of the degree of an accomplice's knowledge as to the principal's intentions. While the latter is about the principal's own knowledge of what they wish to do, the former requires an assessment of what another person knows about another's knowledge.[136]

The issue of the degree of knowledge in Article 25(3)(d) raises the judicial and scholarly debate over whether specific direction is an element of aiding and abetting under customary international law, which has caused much confusion,[137] including whether the requirement relates to *actus reus* or *mens rea*. The so-called 'specific direction' is of limited

---

[135]   *Kouwenhoven* Appeal Judgment, Section L2.1.
[136]   Smith (*supra* n. 92), p. 162.
[137]   Stahn (*supra* n. 48) 114–16.

direct relevance in the Rome Statute context. Nonetheless, some of the concerns that fuelled the proposal of a specific direction requirement have been raised in the Rome Statute context in relation to 'generic contribution[s made] with simple knowledge of the existence of a group acting with a common purpose'.[138] These concerns appear to be ameliorated at the ICC by interpreting complicity in terms of the *specificity* and *degree* of knowledge required. In situations where an arms supplier provides assistance that could be used for lawful and unlawful activities, it will be a question of whether they have sufficiently specific and sufficiently certain awareness of the group's unlawful intentions.

The default definition of the degree of knowledge in the Rome Statute under Article 30(3) is either to be aware that *a circumstance exists* or, alternatively, to be aware that *a consequence will occur in the ordinary course of events*. Since the contributor's knowledge under Article 25(3)(d) (ii) relates to an intention, rather than to criminal consequences, the only plausible reading of Article 30 in relation to the accomplice's knowledge of the principal's *mens rea* is that the contributor must be aware of the existence of the group's intention. Accordingly, the Trial Chamber in *Katanga* found that the contributor must know that the group 'means to cause [the criminal consequence of the crime] or is aware that it will occur in the ordinary course of events'.[139] The Chamber found that the contributor's knowledge should be inferred from relevant facts and circumstances.[140] The assessment of those facts and circumstances will overlap to a significant extent with the assessment of remoteness discussed in Section 6.5.1, since there will often be a strong correlation between the degree of an individual's familiarity with an impending crime and their causal proximity to its commission.

In relation to the accomplice's awareness of the likelihood of the crime occurring, the knowledge that the crime 'will occur in the ordinary course of events' inevitably implies an assessment of the probability or risk that an incident is going to take place. Arguably, there is something distinctive about selling weapons that often increases the risk that violence will follow, when compared to other forms of assistance. The English case of *NCB* v. *Gamble* chose the example of an arms supplier to describe knowledge in terms of a lack of purpose or an 'indifference' as to the principal's criminal intentions:

---

[138] *Katanga* Trial Judgment (*supra* n. 56), Minority Opinion of Judge Christine Van den Wyngaert, para. 287.

[139] *Katanga* Trial Judgment, ibid., paras. 774–7, 1641.

[140] *Katanga* Trial Judgment, ibid., para. 1642.

Evidence of an intent in the crime or of an express purpose to assist it will greatly strengthen the case for the prosecution. But an indifference to the result of the crime does not of itself negative abetting. If one man deliberately sells to another a gun to be used for murdering a third he may be indifferent about whether the third man lives or dies and interested only in the cash profit to be made out of the sale, but he can still be an aider and abettor. To hold otherwise would be to negative the rule that mens rea is a matter of intent only and does not depend on desire or motive.[141]

The sale of a gun is a carefully chosen illustration of blameworthy complicit knowledge, since the disinterested accomplice cannot avoid the awareness that the gun may help kill the third man. This distinctive example was also chosen by the UK Supreme Court in its reasoning in *Jogee* to typify the situation where an accomplice lacks the positive intent that a particular offence will be committed and where, at the time the contribution is made, 'it remains uncertain what [the perpetrator] will do'.[142] All other things being equal, 'what the perpetrator may do' is inherently more certain when you hand him or her a gun, compared to providing finance or food. In the case of finance or food, it will often be less clear whether an accomplice's lack of desire for the principal offence negates *mens rea*.[143] The sale of a gun holds an inherent potential for violence, increasing the risk assented to by the seller upon making the sale.

As mentioned earlier in this section, there are practical limitations to the conceivable degree of knowledge, since, as Smith observes, 'an accessory cannot "know" something yet to occur' in the same way that the principal can know his own intentions.[144] In situations of mass atrocity, this is exacerbated by the complexity of international crimes, perpetrated collectively with physical and structural distance separating the contributor from the point of commission. For instance, in *Kouwenhoven*, the Court of Appeal found that the defendant 'must have been aware that "in the ordinary cause [sic] of events" weapons and ammunition would be used' to commit atrocity.[145] But only a weak analogy can be made between international crimes and a municipal violent crime where, for instance, accomplice A hands perpetrator B a

---

[141] Although there is English jurisprudence to the contrary, this standard was largely reaffirmed in subsequent cases. See *Bryce* [2004] EWCA Crim 1231.

[142] *Jogee* (*supra* n. 117), para. 10.

[143] A. P. Simester et al., *Criminal Law: Theory and Doctrine* (6th ed., Hart, 2016), p. 232.

[144] Smith (*supra* n. 92), p. 181.

[145] *Kouwenhoven* Appeal Judgment, Section L2.1.

knife while standing next to anticipated victim C. The assessment of probability is central to criminal law standards of complicit knowledge, essentially describing different gradations of mental acceptance of risk. Even the standard of 'occurrence in the ordinary course of events' simply describes a degree of risk.

Similarly, while the Rome negotiations rejected a recklessness standard from the requirements of Article 25, the differences between 'knowledge' and 'recklessness' may in practice be difficult to distinguish in scenarios of complicit assistance.[146] Common law systems tend to treat 'virtual certainty' and 'recklessness' as sharing the same *qualities*, with the difference between them being quantitative points on a spectrum, from the accomplice being certain to the accomplice seeing a remote possibility.[147] Seen in this light, a difficulty with interpreting the required degree of knowledge under Article 25(3)(d)(ii) is not so much a formalistic question of how best to describe and name the appropriate standards of 'knowing the intention of the group'; rather, it concerns how best to understand the level of risk under which it is acceptable for the contributor to make an arms transfer and how best to apply this notion of acceptable risk to concrete cases.

In the Court's current interpretation of the degree of knowledge under Article 25(3)(d)(ii), an arms supplier must know that the crime 'will occur in the ordinary course of events', requiring a factual assessment of the contributor's awareness of the risk that the group intends to use the weapons to commit the crime. Although beyond the scope of this chapter, an in-depth application of the Rome Statute to arms transfers should be based on analyses of what is considered an unacceptable degree of knowledge in other bodies of global arms trade law that criminalise arms transfer conduct, including domestic licensing regimes for arms exports, the international obligations in the Arms Trade Treaty, the potential for state complicity on the basis of arms supplies, the standards of UNSC and EU arms embargoes, international and national prohibitions on material assistance to terrorism, as well as non-binding commercial standards in the arms trade.[148] These standards constitute subsidiary sources of applicable ICC law, as well as offering decision-makers a wealth of legal criteria and factual precedents when interpreting and applying the acceptable level of risk.

---

[146] Smith (*supra* n. 92), p. 181.
[147] Smith (*supra* n. 92), pp. 182–3.
[148] Section 2.

6.7   Conclusion

A broad range of arms transfer conduct is criminalised by the mode of liability in Article 25(3)(d)(ii) of the Rome Statute. Exactly how far this range extends will depend on the interpretation and application of the *actus reus* and *mens rea*. Notwithstanding some interpretive difficulties (perhaps due to the fact that 'the overall structure of Article 25 was incompletely theorized by its drafters and was the product of negotiated compromises and drafting by committee'[149]), a coherent interpretation of Article 25(3)(d)(ii), based on a literal and purposive reading of the text and its place in the Court's framework for liability, is possible.

First, not only does Article 25(3)(d)(ii) apply to non-group members, it was in fact those individuals who appear to have been primarily envisaged by the drafters when they followed the wording of Article 2(3)(c) of the Terrorist Bombing Convention 1997 and Article 3(4) of the EU Extradition Convention 1996, two treaty provisions aimed at curtailing the activities of the external actors who assist terrorists and organised crime, rather than the terrorists and criminal gangs themselves (who were addressed by other modes of liability). The Prosecutor may therefore wish to consider using Article 25(3)(d)(ii) primarily as a tool to prosecute external actors such as arms traders.

Second, Article 25(3)(d)(ii) requires a contribution that is significant in the sense that there is a tangible causal connection *to the commission or attempted commission* of the crime. The contribution must be causal in the sense that the perpetration of the crime would not have occurred in the way that it did, *but for* the existence of the contribution. As such, a nexus with the manner of commission of the crime may be sufficient, without any direct causal connection between the contribution and the crime itself, and, accordingly, the fungible and interchangeable nature of arms is no barrier to liability. Furthermore, although the contribution may in theory be infinitesimally small, a threshold is provided by the requirement of remoteness: the contribution must be sufficiently proximate in the causal sense. In determining causation, it is not necessary to show that a particular weapon or piece of ammunition was used in a particular incident of violence. Moreover, causation may be present even where crimes of sexual and gender-based violence are based on an element of force due to the threatening presence of weaponry.

---

[149] Ohlin (*supra* n. 55) 417.

Additionally, the causal link may be to the mental, as well as material, elements of crimes, as in the situation where the supply of guns encourages or emboldens the perpetrators.

Third, an arms trader will not be liable under Article 25(3)(d)(ii) unless they know enough specific information about the predicted usage of the weapons, such that they can be said to be aware of the *essential matters* of the impending crime; in other words, they must know what the crime's basic factual contours are going to be. In addition, they must be proven to have believed that, *in the ordinary course of events,* the group's intention to commit the crime would be realised, a test that is inevitably based on a prediction of the likely future usage of the weapons. As such, the standard will be satisfied where the arms trader takes on an unacceptably high degree of risk that the end-user group intends to commit the charged crime in the ordinary course of events.

The ramifications of this interpretation and application of Article 25(3)(d)(ii) for the commercial arms trade are significant. Liability under Article 25(3)(d)(ii) applies to an arms supplier who transfers weapons to a group of which they are not a member and to whose aims and intentions they are utterly indifferent. Even where only a relatively small quantity of arms is supplied, for example, relative to the total amount of weaponry used in a large-scale attack, liability may exist for the provider where there is a non-remote causal impact on the commission or attempted commission of the crimes. In this regard, evidence that a shipment of weapons affected the manner of commission of a crime would be sufficient. Furthermore, it would be unnecessary to tender evidence identifying the very same weapons from the shipment that were fired or otherwise used in a particular criminal incident. This means that a judicial finding that the sale of a package of ammunition to a militia group that contributes to increasing the scale of an assault on a village would satisfy liability under Article 25(3)(d)(ii) for, say, a crime against humanity of murder, even if there is no evidence that a specific killing was carried out using one of the vendor's bullets.

Arms brokers may be exposing themselves to liability if they decide to trade weapons in a scenario where there is unavoidable information about the future usage of their weapons or ammunition. It is unnecessary that they know exactly which criminal incident will follow, but they must be in an undeniable position of being aware that a crime, for instance a war crime of rape, is intended to take place. Often then, liability will be imposed under this provision where there is an egregious and widely known situation of attacks against civilians or violations of humanitarian law, creating a scenario where a trader cannot plausibly deny that selling weapons is going to contribute to the occurrence of more crimes. The presence of widespread reports of previous atrocities, or an arms embargo, would no doubt be relevant indicia of the supplier's constructive knowledge.

The Court's current interpretations of Article 25(3)(d)(ii) leave some ambiguity as to how the provision would be applied in an arms transfer case. The text is unlikely to receive amendment by the Assembly of States Parties in the near future, and the limited ICC jurisprudence on Article 25(3)(d)(ii) has not ruled on all its elements, nor has it been applied to commercial conduct. Still less has Article 25(3)(d)(ii) been applied to a sufficiently broad range of fact patterns across multiple cases, and repeated before a sufficient number of judicial benches to constitute a truly constant line of case law that could be relied upon to predict the boundaries of liability. The specific interpretations of individual judges are relatively impermanent glosses on the terms of the Rome Statute and, in centuries from now, ICC Judges may look back on the Court's ancient jurisprudence as a minutia in a long stream of case precedent. To date, the limited jurisprudence on Articles 25 and 28 has not fixed anything in stone. Ultimately, the existing passages of jurisprudence interpreting Article 25(3)(d) have considered only a narrow range of factual scenarios, especially when one considers the broad variety of complicit conduct that may constitute 'any other contribution'. This observation has ramifications not only for the Court's interpretation of the law but moreover for interpretations of the Rome Statute as a source of customary international law.

The lack of legal certainty limits the ability of those working in the arms trade to predict the permissible boundaries of non-criminal commercial conduct. It also renders the law of limited utility to decision-makers in the ICC and domestic criminal justice systems. A reasonable degree of certainty for making commercial decisions is likely to be realised only through an ICC case involving arms transfer conduct since the ICC has not developed any mechanism analogous to the International Court of Justice's issuance of advisory opinions, nor has the majority of ICC judges tended to give *obiter dicta* views on hypothetical matters. Clarifying how Article 25(3)(d)(ii) applies to commercial arms transfer conduct would enhance the ICC's deterrent effect on arms transfer conduct by identifying what forms of individual behaviour fall within the Statute's ambit. It would deter individuals directly, as well as through the indirect effects of complementarity on national criminal justice systems. Ensuring that the Court acts as an effective deterrent for the arms transfer conduct that it prohibits is a question not only of ensuring that the extent of the law is predictable but also of deciding practically how this information is disseminated, and, as David Scheffer has noted, the effects of Rome Statute liability are yet to be integrated into mainstream commercial law education.[150] An aspect of the deterrent function for corporate entities in the arms trade is therefore in promulgating awareness of the ICC's regulatory role, informing individuals about the extent of their personal liabilityas well as making the international legal community more aware of the reach of the Rome Statute.

'Any other contribution' is a fair label for arms transfer complicity and the ICC Prosecutor and ICC Chambers would be respecting the intentions of the drafters of Article 25(3)(d)(ii) by bringing and confirming charges against arms traders whose relatively peripheral form of participation in crimes is fairly represented by this residual label. Demanding that the modes of liability be used to fairly represent the conduct of the accused is not inconsistent with arguments about the legal correctness and utility of a 'hierarchical reading' of Article 25.[151] Fair labelling does not require fixed and mutually exclusive categories, and, without going as far as to invent a strict taxonomy of liability, different modes can nonetheless be associated with certain forms of participation.

The Prosecutor of the ICC might identify arms transfers as a subject of thematic prosecution in their policy documents. Indeed, the first Prosecutor announced that arms traders were amongst the targets under consideration in the Court's investigations in the DRC and that 'those who provide weapons ... could also be authors' of international crimes 'even if they are based in other countries'.[152] Prioritising case selection on the basis of such a policy, the Prosecutor might then choose a relatively simple commercial arms transfer case against a 'small fish' broker, probably involving low-volume shipments of small arms and light weapons and ammunition. Even a single case against a minor actor would have significant deterrent effects on rationally minded

---

[150] D. Scheffer, 'Corporate Liability under the Rome Statute' (2016) 57 *Harvard International Law Journal* 35, 37.

[151] *Ruto* Confirmation Decision, para. 354. The Chamber did not explain legal basis for reading Article 25 as a 'hierarchy'. E. Van Sliedregt, 'International Criminal Law: Over-studied and Underachieving?' (2016) 29(1) *Leiden Journal of International Law* 1–12, 8–9.

[152] Second Assembly of States Parties to the Rome Statute of the International Criminal Court Report of the Prosecutor of the ICC, Mr Luis Moreno-Ocampo on 8 September 2003.

traders, as well as substantial expressive effects.[153] In a suitable ICC situation, an investigation into arms transfers could take place in synergy with cases against other actors. Indeed, it is not unlikely that the Office of the Prosecutor already has in its possession or is aware of substantial evidence against arms traffickers or sole-trading arms brokers arising from its previous investigations. The arms transfer conduct of these individuals would be eminently suited to the label of Article 25(3)(d) (ii) 'knowingly contributing to an international crime'.

[153] See M. deGuzman, 'Giving Priority to Sex Crime Prosecutions: The Philosophical Foundations of a Feminist Agenda' (2011) 11 *International Criminal Law Review* 515–28.

PART III

Developing the Available Law

Economic War Crimes and Crimes against Humanity

The Prohibition of Pillage in International Humanitarian Law

EVE LA HAYE [*]

This chapter provides a brief historical overview of the concept of pillage and shows how the prohibition of pillaging developed into an absolute prohibition in international humanitarian law, in both international and non-international armed conflict. The chapter discusses a possible definition of pillage and its material elements, which have developed through decisions of international tribunals since World War II.

The prohibition of pillage was born of the need to maintain discipline among troops. The practice of pillage 'disrupts units and disturbs orderly procedure toward the essential end – the correct and efficient conduct of military operations'.[1] Individual soldiers who violated this principle were often severely punished.[2] If booty of war, being a state's taking of movable public property belonging to the enemy, has always been accepted practice in international armed conflicts, the need to protect civilians from the taking of their property in wartime was gradually recognized and included in the first modern compilations of the law of

---

[*] This chapter draws on the discussion of the prohibition of pillage published in the ICRC Commentary on the First Geneva Convention, 2nd edn, 2016, paras. 1492–9 and a paper presented by Larry Maybee, then Deputy Head of Regional Delegation – East Asia, International Committee of the Red Cross, at the conference on 'The International Criminal Responsibility of War's Funders and Profiteers' in Hong Kong in June 2017. The views expressed in this chapter are those of the author and do not necessarily reflect the position of the ICRC.

[1] E. Colby, 'The Military Value of the Laws of War' (1926–1927) 15 *Georgetown Law Journal* 24–34, 25. On this point, see also T. Meron, 'Shakespeare's Henry the Fifth and the Law of War' (1992) 86 *American Journal of International Law* 1–45, 31–4; E.H. Wayne, 'The Third Priority: The Battlefield Dead' (1996) 3 *Army Law* 3–20, 14–15.

[2] See even some early cases of prosecutions and punishment in Meron (*supra* n. 1) 32–3. Christine de Pisan, who compiled the medieval laws of war and customs of chivalry in 1408–1409, supported the death penalty for soldiers committing pillage (Meron (*supra* n. 1) 32).

armed conflict such as the Lieber Code, the Brussels Declaration and the Oxford Manual.[3]

Despite being one of the oldest prohibitions under the law of armed conflict, the practice of pillage has unfortunately been a feature of many armed conflicts to this day. The humanitarian consequences for the affected population are manifold, ranging from short-term problems caused by the pillage of their goods to long-term problems caused by lack of income or the theft of means of production such as seed. Even the goods delivered as part of humanitarian assistance have not been spared pillage in a number of situations.[4] Practice over the centuries has shown the continuing need to protect civilians from the intentional taking of their property against their will and to focus on the use-value of civilian property[5] in order to alleviate the suffering of the civilian population.

7.1   Main Elements of a Definition of Pillage in International Humanitarian Law

Articles 28 and 47 of the 1907 Hague Regulations prohibit pillage during the conduct of hostilities and during occupation.[6] Pillage is also prohibited by Article 15 of the First Geneva Convention of 1949, Article 33(2) of the Fourth Geneva Convention and Article 4(2)(g) of Additional Protocol II (applicable in non-international armed conflicts). Pillage is further prohibited in Article 4(3) of the 1954 Cultural Property Convention and Article 9 of the Second Optional Protocol to this Convention.[7] However, none of these instruments provides a definition of pillage. The terms 'pillage', 'plunder', 'looting' and 'sacking' are often

---

[3] See Lieber Code (1863), Article 44; Brussels Declaration (1874), Articles 18 and 39; Oxford Manual (1880), Article 32.

[4] See e.g. ICRC, Press release on the situation in the DRC, 27 April 2007; Press release on the situation in Iraq, 11 April 2003; Operational update on Afghanistan, 8 November 2001.

[5] On this issue, Brilmayer and Chepiga note that, in a major shift from the 1907 Hague Regulations, the 1949 Geneva Conventions, and more clearly Additional Protocol I, not only protect the ownership rights of civilians but also the use value of the property to the population at large. See L. Brilmayer and G. Chepiga, 'Ownership or Use? Civilian Property Interests in International Humanitarian Law' (2008) 49 *Harvard International Law Journal* 413–46. In Additional Protocol I, objects that are in use by civilians are protected, regardless of who owns them.

[6] Article 28, which applies during the conduct of hostilities, reads: 'The pillage of a town or place, even when taken by assault, is prohibited.' Article 47, which applies in occupied territory, reads: 'Pillage is formally forbidden.'

[7] See Second Protocol for the Protection of Cultural Property in the Event of Armed Conflict, The Hague, 26 March 1999.

used synonymously, without being clearly defined as separate concepts in international law.[8] In many trials following World War II, the terms 'pillage', 'plunder' and 'spoliation' were used interchangeably.[9]

Nonetheless, it is possible to identify the commonly accepted elements of a definition of pillage. Pillage can be defined as the appropriation or obtaining of public or private property by an individual without the owner's consent in violation of international humanitarian law.[10] The appropriation or obtaining of the property is not necessarily done by force or violence[11] but is carried out against the owner's implied or express consent.[12] The absence of consent can be deduced from the

---

[8] For a discussion of a definition of pillage, see, for example, K. Dörmann, *Elements of War Crimes Under the Rome Statute of the International Criminal Court* (Cambridge University Press, 2002), p. 273; A. A. Steinkamm, 'Pillage', in R. Bernhardt (ed.), *Encyclopaedia of Public International Law*, Vol. III (North-Holland Publishing, 1997), pp. 1029–30; J. G. Stewart, *Corporate War Crimes: Prosecuting the Pillage of Natural Resources* (Open Society Justice Initiative, 2011), pp. 15–17.

[9] See, in particular, US Military Tribunal at Nuremberg, *I.G. Farben Trial* (1948) and *Krupp Trial* (1948), UN War Crimes Commission, Law Reports of Trials of War Criminals, Vol. X, 1949. See also Digest of Laws and Cases, UN War Crimes Commission, Law Reports of Trials of War Criminals, Vol. XV, 1949, p. 126. The ICTY discussed the definition of plunder or pillage in the following judgments: *Prosecutor v. Delalić et al.*, IT-96–21-T, Trial Judgment, 16 November 1998 (*Delalić* Trial Judgment), paras. 587–91; *Prosecutor v. Jelisić*, IT-95–10-T, Trial Judgment, 14 December 1999 (*Jelisić* Trial Judgment), para. 48; *Prosecutor v. Simić*, IT-95–9-T, Trial Judgment, 17 October 2003 (*Simić* Trial Judgment), para. 99; *Prosecutor v. Kordić and Čerkez*, IT-95–14/2-A, Appeal Judgment, 17 December 2004, paras. 79–84; *Prosecutor v. Naletilić and Martinović*, IT-98–34-T, Trial Judgment, 31 March 2003 (*Naletilić* Trial Judgment), paras. 612–15; *Prosecutor v. Blaškić*, IT-95–14-T, Trial Judgment, 3 March 2000, paras. 75–6, 184; *Prosecutor v. Martić*, IT-95–11-T, Trial Judgment, 12 June 2007 (*Martić* Trial Judgment), para. 104; *Prosecutor v. Hadžihasanović and Kubura*, IT-01–47-T, Trial Judgment, 15 March 2006 (*Hadžihasanović* Trial Judgment), paras. 49–51. The SCSL discusses the war crime of pillage in e.g. the following cases: *Prosecutor v. Brima, Kamara and Kanu*, SCSL-04–16-T, Trial Judgment, 20 June 2007 (*Brima* Trial Judgment), para. 754; *Prosecutor v. Fofana and Kondewa*, SCSL-04–14-T, Trial Judgment, 2 August 2007 (*Fofana* Trial Judgment), para. 160; *Prosecutor v. Taylor*, SCSL-03–01-T, Trial Judgment, 18 May 2012, para. 452. See also *Situation in the Central African Republic, In the Case of the Prosecutor v. Jean-Pierre Bemba Gombo*, ICC-01/05–01/08, Judgment pursuant to Article 74 of the Statute, 21 March 2016, para. 114.

[10] ICRC, *Commentary on the First Geneva Convention*, 2nd edn, 2016, Article 15, paras. 1492–9, 1494.

[11] See ICRC, *Commentary on the First Geneva Convention*, 2nd edn, 2016, Article 15, para.1494. *Delalić* Trial Judgment (*supra* n. 9), para. 591. See also Permanent Military Tribunal at Metz, *Bommer case*, 1947. During the negotiation of the elements of the war crime of pillage under the ICC Statute, states rejected the element of 'force', concentrating instead on the 'absence of consent'.

[12] On the issue of consent, the US Military Tribunal at Nuremberg in the *I.G. Farben* case found that 'action by the owner is not voluntary because his consent is obtained by threats, intimidation, pressure, or by exploiting the position and power of the military

surrounding circumstances, such as the threat of force, violence, duress, detention, psychological oppression or abuse of power. The absence of consent must also be presumed in the case of persons incapable of giving genuine consent, for example if they are deceased or affected by natural, induced or age-related incapacity.[13]

The prohibition of pillage covers both cases of organized pillage, such as authorized or ordered forms of pillage, and individual acts.[14] Pillage can be carried out either by combatants or by civilians. In the words of the ICTY Trial Chamber, the prohibition of pillage 'extends both to acts of looting committed by individual soldiers for their private gain, and to the organised seizure of property undertaken within the framework of a systematic economic exploitation of occupied territory'.[15]

During the negotiation of the elements of the war crime of pillage for the ICC Statute, states defined pillage slightly differently.[16] Pillaging under the Statute is the act of appropriation of certain property without the consent of the owner, with the intent to deprive the owner of the property and to appropriate it for private or personal use.[17] This mental

occupant under circumstances indicating that the owner is being induced to part with his property against his will' (Law Reports of Trials of War Criminals, Vol. X, p. 47).

[13] This definition of absence of consent is inspired by the elements of the war crime of rape under the ICC Statute. See ICC Elements of Crimes (2000), Article 8(2)(b)(xxii)(1).

[14] See ICRC, *Commentary on the First Geneva Convention*, 2nd edn, 2016, Article 15, para. 1495. *Delalić* Trial Judgment (*supra* n. 9), para. 590. As an example of organized pillage, see the case against Rosenberg before the International Military Tribunal. Rosenberg was found responsible for a system of organized plunder of both public and private property throughout the invaded countries of Europe (Trial of the Major War Criminals before the IMT, Nuremberg, 14 November 1945–1 October 1946).

[15] *Delalić* Trial Judgment (*supra* n. 9), para. 590. For a discussion of the definition of pillage, see also: *Jelisić* Trial Judgment (*supra* n. 9), paras. 46–9; *Martić* Trial Judgment (*supra* n. 9), paras. 100–4; *Simić* Trial Judgment (*supra* n. 9), paras. 98–102. In the *Hadžihasanović* case, the ICTY found that plunder covers 'all forms of unlawful appropriation of property in armed conflict for which individual criminal responsibility attaches under international law, including those acts traditionally described as "pillage"' and extends to 'both widespread and systematised acts of dispossession and acquisition of property in violation of the rights of the owners and isolated acts of theft or plunder by individuals for their private gain' (*Hadžihasanović* Trial Judgment (*supra* n. 9), para. 49).

[16] When defining the elements of crimes, states realized that there was an overlap between the war crime of 'pillaging' and the war crime of 'seizing the enemy's property unless such destruction or seizure be imperatively demanded by the necessities of war'. They attempted to differentiate them when defining the constitutive elements of each war crime.

[17] The ICC Elements of Crimes (2000) for the war crime of pillaging read as follows:

The perpetrator appropriated certain property.
The perpetrator intended to deprive the owner of the property and to appropriate it for private or personal use.

element ('with the intent to') could be seen as unduly restrictive as a number of situations qualified as pillage or plunder by courts and tribunals after World War II would not qualify as pillage under this definition.[18] In these cases, authorized or ordered pillage of natural resources or the systematic economic exploitation of a territory was carried out in furtherance of the war effort and not purely for private or personal use or gain.[19]

In international humanitarian law, pillage is committed if a link can be established between the act of pillage and the armed conflict. This nexus or link is what distinguishes pillage from theft under domestic law. The prohibition of pillage is not contained only in treaty law; it is also widely recognized to be a rule of customary international law in both international and non-international armed conflict.[20]

7.2 Appropriation in Violation of the Rules of International Humanitarian Law

It is important to distinguish between unlawful appropriation of property that amounts to pillage, on the one hand, and appropriation of property that is considered lawful under international humanitarian law, on the

The appropriation was without the consent of the owner.

    See H. B. Hosang, 'Pillaging', in R. Lee (ed.), *The International Criminal Court: Elements of Crimes and Rules of Procedure and Evidence* (Transnational Publishers, 2001), pp. 176–7; C. Byron, *War Crimes and Crimes against Humanity in the Rome Statute of the International Criminal Court* (Manchester University Press, 2010), pp. 127–9; R. O'Keefe, 'Protection of Cultural Property Under International Criminal Law', (2010) 11 *Melbourne Journal of International Law* 339–80, 356. For a commentary on this element, see Dörmann (*supra* n. 8), pp. 272–3.

[18] The SCSL has taken the view that 'the requirement of "private or personal use" is unduly restrictive and ought not to be an element of the crime of pillage'. See *Brima* Trial Judgment (*supra* n. 9), para. 754, and *Fofana* Trial Judgment (*supra* n. 9), para. 160.

[19] See Stewart, 2011 (*supra* n. 8), p. 20, citing Singapore, Court of Appeal, *The Singapore Oil Stocks case*, Judgment, 1956. In the *Krupp* case, the Prosecutor alleged that 'acts of plunder and spoliation were carried out in consequence of a deliberate design and policy on behalf of the German Government'. Some properties were seized and used in the occupied territories or in Germany in the interest of the German war effort (*Krupp Trial* (*supra* n. 9), p. 73). In the *I.G. Farben* case, the indictment alleged that '[Farben] used its expert technical knowledge and resources to plunder and exploit the chemical and related industries of Europe, to enrich itself from unlawful acquisitions, to strengthen the German war machine and to assure the subjugation of the conquered countries to the German economy' (*I.G. Farben Trial* (*supra* n. 9), p. 4).

[20] Henckaerts/Doswald-Beck, ICRC Study on Customary International Humanitarian Law, 2005, Rule 52, pp. 182–5.

other.[21] First, there is a recognized right in international armed conflicts to capture as war booty any movable property belonging to the enemy state.[22] Booty of war covers all types of enemy movable public property that can be used for military operations, such as arms and munitions but also money and food supplies.[23] Private enemy property is immune from capture. It is permissible, however, to seize as war booty on the battlefield weapons, ammunition, non-protective military equipment and military papers belonging to private individuals.[24] War booty must, however, be handed over to the authorities; if any property is kept by individual soldiers, this act might amount to pillage.[25]

Second, in international armed conflicts, the prohibition of pillage does not affect the right of an occupying power to use the resources of the occupied territory for the maintenance and needs of the army of occupation within the limits of the law of occupation.[26] Under the law of

[21] ICRC, *Commentary on the First Geneva Convention*, 2nd edn, 2016, Article 15, para. 1496. This is without prejudice to the law applicable respectively in naval and aerial warfare. In both contexts, under certain circumstances, capture as prize of enemy or neutral property is considered lawful. See *Manual on International Law Applicable to Air and Missile Warfare* (2009), Section U; *San Remo Manual on International Law Applicable to Armed Conflicts at Sea* (1994), Rules 135–58.

[22] See ICRC Study on Customary International Humanitarian Law (*supra* n. 20), Rule 49: 'The parties to the conflict may seize military equipment belonging to an adverse party as war booty.' The title of captured enemy public property susceptible of becoming war booty passes from the enemy to the capturing state immediately upon the effective seizure, without the need for an adjudication by a court as is required in the case of prizes captured at sea or during aerial warfare.

[23] 'The purpose of the law of booty is to enable a belligerent to take possession of all property which his enemy can make use of for the purpose of waging war, and under modern conditions there is very little which does not come within this definition.' H. A. Smith, 'Booty of War' (1946) 23 *British Year Book of International Law* 227–39, 231. See also W. G. Downey, 'Captured Enemy Property: Booty of War and Seized Enemy Property' (1950) 44 *American Journal of International Law* 488–504; E. K. D. Santerre, 'From Confiscation to Contingency Contracting: Property Acquisition On or Near the Battlefield' (1989) 124 *Military Law Review* 111–61 and Y. Dinstein, 'Booty in Land Warfare', in R. Wolfrum (ed.), *Max Planck Encyclopedia of Public International Law* (Oxford University Press, 2008), online edition, www.mpepil.com.

[24] See Downey (*supra* n. 23) 494–5. See also UK, *Military Manual*, 1958, para. 615; UK, *Manual of the Law of Armed Conflict*, 2004, para. 8.25; US, *Field Manual*, 1956, para. 59; these specify that arms, ammunition, non-protective military equipment and military papers belonging to an individual can be taken as booty of war.

[25] A number of pieces of national legislation and military manuals specify that war booty must be handed over to the authorities. See Dörmann (*supra* n. 8), p. 278.

[26] On this issue, see Santerre (*supra* n. 23) 117–22; Downey (*supra* n. 23) 496–9; R. Dolzer, 'Requisitions', in R. Bernhardt (ed.), *Encyclopedia of Public International Law*, Vol. III, (North-Holland Publishing, 1997), pp. 205–8; A. McDonald and H. Brollowski,

occupation, all public movable enemy property that may be used for military operations may be confiscated and no compensation needs to be paid.[27] In contrast, private property may be seized or requisitioned but may not be confiscated.[28] Private property that can be characterized as war material, such as ammunition and means of transport or communication, may be seized, but compensation must be paid at the end of the war. Other private property may be requisitioned, but fair value must be paid as soon as possible.[29] The rights of requisition and seizure are governed by Articles 52, 53 and 55 of the 1907 Hague Regulations.[30] This has given rise to numerous examples of case law following World War II and relating to other situations of occupation.[31]

Third, in the conduct of hostilities, there are situations of lawful appropriation of property that are derived from Article 23(g) of the 1907 Hague Regulations. This provision provides that 'it is especially forbidden ... [t]o destroy or seize the enemy's property unless such destruction or seizure be imperatively demanded by the necessities of war'. This rule amounts to a customary law principle applicable in both international and non-international armed conflict.[32] International law applicable in armed conflicts therefore allows the seizure of enemy property when such seizure is imperatively demanded by the necessities of war.

Other than the previously listed exceptions, appropriation of property during armed conflict without the consent of the owner constitutes pillage.[33] The prohibition of pillage under the Geneva Conventions is absolute and pillage cannot be justified by military necessity.[34]

'Requisitions', in *Max Planck Encyclopaedia of Public International Law* (Oxford University Press, 2008–), online edition, www.mpepil.com.

[27] See Santerre (*supra* n. 23) 120; Downey (*supra* n. 23) 496.

[28] Article 46 of the 1907 Hague Regulations reads: 'Private property cannot be confiscated.'

[29] Note also Articles 55 and 57 of the Fourth Convention. Article 55 clarifies the conditions under which food and medical supplies can be requisitioned and Article 57 regulates the requisitioning of civilian hospitals. See also Articles 33 and 34 of the First Convention.

[30] Together with Articles 55 and 57 of the Fourth Convention, Articles 33 and 34 of the First Convention and Article 14 of Additional Protocol I.

[31] See, in particular, *Krupp Trial* (*supra* n. 9), pp. 132–8, and Israel High Court, *Al-Nawar v. Minister of Defence*, Case H.C. 574/82, Judgment, 11 August 1985, summarized in (1986) *Israel Yearbook on Human Rights*, Vol. 16, pp. 321–8.

[32] See ICRC Study on Customary International Humanitarian Law (*supra* n. 20), pp. 175–7.

[33] ICRC, *Commentary on the First Geneva Convention*, 2nd edn, 2016, Article 15, para. 1496. This presupposes, of course, that a link can be established between the act of pillage and the armed conflict. This nexus is what distinguishes pillage from theft in domestic law.

[34] During the negotiation of the ICC Elements of Crimes (2000), many states supported the view that pillage cannot be justified by military necessity and that pillage is forbidden in all circumstances. Footnote 47 was nonetheless added in the Elements of Crimes and

7.3   Nature of the Property Appropriated

It is widely recognized that the prohibition of pillage extends to the appropriation of all types of property, whether it belongs to private persons, to communities or to a state. The use of the word 'property' implies that the object appropriated must be the subject of ownership in order to be protected. The appropriation of a wide variety of public or private property has been recognized as amounting to pillage, including the theft of valuables from detainees in a prison camp,[35] the systematic extraction of oil stocks,[36] the illegal transfer of shareholdings in privately owned companies[37] and the unlawful exploitation of natural resources such as gold and diamonds.[38] Cultural property also falls within the ambit of property protected against pillage. The 1954 Hague Convention for the Protection of Cultural Property enjoins states to prohibit, prevent and, if necessary, put a stop to any form of theft, pillage or misappropriation of cultural property.[39]

In most cases, and in order to establish the nexus between pillage and the armed conflict, the pillaged property will belong to individuals or entities who are aligned with or whose allegiance is to a party to the conflict who is adverse or hostile to the perpetrator.[40] It can also happen

---

reads: 'As indicated by the use of the term "private or personal use", appropriations justified by military necessity cannot constitute the crime of pillaging.' Appropriations justified by military necessity are lawful appropriations of property and cover the cases explained in section 2 of the commentary on this article.

[35] See *Jelisić* Trial Judgment (*supra* n. 9), para. 49.

[36] See *Singapore, Bataafsche Petroleum v. The War Damage Commission*, Singapore Court of Appeal, 13 April 1956, cited in (1957) 51(4) *American Journal of International Law* 802–15.

[37] *I.G. Farben Trial* (*supra* n. 9), pp. 49–50.

[38] *Case concerning Armed Activities on the Territory of the Congo (Democratic Republic of the Congo v. Uganda)*, Judgment, 19 December 2005, para. 250.

[39] Hague Convention for the Protection of Cultural Property (1954), Article 4(3). On the protection of cultural property and the prohibition of pillage, see H. Abtahi, 'The Protection of Cultural Property in Times of Armed Conflict: The Practice of the ICTY' (2001) 14 *Harvard Human Rights Journal* 1–32; O'Keefe (*supra* n. 17) 339–80; V. Birov, 'Prize or Plunder: The Pillage of Works of Art and the International Law of War' (1997–1998) 30 *New York University Journal of International Law and Politics* 201–49.

[40] The ICC took the view that the 'pillaged property must belong to individuals or entities who are aligned with or whose allegiance is to a party to the conflict who is adverse or hostile to the perpetrator'. See *Situation in the Democratic Republic of the Congo, In the Case of the Prosecutor v. Germain Katanga and Mathieu Ngudjolo Chui*, ICC-01/04–01/07, Decision on the Confirmation of Charges, 30 September 2008, para. 329. This element does not appear, however, as an element of the war crime of pillaging under the ICC Statute.

that property belonging to private citizens of neutral states or to National Red Cross or Red Crescent Societies of neutral states is subjected to acts of pillage.

7.4   Direct versus Indirect Appropriation

It has been found that the prohibition of pillage covers cases of both direct and indirect unlawful appropriation of property. Appropriation is direct when an individual seizes a good directly from the owner.[41] It is indirect when an individual purchases or receives a good acquired illegally during an armed conflict.[42] For example, the UN War Crimes Commission noted in 1949: 'If wrongful interference with property rights has been shown, it is not necessary to prove that the alleged wrongdoer was involved in the original wrongful appropriation.'[43] To reach this conclusion, the Commission relied on the statements or findings of the tribunals that conducted the *Flick, I.G. Farben* and *Krupp* trials after World War II.[44]

7.5   Criminalization of Pillage

Pillage constitutes an offence under the legislation of many states.[45] Pillage appears in the first list of war crimes produced by the 1919 Commission on Responsibility.[46] It is today widely accepted that individual criminal responsibility for the war crime of pillage is established in customary international law in both international and non-international armed conflicts.[47]

---

[41] See Stewart, 2011 (*supra* n. 8), p. 34.

[42] See e.g. Permanent Military Tribunal at Metz, *Bommer case*, 1947, in which the daughters were found guilty of the war crime of pillage, having received stolen goods from their parents. Stewart argues that at least twenty-six pillage cases have involved receiving stolen property during armed conflict (Stewart, 2011 (*supra* n. 8), p. 36).

[43] Digest of Laws and Cases (*supra* n. 9), p. 130.

[44] Law Reports of Trials of War Criminals, Vol. X, 1949, p. 166. While these cases concerned situations of international armed conflict, the same reasoning could apply in non-international armed conflict. So far, however, there is no recent case law to confirm this interpretation in non-international armed conflict.

[45] See ICRC Study on Customary International Humanitarian Law (*supra* n. 20), Rule 52, p. 182, footnote 67.

[46] Report submitted to the Preliminary Conference of Versailles by the Commission on Responsibility of the Authors of the War and on Enforcement of Penalties, Versailles, 29 March 1919.

[47] This was reaffirmed by the ICTY Appeals Chamber in 2005 when it stated that 'violations of the prohibition against "plunder of public or private property" under Article 3(e) entail, under customary law, the individual criminal responsibility of the person

The Nuremberg Charter already contained the war crime of plunder of public or private property[48] and the International Military Tribunal for Germany found the accused Göring, Rosenberg and Frank guilty of the war crime of plunder.[49] Numerous trials were conducted by the military tribunals established under Control Council Law No. 10 throughout Europe at the end of World War II.[50] Individuals were found guilty of 'widespread and systematized acts of dispossession and acquisition of property in violation of the rights of the owners, which took place in territories under the belligerent occupation or control of Nazi Germany during World War II'.[51] The ICTY Statute also lists among the war crimes applicable in international and non-international armed conflict the crime of plunder of public or private property.[52]

In current international criminal law, an individual who unlawfully appropriates public or private property can be prosecuted under various categories of crime. First, if this person extensively appropriates property protected under the Geneva Conventions, such as medical material belonging to aid societies requisitioned without respecting the prescribed conditions spelled out in Article 34, he or she can be prosecuted pursuant

---

breaching the rule' (*Prosecutor* v. *Hadžihasanović*, IT-01–47-AR73.3, Decision on Joint Defence Interlocutory Appeal of Trial Chamber Decision on Rule 98*bis* Motions for Acquittal, 11 March 2005, para. 38).

[48] See Nuremberg Charter (1945), Article 6(b).

[49] International Military Tribunal for Germany, *Case of the Major War Criminals*, 1946, pp. 299, 314, 316.

[50] Among these, the following cases made an explicit reference to pillage: *Szabados case* (1946), UN War Crimes Commission, Law Reports of Trials of War Criminals (1949), Vol. IX, p. 60, in which the Permanent Military Tribunal at Clermont-Ferrand found the accused guilty under Article 440 of the French Penal Code of the looting of personal belongings and other property of civilians evicted from their homes prior to their destruction; *Holstein case* (1947), ibid., Vol. VIII, p. 31, in which the Permanent Military Tribunal at Dijon found the accused guilty under Article 221 of the French Code of Military Justice of pillage committed in gangs by military personnel with arms or open force; *Rust case* (1948), ibid., Vol. IX, p. 71, in which the Permanent Military Tribunal at Metz found the accused guilty of abusive and illegal requisitioning of French property, a case of pillage in time of war, under Article 221 of the French Penal Code of Military Justice and Article 2(8) of the Ordinance of 1944 concerning the Prosecution of War Criminals.

[51] *I.G. Farben Trial* (*supra* n. 9), p. 44.

[52] ICTY Statute (1993), Article 3(e). For examples of convictions for the crime of plunder, see, in particular, ICTY, *Delalić* Trial Judgment (*supra* n. 9), paras. 587–91; *Jelisić* Trial Judgment (*supra* n. 9), para. 48; *Prosecutor* v. *Kordić and Čerkez*, IT-95–14/2-T, Trial Judgment, 26 February 2001, para. 352; *Naletilić* Trial Judgment (*supra* n. 9), paras. 612–15; *Blaškić* Trial Judgment (*supra* n. 9), paras. 75–6, 184; *Martić* Trial Judgment (*supra* n. 9), para. 104.

to Article 147 of the Fourth Convention.[53] Provided that these acts are not justified by military necessity and carried out unlawfully and wantonly, they can amount to the grave breach of extensive appropriation of property.[54]

Provided that the ICC's jurisdictional requirements are fulfilled, the individual can also be prosecuted by the ICC under the crime of 'destroying or seizing the enemy's property unless such destruction or seizure be imperatively demanded by the necessities of war'. This offence originates from Article 23(g) of the 1907 Hague Regulations and is contained in Article 8(2)(b)(xiii) of the ICC Statute as a war crime applicable in international armed conflict.

Lastly, an individual who unlawfully appropriates public or private property can also be prosecuted by the ICC under Article 8(2)(b)(xvi) of its Statute for the crime of 'pillaging a town or place, even when taken by assault'.[55]

It is important to note that pillage of cultural property can be prosecuted by national courts or tribunals under Article 15(1)(e) of the 1999 Second Protocol to the Hague Convention for the Protection of Cultural Property.[56] This article provides for the criminal responsibility of persons who have committed pillage under this protocol.[57]

7.6   Conclusion

The numerous prosecutions by international courts and tribunals of individuals for the war crime of pillage illustrate the cardinal importance and the continued relevance of the protection of private and public property from unlawful appropriation during armed conflict. A recent trend can also be noted: a number of armed conflicts throughout the

---

[53] Such a person could be prosecuted by international tribunals such as the ICC or the ICTY (Article 2 of the ICTY Statute) or by national courts under the national implementing provisions of Article 147 of the Geneva Conventions.

[54] See the commentary on Article 147 of the Fourth Geneva Convention.

[55] The formulation of this crime originates from Article 28 of the 1907 Hague Regulations. To date, a number of accused persons are currently indicted by the ICC for allegedly having committed pillage in the armed conflicts that took place in the DRC, Uganda and Darfur (Sudan).

[56] Under Article 15(1)(e) of the Protocol, 'theft, pillage or misappropriation of, or acts of vandalism directed against cultural property protected under the [Hague] Convention' are serious violations of the Protocol if committed 'intentionally and in violation of the Convention or this Protocol'. Obviously, only states parties to the Protocol will be obliged to prosecute individuals under the conditions provided for in Article 16 of this Protocol.

[57] On this issue, see in general O'Keefe (*supra* n. 17) 339–80 and Birov (*supra* n. 39) 201–49.

world are fuelled by the illegal exploitation and pillage of natural resources. After World War II, some companies' managers were found guilty of the war crime of pillage for their role in the exploitation of natural resources of occupied territories. The war crime of pillage as a property crime could extend to the prosecutions of managers of companies, who nowadays plunder the natural resources of war-torn countries.[58]

---

[58] On these issues, see in particular M. A. Lundberg, 'The Plunder of Natural Resources during War: A War Crime?' (2007–2008) 39 *Georgia Journal of International Law* 495–525 and J. G. Stewart, 'Pillage', in A. Cassese (ed.), *The Oxford Companion to International Criminal Justice* (Oxford University Press, 2009), pp. 454–55. For the question of the corporate criminal liability of such companies, see in particular M. A. McGregor, 'Ending Corporate Impunity: How to Really Curb the Pillaging of Natural Resources' (2009–2010) 42 *Case Western Journal of International Law* 469–97.

A Jurisprudential History of the Displacement Crimes Applicable to Corporate Landgrabbing

JAMES G. STEWART[*]

The term "landgrabbing" denotes the illegal forcible eviction of local populations in order to make way for mining, logging, agricultural plantations, infrastructure projects, and other commercial ventures. The phenomenon is a widespread and rapidly growing problem globally, often involving the collusion of political leaders, local businesspeople, representatives of multinational enterprises, and financial institutions.[1] Interestingly, there is a growing interest in employing international criminal justice as a response to these practices. In 2014, for instance, the International Criminal Court (ICC) received a formal communication alleging that corporate actors had colluded with Cambodian officials as part of a massive landgrab.[2] The ICC has also formally expressed an interest in pursuing these cases. After referencing landgrabbing explicitly, a policy paper on case selection and prioritization issued by the ICC's Office of the Prosecutor in 2016 stipulated that "the Office will give particular consideration to prosecuting Rome Statute crimes that are committed by means of, or that result in, inter alia, the destruction of

---

[*] This chapter is a condensed version of a larger doctrinal work that began fifteen years ago as a co-authored piece with Ken Roberts. See K. Roberts and J. G. Stewart, "Defining Deportation, Unlawful Transfer, Forcible Transfer and Forcible Displacement in International Criminal Law: A Jurisprudential History" *African Journal of International Criminal Justice* (Issue 1, 2019). My kind thanks also to Saif Ansari who provided extensive and invaluable research assistance and to Lindsey Israel for her invaluable assistance throughout.

[1] Peter A. Allard School of Law, International Justice and Human Rights Clinic, *Breaking New Ground: Investigating and Prosecuting Land Grabbing as an International Crime* (University of British Columbia, 2018), www.allard.ubc.ca/sites/www.allard.ubc.ca/files/uploads/IJHR/break ing_new_ground_-_allard_ijhr_land_grabbing_manual_-_public_version.pdf.

[2] R. J. Rogers and A. Prezanti, "Communication under Article 15 of the Rome Statute of the International Criminal Court: The Commission of Crimes Against Humanity in Cambodia, July 2002 to Present" (7 October 2014).

the environment, the illegal exploitation of natural resources or the illegal dispossession of land."[3] But landgrabbing itself is not an international crime, meaning that prosecutors would likely seek to charge displacement-type offenses for corporate implication in these practices.

In addition, the ICC recently declared that it enjoyed jurisdiction over the crime of deportation where victims fled from a non-state party in Myanmar to a state party in Bangladesh.[4] On its face, this decision promises a major new role of displacement crimes within international criminal justice. And because acts of displacement are often economically motivated, including in the Myanmar/Bangladesh situation over which the ICC has asserted jurisdiction,[5] using displacement crimes in this way also has important implications for international criminal justice's impact on business and corporations. Therefore, a jurisprudential history of displacement crimes in international criminal law is an important point of departure in assessing the potential and pitfalls of the new weight to be placed on these crimes, either as a basis for expanding international courts' jurisdiction over atrocities or for addressing some of the underlying commercial interests that provide both the means and the motivation for them.

As this chapter shows, the forced displacement of civilian populations is criminalized by a complex set of distinct but overlapping offenses in international criminal law. Deportation and forcible transfer are both different crimes against humanity, although displacement has also been treated as an element of the crime against humanity of persecution and other inhumane acts. Likewise, the Geneva Conventions list "unlawful deportation or transfer" as war crimes, whereas "displacement" is prohibited in non-international armed conflicts. The Statutes of different courts and tribunals adopt slightly different variations of these crimes against humanity and war crimes, making an already elaborate normative overlap all the more difficult to interpret. As a consequence, if one had to point to just one set of international crimes that had required the most judicial attention over the past several decades, these displacement offenses could well lay claim to that title. Moreover, the history is not just

---

[3] International Criminal Court, Office of the Prosecutor, Policy Paper on Case Selection and Prioritisation, 15 September 2016, para. 41.

[4] Decision on the "Prosecution's Request for a Ruling on Jurisdiction under Article 19(3) of the Statute," ICC-RoC46(3)-01/18–37.

[5] D. Wagner, "The Pursuit of Money and Natural Resources: The Untold Story behind Myanmar's Rohingyas" (*Huffington Post*, 2017), www.huffingtonpost.com/entry/the-pursuit-of-money-and-natural-resources-the-untold_us_59c7b9bce4b0b7022a646b53.

lengthy; it also involves a range of important sub-topics that have important global implications, has often involved inconsistent judicial approaches, is full of controversy, and contains more than one radical change in direction.

In this chapter, I leave aside questions of corporate responsibility to focus uniquely on the jurisprudential history of these overlapping crimes. In particular, I am concerned only with the case law emanating from the International Criminal Tribunal for the Former Yugoslavia (ICTY), since this court has spent innumerable hours wrestling with these topics, whereas they have enjoyed only limited application in other jurisdictions.[6] A more comprehensive treatment of this body of case law would add these important cases from other courts to the jurisprudential history from the ICTY I depict here. I have also written this jurisprudential history in chronological order, beginning with the earliest inceptions of displacement crimes at the ICTY then tracing their development into the most contemporary jurisprudence. In so doing, I draw attention to many of the twists and turns this interpretative history has taken across a broad array of sub-issues. My hope is that this method reveals something of the offenses' development, prevents a recurrence of some of the clear interpretative missteps in this history, informs debate about the implications of using displacement to extend jurisdiction in international criminal justice, and is useful to those considering the strengths and weaknesses of cases against corporations or their representatives for landgrabbing.

---

[6] For cases involving or that concern displacement crimes generally at the ICC, see *Prosecutor* v. *Harun and Kushayb*, ICC PT. Ch. I, Decision on the Prosecution Application under Article 58(7) of the Statute, ICC-02/05–01/07–1. Corr, 27 April 2007, paras. 68–75; *Prosecutor* v. *Al Bashir*, ICC PT. Ch. I, Decision on the Prosecution's Application for a Warrant of Arrest against Omar Hassan Ahmad Al Bashir, ICC-02/05–01/09–3, 4 March 2009, paras. 98–101; *Prosecutor* v. *Muthaura et al*, Decision on the Confirmation of Charges Pursuant to Article 61(7)(a) and (b) of the Rome Statute, ICC-01/09–02/11, 29 January 2012, paras. 241–86; *Prosecutor* v. *William Samoei Ruto, Henry Kiprono Kosgey and Joshua Arap Sang*, Decision on Confirmation of Charges Pursuant to Article 61(7)(a) and (b) of the Rome Statute, ICC-01/09–01/11, 23 January 2012, paras. 243–68; *Prosecutor* v. *Hussein*, ICC PT. Ch. I, Public redacted version of "Decision on the Prosecutor's application under Article 58 relating to Abdel Raheem Muhammad Hussein," ICC-02/05–01/12–1-Red, 1 March 2012, paras. 12–13; and *Prosecutor* v. *Bosco Ntaganda*, Decision Pursuant to Article 61(7)(a) and (b) of the Rome Statute on the Charges of the Prosecutor against Bosco Ntaganda, ICC-01/04–02/06, 9 June 2014, paras. 35–68. See also the judgments in 002/01 at the ECCC: *Nuon Chea and Khieu Samphan*, Case 00219–09-2007/ECCC, Trial Judgment, 7 August 2014, paras. 434–657; and Appeal Judgment, 23 November 2016, paras. 255–97.

8.1   Introducing the Crimes

This section sets out the various displacement crimes that may be prosecuted as international offenses by sketching the legal bases for these crimes using the ICTY framework based on customary international law. This case law will be directly relevant to other courts, international and otherwise, seeking to apply custom as a basis for international crimes. Likewise, even though the ICC Statute articulates these offenses in slightly different terms, the ICC has already shown that it will draw on the ICTY case law governing these displacement-type offenses, partly because the ICTY interprets the ICC Statute within its own attempts to define the crimes in customary international law, since custom is a subsidiary interpretative source in the ICC Statute, and as a result of informal interpretative emulation within the interpretation of international criminal law.

The ICTY Statute (the Statute) allowed the Prosecutor to charge acts of illegal displacement in four different ways, either as grave breaches of the Geneva Conventions of 1949 pursuant to Article 2 of the Statute or as crimes against humanity pursuant to Article 5 of the Statute. If four was not enough, the court itself constructed a fifth, all of which use different terminology to specify a set of overlapping crimes. First, the Statute provided for jurisdiction over a war crime called "unlawful deportation or transfer," incorporating aspects of Article 49 of Geneva Convention IV.[7] Second, the section of the Statute dealing with crimes against humanity explicitly listed "deportation" as one. Third, that same article lists persecution as a crime against humanity, and acts of displacement can constitute the physical element of persecution.[8] Fourth, drawing on language from the ICC Statute, a number of ICTY Judgments have characterized what they describe as "forcible transfer" as "other inhumane acts."[9]

---

[7] Individual or mass forcible transfers, as well as deportations of protected persons from occupied territory to the territory of the occupying power or to that of any other country, occupied or not, are prohibited, regardless of their motive.

[8] For example, *Prosecutor* v. *Blaškić*, IT-95-14-T, Judgment, 3 March 2000, para. 234; *Prosecutor* v. *Krstić*, IT-98-33-T, Judgment, 2 August 2001, paras. 519–32; *Prosecutor* v. *Krnojelac*, IT-97-25-T, Judgment, 15 March 2002, para. 197; *Prosecutor* v. *Krnojelac*, IT-97-25-A, Judgment, 17 September 2003, para. 214.

[9] The *Kupreškić* Trial Judgment, for instance, found that the term other inhumane acts "undoubtedly embraces the forcible transfer of groups of civilians (which is to some extent covered by Article 49 of the IVth Convention of 1949 and Article 17(1) of the Additional Protocol II of 1977)." *Kupreškić* Trial Judgment, para. 566. See also *Krstić* Trial Judgment, para. 673 and *Prosecutor* v. *Blagojević et al.*, IT-02-60-T, Judgment, 17 January 2005, para. 629.

Other inhumane acts denote a residual category of crimes against humanity that are not specifically enumerated but that are nevertheless sufficiently similar to explicitly listed crimes against humanity in nature and gravity.[10] The prosecution of "forcible transfer" as an other inhumane act before the ICTY was necessary because, unlike in the ICC Statute, forcible transfer is not explicitly listed within the ICTY's jurisdiction.[11] Fifth, as will become clear, the ICTY constructed a further label of "forcible displacement" to encompass acts of displacement charged as persecution, although that addition was largely an attempt to avoid addressing competing precedents and was unhelpful in that it added further nomenclature to an already confusing area of the law.

Thus, if and when landgrabbing is ever prosecuted as an international crime, the first process will involve disentangling the meaning of deportation, forcible transfer, unlawful transfer, and forcible displacement. This task is complicated by these offenses' significant legal and terminological overlap. Indeed, as will become clear, courts have disagreed as to the existence and extent of any such differentiation. This lack of unanimity has been further complicated by the introduction of related concepts such as "forcible displacement" as a means of describing the concepts more generically. Arguably, however, unlawful transfer, forcible transfer, and deportation each retain autonomous legal meanings under customary international law, as is apparent from a chronological exploration of these crimes' development. Moreover, because the meaning and identity of these offenses have drawn on the ICC Statute at almost every turn, there is good reason to think that the jurisprudential history that follows will be relevant to landgrabbing cases brought on the basis of the ICC Statute, pursuant to customary international law, or before national courts that adopt either of these standards.

---

[10] The *Vasiljević* Trial Judgment clarified that the three criteria include: "(i) the occurrence of an act or omission of similar seriousness to the other enumerated acts under the Article; (ii) the act or omission caused serious mental or physical suffering or injury or constituted a serious attack on human dignity; and (iii) the act or omission was performed deliberately by the accused or a person or persons for whose acts and omissions he bears criminal responsibility" (*Vasiljević* Trial Judgment, para. 234). See also *Prosecutor v. Naletilić & Martinović*, IT-98-34-T, Judgment, 31 March 2003, para. 247; *Kupreškić* Trial Judgment, para. 563; *Kordić* Trial Judgment, para. 271; *Kvočka* Trial Judgment, para. 206.

[11] Article 7(1)(d) of the ICC Statute prohibits "[d]eportation or forcible transfer of population," whereas Article 5(d) of the ICTY Statute contains only the term "deportation."

8.2   Competing Initial Understandings

The ICTY Statute does not elaborate the requisite elements of the various displacement offenses it references.[12] Early judgments at the ICTY were therefore concerned with establishing the exact parameters of these crimes based on definitions inspired from other related international law instruments. In undertaking this task, the judges were restricted by the requirement that the definitions be based upon customary international law as it existed at the time the alleged offenses took place.[13] Nevertheless, at least initially, two competing approaches emerged that collectively announced the arrival of a core legal problem that would require many years to resolve at the ICTY, before it would later spill over into the ICC. There is a wider narrative that explains the various manifestations of these two competing camps at the beginning of these crimes' jurisprudential history, but, for present purposes, they can be explained by reference to just two core judgments.

In 2000, a Trial Chamber considered deportation and forcible transfer as acts underlying the crime against humanity of persecution in the *Blaškić* trial. For the first time, a Trial Chamber made a concerted attempt to define these acts based on previous legal authorities, concluding that deportation and forcible transfer of civilians were both defined as the "forced displacement of the persons concerned by expulsion or other coercive acts from the area in which they are lawfully present, without grounds permitted under international law."[14] On its face, therefore, the position seemed to amalgamate deportation and forcible transfer, making no mention of the need to expel civilians across a national border as a point of demarcation between the two crimes. Importantly, the Trial Chamber made clear that, in its view, this definition derived from the wording of Article 7(2)(d) of the ICC Statute and the conclusions reached

---

[12] A situation that contrasts with the ICC Statute.

[13] This restriction was set out in the Secretary-General's Report of 1993, which stipulated: "In the view of the Secretary-General, the application of the principle *nullum crimen sine lege* requires that the international tribunal should apply rules of international humanitarian law which are beyond any doubt part of customary law so that the problem of adherence of some but not all States to specific conventions does not arise. This would appear to be particularly important in the context of an international tribunal prosecuting persons responsible for serious violations of international humanitarian law." Report of the Secretary-General Pursuant to Paragraph 2 of Security Council Resolution 808 (1993), 3 May 1993, S/25704, para. 34. There is an issue as to whether treaty law would be sufficient to ground jurisdiction where it is proved that the states concerned were both bound by the terms of the treaties in question, but this is beyond the scope of this chapter.

[14] *Blaškić* Trial Judgment, para. 234.

by the International Law Commission's 1996 Articles on the Draft Code of Crimes against the Peace and Security of Mankind (ILC Draft Code).[15] Already, the willingness of the ICTY to draw on the ICC Statute for interpretative guidance speaks to the salience of this jurisprudential history outside the confines of just ad hoc tribunals, which marks a theme that emerges throughout this history. Nonetheless, the validity of this reason was highly debatable and ultimately proved unconvincing when viewing the full span of this jurisprudence in hindsight.

Conversely, a year later, the *Krstić* Trial Judgment adopted a disaggregated approach to these crimes.[16] This case involved charges of deportation as a crime against humanity (both in its own right and as a constitutive element of persecution), as well as forcible transfer as an element of both persecution and other inhumane acts.[17] Already, the doctrinal overlap that landgrabbing cases will have to grapple with was apparent from the outset. The judgment represented a step forward in terms of clarity in the law as the Trial Chamber clearly addressed the definitions by finding that "both deportation and forcible transfer relate to the involuntary and unlawful evacuation of individuals from the territory in which they reside. Yet, the two are not synonymous in customary international law. Deportation presumes transfer beyond State borders, whereas forcible transfer relates to displacements within a State."[18] Having drawn a distinction between deportation and forcible transfer, the *Krstić* Trial Chamber went on to note that "any forced displacement is by definition a traumatic experience which involves abandoning one's home, losing property and being displaced under duress to another location."[19] While this conclusion would appear to be both logical and correct, it sowed the seeds for subsequent confusion.

In short, the initial attempts to address displacement crimes involved competing approaches to whether a complex set of labels described one and the same offense or whether they retained distinct identities one from the other. Moreover, what weight to place on the ICC Statute's definition of these crimes, particularly the inclusion of forcible transfer alongside deportation in the definition of crimes against humanity, sounded the emergence of a second issue that would reappear time and again over the course of the coming years.

---

[15] See ibid., footnote 460.
[16] *Prosecutor* v. *Krstić*, IT-98–33-T, Judgment, 2 August 2001.
[17] *Krstić* Trial Judgment, paras. 519–32.
[18] Ibid., para. 521.
[19] Ibid., para. 523.

8.3   Identifying Customary International Law

Following these earlier judgments, which had provided incomplete and at times contradictory findings regarding the elements of the crimes, the *Krnojelac* Trial Judgment[20] recognized the need for a comprehensive review of the definition in customary international law.[21] The *Krnojelac* Trial Chamber examined the status of the prohibition of deportation under international humanitarian law, focusing first upon post-war jurisprudence. To begin, it referenced the Nuremburg Judgment[22] and the Control Council Law No. 10 cases, in particular the *United States of America* v. *Erhard Milch* in which Judge Phillips stated that "International Law has enunciated certain conditions under which the fact of deportation of civilians from one nation to another during times of war becomes a crime."[23] The Chamber went on to note that deportation was prohibited in a number of international legal instruments, including the Nuremburg Charter,[24] the Tokyo Charter,[25] Control Council Law No. 10,[26] Geneva Convention IV,[27] Additional Protocol I,[28] the International Law Commission Draft Code of Offences against the Peace and Security of Mankind (1996),[29] and the ICC Statute.[30] With a final reference to academic commentary,[31] the Trial Chamber

---

[20] *Prosecutor* v. *Krnojelac*, IT-97–25-T, Judgment, 15 March 2002.

[21] In the *Krnojelac* Trial, acts of deportation were charged within the context of the crime of persecution under Article 5(h). Although forcible transfer was not formally considered, it was used as a point of reference in arriving at a definition of deportation.

[22] *Krnojelac* Trial Judgment, footnote 1429.

[23] *United States of America* v. *Erhard Milch*, Trials of War Criminals Before the Nuernberg Military Tribunals Under Control Council Law No. 10 (1952) Vol. 2, Concurring Opinion by Judge Phillips, p. 865. The Trial Chamber also relied upon *United States of America* v. *Alfried Krupp et al*, Trials of War Criminals Before the Nuernberg Military Tribunals Under Control Council Law No. 10 (1952) Vol. 9, part 2, pp. 1432–3; and *United States of America* v. *Friedrich Flick et al*, Trials of War Criminals Before the Nuernberg Military Tribunals Under Control Council Law No. 10 (1952) Vol. 6, p. 681.

[24] Articles 6(b) and (c).

[25] Article 5(c).

[26] Articles II (1)(b) and (c).

[27] Articles 49 and 147.

[28] Article 85(4)(a).

[29] Articles 18 and 20.

[30] Articles 7(1)(d) and 8(2)(a)(vii).

[31] Cited articles include J.-M. Henckaerts, "Deportation and Transfer of Civilians in Time of War" (1993) 26 *Vanderbilt Journal of Transnational Law* 472, which states with respect to Article 49 of Geneva Convention IV that "[p]resumably, a transfer is a relocation within the occupied territory, and a deportation is a relocation outside the occupied territory"; M. Cherif Bassiouni, *Crimes Against Humanity in International Criminal Law* (2nd rev. ed., Kluwer Law, 1999), p. 312; C. K. Hall, "Crimes against Humanity: Para. 1(d)," in

concluded that deportation was clearly prohibited under international humanitarian law, both as a war crime and as a crime against humanity, the content of the offense remaining the same under each.[32]

Having established deportation as an offense recognized under international law at the time relevant to the indictment, the Trial Chamber endorsed the ICC standard applicable to crimes against humanity (and the definition set out previously in the *Blaškić* Trial Judgment), stipulating that "[d]eportation may be defined as the forced displacement of persons by expulsion or other coercive acts from the area in which they are lawfully present, without grounds permitted under international law."[33] This assertion is unobjectionable insofar as it defines preliminary elements of the offense as a crime against humanity, although the idea that the same definition is equally applicable to the definition of a war crime seems problematic in that it ignores the explicit requirement that deportation as a war crime involves occupied territory.[34]

To some extent, this reasoning appeared to involve an attempt to have things both ways, though, since the Trial Chamber went further to draw a clear distinction between deportation (requiring the displacement of persons across a national border) and forcible transfer (which may take place within national boundaries).[35] Unlike *Krstić*, the Trial Chamber relied on jurisprudence and a number of international instruments which indicated that such a conclusion was, in fact, customary international law at the time the offenses were allegedly committed. In arriving at this conclusion, the *Krnojelac* Trial Judgment expressly rejected the more liberal approach initially adopted in the *Nikolić* Rule 61 Decision. The *Krnojelac* Trial Judgment declared that it "does not accept as persuasive the only previous

---

O. Triffterer (ed.), *Commentary on the Rome Statute of the International Criminal Court* (Nomos Verlagsgesellschaft, 1999), p. 136, with respect to the two terms used in Article 7 of the Rome Statute: "Unfortunately, the Statute does not expressly distinguish between deportation and transfer. However, given the common distinction between deportation as forcing persons to cross a national frontier and transfer as forcing them to move from one part of the country to another without crossing a national frontier, and given the basic presumption that no words in a treaty should be seen as surplus, it is likely that the common distinction was intended."

[32] *Krnojelac* Trial Judgment, para. 473.

[33] Ibid., para. 474.

[34] See Article 49 Geneva Convention IV, in relevant part: "Individual or mass forcible transfers, as well as deportations of protected persons *from occupied territory* to the territory of the Occupying Power or to that of any other country, occupied or not, are prohibited, regardless of their motive." Emphasis added.

[35] *Krnojelac* Trial Judgment, para. 474; *Krstić* Trial Judgment, para. 521.

decision of this Tribunal which states to the contrary, and it notes that this decision did not follow fully litigated trial proceedings."[36]

The *Krnojelac* Trial Chamber further elaborated on other elements of the crime of deportation. In particular, the Chamber found that deportation is illegal only where it is forced,[37] specifying that the term "forced" is not limited to physical force but may also include the "threat of force or coercion, such as that caused by fear of violence, duress, detention, psychological oppression or abuse of power against such person or persons or another person, or by taking advantage of a coercive environment."[38] According to the Chamber, the essential element in establishing that deportation is forced is the involuntary nature of the displacement, where relevant persons had no real choice.[39] Finally, the Trial Chamber noted that forced displacement is illegal only when it takes place without grounds permitted by international law.[40] In all these respects, the *Krnojelac* case built a firmer foundation in custom, and deepened several understandings of this law.

8.4   Challenging Forcible Transfer as an Other Inhumane Act

The *Stakić* Rule 98*bis* Decision was the next installment in the chronological development of displacement-type crimes.[41] In the *Stakić* Rule

---

[36] *Krnojelac* Trial Judgment, para. 474.
[37] Ibid., para. 475.
[38] Ibid., citing *Krstić* Trial Judgment, para. 529.
[39] *Krnojelac* Trial Judgment, para. 475, footnotes 1434, 1435. On the facts of the case, the Trial Chamber concluded that the majority of incidents alleged by the prosecution to constitute deportation did take place. However, it further concluded that the transfer of detainees from one prison camp to another within BiH did not fulfill the legal requirements of deportation, because no national border was crossed (para. 478). Regarding the one instance in which a group of thirty-five men was moved across a national border (to Rozaj in Montenegro), the Chamber decided that this was not involuntary because "there is general evidence that detainees wanted to be exchanged, and that those selected for so-called exchanges freely exercised their choice to go and did not have to be forced" (para. 483). On the facts of the case, the Trial Chamber thus rejected the prosecution submission that the mere fact that the detainees were taken *out* of the KP Dom, wherever else they may have been transferred to, constituted deportation. The prosecution appealed regarding both the Trial Chamber's interpretation of the law as well as the findings on these incidents.
[40] Ibid., para. 475 and footnote 1436.
[41] *Prosecutor* v. *Stakić*, IT-97–24-T, Decision on Rule 98bis Motion for Judgment of Acquittal, 31 October 2002. Rule 98 bis of the ICTY Rules of Procedure and Evidence provided at the time that: "(A) An accused may file a motion for the entry of Judgment of acquittal on one or more offences charged in the indictment within seven days after the close of the Prosecutor's case and, in any event, prior to the presentation of evidence by the defence pursuant to Rule 85 (A)(ii). (B) The Trial Chamber shall order the entry of

98*bis* Decision, the Chamber reiterated the view that "the crime of deportation presumes transfer across State borders, whereas forcible transfer relates to displacement within a State."[42] But while the *Stakić* Trial Chamber was prepared to follow others in defining deportation, it expressed great concern with treating forcible transfer as an "other inhumane act." In particular, the Trial Chamber expressed its "serious concern" with the use of "other inhumane acts" as a crime against humanity to attach criminal liability to forcible transfers, reasoning that "the description of a criminal offence extends beyond the permissible when the form of conduct prohibited cannot be identified."[43] The Trial Chamber considered that "other inhumane acts" subsume a broad range of criminal behavior that could be considered to lack sufficient clarity, precision, and definiteness, as required by the principle *nullum crimen sine lege*.[44] Moreover, the fact that the ICC Statute included deportation and forcible transfer as separate, explicitly enumerated offenses led the Chamber to conclude that the reference to deportation in the ICTY might encompass both these forms of forced displacement in customary international law.[45]

While these misgivings are certainly principled, the logic that a residual clause such as "other inhumane acts" should be interpreted as excluding acts not otherwise enumerated in Article 5 would appear to render the clause redundant and to raise the question of why it was included in the Statute by the drafters. In addition, a large number of cases had applied "other inhumane acts" in practice.[46] Perhaps most intriguingly, the *Stakić* 98*bis* Decision eventually concluded that

---

Judgment of acquittal on motion of an accused or proprio motu if it finds that the evidence is insufficient to sustain a conviction on that or those charges."

[42] Ibid., para. 130.

[43] Ibid., para. 131.

[44] Ibid.

[45] Ibid.

[46] For example, the *Kvočka* Trial Judgment stated that "[m]utilation and other types of severe bodily harm, beatings and other acts of violence, serious physical and mental injury, forcible transfer, inhumane and degrading treatment, forced prostitution, and forced disappearance are listed in the jurisprudence of the Tribunal as falling under this category." *Kvočka* Trial Judgment, para. 208. According to the *Blaškić* Trial Judgment, "serious physical and mental injury – excluding murder – is without doubt an 'inhumane act' within the meaning of Article 5 of the Statute." *Blaškić* Trial Judgment, para. 239. See also *Prosecutor v. Akayesu*, ICTR-96-4-T, Judgment, 2 September 1998, para. 697, for forcing nudity in various public circumstances; *Prosecutor v. Kayishema and Ruzindana*, ICTR-95-1-T, Judgment, 21 May 1999, paras. 154, 583; *Prosecutor v. Niyitegeka*, ICTR-96-14-T, Judgment, 16 May 2003, para. 465, for decapitation, castration, piercing of a victim's skull and sexual desecration of a corpse.

a reasonable Trial Chamber could not dismiss a count at the 98*bis* stage for legal reasons (vagueness), on the basis that the *Kupreškić* Judgment had previously applied the provision to forcible transfers.[47] Accordingly, the Chamber did not follow through with its concerns about treating forcible transfer as an other inhumane act (or the solution it foresaw that involved folding forcible transfer back into deportation). If this conclusion was difficult to reconcile with the Trial Chamber's earlier view that charging forcible transfer as an "other inhumane act" may amount to a violation of the principle of *nullum crimen sine lege*, the tensions apparent in the decision set the stage for a more radical approach that was soon to follow.

8.5   The First Substantive Treatment of Unlawful Transfer as a War Crime

Up until this point in the chronological development of these offenses, all substantive debate about displacement-type crimes had focused on crimes against humanity. In the *Naletilić* Trial Judgment,[48] a Trial Chamber dealt with a charge of unlawful transfer of a civilian as a grave breach of the Geneva Conventions for the first time.[49] This first ICTY articulation of the definition of this war crime was clearly influenced by case law that had interpreted deportation and forced transfer as crimes against humanity, but we should pause briefly to observe the introduction of new terminology that could complicate landgrabbing cases if they move forward in practice: whereas crimes against humanity use the labels deportation and forcible transfer, the war crime speaks of "unlawful" transfer. Just because the word "transfer" is common to both forcible transfer and unlawful transfer, it need not follow that unlawful transfer would come with the same legal meaning.

With respect to the "unlawful" nature of the transfer, the Trial Chamber noted that Article 49 of the Geneva Conventions does not prohibit transfers where motivated by the security of the population or

---

[47] The Trial Chamber stated that "[a]t this point in the proceedings this Chamber is not satisfied that a reasonable Trial Chamber could decline to enter a conviction for legal reasons (vagueness), and, therefore, will not dismiss the count on this basis. The Trial Chamber is fortified in its conclusion by the *Kupreškić Trial Judgment*, in which the same issue in relation to the imprecision of the crime of other inhumane act was raised, but the count was not dismissed for vagueness." *Stakić 98bis Decision*, para. 131.

[48] *Prosecutor* v. *Naletilić and Martinović*, IT-98-34-T, Judgment, 31 March 2003.

[49] *Naletilić* Trial Judgment, para. 513.

imperative military reasons.[50] The Trial Chamber thus arrived at the following definition of unlawful transfer:[51]

i) the general requirements of Article 2 of the Statute are fulfilled [listing the category of war crimes known as grave breaches];

ii) the occurrence of an act or omission, not motivated by the security of the population or imperative military reasons, leading to the transfer of a person from occupied territory or within occupied territory;

iii) the intent of the perpetrator to transfer a person.

The definition is noteworthy for several reasons. First, it stresses that the transfer must take place from or within occupied territory. While it is true that unlawful transfer and deportation as referenced in Article 49 of Geneva Convention IV are limited by a connection to occupied territories, there is some evidence that this limitation may no longer be applicable as a matter of customary international law. A range of state practice positively dispenses with the need for a link to occupied territory in defining the war crimes of deportation and unlawful transfer and thus more closely approximates the definition of these war crimes to the ICC definition for crimes against humanity based on "expulsion or other coercive acts from the area in which [the individuals expelled] are lawfully present." For example, General Assembly Resolution 3318 (XXIX), adopted in 1974, proclaimed that "forcible eviction, committed by belligerents *in the course of military operations* or in occupied territories shall be considered criminal."[52] Other similar constructions can be found in military manuals,[53] domestic criminal codes,[54] and legislation implementing the Geneva Conventions' grave

---

[50] Ibid., para. 518.

[51] Ibid., para. 521.

[52] UN General Assembly, Res. 3318 (XXIX), 14 December 1974, § 5. Emphasis added.

[53] Australia's Commanders' Guide provides that "civilians should not be relocated" and further provides that "unlawfully deporting, transferring … a protected person" constitutes "grave breaches or serious war crimes likely to warrant institution of criminal proceedings"; France's LOAC Summary Note provides that "deportation or illegal transfer of population" constitutes a grave breach, which is a war crime; the Military Instructions of the Philippines provide that emphasis should be placed on allowing the civilian population to remain in their homes, on the basis that the large-scale movement of civilians creates logistical and strategic difficulties for the military.

[54] Azerbaijan's Criminal Code punishes the "driving away [of] the civilian population with other aims from the area where they legally live"; Colombia's Penal Code punishes "anyone who, during an armed conflict, without military justification, deports, expels or carries out a forced transfer or displacement of the civilian population from its own territory."

breach regime.[55] Whether these authorities are sufficient to constitute custom must be subject to some doubt given the plethora of practice insisting on the more traditional link to occupation.[56]

Second, the *Naletilić* Trial Judgment does not expressly mention a forcible aspect to the transfer, despite the fact that the Chamber clearly considered this in its earlier analysis and it was expressly required in earlier jurisprudence addressing displacement within the context of crimes against humanity. It is not immediately clear why this element does not form part of the Chamber's definition when it took the position that transfers motivated by an individual's own genuine wish to leave are lawful. Regardless, considering the link to occupied territory and the absence of a forcible aspect, the definition of unlawful transfer would appear to differ from that of forcible transfer as defined by the ICC Statute.[57] As a result, this would seem to call into question the Trial Chamber's suggestion that unlawful transfer and forcible transfer are in fact interchangeable.

Third, the *Naletilić* Trial Judgment's definition of the *mens rea* requirement demands only "the intent of the perpetrator to transfer a person," even though the same Judgment had previously held that "the intent to have the person (or persons) removed ... implies the aim that the person is not returning."[58] The difference is important since subsequent decisions adopted the requirement of intention to transfer permanently without further analysis, before other tribunals rejected this element. The sole authority provided by the *Naletilić* Trial Judgment to support the requirement for permanent transfer was contained in a footnote

---

[55] Bangladesh's International Crimes (Tribunal) Act states that the "violation of any humanitarian rules applicable in armed conflicts laid down in the Geneva Conventions of 1949" is a crime and also specifies that "war crimes: namely violation of law or custom of war include ... deportation to slave labour or for any other purpose of civilian population in the territory of Bangladesh"; under the Criminal Code of the Federation of Bosnia and Herzegovina, "whoever in violation of rules of international law applicable in time of war, armed conflict or occupation ... orders displacement" of the civilian population commits a war crime; the Criminal Code of the Republika Srpska contains the same provision; China's Law Governing the Trial of War Criminals provides that "mass deportation of non-combatants" constitutes a war crime.

[56] See practice identified in J.-M. Henckaerts and L. Doswald-Beck, *Customary International Humanitarian Law*, Vol. II (Cambridge University Press, 2005), ch. 38.

[57] Article 7(2)(d) of the ICC Statute provides that "[d]eportation or forcible transfer of population means forced displacement of the persons concerned by expulsion or other coercive acts *from the area in which they are lawfully present*, without grounds permitted under international law." Emphasis added.

[58] *Naletilić* Trial Judgment, para. 520.

citing the Geneva Convention's Commentaries.[59] Understandably, the Trial Chamber perceived this statement as being "indicative ... that deportation and forcible transfer are not by their nature provisional, which implies an intent that the transferred persons should not return."[60] Nevertheless, in practical terms, it is difficult to see why a temporary but otherwise unlawful transfer should be exempt from the definitions of deportation or forcible transfer. By requiring an intention that the transfer be permanent, the *Naletilić* Trial Judgment suggests that it would not be a crime for a civilian to be transferred or deported for a finite period of time (with the commensurate *mens rea*), no matter the length of that intended period. This issue, too, would spark further litigation.

8.6   Upending the Initial Definitions

Up until this point in time, the jurisprudential history of displacement crimes was originally bifurcated, then it became uniform but underdeveloped for a period, before a radical reinterpretation was gestured at. At the same time, the confusing overlap of labels was exacerbated by the partially overlapping but distinct war crime of unlawful transfer. Then, in 2003, the *Stakić* Trial Judgment sought to upend these initial foundations by following through with the radical reinterpretation it had hinted at earlier. Nine months after the *Stakić* 98*bis* Decision, the same Trial Chamber rendered its final Judgment, reversing much that came before.[61] The *Stakić* Trial Judgment's radical reinterpretation of deportation would color much of the subsequent case law, and resurfaced in debates about jurisdiction at the ICC fifteen years later. To foreshadow this, however, the Trial Chamber's approach that I discuss here was rejected on appeal then uniformly discontinued thereafter, but it warrants careful consideration so that lessons learned are not repeated in landgrabbing cases.

The *Stakić* Trial Judgment began its analysis by examining the definition of deportation in *Black's Law Dictionary*. The Trial Chamber concluded, based on its reading of the dictionary definition, that: "under Roman law, the term deportation, referred to instances where persons were dislocated from one area to another area also under the control of

---

[59] Ibid., footnote 1362. The citation in question reads: "[unlike] deportation and forcible transfer, evacuation is a provisional measure."

[60] Ibid.

[61] *Prosecutor v. Stakić*, IT-97-24-T, Judgment, 31 July 2003.

the Roman Empire. A cross-border requirement was consequently not envisaged."[62] Although the use of dictionaries is a fairly commonplace occurrence within the jurisprudence of the Tribunal, their use has generally been restricted to specific procedural terms. In the limited circumstances where they have been used to define crimes, their value is clearly auxiliary to or corroborative of a much wider analysis of more authoritative sources.[63] In this case, however, the Trial Chamber apparently disregarded reasoned judgments of the Tribunal based on wide-ranging sources evidencing customary international law for a definition from a dictionary.

The Trial Chamber also relied on policy arguments. In support of its interpretation that a cross-border element is not required in the crime of deportation, it posited that, based on the Secretary General's Report and in particular its reference to "ethnic cleansing," the Tribunal "was established to attach criminal responsibility to those in the former Yugoslavia responsible for this practice."[64] As a basis for dismissing the cross-border requirement, this reasoning would appear to be flawed, most notably because ethnic cleansing per se is not included as a crime in the Statute. Therefore, if the Tribunal were to attach criminal responsibility for the practice, it would need to do so pursuant to crimes that are included in the Statute and that reflect customary international law, such as deportation and forcible or unlawful transfer. As was the case with dictionary definitions, one can only assume that arguments from policy play a secondary role to established law, especially if one's approach is driven by a concern for the sanctity of the *nullum crimen sine lege* principle.

With respect to previous case law, the Tribunal pointed out "that the International Military Tribunal at Nuremberg, on the basis of Article 6(c)

---

[62] *Stakić* Trial Judgment, para. 674.
[63] See for example the *Furundžija* Appeal Judgment's reference to *Black's Law Dictionary* in defining "miscarriage of justice," *Prosecutor* v. *Furundžija*, IT-95-17/1-A, Judgment, 21 July 2000, para. 37; see also the *Blaškić* Trial Judgment's use of a dictionary definition to confirm the meaning of the term "instigating," *Blaškić* Trial Judgment, para. 280; or the *Čelebići* Trial Judgment's reference to dictionary definitions in defining "serious," *Prosecutor* v. *Delalić et al.*, IT-96-21-T, Judgment, 16 November 1998, para. 510. Where the Tribunal has used a dictionary to assist in the definition of the offense of inhuman treatment, it has done so in conjunction with reference to state practice, a host of international instruments, the Commentaries to the Geneva Conventions and other relevant judicial material. See, for example, *Čelebići* Trial Judgment, paras. 516–42.
[64] Ibid., para. 676.

of the Nuremberg Charter referring to 'deportations' as a crime against humanity, applied this provision *de facto* in cases where victims were displaced within internationally recognised borders."[65] Yet, here, too, the reasoning was less than compelling. The fact that civilians were held unlawfully in concentration camps within Germany does not support the conclusion that the Nuremberg Tribunal applied the law of deportation "de facto in cases where victims were displaced within internationally recognised borders." A closer analysis of references to deportation within the Nuremberg Judgment reveals that the majority unambiguously refer to transfers across borders. In particular, the Judgment cites deportations from Poland to Germany,[66] the deportation of "430,000 Jews from Hungary,"[67] and "the mass deportation of almost 120,000 of Holland's 140,000 Jews to Auschwitz, deporting Jews from the Italian occupation zone of France."[68] To the extent that the Judgment does make passing reference to "deportation of Jews from various Axis satellites"[69] and expulsion "to the East,"[70] it is far from clear that such displacements did not involve a cross-border transfer.

Intriguingly, despite its earlier stated opposition to a fixed destination requirement, the Trial Chamber ultimately required that the displacement must cross at a minimum a de facto boundary.[71] Quite what would suffice to constitute a de facto boundary would later give rise to further litigation, but it is worth noting that this position also arose from an attempt to find comparable meanings in crimes against humanity and war crimes: because the Geneva Conventions explicitly listed forced displacement out of occupied territory but within one and the same state as deportation, the idea that occupation operated as a de facto border was applied to all forms of deportation. This again announced an important theme, namely, how to understand a set of displacement-type crimes that partially overlap in terms of both substantive scope and

---

[65] Ibid., para. 684 (footnotes omitted).
[66] The *Nuremberg Judgment* states that "by the middle of April, 1940, compulsory deportation of labourers to Germany had been ordered in the Government General; and a similar procedure was followed in other eastern territories as they were occupied. A description of this compulsory deportation from Poland was given by Himmler." *Trial of Major War Criminals Before the International Military Tribunal*, Nuremberg, 14 November 1945–1 October 1946, Vol. I (1947), p. 244.
[67] Ibid., p. 259.
[68] Ibid., p. 287.
[69] Ibid., p. 271.
[70] Ibid., p. 287.
[71] Ibid., para. 679.

218 RESPONSIBILITY OF WAR'S FUNDERS AND PROFITEERS

nomenclature without transgressing the particularities of the different bodies of law within which they exist. In that vein, it was also notable that the *Stakić* Trial Judgment concluded that the ICC Statute provides for a single category of "deportation or forcible transfer of the population."[72] In this respect, too, this Trial Chamber appeared to be on the wrong side of jurisprudential history, since the ICC itself would later reject that view.[73]

8.7 The Emergence of "Forcible Displacement" as a Generic Label

Mere weeks after the *Stakić* Trial Judgment rendered its decision, the Appeals Chamber was afforded an opportunity to review the Tribunal's approach to the definition of deportation in the context of the *Krnojelac* Appeal Judgment, which considered charges of deportation as grounds for establishing the *actus reus* of persecution. By coincidence, the appeal bench included Judge Schomburg, who had presided on the *Stakić* Trial Judgment. Despite submissions from the prosecution imploring the Appeals Chamber to rule authoritatively on the definition of deportation given the lack of clarity in the jurisprudence,[74] the Appeals Chamber expressly declined the invitation, declaring that "it is not necessary to express a view either supporting or rejecting the Trial Chamber's definition of the terms 'deportation' or 'expulsion',"[75] because the crime at issue on appeal was persecution. Instead, the Appeals Chamber introduced new terminology, in an area already struggling with too much, by creating the generic term "forcible displacement" to cover all forms of displacement when it is considered an aspect of persecution.

---

[72] The ICC Statute defines the crime of "deportation or forcible transfer of population" as the "forced displacement of the persons concerned by expulsion or other coercive acts from the area in which they are lawfully present, without grounds permitted under international law": Article 7(1)(d) as defined in 7(2)(d).

[73] Decision on the "Prosecution's Request for a Ruling on Jurisdiction under Article 19(3) of the Statute," ICC-RoC46(3)-01/18, 6 September 2018. See also S. Ansari and J. G. Stewart, "Part 2 – Rohingya Deportation: Deportation Is a Distinct Crime in the ICC Statute" (2018), http://jamesgstewart.com/rohingya-deportation-post-2-deportation-is-a-distinct-crime-in-the-icc-statute/.

[74] The trial transcripts quote prosecution attorney Norul Rashid as pleading that "[t]he Appeals Chamber must seize this opportunity to try and resolve this issue, because even at the trial level, the position is still unclear." *Krnojelac* Transcripts, 14 May 2003, p. 89, www.un.org/icty/transe25/030514ED.htm.

[75] *Krnojelac* Appeal Judgment, para. 224.

In the Appeals Chamber's estimation, for the purposes of the crime of persecution it was preferable to qualify as "forcible displacement" acts that, when charged independently, would be qualified as crimes of deportation or forcible transfer.[76] This approach gives rise to the question of how deportation can be considered as a "general" or "generic" term. True, an act underlying the crime of persecution can be either a crime in and of itself or an act which does not independently amount to a crime,[77] but in a situation where the act does amount to a crime, as is the case with deportation, it is unclear why it should be interpreted as a general term rather than the crime that it is. As a result, deportation may have one meaning when analysed as a crime in its own right, and a different meaning within the context of the crime of persecution. Nonetheless, this position allowed the Appeals Chamber to avoid the controversy about the meaning of these crimes by developing a new label whose origins are unclear, but that would avoid the border issue altogether. The Appeals Chamber even announced the legal interests protected by this generic label.[78]

In sum, rather than providing needed clarity regarding the cross-border nature of displacement-type crimes, the *Krnojelac* Appeal Judgment avoided the issue by introducing a generic term of "forcible displacement." Quite apart from the dubious legal basis for reaching this conclusion, the introduction of more overlapping terminology muddied the waters further, creating new ambiguities subsequent decisions would need to wade through. Hopefully, landgrabbing cases can avoid some of these pitfalls by emulating interpretations that won out over time at the ICTY, rather than replicating approaches that add more confusion than

---

[76] *Krnojelac* Appeal Judgment, para. 214.

[77] See K. Roberts, "The Law of Persecution Before the International Criminal Tribunal for the Former Yugoslavia" (2002) 15 *Leiden Journal of International Law* 623–39. On its face, the *Krnojelac* Appeal Judgment appears to be at odds with this established jurisprudence when it states in paragraph 219 that "the crime of persecution may take different forms. It may be one of the other acts constituting a crime under Article 5 of the Statute or one of the acts constituting a crime under other articles of the Statute," thus suggesting that the underlying act must be a crime. The context suggests that the Appeals Chamber was not actually taking this position from the very fact that it considered the underlying act of deportation not to be a crime.

[78] Ibid., para. 218. The Appeals Chamber found that: "The prohibition against forcible displacements aims at safeguarding the right and aspiration of individuals to live in their communities and homes without outside interference. The forced character of displacement and the forced uprooting of the inhabitants of a territory entail the criminal responsibility of the perpetrator, not the destination to which these inhabitants are sent."

clarity to an area of law that consumed an undue amount of time and resources there.

8.8   An Emerging Consensus

A consensus gradually emerged within the subsequent case law, providing the clarity the Appeals Chamber was unable to deliver initially. That consensus sided with the earlier analysis that customary international law required forced displacement across a border to establish deportation. This reversion to pre-*Stakić* reasoning would make *Stakić* an outlier rather than a turning point towards a new legal approach. The new consensus also incorporated the term "forcible displacement" for persecution cases, even though the legal arguments for this view were contentious and the practicality of the development was dubious given that it added yet another label to a field struggling to understand the multiplicity of overlapping terminology it already had. Further, while the new consensus laid a bedrock for subsequent decisions, it did not resolve all problems.

Importantly, the *Milošević* 98 *bis* Decision undertook what is, arguably still, the most extensive Tribunal analysis of deportation's cross-border element. It noted that "in the aftermath of the war, deportation was included in [Article 6(c) of] the Charter of the International Military Tribunal [IMT] as a crime against humanity, giving the IMT jurisdiction over acts committed against persons of the same nationality as the principle offenders."[79] Similarly, deportation was included as a crime against humanity in Control Council Law No. 10 and Principle VI of the Nuremberg Principles. The Chamber made further reference to the IMT Judgment[80] and to *United States of America* v. *Milch*[81] in reaching the

---

[79] *Prosecutor* v. *Milošević*, IT-02-54-T, Decision on Motion for Judgment of Acquittal, 16 June 2004, para. 49.

[80] In particular Von Schirach's conviction for deportation as a crime against humanity for his part in the removal of tens of thousands of Jews from Vienna to the "Ghetto of the East," ghettos in Poland: ibid., para. 50.

[81] Ibid., para. 51. The Chamber cited the following passage from the concurring opinion of Judge Philips in this Control Council Law No. 10 case: "Displacement of groups of persons from one country to another is the proper concern of international law in as far as it affects the community of nations. International law has enunciated certain conditions under which the fact of deportation of civilians from one nation to another during times of war becomes a crime ... [D]eportation of the population is criminal whenever there is no title in the deporting authority or whenever the purpose of the displacement is characterised by inhumane or illegal methods."

conclusion that the IMT dealt with deportation as a crime involving cross-border transfer.[82] While the Chamber's analysis is probably correct, there is no express reference in the IMT judgment to Poland in respect of Von Schirach's conviction, thus making it impossible to conclude with certainty that there was a cross-border element to the crime in that case. Further, while *Milch* generally supports the view that deportation requires a cross-border element, it was a Control Council Law No. 10 case with no impact on the IMT judgment.

In addressing displacement as a war crime, the *Milošević* Trial Chamber further noted Article 49 of Geneva Convention IV and Article 17 of Additional Protocol II to the Geneva Conventions, the latter building on the provisions of the former. It found that "although Additional Protocol II does not deal with the crimes of deportation and forcible transfer in express terms, Article 17, paragraph 1 may be construed as referring to forcible transfer within the territory of a state, *i.e.* internal displacement, and paragraph 2 may be interpreted as referring to deportation outside the territory of a state, *i.e.* external displacement."[83] The Chamber's interpretation of Article 17 seems to imply that forcible transfer is restricted to movements within the territory of a state, rather than applying to movements both within and outside a state. It is also noticeable that the Chamber did not declare that a violation of Article 17 of Additional Protocol II constitutes a crime in customary international law.

The Chamber's analysis continued with an acknowledgment of the cross-border requirement set out in the 1996 Draft Code, although without any reference as to the weight to be accorded to this source of law. Reviewing the jurisprudence of the ICTY, the Chamber found that *Stakić* was the only case in which transfer across national borders was not a requirement of the crime of deportation.[84] Finally, the Chamber addressed Article 7(2)(d) of the ICC Statute and, despite coming to the conclusion that "the terms deportation and forcible transfer appear to be given the same meaning," noted that one commentator took the view that

---

[82] Ibid., para. 52.
[83] Article 17 of Additional Protocol II reads in relevant part:

> (1) The displacement of the civilian population shall not be ordered for reasons related to the conflict unless the security of the civilians involved or imperative military reasons so demand . . .
> (2) Civilians shall not be compelled to leave their own territory for reasons connected to the conflict.

[84] *Milošević 98 bis Decision*, para. 64.

a distinction between the two crimes was intended, based on the cross-border element.[85] The Trial Chamber also cited two other commentators, involved in the preparatory work for the ICC Statute and Elements of Crimes, in support of the same assertion.[86] According to the Trial Chamber, the "correctness of this interpretation must be a matter of dispute, since it contradicts what appears to be the plain meaning of Article 7(2) (d)."[87] However, these views were later rejected by the ICC itself, which concluded that the two traditionally separate crimes were simply housed within one and the same provision of the ICC Statute without compromising their independent status.[88] The willingness to pronounce on the meaning of the ICC Statute does suggest, however, that this jurisprudential history is likely to inform legal analyses in all ranges of fora moving forward, including in landgrabbing cases if they ever come to pass.

The *Brđanin* Trial Judgment largely followed the conclusions set out in the *Milošević* 98 *bis* Decision. With respect to the issue of the cross-border requirement, the majority of the Trial Chamber supported the distinction that deportation requires a cross-border transfer whereas forcible transfer may consist of forced displacement within state borders.[89] The Trial Chamber considered the alternative approach supported in the *Stakić* case, but was "not convinced that this reflects customary international law as it stood at the relevant time. It is customary international law, and not policy, which the Trial Chamber is bound to apply."[90] Moreover, the Trial Chamber affirmed the position that "displacement within the boundaries of a State constitutes 'forcible transfer', punishable as 'other inhumane acts' pursuant to Article 5(i) of the Statute."[91] For both deportation and forcible transfer, the *Brđanin* Trial Judgment again found that the displacement must take place under coercion, a fact which may be established where the displacement is involuntary in nature and where the persons concerned had no real

---

[85] Ibid., para. 66, referring to Hall in Triffterer (ed.), 1999 (*supra* n. 32), p. 136.
[86] Ibid., referring to H. von Hebel and D. Robinson, "Crimes within the Jurisdiction of the Court," in R. Lee (ed.), *The International Criminal Court: The Making of the Rome Statute – Issues, Negotiations, Results* (Kluwer Law, 1999), p. 99 (stating that "Forcible transfer of population" was added as an alternative to "deportation" so as to encompass large-scale movements within a country's borders).
[87] Ibid., para. 67.
[88] Decision on the "Prosecution's Request for a Ruling on Jurisdiction under Article 19(3) of the Statute," ICC-RoC46(3)-01/18, 6 September 2018.
[89] Ibid., para. 540.
[90] Ibid., para. 542.
[91] Ibid., para. 544.

choice. In addition, it was again noted that the displacement must be unlawful[92] and that for both crimes the required intent is that the removal of the person or persons be permanent, although this latter aspect would later be overturned.[93]

The *Blaškić* Appeal Judgment's contribution to bringing clarity to the area was limited to assessing deportation as an act underlying persecution, charged under Article 5(h) of the Statute. Following a cursory review of the basis for the *Blaškić* Trial Chamber's conclusions, a survey of relevant provisions of Geneva Convention IV and the Additional Protocols, and reference to the *Krnojelac* Appeal Judgment, which had introduced the generic term "forcible displacement," the Appeals Chamber concluded that "at the time relevant to the Indictment in this case, deportation, forcible transfer, and forcible displacement constituted crimes of equal gravity to other crimes listed in Article 5 of the Statute and therefore could amount to persecutions as a crime against humanity."[94] While this conclusion added little to the debate, it was of note for its approach when considering deportation or forcible transfer as persecution. Although the *Krnojelac* Appeal Judgment had expressly avoided considering the underlying act of deportation as a crime, preferring instead the view that deportation had been charged in its "generic" sense, the *Blaškić* Appeals Chamber expressly considered the underlying act of deportation as a crime alongside forcible transfer and the generic term forcible displacement. As such, the *Blaškić* Appeals Judgment's reasoning was potentially significant in watering down the need for reliance on forcible displacement.

8.9 Confirmation

In the *Stakić* Appeal Judgment,[95] the ICTY Appeals Chamber was presented with another opportunity to provide clarity with respect to the crimes of deportation and forcible transfer as an other inhumane act. In this instance, the Appeals Chamber comprised a different set of judges from those who avoided the issue in the *Krnojelać* Appeal, and the recomposition evidently affected the willingness to address the complexity that had emerged in this area of law. To begin, the Appeals Chamber found that the Trial Chamber had erred in convicting Stakić of

---

[92] *Brđanin* Trial Judgment, para. 543.
[93] Ibid., para. 545.
[94] *Prosecutor v. Blaškić*, IT-94-14-A, Judgment, 29 July 2004, para. 153.
[95] *Prosecutor v. Stakić*, IT-97-24-A, Judgment, 22 March 2006.

deportation only as an act amounting to persecution and not separately for the crime of deportation. As a result, the *Stakić* Appeals Chamber concluded that the "question whether the Appellant should be liable for deportation as a crime against humanity is not moot,"[96] paving the way for a re-examination of the issue. In its analysis, the Appeals Chamber majority clearly set out the definition of deportation as a crime against humanity, stating that "[t]he *actus reus* of deportation is the forced displacement of persons by expulsion or other forms of coercion from the area in which they are lawfully present, across a *de jure* state border or, in certain circumstances, a *de facto* border, without grounds permitted under international law."[97]

Consistent with the emerging consensus, the Appeals Chamber thus found that there was a requirement of a cross-border transfer. In coming to this conclusion, the Chamber examined World War II-related jurisprudence,[98] the Geneva Conventions and Additional Protocols, the 1991 precursor to the 1996 ILC Draft Code of Crimes, the ICRC study on customary international law and the jurisprudence of the Tribunal.[99] Following this survey of relevant sources of law, the Appeals Chamber concluded that: (a) displacement requires the displacement of individuals across a border; (b) normally a *de jure* border is required but displacement across a *de facto* border may be sufficient in some circumstances; and (c) "whether a particular *de facto* border is sufficient for the purposes of the crime of deportation should be examined on a case by case basis in light of customary international law."[100] Thus, the Appeals Chamber definitively ruled that a cross-border transfer is necessary for the

---

[96] *Stakić* Appeal Judgment, para. 275.

[97] Ibid., para. 278. Judge Shahabuddeen dissented on the issue of deportation. See Partly Dissenting Opinion of Judge Shahabuddeen, pp. 149–67, para. 21, in which he sets out the arguments that "(i) that customary international law did not confine 'deportation' to the crossing of a border – rather, the crossing of a front line was enough, whether or not it was a border; (ii) that, even if customary international law always used the term 'deportation' in relation to the crossing of a border, the term was reasonably capable of applying to a front line; (iii) that in any event the question is how the Security Council used the term 'deportation' in article 5(d) of the Statute; (iv) that there can be a deportation even across a constantly changing front line; (v) that this view does not conflict with the principle *nullum crimen sine lege*; and (vi) that it accords with the substance of customary international law."

[98] Notably making a number of references to the IMT Judgment and referring to the Control Council Law No. 10 cases *United States of America* v. *Milch* and *United States of America* v. *Alfried Krupp et al*: see *Stakić* Appeal Judgment, paras. 290–1.

[99] See *Stakić* Appeal Judgment, paras. 288–99 for the Appeals Chamber's survey of the relevant law on this issue.

[100] *Stakić* Appeal Judgment, para. 300.

purposes of the crime of deportation. It further found on the facts of the case that the "constantly changing frontlines" at issue were not sufficient under customary international law to ground a conviction for deportation.[101]

The *Stakić* Appeal Judgment also addressed the requisite *mens rea* for deportation. In so doing, it questioned whether the ICRC Commentary on Article 49 of Geneva Convention IV should properly be interpreted as requiring intent to displace permanently.[102] On this issue, the Appeals Chamber departed from the majority of trial jurisprudence in finding that there is no requirement of intent to displace permanently. According to the Appeals Chamber, Article 49 of Geneva Convention IV makes no mention of the motive behind deportation. Dismissing a passage from the Commentaries to the Geneva Conventions that might suggest otherwise, the Appeals Chamber concluded that in the absence of any explicit indication that deportation required an intent to displace permanently, an intention to displace temporarily could still satisfy the elements of the offense. This interpretation has potentially far-reaching implications for a number of fields, including corporate practices that amount to what are colloquially known as landgrabbing. This jurisprudential turn away from previous case law, therefore, revealed the rise of new issues even as the basic approach to this class of crimes was solidifying.

Thus, the Appeals Chamber stood by its earlier judgments in providing what amounted to a definitive ruling with respect to deportation within the jurisprudence of the Tribunal. In fact, following the *Stakić* Appeal Judgment, the Tribunal shifted to applying the now-established framework, giving rise to a set of further issues discussed below.

8.10   Applying the Framework, Developing Nuance

If the *Stakić* Appeal Judgment finally brought a degree of clarity about the scope and intersection of deportation, unlawful transfer, forcible transfer, and forced displacement, this did not mark the end of interpretative controversies as new nuanced sub-areas emerged within the new normative

---

[101] *Stakić* Appeal Judgment, para. 303.
[102] The relevant passage in the Commentary states: "Unlike deportation and forcible transfers, evacuation is a provisional measure entirely negative in character, and is, moreover, often taken in the interests of the protected persons themselves." See ICRC Commentary (GC IV), p. 280.

framework. After *Stakić*, the Tribunal handed down approximately twenty-five further judgments on deportation and forcible transfer. These cases systematically upheld the cross-border requirement as the element distinguishing between deportation and forcible transfer, relying on the *Stakić* Appeal Judgment as authority for this proposition.[103] While this primary issue was thus resolved, ambiguities remained related to identifying the protected interests underlying the crimes, the requisite extent of removal from an area, and the ambit of de facto borders. All of these issues could well be relevant to cases against corporations and/or their representatives.

Addressing the interests protected by the crimes, the *Martić* Trial Judgment held that deportation and forcible transfer are similar precisely because they both protect "the right of victims to stay in their home and community and the right not to be deprived of their property by being forcibly displaced to another location."[104] The *Prlić* Appeal Chamber held not only that deportation and forcible transfer did protect the same interests, but also that criminal liability is attached solely to the fact that the victim was uprooted from their home, and not to their final destination.[105] This reasoning was unsubstantiated and seemingly challenged the core distinction between the two crimes as set out in the framework put in place by the *Stakić* Appeal Judgment. More recently, the ICC has rejected that view, finding that deportation and forcible transfer protect overlapping but distinct interests.[106] In my view, that position is easiest to reconcile with the structure of the framework the *Krnojelać* Appeals Chamber adopted after the long period of litigation I have documented.

With respect to the required extent of removal from an area, the *Prlić* Trial Chamber held that "[g]iven that the prohibition on forcible removals seeks to protect the right of individuals to live in their

[103] See e.g. *Popović* Trial Judgment, para. 892; *Mladić* Trial Judgment, para. 3118; *Gotovina* Trial Judgment, para. 1738; *Martić* Trial Judgment, para. 107; *Milutinović* Trial Judgment, para. 164; *Zuplijanin* Trial Judgment, para. 61; *Karadžić* Trial Judgment, para. 488; *Stanišić* Trial Judgment, para. 992; *Tolimir* Trial Judgment, para. 793. See also *Dordević* Trial Judgment (compare paras. 1604 on deportation and 1613 on forcible transfer).
[104] *Martić* Trial Judgment, para. 106.
[105] *Prlić* Appeal Judgment, para. 491 ("[t]he prohibition against forcible displacements aims at safeguarding the right and aspiration of individuals to live in their communities and homes without outside interference. The forced character of displacement and the forced uprooting of the inhabitants of a territory entail the criminal responsibility of the perpetrator, not the destination to which these inhabitants are sent," citing the appeal judgment in *Krnojelac*, para. 218). See also *Župlijanin* Trial Judgment, para. 60.
[106] Decision on the "Prosecution's Request for a Ruling on Jurisdiction under Article 19(3) of the Statute," ICC-RoC46(3)-01/18-37, para. 17.

communities and in their homes and not be deprived of their property," "there is a 'removal from an area' within the meaning of Article 5 of the Statute when the location to which the victims are sent is so remote that they are no longer able to effectively enjoy these rights."[107] The Appeals Chamber in this same case further specified that there is no distance requirement such that even transfers between detention centers might constitute forced displacement. Further, it clarified that that there is no size requirement for deportation or forcible transfer; even one victim suffices.[108]

With respect to de facto borders, most subsequent judgments confirmed the holding from the *Stakić* Appeal Judgment that deportation may take place "in certain circumstances, which must be examined on a case by case basis and in light of customary international law, [across] a de facto border." For example, the Appeals Chamber in *Đorđević* held that a de facto border suffices, depending on the facts of the case and customary international law.[109] However, not all judgments agreed on the type of de facto border that would fall into this category. In *Tolimir*, the Trial Chamber added an additional requirement that the de facto border be between states.[110] The *Prlić* Trial Chamber, on the basis that "by 'de facto border', the Appeals Chamber [in *Stakić*] had in mind forcible removal beyond occupied territory,"[111] found that the frontline between East and West Mostar constituted a de facto border for purposes of the war crime of unlawful deportation of civilians, without elaborating further.[112]

The most significant subsequent refinement on this issue took place in the *Đorđević* case, in which the Appeals Chamber examined whether the accused could be convicted of deportation from Kosovo to Montenegro.[113] At the relevant time, Kosovo was an autonomous province of the Republic of Yugoslavia, and Montenegro a constituent republic. Therefore, the Appeals Chamber held that at most there was a de facto border between Kosovo and Montenegro. After considering various sources, the Appeals Chamber concluded that the border between Kosovo and Montenegro did not constitute a de facto border for purposes of deportation, reasoning that the sources in question discuss deportation only from occupied territory

---

[107] *Prlić* Trial Judgment, para. 49, vol. 1.
[108] *Krajisnik* Appeal Judgment, para. 333.
[109] *Đorđević* Appeal Judgment, para. 532.
[110] *Tolimir* Trial Judgment, para. 793.
[111] *Prlić* Trial Judgment, para. 54, vol. 1.
[112] Ibid., para. 813, vol. 3.
[113] *Đorđević* Appeal Judgment, paras. 533–7.

228 RESPONSIBILITY OF WAR'S FUNDERS AND PROFITEERS

or across disputed borders, neither of which was at issue in *Đorđević*.[114] While not definitely resolving the question, the decision of the Appeals Chamber clearly narrowed the scope for what might constitute a de facto border for the purposes of deportation.

With respect to the crime of persecution, post-*Stakić* jurisprudence has retained the concept of "forcible displacement" to characterize all types of displacement charged as underlying acts. For example, the *Simić* Appeal Judgment found that "for the purposes of a persecutions conviction, it is not necessary to distinguish between the underlying acts of 'deportation' and 'forcible transfer' because the criminal responsibility of the accused is sufficiently captured by the general concept of forcible displacement." Most recently, the trial judgment in *Milutinović* held that "[a] number of elements of these offences are the same and are discussed herein under the heading 'forcible displacement.'"[115] While the logic behind this approach is questionable and it remains to be seen whether this approach will be carried over to other international courts, forcible displacement is a confirmed feature of the ICTY's interpretation of the customary international law framework for displacement-type crimes.

Subsequent case law has further explored the limits of the forced nature of displacement, solidifying the previous approach. In *Krajišnik*, the Appeals Chamber confirmed that coercive acts need not be physical and may include threats, psychological duress and abuse of power, as well as exploitation of an environment that is already coercive.[116] The *Milutinović* Trial Judgment confirmed that a lack of genuine choice may be inferred from "threatening and intimidating acts that are calculated to deprive the civilian population of exercising its free will, such as the shelling of civilian objects, the burning of civilian property, and the commission of or the threat to commit other crimes 'calculated to terrify the population and make them flee the area with no hope of return.'"[117] The same Trial Chamber found that alleged consent does not render the displacement voluntary if it is found that the circumstances surrounding

---

[114] Ibid., para. 535.

[115] *Milutinovic* Trial Judgment, para. 163.

[116] *Krajisnik* Appeal Judgment, paras, 759, 319. See also *Đorđević* Trial Judgment, para. 1605 (holding that non-physical types of coercion, such as threats and exploitation of an already coercive environment, suffice, and finding that whether consent is "real" and "voluntary" has to be assessed in light of the circumstances); *Perišić* Trial Judgment, para. 114 (holding "[f]ear of violence, duress, detention, psychological oppression, and other such circumstances may create an environment where there is no choice but to leave, thus amounting to the forced displacement of persons").

[117] *Milutinović* Trial Judgment, para. 165, citing the *Simić* Trial Judgment, para. 126.

the consent "deprive [it] of any value."[118] The Trial Chamber in *Đorđević* specified that non-physical coercion also includes making an area so inhospitable to live in that people have no choice but to leave.[119]

With respect to the *mens rea* element of displacement-type crimes, subsequent cases followed the holding in the *Stakić* Appeal Judgment that deportation does not require an intent to displace permanently.[120] In a further development, the *Milutinović* Trial Chamber expressly held that the relevant *mens rea* accords with the cross-border requirement, requiring "intent to displace . . . the victims within the relevant national border (as in forcible transfer) or across the relevant national border (as in deportation)."[121]

In sum, the cases since the *Stakić* Appeal Judgment have raised some important new normative issues, but have largely applied the established framework governing the relationships between deportation, unlawful transfer, forcible transfer and forced displacement.

8.11   Conclusions

In recent years, the ICC has placed new and important emphasis on one of the most litigated sets of crimes before the ICTY. By first announcing that it would consider pursuing what is colloquially known as "land-grabbing" as part of its prosecutorial strategy, then employing deportation as a basis for asserting jurisdiction over offenses that occur in non-state parties if they result in displacement to state parties, the ICC has effectively made displacement crimes a central component of its work moving forward. Both of these developments have important implications for corporations and their representatives. Moreover, at a certain level, this reality should be unsurprising; displacement crimes were a central aspect of the "ethnic cleansing" the ICTY was called to address and are a recurrent feature of atrocities the world over. It stands to reason, therefore, that a jurisprudential history of the ICTY's treatment of these crimes is an initial first step in plotting how commerce interfaces with these offenses. This reality is all the more true when the various displacement offenses addressed at the ICTY have involved such a long

---

[118] Ibid.

[119] *Popović* Trial Judgment, para. 917.

[120] For example, see *Đorđević* Trial Judgment, para. 1604; *Milutinović* Trial Judgment, para. 164, citing *Martić* Trial Judgment, para. 111 and *Stakić* Trial Judgment, paras. 278, 307, 317.

[121] *Milutinović* Trial Judgment, para. 164.

and complex interpretative history. In this chapter, I have provided a chronological overview of this history in the hope that it informs businesses, judges, and lawyers about the scope of these crimes, and that it influences debates about the merits of using these offenses to address one area where economic interests enable atrocities.

The crimes' jurisprudential history is complex. As I have shown, early attempts at defining displacement crimes at the ICTY drew on a range of sources, including the work of the ILC and the ICC Statute, to define the offenses in broad, largely undifferentiated terms. Soon thereafter, the Tribunal undertook a more rigorous process focused on defining the precise meaning of the offenses in customary international law. This analysis was brought about by the need to ascertain whether deportation and forcible transfer were largely indistinguishable in that they shared a single legal meaning, or whether a destination requirement separated the two, meaning that deportation required expulsion across a border whereas forcible displacement did not. Simultaneously, the overlap between war crimes and crimes against humanity, and, in the ICTY's instance, the need to charge forcible transfer as an "other inhumane act" because of the absence of an explicit reference to the term in the ICTY Statute, added further layers of legal complexity. Then, an emerging set of answers to these questions was temporarily stalled when the *Stakić* Trial Judgment adopted a radical new approach, amalgamating forcible transfer and deportation into a single offense out of a concern about the overreach of "other inhumane acts."

Initially, the confusion this about-turn brought about was exacerbated by a decision of the Appeals Chamber to avoid the controversy. At first, instead of adjudicating whether the about-turn was justified, the Appeals Chamber avoided the issue by creating a new category it called "forcible displacement," which it used to describe acts of expulsion in the context of the crime against humanity of persecution. The resulting disarray left Trial Chambers then a reconstituted Appeals Chamber to bring a degree of interpretative order back to the area by carefully distinguishing the underlying crimes, overturning *Stakić*, and instituting a framework that defined deportation as involving a cross border element. Once this framework was set, the Tribunal set about applying this much-litigated understanding of displacement crimes in a range of cases thereafter, thereby reaffirming the new consensus while simultaneously raising a range of new, more nuanced controversies. These new controversies ranged from further debate about whether the border requirement for deportation would require a *de jure* border, or whether and when a de facto border might suffice, to questions about whether victims were consenting to their relocation. All in all, this long jurisprudential history marks a set of issues that are hopefully settled as well as others that will certainly resurface with time.

An understanding about the relationships among commerce, atrocity, and international criminal law (ICL) is still emerging. In many quarters, there is a perception that complicity is the one and only aspect of ICL that gives rise to potentially serious criminal responsibility of businesspeople and their corporations, but this notion misconceives the full scope of ICL, in this instance, by overlooking the ways in which different international crimes impact corporate actors. Although this chapter has not offered a comprehensive history of displacement crimes across all international and national courts, let alone attempted to plot the relationship between displacement crimes and corporate roles in landgrabbing, it has offered a first articulation of the history of the crimes that will likely cover these practices. My aspiration is that those involved in thinking about the phenomenon of landgrabbing, and indeed about the role of displacement crimes more broadly, will find in this history a series of interpretations worth emulating as well as others that should not be repeated.

The International Responsibility of War Profiteers for Trafficking in Persons

MICHAEL RAMSDEN

9.1 Introduction

War often promotes the 'ideal' conditions for traffickers to exploit vulnerable civilians for profit, including human displacement, economic desperation, and erosion of the rule of law. Some militia will use human trafficking as a means to fund their military campaign or efforts at state building, whereas others, being private profiteers not affiliated to any side of the conflict, will act simply to take advantage of the situations of vulnerability arising out of war.[1] Trafficking in persons profiteers vary in size and composition: from small-scale criminal enterprises (as well as economically vulnerable family members) to large state-like entities that control territory (such as the Islamic State of Iraq and the Levant (ISIL), Boko Haram, Al-Shabaab, and the Lord's Resistance Army).

Not all acts of trafficking during war are in pursuit of profit, although it remains an important underlying factor. There has been increasing scholarly attention on ascertaining the political and economic incentives which have been driving the trafficking in persons 'markets'.[2] In this regard, trafficking may further other ends than profit, being used as a 'weapon of war', such as with the ethnic cleansing or rape of civilian populations in the Balkans in the 1990s, or as a means to use exploited persons towards the war effort, as with the recruitment of child soldiers

---

[1] For recent examples of such practices, see e.g. International Centre for Migration Policy Development, *Targeting Vulnerabilities: The Impact of the Syrian War and Refugee Situation on Trafficking in Persons* (Vienna, 2015).

[2] For a recent study of this nature, see E. Saville, *Human Trafficking as a Weapon of War: Sudan* (LAP Lambert, 2016).

and use of forced labour in numerous conflicts.[3] Trafficking in persons may also be used as 'part of the strategic objectives and ideology of . . . certain terrorist groups'.[4] Not all trafficking can thus be attributed to 'greedy' profiteering, although there is clearly a need to consider the link between trafficking and profit during conflict. As this literature develops, it will lend insight into the scale of the problem facing states and international institutions in addressing the connection between war economics and trafficking in persons.

In doing so, concerned actors will require an effective response, particularly as this issue has now commanded the attention of the International Criminal Court (ICC). The Office of the Prosecutor (OTP) noted in its Policy Paper on Sexual and Gender-Based Crimes that it 'has elevated this issue to one of its key strategic goals'.[5] Building on this commitment, the Prosecutor in May 2017 indicated that she would be examining the 'credible accounts that Libya has become a marketplace for the trafficking of human beings'.[6] As international prosecutions are contemplated, it is therefore timely to consider the applicable legal framework that gives rise to the international criminal responsibility for trafficking in persons, with particular reference to norms under the ICC Statute. Accordingly, this will clearly have implications for war profiteers who are engaged in such trafficking practices. This chapter will consider this question with an examination of the legal frameworks of international humanitarian law (IHL) and international criminal law (ICL).

The assumption underpinning this analysis is that there is benefit in characterising trafficking in persons as a crime that gives rise to international responsibility for its perpetrators. Much of the efforts at forging a proscription of such trafficking practices so far have concentrated on securing state compliance and, even then, the requirements on states have been to criminalise trafficking as an 'ordinary' crime, with its distinguishing feature being that it sometimes occurs 'transnationally'.[7]

---

[3] See e.g. R. Friman and S. Reich, *Human Trafficking, Human Security and the Balkans* (University of Pittsburgh Press, 2008); S. Tiefenbrun, 'Child Soldiers, Slavery and the Trafficking of Children' (2007) 31 *Fordham International Law Journal* 415.

[4] UN Security Council Resolution 2331 (2016), Preamble.

[5] ICC Office of the Prosecutor, *Policy Paper on Sexual and Gender-Based Crimes*, 20 June 2014, para. 2.

[6] ICC, Statement of ICC Prosecutor to the UNSC on the Situation in Libya, 9 May 2017, www.icc-cpi.int/pages/item.aspx?name=170509-otp-stat-lib.

[7] See in particular the Protocol to Prevent, Suppress and Punish Trafficking in Persons, Especially Women and Children, Supplementing the United Nations Convention Against Transnational Organised Crime 2000 ('Trafficking Protocol'), Article 5 (which creates

Acknowledging that trafficking can give rise to international criminal responsibility can in turn provide the impetus to exert pressure on states to prosecute offenders under the framework of IHL/ICL. Institutionally, too, a change of impetus, such as in the United Nations Security Council (UNSC) acknowledging that trafficking in persons can give rise to international responsibility as a facet of a war crime, could in turn help build momentum in support of future referrals to the ICC.[8] Furthermore, by drawing a conceptual link between trafficking in persons and international crimes, it provides the impetus for argument that such conduct is of a gravity and magnitude that support universal prosecution and repression, and with this, the exercise of universal jurisdiction by concerned states.

While it is valuable to characterise trafficking in persons as an international crime, it should also be acknowledged that the prosecution of traffickers is amongst a range of strategies available to states and international organisations to combat the impunity of such practices. In this regard, the investigation of trafficking in persons during armed conflict has been linked to UN recommendations to promulgate national legislation to address a variety of trafficking activities and financial crimes, including anti-money-laundering, anti-corruption and anti-bribery laws, and, where appropriate, counter-terrorism laws.[9] At the international institutional level, one possible area for future extension of the UN sanctions regimes is to known traffickers. Thus, the Security Council noted that any persons or entities that transfer funds to ISIL 'in connection with such exploitation and abuse would be eligible for listing' by the sanctions committee.[10] Moreover, it also expressed an intention to consider 'targeted sanctions for individuals and entities involved in trafficking in persons in areas affected by armed conflict and in sexual violence in conflict'.[11] In 2018, these were issued for the first time by the Security Council against six wealthy individuals allegedly responsible for human

---

a requirement that states make criminal offences the conduct outlined previously in Article 3 but does not refer to such conduct as amounting to any of the core international crimes).

[8] Indeed, there is some evidence of correlation between the characterisation of a situation (as amounting to 'crimes') and subsequent action by the Security Council: M. Ramsden and T. Hamilton, 'Uniting against Impunity: The UN General Assembly as a Catalyst for Action at the ICC' (2017) 66(4) *International and Comparative Law Quarterly* 893, 897–900.

[9] UN Security Council Resolution 2331 (2016), para. 2.

[10] Ibid., Preamble.

[11] Ibid., para. 12.

trafficking from Libya.[12] There are, then, a range of measures available to address the financing and profiteering from trafficking in persons during armed conflict; but the focus here will be on establishing the foundations for the proposition that such activities can in fact give rise to international criminal responsibility.

Accordingly, this chapter is structured in three parts. It will first provide a survey of existing sources of IHL and ICL to identify correlates between these norms and the internationally accepted definition of trafficking in persons. It will then move on to consider the scope to prosecute trafficking in persons as a crime against humanity under Article 7 of the Rome Statute establishing the ICC (ICC Statute). A focus on this provision is warranted given that it is the first in the history of ICL/IHL to explicitly acknowledge that 'trafficking in persons' can give rise to international responsibility. Finally, the chapter will consider some of the common obstacles to securing prosecutions that arise both domestically and internationally, with particular reference to the ICC.

9.2 Surveying the Legal Framework for Trafficking in Persons during Armed Conflict

There is little doubt that some of the most abhorrent practices of armed conflict can be characterised as falling within the internationally agreed legal definition of trafficking, if not in whole then at least in part. In particular, the 'Trafficking Protocol' defines trafficking in persons to comprise three elements.[13] The first is that the perpetrator takes action, being the 'recruitment, transportation, transfer, harbouring or receipt of persons'. Second, that the perpetrator adopts one of a number of means, being any of 'the threat or use of force or other forms of coercion, of abduction, of fraud, of deception, of the abuse of power or of a position of vulnerability or of the giving or receiving of payments or benefits to achieve the consent of a person having control over another person'. Finally, the trafficking activities must be taken for the purpose of 'exploitation', which 'shall include, at a minimum, the exploitation of the prostitution of others or other forms of sexual exploitation, forced labour or services, slavery or practices similar to slavery, servitude or the

---

[12] See further documents in UN Security Council, Security Council Committee established pursuant to resolution 1970 (2011) concerning Libya, www.un.org/securitycouncil/sanctions/1970.

[13] Trafficking Protocol (*supra* n. 7), Article 3.

removal of organs'. It is apparent on its face that many acts of criminality perpetrated during armed conflict, including those for profit, such as the forced labour of civilians and sexual exploitation of women and girls, would satisfy the elements of 'action', 'means' and 'purpose' set out in the Trafficking Protocol.

It is perhaps surprising, therefore, that human trafficking generally finds no clear and explicit prohibition either in IHL or in ICL. None of the IHL conventions provides any mention of 'trafficking in persons', nor do contemporary international studies into customary IHL.[14] The United Nations General Assembly, an important incubator for norm formation, has similarly failed, so far, to clearly define trafficking as an international crime.[15] The clearest reference to a prohibition is provided in Article 7(2)(c) of the Rome Statute where, in defining the crime against humanity of enslavement, it notes this to mean 'the exercise of any or all of the powers attaching to the right of ownership over a person and *includes* the exercise of such power *in the course of trafficking in persons, in particular women and children'*. Whether this means that trafficking can be prosecuted generally (the broad view) or only within the parameters of the crime of enslavement (the narrow – and textually consistent – view) remains an open question until it is resolved at the ICC. The drafting of the Rome Statute reveals an unsuccessful attempt by civil society to delineate trafficking as an independent crime against humanity so as to draw a clearer division between slavery and the practices that trafficking entails, such as systematic recruitment and forced labour.[16] Given this, the most appropriate focus is therefore in defining the

---

[14] See e.g. International Committee of the Red Cross, *Customary International Humanitarian Law* (Cambridge University Press, 2009).

[15] See e.g. UN General Assembly Res. 72/1 (2017), para. 4 (where the plenary reiterated that trafficking in persons 'constitutes a crime' but did not specify whether this was 'transnational' or 'international' in character). Although the Security Council has done so in relation to established international crimes, see Resolution 2331 (2016), Preamble ('*nders-coring* that certain acts or offences associated with trafficking in persons in the context of armed conflict may constitute war crimes . . .').

[16] The Advocacy Project, *On the Record: Your Link to the Rome Conference for the Establishment of an International Criminal Court* 1(14), 7 July 1998, www .advocacynet.org/wp-content/uploads/2015/06/Issue-14-ICC.pdf. (Specifically, it noted: 'Women's groups welcome the fact that the Italian proposal would make a specific reference to women and children, but they feel it would be much stronger if it was separated from enslavement and was broader than sexual exploitation. Human rights groups feel that trafficking includes a broad range of slavery and slavery-like practices, including systematic recruitment and forced labor. The women's groups also object to the wording "the right of ownership."')

parameters of enslavement to ascertain whether it is indeed broad enough to cover all aspects of the trafficking in persons definition. Before doing so, it is also important not to focus the enquiry too narrowly on finding a textually explicit criminal prohibition of trafficking in persons in the IHL and ICL instruments. It is readily apparent that these instruments do, albeit in different forms and manifestations, contain various proscriptions that correspond to aspects of the three-part definition in Article 3 of the Trafficking Protocol. In this sense, the description 'trafficking in persons', while not formally relevant in the application of IHL and ICL instruments, offers a useful analytical tool and method to draw connections between a variety of international jurisprudence, and instruments, in response to exploitative practices that derive from systems of human trafficking.

First, the different forms of 'exploitation' rooted in the trafficking in persons definition – namely, sexual exploitation, forced labour, slavery, and the removal of organs – give rise to criminal responsibility in multiple IHL and ICL instruments, as well as in customary international law.[17] The nuances of such proscriptions differ slightly depending on whether such exploitative practices are framed as an element of a war crime, crimes against humanity or genocide, or indeed whether they occur during an international or non-international armed conflict.[18] Still, there is a general recognition that such exploitative practices are crimes. The ICC Statute, in this respect, criminalises sexual exploitation in various guises, which include sexual slavery, enforced prostitution, forced pregnancy, and enforced sterilisation.[19] The role of the ICC and ad hoc tribunals in developing more precise standards for addressing instances of exploitation in armed conflict must also be acknowledged, especially with respect to sexual exploitation.[20] Indeed, the scope for

[17] See generally ICRC (*supra* n. 14).
[18] Compare, for e.g., the elements of the war crime of enforced prostitution and the crime against humanity of sexual slavery (the former not requiring it to be proven that the perpetrator exercised 'any or all of the powers attaching to the right of ownership over one or more persons': ICC Elements of Crime, Articles 71(g)(2), 8(2)(b)(xxii).
[19] ICC Statute, Articles 7(1)(g), 8(2)(b)(xxii).
[20] These landmark cases include *Bemba* Appeal Judgment, ICC-01/05-01/08 A, 8 June 2018 (rape as a crime against humanity); *Kunarac* Appeal Judgment, IT-96-23, Appeals Chamber, 12 June 2002 (sexual enslavement and rape as crime against humanity); *Krstić* Trial Judgment, IT-98-33-T, 19 April 2001 (connection between rape and ethnic cleansing); *Mucić* Trial Judgment, IT-96-21-T, 16 November 1998 (rape as torture); *Tadić* Trial Judgment, IT-94-1-T, 7 May 1997 (first trial for sexual violence against men). See further S. Brammertz and M. Jarvis (eds.), *Prosecuting Conflict-Related Sexual Violence at the ICTY* (Oxford University Press, 2016).

evolution is partly made possible by the incorporation of broad provisions to provide some degree of interpretive latitude to embrace 'modern'
forms of exploitation, as with Article 7(1)(k) of the ICC Statute, which
includes 'other inhumane acts' as a crime against humanity. Most
recently, the ICC Pre-Trial Chamber II, in confirming charges in
Ongwen, regarded the practice of 'forced marriage' to constitute an
'other inhumane act', with the fact that the marriage is 'factually imposed
on the victim, with the consequent social stigma' being an important
consideration for its inclusion as an Article 7(1)(k) crime.[21]

Second, there are also crimes that are analogous to trafficking in
persons in relation to the 'action' element of the definition in the
Trafficking Protocol (which includes 'recruitment, transportation, transfer, harbouring or receipt of persons'). In various instruments, it is
prohibited to forcibly 'transfer' or 'deport' a civilian,[22] and to 'enlist'
children into the armed forces.[23] In this regard, some crimes focus only
on the conduct of state actors, such as the crime against humanity of
'enforced disappearance', carried out with the authorisation, support or
acquiescence of a state or political organisation.[24] By contrast, no such
link to a state is required for 'forcible transfer'.[25] But 'action' that is akin
to those contained in the Trafficking Protocol may also be found in
accessorial modes of liability in instruments such as the ICC Statute,
where an individual can bear responsibility for facilitating the commission of a crime and 'aids, abets or otherwise assists in its commission or
its attempted commission, including providing the means for its
commission'.[26] Thus, for example, if an individual knowingly transferred
a victim of trafficking to a destination where they were to be subsequently
subject to enslavement or sexual exploitation, then the act of transfer
would constitute a form of aid or assistance to these underlying
offences.[27] Similarly, concepts such as joint criminal enterprise enable

---

[21] *Ongwen* (Decision on the confirmation of charges), Pre-Trial Chamber II, ICC-02/04-01/
15, 23 March 2016, paras. 87–95.

[22] ICC Statute, Articles 6(e), 7(1)(d), 8(2)(a)(vii), 8(2)(b)(viii); Fourth Geneva Convention,
Article 49(1). See also IMT Charter (Nuremberg) Art. 6(b) ('deportation to slave labour or
for any other purpose of civilian population of or in occupied territory constitutes a war
crime').

[23] ICC Statute, Articles 8(2)(b)(xxvi), 8(2)(e)(vii).

[24] ICC Elements of Crime, Article 7(1)(i).

[25] Ibid., Article 8(2)(a)(vii).

[26] ICC Statute, Article 25(3)(c).

[27] The requirement is that the act 'significantly facilitated the perpetration of the crime':
ICTY, *Krstić* Trial Judgment, 19 April 2001, para. 601.

a link to be drawn between such forms of action and the exploitative conduct that is criminalised, where a common purpose between the various parties can be established.[28]

Third, it is apparent that the 'means' specified in the Trafficking Protocol also form part of the elements of many international crimes linked to exploitation, particularly in exerting coercion over another. In this regard, it is apparent that many international crimes include in their elements the use or threat of force, or coercion. For example, the crime against humanity of forcible transfer is defined as the 'forced displacement of the persons concerned by expulsion or *other* coercive acts from the area in which they are lawfully present, without grounds permitted under international law'.[29] Indeed, the ICC Elements of Crimes define 'forcibly' as not being limited to physical force but including the threat of force or coercion, such as that caused by fear of violence, duress, detention, psychological oppression or abuse of power against such person or persons or another person, or by taking advantage of a coercive environment.[30] This raises a sub-issue as to the relevance of consent where such means are established. The exercise of the 'rights of ownership' inherently renders consent irrelevant to the crimes of enslavement and sexual slavery.[31] Similarly, consent to sexual intercourse is also irrelevant where it is proven that the perpetrator used force, threatened it, or otherwise took advantage of a coercive environment.[32] Outside of such acts or environment, consent appears to bear some relevance to the crimes of rape, enforced prostitution or sexual violence under the ICC Statute, in that the court is directed to consider whether the bodily invasion was committed against a person 'incapable of giving genuine consent'.[33] By contrast, consent will never be relevant for the crime of mutilation (including organ removal) under the ICC Statute, as is also true in relation to the prohibition against the removal of organs under the Trafficking Protocol.[34] Therefore, there is some correspondence between the 'means' in the Trafficking Protocol and instruments such as the ICC

---

[28] For an explication of the relevant principles, see L.Marsh and M. Ramsden, 'Joint Criminal Enterprise: Cambodia's Reply to *Tadić*' (2011) 11(1) *International Criminal Law Review* 137.

[29] ICC Statute, Article 7(2)(d). Emphasis added.

[30] Elements of Crimes, Article 7(1)(d), note 12.

[31] See e.g. *Kunarac* (Appeal), IT-96-23, Appeals Chamber, 12 June 2002, para 120; *Kunarac* (Judgment), IT-96-23 and IT-96-23/1-T, Trial Chamber, 22 February 2001, para. 542.

[32] *Bemba* (Judgment), ICC-01/05-01/08, Trial Chamber, paras. 105–6.

[33] Elements of Crimes, Article 7(1)(g)1–3, 6.

[34] ICC Statute, Article 8(2)(b)(x), note 46; Trafficking Protocol, Article 3(b).

Statute, the latter rendering consent irrelevant in many instances 'on the basis that such a requirement would, in most cases, undermine efforts to bring perpetrators to justice'.[35]

It can therefore be said with some caution that the contemporary international criminal law of trafficking in persons can be constructed from multiple instruments and principles forged over many decades of state and judicial practice. That said, it is clear that the existing IHL/ICL framework does not capture every aspect of the law of trafficking in persons. For example, to establish the war crime of 'deportation' it is necessary for the victim to be lawfully present in the state where the act occurred, which is unproblematic in most cases but is of concern where the victim is stateless or entered illegally.[36] More generally, trafficking can be prosecuted only where the general requirements of these crimes are established: for war crimes, for example, being the existence of an international or non-international armed conflict. This inevitably limits the scope for the prosecution of trafficking (at least as international crimes) and has led some authors to argue for trafficking in persons to become a separate core international crime so as to be free from the doctrinal constraints of the other core crimes.[37] This is ultimately a question for states as to whether they seek to forge international agreement on a new core crime; however, the opportunity to do so presented itself at the Rome Conference without success, with human trafficking being subsumed under the crime against humanity of enslavement.[38] This raises the question of whether and to what extent doing so limits the possibility of trafficking in persons being prosecuted in the future under the ICC Statute, to which this chapter now turns.

9.3 Trafficking in Persons as a Crime Against Humanity Under the Rome Statute

The inclusion of the phrase 'trafficking in persons' in the Rome Statute, set against the above framework, is significant in offering the first

---

[35] *Bemba* (Judgment), para. 105.
[36] *Stakić* (Appeal), IT-97-24-A, Appeals Chamber, 22 March 2006, para. 278.
[37] C. F. Moran, 'Human Trafficking and the Rome Statute of the International Criminal Court' 3 *The Age of Human Rights Journal* (December 2014) 32.
[38] See further J. Kim, 'Prosecuting Human Trafficking as a Crime against Humanity Under the Rome Statute', *Columbia Law School Gender and Sexuality Online* (2011), http://blogs .law.columbia.edu/gslonline/files/2011/02/Jane-Kim_GSL_Prosecuting-Human-Trafficking -as-a-Crime-Against-Humanity-Under-the-Rome-Statute-2011.pdf.

recognition that this practice could directly give rise to international criminal responsibility. It is thus relevant to consider the possible scope of this provision and the responsibility of war profiteers who engage in trafficking. Technically, as noted, it is incorrect to assert that trafficking in persons can be generally prosecuted; rather, Article 7(2) simply foresees that the act of trafficking in persons can be a vehicle for the exercise of a power attaching to the right of ownership of the kind to amount to enslavement (the phrase 'includes in the exercise of such power' in Article 7(2) seems to make this clear).[39] Similarly, while Article 7(2) has in mind exploitative practices against a particular set of victims (i.e. women and children), this is not exclusively so (as the words 'in particular' establishes). The core issue, rather, is what constitutes 'enslavement' and, in turn, whether this would limit the scope of the trafficking in person offences that can be prosecuted under Article 7(2). On its face, this would appear to be the case: enslavement, after all, is a form of exploitation embraced by the trafficking definition, but it is by no means the only one. Conversely, the issue is whether the enslavement definition in Article 7(2) is sufficiently malleable to incorporate trafficking as a wider legal concept. Furthermore, it must also be considered whether the structure of a crime against humanity also necessarily limits the forms of human trafficking that can be prosecuted, and the ability to prosecute those who profit from trafficking.

9.3.1 Trafficking as Enslavement

In this regard, the formulation in Article 7(2) that defines enslavement as 'exercise of any or all of the powers attaching to the right of ownership over a person' provides a clear reference and link to the definition of slavery as contained in the Slavery Convention 1926. The limitation of such a definition is that it is linked to complete 'ownership' rather than 'exploitation' as such, evidenced by the showing of an 'intent to reduce persons to slavery'.[40] The Slavery Convention thus was focused on permanent ownership over persons and did not cover more volatile

---

[39] A. Gallagher, *The International Law of Human Trafficking* (Cambridge University Press, 2010), p. 216.

[40] Article 1(2), Slavery Convention. In this regard, the Trafficking Protocol differentiates itself from the Slavery Convention by focusing the requisite intention on exploitation rather than ownership as such, of which see Article 3.

activities to acquire benefits from the temporary commercial exploitation of persons.[41] Seen in this light, the idea of 'ownership' in Article 7(2) would seem to place a more stringent standard than is applicable under the Trafficking Protocol, which is focused on the 'control over the other person, for the purposes of exploitation' rather than ownership.[42] Of course, the subsequent exploitation of trafficking victims can easily be regarded as slavery because the right of ownership will then be fully exercised and retained when such victim is exploited in their place of destination.[43] But at least in terms of the traditional definition of slavery, 'ownership' is not necessarily exercised by traffickers who are engaged in the transportation and trading of victims. However, there are at least two reasons why this interpretation of Article 7(2) should be rejected.

First, it is apparent that the text of the Rome Statute also references modern instruments that address exploitative practices known as 'modern' forms of slavery. In this regard, the accompanying notes to the ICC Elements of Crimes also explain that the concept of 'deprivation of liberty' in Article 7(2) 'may in some circumstances, include exacting forced labour or otherwise reducing a person to a servile status' as defined in the 1956 Supplementary Slavery Convention: this instrument includes debt bondage, forced marriage, child exploitation and serfdom as acts that might constitute 'deprivations of liberty'.[44] Furthermore, the reference to 'trafficking' in Article 7(2) should be read in line with the accepted definition in international law: while the Trafficking Protocol took effect after the Rome Statute, it offers an authoritative contemporary definition of trafficking to encompass 'modern' forms of slavery that are not limited to chattel slavery, as seen above.

Second, the ICTY Trial Chamber in *Kunarac* considered at length the nature of enslavement as a crime against humanity, embracing an interpretation that went beyond traditional slavery to including trafficking in

---

[41] H. van der Wilt, 'Trafficking in Human Beings, Enslavement, Crimes against Humanity: Unravelling the Concepts' (2014) 13 *Chinese Journal of International Law* 297, 301; N. Boister, *An Introduction to Transnational Criminal Law* (Oxford University Press, 2012), p. 40: 'The requirement in both the 1926 Slavery Convention and the 1956 Supplementary Convention that slave trade be carried out with "an intent to reduce persons to slavery" was difficult to meet when the trafficker's purpose was temporary commercial exploitation, not ownership.'

[42] Trafficking Protocol (*supra* n. 7), Article 3.

[43] T. Obokata, 'Trafficking of Human Beings as a Crime against Humanity: Some Implications for the International Legal System' (2005) 54(2) *International and Comparative Law Quarterly* 445, 449.

[44] ICC Elements of Crimes, Article 8(2)(b)(xxii)2, note 53.

persons.[45] *In Kunarac*, the defendants were charged with the rape and enslavement of Muslim women whom they had detained for six months for their own sexual gratification. The Trial Chamber held that 'enslavement as a crime against humanity' might be 'broader than the traditional and sometimes apparently distinct definitions of slavery, the slave trade and servitude or forced or compulsory labour found in other areas of international law'.[46] The Trial Chamber proceeded to identify a number of examples of exploitation, including 'the exaction of forced or compulsory labour or service, often without remuneration and often, though not necessarily, involving physical hardship, sex, prostitution and human trafficking'.[47] It also noted the irrelevance of consent, the use or threat of force and the purpose of exploitation, aspects that resemble the definition of trafficking set out in the Trafficking Protocol.[48]

While the crime against humanity of 'enslavement' encompasses modern forms of slavery, including human trafficking, it still raises some questions about the responsibility of traffickers at different stages of the supply chain, be it those individuals who engage in buying, selling or otherwise trading in persons. This will turn on the judicial construction of 'rights of ownership' in Article 7(2) and whether it covers all the activities of trafficking (be it the 'recruitment, transportation, transfer, harbouring or receipt of persons' as noted in the Trafficking Protocol). Traffickers, in this regard, come in different forms. Some might engage in the trading of victims as 'agents' but have not subjected victims to deprivation of liberty in the sense of holding them in detention facilities. There are also traffickers who actually detain or transport victims for varying lengths of time for their subsequent sale to a third party. Traffickers therefore exercise varying degrees of ownership/control over victims such that it raises an issue whether all such trafficking perpetrators can be responsible for the crime against humanity of enslavement.

In this regard, establishing responsibility for traffickers is a question of establishing the point at which it could be said that they exercised a 'right of ownership' over another.[49] The ICC Elements of Crime provide

---

[45] *Kunarac* Trial Judgment, para. 542.
[46] Ibid.
[47] Ibid.
[48] Van de Wilt (*supra* n. 41) 305.
[49] *Kunarac* Appeal Judgment, para. 117. ('In the case of these various contemporary forms of slavery, the victim is not subject to the exercise of the more extreme rights of ownership associated with "chattel slavery", but in all cases, as a result of the exercise of any or all of

further elucidation on the meaning of 'right of ownership', which includes 'purchasing, selling, lending or bartering such a person or persons, or by imposing on them a similar deprivation of liberty'.[50] Some might suggest, on the basis of this definition, that the transactional aspects of trafficking alone would suffice to establish an exercise of the right of ownership. However, this definition is qualified by the final clause, being the imposition of 'a similar deprivation of liberty'. This suggests that the trafficker deprived the victims of their physical liberty in addition to engaging in one or more of the transactions listed (i.e. 'purchasing, selling, lending or bartering').

This interpretation seems to be consistent with the Trial Chamber's approach in *Kunarac*, which noted that the 'mere ability to buy, sell, trade or inherit a person or his or her labours or services could be a relevant factor'.[51] The Trial Chamber further noted that the 'control of someone's movement, control of physical environment, psychological control, measures taken to prevent or deter escape' are important indicia of enslavement.[52] Similarly, the duration of the powers attaching to the right of ownership can also be taken into account 'when determining whether someone was enslaved'.[53] These statements imply that the mere transactional aspects of trafficking would not constitute enslavement where they are not accompanied with any corresponding deprivation of liberty.[54] Again, where both elements are present (the transaction and deprivation of liberty), such perpetrators would fall within Article 7(2); but this crime would appear to exclude those who engage purely in the transactional aspects of trafficking in persons, such as agents.[55]

the powers attaching to the right of ownership, there is some destruction of the juridical personality; the destruction is greater in the case of "chattel slavery" but the difference is one of degree.')

[50] ICC Elements of Crime, Article 7(1)(c). See further D. Robinson, 'The Elements for Crimes against Humanity', in R. S. Lee (ed.), *The International Criminal Court: Elements of Crimes and Rules of Procedure and Evidence* (Transnational Publishers, 2001), ch. 4, pp. 57, 85.

[51] *Kunarac* Trial Judgment, para. 543.

[52] Ibid, para. 541.

[53] Ibid, para. 543.

[54] Obokata (*supra* n. 43), 449.

[55] An alternative way to construct trafficking as an international crime is as 'other inhumane acts' under Article 7(1)(k). Such acts must be similar in character to those outlined in Article 7 and involve the intentional causing of great suffering or serious injury to body or to mental or physical health. In this respect, Article 7(1)(k) might be used to address suffering to victims as a result of trafficking not otherwise covered by the crime of enslavement. This might include, for example, the inhumane conditions that trafficking victims are subject to as a result of travelling in overcrowded trucks and shipping

9.3.2   Crime Against Humanity Elements and Human Trafficking

In addition to the limitations imposed in defining trafficking within the framework of enslavement, further limits are placed by the contextual elements of the crime.[56] In this respect, it is the elements pertaining to the definition of 'widespread or systematic attack' and the need for there to be a 'State or organisational policy' that poses some challenges in relation to the prosecution of trafficking in persons (or indeed the extent to which such offence can be prosecuted).

The first issue, then, is whether trafficking in persons can be regarded as a 'widespread or systematic attack', being disjunctive concepts albeit often impractical to separate.[57] It is apparent from ICC and ad hoc jurisprudence that 'widespread' refers to a large-scale attack directed at a multiplicity of victims.[58] This test would likely preclude many acts of trafficking, which, while planned, may not have occurred on such a scale, given that most traffickers typically run small-scale operations that traffic in victims totalling in the dozens rather than thousands (a victim count that is more typical in the international tribunals). That said, much depends on how the trafficking market in a given situation is constructed; if the actions of one small-scale trafficking profiteer can be linked to a broader trafficking market, and actors within it, through the doctrines of joint or accomplice liability, then this would assist in establishing the 'widespread' nature of such attacks by drawing upon the cumulative number of trafficking victims. Instead, characterising the trafficking operation as 'systematic' would be, from a prosecutorial perspective, easier to establish. An attack is 'systematic' where it is shown to be 'thoroughly organised and following a regular pattern on the basis of a common policy involving substantial public or private resources'.[59] Trafficking operations vary in size and complexity, but there is little doubt that many that occur on a large scale are highly organised

---

containers for periods of time as they are being transported to their country of destination.

[56] These elements being (i) the perpetration of acts enumerated in Articles 7(1)(a)–(k); (ii) an act committed as part of a 'widespread or systematic attack'; (iii) such attack being directed at a 'civilian population'; (iv) in furtherance of a state or organisational policy; (v) with a 'nexus' between the acts and the attack; (vi) and the perpetrator knowing that their conduct was part of or intended to be a part of such attack.

[57] *Blaškić* (Judgment), ICTY Trial Chamber IT-95-14-T, 3 March 2000, para. 207.

[58] *Al Bashir* (Arrest Warrant Decision), ICC Pre-Trial Chamber I, ICC-02/05-01/09-3, 3 March 2009, para. 81; *Akayesu* (Judgment), ICTR Trial Chamber ICTR-96-4-T, 2 September 1998, para. 208.

[59] *Akayesu* (Judgment), para. 219; *Al Bashir* (Arrest Warrant Decision), para. 85.

operations involving the identification, recruitment, coercion, control, and exploitation of trafficked persons. The process will involve developed supply lines for the sale of trafficked persons particularly which, when traded transnationally, will likely require a high degree of coordination between different actors across international frontiers. It therefore seems plain that many acts of trafficking by profiteers would indeed constitute a 'systematic' attack.

Still, the second issue is whether the acts of trafficking profiteers form part of a 'State or organisational policy'.[60] If crimes against humanity could be committed only by those exercising powers on behalf of a state (or a state-like entity such as ISIS) that would obviously preclude the responsibility of private profiteers who, it may be reasonably surmised, make up the majority of trafficking offenders. The question is whether 'State or organisational' is suggestive of a sufficient difference to capture within its ambit not only state entities but also (as relevant in our case) private profiteers. A narrow reading of 'organisational' in this context is that it refers to a group of 'quasi-State' abilities, such as control over territory; 'State' therefore modifies 'organisation' in Article 7 and see- mingly imposes a more demanding requirement such that the vast majority of criminal organisations, let alone small-scale enterprises, would not meet the threshold.[61] A broad(er) approach in the jurispru- dence, such as by the Pre-Trial Chamber in *Bemba*, on the other hand, defines organisation as referring to any group of persons 'with the *capability* to commit a widespread or systematic attack against a civilian population'.[62] 'Capability', in this context, could be identified by a number of non-exhaustive factors, including whether the group has an established hierarchy; a criminal purpose; the means to carry out a widespread or systematic attack directed against a civilian population; a declared intention to so direct such an attack; or territorial control.[63]

Often there will be little practical difference between the narrow and the broad readings, but in the case of trafficking in persons, concerned often with private transnational groups operating for profit and without

---

[60] ICC Statute, Article 7(2)(a).
[61] See the approaches set out in *Ruto* ('Decision Pursuant to Article 15 of the Rome Statute on the Authorization of an Investigation into the Situation in the Republic of Kenya'), Pre-Trial Chamber II, ICC-01/09-19-Corr, 31 March 2010, paras. 51–53 (Judge Kaul) (dissenting); van der Wilt (*supra* n. 41) 306–8.
[62] See e.g. *Bemba* (Decision on Charges), Pre-Trial Chamber, ICC-01/05-01/08, 15 June 2009, para. 81.
[63] *Katanga* Trial Judgment, ICC Trial Chamber, 7 March 2014, paras. 1117–22.

any territorial control, it evidently matters. Leaving aside whether the broader approach would assist in trafficking prosecutions for a moment, there are good arguments to support treating 'State' and 'organisational' as independent concepts. For a start, it is a presumption of treaty interpretation, which applies to the ICC Statute, that terms be given their ordinary meaning and be interpreted in their context.[64] The conjunction 'or' textually denotes concepts that are and must remain distinct; the organisation is not the state.[65] Further, the presumption against redundancy requires every word in a treaty to have meaning; it would render the 'organisational' term in Article 7(2)(a) redundant if crimes against humanity could be committed only by a state or a state-controlled entity.[66] 'Organisation' ordinarily refers to a group of people structured in a specific way to achieve shared goals.[67] This also ties into the word that accompanies 'organisational', being 'policy', which itself is interpreted as a planned, directed, or organised crime, as opposed to spontaneous, isolated acts of violence.[68] The focus on the group's capability rather than its formal designation within a state is also preferable given the need to afford protection to victims of crimes against humanity. Finally, in this regard, support can be found in the observations of the International Law Commission in the drafting of an analogous provision to Article 7(2)(a), which did not 'rule out the possibility that private individuals with de facto power or organized in criminal gangs or groups might also commit the kind of systematic or mass violations of human rights covered by the article'.[69]

While there are points of difference between 'State' and 'organisational', it is arguable that the definition placed on the latter by the pre-trial majority in *Bemba* would itself be highly restrictive of the types of criminal enterprise that would be deemed 'capable' of committing crimes against humanity. Specifically, the indicium that the organisation has

---

[64] Vienna Convention on the Law of Treaties, Article 31(1); *Situation in the Democratic Republic of Congo* (Judgment on the Prosecutor's Application for Extraordinary Review of the Pre-Trial Chamber I's 1 March 2006 Denying Leave to Appeal), Pre-Trial Chamber I, ICC-01/04, 13 July 2006, para. 33.

[65] *Katanga* Trial Judgment, paras. 1117–22.

[66] A. Orakhelashvili, *The Interpretation of Acts and Rules in Public International Law* (Oxford University Press, 2008), p. 422.

[67] *Black's Law Dictionary* (10th edn, Thomson West, 2014).

[68] *Ruto* ('Decision on the confirmation of charges'), Pre-Trial Chamber, ICC-01/09-01/11, 23 January 2012, para. 210.

[69] 2(2) *Yearbook of the International Law Commission* (1991), A/ CN.4/Ser.A/1991/ Add. 1 (Pt. 2), 103.

a hierarchical command and controls territory, in effect, incorporates state-like elements into the 'organisational' definition or, at least, uses the structure of an armed group as strongly indicative of an organisation under Article 7. However, there is no justification for so limiting 'organisational' in this manner. It is equally possible that loosely structured transnational groups have the 'capability' to commit a widespread or systematic attack. Indeed, a better approach would be to read 'organisational' harmoniously with how this term is used in an organised crime context. Article 2 of the United Nations Convention Against Transnational Organised Crime, for example, defines 'organised criminal group' as 'a structured group of three or more persons, existing for a period of time and acting in concert with the aim of committing one or more serious crimes or offences'. This definition is less stringent than the factors stated in *Bemba*, such as the existence of organised command, and thus would more readily accommodate enterprises that exist for profit but that are not so highly structured. On this basis, it is submitted that it is the capacity of the group to commit serious crimes that should matter, not its quasi-state qualities or functions.

9.4 Criminal Enforcement Against War Profiteers for Human Trafficking

Having outlined the legal framework under the ICC Statute for the international criminalisation of trafficking in persons, the more difficult issue, as with international crimes generally, is finding ways to ensure their effective prosecution. The development of international norms on trafficking in persons has moved at a remarkable pace generally over the past two decades, with previously reticent regions such as ASEAN even adopting a convention for, amongst other things, the prosecution of human trafficking.[70] It seems that the difficulty is not in finding general agreement as to the need to criminalise human trafficking, either specifically or via other established crimes that contain the various elements of trafficking, but in ensuring that effective mechanisms are instituted to prosecute offenders and combat impunity. Recent developments in both the ICC OTP and the Sanctions Committee of the Security Council, in placing attention on trafficking in Libya, are a cause for some optimism that the prosecution of this crime will receive greater priority in the

---

[70] See ASEAN Convention Against Trafficking in Persons, Especially Women and Children (in force 6 February 2017).

future. That said, there remain a number of conceptual and practical hurdles to securing the prosecution of traffickers before the ICC.

The first concerns the transnational nature of the crimes, raising jurisdictional questions. It is common, no less during armed conflict, for the different phases of the trafficking process to occur in different jurisdictions: this is the case, for instance, with Syrian women and girls who have been trafficked into Lebanon, or Nigerian women trafficked into Libya.[71] This not only creates practical evidentiary difficulties but also impedes the exercise of criminal jurisdiction, specifically where national courts are confronted with trafficking conduct that occurred in another jurisdiction from its own (leaving aside the question of whether trafficking justifies the invocation of universal jurisdiction by a national court). In this respect, there seems a clear basis for the exercise of jurisdiction in national criminal courts: the objective territorial principle, long established in customary international law, allows a state to exercise jurisdiction where a constituent element of a crime occurred within its territory.[72] Similarly, it is also possible to characterise trafficking as a continuing crime; thus, even if a transaction occurred in another territory (i.e. selling), the act continued into the destination country.[73]

At the ICC, jurisdictional issues may arise in the circumstance where a national of a non-ICC Statute party commits an act of trafficking in the territory of such a non-party but where the destination country of the trafficked person is an ICC Statute party. If this was the case, the court would be confronted with the text of Article 12(2)(a), which allows it to exercise jurisdiction in relation to a situation in 'the State on the territory of which the conduct in question occurred'. However, the 'conduct' that is sought to be tried (such as the act of selling) may have taken place in another (non-party) state. This would limit the ambit for trafficking prosecutions to those involved in the enterprise in the destination country. To overcome this seemingly plain wording, it might be that an appeal to the object and purpose of the ICC Statute, to end impunity, is invoked, particularly the need to prevent transnational actors from using cross-border crimes as a shield from accountability. Equally, a gentle remedying of some of the apparent inconsistencies in terminology in the ICC Statute (such that 'conduct' in Article 12(2)(a) is given a broader

---

[71] For further details, see *Targeting Vulnerabilities* (n. 1).

[72] Van der Wilt (*supra* n. 41) 317–21 (and citations there). It is also recognised in Article 15(2) of the United Nations Convention against Transnational Organized Crime Convention, the parent treaty to the Trafficking Protocol.

[73] Ibid.

construction to encompass the different elements of a 'crime'[74]) would provide a basis for the objective territorial principle to be applied. Indeed, recently, the ICC Pre-Trial Chamber I adopted such a purposive reading of Article 12(2)(a) in the context of the deportation of Rohingya from Myanmar (a non-state party) to Bangladesh (a state party).[75] Drawing upon the objective territorial principle, the Pre-Trial Chamber noted 'that the preconditions for the exercise of the Court's jurisdiction pursuant to article 12(2)(a) of the Statute are, as a minimum, fulfilled if at least one legal element of a crime within the jurisdiction of the Court or part of such a crime is committed on the territory of a State Party'.[76] This finding, provided it is upheld on appeal, would certainly remove one of the major obstacles to prosecuting trafficking in persons at the ICC.

At the ICC, there are also issues pertaining to the admissibility of trafficking cases. Article 17(1)(d) of the Rome Statute requires a situation to be of 'sufficient gravity' to justify action at the ICC. In this regard, there are two key features to determine gravity. First, the 'subject of a case must be either systematic (pattern of incidents) or large-scale', thereby excluding isolated instances of criminal activity.[77] Second, the gravity assessment should give regard 'to the social alarm such conduct may have caused in the international community'.[78] These factors would inevitably exclude the many smaller-scale enterprises that make up the majority of trafficking operations.[79] The OTP's examination into trafficking in Libya perhaps provides an indication of the types of case that the ICC will be considering in the future and which would most certainly meet the gravity threshold on any measure. In Libya, there are estimates that

---

[74] 'Conduct' in Article 12(2)(a) was equated to 'crime' by the ICC in *Kenya* and *Côte d'Ivoire*: *Situation in Republic of Kenya* (Authorisation of an Investigation Decision), Pre-Trial Chamber II, ICC-01/09, 31 March 2010, para. 175; *Situation in the Republic of Côte d'Ivoire* (Authorisation of an Investigation Decision), Pre-Trial Chamber III, ICC-02/11, 3 October 2011, para. 10. The significance of this is that Article 30 of the ICC Statute and the ICC Elements of Crime note that 'crime' includes 'conduct', 'consequence' and 'circumstance'.

[75] Request Under Regulation 46(3) of the Regulations of the Court, 'Decision on the "Prosecution's Request for a Ruling on Jurisdiction under Article 19(3) of the Statute"', 6 September 2018.

[76] Ibid.

[77] *Prosecutor* v. *Thomas Lubanga* (Case No. ICC-01/04-01/06), ICC Pre-Trial Chamber I, Decision Concerning Pre-Trial Chamber I's Decision of 10 February 2006 and the Incorporation of Documents into the Record of the Case against Mr. Thomas Lubanga Dyilo, 24 February 2006, Annex 1, para. 46.

[78] Ibid.

[79] Kim (*supra* n. 38) 30–1.

around 400,000 to 700,000 migrants have been held in often inhumane conditions in more than 40 detention camps.[80] There is evidence that these trafficking activities are highly organised, involving associations among militias, governmental (or quasi-governmental) officials controlling key infrastructure such as the coastal ports, and leaders of large transnational trafficking networks.[81] If this is the standard by which future cases of this kind are to be judged, it will inevitably limit the scope for the ICC to address trafficking in persons as it occurs on a smaller scale involving private criminal enterprises without elements of military and governmental collusion.

9.5   Conclusion

Trafficking in persons is a common occurrence in armed conflict for a variety of purposes, including for profit. It is apparent that the laws of IHL and ICL prohibit and criminalise, in various guises, the exploitative practices that form part of the international definition of trafficking in persons. Such practices – which correlate to the 'means', 'action' and/or 'exploitation' elements of trafficking in persons – have indeed been prosecuted as war crimes, crimes against humanity and genocide in the international tribunals, albeit without specific reference to 'trafficking' as an element or organising concept. Although capturing many of the elements of trafficking in persons, there are limitations in treating this conduct as a subset of the existing core crimes rather than as a core crime in its own right. This includes the need to meet the general doctrinal requirements of these core crimes, such as finding the existence of an armed conflict or a 'widespread or systematic attack', which greatly curtails the ability to bring international prosecutions against those responsible for trafficking in persons, as does considerations of gravity at the admissibility stage of ICC proceedings.

Article 7(2) of the ICC Statute offers the first direct reference to 'trafficking in persons' as a facet of an international crime and thus provides an opportunity to give greater expression to this offence as a crime against humanity. However, much will depend on the relationship between 'enslavement' and trafficking, particularly whether all the practices associated with the latter can be sufficiently accommodated

---

[80] UN News, 'As Security Council Imposes Sanctions on Six Human Traffickers in Libya, UN Chief Calls for More Accountability' (8 June 2018), https://news.un.org/en/story/2018/06/1011751.

[81] Ibid.

within the former. The Libya case provides the first opportunity for the ICC to clarify this relationship. With the Security Council now taking trafficking seriously, in imposing sanctions against high-level traffickers, the opportunity presents itself for the ICC to break new ground and try individuals for the first time for trafficking as a subset of a crime against humanity. In doing so, the ICC would not only demonstrate that the 'trafficking in persons' reference in Article 7(2) is not merely theoretical but also aid in progressing the conversation on trafficking as an 'international', and not merely a 'transnational', crime. This would certainly augment national and international efforts to end the impunity of war profiteers for trafficking in persons.

PART IV

Where Should the Buck Stop?

The Legal Framework for Economic Aiders and Abettors

Charles Taylor Inc.: Lessons from the Trial of a President, Businessman and Warlord

NINA H. B. JØRGENSEN[*]

10.1 Introduction

Liberia was sometimes referred to as *Charles Taylor Inc.* during Taylor's time as president from 1997 to 2003.[1] His reign was defined by the misuse of state power, corruption, nepotism and the monopolization of business for personal financial gain.[2] Regarded as the archetypical 'Big Man', even that 'overworked cliché of African reportage' is inadequate to capture Taylor's ambitions.[3] He is currently serving a fifty-year sentence in Frankland Prison in the northern English city of Durham after being convicted by the Special Court for Sierra Leone (SCSL) of aiding and abetting, and planning war crimes and crimes against humanity during Sierra Leone's armed conflict in the 1990s. Taylor's trial and fall from grace carried special significance for West Africans who had become used to seeing powerful individuals escape accountability.[4] However, the scope of the trial was necessarily limited to events in Sierra Leone and Taylor has never properly been held to account for his excesses at home in Liberia. Further, while the case before the SCSL addressed certain economic aspects of Taylor's conduct, including the exchange of arms for diamonds, pillage of Sierra Leone's diamond resources was treated as

---

[*] The author wishes to thank Harry Annison and Tom Hamilton for their helpful comments on an earlier draft.

[1] L. Polgreen, 'A Master Plan Drawn in Blood', *The New York Times*, 2 April 2006.

[2] A. Tejan-Cole, 'A Big Man in a Small Cell: Charles Taylor and the Special Court for Sierra Leone', in E. Lutz and C. Reiger (eds.), *Prosecuting Heads of State* (Cambridge University Press, 2008), pp. 205–32, 207.

[3] Polgreen (*supra* n. 1).

[4] Human Rights Watch, 'Even a "Big Man" Must Face Justice: Lessons from the Trial of Charles Taylor', 25 July 2012, www.hrw.org/report/2012/07/25/even-big-man-must-face-justice/lessons-trial-charles-taylor.

a motive or objective rather than as a core crime. This meant that Taylor's role as a 'financier and facilitator of international crimes'[5] was only partly exposed.

The *Taylor* case before the SCSL illustrates that what might be termed the political, military and economic 'pillars' of international crimes are often intertwined. The case also supports the contention that since the Nuremberg-era trials, the political and military pillars have tended to be prioritized.[6] There does not yet appear to be a sustained effort to direct prosecutorial attention towards the economic pillar and consequently there is an absence of modern precedents.[7] This may be due partly to prosecutorial policy whereby the political and military pillars are viewed as being more grave, and partly to issues of proof when the alleged perpetrator is 'remote' from the physical commission of the crimes. Furthermore, under the economic pillar, 'the causal, motivational, organizational and structural nexus between the economic actor's conduct and the crime may be more tenuous than under other pillars'.[8] The geographical nexus might be added to the list of evidential hurdles. Taylor was 'alleged to have participated in the civil war without being physically present on the territory of Sierra Leone'.[9] He did not formally hold a position of authority over the leaders of the rebel group known as the Revolutionary United Front (RUF). In order to hold Taylor criminally responsible for the RUF's conduct, it was necessary for the prosecution to prove the factual nexus linking him to the crime base in Sierra Leone – a different country – and the legal nexus allowing liability to be attributed, which in turn meant establishing all the 'missing links' represented by the potential middlemen in between.[10]

This chapter considers how the SCSL approached the question of liability in Taylor's case leading to convictions on all eleven counts of the indictment. It aims to identify lessons from the story of *Charles*

---

[5] J. Kyriakakis, 'Developments in International Criminal Law and the Case of Business Involvement in International Crimes' (2012) 94(887) *International Review of the Red Cross* 981–1005, 999.

[6] See C. Burchard, 'Ancillary and Neutral Business Contributions to "Corporate-Political Core Crime"' (2010) 8 *Journal of International Criminal Justice* 919–46, 920.

[7] Kyriakakis (*supra* n. 5) 981; N. Farrell, 'Attributing Criminal Liability to Corporate Actors: Some Lessons from the International Tribunals' (2010) 8 *Journal of International Criminal Justice* 873–94.

[8] Burchard (*supra* n. 6) 921.

[9] *Prosecutor v. Charles Ghankay Taylor*, SCSL-03-01-T, Judgment, Trial Chamber, 18 May 2012 (*Taylor* Trial Judgment), para. 19.

[10] Farrell (*supra* n. 7) 879.

Taylor Inc. that might assist in addressing the economic pillar of international crimes in the future. The chapter begins with a brief introduction to the personality of Charles Taylor and his role in the conflicts in
Sierra Leone and Liberia. It proceeds to consider the modes of liability
applied by the SCSL, namely aiding and abetting and planning, and
rejected, namely joint criminal enterprise and superior responsibility,
and reflects on the proper characterization of Taylor as an accomplice or
(co-)perpetrator. The fact that Taylor was head of state for most of the
period relevant to the indictment raises the question of the responsibility
of the Liberian state, despite the SCSL's finding that Taylor acted privately, that is, independently of the state structure, when he participated
in international crimes. This question is highlighted as one that remains
under-explored in the academic literature, perhaps reflecting the absence
of any practical incentive on Sierra Leone's part to hold Liberia to
account for Taylor's conduct while head of state. Finally, the chapter
analyzes the economic aspects of Taylor's roles as president, businessman, warlord and war criminal that were outside the mandate of the
SCSL but that led to the freezing of his assets and were the subject of
detailed consideration by the Liberian Truth and Reconciliation
Commission.

10.2   A Brief Biography of Charles Taylor

Born outside Monrovia, Taylor became a student activist in the 1970s and
protested against William Tolbert's corrupt regime. He studied economics at Bentley College in Massachusetts.[11] He returned to Liberia in 1980
just as Samuel Doe overthrew, and murdered, Tolbert. After allying
himself with Doe's government, Taylor was accused of embezzling
a million US dollars and escaped to the United States where he was
detained at Plymouth County House of Correction in Massachusetts
under a Liberian extradition warrant. He escaped from prison either by
sawing through the bars of his cell, or, less imaginatively, with the help of
influential Americans who had earmarked him as someone who could
overthrow Doe's regime. Toppling Doe was precisely what he attempted
to do after meeting with fellow revolutionaries in Burkina Faso, Ivory
Coast and Libya.[12] Doe met with a brutal end just like his predecessor.

---

[11] *Taylor* Trial Judgment (*supra* n. 9), para. 4.
[12] Polgreen (*supra* n. 1).

Taylor never quite transitioned from warlord to statesman. As president, 'Taylor turned his government into an illegal money-making machine' and Liberia became 'a huge arms bazaar'.[13] After his first year in office, corruption was prominent and there was 'a fine line between personal and public assets', in part due to illegal mining and smuggling of diamonds through the country's porous borders with little revenue being accrued to the state.[14] According to his successor, he ran the country 'like it was his personal fiefdom'.[15] This degree of personal rule, which alienated the Liberian population, was 'unprecedented in the history of the country'.[16]

Based on a review of the SCSL trial record, it has been observed that: 'One of the few points of agreement between the prosecution and the defence appears to be that Taylor is an educated, intelligent and strategic thinker, a rational man not motivated by revenge, sadism or other irrational sentiments.'[17] The SCSL never clearly established Taylor's motives for assisting the RUF, which are unlikely to have been as simple as pure greed. A beguiling protagonist in a self-made drama, Taylor nonetheless defies any stereotype of the rational economic actor.

10.3   The Conflicts in Liberia and Sierra Leone

In 1989, insurgents led by Taylor and calling themselves the National Patriotic Front of Liberia (NPFL) attacked Liberia from neighbouring Côte d'Ivoire, triggering a seven-year civil war in Liberia. The conflict escalated after Doe's murder in 1990. Armed groups such as the United Liberation Forces of Liberia (ULIMO) formed of Doe loyalists joined in the fighting. A regional military force known as the Economic Community of West African States Cease-Fire Monitoring Group

---

[13] S. Lovgren, 'Liberia President Taylor's Life of Crime', *National Geographic News*, 25 July 2003.

[14] A. Onadipe, 'Liberia: Taylor's First Year Report Card', *Contemporary Review*, November 1998, 237. See also C. M. Waugh, *Charles Taylor and Liberia: Ambition and Atrocity in Africa's Lone Star State* (Zed Books, 2011), p. 249: 'Often, just as in his days in Gbarnga, government business would help finance personal deals – that is, in those cases where it was possible to tell which was which.'

[15] D. Carvajal, 'Hunting for Liberia's Missing Millions', *The New York Times*, 30 May 2010, www.nytimes.com/2010/05/31/world/africa/31taylor.html?pagewanted=all&_r=0, citing interview with Ellen Johnson-Sirleaf.

[16] T. Jaye, 'Liberia: An Analysis of Post-Taylor Politics' (2003) 98 *Review of African Political Economy* 643–86, 644.

[17] M. Glasius and T. Meijers, 'Constructions of Legitimacy: The Charles Taylor Trial' (2012) 6 *International Journal of Transitional Justice* 229–52, 239.

(ECOMOG) intervened. During the battle, 'the country's natural and economic resources became a private enterprise for Taylor and many of the other warlords'.[18]

In March 1991, a group of NPFL-trained Sierra Leonean fighters led by former Sierra Leone Army Corporal Foday Sankoh invaded Bomaru, a small town in Sierra Leone's Kailahun District, and announced the formation of the RUF. It has been noted that 'Charles Taylor acted as mentor, patron, banker, and weapons supplier for this motley collection of Sierra Leonean dissidents, bandits and mercenaries'.[19] The RUF claimed to want to expand access to Sierra Leone's economic resources but instead unleashed war on ordinary citizens to gain control of the country's diamond wealth.

A ceasefire and power-sharing agreement was reached among the warring factions in the Liberian conflict at Abuja on 19 August 1995. Taylor won 75 per cent of the vote in elections held in July 1997 to become President. By this point Liberia's economy had been devastated. For their part, the RUF and the democratically elected government of Sierra Leone under Ahmad Tejan Kabbah reached a peace agreement at Abidjan on 30 November 1996. This failed and on 25 May 1997 a group of Sierra Leone Army Officers – the Armed Forces Revolutionary Council (AFRC) led by Johnny Paul Koroma – staged a successful coup and invited the RUF to share power. ECOMOG intervened and restored Kabbah's government on 10 March 1998. A new peace accord was signed at Lomé in July 1999, according to which the RUF and Kabbah's government agreed to share power, making Sankoh chairman of a commission on natural resources that effectively gave him control of Sierra Leone's diamonds. The Lomé Peace Accord also provided for the establishment of a Truth and Reconciliation Commission and granted a broad amnesty.

The seeds of a second civil war in Liberia were sown in 1999 when a rebel group known as the Liberians United for Reconciliation and Democracy (LURD) entered Liberia from Guinea. This resulted in a brutal crackdown by Taylor's government. By 2003, however, LURD forces threatened the capital, Monrovia. In the meantime, the peace in Sierra Leone had not held and in 2000 a group of UN peacekeepers was taken hostage, leading to Foday Sankoh's arrest. Kabbah requested the UN's assistance in establishing an independent judicial mechanism and, in 2002, the SCSL was born in Freetown.

---

[18] Tejan-Cole (*supra* n. 2), p. 206.
[19] Ibid., p. 208.

On the opening day of talks to resolve the Liberian conflict held in Accra, Ghana, on 4 June 2003, the SCSL Prosecutor unsealed an indictment against Taylor causing a diplomatic incident. Taylor was enabled to return speedily to Liberia while talks continued for seventy-six days before agreement on the terms of peace could be reached. These terms included the removal of Taylor from office. He was granted asylum in Nigeria and left Liberia on 11 August 2003. Pressure to surrender Taylor to the SCSL mounted after Ellen Johnson-Sirleaf won the Liberian presidential elections in 2005. Taylor touched ground in Monrovia on 29 March 2006 – a brief stopover on his way to the SCSL – following his arrest on the Cameroonian border after twenty-four hours on the run from his luxury residence in Calabar. He was reportedly in possession of 220,000 USD provided to him to aid his escape.[20] After spending several months in Freetown, Taylor was transported to The Hague to stand trial due to the risk that his presence in the region might prove a destabilizing factor.

10.4   Taylor's Liability for Crimes Committed in Sierra Leone

The SCSL Prosecution argued that Taylor was criminally responsible for the crimes set out in the indictment through his participation in a joint criminal enterprise (JCE). Emphasis was placed on this mode of liability throughout the case although planning, instigating, ordering, aiding and abetting, and superior responsibility were also included in the indictment. Taylor was charged with five counts of crimes against humanity (murder, rape, sexual slavery, other inhumane acts (mutilations), and enslavement), five counts of violations of Article 3 Common to the Geneva Conventions and of Additional Protocol II (acts of terrorism, murder, outrages upon personal dignity, cruel treatment, pillage) and the conscription, enlistment and use of child soldiers.

The Trial Chamber convicted Taylor of all eleven counts in the indictment under the modes of liability of aiding and abetting and planning. The aiding and abetting conviction related to the whole indictment period while the planning conviction concerned only the attacks on Kono and Makeni in December 1998, and the invasion of and retreat from Freetown, between December 1998 and February 1999. The Trial Chamber defined the *actus reus* of aiding and abetting as the provision of

---

[20] Ibid., p. 218.

'practical assistance, encouragement, or moral support which had a substantial effect upon the commission of the crimes'.[21] The *mens rea* constituted 'knowledge that these acts or omissions would assist the commission of the crime, or awareness of the substantial likelihood that these acts would assist the commission of the crime, and awareness of the "essential elements" of the crime committed by the principal offender, including the state of mind of the principal offender'.[22]

The Trial Chamber found that Taylor had provided arms and ammunition,[23] military personnel,[24] operational support (including communications, housing for the rebels, transport and monetary donations)[25] as well as encouragement and moral support (for example giving direction while being in a position of authority).[26] The supply of arms and ammunition was considered a major form of support to the RUF and AFRC:

> [T]he Accused directly or through intermediaries supplied or facilitated the supply of arms and ammunition to the RUF/AFRC. The Accused sent small but regular supplies of arms and ammunition and other supplies to the RUF from late 1997 to 1998 via his subordinates, and substantial amounts of arms and ammunition to the AFRC/RUF from 1998 to 2001. The Accused facilitated much larger shipments of arms and ammunition from third party states to the AFRC/RUF, including the Magburaka shipment of October 1997 and the Burkina Faso shipment of November/December 1998.[27]

The Trial Chamber overcame the problem of establishing which forms of assistance contributed to criminal activity and which forms of assistance were aimed at conducting a lawful military operation by finding an 'inextricable link' between the operational strategy of the RUF and AFRC which amounted to 'a campaign of crimes against the Sierra Leonean civilian population, including murders, rapes, sexual slavery, looting, abductions, forced labour, conscription of child soldiers, amputations and other forms of physical violence and acts of terror'[28] and the military operations themselves. This meant that '*any* assistance towards these military operations of the RUF and RUF/AFRC constitutes direct

---

[21] *Taylor* Trial Judgment (*supra* n. 9), para. 6904.
[22] Ibid.
[23] Ibid., para. 6910.
[24] Ibid., para. 6924.
[25] Ibid., para. 6936.
[26] Ibid., paras. 6940–5.
[27] Ibid., para. 6910.
[28] Ibid., para. 6905.

assistance to the commission of crimes by these groups'.[29] The Trial
Chamber found that the various forms of support provided by
Taylor were used by the RUF and AFRC during military operations
so that his support amounted to practical assistance to the commission of crimes.[30]

In answering the question of whether the 'provision and facilitation of
the supply of arms and ammunition to the RUF/AFRC had a substantial
effect on the commission of crimes charged in the Indictment', the Trial
Chamber found that 'the additional sources of supply which the RUF/
AFRC had could not provide sufficient quantities of materiel to sustain
the existence and military operations of the rebels'.[31] The rebels relied
'heavily and frequently' on the assistance given by Taylor and 'on
a number of occasions the arms and ammunitions which he supplied
or facilitated were in fact indispensable for the RUF/AFRC military
offensives'.[32] Similar conclusions were reached with regard to the provision of military personnel.[33]

Finally, as regards the *mens rea*, Taylor was found to have been fully
informed of events in Sierra Leone at the relevant time, including criminal activities of the RUF and AFRC through daily press and intelligence
briefings and in his capacity as member of the Economic Community of
West African States. Additionally, Taylor had himself testified as to his
awareness of news reports describing a violent campaign against the
civilian population of Sierra Leone which he had even condemned. The
Trial Chamber found that Taylor knew that his support would contribute
towards the commission of crimes and nonetheless continued to provide
such support[34] and that he was aware of the 'essential elements' of the
crimes to which he was contributing, including the state of mind of the
perpetrators.

The SCSL Appeals Chamber upheld the Trial Chamber's findings. In
addition, the Appeals Chamber explicitly rejected the requirement of
'specific direction' as an element of the *actus reus* of aiding and abetting
that had been put forward in the *Perišić* case before the ICTY, disagreeing

[29] Ibid., emphasis added.
[30] Ibid., paras. 6911–12.
[31] Ibid., para. 6913.
[32] Ibid., para. 6914. See also the critique of this evidentiary assessment in K. Ambos and
O. Njikam, 'Charles Taylor's Criminal Responsibility' (2013) 11 *Journal of International
Criminal Justice* 789–812, 801.
[33] *Taylor* Trial Judgment (*supra* n. 9), see discussion at paras. 6916–24.
[34] Ibid., paras. 6947–9.

that such a requirement was needed in addressing cases where the accused lacked physical proximity to the crime.[35] The requirement of 'substantial effect' was seen to ensure 'a sufficient causal link – a criminal link – between the accused and the commission of the crime before an accused's conduct may be adjudged criminal'.[36]

The Appeals Chamber placed considerable emphasis on the *actus reus* requirement of substantial effect, separating this element from the 'particular manner in which [the] assistance is provided'.[37] Contrary to arguments presented by the defence, it did not need to be shown that 'Taylor provided assistance to the physical actor who committed the *actus reus* of each specific underlying crime or that such assistance was used by the physical actor in the commission of each specific crime'.[38] The Appeals Chamber also stressed that the question of whether the acts of the accused had a substantial effect on the commission of the crime was 'to be assessed on a case-by-case basis in light of the evidence as a whole'.[39] This meant that in cases of isolated crimes in combination with fungible means of assistance, it might be difficult to establish a sufficient connection between the acts of the accused and the alleged crime. Similarly, an insignificant or insubstantial contribution to the 'causal stream leading to the commission of the crime' might preclude a finding of substantial effect.[40] This assessment allowed the Appeals Chamber to distinguish its conclusion in another case before the SCSL that the provision of logistics was not sufficient to establish beyond reasonable doubt that the accused in that case 'contributed as an aider and abettor to the commission of specific criminal acts in Bo District'.[41]

In this context, the Trial Chamber's finding of an 'inextricable link' between the operational strategy of the fighting forces which involved the

---

[35] *Prosecutor* v. *Charles Ghankay Taylor*, SCSL-03-01-A, Judgment, Appeals Chamber, 26 September 2013 (*Taylor* Appeal Judgment), paras. 478–80, 486. The Trial Chamber had similarly found that '[t]he actus reus of aiding and abetting does not require "specific direction"'. *Taylor* Trial Judgment (*supra* n. 9), para. 484 and see footnote 1141.

[36] *Taylor* Appeal Judgment (*supra* n. 35), para. 390.

[37] Ibid., para. 401.

[38] Ibid., para. 401.

[39] Ibid., para. 370.

[40] Ibid., para. 391.

[41] *Prosecutor* v. *Moinina Fofana and Allieu Kondewa*, SCSL-04-14-A, Judgment, Appeals Chamber, 28 May 2008, para. 102. See also S. Meisenberg, 'The Final Judgement in the Trial of Charles Taylor', *OUPBlog*, 23 September 2013, https://blog.oup.com/2013/09/charles-taylor-trial-judgement-special-court-sierra-leone-pil/.

use of terror as the 'primary modus operandi' to achieve the political and military goals of the RUF and AFRC 'at any civilian cost' was accepted by the Appeals Chamber.[42] The establishment of such an inextricable link between military strategy and criminal conduct appeared essential in Taylor's case in view of the magnitude of crimes alleged against him as a senior leader, with the indictment encompassing all the major criminal conduct attributed to the RUF and AFRC. This approach precluded an individualized assessment of which of Taylor's contributions supported legitimate military operations and which forms of assistance were directed towards crimes. However, since the notion of 'specific direction' had been rejected as a requirement under customary international law and none of the RUF/AFRC military operations was deemed to be legitimate, the SCSL's conclusions appear legally justifiable. It is questionable whether this precise set of circumstances is likely to arise in future cases, casting doubt on the transferability of the approach in Taylor to similar instances of high-level actors potentially incurring liability under the economic pillar.

A related feature of the Trial Chamber's judgment, upheld by the Appeals Chamber, was the cumulation of the forms of support that gave rise to a substantial effect on the crimes. Out of the four categories of aid and assistance considered by the chambers, only the supply of arms and ammunition to the RUF/AFRC was independently seen to have such an effect.[43] The instances of military personnel provided by Taylor were taken cumulatively, and 'in addition to the arms and ammunition' he provided.[44] Similarly, instances of operational support were taken cumulatively, 'having regard to the military support', as were instances of encouragement and moral support, 'considering the other forms of practical assistance'.[45] This bunching together of the instances of aid and assistance to establish an overall substantial effect means that no guidance is given as to the threshold for particular forms of assistance. For example, the Trial Chamber found that Taylor provided financial support to the RUF/AFRC including amounts of '[US] $10,000 to $20,000 at a time, on multiple occasions for the purchase of arms'.[46] It seems doubtful whether supplying these funds would independently have secured

[42] *Taylor* Appeal Judgment (*supra* n. 35), para. 399.
[43] *Taylor* Trial Judgment (*supra* n. 9), para. 6915.
[44] Ibid., para. 6924.
[45] Ibid., paras. 6937, 6946.
[46] Ibid., para. 6932.

a conviction for aiding and abetting in the broader context of the *Taylor* case, but arguably in different circumstances the substantial effect test could be met by this type of contribution alone.

Indeed, in considering the international jurisprudence on aiding and abetting liability, the Appeals Chamber commented on the 'infinite variety of ways' in which the conduct of accused persons had been found to have a substantial effect on the commission of crimes and noted that this included the provision of financial support to an organization engaged in the commission of crimes.[47] Nevertheless, it was clearly stated that the RUF/AFRC had not been found to be a criminal organization in the sense envisaged by Articles 9 and 10 of the Nuremberg Charter.[48]

Article 6(3) of the SCSL Statute provides for criminal responsibility if a superior knew or had reason to know that his or her subordinate was about to commit crimes prohibited by the Statute or had done so, and the superior failed to take the necessary and reasonable measures to prevent such crimes or punish the perpetrators. It has been observed that 'Taylor's only formal, public relationship with the leadership of the RUF was that of ECOWAS-appointed negotiator' or 'point president for peace'.[49] The prosecution drew on ideas of patrimony, presenting Taylor as being in a father-son relationship with the leaders of the RUF.[50] At times he was described as the 'godfather' of the RUF.[51] However, he was not formally in command of the group. The Trial Chamber did not find Taylor liable on the basis of his superior position. Taylor's 'substantial influence over the leadership of the RUF, and to a lesser extent that of the AFRC' was noted, but the Trial Chamber considered that his substantial influence over the conduct of others fell short of effective control.[52]

---

[47] *Taylor* Appeal Judgment (*supra* n. 35), para. 369, referring to the post-World War II *Flick* case and the *Bagaragaza* case before the ICTR. *Bagaragaza*, who held a prominent position in Rwanda's tea industry (controlling 11 tea factories employing about 55,000 persons) and was a member of the *Akazu* group which held financial power in Rwanda, pleaded guilty to complicity in genocide, inter alia, on the basis of providing substantial funds to buy alcohol to motivate the Interahamwe to kill Tutsis. *Prosecutor v. Bagaragaza*, ICTR-2005–86-S, Sentencing Judgment, 17 November 2009, para. 25.
[48] *Taylor* Appeal Judgment (*supra* n. 35), para. 399.
[49] Glasius and Meijers (*supra* n. 17) 237.
[50] Ibid. 239.
[51] SCSL-2003–01-T, Trial Transcript, 9 April 2009, 24181/14; 8 February 2011, 49152/3.
[52] *Taylor* Trial Judgment (*supra* n. 9), paras. 6979, 6986.

10.5 Joint Criminal Enterprise and the Characterization of Taylor's Conduct

The original indictment presented in 2003 described a joint criminal enterprise between the RUF and AFRC, in which Taylor was alleged to have participated, as follows:

> The RUF and the AFRC shared a common plan, purpose or design (joint criminal enterprise) which was to take any actions necessary to gain and exercise political power and control over the territory of Sierra Leone, in particular the diamond mining areas. The natural resources of Sierra Leone, in particular the diamonds, were to be provided to persons outside Sierra Leone in return for assistance in carrying out the joint criminal enterprise.[53]

The alleged JCE was expressed in similar terms in the amended indictment of 2006 which went on to state:

> The ACCUSED participated in this common plan, design or purpose as part of his continuing efforts to gain access to the mineral wealth of Sierra Leone, in particular diamonds, to destabilize the Government of Sierra Leone in order to facilitate access to such mineral wealth and to install a government in Sierra Leone that would be well disposed toward, and supportive of, the ACCUSED's interests and objectives in Liberia and the region.[54]

The Second Amended Indictment of 2007 alleged that:

> Members of the [RUF], [AFRC], AFRC/RUF Junta or alliance, and/or Liberian fighters, including members and ex-members of the NPFL (Liberian fighters), assisted and encouraged by, acting in concert with, under the direction and/or control of, and/or subordinate to the ACCUSED, burned civilian property, and committed the crimes set forth below . . ., as part of a campaign to terrorize the civilian population of the Republic of Sierra Leone.[55]

A case summary accompanying the indictment provided further particulars of the JCE:

> Between about 1988 and about 18 January 2002, the Accused and others agreed upon and participated in a common plan, design or purpose to

---

[53] *Prosecutor* v. *Charles Ghankay Taylor*, SCSL-2003–01-I, Indictment, 7 March 2003, para. 23.

[54] *Prosecutor* v. *Charles Ghankay Taylor*, SCSL-2003–01-I, Amended Indictment, 16 March 2006, para. 44.

[55] *Prosecutor* v. *Charles Ghankay Taylor*, SCSL-2003–01-I, Second Amended Indictment, 29 May 2007, para. 5. See also para. 33.

carry out a criminal campaign of terror, as charged in the Second Amended Indictment, in order to pillage the resources of Sierra Leone, in particular the diamonds, and to forcibly control the population and territory of Sierra Leone.[56]

In its final brief, the prosecution claimed that the JCE involved the use of 'criminal means' in the form of a 'campaign of terror encompassing the Indictment Crimes, in order to achieve the *ultimate objective* of the JCE, to forcibly control the population and territory of Sierra Leone and to pillage its resources, in particular diamonds'.[57]

In closing arguments, the prosecution summed up its position as follows:

> Charles Taylor, this intelligent, charismatic manipulator had his proxy forces and members of his Liberian forces carry out these crimes against helpless victims in Sierra Leone to achieve the objectives he shared with other members of the joint criminal enterprise in which he participates, to forcibly control the people and territory of Sierra Leone and to pillage its resources, in particular its diamonds. And they would do this through their agreed criminal means, the campaign of terror he waged on the innocent people of Sierra Leone with all its attendant crimes.[58]

The SCSL Appeals Chamber had previously held that the common purpose comprises both the objective of the JCE and the means contemplated to achieve that objective.[59] But throughout the trial the prosecution, defence and judges were engaged in a tug of war over the precise contours of the JCE resulting in an evolving framework that was ultimately to the detriment of the prosecution case. The Trial Chamber noted in its judgment that the theory of JCE presented by the prosecution had 'evolved and shifted over the course of the proceedings'.[60] The Trial Chamber settled on its understanding of the common purpose of the JCE

---

[56] *Prosecutor* v. *Charles Ghankay Taylor*, SCSL-2003–01-T, Prosecution Notification of Filing of Amended Case Summary, Case Summary accompanying the Second Amended Indictment, 3 August 2007, para. 42.

[57] *Charles Ghankay Taylor*, SCSL-2003–01-T, Prosecution Final Trial Brief, 8 April 2011, para. 574, emphasis added. See also *Taylor* Trial Judgment (*supra* n. 9), para. 6893.

[58] SCSL-2003–01-T, Trial Transcript, 8 February 2011, 49149/19–29-49150/4.

[59] *Prosecutor* v. *Charles Ghankay Taylor*, SCSL-2003–01-T, Decision on 'Defence Notice of Appeal and Submissions regarding the Majority Decision concerning the Pleading of JCE in the Second Amended Indictment', 1 May 2009, para. 25.

[60] *Taylor* Trial Judgment (*supra* n. 9), para. 6893. See also *Prosecutor* v. *Charles Ghankay Taylor*, SCSL-03–1-T, Decision on Urgent Defence Motion regarding a Fatal Defect in the Prosecution's Second Amended Indictment relating to the Pleading of JCE, 27 February 2009.

as being 'a campaign to terrorize the civilian population of the Republic of Sierra Leone, of which the crimes charged in Counts 2–11 of the Indictment were either an integral part, or a foreseeable consequence thereof'.[61]

The Trial Chamber considered that the prosecution had failed to prove that Taylor's support was provided pursuant to a common plan to terrorize the civilian population of Sierra Leone. Taylor's relationship with the RUF was viewed by the Trial Chamber as having intensified during his tenure as president, but the trading of arms for diamonds was ultimately found to have been based on a quid pro quo rather than a common criminal plan.[62] The trading of arms for diamonds was seen to be the clearest example of the quid pro quo in the relationship between Taylor and the RUF, 'and a number of statements attributed to the Accused indicate the interest he had in providing weapons or facilitating the provision of weapons to the RUF in exchange for diamonds'.[63]

Despite these findings, it was never clearly established why Taylor supported the RUF's cause. Possible explanations included the potentially lucrative trade deals, Taylor's anger against Sierra Leone for backing ULIMO and hosting ECOMOG, or his wish to honour an agreement with Sankoh made in Libya in the 1980s. The last possibility seemed to be the main prosecution focus in terms of establishing the meeting of minds necessary for a JCE.[64] However, the Trial Chamber found that the prosecution had failed to prove that 'prior to 1996 the Accused, Foday Sankoh and Kukoi Samba Sanyang (a.k.a. Dr Manneh), participated in any common plan involving the commission of the crimes alleged in the Indictment, nor that the alleged meetings in Libya, Burkina Faso and Voinjama, where the common plan is alleged to have been established, ever took place'.[65]

It is possible to speculate only whether a more consistent approach to the pleading of the JCE, avoiding any fluctuation over the objective, 'ultimate' objective and means, may have led to a conviction under JCE liability. The Trial Chamber did not fully explain whether a quid pro quo arrangement and a JCE were mutually exclusive. According to the Chamber, the evidence showed that Taylor and the RUF were 'military allies and trading partners'.[66] The Chamber seemed to treat such an

---

[61] *Taylor* Trial Judgment (*supra* n. 9), para. 6892.
[62] Ibid., para. 6898.
[63] Ibid.
[64] See ibid., para. 6889.
[65] Ibid., para. 6894.
[66] Ibid., para. 6899.

alliance as conceptually different from a JCE as opposed to evidence from which the existence of a JCE could in principle be inferred.

The prosecution did not appeal the Trial Chamber's failure to find a JCE and this issue was therefore never considered by the Appeals Chamber.[67] Taylor's conviction under the category of aiding and abetting as opposed to JCE raises the question whether the level of his responsibility was adequately captured by the legal characterization. In other words, was it appropriate to portray Taylor as an accomplice? It has been suggested that 'the sheer range of participants' contributions – from the intellectual authors of the crime to ordinary citizens who voted them into office, from the general who gives the order to a private who stands guard outside the prison camp – points to a graded understanding of moral responsibility'.[68] JCE liability and the concepts of co-perpetration applied by the International Criminal Court (ICC), especially co-perpetration through an organization, are designed to 'capture the "arm-chair" perpetrator as a principal rather than an accessory to a crime'.[69] These modes of liability are often considered to reflect the idea that moral blameworthiness is greater in respect of principal perpetrators, although this conception is open to challenge.[70] Taylor's exploitation of the conflict in Sierra Leone for financial gain was taken into account as an aggravating factor in sentencing.[71] His fifty-year sentence was the second highest to be given by the SCSL. Former ICC Judge van der Wyngaert has expressed the opinion that Taylor's fifty-year sentence was an expression of his perceived blameworthiness, reflecting his position of leadership.[72] It is perhaps unlikely that he would have received the eighty-year sentence requested by the prosecution even if JCE liability had been established, although possibly his sentence would then at least have been equivalent to the fifty-two years imposed on RUF leader Issa Sesay.

---

[67] See *Prosecutor* v. *Charles Ghankay Taylor*, SCSL-03-01-A, Prosecution's Notice of Appeal, 19 July 2012.

[68] M. Jackson, 'The Attribution of Responsibility and Modes of Liability in International Criminal Law' (2016) 29 *Leiden Journal of International Law* 879–95, 886.

[69] Kyriakakis (*supra* n. 5) 993.

[70] Cf. Concurring Opinion of Judge Christine van den Wyngaert, *Prosecutor* v. *Mathieu Ngudjolo Chui*, Judgment pursuant to Article 74 of the Statute, 1 December 2012, para. 24: 'I fail to see an inherent difference in blameworthiness between aiding and abetting and committing a crime.'

[71] *Prosecutor* v. *Charles Ghankay Taylor*, SCSL-03-01-T, Sentencing Judgment, 30 May 2012, para. 99.

[72] Concurring Opinion of Judge Christine van den Wyngaert (*supra* n. 70), para. 26.

10.6   Taylor's Responsibility as Head of State

Taylor was President of Liberia from 2 August 1997 until his resignation on 11 August 2003. The SCSL indictment covered the period from 30 November 1996 to 18 January 2002 and was therefore mainly concerned with Taylor's involvement in the Sierra Leone conflict while head of state. At an early stage of the proceedings, when Taylor claimed immunity as a serving head of state after the unsealing of the indictment, the prosecution put forward the perspective that state officials may be acting in a private rather than an official capacity when engaging in criminal conduct. This would exclude attribution of their conduct to the state. The SCSL Appeals Chamber, in its decision concerning Taylor's immunity, summed up an argument of the prosecution as follows: '[T]he prosecution maintains that from an early stage and *acting in a private rather than an official capacity* [Taylor] resourced and directed rebel forces, encouraging them in campaigns of terror, torture and mass murder, in order to enrich himself from a share in the diamond mines that were captured by the rebel forces.'[73] Nothing more was made of this distinction between acting in a private or official capacity in the immunity context because the Appeals Chamber concluded, relying on the *Arrest Warrant* case before the International Court of Justice,[74] that the SCSL was an international court before which an incumbent head of state had no immunity, as also provided in Article 6(2) of the SCSL Statute.[75]

For the purpose of attribution of the act of a state organ to the state, it can be difficult to distinguish private and official conduct, especially where an individual head of state manipulates the state bureaucratic apparatus in order to achieve criminal aims. An abuse of public power will generally still render the state liable. As the Commentary to Article 4 of the International Law Commission's Articles on State Responsibility (conduct of organs of a state) notes:

> A particular problem is to determine whether a person who is a State organ acts in that capacity. It is irrelevant ... that the person concerned may have had ulterior or improper motives or may be abusing public

[73] *Prosecutor* v. *Charles Ghankay Taylor*, SCSL-2003–01-I, Decision on Immunity from Jurisdiction, 31 May 2004, para. 5, emphasis added.
[74] *Case concerning the Arrest Warrant of 11 April 2000 (Democratic Republic of the Congo* v. *Belgium)*, Judgment of 14 February 2002, 2002 ICJ Rep 3.
[75] Statute of the Special Court for Sierra Leone, 16 January 2002.

power. Where such a person acts in an apparently official capacity, or under colour of authority, the actions in question will be attributable to the State.[76]

Since the SCSL was concerned with individual criminal responsibility, the issue of the capacity in which Taylor acted never resurfaced directly. Taylor attempted to argue that assistance to the RUF and AFRC in self-defence was a justified purpose under customary international law,[77] and that states could 'pursue national security interests by supplying materiel to the armed forces of a State or a party to an internal conflict, even if there is evidence of a recurring pattern of crimes committed by those armed forces'.[78] The Appeals Chamber was not swayed by these arguments.[79] It correctly pointed out that the criminality of state action was outside the SCSL's jurisdiction and left it to 'those bodies and tribunals which properly have authority over States to interpret the law on state responsibility'.[80]

The Appeals Chamber rejected the Trial Chamber's finding that Taylor's violation of the state's obligation of military non-intervention could constitute an aggravating factor in sentencing, but it accepted that 'the extraterritorial nature and consequences of Taylor's acts and conduct are directly related to Taylor and the gravity of his culpable conduct'.[81] In this respect, the approach of the Appeals Chamber appears correct, as one of the SCSL's purposes was to individualize guilt. However, Taylor's individual criminal responsibility does not exclude state responsibility where attribution can be established.[82] While Taylor may have viewed the Liberian state as his personal economic playground, the extent to

[76] Draft Articles on Responsibility of States for Internationally Wrongful Acts, with commentaries, *Yearbook of the International Law Commission*, 2001, Vol. II, Part Two, Commentary to Article 4, para. 13.
[77] *Prosecutor v. Charles Ghankay Taylor*, SCSL-03–01-A, Notice of Appeal of Charles Ghankay Taylor, 19 July 2012, para. 100, Ground 35.
[78] *Prosecutor v. Charles Ghankay Taylor*, SCSL-2003–01-A, Public with Confidential Annex A and Public Annexes B and C Appellant's Submissions of Charles Ghankay Taylor, 1 October 2012, para. 268.
[79] *Taylor* Appeal Judgment (*supra* n. 35), paras. 456–65.
[80] Ibid., para. 456.
[81] Ibid., para. 683. See also *Prosecutor v. Charles Ghankay Taylor*, SCSL-03–01-T, Sentencing Judgment (*Taylor* Sentencing Judgment), 30 May 2012, para. 27.
[82] See further A. Clapham, 'The Complexity of International Criminal Law: Looking beyond individual responsibility to the responsibility of Organizations, Corporations and States', in R. Thakur and P. Malcontent (eds.), *From Sovereign Impunity to International Accountability: The Search for Justice in a World of States* (United Nations University Press: 2004), pp. 233–53, 246–7.

which he also engaged the responsibility of the state through his activities remains unexplored. This reflects the widely held sentiment in Sierra Leone that Taylor himself, state-like in his power, personality and influence, was the source of the country's woes while the state of Liberia, which was experiencing unrest of its own, was not to blame.[83]

10.7   Taylor's Diamonds and 'Flying Money'

A report of a UN Panel of Experts on 'Sierra Leone Diamonds and Arms' submitted prior to the SCSL proceedings in 2000 stated that diamonds were 'a major and primary source of income' for the RUF and that the 'volume' varied from 25 million USD to 125 million USD per annum.[84] The bulk of RUF diamonds were found to have left Sierra Leone via Liberia with the knowledge and involvement of key Liberian government officials.[85] According to the report, 'President Charles Taylor is actively involved in fuelling the violence in Sierra Leone, and many businessmen close to his inner-circle operate on an international scale, sourcing their weaponry mainly in Eastern Europe.'[86] Liberia was found to be breaching Security Council arms embargoes and importing arms into its own territory and into Sierra Leone. As a result of diamonds coming in from Sierra Leone, Guinea and even Angola, Liberia became the 'official export source for many more times the quantity of diamonds than it actually produced'.[87]

A whole chapter of the Judgment of the SCSL Trial Chamber in the *Taylor* case is headed 'Diamonds', running from pages 2046 to 2173 of one of the longest judgments issued by an international tribunal (and following from a chapter on 'Arms and Ammunition'). The sustained

---

[83] See further, K. A. Hardtke, 'The Actions of One, The Responsibility of a Nation: Charles Taylor's Conviction by the Special Court for Sierra Leone and Its Impact on State Responsibility Claims against Liberia' (2014) 31 *Wisconsin International Law Journal* 909–33, 932, citing a news report where Prosecutor Brenda Hollis is reported to have stated 'it's not Liberia versus Sierra Leone, it's Sierra Leone versus Charles Ghankay Taylor'.

[84] Report of the Panel of Experts established by Security Council Resolution 1306 (2000), S/2000/1195, 20 December 2000, para. 1.

[85] Ibid., para. 2.

[86] Ibid., para. 23. Reference is made to Lebanese businessman Talal El-Ndine as the inner circle's paymaster who paid Liberians fighting alongside the RUF and bringing diamonds out of Sierra Leone personally, and also paid pilots and crew of the aircraft used for clandestine shipments in or out of Liberia. This name is not mentioned in the *Taylor* Trial Judgment.

[87] Waugh (*supra* n. 14), p. 188.

focus on the trade in diamonds for arms to fuel the conflict in Sierra Leone is not surprising as diamond wealth was a dominant theme in the prosecution discourse presented at trial.[88] However, there was limited evidence of Taylor's personal receipt of diamonds. Supermodel Naomi Campbell and actress Mia Farrow were called as witnesses in an attempt to fill this gap. The Trial Chamber accepted a version of the story that two strangers knocked on Campbell's door in the middle of the night after a charity dinner at Nelson Mandela's presidential residence. 'A gift for you,' they said and gave Campbell a pouch.[89] The 'pouch' contained rough diamonds that resembled pebbles to Campbell who had not seen diamonds in that state previously. At breakfast the following day she told the story to Mia Farrow and her ex-model agent and they responded that the gift was obviously from Taylor, an explanation which Campbell accepted. The difficulty for the Court was that the origin of the diamonds could not be proved, so while the witnesses brought media attention to the proceedings, their stories had little real evidential value. The Trial Chamber did, however, find it proven that diamonds mined in Sierra Leone, for example in Kono and Tongo Fields, were delivered from the AFRC/RUF to Taylor through various agents and during different time frames in exchange for arms and ammunition.[90] Presumably Taylor, as an astute businessman, received a good deal from the RUF in the sense that the diamonds he received were worth more than the arms he provided. Indeed, he appeared to use the profits to procure further arms, especially as the threat to his regime intensified.

In March 2004, Taylor's assets were frozen in the belief that he was still able to access them from his refuge in Nigeria. The UN Security Council (UNSC) noted that Taylor's depletion of Liberian resources and misappropriation of funds and assets and their removal abroad was undermining the transition to democracy in Liberia. It was therefore decided:

> [T]o prevent former Liberian President Charles Taylor, his immediate family members, in particular Jewell Howard Taylor and Charles Taylor, Jr., senior officials of the former Taylor regime, or other close allies or associates . . . from using misappropriated funds and property to interfere in the restoration of peace and stability in Liberia and the sub-region, all States in which there are, at the date of adoption of this resolution or at any time thereafter, funds, other financial assets and economic resources owned or controlled directly or indirectly by Charles Taylor, Jewell

---

[88] Glasius and Meijers (*supra* n. 17) 238.

[89] SCSL-2003–01-T, Trial Transcript, 5 August 2010, 45468/27.

[90] See *Taylor* Trial Judgment (*supra* n. 9), paras. 5874, 5948, 5990, 6057, 6058, 6076.

Howard Taylor, and Charles Taylor, Jr. ... shall freeze without delay all
such funds, other financial assets and economic resources, and shall
ensure that neither these nor any other funds, other financial assets or
economic resources are made available, by their nationals or by any
persons within their territory, directly or indirectly, to or for the benefit
of such persons.[91]

It is believed that Liberia's civil war made Taylor very wealthy.[92] Yet it has
never been established where the wealth Taylor supposedly amassed
actually ended up or precisely how it was dissipated.[93] Total figures are
unknown, with one unsubstantiated estimate being that Taylor put aside
an excess of 100 million USD per year as president.[94] Like the first paper
money used in China's ancient history that led to the coining of the term
'flying money',[95] Taylor's assets appear simply to have flown away.

10.8   Unfinished Business in Liberia

Taylor's plundering of Liberia's resources both during his armed struggle
and as president has been well-documented, including by the Liberian
Truth and Reconciliation Commission. The NPFL's first major business
deal was apparently the cannibalization of the Bong iron ore mine that
had been abandoned by a German-owned enterprise.[96] Taylor had
already secured international cooperation before assuming power.
Timber went through Côte d'Ivoire where it was handled by French
and Lebanese businesses.[97] When Taylor took over the presidency, he
used the state apparatus to further his economic aims.

An entire section of the report of the Truth and Reconciliation
Commission published on 30 June 2009 is devoted to 'Economic Crimes
and the Conflict, Exploitation and Abuse'. Part of the TRC's mandate was to
'investigate economic crimes, such as the exploitation of natural or public
resources to perpetuate armed conflicts, during the period January 1979 to

---

[91] UN Security Council Resolution 1532 (2004), 12 March 2004.
[92] Lovgren (*supra* n. 13).
[93] See D. Carvajal, 'Hunting for Liberia's Missing Millions', *The New York Times*,
      30 May 2010, www.nytimes.com/2010/05/31/world/africa/31taylor.html?pagewante
      d=all&_r=0: 'the search has stretched from the mangrove swamps and diamond fields
      of West Africa to Swiss banks and shell corporations'. Taylor was declared partly indigent
      by the SCSL, which meant that the bulk of his legal fees were covered by the Court.
[94] Polgreen (*supra* n. 1).
[95] See Introduction to this volume.
[96] Waugh (*supra* n. 14), p. 184.
[97] Ibid., p. 187.

October 14, 2003; determine whether these were isolated incidents or part of a systemic pattern; establish the antecedents, circumstances, factors and context of such violations and abuses; and determine those responsible for the commission of the violations'.[98] According to the TRC:

> Successive governments, including the Taylor regime, established a massive patronage system with domestic and foreign-owned corporations in several critical economic sectors, such as timber, mining and telecommunications, and granted illegal benefits to the corporations in exchange for financial and military support. Corporations and private individuals engaged in a host of illegal and anti-competitive activities such as tax evasion, bribery, looting, forced displacement of civilians, money laundering, arms smuggling, and illegal price fixing.[99]

The role of corporations in perpetrating economic crimes in Liberia was singled out for special attention. The TRC attempted to define 'economic crime', noting that there was no generally accepted definition and that the scope of the term was potentially very broad, covering most instances where the aim was to generate an illicit profit. The TRC report provides a list of individuals and corporate actors/public agencies that the TRC determined had committed economic crimes as well as a list of individuals and corporate actors/public agencies that were suspected of economic crimes and should be investigated further. The TRC reached the conclusion that: 'The perpetration of economic crimes in Liberia fuelled violent conflict both domestically and throughout the region. Warring factions used natural resources, such as timber, diamonds and other minerals, and rubber to finance war efforts. The illegal exploitation of natural resources by warring factions greatly contributed to the procurement and distribution of weapons throughout the sub-region.'[100]

Among other recommendations, it was suggested that the Liberian government 'must aggressively pursue civil and criminal actions against alleged perpetrators'.[101] The report set out an array of relevant domestic laws, although it noted that Liberian law needed to be reformed to include sufficient criminal penalties for illicit mining of mineral resources other than diamonds. The TRC also called for the establishment of a Reparations Trust Fund to compensate victims of economic crimes in Liberia, for which sources of funding would include tax arrears

[98] Final Report of the Truth and Reconciliation Commission of Liberia (TRC Report), Vol. III, Title III (Economic Crimes and the Conflict, Exploitation and Abuse), para. 1.
[99] Ibid., para. 4.
[100] Ibid., para. 134.
[101] Ibid., para. 140.

from timber, mining, petroleum and telecommunications companies that evaded tax liability under the Taylor regime; restitution or fines ordered by a Liberian court; and criminal and civil confiscation schemes in foreign jurisdictions to repatriate Liberian assets. At the level of international crimes, the TRC recommended that if a court with specialized jurisdiction were established, the prosecution of grave economic crimes should be included in its mandate and could be brought under the heading of pillage. Finally, the international community was recommended to investigate economic crimes related to the TRC's temporal mandate where it has jurisdiction, including under the principle of universal jurisdiction.[102]

Domestic prosecutions, although limited, have included some members or former members of Taylor's family circle. Taylor's first son, McArthur 'Chuckie' Taylor, who is a US citizen, was placed in charge of a special security unit during his father's presidency. He was convicted in the United States of torture committed in Liberia and sentenced to ninety-seven years' imprisonment in 2009.[103] One of Taylor's ex-wives, Agnes Reeves Taylor, recently had eight charges of torture and conspiracy to commit torture dismissed before the English courts in respect of acts allegedly committed in her official capacity at the start of the rebellion led by Taylor at the end of the 1980s.[104] Proceedings have commenced in Switzerland against Alieu Kosiah, a former ULIMO commander, and Martina Johnson has been indicted in Belgium for alleged international crimes committed in her role as an NPFL commander during Liberia's first civil war.[105] Most notably, perhaps, from a jurisprudential perspective, Guus Kouwenhoven was tried in the Netherlands and sentenced to a term of imprisonment of nineteen

---

[102] Ibid., para. 171.

[103] 'Taylor's Son Sentenced in US for Torture in Liberia', *The Guardian*, 9 January 2009, www.theguardian.com/world/2009/jan/09/charles-taylor-jr-torture-liberia.

[104] 'Britain drops war crimes case against Charles Taylor's former wife', *The Telegraph*, 6 December 2019, https://www.telegraph.co.uk/news/2019/12/06/britain-drops-war-crimes-case-against-charles-taylors-former/; 'Charles Taylor's Ex-wife Charged with Torture in Britain', *The Telegraph*, 3 June 2017, www.telegraph.co.uk/news/2017/06/03/charles-taylors-ex-wife-charged-torture-britain/. In June 2019, the UK Supreme Court heard a preliminary legal issue in the case concerning the interpretation of the term 'person acting in an official capacity' in section 134(1) of the Criminal Justice Act 1988.

[105] A. Mudukuti, 'Universal Jurisdiction – Opportunities and Hurdles', *Opinio Juris Blog*, 9 April 2019, http://opiniojuris.org/2019/04/09/universal-jurisdiction-opportunities-and-hurdles/. Mohammed Jabbateh and Thomas Woewiyu have also faced proceedings in the United States for immigration fraud.

years for complicity in war crimes based on his involvement with Taylor as a timber merchant and arms trader.[106]

The TRC report states that, in July 2001, Aziz Nassour allegedly paid Charles Taylor 1 million USD in cash to hide two Al-Qaeda operatives in Camp Gbatala near Taylor's farm and that, in the same month, Issa Sesay informed Taylor that the RUF would follow his recommendation and sell all of its diamonds to Nassour.[107] However, neither the TRC report nor the SCSL trial judgment throws much light on the possible links among Taylor, the RUF, the diamond trade and international terrorism.[108]

10.9   Conclusion

There was an expectation that the SCSL would try dozens rather than fewer than a dozen alleged perpetrators bearing the greatest responsibility for international crimes in Sierra Leone.[109] Charles Jalloh has noted that, alongside commanders and heads of state, the list of candidates for trial could have included 'the Belgian, Dutch, Italian, Israeli, Lebanese, and other foreign businessmen and profiteers who allegedly played an equally critical role by financing the war from a distance and amassing the loot'.[110] In Jalloh's view, '[t]hese are, in many ways, the real financial beneficiaries of the war'.[111] Apart from suggesting that the SCSL's record was disappointing in terms of the number of indictments, this comment points to the desirability of dividing a case such as Taylor's, which combined the political, military and economic pillars, into its separate themes, allowing for a prioritization of the economic pillar where appropriate.

The SCSL's indictment against Taylor failed fully to expose the economic aspect of the alleged criminal activity, further highlighting the need to bring attention to the economic pillar in developing charging practices. The allegations of pillage did not in fact relate to the theft of Sierra Leone's diamond resources, even though the objective of the JCE

---

[106] See further Chapter 12 in this volume.
[107] TRC Report (*supra* n. 98), para. 103.
[108] See further Waugh (*supra* n. 14), pp. 226–7. See also Lovgren (*supra* n. 13).
[109] C. C. Jalloh, 'Special Court for Sierra Leone: Achieving Justice?' (2011) 32(3) *Michigan Journal of International Law* 395–460, 420.
[110] Ibid., 424. Subsequent to his term as the first SCSL Prosecutor, David Crane apparently grouped Sammy Osally, Ibrahim Bah, Victor Bout, Vladimir Menin, Aziz Nasur and Gus Kouwenhoven in a 'West African Joint Criminal (Business) Enterprise'. Ibid., footnote 145.
[111] Ibid. 424.

was purportedly to 'pillage' Sierra Leone's natural resources. Count 11 charging pillage concerned rather mundane facts by comparison, including the looting of sheep and watches. Arguably the most significant allegation related to so-called 'Operation Pay Yourself' declared by Johnny Paul Koroma after ECOMOG dislodged the junta from Freetown in February 1998 and when there was no money to pay the AFRC/RUF fighters.[112] Notably, the pillage of civilian property that occurred in various districts was not found to have been perpetrated with the primary purpose of spreading terror.

The *Taylor* case before the SCSL demonstrates that the legal framework for establishing individual criminal responsibility for international crimes under the economic pillar exists, but that it is still evolving. Stepping back from any evidential gaps or inconsistencies, or factual issues in dispute between the parties in *Taylor*, the legal conclusion that providing arms and ammunition, personnel and funding to sustain military operations can lead to liability (provided all other requirements are met) where the recipient's modus operandi involves a campaign to terrorize the civilian population and the crimes charged are inextricably linked to this campaign appears reasonable within the context of the SCSL Statute and customary international law. In other words, *Taylor* suggests that the remote perpetrator supplying arms, personnel and even money from a different country can be held to account where there is proof that crimes are inextricably linked to the supported war aims and that the perpetrator has knowledge of the broad nature and scope of those crimes. But, as demonstrated in the chapters that follow, the definition of aiding and abetting differs from jurisdiction to jurisdiction and is sometimes open to different interpretations within a single jurisdiction (such as the ICTY). It therefore remains to be seen whether the approach in *Taylor* will be followed in other cases.

There is an ongoing debate over the scope of JCE liability and its ICC competitor, co-perpetration, both of which tend to be favoured by international prosecutors when charging those in senior leadership roles with international crimes. As these are forms of principal perpetration, it has been questioned whether 'secondary liability [will] ever be the correct characterization of responsibility in ICC proceedings'.[113] The *Taylor* case suggests that secondary liability may be the correct characterization even as it concerns leading 'economic' architects, although this finding by the

---

[112] *Taylor* Trial Judgment (*supra* n. 9), para. 1878.
[113] Kyriakakis (*supra* n. 5) 998.

Trial Chamber contradicted the main theory of the prosecution's case. As it concerns superior responsibility, the outcome in *Taylor* combined with the recent acquittal of Jean-Pierre Bemba Gombo by the Appeals Chamber of the ICC may lead to a greater reluctance to bring charges under this heading.[114] Bemba's responsibility for crimes against humanity and war crimes, including pillage, committed by *Mouvement de libération du Congo* troops in the Central African Republic, had been assessed exclusively under Article 28(a) of the ICC Statute concerning military commanders. Despite the apparent relevance of the concept of superior responsibility, it may be difficult to link 'remote' perpetrators to criminal activity of an economic nature under this concept due to the requirement of effective control.

Thirty-two of the ninety-four witnesses in *Taylor* were described as linkage witnesses (individuals who testified to links between Taylor and the underlying crimes), but there was nevertheless a strong emphasis on presenting the crime base. Indeed, in view of the Trial Chamber's finding that the RUF/AFRC's operations were 'inextricably linked' to crimes, this may have been important. However, presenting the full picture of atrocities may not be necessary or helpful in cases focused on the economic pillar provided the linkage evidence is available. The problem is that the linkage is often difficult to establish in cases of what are sometimes termed 'neutral'[115] or 'dual purpose' contributions, such as pure financial donations to a 'criminal' regime, or profiting from the proceeds of crime that have been 'laundered' in several steps (for example, the jewellery shop selling necklaces containing diamonds that were the product of slave labour in the mines of Kono). This difficulty is illustrated by the challenges that the SCSL prosecutor faced when attempting to prove Taylor's personal receipt of diamonds. Furthermore, establishing linkages may require sometimes controversial reliance on insider witnesses who have themselves engaged in criminal conduct.[116]

---

[114] ICC-01/05–01/08A, *Situation in the Central African Republic, Prosecutor v. Jean-Pierre Bemba Gombo*, Judgment on the appeal of Mr Jean-Pierre Bemba Gombo against Trial Chamber III's 'Judgment pursuant to Article 74 of the Statute', 8 June 2018.

[115] Burchard (*supra* n. 6) 921, referring to the use of the term in German criminal law theory.

[116] While it may be an exaggeration, it has been suggested that: 'The only direct evidence linking murder, maiming, rape and pillage in Sierra Leone to Taylor comes from the testimony of the president's blood-steeped former accomplices, such as convicted RUF leader Issa Sesay and Liberian commander Zigzag Marzah.' See Glasius and Meijers (*supra* n. 17) 249. See also Human Rights Watch (*supra* n. 4).

Taylor's trial before the SCSL, while arguably providing justice for his victims in Sierra Leone, 'left lingering questions for his victims in Liberia where he may have committed worse crimes'.[117] This demonstrates both the possibilities and the limitations of international criminal trials and the prosecutorial emphasis on the most senior leaders. It is doubtful whether the Liberian TRC process is adequate to provide justice for the victims in Liberia unless its recommendations are fully implemented. Indeed, it is in Liberia more than in Sierra Leone that Taylor acted as a 'homo oeconomicus who follows the logic of financial profit rather than of humanity'.[118] With the limitations of the SCSL process and the recommendations of the TRC in mind, there is a need for further attention to be paid to the complementary nature of different regulatory frameworks, domestic and international, and a further exploration of individual, state, organizational and corporate responsibility with respect to activities under the economic pillar of international crimes. Attention is also turning to the goal of ensuring that in future cases the 'flying money' is netted and provided to the victims.

[117] Tejan-Cole (*supra* n. 2), p. 205.
[118] Burchard (*supra* n. 6) 928.

A Different Type of Aid

Funders of Wars as Aiders and Abettors under International Criminal Law

JAN WOUTERS AND HENDRIK VANDEKERCKHOVE

11.1 Introduction

Article 25(3)(c) of the Rome Statute of the International Criminal Court[1] (Rome Statute) provides that 'a person shall be criminally responsible and liable for punishment for a crime within the jurisdiction of the Court if that person, . . . for the purpose of facilitating the commission of such a crime, aids, abets or otherwise assists in its commission or its attempted commission, including providing the means for its commission'.

However, while the Rome Statute and general international criminal law contain intricate rules on both the *actus reus* and *mens rea* requirements regarding aiding and abetting, this body of law fails to elaborate on the ways in which aiding and abetting take place. For instance, if a company engages in the sale of weapons to a terrorist organisation, may courts qualify the provision of weapons as aiding and abetting criminal acts committed by members of the organisation? What if a company purchased oil from a terrorist group knowing that the revenues accumulated would be used to detrimentally affect civilians? Would such business activity be interpreted as an indirect provision of aid? Or would a company have to pay an above-market price for the commodities, in order for the payment to constitute a form of aiding and abetting, as perhaps it could then be seen as an indirect and intentional way of financing terrorism? This chapter aims to provide answers to these questions, by assessing whether corporate actors in positions to make

---

[1] Rome Statute of the International Criminal Court, Rome, 17 July 1998, in force 1 July 2002 (Rome Statute).

relevant determinations can be held liable as aiders and abettors of international crimes.

First, the chapter provides an overview of the relevant legal rules and the international case law with respect to aiding and abetting. Additionally, these rules are applied to funders of wars who provide financial support to a party to an armed conflict, in order to evaluate whether the funders can be held liable as aiders and abettors for international crimes. Second, the complex issue of corporate criminal liability will be addressed. While the first part relates to the liability of individual corporate actors, companies can equally be direct funders of wars. However, they cannot yet be held criminally accountable at the international level. Numerous individual states, on the other hand, have enacted legislation to enable their domestic courts to determine corporate criminal liability. In light of this development, in the second part of the chapter the authors seek to evaluate whether reverting to domestic judicial systems can be viewed as an effective alternative solution to hold corporate funders of wars accountable for their involvement in the commission of international crimes.

11.2   War's Funders as Aiders and Abettors

International crimes are often committed in a multi-perpetrator setting and the extent to which one specific perpetrator is responsible depends on the often convoluted circumstances of the case. Therefore, and in order to ensure the accountability of all persons involved in the criminal act, several modes of liability have been devised in international criminal law. These modes correspond to the specific degrees of international criminal responsibility that are imposed on certain perpetrators.[2] For instance, Article 25 of the Rome Statute lists six different modes, including 'aiding and abetting or otherwise assisting'.[3] Furthermore, international criminal law stipulates

---

[2] K. Ambos, 'Article 25: Individual Criminal Responsibility', in O. Triffterer and K. Ambos (eds.), *Rome Statute of the International Criminal Court: A Commentary* (3rd ed., Hart Publishing, 2016), p. 984; H. Olasolo and E. Carnero Rojo, 'Forms of Accessory Liability Under Article 25(3)(b) and (c)', in C. Stahn (ed.), *The Law and Practice of the International Criminal Court* (Oxford University Press, 2015), p. 557; C. Plomp, 'Aiding and Abetting: The Responsibility of Business Leaders under the Rome Statute of the International Criminal Court' (2014) 30(79) *Utrecht Journal of International and European Law* 4–29, 7; A. Eser, 'Individual Criminal Responsibility', in A. Cassese, P. Gaeta and J. R. W. D. Jones (eds.), *The Rome Statute of the International Criminal Court: A Commentary*, Vol. 1 (Oxford University Press, 2002), p. 788.

[3] Article 25(3) Rome Statute.

several distinct requirements (relating to both the *mens rea* and the *actus reus*) which are to be fulfilled in order for a particular mode to be applicable.

Generally, and as was construed in the 1997 *Tadić* trial chamber judgment of the International Criminal Tribunal for the Former Yugoslavia (ICTY), 'aiding and abetting includes all acts of assistance by words or acts that lend encouragement or support, as long as the requisite intent is present'.[4] Throughout the subsequent years, international criminal courts and tribunals have been confronted with cases involving aiders and abettors and have shaped international criminal law and the *actus reus* and *mens rea* requirements with regard to this mode of liability.

In this first part, a short overview is given of the international legal requirements that should be fulfilled in order for an accused to be held criminally responsible as an aider and abettor. Additionally, each requirement is applied to the funders of war, who provide financial support to a party to an armed conflict, in order to evaluate whether the funders can be held liable as aiders and abettors for international crimes.

11.2.1 Actus Reus

11.2.1.1 Substantial Contribution: What, Where and When?

The *actus reus* – or physical element – required for 'aiding and abetting' relates to the provision of substantial practical assistance, encouragement or support to the principal offender.[5] First, it would need to be established that an act of practical assistance, encouragement or support was in fact carried out.[6] In addition, this act must have had a substantial effect

---

[4] International Criminal Tribunal for the Former Yugoslavia (ICTY), *Tadić* Trial Judgment of 7 May 1997, ICTY-94–1-T, para. 689.

[5] ICTY, *Vasiljević* Trial Judgment of 29 November 2002, ICTY-98–32-T, para. 70; ICTY, *Furundžija* Trial Judgment of 10 December 1998, ICTY-95–17/1-T, paras. 235, 249; Ambos (*supra* n. 2), p. 1003; K. Ambos, 'The ICC and Common Purpose: What Contribution Is Required Under Article 23(3)(d)', in C. Stahn (ed.), *The Law and Practice of the International Criminal Court* (Oxford University Press, 2015), p. 598; Olasolo and Carnero Rojo (*supra* n. 2), pp. 579–80; A. Cassese and P. Gaeta, *International Criminal Law* (3rd ed., Oxford University Press, 2013), p. 193; W. A. Schabas, *The International Criminal Court: A Commentary on the Rome Statute* (Oxford University Press, 2010), p. 434; A. Eser (*supra* n. 2), pp. 800–1.

[6] ICTY, *Vasiljević* (*supra* n. 5), para. 70; ICTY, *Furundžija* (*supra* n. 5), paras. 235, 249; Ambos (*supra* n. 2), p. 1004; Olasolo and Carnero Rojo (*supra* n. 2), p. 579.

on the perpetration of the crime.[7] The ICTY confirmed in its *Vasiljević* trial judgment of 2002 that 'the act of assistance need not have caused the act of the principal offender, but it must have had a substantial effect on the commission of the crime by the principal offender'.[8]

Other thresholds have likewise been applied by the ICTY when elaborating on the *actus reus*, namely those of directness[9] and of specific direction.[10] However, both have been rejected in later judgments of the ICTY and the Special Court for Sierra Leone (SCSL).[11] Moreover, the International Criminal Court (ICC) seems also to be a proponent of adhering to the threshold of substantial contribution. Even though the ICC has not yet definitively decided on a case involving prosecutorial allegations of aiding and abetting,[12] the Pre-Trial Chamber commented in its Confirmation of Charges decision in *Mbarushimana* that 'the application of analogous modes of liability at the ad hoc tribunals suggests that a substantial contribution to the crime may be contemplated'.[13] While the ICTY had not yet conclusively discarded the threshold of specific direction at the time of the Confirmation of Charges decision, it has done so now.[14] Therefore, the Pre-Trial Chamber's reasoning is

---

[7] International Criminal Tribunal for Rwanda (ICTR), *Ntakirutimana and Ntakirutimana* Trial Judgment of 21 February 2003, ICTR-96-10 & ICTR-96-17-T, para. 787; ICTY, *Vasiljević* (*supra* n. 5), para. 70; ICTR, *Bagilishema* Trial Judgment of 7 June 2001, ICTR-95-1A, para. 33; ICTY, *Blaškić* Trial Judgment of 3 March 2000, ICTY-95-14-T, para. 285; ICTR, *Musema* Trial Judgment of 27 January 2000, ICTR-96-13, para. 126; ICTR, *Rutaganda* Trial Judgment of 6 December 1999, ICTR-96-3, para. 43; ICTY, *Furundžija* (*supra* n. 5), para. 234; ICTY, *Tadić* (*supra* n. 4), para. 691; Ambos (*supra* n. 2), p. 1004; Olasolo and Carnero Rojo (*supra* n. 2), p. 580; A. Eser (*supra* n. 2), p. 800.

[8] ICTY, *Vasiljević* (*supra* n. 5), para. 70.

[9] ICTY, *Tadić* (*supra* n. 4), para. 691.

[10] ICTY, *Perišić* Appeal Judgment of 28 February 2013, ICTY-04-81-A, paras. 32–6.

[11] Regarding the threshold of directness, see ICTY, *Furundžija* (*supra* n. 5), para. 232. Regarding the threshold of specific direction, see ICTY, *Šainović* Appeal Judgment of 23 January 2014, ICTY-05-87-A, paras. 1617–25, 1650 and Special Court for Sierra Leone (SCSL), *Taylor* Appeal Judgment of 26 September 2013, SCSL-03-01-A, paras. 471–81.

[12] However, the *Lubanga* Trial Chamber did address the contribution threshold requirement of subparagraph (c) in relation to defining the contribution threshold for Article 25(3)(a) as a principal actor versus an accessorial actor (ICC, *Lubanga* Judgment of 14 March 2012, ICC-01/04-01/06-2842, para. 997).

[13] ICC, *Mbarushimana*, Decision on the confirmation of charges of 16 December 2011, ICC-01/04-01/10-465-Red, para. 279.

[14] While the ICTY had dismissed the 'specific direction' threshold, as applied in the *Tadić* appeal judgment (ICTY, *Tadić* Appeal Judgment of 15 July 1999, IT-94-1-A), in its *Mrkšić and Šljivančanin* appeal judgment, its *Blagojevic and Jokic* appeal judgment and its *Lukić and Lukić* appeal judgment, the threshold appeared once again in the ICTY's 2013 *Perišić* appeal judgment, which was considered to be incorrect only in September 2013 (*supra*

currently still valid, allowing the ICC to apply the 'substantial contribution' criterion. Besides, the ICC appears to have implicitly assumed or endorsed this standard in its *Lubanga* judgment where it addressed the contribution threshold for accessorial actors in relation to defining the contribution threshold for principal actors. In brief, the Trial Chamber in *Lubanga* relied on the threshold of a substantial contribution and suggested that 'if accessories must have had a substantial effect on the commission of the crime to be held liable, then co-perpetrators must have had . . . more than a substantial effect'.[15]

Second, the aider and abettor is not required to be present at the scene of the crime to be subject to accessory liability.[16] However, while the mere presence of the aider and abettor is not conclusive of aiding and abetting, the geographical connection – that is, presence – can be considered as such when it is demonstrated to have had a significant encouraging effect.[17] The encouraging or supporting effect can, for example, be deduced – whilst not necessarily in a conclusive manner – from the presence of a person with superior authority, as the latter's presence can, in some circumstances, be interpreted as an approval of the conduct.[18]

Third, the assistance may be given before, during or after the crime has been committed.[19] Nevertheless, it must be noted that, especially when assistance *ex post facto* is concerned, the 'substantial contribution' threshold still ought to be met.[20]

---

n. 11) – two years after the *Mbarushimana* Pre-Trial Chamber's 2011 confirmation of charges decision (*supra* n. 13).

[15] ICC, *Lubanga* (*supra* n. 12), para. 997.

[16] ICTR, *Bagilishema* (*supra* n. 7), para. 33; ICTY, *Blaškić* (*supra* n. 7), para. 285; ICTR, *Musema* (*supra* n. 7), para. 125; ICTR, *Rutaganda* (*supra* n. 7), para. 43; ICTR, *Kayishema and Ruzindana* Trial Judgment of 21 May 1999, ICTR-95-1, para. 200; ICTR, *Akayesu* Trial Judgment of 2 September 1998, ICTR-96-4-T, para. 484; ICTY, *Tadić* (*supra* n. 4), para. 691; Ambos (*supra* n. 2), p. 1007; Olasolo and Carnero Rojo (*supra* n. 2), p. 580.

[17] ICTR, *Semanza* Trial Judgment of 15 May 2003, ICTR-97-20, paras. 385, 386; ICTY, *Vasiljević* (*supra* n. 5), para. 70; ICTY, *Kunarac, Kovac and Vukovic* Trial Judgment of 22 February 2001, ICTY-96-23 & 23/1, para. 393; *Aleksovski* Trial Judgment of 25 June 1999, ICTY-95-14/1, para. 64; ICTR, *Kayishema and Ruzindana* Trial Judgment of 21 May 1999, ICTR-95-1, paras. 200–1; Ambos (*supra* n. 2), p. 1007.

[18] ICTR, *Niyitegeka* Trial Judgment of 16 May 2003, para. 461; ICTR, *Bagilishema* (*supra* n. 7), para. 34; ICTY, *Blaškić* (*supra* n. 7), para. 284; ICTY, *Aleksovski* (*supra* n. 17), para. 65; Ambos (*supra* n. 2), p. 1007.

[19] ICTR, *Semanza* (*supra* n. 17), para. 385; ICTY, *Vasiljević* (*supra* n. 5), para. 70; ICTR, *Bagilishema* (*supra* n. 7), para. 33; ICTY, *Blaškić* (*supra* n. 7), para. 285; ICTY, *Aleksovski* (*supra* n. 17), para. 62; Olasolo and Carnero Rojo (*supra* n. 2), p. 581.

[20] Cassese and Gaeta (*supra* n. 5), p. 193.

11.2.1.2   Aiding v. Abetting v. Otherwise Assisting
v. Providing the Means: Differences *Qua Actus Reus*?

So far, we have discussed the two forms of assistance, aiding and abetting, in tandem. However, as the International Criminal Tribunal for Rwanda (ICTR) noted in the *Akayesu* trial judgment, the terms "'aiding" and "abetting" are not synonymous'.[21] The ICTR specified that 'aiding' involves giving assistance to someone while 'abetting' relates to the facilitation of 'the commission of an act by being sympathetic thereto'.[22] This line of reasoning has been confirmed in subsequent judgments of both the ICTY and the ICTR.[23] However, in practice, international criminal courts and tribunals do not seem to have adapted their case law to the finding in *Akayesu* and it makes sense to consider both concepts together as one mode of liability. Doing so ensures, for example, that perpetrators who are showing their willingness to help (i.e. abettors), but whose willingness did not materialise in objective aid, are equally subject to criminal liability, without the prosecutor having to specify the discrete type of assistance beforehand.[24] In conclusion, while the two concepts can be distinguished, the difference is hardly ever genuinely considered in practice. Neither are different *actus reus* requirements applicable.

The Rome Statute introduced two new, related concepts in its Article 25(3)(c). This provision speaks of 'otherwise assisting' and 'providing the means for the commission of a crime', in addition to referring to 'aiding' and 'abetting'. These new terms should not, however, be regarded as innovative, distinct concepts relating to an independent mode of liability. The former term merely constitutes an umbrella term that encompasses both aiding and abetting and other possible forms of assistance. The latter concept, on the other hand, simply involves an example of how one can provide assistance.[25]

11.2.1.3   War's Funders: Substantially Contributing
v. Financially Contributing

While international criminal law clearly encompasses intricate rules on the *actus reus* requirements regarding aiding and abetting, it fails to

---

[21] ICTR, *Akayesu* (*supra* n. 16), para. 484.
[22] Ibid.
[23] ICTR, *Semanza* (*supra* n. 17), para. 384; ICTR, *Ntakirutimana and Ntakirutimana* (*supra* n. 7); ICTY, *Kvočka et al.* Trial Judgment of 2 November 2001, ICTY-98-30/1, para. 254.
[24] Plomp (*supra* n. 2) 9.
[25] Eser (*supra* n. 2), p. 799.

elaborate on the ways in which one aids or abets. Nevertheless, examples of convictions on the basis of aiding and abetting are abundant and can be relied upon in order to shed light on the issue. For example, in 1946 a British Military Court convicted German industrialist B. Tesch for aiding and abetting the Nazi SS in murdering allied nationals in concentration camps. The Court was of the opinion that Mr. Tesch assisted the SS when supplying poison gas, and, further, that he was aware of the fact that the SS used the specific goods to perpetrate the concerned crimes.

By analogy, if a company executive engages in the sale of weapons with a designated criminal organisation, courts may equally qualify the provision of weapons as a form of aiding and abetting. However, what if an entrepreneur provides mere financial support to a party to an armed conflict, for instance by way of providing a loan, making direct payments or purchasing commodities? Would such business activities be considered to qualify as the provision of aid? In this section the well-established rules on aiding and abetting are applied to individual funders of war and it will be evaluated whether more common forms of corporate financial contribution[26] fulfil the *actus reus* requirements.

Providing Funds   Companies often provide loans to the principal perpetrators of international crimes, be it dictatorial regimes or individual militia members.[27] For example, some banks provided considerable loans to the Argentinian junta and the South African apartheid regimes. Hence, the banks concerned were accused of having aided and abetted the said regimes as, allegedly, without these loans the regimes could not have supported their systemic human rights abuses and torture apparatus.[28] In addition, companies can provide funds to perpetrators by way of making direct payments to them. Chiquita Brands, for instance, admitted to having made payments to a paramilitary organisation, the United Self-Defense Forces of Colombia, which has been held responsible for killing several thousand civilians.[29]

---

[26] See W. Kaleck and M. Saage-Maass, 'Corporate Accountability for Human Rights Violations Amounting to International Crimes' (2010) 8 *Journal of International Criminal Justice* 699–724, 702–9 for an overview of how companies can be and have been involved in international crimes.

[27] Ibid. 706.

[28] Ibid.

[29] Ibid. 708. Another example is the *Lafarge* case relating to a cement supplier which, on the basis of its financial dealings with the Islamic State (IS), is being accused of aiding and abetting war crimes and crimes against humanity by financing the group (European

288 RESPONSIBILITY OF WAR'S FUNDERS AND PROFITEERS

Nonetheless, the question remains whether the provision of such funds can amount to substantial assistance to the principal offender. In the *In re South African Apartheid Litigation* case, the US Southern District Court of New York held that a distinction must be drawn between the provision of means by which a violation of international law was committed and the provision of funds.[30] On the basis of the *Ministries* and *Zyklon B* cases, the District Court concluded that 'the distinction between these two cases is the quality of the assistance provided to the primary violator. . . . The provision of goods . . . bear[s] a closer connection to the principal crime than the . . . provision of loans. . . . Therefore, in the context of commercial services, provision of the means by which a violation of the law is carried out is sufficient to meet the actus reus requirement of aiding and abetting liability under customary international law.'[31] The provision of funds, by contrast, could not be considered sufficient to meet the requirement.

While it might have been correct for the District Court to note that a closer connection exists between the provision of goods and the principal crime, it is submitted that this does not imply necessarily that the provision of funds cannot be considered a kind of substantial assistance. Whether that is the case depends on the evidence. There is no principled legal reason to exclude the provision of funds from being considered substantial with respect to the law on aiding and abetting.[32] What would still need to be determined, though, is what 'substantial' means.

Unfortunately, a generally accepted definition of the term 'substantial' does not exist. Hence, reliance on the case law of international criminal courts and tribunals is warranted. In its *Blagojević and Jokić* judgment, the ICTY concluded that the act of deploying engineering resources to mass execution sites could be considered substantial, while the act of relaying information could not.[33] In the same decision, the Tribunal held that the scope of the contribution, compared to the scope of the entire crime, is irrelevant. What is relevant, according to the Tribunal, is

---

Center for Constitutional and Human Rights, *Case Report: Lafarge in Syria: Accusations of Complicity in War Crimes and Crimes Against Humanity*, www.ecchr.eu).

[30] *In re South African Apartheid Litigation*, WL 960078 (2009), p. 21; Farrell, 'Attributing Criminal Liability to Corporate Actors: Some Lessons from International Tribunals' (2010) 8 *Journal of International Criminal Justice* 873–94, 890–1

[31] Farrell, 890–1.

[32] Farrell (*supra* n. 30) 891.

[33] ICTY, *Blagojević and Jokić* Trial Judgment of 17 January 2005, ICTY-02-60-T, paras. 763–4.

whether the contribution, be it with a limited or broad scope, had a substantial effect on the commission of the crime.[34] Consequently, as no principled legal difference should be drawn between the provision of goods and the provision of funds, and as the provision of goods can amount to substantial assistance, so can the provision of funds, regardless of the scope of the financial contribution.

Still, it is not clear *when* a financial contribution has a substantial effect on the commission of the crime. As the case law provides examples only on a case-by-case basis, one should turn to general theories of attribution.[35] On that basis, for the aider and abettor to be subject to accessory liability, he or she would need to create or increase the risk that the crime will be committed.[36] Further, there must be a causal link between, on the one hand, the creation or increase of the risk and, on the other, the commission of the crime.[37] Admittedly, this standard resembles, to a large extent, the 'specific direction' criterion.[38] However, rather than a causal link between the assistance and the crime,[39] general theories of attribution require merely a causal link between the assistance and the creation or increase of the risk that the crime will be committed.[40] In other words, a two-pronged test will need to be met: (i) the assistance would have to lead to the creation or increase of risk that the crime will be committed and (ii) this specific creation or increase of risk would, in turn, have to entail the actual commission of the crime.

In conclusion, the *actus reus* requirement could be fulfilled by way of providing funds if the latter act creates or increases the risk that a crime be committed. However, one notable issue remains unsolved: it continues to be difficult to prove that (financial) resources created or increased the risk of the principal committing a crime.[41] This evidentiary issue arose in two Dutch cases, namely the *van Anraat* and the *Kouwenhoven* cases.[42] In the former case, the prosecution had to prove

---

[34] ICTY, *Blagojević and Jokić* (*supra* n. 33), para. 765; ICTY, *Blagojević and Jokić* Appeal Judgment of 9 May 2007, IT-02-60-A, paras. 309–10.

[35] Ambos (*supra* n. 2), p. 1008.

[36] Ibid.; Ambos (*supra* n.) 5, p. 606.

[37] Ambos (*supra* n. 2), p. 1008; Ambos (*supra* n. 5), p. 606.

[38] ICTY, *Perišić* (*supra* n. 10), para. 44; see *supra* n. 13 and n. 14 on the acceptance and subsequent rejection of the 'specific direction' threshold.

[39] Plomp (*supra* n. 2).

[40] Ambos (*supra* n. 2), p. 1008; Ambos (*supra* n. 5), p. 606.

[41] Farrell (*supra* n. 30) 893.

[42] Court of Appeal in The Hague, *In the case of Frans van Anraat*, Judgment of 9 May 2007, Case No. 2200050906-2 and Court of Appeal in The Hague, *In the case of Guus*

that the provision of chemicals by the defendant, through his company, created or increased the risk of Saddam Hussein's government of Iraq committing war crimes and that the Iraqi government had in fact used the chemicals in committing war crimes.[43] In the latter case, the prosecution faced a similar problem: it had to prove that Guus Kouwenhoven delivered weapons to the Charles Taylor regime and that, by providing the risk-increasing assistance, he enabled the regime to commit international crimes.[44] Finally, while this hurdle is not necessarily impossible to overcome, as exemplified by the *van Anraat* case where the prosecution succeeded in meeting the two-pronged threshold,[45] it is a challenging one that will have to be surmounted on a case-by-case basis.[46]

Purchasing Commodities In 2000, the United Nations Security Council (UNSC) requested the Secretary-General (UNSG), K. Annan, to establish a Panel of Experts on the Illegal Exploitation of Natural Resources and Other Forms of Wealth of the Democratic Republic of the Congo (DRC).[47] The Panel's initial mandate was to investigate the links between the exploitation of natural resources and other forms of wealth in the DRC. In 2001, after the submission of its first final report, the Panel's mandate was renewed to include the preparation of a report on the possible actions that could be taken by the UNSC to help bring to an end the plundering of natural resources of the DRC.[48]

Kouwenhoven, Judgment of 10 March 2008, Case No. 220043306. The latter judgment has been quashed, however, by the Supreme Court of the Netherlands (see Supreme Court of the Netherlands, *In the case of Guus Kouwenhoven*, Judgment of 20 April 2010, Case No. 08/01322). Subsequently, the case had to be retried before the Court of Appeal in The Hague which eventually decided that there was sufficient evidence, at the time of its new decision, to establish that the principal perpetrator used Kouwenhoven's goods (see Court of Appeal in The Hague, *In the case of Guus Kouwenhoven*, Judgment of 21 April 2017, Case No. 20-001906-10). The case was, once again, brought before the Supreme Court of the Netherlands, yet this time the Supreme Court upheld the (second) conviction by the Court of Appeal (Supreme Court of the Netherlands, *In the case of Guus Kouwenhoven*, Judgment of 18 December 2018, Case No. 17/02109).

[43] Court of Appeal in The Hague, *In the case of Frans van Anraat* (*supra* n. 42).
[44] Court of Appeal in The Hague, *In the case of Guus Kouwenhoven*, Judgment of 10 March 2008 (*supra* n. 42).
[45] Court of Appeal in The Hague, *In the case of Frans van Anraat* (*supra* n. 42).
[46] Farrell (*supra* n. 30) 893.
[47] United Nations Security Council (UNSC), Statement by the President of the Security Council, 2 June 2000, S/PRST/2000/20.
[48] UNSC, Statement by the President of the Security Council, 19 December 2000, UN Doc. No. S/PRST/2001/39.

The UN Panel of Experts indicated in the second final report that companies not only provide loans to parties to an armed conflict, which possibly commit international crimes, but also finance them indirectly by way of purchasing their commodities. For instance, in 2001, a number of licensed diamond businesses in Antwerp procured several diamonds, for a value of 150 million USD, from the DRC.[49] The Panel confirmed that the revenues were, in turn, used to acquire weapons for the DRC's Armed Forces,[50] which are deemed to have committed several human rights violations. More specifically, the United Nations Joint Human Rights Office held that the Armed Forces were responsible, inter alia, for several arbitrary killings.[51]

It will be for a prosecutor to establish that the purchasing of commodities may have been a form of substantial assistance. It should be noted, however, that there is not much of a difference when compared to the provision of funds: both acts will allow the principal perpetrator to purchase the means for the commission of a crime. Regardless of whether the perpetrator has an amount of money at his disposal due to a loan or a sale, with it he will be able to acquire the means for the commission of a crime. Furthermore, it is not necessary for the buyer to overestimate the value of the commodities and, in turn, to pay an excessive price in order for his purchase to be considered a form of substantial aid. A regular price would be sufficient to allow the perpetrator to use the financial gains to purchase the means for the commission. As indicated above, the ICTY has held that the scope of the contribution, compared to the scope of the entire crime, is irrelevant.[52]

Therefore, the *actus reus* requirement may also be fulfilled by way of purchasing commodities from the perpetrator if the latter act creates or increases the risk that a crime be committed. Nonetheless, the major difficulty lies not with the fulfilment of the *actus reus* requirement but with evidencing the existence of the *mens rea* element. Indeed, as is the

[49] Panel of Experts on the Illegal Exploitation of Natural Resources and Other Forms of Wealth of the Democratic Republic of the Congo, *Final Report of the Panel of Experts on the Illegal Exploitation of Natural Resources and Other Forms of Wealth of the Democratic Republic of the Congo*, 16 October 2002, UN Doc. No. S/2002/1146, para. 34.
[50] Ibid., para. 54.
[51] United Nations Joint Human Rights Office (UNJHRO) MONUSCO-OHCHR, *Report on Human Rights Violations in the Democratic Republic of the Congo in the Context of the Events of 19 December 2016*, February 2017, paras. 18–19.
[52] ICTY, *Blagojević and Jokić* (*supra* n. 33), para. 765; ICTY, *Blagojević and Jokić* (*supra* n. 34), paras. 309–10.

case for aiding and abetting in general, a relatively low objective threshold but a rather high subjective threshold applies.[53]

11.2.2   Mens Rea

The *mens rea* – or mental element – required for 'aiding and abetting'
relates to the knowledge that one's 'actions assist the perpetrator in the
commission of a crime'.[54]

11.2.2.1   Knowledge, in the Sense of Awareness, at Least

First, the aider and abettor is required to have intended to provide the
assistance.[55] Or, at least, he or she would need to have accepted that his or
her conduct could result in de facto assistance.[56]

Second, the aider and abettor must know that his or her actions will
assist the perpetrator in the commission of a crime.[57] The SCSL has
further elucidated that an individual might be considered an aider and
abettor when it is evidenced that 'he was aware of the substantial likelihood that his acts would assist the commission of a crime by the
perpetrator'.[58] Additionally, the Rome Statute stipulates that 'knowledge'
means 'awareness that … a consequence will occur in the ordinary
course of events'.[59] Some degree of probability is, however, required
before one can be held to be aware of the fact that a consequence *will
occur*: one would need to be virtually certain that the consequence will
materialise, unless extraordinary circumstances intervene.[60] By way of

---

[53] Ambos (*supra* n. 2), p. 1009; Eser (*supra* n. 2), p. 801.

[54] ICTY, *Mrkšić and Šljivančanin* Appeal Judgment of 5 May 2009, ICTY-95-13/1-A, paras.
49, 63; ICTY, *Simić* Appeal Judgment of 28 November 2006, ICTY-95-9-A, para. 86;
ICTY, *Vasiljević* Appeal Judgment of 25 February 2004, IT-98-32-A, para. 102; ICTY,
Blaškić Appeal Judgment of 29 July 2004, IT-95-14-A, paras. 45, 49; ICTY, *Furundžija*
(*supra* n. 5), paras. 236–49; Olasolo and Carnero Rojo (*supra* n. 2), pp. 586–7.

[55] ICTR, *Bagilishema* (*supra* n. 7), para. 32; ICTY, *Blaškić* (*supra* n. 7), para. 286.

[56] ICTR, *Bagilishema* (*supra* n. 7), para. 32; ICTY, *Blaškić* (*supra* n. 7), para. 286.

[57] ICTY, *Vasiljević* (*supra* n. 5), para. 71; ICTR, *Bagilishema* (*supra* n. 7), para. 32; ICTY,
Blaškić (*supra* n. 7), para. 286; ICTY, *Furundžija* (*supra* n. 5), paras. 245, 249; Olasolo and
Carnero Rojo (*supra* n. 2), pp. 586–7.

[58] SCSL, *Brima et al.* Trial Judgment of 20 June 2007, SCSL-2004-16-A, para. 776.

[59] Article 30 of the Rome Statute, which equally refers to the 'awareness that a circumstance
exists'. However, in practice, 'knowledge' within the framework of aiding and abetting
relates only to the awareness that a consequence of one's act (i.e. the act of substantial
practical assistance, encouragement or support) will occur.

[60] ICC, *Katanga* Judgment pursuant to Article 74 of the Statute of 7 March 2014, paras.
770–9; ICC, *Bemba Gombo*, Decision on the confirmation of charges of 3 July 2009, paras.
352–69; L. Ferro, '"Brothers-in-Arms": Ancillary State Responsibility and Individual

example, a soldier who aims to destroy a building, while not wishing to kill the civilians that he knows are in the building, is said to intend the killing of the civilians if the building is in fact destroyed and the civilians are killed.[61] In that case, the *mens rea* requirement will be fulfilled.

This mental element does not oblige the aider to share the principal perpetrator's intent in order for him to be subject to accessory liability.[62] Yet, what must be shown is that the accomplice was, at least, aware of the essential elements of the crime, including the principal's mental state.[63]

Third, neither is it required for the aider and abettor to have been aware of which precise crime was intended or which crime would eventually be committed by the principal perpetrator.[64] As the ICTY stated in its *Furundzija* trial judgment, 'if he is aware that one of a number of crimes will probably be committed, and one of those crimes is in fact committed, he has intended to facilitate the commission of that crime, and is guilty as an aider and abettor'.[65]

Finally, as it is particularly difficult to establish whether a person knew or was aware of a fact, international criminal courts and tribunals have established that the *mens rea* may be deduced from factual circumstances.[66]

11.2.2.2 'For the Purpose of Facilitating the Commission of Such a Crime'

Article 25(3)(c) of the Rome Statute introduced new concepts relating to both the *actus reus* and the *mens rea* requirements for aiding and

---

Criminal Liability for Arms Transfers to International Criminals' (2017) 54(1) *Military Law and the Law of War Review* 139–87, 152; D. K. Pigaroff, 'Article 30. Mental Element', in O. Triffterer and K. Ambos (eds.), *Rome Statute of the International Criminal Court: A Commentary* (3rd ed., Hart Publishing, 2016), p. 1122.

[61] G. Werle and F. Jessberger, '"Unless Otherwise Provided": Article 30 of the ICC Statute and the Mental Element of Crimes under International Criminal Law' (2005) 3 *Journal of International Criminal Justice* 35–55, footnote 34.

[62] ICTY, *Vasiljević* (*supra* n. 5), para. 71; ICTY, *Aleksovski* Appeal Judgment of 24 March 2000, IT-95-14/1-A, para. 162; ICTY, *Furundžija* (*supra* n. 5), para. 245. An exception applies when the crime of genocide is concerned, however. The ICTR stated in its 1998 Akayesu trial judgment that 'when dealing with a person accused of having aided and abetted in the planning, preparation and execution of genocide, it must be proven that such a person did have the specific intent to commit genocide'. See ICTR, *Akayesu* (*supra* n. 16), para. 485.

[63] ICTY, *Vasiljević* (*supra* n. 5), para. 71; ICTY, *Aleksovski* (*supra* n. 62), para. 162; ICTY, *Furundžija* (*supra* n. 5), para. 245; Olasolo and Carnero Rojo (*supra* n. 2), p. 587.

[64] ICTY, *Kvočka et al.* (*supra* n. 23), para. 255; ICTY, *Furundžija* (*supra* n. 5), para. 246.

[65] ICTY, *Furundžija* (*supra* n. 5), para. 246.

[66] ICTY, *Aleksovski* (*supra* n. 17), para. 65; ICTR, *Akayesu* (*supra* n. 16), para. 478; ICTY, *Tadić* (*supra* n. 4), para. 676; Ambos (*supra* n. 2), p. 1009; Schabas (*supra* n. 5), p. 436.

abetting. The provision begins with the phrase 'for the purpose of facilitating the commission of . . . a crime'. Some scholars have interpreted this
phrase as a separate requirement, additional to intent and knowledge[67], the
latter two elements being the main mental elements according to Article
30(1) of the Rome Statute. The question then arises, to what extent does
this additional requirement affect the well-established *mens rea* criteria for
aiding and abetting? Cassese correctly notes that application of this additional requirement would significantly narrow the mode of liability as it
stands now under international criminal law.[68] Further, he states that
'requiring the aider and abettor to act with purpose to facilitate the crime
is tantamount to requiring shared intent',[69] a requirement that is categorically rejected by the ad hoc tribunals.[70]

Moreover, having to adhere to this additional requirement could entail
some absurd consequences, as indicated by Cassese. For instance,
a person who would otherwise be considered an aider and abettor in
line with settled rules of international criminal law could avoid conviction by the ICC on the basis of the new requirement if they were able to
show that they assisted for a purpose other than facilitating the crime,
such as the increase of profits.[71] An aider and abettor could be convicted,
in line with the new requirement, only if he or she intended to bring
about the crime or to, at least, assist in the commission thereof[72] and,
strangely enough, not if he or she is virtually *certain* of the fact that his or
her act would assist the perpetrator in the commission of a crime.

Finally, an additional mental requirement would not be useful in light
of the legal rationale behind the insertion of the phrase. The expression
'for the purpose of facilitating' was copied from the US Model Penal
Code, where the expression imposes a subjective requirement stricter
than mere knowledge.[73] Logically, the same rationale lies behind the

---

[67] S. Finnin, 'Mental Elements under Article 30 of the Rome Statute of the International
    Criminal Court: A Comparative Analysis' (2012) 61(2) *International Comparative Law
    Quarterly* 325–59, 357.

[68] Cassese and Gaeta (*supra* n. 5), p. 195.

[69] Ibid.

[70] ICTY, *Mrkšić and Šljivančanin* (*supra* n. 54), paras. 49, 63; ICTY, *Vasiljević* (*supra* n. 5),
    para. 71; ICTY, *Aleksovski* (*supra* n. 62), para. 162; ICTY, *Furundžija* (*supra* n. 5),
    para. 245.

[71] Cassese and Gaeta (*supra* n. 5), p. 195.

[72] Olasolo and Carnero Rojo (*supra* n. 2), pp. 584–5.

[73] Article 2.06(3)(a) of the US Model Penal Code, American Law Institute, 1985; Ambos
    (*supra* n. 2), p. 1009; H. Vest, 'Business Leaders and the Modes of Individual Criminal
    Responsibility under International Law' (2010) 8(3) *Journal of International Criminal
    Justice* 851–72, 861.

insertion of the expression in Article 25(3)(c) of the Rome Statute.[74] Consequently, it is only if the general rules on the mental element do not have the effect of imposing a stricter subjective requirement at the level of the ICC that the additional mental requirement is truly required. The provision of the Rome Statute that deals with the *mens rea* requirements in general is Article 30. In particular, it stipulates that 'a person shall be criminally responsible if the material elements are committed with intent and knowledge'. Since Article 30 of the Rome Statute does not require mere knowledge but also intent, it can be argued that in fact it already imposes a stricter subjective requirement.[75] Consequently, as Article 25(3)(c) does not include a truly *additional* requirement, it cannot be deemed a deviation from the default rule that is Article 30 and should, therefore, be considered superfluous. In addition, as was noted by Pigaroff, such phrases are often included merely to reiterate that the *actus reus* is indeed performed intentionally.[76]

In conclusion, the new concepts and phrases inserted in Article 25(3)(c) of the Rome Statute do not necessarily entail a major evolution of the law on aiding and abetting at the international level. However, it all depends on how the ICC eventually deals with these novelties.

11.2.2.3 War's Funders: Virtually Certain of Consequences of Assistance

A person providing funds to or purchasing commodities from a warring party can obviously do so intentionally – meaning that the person 'means to engage in the conduct',[77] rather than doing so by accident. However, it would arguably even suffice if he or she merely accepts that the de facto provision of funds would be 'a possible and foreseeable consequence of his conduct', while at the same time not specifically intending to provide funds.[78] This 'acceptance of risk' threshold is especially relevant when it comes to persons purchasing commodities who might not have intended to fund the principal perpetrator directly but who still purchase the latter's commodities, which clearly entails the de facto provision of funds.

---

[74] 'Nothing in the *travaux* to assist in construing the specific language' (see Schabas (*supra* n. 5), p. 431). Yet, Commentaries to the Rome Statute do confirm that the expression was 'borrowed' from the US Model Penal Code (see Ambos (*supra* n. 2), p. 1009).

[75] Plomp (*supra* n. 2) 15.

[76] Pigaroff (*supra* n. 60), p. 1117.

[77] Article 30 of the Rome Statute.

[78] Article 30 of the Rome Statute; ICTR, *Bagilishema* (*supra* n. 7), para. 32; ICTY, *Blaškić* (*supra* n. 7), para. 286.

Additionally, the aider and abettor must have been virtually certain of the fact that his or her act would entail the commission of the principal perpetrator's crime. By way of example, employees of banks who provide loans to people – in a normal scenario – do not know per se that their loans enable the borrower to commit crimes. The same goes for individual corporate actors who decide to make direct payments to or purchase commodities from a party to an armed conflict for a certain amount of money. However, depending on the circumstances, corporate actors might be considered to be virtually certain of the consequences of providing funds to a warring party that is known for committing international crimes: the provision of funds will enable the party to do so again. This line of reasoning has been confirmed by the SCSL. In its *Brima and others* trial judgment, it relies several times on 'the systematic pattern of crimes committed by the [Armed Forces Revolutionary Council] troops'[79] to establish that the accused certainly had to be aware of the consequences of his acts.

Concluding this part, we can say that providing funds to a warring party is, in and of itself, not necessarily a criminal act. However, when companies are substantially supporting – be it by way of providing loans, making direct payments or purchasing commodities – a party to an armed conflict that is known for committing international crimes, their individual executives may be held accountable as aiders. Yet, the *mens rea* requirement must still be met. While this subjective threshold usually is rather high,[80] it is met more easily when assistance to a party to an armed conflict that is known for systematically committing international crimes (such as Daesh) is concerned. After all, in such a situation, it can hardly be possible for an aider and abettor to be unaware of the violations.

11.3   Recourse to Domestic Corporate Criminal Liability for International Crimes

In the previous sections we mainly focused on the responsibility of individual corporate actors as aiders and abettors. However, companies themselves can equally act as direct funders of wars. Yet, legal persons currently cannot be held criminally accountable at the international level. Numerous individual states, on the other hand, have enacted legislation to enable their domestic courts to determine corporate criminal liability in such situations. In light of this development, this section seeks to

---

[79] SCSL, *Brima et al.* (*supra* n. 58), paras. 1786, 1940.
[80] Ambos (*supra* n. 2), p. 1009; Eser (*supra* n. 2), p. 801.

evaluate whether reverting to domestic judicial systems can be a proper alternative solution to hold corporate funders of wars accountable for their involvement in the commission of international crimes

11.3.1 Origins, Scope Ratione Materiae *and Objectives of Corporate Criminal Liability*

The concept of corporate criminal liability originated in the United States in the early 1900s and spread quickly to other common law countries.[81] The original doctrine entailed that 'masters were criminally liable for their servant's public nuisance'[82] and that governmental bodies were liable for acts of local officials.[83] In the subsequent decades, the scope of this particular form of liability was widened significantly.[84] Following the acceptance of criminal intent of companies in 1909 by a US court,[85] restrictions *ratione materiae* of corporate criminal liability were gradually abolished,[86] ultimately even allowing corporate liability for homicide.[87] Furthermore, despite several legal obstacles, many civil law countries equally enacted legislation with respect to corporate criminal liability, albeit only towards the end of the twentieth century.[88]

Both civil law and common law countries have since broadened the scope of corporate criminal liability, thereby encompassing liability not only for homicide but also for international crimes.[89] Consequently, the criminal liability of companies for international crimes can today be determined in

---

[81] S. Beck, 'Corporate Criminal Liability', inM. D. Dubber and T. Hörnle (eds.), *Oxford Handbook of Criminal Law* (Oxford University Press, 2014), p. 562. A long-lasting tradition of corporate criminal liability can be found in many common law countries such as the UK (see M. Pieth and R. Ivory (eds.), *Corporate Criminal Liability: Emergence, Convergence, and Risk* (Springer, 2011), pt II, chs. 3, 4) but also in India, South Africa, Australia, New Zealand and Canada (see M. Engelhart, 'Unternehmensstrafbarkeit im europäischen und internationalen Recht' (2012) 3 *Eucrim* 110–23).

[82] Beck (*supra* n. 81), p. 562.

[83] Ibid.

[84] Ibid.

[85] *New York Central & Hudson River Rail Road Co.* v. *U.S.*, 212 US 481 (1909); Beck (*supra* n. 81), p. 563.

[86] Beck (*supra* n. 81), p. 563.

[87] *State of Indiana* v. *Ford Motor Co.*, (1978) 47 *United States Law Week* 2514, at 2515; Beck (*supra* n. 81), p. 563.

[88] Beck (*supra* n. 81), p. 565; G. Heine, '§ 27 StGB: Beihilfe', in A. Schönke and H. Schröder (eds.), *Strafgesetzbuch Kommentar* (2nd ed., Beck, 2014), paras. 25 ff., 122 with further references; Engelhart (*supra* n. 81) 110, footnotes 2–4; Pieth and Ivory (*supra* n. 81), p. 9.

[89] J. G. Stewart, 'The Turn to Corporate Criminal Liability' (2014) 47(1) *New York University Journal of International Law and Politics* 121–206, 161.

many Western countries.[90] However, national laws still differ significantly from state to state with respect to, amongst others, included entities and actors.[91] Nonetheless, the doctrine of corporate criminal liability is currently firmly embedded in many domestic legal systems[92] and allows for the prosecution of companies involved in international crimes.[93]

The doctrine of corporate criminal liability strives to attain several objectives. First, companies are deemed to have more means to commit international crimes than individuals[94] and consequently pose a considerably higher risk.[95] Corporate criminal liability aims at effectively reducing that risk. Accordingly, the doctrine is deterrent-based, like most corporate crime theories.[96] Moreover, focusing on the liability of companies is in fact 'more effective than exclusively penalizing individuals and other means of regulation because it should have a stronger preventive effect by addressing the real decision-maker(s)',[97] considering that criminal punishment has a greater deterrent effect.[98] Besides, corporate criminal liability is characterised by specific criminal financial penalties such as fines and the dissolution of a company, which could be more effective in halting the company's malicious practices.[99] Second, a company is in some cases designed specifically to shield its executives from liability.[100] Subjecting the company to criminal liability is therefore

---

[90] Ibid. 161–3.

[91] Beck (*supra* n. 81), p. 566; M. Pieth, 'Ein europäisches Unternehmensstrafrecht', in E. Kempf, K. Lüderssen and K. Volk (eds.), *Unternehmensstrafrecht* (Beck, 2012), 397 ff.

[92] Beck even speaks of an '(almost) worldwide introduction of corporate criminal liability' (*supra* n. 81), p. 566.

[93] Beck (*supra* n. 81), p. 566; Stewart (*supra* n. 89) 161–3; Pieth and Ivory (*supra* n. 81), p. 13.

[94] Plomp (*supra* n. 2) 22; H. van der Wilt, 'Corporate Criminal Responsibility for International Crimes: Exploring the Possibilities' (2013) 12 *Chinese Journal of International Law* 43–77, 73.

[95] Beck (*supra* n. 81), p. 567.

[96] P. Cartwright, 'Publicity, Punishment and Protection: The Role(s) of Adverse Publicity in Consumer Policy' (2012) 32(2) *Legal Studies* 179–201, 181; C. Wells, *Corporations and Criminal Responsibility* (2nd ed., Oxford University Press, 2001), p. 31.

[97] Beck (*supra* n. 81), p. 567. See also A. Pinto and M. Evans, *Corporate Criminal Liability* (3rd ed., Sweet and Maxwell, 2013), p. 4.

[98] Beck (*supra* n. 81), p. 567; N. Gotzmann, 'Legal Personality of the Corporation and International Criminal Law: Globalisation, Corporate Human Rights Abuses and the Rome Statute' (2008) 1(1) *Queensland Law Student Review* 38–54, 43; J. Gobert and M. Punch, *Rethinking Corporate Crime* (Cambridge University Press, 2003), pp. 50 ff; J. Braithwaite, 'The Limits of Economism in Controlling Harmful Corporate Conduct' (1981–1982) 16 *Law and Society Review* 481–504.

[99] Plomp (*supra* n. 2) 22; Gotzmann (*supra* n. 98) 44.

[100] Plomp (*supra* n. 2) 22; Gotzmann (*supra* n. 98) 43.

meant to prevent business leaders from hiding behind the so-called corporate veil.[101] Moreover, corporate criminal liability tries to ensure that problems of evidencing the actions and intentions of separate individual members are avoided or overcome.[102] Finally, addressing the collective entails that it is not only the material, individual perpetrator but also those that are benefiting from the crime who are being punished. A third important objective of prosecuting companies is to achieve a result that is 'not only effective but also just and equitable'.[103]

11.3.2 Domestic Corporate Criminal Liability for International Crimes: A Waste of Precious Time or a Worthwhile Investment?

Admittedly, the responsibility to prosecute and punish perpetrators of international crimes presently lies primarily with states.[104] Yet, can domestic courts and tribunals effectively contribute to the achievement of the goals of corporate criminal liability when faced with cases involving companies that have aided and abetted the principal perpetrator of an *international* crime?

Regarding the fulfilment of the first objective of corporate criminal liability (i.e. the application of a deterrence-based doctrine), regardless of whether an international or domestic crime has been committed, a conviction of a company by a national court can usually be deemed an effective deterrent. While it might be accurate to state that criminal punishment does not necessarily deter the convicted or other companies and that specific penal, financial sanctions 'have insignificant preventive effect vis-à-vis powerful corporations, which may already factor in possible sanctions in their cost-benefit analyses',[105] the same critics

---

[101] Ibid.

[102] Beck (*supra* n. 81), p. 567.

[103] Beck (*supra* n. 81), p. 568; H. J. Hirsch, *Die Frage der Straffähigkeit von Personenverbänden* (Springer, 1993), p. 6; H. Otto, *Die Strafbarkeit von Unternehmen und Verbänden* (De Gruyter, 1993), pp. 8, 25; R. Busch, *Grundfragen der strafrechtlichen Verantwortlichkeit der Verbände* (Weicher, 1933), p. 116 ff.

[104] Articles 1 and 17, and Preamble of the Rome Statute: 'Emphasizing that the International Criminal Court established under this Statute shall be complementary to national criminal jurisdictions.'

[105] O. K. Fauchald and J. Stigen, 'Corporate Responsibility before International Institutions' (2009) 40 *George Washington International Law Review* 1025–1100, 1042. See also: Beck (*supra* n. 81), p. 568; W. Hassemer, 'Die Basis des Wirtschaftsstrafrechts', in E. Kempf, K. Lüderssen and K. Volk (eds.), *Die Handlungsfreiheit des Unternehmers—wirtschaftliche Perspektiven, strafrechtliche und ethische Schranken* (De Gruyter, 2009), p. 29 ff., 40;

acknowledge that 'adverse publicity may well be the most effective deterrent as it affects both the corporation's prestige and financial success'.[106] Nonetheless, judicial convictions – which entail specific penal financial sanctions – are consistently accompanied by adverse publicity and public stigma, be it through subsequent media coverage or published court reports.[107]

Furthermore, the second objective (i.e. removing the corporate veil) will be reached as well if domestic courts impose penal economic sanctions, regardless of whether an international or domestic crime has been committed. Indeed, any punishment within the framework of corporate criminal liability will affect the entire company, including the individual corporate actor, the corporate veil notwithstanding. In any case, responsible actors will never be able to hide behind the said veil when facing criminal charges.[108]

Moreover, it has been noted that economic sanctions 'might appear totally inadequate compared to the harm caused by international crimes',[109] and that the third goal (i.e. a just and equitable outcome) thus can never be truly achieved through corporate criminal liability. If, however, one agrees with this line of argument, then neither can regular, non-economic criminal sanctions ever be considered adequate, just or equitable compared to the harm caused by international crimes. Indeed, both economic and non-economic sanctions merely aim at ensuring that the perpetrator of the crime is being punished. Furthermore, economic sanctions might even be considered more adequate, just and equitable as not only the perpetrator but all beneficiaries are subject to punishment.[110] Therefore, imposing economic sanctions on the collective would lead to a result that is, at least, as adequate, just and equitable as if regular, non-economic penalties had been imposed.

S. S. Simpson, *Corporate Crime, Law and Social Control* (Cambridge University Press, 2005), p. 5; G. Eidam, *Straftäter Unternehmen* (Beck, 1997), p. 91 ff. Moreover, classic economics assumes this situation as long as the anticipated benefits exceed the anticipated costs (see Cartwright (*supra* n. 96) 182).

[106] Fauchald and Stigen (*supra* n. 105) 1042. See also Cartwright (*supra* n. 96) 182; R. Macrory, *Regulatory Justice: Making Sanctions Effective, Final Report*, Macrory Review, Cabinet Office, 2006, para. E7.

[107] Cartwright (*supra* n. 96) 187; Macrory (*supra* n. 106).

[108] The corporate veil applies only when tort law or civil law procedures are concerned (see A. Pinto and M. Evans, *Corporate Criminal Liability* (2nd ed., Sweet and Maxwell, 2008), pp. 71–3).

[109] Fauchald and Stigen (*supra* n. 105) 1042.

[110] Beck (*supra* n. 81), p. 568; Hirsch (*supra* n. 103), p. 6; Otto (*supra* n. 103), pp. 8, 25; Busch (*supra* n. 103), p. 116 ff.

On the other hand, innocent shareholders – the ones who most likely will bear the costs of the economic sanction[111] – are equally and, according to some, unjustly affected. However, classic economics dictates that 'an efficient market would price in the risk that a company will get caught committing a crime, making the shareholder's loss in a particular case simply one of many perils associated with investing'.[112] Admittedly, the same counter-argument does not hold true for employees and customers who are affected indirectly by the punishment. Nevertheless, by way of analogy, the incarceration of a wrongdoer likewise affects the latter's innocent family members, yet no one doubts the equitability of imprisonment per se.[113]

In conclusion, domestic courts can be legally competent and can theoretically contribute to the achievement of the goals of corporate criminal liability when faced with cases involving companies that have aided and abetted the principal perpetrator of an international crime. Admittedly, numerous practical issues come with the domestic prosecution of perpetrators of international crimes, especially when the forum state is not the state on whose territory the international crime was committed. Yet, with a view to a genuine contribution to international criminal justice, domestic corporate criminal liability for international crimes is worth the investment. Resources should hence be made available for domestic judicial systems to be able to address a company's involvement in international crimes. Otherwise, as long as the international community is not apt to exercise criminal jurisdiction and impose penalties on companies, business enterprises would escape justice and impunity would endure. Moreover, in practice, the first steps have already been taken. In recent years, the Swiss and Dutch prosecutors, for instance, have opened investigations following complaints against companies for allegedly having been involved, to some extent, in the commission of international crimes.[114] While the cases were ultimately

---

[111] J. Fisch, 'Criminalization of Corporate Law: The Impact on Shareholders and Other Constituents' (2007) 2(1) *Journal of Business & Technology Law* 91–6, 93.

[112] X., *Corporate Criminal Liability Serves the Purposes of Punishment*, Manhattan Institute, 2009, www.pointoflaw.com/feature/archives/2009/07/corporate-criminal-liability-s.php.

[113] Ibid.

[114] Stewart (*supra* n. 89) 125, 127. Furthermore, on 28 June 2018, a cement company called HolcimLafarge was indicted by a French investigative judge for complicity in crimes against humanity (Business and Human Rights Resource Center, 'Lafarge Lawsuit (re Complicity in Crimes Against Humanity in Syria)', www.business-humanrights.org/en/lafarge-lawsuit-re-complicity-in-crimes-against-humanity-in-syria. However, while the

shelved,[115] these attempts to bring about justice could serve as a prelude to corporate criminal liability for international crimes.

Another option in the fight against impunity would be to empower the ICC and to ensure that it can determine corporate criminal liability. Indeed, international criminal courts were specifically established in order to avoid the difficulties involved in national prosecutions of international crimes,[116] and the same reasoning could be at the basis of a further expansion of the powers of the ICC. Moreover, already in 1998, the French delegation to the Rome Diplomatic Conference for an International Criminal Court proposed that an individual be convicted too, as a *sine qua non* of corporate liability.[117] Nonetheless, at the time, the proposal was turned down. If it were submitted today, things could be different. Compared to 1998, many more states have adopted legislation providing for corporate criminal liability[118], and these states may nowadays be more inclined to accept an international court with the competence to determine corporate criminal liability.

11.4   Conclusion

As has been evidenced throughout the first part of the chapter, corporate actors in positions to make relevant decisions can in fact be held personally liable as aiders and abettors when their institutions provide financial support to a party to an armed conflict that commits international crimes. Indeed, the *actus reus* requirements can be fulfilled by way of providing funds to or by way of purchasing commodities from the perpetrator if the act amounts to a substantial form of assistance, that is, it creates or increases the risk that a crime be committed. The fulfilment of the *actus reus* requirement is thus rather easily evidenced. Demonstrating the existence of the *mens rea* elements, on the other hand, frequently proves to be difficult. Nonetheless, the threshold with

---

case is not yet shelved, neither has a French court definitively held the company criminally liable.

[115] Stewart (*supra* n. 89) 127; AFP, 'Swiss Slammed for Closing DR Congo "Dirty Gold" Case', www.dailymail.co.uk/wires/afp/article-3107021/Swiss-slammed-closing-DR-Congo-dirty-gold-case.html.

[116] N. Roht-Arriaza, 'Just a "Bubble"? Perspectives on the Enforcement of International Criminal Law by National Courts' (2013) 11 *Journal of International Criminal Justice* 537–43, 537.

[117] Working Paper on Article 23, paras. 5–6, A/Conf.183/C.1/WGGP/L.5/Rev.2, 3 July 1998; Plomp (*supra* n. 2) 22; van der Wilt (*supra* n. 94) 46–8.

[118] Beck (*supra* n. 81), p. 565.

respect to the latter elements is met more easily when assistance to a party to an armed conflict that is known for systematically committing international crimes (such as Daesh) is concerned. After all, in such a situation, it can be more or less assumed that an aider and abettor is aware of the violations.

In the second part of the chapter, the complex issue of corporate criminal liability was addressed. Despite the fact that companies can be direct funders of wars, they cannot be held criminally accountable at the international level as of yet. Numerous individual states, on the other hand, have enacted legislation to enable their domestic courts to determine corporate criminal liability. It has been shown that domestic courts can be competent, both legally and theoretically, to contribute to the achievement of the goals of corporate criminal liability, when faced with cases involving companies having aided and abetted the principal perpetrator of an international crime. Admittedly, domestic courts would be confronted with several practical issues when initiating proceedings involving corporate criminal liability for international crimes. Yet, today it is the only option to fight the impunity that business enterprises would otherwise enjoy – unless, of course, the international community were to empower the ICC and allow it to determine corporate criminal liability.

Aiding and Abetting and Causation in the Commission of International Crimes

The Cases of Dutch Businessmen van Anraat and Kouwenhoven

GÖRAN SLUITER AND SEAN SHUN MING YAU[*]

Introduction

An increasing amount of attention is being paid to the roles of companies and businessmen assisting in the commission of international crimes, for example through the delivery of weapons. The mode of criminal liability that corresponds to unlawful assistance in the commission of crimes is generally referred to as aiding and abetting. It requires an act of assistance that has contributed to the commission of the crime (*actus reus*) and that the suspect has done so with the requisite degree of intent or knowledge (*mens rea*).

This chapter will focus on the *actus reus*; to be more specific, the standard of causation, in the context of companies and businessmen who contribute to mass atrocities. It will do so through the lens of two well-known Dutch cases, concerning two businessmen, Mr van Anraat and Mr Kouwenhoven, who delivered weapons in situations of armed conflict and mass atrocities (Iraq in the 1980s and Liberia in the 1990s). While both men have been convicted for aiding and abetting war crimes, the requisite standard of contribution appears to differ considerably between the two cases. This chapter addresses the question as to what the degree of causation should be for aiding and abetting liability of companies and businessmen who have assisted in the commission of mass atrocities. This question will be answered in the context of aiding and abetting in Dutch domestic criminal law and international criminal law.

[*] This chapter is part of the VICI research project on Secondary Liability for International Crimes (see rethinkingslic.org), funded by the Netherlands Organization for Scientific Research (NWO). Sean Shun Ming Yau contributed to this chapter as a former participant in the VICI project.

In order to answer this question, it will first be necessary to provide, as a background, a short introduction to the theoretical debate on causation as a requirement for liability of aiders and abettors. Next follows an analysis of the requisite standards for causation under both Dutch and international criminal law. The cases of van Anraat and Kouwenhoven – and the diverging approaches in these cases – will be analysed in the subsequent section against the backdrop of these theories and legal standards. As a synthesis of the preceding sections, we will offer some reflections on the need for a revised or *sui generis* approach to the standard of causation in case of complex situations of assistance in atrocity crimes. The last section will contain concluding observations.

Theory on Causation in Aiding and Abetting

There is an interesting theoretical debate among scholars, especially legal philosophers, as to the required degree of causation in situations of complicity. For our purposes it suffices to address the two contrasting views on causation, one in which causation matters and the other in which it does not. This requires a consideration of the underlying rationales and theoretical justifications for these diverging views.

Gardner is among the scholars who argue that complicity can exist only where a suspect participates in the wrongs of others by making a causal contribution to them.[1] He takes the view that only assistance which has made a difference to the overall incidence of wrongdoing should result in (accomplice) liability. The fundamental issue is thus whether as a result of the assistance there are more wrongs in the world than without it. If this is not the case, there should not be any criminal liability, 'because it seems odd that someone should be expected to pay attention (in her practical reasoning) to features of the world that will come out no better whatever she does'.[2]

Gardner's philosophical and moral justification for causation in complicity appears to have received considerable support. Stewart, for example, has argued that there should be actual causation, namely whether the accomplice's help could have contributed to the criminal action of the principal.[3] Moore has taken the position that causation is crucial for

---

[1] J. Gardner, 'Complicity and Causality' (2007) 1 *Criminal Law and Philosophy* 127.
[2] Ibid. 138.
[3] J. G. Stewart, 'Complicity', in M. D. Dubber and T. Hörnle (eds.), *The Oxford Handbook of Criminal Law* (Oxford University Press, 2014), p. 18.

responsibility.[4] Petersson has argued that 'undetectability of causal links between acts and effects should make us cautious before assigning responsibility, precisely because the causal involvement condition is an essential and practically important element in our practices of holding agents morally to account for events that have made the world worse'.[5]

Contrary to Gardner, Kutz has argued in 'Causeless Complicity' that accomplice liability does not require causation.[6] One can be an accomplice in various ways; some situations require causation and others not. Kutz offers the example of a guard who can render himself complicit in a burglar's theft by doing nothing, deliberately failing to sound the alarm.[7] What binds together all the complicity cases is the mental state of the accomplice – a mental state directed both towards the accomplice's own agency (including the agency involved in refraining) and towards the agency of the principal.'[8]

There is considerable support for Kutz's position on causeless complicity. Lawson has argued that '[b]y centering on the wills of individual partici-pants, the complicity principle is able to take note of the fact that individual contributions vary in terms of how closely they resemble the collective goal', and 'causal contributions can still be relevant, but only within the context of the kind of role played by the participants'.[9] It has also been said that 'aiding is required, but the degree of influence is immaterial'.[10] Farmer supports Kutz, by arguing that various types of (non-causal) contribution may sustain, intensify or legitimate the wrong in legally relevant ways, and while some of these may be reconstructed in causal terms, it would seem both artificial and unduly constraining to do so.[11]

The two opposing views on the role of causation in accomplice liability can in our view be described as a harm-caused doctrine on the one hand and a risk-based doctrine on the other. The essential question for this chapter is whether the unique nature of international crimes, notably the core crimes as set out in the International Criminal Court (ICC)

---

[4] M. Moore, 'Causing, Aiding, and the Superfluity of Accomplice Liability' (2009) 156 *University of Pennsylvania Law Review* 395, 397.

[5] B. Petersson, 'Co-Responsibility and Causal Involvement' (2013) 41 *Philosophia* 847, 865.

[6] C. Kutz, 'Causeless Complicity' (2007) 1 *Criminal Law and Philosophy* 289.

[7] Ibid. 300.

[8] Ibid.

[9] B. Lawson, 'Individual Complicity in Collective Wrongdoing' (2013) 16 *Ethical Theory and Moral Practice* 227, 242.

[10] J. Dressler, 'Reassessing the Theoretical Underpinnings of Accomplice Liability: New Solutions to an Old Problem' (1985) 37 *Hastings Law Journal* 91, 102.

[11] L. Farmer, 'Complicity beyond Causality: A Comment' (2007) 1 *Criminal Law and Philosophy* 151, 155.

Statute,[12] could lead to a preference for either school of thought on causation.

Two aspects of mass atrocities that are relevant in answering this question need to be mentioned. First, international crimes generally result in extreme harm. They tend to be characterized by extreme brutality and numerous victims. This certainly sets the core crimes apart from many of the examples of 'ordinary' criminal wrongdoing that have been discussed in the scholarly literature on the theory of causation and complicity, and which do not result in a similar degree of harm. Second, core crimes often manifest themselves in a widespread and systematic manner, and involve a high plurality of actors, which is generally not the case with the commission of 'ordinary' crimes. The commission of core crimes is often a form of 'system criminality', involving the state or a similarly organized group such as a rebel army; this results in a very high number of principals committing a high number of crimes.[13] It almost goes without saying that the number of possible accomplices who provide various forms and degrees of assistance can be extremely high.

One could argue that these unique aspects of the core crimes support the school of thought in favour of complicity liability without causation, for two reasons. First, there is an undeniable and very clear correlation between the seriousness of the crime, or the harm occasioned by the crime, and the penalization of risk-based conduct. This correlation is already part of international criminal law in, for example, the criminalization of incitement to commit genocide, without necessarily having caused the genocide. In this case the mere risk-enhancing nature of incitement suffices.[14] The crime of terrorism provides another example. We see that, in respect of the crime of terrorism, conduct which increases the risk of a terrorist attack, such as publicly praising terrorism, or

---

[12] The core crimes are set out in Article 5 (1) of the ICC Statute: (a) The crime of genocide; (b) Crimes against humanity; (c) War crimes; (d) The crime of aggression. The crime of aggression raises particular causation issues and can also on other levels be distinguished from the other crimes in the ICC's jurisdiction. When reference is being made in this chapter to mass atrocities, it thus does not refer to the crime of aggression but connotes the – multiple – commission, on a widespread and systematic basis, of genocide, crimes against humanity or war crimes.

[13] See on the various dimensions and complexities related to system criminality, A. Nollkaemper and H. van der Wilt (eds.), *System Criminality in International Law* (Cambridge University Press, 2009).

[14] W. Schabas, *Genocide in International Law: The Crime of Crimes* (Cambridge University Press, 2009), p. 319.

apologie du terrorisme, which is broader than incitement, has triggered criminalization, without requiring actual causation in relation to a terrorist attack.[15] In light of these non-exhaustive examples of criminalizing risk-enhancing conduct in respect of very serious crimes, it may seem defensible that a person who has acted in a way that could have assisted in the commission of mass atrocities should be punishable on that basis, without this assistance needing to have made any difference to the crime's actual commission.

The second reason why aiding and abetting without causation could be justifiable in cases of mass atrocities has to do with the plurality of crimes and actors involved and the impossibility of proving causation in certain scenarios. Take for example the selling of weapons to parties to an armed conflict that is characterized by war crimes and crimes against humanity. In case of multiple suppliers of weapons and bearing in mind the chaos that generally reigns in situations of armed conflict, it may be as good as impossible to prove which arms supplier's assistance has caused a specific war crime or crime against humanity. Given that an indictment shall contain clear and specific charges, the causation question – that is, whether or not the indicted arms dealer made a difference for that particular charge – is answerable through the fact that his or her weapons were used in the commission of crimes. It seems hard to swallow under these circumstances, in which the beyond reasonable doubt standard is unlikely to be met, that all arms suppliers would have to be acquitted as accomplices. A risk-based approach towards accomplice liability, without actual causation being necessary, could resolve this problem. It would then be sufficient that the weapons dealer in question has acted, that is, has supplied weapons, with the risk that they would be used in the commission of extremely serious crimes.

Causation in Aiding and Abetting under Dutch Criminal Law and International Criminal Law

Dutch Criminal Law

Article 48 of the Dutch Penal Code (DPC) provides for two types of accomplice liability and attaches criminal liability to:

---

[15] See B. Saul, 'Speaking of Terror: Criminalising Incitement to Violence' (2005) 28 *UNSW Law Journal* 868.

1. any persons who intentionally aid and abet the commission of the serious offence;
2. any persons who intentionally provide opportunity, means or information for the commission of the serious offence.

On the face of the text, the first paragraph appears to have a broader construction – aiding and abetting generally – than in the second paragraph, which specifies certain forms of assistance. The Dutch Supreme Court has addressed this tenuous distinction and taken the view that the two categories of assistance in Article 48 cannot be strictly distinguished.[16]

For an act of assistance to qualify as aiding and abetting under Article 48, it must satisfy the requirement of causality. The Supreme Court has elaborated on this *actus reus* element to require that the assistance furthered, facilitated or enabled the commission of the offences.[17] The assistance need not be decisive, substantial or indispensable (*condicio sine qua non*) for the commission.[18] Neither must the accomplice have made an 'adequate causal contribution' to the crimes.[19] Instead, the accomplice's assistance must have 'had a certain effect' on the offence, which is a relatively low threshold.[20] In practice, what it means is that the accomplice supported the crime or made it easier for the principal perpetrator to commit the crime.[21] Further, it is not required that the accomplice be physically present at the time of commission, or that he or she cooperated with the principal perpetrator in any way.[22]

---

[16] Supreme Court, 22 March 2011, ECLI:NL:HR:2011:BO2629, para. 2.2. See also P. J. P. Tak, *The Dutch Criminal Justice System: Organization and Operation* (Boom Juridische Uitgevers, 2003), p. 47.

[17] Supreme Court, 10 June 1996, ECLI:NL:HR:1997:ZD0749. In addition, note that the Dutch criminal law distinguishes between serious offences (*misdrijven*) and lesser offences (*overtredingen*). The qualifier 'serious' is found in Articles 92–206 of the DPC. Furthermore, the crimes enumerated in the International Crimes Act, according to its Article 2(2), are equated to serious offences, thus rendering Article 48 applicable to international crimes cases.

[18] Supreme Court, 8 January 1985, ECLI:NL:HR:1985:AC0143.

[19] Ibid.

[20] As seen later, this 'certain effect' threshold is comparatively lower than that adopted at the ad hoc criminal tribunals, i.e. substantial contribution to the crime but may be similar to the under-developed standard at the ICC.

[21] Supreme Court, 22 March 2011, ECLI:NL:HR:2011:BO2629. See also J. de Hullu, *Materieel strafrecht. Over algemene leerstukken van strafrechtelijke aansprakelijkheid naar Nederlands recht* (Wolters Kluwer, 2015), p. 495.

[22] de Hullu (n. 21), p. 496.

The Ad Hoc International Criminal Tribunals

Aiding and abetting is criminalized in Article 7(1) of the Statute of the International Criminal Tribunal for the Former Yugoslavia (ICTY) and Article 6(1) of the Statute of the International Criminal Tribunal for Rwanda (ICTR). The debate in ICTY and ICTR case law has focused on two issues: the meaning of 'substantial effect' and whether the assistance must be 'specifically directed' at the commission of the crime. For the purpose of this chapter, the former is determinative of the requisite level of causation in aiding and abetting.

The threshold of 'substantial effect' was first developed in the *Tadić* case. There, the prosecution argued that even 'the most marginal act of assistance' could constitute aiding and abetting. The Trial Chamber rejected this proposition. Having reviewed a number of Nuremberg judgments and the Draft Code of Crimes against the Peace and Security of Mankind, it concluded that the act of assistance must have 'a substantial and direct effect on the commission' of the crime.[23] A year later, another Trial Chamber in *Furundžija* re-examined the causality standard in aiding and abetting and concluded that, according to customary international law, the accomplice's assistance must have 'a substantial effect on the perpetration' of the crime.[24] In doing so, the Chamber essentially left out the qualifier 'direct'.[25] It justified the modification by rejecting the formulation in the 1996 ILC Draft Code on which the *Tadić* finding was based, requiring that the accomplice must participate 'directly and substantially'.[26] On this note, the ILC Commentary further explained that 'participation of an

---

[23] ICTY, *Prosecutor v. Tadić*, Judgment, Case No. IT-94-1-T, 7 May 1997, para. 688, referring to Draft Code of Crimes Against the Peace and Security of Mankind (1996), U.N. Doc. A/CN.4/SER.A/1996/Add.1 (Part 2).

[24] ICTY, *Prosecutor v. Furundžija*, Judgment, Case No. IT-95-17/1-T, 10 December 1998, para. 234, followed by the ICTR in e.g. *Prosecutor v. Kayishema & Ruzindana*, Judgment, Case No. ICTR-95-1-A, A. Ch., 1 June 2001, para. 201; *Prosecutor v. Ntakirutimana and Ntakirutimana*, Case Nos. ICTR-96-10-A and ICTR-96-17-A, A. Ch., 13 December 2004, para. 530 ('This support must have a substantial effect upon the perpetration of the crime').

[25] This approach was subsequently followed in case law, including the *Tadić* Appeal Judgment. See ICTY, *Prosecutor v. Tadić*, Judgment, Case No. IT-94-1-A, A. Ch., 15 July 1999, para. 229, requiring 'a substantial effect upon the perpetration', repeated in ICTY, *Prosecutor v. Vasiljević*, Judgment, Case No. IT-98-32-A, A. Ch., 25 February 2004, para. 102; ICTY, *Prosecutor v. Blaškić*, Judgment, Case No. IT-95-14-A, A. Ch., 29 July 2004, para. 46.

[26] See 1996 Draft Code of Crimes Against the Peace and Security of Mankind, Report of the International Law Commission to the General Assembly, UN Doc. A/51/10 (1996), Article 2, para. 3(d).

accomplice must entail assistance which facilitates the commission of a crime in some significant way'.[27] The *Furundžija* Trial Chamber considered such standard to be overly restrictive. It concluded: 'In view of this, the Trial Chamber believes the use of the term "direct" in qualifying the proximity of the assistance and the principal act to be misleading as it may imply that assistance needs to be tangible, or to have a causal effect on the crime.'[28]

But what does it mean for the assistance to have a 'substantial effect' on the perpetration of the crime? It is generally agreed that the threshold is not one of 'but for', that is, it is not required to prove that the crime would not have occurred had the accomplice not assisted. While the ad hoc tribunals have used 'substantial effect' interchangeably with 'substantial contribution'[29] or sometimes 'significant contribution',[30] these terms suggest that the assistance need not be a *condicio sine qua non* for the commission of the crime.[31] The ICTY Appeals Chamber in the case concerning *Prosecutor* v. *Blaškić* concurred with the Trial Chamber's holding that aiding and abetting requires no causal effect on the perpetration of the crime.[32] It stated: 'In this regard, it agrees with the Trial Chamber that proof of a cause–effect relationship between the conduct of the aider and abettor and the commission of the crime, or proof that such conduct served as a condition precedent to the commission of the crime, is not required.'[33] What is required instead is that the effect of assistance produced on the realization of the crime is substantial,[34] or that it substantially contributes to the crime's commission.[35] The *Tadić* Trial Chamber understood the term 'substantial' to require that the

---

[27] Report of the I.L.C., p. 24; *Furundžija* Trial Judgment (n. 24), para. 231.

[28] *Furundžija* Trial Judgment (n. 24), para. 232. Furthermore, the Trial Chamber found support from the absence of the term 'direct' from Article 25(3)(c) of the Rome Statute. However, it has been criticized that such interpretation appears weak since at the ICTY the causation standard was also not in the text but rather developed in case law.

[29] ICTY, *Prosecutor* v. *Mrkšić and Šljivančanin*, Judgment, Case No. IT-95–13/1-A, A. Ch., 5 May 2009, para. 81.

[30] ICTY, *Prosecutor* v. *Blagojević and Jokić*, Judgment, Case No. IT-02–60-A, A. Ch., 9 May 2007, para. 1.

[31] Ibid., para. 134, citing ICTY, *Prosecutor* v. *Simić*, Judgment, Case No. IT-95–9-A, A.Ch., 28 November 2006, para. 85 and ICTY, *Prosecutor* v. *Blaškić*, Judgment, Case No. IT-95–14-A, A. Ch., 29 July 2004, para. 48.

[32] ICTY, *Prosecutor* v. *Blaškić*, Judgment, Case No. IT-95–14-T, 3 March 2000, para. 285.

[33] *Blaškić* Appeal Judgment (n. 25), para. 48.

[34] *Mrkšić and Šljivančanin* Appeal Judgment (n. 29), para. 49; ICTY, *Prosecutor* v. *Orić*, Judgment, Case No. IT-03–68-A, A. Ch, 3 July 2008, para. 43.

[35] *Mrkšić and Šljivančanin* Appeal Judgment (n. 29), para. 202.

contribution 'in fact has an effect on the commission of the crime'.[36] The *Aleksovski* Trial Chamber required that the effect of the assistance for the perpetration must be 'important'.[37] In *Furundžija*, the Trial Chamber endorsed the position from the Nuremberg cases that the contribution must 'make a significant difference to the commission' of the crime and that '[h]aving a role in a system without influence would not be enough'.[38] Overall, it considered an act of assistance substantial if 'the criminal act most probably would not have occurred in the same way had not someone acted in the role the accused in fact assumed'.[39]

This requires a case-by-case assessment of the factual context.[40] The contextual factors probative of the significance of the assistance in the commission of the crime include, inter alia, the accused's position of authority and the nature of his other tasks,[41] the ability to exercise independent initiative, and whether the accused has acted to make resources available for the perpetration of the crime.[42] Thus, in *Blagojević and Jokić*, the Appeals Chamber found that Mr Jokić, in coordinating, sending and monitoring the brigade resources and equipment involved in a mass execution, assisted in carrying out the orders of the commander and thus in the commission of the crime.[43] This is notwithstanding that assistance by way of relaying orders would produce a sufficient effect on the commission of the crimes and is consequently criminal, only if the crimes committed are at least implicit in the order.[44] In order for the contribution to be substantial, the assistance must have

---

[36] *Tadić* Trial Judgment (n. 23), para. 688. O. Triffterer and K. Ambos (eds.), *The Rome Statute of the International Criminal Court: A Commentary* (Hart Publishing, 2016), p. 1004, interpreting this finding as requiring 'a causal relationship with the result'. It may be recalled, however, that the ad hoc tribunals have unequivocally rejected the need for a 'cause–effect relationship'. See e.g. *Blaskic* Trial Judgment (n. 32), para. 285.

[37] ICTY, *Prosecutor v. Aleksovski*, Judgment, Case No. IT-95–14/1-T, 25 June 1999, paras. 60–1.

[38] *Furundžija* Trial Judgment (n. 24), para. 233.

[39] *Tadić* Trial Judgment (n. 23), para. 688.

[40] *Mrkšić and Šljivančanin* Appeal Judgment (n. 29), para. 200. See also ICTR, *Kalimanzira v. Prosecutor*, Judgment, Case No. ICTR-05–88-A, A. Ch., 20 October 2010, para. 86.

[41] *Blagojević and Jokić* Appeal Judgment (n. 30), para. 198; ICTY, *Prosecutor v. Lukić and Lukić*, Judgment, Case No. IT-98–32/1-A, A. Ch., 4 December 2012, para. 438.

[42] *Blagojević and Jokić* Appeal Judgment (n. 30), paras. 747, 755. See also ICTY, *Prosecutor v. Krstić*, Judgment, Case No. IT-98–33-A, A. Ch., 19 April 2004, paras. 135–8.

[43] *Blagojević and Jokić* Appeal Judgment, ibid., paras. 195, 198.

[44] ICTY, *Prosecutor v. Strugar*, Judgment, Case No. IT-01–42-T, A. Ch., 31 January 2005, para. 354: 'The Chamber also found that the deliberate and unlawful shelling . . . was not implied in the Accused's order. In the Chamber's view, therefore, the Accused's order to attack Srd did not have a substantial effect on preparations for the crimes.'

made it easier or more likely for the crime to be realized. This can be done by, for instance, directing victims to the crime scene or providing the means of perpetration.[45] The ad hoc tribunals' jurisprudence thus suggests that although the accomplice's assistance need not be criminal in and of itself, it must pertain to the criminality of the principal's act, in the sense that it is one of the factors in the chain of events cumulatively leading to the commission.[46]

This being said, the focus remains on the effect of the accomplice's assistance upon the act of the principal perpetrator.[47] The fact that the accused provided comparatively more limited assistance to the commission of the crime than others does not preclude fulfilment of the requirement of substantial effect.[48] It is also irrelevant whether the principal perpetrator coordinated with the accomplice or was aware of the accomplice's contribution.[49]

This legal standard on causality applies *mutatis mutandis* in situations where the crime has been perpetrated by a plurality of actors.[50] This is particularly important for cases of international crimes where the ultimate commission is made possible almost always by a network of persons, remotely and at the scene. In such cases, whether the assistance of the accused may fulfil the *actus reus* of aiding and abetting depends on the effect of the accomplice's conduct assessed in itself, not from the perspective of the plurality of actors.

[45] ICTR, *Ntawukulilyayo* v. *Prosecutor*, Judgment, Case No. ICTR-05–82-A, A. Ch., 14 December 2011, para. 216.

[46] Ambos has drawn the analogy to the English 'concerned in the killing' theory. See K. Ambos, 'Individual Criminal Responsibility', in O. Triffterer and K. Ambos (eds.), *The Rome Statute of the International Criminal Court: A Commentary* (Hart Publishing, 2016), p. 1004. See also G. Werle, 'Individual Criminal Responsibility in Article 25 ICC Statute' (2007) 5 *Journal of International Criminal Justice* 953, 967, making the comparison that 'unlike the mere aider and abettor, the instigator sets in motion a chain of events that eventually leads to the commission of the crime'.

[47] Ambos (n. 46), p. 1004.

[48] *Blagojević and Jokić* Appeal Judgment (n. 30), para. 134.

[49] *Tadić* Appeal Judgment (n. 25), para. 229. It is therefore irrelevant whether the principal is identified. See ICTY, *Prosecutor* v. *Perišić*, Judgment, Case No. IT-04–81-T, 6 September 2011, para. 127.

[50] ICTY, *Prosecutor* v. *Kvočka et al.*, Judgment, Case No. IT-98–30/1-A, A. Ch., 28 February 2005, para. 90 ('The requirement that an aider and abettor must make a substantial contribution to the crime in order to be held responsible applies whether the accused is assisting in a crime committed by an individual or in crimes committed by a plurality of persons').

The International Criminal Court

The Rome Statute of the ICC has codified aiding and abetting as a mode of liability in Article 25(3)(c). This provision appears to distinguish among 'aiding', 'abetting' and 'otherwise assisting' as three disjunctive terms. In practice, the Court has rejected the distinction as 'inconsequential' in judicial determination and has treated them as a single mode of liability.[51]

Like the law of the ad hoc tribunals, Article 25(3)(c) is silent on the causal link required. The same debate on how to qualify aiding and abetting thus arose in the early decisions of the Court. On the one hand, the ICC has followed the ad hoc tribunals' jurisprudence in that it considered it unnecessary for the accomplice's assistance to be a *condicio sine qua non*.[52] On the other hand, the level of assistance needed to satisfy the *actus reus* in Article 25(3)(c) remains unsettled. There are three conflicting approaches.

First, various chambers have followed the 'substantial effect' standard set out by the ad hoc tribunals. The Pre-Trial Chamber in *Mbarushimana* held that 'a substantial contribution to the crime may be contemplated'.[53] The Trial Chamber in *Lubanga* determined that Article 25(3)(c) required a 'substantial' contribution from the accomplice.[54] Scholars in favour of this approach, such as Ambos and Schabas, posit that since aiding and abetting is a general principle of criminal law, it should be interpreted consistently without departure from the well-established standard at the ad hoc tribunals.[55]

The second approach requires that the accomplice's assistance 'has an effect [only] on the commission' of the crime.[56] The *Bemba et al.* Trial Chamber departed from the jurisprudence of the ad hoc tribunals and held that '[t]he plain wording of the statutory provision [i.e. Article 25(3) (c)] does not suggest the existence of a minimum threshold'.[57] It reasoned

---

[51] ICC, *Prosecutor v. Bemba et al.*, Judgment, Case No. ICC-01/05–01/13, 19 October 2016, para. 87, confirmed by ICC, *Prosecutor v. Bemba et al.*, Judgment, Case No. ICC-01/05–01/13, A. Ch., 8 March 2018, para. 1324.

[52] ICC, *Prosecutor v. Blé Goudé*, Decision on the confirmation of charges, ICC-02/11–02/11, 11 December 2014, para. 167.

[53] ICC, *Prosecutor v. Mbarushimana*, Decision on the confirmation of charges, ICC-01/04–01/10, 16 December 2011, para. 280.

[54] ICC, *Prosecutor v. Lubanga*, Judgment, ICC-01/04–01/06, 14 March 2012, para. 997.

[55] Ambos (n. 46), p. 1008, citing W. Schabas, *Introduction to the International Criminal Court* (Cambridge University Press, 2011), p. 228.

[56] ICC, *Prosecutor v. Bemba et al.*, Decision pursuant to Article 61(7)(a) and (b) of the Rome Statute, ICC-01/05–01/13–749, 11 November 2014, para. 35.

[57] *Bemba* Trial Judgment (n. 51), para. 93.

that if the drafters so intended, they would have included qualifying elements such as in the 1996 ILC Draft Code, which requires accomplices to assist 'directly and substantially'.[58] According to the Trial Chamber, the assistance must be 'causal' but need not reach the level of substantiality, for a number of reasons. One is that while principal forms of responsibility in Article 25(3)(a) adopt the 'control over the crime' theory[59] requiring principal perpetrators to have the ability to frustrate the commission through withdrawing participation, Article 25(3)(c) does not.[60] In terms of causality, this means that while principal perpetrators have the power to frustrate the commission of the offence by not performing their tasks ('control over the crime'), the accomplice has no such power or control over the realization of the crime. In this sense, the accomplice 'merely contributes to' the offence.[61] Thus, unlike at the ad hoc tribunals, assistance in the sense of Article 25(3)(c) of the Rome Statute can in theory be peripheral or marginal.[62]

Another reason why the Trial Chamber rejected the substantiality requirement was that it deemed the textual construction of Article 25(3)(c) sufficient to filter out contribution not encompassed by aiding and abetting. This is done, firstly, by requiring a causal relationship in that the assistance must have furthered, advanced or facilitated the commission.[63] Furthermore, the Chamber observed that the *mens rea* in article 25(3)(c) ('[f]or the purpose of facilitating') 'goes beyond the ordinary *mens rea* standard encapsulated in Article 30', thus justifying a lower requisite level of assistance than that at the ad hoc tribunals.[64]

In the third and last approach, the Court has focused on the plain text of Article 25(3)(c) and rejected on numerous occasions the need for any qualification to satisfy the *actus reus* of aiding and abetting. According to this approach, assistance need not produce any effect at all. In the *Ongwen* Confirmation of Charges Decision – in line with the pronouncements in *Ble Goude* and *Al Mahdi*[65] – the Pre-Trial Chamber endorsed a strictly textual interpretation:

---

[58] Ibid.
[59] ICC, *Prosecutor v. Lubanga*, Confirmation Decision, para. 338; *Prosecutor v. Lubanga*, Appeal Judgment, para. 469.
[60] *Bemba* Trial Judgment (n. 51), para. 85.
[61] Ibid.
[62] Ibid., para. 86: '[T]he assistant's contribution hinges on the determination of the principal perpetrator to execute the offence.'
[63] Ibid., para. 94.
[64] Ibid.
[65] See ICC, *Prosecutor v. Al Mahdi*, Decision on the confirmation of charges, ICC-01/12–01/15, 2016, para. 26 (quoting *Ongwen* decision); *Goudé* Decision on the confirmation of

'It is nowhere required, contrary to the Defence argument, that the assistance be "substantial" or anyhow qualified other than by the required specific intent to facilitate the commission of the crime.'[66]

More recently, the *Bemba et al.* Appeal Judgment again suggested the theoretical possibility that no effect whatsoever is required. At the outset, the Appeals Chamber made clear that it was not bound by the ad hoc tribunals' jurisprudence.[67] It then recalled that the text of Article 25(3)(c) does not indicate 'whether the conduct must have also had an effect on the commission of the offence'.[68] It nonetheless did not exclude per se such a situation:

'Whether a certain conduct amounts to "assistance in the commission of the crime" within the meaning of article 25(3)(c) of the Statute even without the showing of such an effect can only be determined in light of the facts of each case.'[69]

Causation in Aiding and Abetting in the Cases of van Anraat and Kouwenhoven

The Dutch criminal cases against van Anraat and Kouwenhoven are well-known and share a number of unique features. Both cases deal with businessmen who have been prosecuted and convicted for aiding and abetting the commission of war crimes committed outside the Netherlands. In addition, both cases raise the complex issue of causation in the context of assisting in mass atrocities: in the case of van Anraat the chemical weapon attacks committed in the 1980s by Saddam Hussein's regime in Iraq and in the case of Kouwenhoven the war crimes committed by former Liberian president Charles Taylor and his armed forces. We will look at both cases, in chronological order, and analyze the Dutch courts' approach towards causation in the context of aiding and abetting in mass atrocities.

---

charges (n. 52), para. 167 ('In essence, what is required for this form of responsibility [in Article 25(3)(c)] is that the person provides assistance to the commission of a crime and that, in engaging in this conduct, he or she intends to facilitate the commission of the crime').

[66] ICC, *Prosecutor v. Ongwen*, Decision on the confirmation of charges, Case No. ICC-02/04–01/15, 23 March 2016, para. 43.

[67] ICC, *Prosecutor v. Bemba et al.*, Judgment, Case No. ICC-01/05–01/13, A. Ch., 8 March 2018, para. 1325.

[68] Ibid., para. 1327.

[69] Ibid.

The van Anraat *Case*

Frans van Anraat, a Dutch national, traded in chemicals. He was charged with aiding and abetting the commission of war crimes and genocide (the latter concerning the Kurdish population in Iraq) by Saddam Hussein, through the use of chemical weapons in the attacks against three Kurdish villages in Iraq and five villages in Iran, resulting in numerous deadly casualties and severe bodily harm. The attacks with chemical weapons occurred in the years 1987 and 1988, the attack on the Kurdish village of Halabja on 16 March 1988 being the most known. Van Anraat was accused of having assisted these attacks by arranging the deliveries of large quantities of thiodiglycol (TDG), an important chemical component of mustard gas.[70]

Van Anraat was acquitted of aiding and abetting in the commission of genocide on the Kurdish population for lack of proof of the requisite knowledge of the genocidal intent. On 23 December 2005 he was convicted in first instance for aiding and abetting in the commission of war crimes and sentenced to fifteen years' imprisonment.[71] His conviction was maintained on appeal and the sentence was increased by two years, to seventeen years' imprisonment.[72] The Dutch Supreme Court left the conviction unaltered, but reduced the sentence slightly, to sixteen years and six months.[73]

Throughout the proceedings in the *van Anraat* case, significant attention was paid to the issue of causation. The question that arose was whether the chemicals supplied by van Anraat had contributed to the attacks with chemical weapons as charged in the indictment. The District Court explicitly stated that criminal liability for aiding and abetting can be found only when the chemicals delivered by van Anraat had in fact facilitated the specific attacks charged in the indictment.[74] According to the District Court, this requirement of facilitation means that it must be proven that the chemicals of van Anraat have been used in the attacks as charged in the indictment. We will later discuss whether this is the correct standard for causation. In this particular case, there was strong evidence (including an expert-witness involved in the UN monitoring of disarmament after the Iran–Iraq war) regarding the administration of incoming chemicals and their subsequent use in fabrication of chemical weapons. There was also

---

[70] District Court of 's-Gravenhage, 23 December 2005, ECLI:NL:RBSGR:2005:AU8685.
[71] Ibid.
[72] Court of Appeal 's-Gravenhage, 9 May 2007, ECLI:NL:GHSGR:2007LBA4676.
[73] Supreme Court, 30 June 2009, ECLI:NL:HR:2009:BG4822.
[74] District Court of 's-Gravenhage, 23 December 2005, ECLI:NL:RBSGR:2005:AU8685, para. 13.

evidence that van Anraat was a significant supplier of the raw materials necessary for the fabrication of chemical weapons. As a result of this evidence, it was indeed possible to meet the standard of causation as the District Court required it. The Court determined that the charged attacks, which started in the middle of April 1987, had been made possible or at least facilitated by the use of the chemicals supplied by the accused.[75]

In the appeals proceedings – which is a trial *de novo* in the Netherlands – the Court of Appeals appears to continue on the path set by the District Court. In setting out the applicable legal framework for aiding and abetting, the Court also indicates that, in terms of causation, the question is whether the accused has contributed to the attacks as charged in the indictment.[76] The Court emphasises next, in accordance with the Dutch standards on causation, that the assistance need not be indispensable or adequate; merely facilitating suffices.[77] Quite puzzling is the unsubstantiated statement by the Court of Appeals that the requirements in international criminal law are not stricter in this regard.[78] As discussed in the previous section, international criminal tribunals have at times required a substantive contribution for aiding and abetting, which is obviously more demanding than the Dutch standard of 'merely facilitating', and which should have merited more discussion in the appeals judgment. This is especially the case when one bears in mind the year in which the appeals judgment was issued, 2007, in which more flexible ICTY, ICTR or ICC jurisprudence on causation was not yet available.

In its concluding observations on the matter of causation, the Court of Appeals appears slightly torn between the strict causation requirement as articulated by the District Court and a looser approach (which could be a first step in the direction of a risk-based approach towards causation). On the one hand, the Court of Appeals emphasizes that van Anraat was a very important tradesman and delivered at least 38 per cent of the TDG to Iraq in the period 1980–1988, and where others stopped delivering in 1984, the accused continued to do so until spring 1988.[79] On that basis, the Court considers it *plausible* that the chemicals of van Anraat were used in the charged attacks in 1987 and 1988.[80] On the other hand, the ultimate conclusion by the Court of Appeals on this point of causation is that the

---

[75] Ibid.
[76] Court of Appeal of The Hague, 9 May 2007, ECLI:NL:GHSGR:2007:BA6734, para. 12.4.
[77] Ibid.
[78] Ibid.
[79] Ibid., para. 12.5.
[80] Ibid.

essential role of the deliveries of TDG by the accused since 1985 for the chemical weapons programme of the regime renders the accused guilty of aiding and abetting in the commission of the attacks as charged in the indictment.[81] One could read this final conclusion as an indication that actual use of the aider and abettor's chemicals in the attacks as charged in the indictment is no longer strictly required, as long as in the relevant period, 1987 and 1988, the chemicals delivered by the accused amounted to an essential contribution to the chemical weapons programme as a whole.

The proceedings at the Supreme Court may be seen to give some support to a less strict causation requirement. As happens regularly in proceedings at the Dutch Supreme Court, the more thorough treatment of this matter can be found in the independent advice of the Advocate-General to the Supreme Court and not in the Supreme Court judgment itself. The Advocate-General supports the reasoning and conclusions by the Court of Appeals related to causation. According to the Advocate-General, the reasoning of the Court was that, as time progressed after 1984, the part of the only remaining supplier of TDG – the accused – in the totality of TDG available became increasingly higher and even essential.[82] In conclusion, the Advocate-General said: 'This reasoning is understandable and can substantiate the conclusion that the suspect has actually contributed to the use of mustard gas in 1987 and 1988 by his deliveries.'[83]

One may infer from this that in order to establish causation it is apparently sufficient for the Advocate-General that the accused was at a certain point in time an important supplier in a policy or programme as a whole (in the present case a chemical weapons programme, but it could also be a programme or policy of crimes against humanity), without having to prove beyond a reasonable doubt that the assistance has actually contributed to certain specific elements of the relevant programme, namely, the specific attacks as charged in the indictment.

However, such a view has not been further elaborated on in the *van Anraat* proceedings. Therefore, many questions remain unanswered. To start with, it has never been explicitly stated in these proceedings that the standard of the District Court on strict causation in relation to the specific charges was incorrect. The correct standard in these types of case therefore remains uncertain. If the connection between causation and the commission of crimes by the principal can be slightly looser, then

---

[81] Ibid.

[82] Supreme Court, Attorney-General Conclusion, 30 June 2009, ECLI:NL:PHR:2009: BG4822, para. 6.18.

[83] Ibid.

the question arises of under what circumstances? Is this restricted to situations of grave harm, international crimes, and multiple aiders and abettors, or can it also apply to other scenarios? The question also arises as to whether van Anraat would have escaped criminal liability in case of a less essential contribution to the Iraqi chemical weapons programme. The *Kouwenhoven* case offers another opportunity to reflect on the theoretical and moral justification for the distinction.

The Kouwenhoven *Case*

A considerable part of the criminal case against Guus Kouwenhoven was prosecuted in the Netherlands after the *van Anraat* case. Kouwenhoven was active through two companies in the logging industry in Liberia between 1999 and 2003. It was concluded that the business interests of Kouwenhoven were closely intertwined with the political, financial and private interests of the then president of Liberia, Charles Taylor.[84] The charges concentrated, amongst others, on the deliveries of weapons (such as AK47s) by the accused, making staff available for the armed conflict, making means of transport available for the armed conflict, and allowing company premises to be used as a meeting place for Taylor's armed forces. The assistance provided by the accused was, according to the charges, instrumental to the commission of several war crimes, including murders and rapes, in the villages of Guéckédou (Guinea), Voinjama and Kolahun (Liberia), in the years 2000, 2001 and 2002. Kouwenhoven was charged under the following alternative modes of liability in respect of his acts: co-perpetration, solicitation, aiding and abetting and command responsibility.[85]

The *Kouwenhoven* proceedings were lengthy and complex. The Hague District Court convicted Kouwenhoven on 7 June 2006, not for criminal involvement in war crimes but for violations of trading prohibitions, as penalized under Dutch law in the Sanctions Act of 1977 in respect of which he was sentenced to eight years' imprisonment.[86] In the appeals proceedings that followed, Kouwenhoven was fully acquitted by The Hague Court of Appeals, because there were serious problems with the investigations and evidence, especially the eye-witnesses.[87] The

---

[84] Court of Appeal of 's-Hertogenbosch, 21 April 2017, ECLI:NL:GHSHE:2017:1760, section Q.

[85] Ibid, section 1A–2A.

[86] District Court of The Hague, 7 June 2006, ECLI:NL:RBSGR:2006:AY5160.

[87] Court of Appeal of The Hague, 10 March 2008, ECLI:NL:GHSGR:2008:BC6068, para. 9.17.

prosecution service appealed this acquittal before the Supreme Court. On 20 April 2010, the Supreme Court quashed the acquittal because the Appeals Court had improperly refused to receive further evidence adduced by the prosecution service and the case was remitted to the Court of Appeals of 's Hertogenbosch to be retried.[88] On 21 April 2017, the Court of Appeals of 's Hertogenbosch convicted Kouwenhoven to nineteen years' imprisonment for aiding and abetting war crimes committed by Taylor and his co-accused in the aforementioned villages in Guinea and Liberia.[89] Recently, on 18 December 2018, the Dutch Supreme Court fully confirmed this conviction and sentence, which are therefore now final.[90]

Like the *van Anraat* case, the *Kouwenhoven* case raises the important and complex issue of causation for those who aid and abet in the commission of mass atrocities. However, the matter received far less attention in the *Kouwenhoven* proceedings, essentially because this was not raised by the defence. It is only in the judgment of the Court of Appeals of 's Hertogenbosch of 21 April 2017 that the issue of causation was marginally addressed, in the context of the *proprio motu* obligation for the Court to provide sufficient grounds and reasons for a conviction. This limited attention is, as we will discuss later, not satisfactory for those who would like to gain a greater understanding of the requisite causation standard in these types of situation.

In Section L of the judgment, the Court sets out a number of evidentiary conclusions, such as the accused having an active role in the delivery of weapons, making staff available for the armed conflict, allowing his business premises in Liberia to be used as a hiding place for weapons and encouraging the soldiers to loot. On the basis of these facts, the Court concludes that the accused actively contributed to the acts of war.[91] Later on, the Court simply concludes in respect of the *actus reus* that the accused assisted the persons mentioned in the indictment in respect of the acts charged in the indictment.[92]

This succinct reasoning, almost absent reasoning in respect of causation, is troubling. In light of van Anraat's precedent, one would have expected

---

[88] Supreme Court, 20 April 2010, ECLI:NL:HR:2010:BK8132.
[89] Court of Appeal of 's-Hertogenbosch, 21 April 2017, ECLI:NL:GHSHE:2017:1760; Kouwenhoven was also convicted for violation of the trading sanctions, criminalized under the Sanctions Act of 1977, but this matter does not seem to have had any significant impact on the sentence.
[90] Supreme Court, 18 December 2018, ECLI:NL:HR:2018:2336.
[91] Court of Appeal of 's-Hertogenbosch, 21 April 2017, ECLI:NL:GHSHE:2017:1760, Section L.1.
[92] Ibid., Section M.

the Court to be more specific on the issue of causation. It should be mentioned that the indictment in the *Kouwenhoven* case is quite general. Covering a relatively long period, three years, the indictment states that several war crimes have been committed, by, amongst others, acts of killing, torture or rape. No individual victims are mentioned; nor are any specific incidents singled out. In comparison, the charges formulated in the *van Anraat* case, mentioning specific attacks with chemical weapons, on specific villages, on specific dates, are clearly far more concrete. As explained by Fry, the complex nature of international crimes has been stated as a reason to forgive lowering standards of specificity of charges throughout the history of international criminal courts and tribunals. Fry has criticized the use of unspecific charges in international crimes cases, from the perspective of both challenges in fact-finding and the rights of the accused to be put on notice.[93] In addition to that general concern, unspecific charges regarding the crimes committed by the principal should merit further attention from the perspective of the causation requirement when someone is charged with aiding and abetting. Could a situation of relatively broad mentioning of the crimes of the principal spill over into a lower requirement with respect to causation, when charging aiding and abetting? Or, to be more concrete, would it, in order to establish causation in relation to many crimes committed over a longer period of time, be sufficient that the accused's assistance has actually contributed to *some* of these crimes? And, if so, what portion would justify tying the accused's assistance to all crimes as they are being broadly charged?

Another concern with the Court's approach in the *Kouwenhoven* case on causation has to do with the apparent conflation between assistance in acts of war and assistance in war crimes. Under a strict causation approach, the selling of weapons in a situation of armed conflict would not necessarily contribute to the commission of war crimes, because weapons supplied by the accused can also be used in legitimate acts of war. In order to establish causation, one would have expected these two matters to have received proper attention.

First, it seems imperative to have some idea of the percentage of war crimes in the overall military operations in which the accused's weapons have been used. The answer to this question is helpful for the determination of the accused's *mens rea*; a known high frequency of war crimes in an armed conflict means that the accused knew or should have known that the

---

[93] E. Fry, *The Contours of International Prosecutions: As Defined by Facts, Charges, and Jurisdictions* (Eleven International Publishing, 2015), pp. 79–80.

weapons he delivered would not only be used in lawful military operations. However, to determine the degree to which deliveries of weapons have in fact been used in the commission of crimes, or have met the standard of causation, information on the proportion between legitimate and unlawful military operations appears important. Here we can discern an essential factual difference from the *van Anraat* case. Once chemical weapons are being used in populated areas, this by definition amounts to a war crime; there is no possible legitimate use in such circumstances. The Appeals Court in *Kouwenhoven* appears to equate assistance in acts of war with assistance in war crimes. This follows from the Court's conclusion that the accused has made an active contribution to the acts of war as a basis for aiding and abetting liability. This may be regarded as fully embracing a risk-based view on causation, in the sense that war crimes are likely to be committed in *any* armed conflict and that *any* delivery of weapons in that situation then satisfies the causation standard. However, if the Court adopts this position, further argumentation and substantiation are needed. An alternative explanation for how the Court has handled this is that it has simply overlooked, in respect of causation, the possibility of the weapons delivered by the accused not being used in the commission of war crimes but essentially, or only, in lawful military operations.

A second issue that required the Court's attention in our view is the following: How many of the totality of the weapons used by the armed forces of Charles Taylor in the period set out in the indictment were delivered by the accused? In comparison, the fact that van Anraat delivered a very large portion and at some point in time was even the only supplier of chemicals appeared to be an important factor in proving causation in his criminal case. The *Kouwenhoven* judgment does not give us any information on the importance of the quantities delivered by the accused in the overall weapons arsenal of the armed forces of Charles Taylor. The judgment does inform us that weapons have been delivered and there is evidence that these weapons have been transported to the combat areas. But we have no idea how many in a totality of weapons and therefore cannot determine, or even make an educated guess, about the chances of Kouwenhoven's weapons being used in the war crimes as charged in the indictment. If the determination of these chances does not matter according to the Court, then this strongly suggests a risk-based approach regarding causation. While there may be arguments in favour of such a position, it needs more argumentation and substantiation on the part of the Court.

In conclusion, it can be said that the preference of the Court of Appeals for 'causeless complicity' in the *Kouwenhoven* case could be inferred from the conviction of Kouwenhoven for aiding and abetting in war crimes, and the absence of any discussion on the causation requirement. It is of interest to note that a risk-based approach towards aiding and abetting also resonates in some of the Court's findings on the *mens rea* of Kouwenhoven. Making use of a *dolus eventualis* construction, the Court concludes that by delivering weapons and being aware of the violent character of the Taylor regime, the accused knowingly accepted the risk that these weapons would be used in a variety of war crimes, not only war crimes that are directly the result of the use of weapons, such as killings, but also war crimes committed under threat of weapons, such as looting and rape.[94]

Although it is beyond the scope of this chapter to address the *mens rea* aspects of aiding and abetting, this part of the *Kouwenhoven* case demonstrates both the promise and the pitfalls of the risk-based approach towards causation, especially when combined with a 'broad' *mens rea* construction, such as that of *dolus eventualis*. The consequence may be that the *actus reus* and *mens rea* requirements are merged into one. Of course, some act of potential assistance will always be required. But if the risk that the accused takes that this assistance could have been used in the commission of crimes is ultimately decisive for criminal liability, it can be said that the *actus reus* has very limited independent value, as this same risk is also at the heart of the *mens rea* determination (using *dolus eventualis*). The question arises as to whether Kouwenhoven's conviction in relation to all these crimes, including rapes, is really justifiable on this basis. Conversely, it may also be difficult to accept a full acquittal of Kouwenhoven as a reasonable outcome, as a result of the mere impossibility of proving actual causation in mass atrocity situations. We will reflect more on this dilemma in the following paragraph.

A *Sui Generis* Standard of Causation in Case of Powerful Actors (Companies and Business Owners) Contributing to Mass Atrocities?

Through the lens of the causation problems as they occurred in the *van Anraat* and *Kouwenhoven* cases, we attempt to offer some thoughts on whether there is, or should be, a revised standard of causation in cases of mass atrocities. With aiding and abetting – a mode of liability having its origin in domestic criminal law for ordinary offences – we see a continuous

---

[94] Court of Appeal of 's-Hertogenbosch, 21 April 2017, ECLI:NL:GHSHE:2017:1760, Section L.2.5.

struggle in case law dealing with mass atrocities to depart from the strict requirement of a cause–effect relationship. The justice systems we have examined appear to already show a new direction towards which a revised standard of causality is emerging, even if this is not always recognized as such explicitly.

We see that each court and tribunal has attempted to formulate its own approach *de novo*. Among the ICTY, ICTR, the ICC and the Dutch systems – and among chambers and courts within each separate justice system – there appears to be a tendency not to follow precedents in the majority of cases. Courts at times chose to develop the causation standard as they deemed fit, from the plain text of their law or statute. This is particularly true for the international criminal tribunals. At the ICC, the *Bemba et al.* Trial Chamber consequently rejected any qualification of causality from the ICTY and the ICTR, especially because the drafters of the Rome Statute consciously adopted a higher *mens rea* threshold for aiding and abetting in Article 25(3)(c).[95]

For now, it suffices to note that the Dutch courts and international criminal tribunals are heading in a general, normative direction. The baseline they have all agreed on is that the act of assistance need not be the *condicio sine qua non*, that is, there is no need to prove that hypothetically the perpetration would have failed but for the assistance. In a comparative perspective, this is also why aiding and abetting as a mode of individual criminal responsibility has been set apart, legally and conceptually, from principal perpetration. The latter requires a sufficient level of control effected upon the crimes, in such a way that the principal's conduct is capable of frustrating the commission.[96] Building on this common foundation of what the assistance need not be, the question remains what effect the assistance must have had on the principal perpetration. In order to draw out the contours of a *sui generis* standard of causality, we would like to make the following points.

The first relates to the dilemma between the causation and the risk-based approaches. Previously, we have pointed out that because of the nature of mass atrocities (enormous harm and high plurality of actors) this can be an additional reason in favour of a risk-based approach towards causality, in contrast to situations of 'common criminality'.

---

[95] Ambos (n. 46), p. 1009.

[96] ICC, *Prosecutor v. Thomas Lubanga Dyilo*, Decision on the confirmation of charges, ICC-01/04–01/06–803-tENG, 14 January 2007, para. 322. See also Ambos (n. 46), p. 479.

However, we are convinced that actual causation, that is, effect, is the primary method of attributing criminal responsibility with regards to acts of assistance, and the risk-based approach towards causation should have a subsidiary role only. This is probably already the way courts go about it: if the *Kouwenhoven* case had generated evidence proving that the weapons of the accused were used in the indicted crimes like in the *van Anraat* case, the court would certainly have mentioned this and would have used this to substantiate an actual effect on the principal crimes. However, in the interests of legal certainty and securing the rights of the defence, it is recommended that the impossibility to establish actual causation is explicitly mentioned, and the transition to applying a risk-based causation standard is visible to all.

A related, logically subsequent point is that the move from the causation-based to a risk-based approach should be explicitly justified and motivated. By that, we mean that a court should deviate from actual causation *only* when the circumstances at hand justify doing so and under strict conditions. The bottom line, in our opinion, is that a risk-based approach towards causation could justify the establishment of a causal link only if the risk-enhancing act of assistance was substantial or of significant weight and significant potential impact. We propose a (rough) test that could assist the courts in making such a determination.

The purpose of a *sui generis* causation test in aiding and abetting liability for mass atrocities is to distinguish between those who have taken significant risks by their acts of assistance and have been in a position to have actually made a difference and those who have done less and hold less prominent positions. Or, to make it more concrete, risk-based causation may be justifiable in cases of companies and businessmen delivering significant quantities of weapons with which war crimes could have been committed, but not so in cases of assistance of far less significance, or of a more remote or indirect nature. Going back to the *van Anraat* and *Kouwenhoven* cases, one can think of examples of those having assisted these accused in their (commercial) activities. Let us take the example of banks that have financed, through loans, the relevant business operations of van Anraat and Kouwenhoven, and let as assume that these banks' *mens rea* requirement in respect of their assistance in the war crimes via assisting the aiders and abettors would have been fully satisfied. Continuing on an ever-expanding path of risk-based causation and by consistently applying the same logic, one could argue in favour of complicity liability for these banks. Yet, one could equally feel compelled to draw the line here and to consider this assistance of banks too remote, too indirect, or simply too insignificant to be within the reach of a justifiable and reasonable risk-based causation approach.

Taking this complex example, it would be impossible as well as undesirable to develop hard criteria distinguishing with precision between situations of accepting and denying risk-based causation. Instead, we suggest that in cases of aiding and abetting mass atrocities, courts, in deciding on (risk-based) causation, are obliged to take a number of factors into account. The four-pronged test for risk-based causation in cases of mass atrocities would be as follows: a) whether or not the assistance provided was capable of making a difference to the crimes committed by the principal; b) whether or not the assistance provided could also be used only or essentially for lawful purposes and how likely this was in light of the evidence; c) whether or not the assistance was provided directly to the principal; and d) how important the acts of assistance provided by the accused were in comparison to the assistance provided by others.

Whether or not, and to what degree, one of these factors applies should in our view not be decisive for establishing (risk-based) causation. It is for a court, taking all these factors into account holistically and providing sufficient reasoning, to determine whether (risk-based) causation can be established in a concrete case. The aforementioned test could assist courts in distinguishing between reasonable situations of causeless complicity and endless complicity. The latter may happen if every situation of risk-enhancing assistance, however minor it may be, leads to causation and therefore criminal liability. This is neither necessary nor desirable.

Conclusion

The criminal cases against Dutch businessmen van Anraat and Kouwenhoven offer a fascinating starting point for an inquiry into the required degree of causation in situations of providing assistance in the commission of international crimes. In other words, and repeating the research question: what should the degree of causation be for aiding and abetting liability of companies and businessmen who have assisted in the commission of mass atrocities? This matter continues to pose challenges for both courts and scholars, especially in complex situations of commission of mass atrocities, in which the actual effect of assistance on the commission of crimes often cannot be discerned, but in which the ultimate harm is enormous.

In our endeavour to answer the research question, we have first looked at the views and approaches of legal and moral philosophers in respect of causation. The two contrasting views on causation are one in which actual causation matters and the other in which it does not. Especially when looking at the commission of mass atrocities, in which many aiders and abettors can be involved, the theoretical justifications underlying causeless complicity or risk-based causation appear to be more appealing.

We have then examined what the approach is in the law and practice in the Netherlands and at the international criminal tribunals when it comes to determining causation. While all systems reject a 'but for' (or: *condicio sine qua non*) standard of causation, the approaches differ widely. In the Netherlands, the consistent case law in respect of ordinary crimes is the mere facilitation effect of the assistance provided. At the international criminal tribunals, the initial case law, that of the ICTY, required a substantial effect of the assistance on the commission of the crime. However, the trend within the ICC appears to go in the direction of not requiring any effect at all (causeless complicity).

The analysis of the *van Anraat* and *Kouwenhoven* cases only adds to the confusion. In the *van Anraat* case, actual causation was – certainly initially – a strict requirement, whereas in the *Kouwenhoven* case the accused was convicted without proof of effect of his assistance – the delivery of weapons – on the crimes as charged in the indictment. The diverging approaches and unclear or occasional absence of reasoning fuel the assumption that, even in a well-developed criminal justice system such as that of the Netherlands, there may be a need for a revised, *sui generis* causation standard in the prosecution of mass atrocities.

We have offered a proposal for this *sui generis* standard, taking into account the unique circumstances of mass atrocities and the enormous harm occasioned thereby. Our conclusion is that a risk-based causation standard, that is, one in which assistance need not actually have made but could have made a difference to the commission of the crime, is the most appropriate one in cases of mass atrocities. The attention should focus on the degree to which the assistance provided enhances the risk. In our view, only assistance of significant potential impact could meet the causation requirement. In order to determine 'significant potential impact', we have proposed a four-pronged test that may assist courts in making the causation determination. While this test will not draw a hard line between causation and non-causation, and thus between liability and non-liability, it will in all cases assist courts in better distinguishing between situations where causation is reasonable and those where it is not.

PART V

Criminal Accountability and Beyond

Future Directions for Individual and Corporate Responsibility

On Criminal Responsibility for Terrorist Financing

An Analysis of the International Convention for the Suppression of the Financing of Terrorism

LIU DAQUN

13.1 Introduction

Ever since the beginning of this century, especially after the 9/11 terrorist attack, the spectre of terrorism has engulfed the world, especially in Asia and the Middle East. Al-Qaeda and the so-called Islamic State (IS) became serious threats to international peace and security.[1] IS reportedly once controlled 88,000 square kilometres of territory in Syria and Iraq with almost eight million inhabitants, 'generating billions of dollars in revenue from oil, extortion, robbery and kidnapping'.[2] Terrorist organizations and groups require significant funds to support their criminal activities and maintain an infrastructure of organizational revenues. Without the necessary financial support, terrorist activities and organizations could not possibly be sustained.

According to a Report on Terrorist Financing prepared by the intergovernmental Financial Action Task Force (FATF) in 2008, there are three major sources for terrorist financing. The first is described as 'legitimate sources' as terrorist organizations may receive funding from charities and businesses and in many cases are funded from legitimate employment, savings and social welfare payments. The second source is 'criminal activities', such as arms trafficking, drug trafficking, money laundering, kidnap-for-ransom, extortion and racketeering. The third

---

[1] UN Security Council Resolution 1373, S/RES/1373 (2001), 28 September 2001.
[2] 'IS "Caliphate" Defeated but Jihadist Group Remains a Threat', *BBC News*, 23 March 2019, www.bbc.com/news/world-middle-east-45547595.

source is 'State sponsors' and especially failed states continue to represent crucial sources of support for terrorist organizations today.[3]

The international community has made a concerted effort to address the crime of financing terrorism. The United Nations Security Council (UNSC) and the UN General Assembly (UNGA) have adopted many resolutions addressing the problem of terrorism in the past years.[4] In 1997, UNGA adopted the International Convention for the Suppression of Terrorist Bombings ('Terrorist Bombings Convention') designed to criminalize participation in terrorist bombings.[5] This convention lays a very solid foundation for the later international counter-terrorism treaties and conventions, especially for the adoption of the International Convention for the Suppression of the Financing of Terrorism ('Terrorism Financing Convention' or 'Convention') on 9 December 1999 by UNGA resolution.[6] There are currently 188 contracting parties to the Convention.[7] The Convention is a universal legal document specially addressing the criminal acts of terrorist financing and also seeking to promote police and judicial cooperation to prevent, investigate and punish the crime of terrorist financing.

13.2   The Terrorist Acts and the Crime of Terrorist Financing

The Terrorism Financing Convention was the first international legal instrument specializing in the criminalization of terrorist financing. It stipulates two separate but related elements of the offences set out in Article 2, namely, the crime of terrorist financing and the acts of terrorism themselves. These two elements will be addressed in turn.

---

[3] Financial Action Task Force (FATF), 'Terrorist Financing', 29 February 2008, www.fatf-gafi.org/media/fatf/documents/reports/FATF%20Terrorist%20Financing%20Typologies%20Report.pdf. See also FATF, 'Emerging Terrorist Financing Risks', October 2015, www.fatf-gafi.org/media/fatf/documents/reports/Emerging-Terrorist-Financing-Risks.pdf.

[4] See UNGA Res. 49/60 of 9 December 1994; UNGA Res. 50/6 of 24 October 1995; UNGA Res. 1/210 of 17 December 1996; UNGA Res 52/165 of 15 December 1997; UNGA Res. 53/108 of 8 December 1998; UNSC Res 1269 (1999) of 19 October 1999 and UNSC Res 1368 (2001) of 12 September 2001.

[5] UN General Assembly, Resolution 52/164, International Convention for the Suppression of Terrorist Bombings, 15 December 1997, entered into force on 23 May 2001.

[6] UN General Assembly, Resolution 54/109, International Convention for the Suppression of the Financing of Terrorism, 9 December 1999, entered into force on 10 April 2002.

[7] United Nations Treaties Collection, Chapter XVIII:11, https://treaties.un.org/Pages/ViewDetails.aspx?src=IND&mtdsg_no=XVIII-11&chapter=18&clang=_en.

13.2.1   The Terrorist Acts

As for the definition of a terrorist act, the Convention adopts two approaches. The first one is to annex a list of nine anti-terrorism conventions adopted between 1970 and 1997.[8] Since not all the state parties are parties to these nine conventions and a treaty only has binding force over the contracting parties, the Convention designs an opt-in and opt-out scheme in order to solve this problem.

Article 2.2 of the Convention stipulates that on depositing its instrument of ratification, acceptance, approval or accession, a state party which is not a party to a treaty listed in the annex may declare that the treaty shall be deemed not to be included in the annex. The declaration shall cease to have effect as soon as the treaty enters into force for the state party. When a state party ceases to be a party to a treaty listed in the annex, it may make a declaration that the treaty is no longer regarded as being in the list of the Convention for that state. A contracting state may also declare that certain listed treaties are not applicable to certain territories, because those territories may have different legal systems according to the state's Constitution. For instance, China declared that three listed treaties did not apply in the Macao Special Administrative Region when China became a state party to the Convention.[9] If

---

[8] Those Conventions are: 1. Convention for the Suppression of Unlawful Seizure of Aircraft, done at The Hague on 16 December 1970; 2. Convention for the Suppression of Unlawful Acts against the Safety of Civil Aviation, done at Montreal on 23 September 1971; 3. Convention on the Prevention and Punishment of Crimes against Internationally Protected Persons, including Diplomatic Agents, adopted by the UNGA on 14 December 1973; 4. International Convention against the Taking of Hostages, adopted by the UNGA on 17 December 1979; 5. Convention on the Physical Protection of Nuclear Material, adopted at Vienna on 3 March 1980; 6. Protocol for the Suppression of Unlawful Acts of Violence at Airports Serving International Civil Aviation, supplementary to the Convention for the Suppression of Unlawful Acts against the Safety of Civil Aviation, done at Montreal on 24 February 1988; 7. Convention for the Suppression of Unlawful Acts against the Safety of Maritime Navigation, done at Rome on 10 March 1988; 8. Protocol for the Suppression of Unlawful Acts against the Safety of Fixed Platforms located on the Continental Shelf, done at Rome on 10 March 1988; 9. International Convention for the Suppression of Terrorist Bombings, adopted by the General Assembly of the United Nations on 15 December 1997.

[9] When China ratified the Convention, it made the following declaration: 'As to the Macao Special Administrative Region of the People's Republic of China, the following three Conventions shall not be included in the annex referred to in Article 2, paragraph 1, subparagraph (a) of the Convention: (1) Convention on the Physical Protection of Nuclear Material, adopted at Vienna on 3 March 1980. (2) Convention for the Suppression of Unlawful Acts against the Safety of Maritime Navigation, done at Rome on 10 March 1988. (3) Protocol for the Suppression of Unlawful Acts against the Safety of Fixed Platforms located on the Continental Shelf, done at Rome on 10 March 1988.'

a subsequent treaty comes into force, the annex may be amended to include that treaty in the list according to the procedure laid down in Article 23 of the Convention.

Up to now, the international community has not reached an agreement on a comprehensive counter-terrorism convention. All the international anti-terrorism treaties deal only with specific terrorist acts, such as the hijacking of an aeroplane and taking of hostages. In order to fill this lacuna, the second approach of the Convention is to contain a definition of a terrorist act as 'any other act intended to cause death or serious bodily injury to a civilian, or to any other person not taking an active part in the hostilities in a situation of armed conflict, when the purpose of such act, by its nature or context, is to intimidate a population, or to compel a government or an international organization to do or to abstain from doing any act'. This definition is the most authoritative one which has been followed by the ad hoc international tribunals, such as the International Criminal Tribunal for the former Yugoslavia (ICTY).[10]

There is no specific definition of an 'other act'. It would appear to include all relevant ordinary crimes such as murder, kidnapping, torture, rape, bombing and taking hostages, etc. The crime of terrorism requires special intent, that is, *dolus specialis*, since the purpose of such act, by its nature or context, is to intimidate a population, or to reach a political objective. Arguably, the threshold for a terrorist act in the Convention is too high. Although the definition does not include terrorist threats, it adds the requirement of physical harm. Serious trauma or psychological harm to the general population would appear to be more essential. It is submitted that terrorist acts need not necessarily be violent so long as they fulfil the purpose of the crime.

The act of terror in the Convention ostensibly envisages two sets of victims, namely, the direct victims of the attack and those who are terrorized as a result of the attack. According to the ICTY Appeals Chamber in the *Dragomir Milošević* case: 'Causing death or serious injury to body or health represents only one of the possible modes of

---

[10] In the ICTY, the Trial Chamber in *Galić* defined the crime of terror against the civilian population as follows: '1. Acts of violence directed against the civilian population or individual civilians not taking direct part in hostilities causing death or serious injury to body or health within the civilian population. 2. The offender wilfully made the civilian population or individual civilians not taking direct part in hostilities the object of those acts of violence. 3. The above offence was committed with the primary purpose of spreading terror among the civilian population.' *Prosecutor v. Galić*, IT-98-29-T, Judgment, Trial Chamber, 5 December 2003, para. 137.

commission of the crime of terror, and thus is not an element of the offence *per se*.'[11] In the same case, the ICTY Appeals Chamber stated: 'What is required, however, in order for the offence to fall under the jurisdiction of this Tribunal, is that the victims suffered grave consequences resulting from the acts or threats of violence; such grave consequences include, but are not limited to death or serious injury to body or health.'[12] This means that so long as an unlawful act satisfies the purpose requirement of the offence, that is, intimidating a population or compelling a government or an international organization to do or to abstain from doing any act, even if there is no direct victim of the attack, the crime of terror could still be proved. Most often, terrorists simply use the direct victim as a means to realize their criminal purpose. The real victims are the civilians who suffer serious trauma or psychological harm.

Terrorist acts are not limited to violent attacks. There are various ways to fulfil the purpose requirement of the terrorist act, for instance via cyber-attacks and information and propaganda warfare, which have an equally devastating effect. These acts may not cause death or serious injury to body or health. Therefore, the definition of a terrorist act could be simplified, being composed of three parts, namely conduct (*actus reus*), mental element (*mens rea*) and result. As for the *actus reus*, there must be the commission of an unlawful act[13] which is not necessarily violent. As for *mens rea*, the mental state of *dolus specialis* is required. The offender should have the specific intent to spread terror among the civilian population or individual civilians or to fulfil a political, religious or military objective. Finally, the result should be that the unlawful act or threat led to serious trauma or psychological harm among the victims.

13.2.2   The Crime of Terrorist Financing

Terrorist financing is a non-violent crime. In most situations, there are no direct victims. In different jurisdictions, 'the modalities by which states have proceeded to the criminalization of terrorist financing vary a great deal. In some instances, terrorist financing, although not a distinct crime, is punished as "participation" in the main criminal offence of terrorism, subject to a penalty that varies depending on the gravity of the

---

[11] *Prosecutor* v. *Dragomir Milošević*, IT-98-29/1-A, Judgment, Appeals Chamber, 12 November 2009, para. 33.
[12] Ibid.
[13] The 'unlawful act' requirement would comprehend all unlawful acts amounting to violations of international law.

latter offence.'[14] In other states, it has been regarded as a mode of liability, such as aiding and abetting, or complicity. This means that if the substantive crime (terrorist acts) did not occur, those who engage only in providing and collecting funds for terrorism could not be prosecuted and convicted.

According to the definition of terrorist financing in Article 2.1 of the Convention, 'any person commits an offence within the meaning of this Convention if that person, by any means, directly or indirectly, unlawfully and wilfully, provides or collects funds with the intention that they should be used or in the knowledge that they are to be used, in full or in part, in order to carry out' a terrorist act as listed in Article 2.1(a) and (b).

The *actus reus* of the crime of terrorist financing consists of providing or collecting funds, which includes the whole process of the liquidity of the funds. Provision of funds refers to the outflow of funds, while collection concerns incoming funds. 'Unlawful' must mean that the act is in violation of international law rather than domestic law, since some states may sponsor or engage in terrorist financing themselves. Nonetheless, it is submitted that the 'unlawful' standard is either too high or unnecessary since the lawfulness of the contribution is determined by the criminal nature of the principal's offence.

Like other crimes of complicity, the crime of terrorist financing requires double *mens rea*. One is the intent to provide and collect funds, and the other is knowledge that when the accused provides or collects funds, those funds are to be used, in whole or in part, in order to carry out a terrorist act. This low *mens rea* standard of simple knowledge as to the use of the funds in a terrorist act is stipulated in the provision of Article 2(5)(c)(ii) of the Convention requiring 'knowledge of the intention of the group to commit an offence'. According to the Rome Statute of the International Criminal Court ('Rome Statute' or 'ICC Statute'), knowledge means awareness that a circumstance exists or a consequence will occur in the ordinary course of events.[15]

Attention should be paid to the nature and character of the crime of terrorist financing, which are different from international crimes *strictu sensu*. The definition of crimes against humanity requires the context of a widespread or systematic attack against any civilian population, while the nature of genocide means that it will usually involve propaganda,

[14] A. Bianchi, 'Security Council Anti-Terror Resolutions and Their Implementation by Member States: An Overview' (2006) 4(5) *Journal of International Criminal Justice* 1052.
[15] Rome Statute of the International Criminal Court (ICC Statute), UN Doc. A/CONF.183/9, 17 July 1998, Article 30.

mobilization, organization and coordination of the perpetrators. However, unlike the above two categories of international crimes, terrorist financing and terrorist acts are mostly concealed, disguised or committed under cover. Before the terrorist act, or the provision and collection of funds, occurs, the less people know about it, the greater the likelihood that the crime will be completed. Therefore, it might be difficult to establish the requisite standard of proof in terms of the knowledge of the provider or collector, especially when the crime does not require that the funds are actually used to carry out terrorist acts and especially in scenarios where the funds are mixed with legitimate funding.

In the situation of terrorist financing, it is necessary to distinguish *mens rea* from motive. The ICTY Appeals Chamber in the *Blaškić* case stated: '*Mens rea* is the mental state or degree of fault which the accused held at the relevant time. Motive is generally considered as that which causes a person to act.'[16] The Appeals Chamber went on to cite its own jurisprudence to the effect that 'as far as criminal responsibility is concerned, motive is generally irrelevant in international criminal law, but it "becomes relevant at the sentencing stage in mitigation or aggravation of the sentence"'.[17] To take a hypothetical example: an offender's son is killed in an anti-terrorist campaign and, motivated by revenge, the offender provides funds to a terrorist group which he believes can carry out an attack to avenge his lost son. If the offender in this scenario has the intention that the funds he provides are to be used to carry out a terrorist act or he has the knowledge that the funds are to be used in this way, in full or in part, the offender could still be prosecuted and convicted regardless of his motive. Another example is that of an offender who provides funds to a group of people with the motive to support a national liberation movement or a legitimate war. If the offender knows that the group is also engaging in terrorist activities and his funds are used for such activities, he might incur criminal liability.

Article 2.3 of the Convention provides that 'for an act to constitute an offence set forth in paragraph 1, it shall not be necessary that the funds were actually used to carry out an offence referred to in paragraph 1, subparagraphs (a) or (b)'. This demonstrates that for the crime of terrorist financing to be established, it is not necessary to prove that the financing is causally connected to a criminal result, or even that any

[16] *Prosecutor* v. *Blaškić*, IT-95-14-A, Judgment, Appeals Chamber, 29 July 2004, para. 694.
[17] Ibid.

offence occurred. So long as the accused provides and collects the funds with the requisite *mens rea*, the crime of terrorist financing is constituted.

If proof of a result is not required, there will often be some difficulty in establishing the *mens rea* of the offender except in two particular scenarios. The first is that the offender provides funds to an insurgent group or organization which has as its sole purpose the engagement in terrorist activities, such as IS or Al-Qaeda. The second situation is that the accused provides funds knowing that they will be used to buy widely destructive weapons, such as nuclear or chemical weapons. Those weapons could not be used legitimately during armed conflict, let alone in times of peace, as the only purpose for their use is to engage in unlawful actions and, when in the hands of a designated terrorist group, their only conceivable use is in a terrorist act.

Another issue is the degree of knowledge of the offender. How could he or she distinguish a terrorist act from legitimate fighting, for instance, by a national liberation movement? Since a national liberation movement should use legitimate means or methods for the purpose of decolonization, if participants in the movement kill civilians with the aim of spreading terror among the civilian population, the conduct may meet the definition of a terrorist activity. The offender for the purpose of terrorist financing must know that the funds are being used for a terrorist action, but they are not required to know the details of the terrorist activities. The ICTY has also pointed out that 'the accused need not know the details of the attack .... The accused merely needs to understand the overall context in which his or her acts took place.'[18]

It is true that sometimes it is difficult to distinguish legitimate from criminal activities, for the funds could be used for both legitimate and illegal purposes. The most pertinent case before the ICTY is the *Perišić* case. *Perišić* was the Chief of the General Staff in the Yugoslavia Army during the Bosnian War. He was charged with aiding and abetting crimes in Sarajevo and Srebrenica for his role in facilitating the provision of military and logistical assistance to the Serb Army in Bosnia. The Trial Chamber found that the assistance provided by Perišić 'sustained the very life line of the Serbian Army and created the conditions for it to implement a war strategy that encompassed the commission of crimes against civilians'.[19] The Trial Chamber was satisfied that it had the evidence to

[18] *Prosecutor* v. *Limaj et al.*, IT-03-66-T, Judgment, Trial Chamber, 30 November 2005, para.190.
[19] *Prosecutor* v. *Perišić*, IT-04-81-T, Judgment, Trial Chamber, 6 September 2011, para. 1623 (emphasis added).

show that Perišić knew that 'without the regular supply of considerable quantities of ammunition and other weaponry, as well as fuel, technical expertise, repair services and personnel training, the VRS (Serb Army) would have been hampered in conducting its operations in Sarajevo and Srebrenica'.[20] The Trial Chamber found him guilty of aiding and abetting VRS crimes in Sarajevo and Srebrenica, since the evidence showed that he knew that the armed forces were using the funds and military supplies to commit the crimes in these locations. He was sentenced to twenty-seven years' imprisonment.[21] Here, *mens rea* is an essential issue since the *actus reus* is the same in regard to a legitimate activity and a criminal offence.

Article 2.3 of the Convention also criminalizes attempts as the majority of states had already done so in their domestic law. The concept of 'attempt' was not included in the Nuremberg Charter or the Tokyo Charter. The Statutes of the ICTY and the International Criminal Tribunal for Rwanda (ICTR) criminalize attempts only in cases of genocide,[22] while in the ICC Statute attempt may be applicable to all crimes. 'Attempt' is an inchoate crime as defined in Article 25(3)(f) of the ICC Statute as follows: 'taking action that commences [the crime's] execution by means of a substantial step, but the crime does not occur because of circumstances independent of the person's intentions'.[23] The same provision goes on to provide the following qualification: 'However, a person who abandons the effort to commit the crime or otherwise prevents the completion of the crime shall not be liable for punishment under this Statute for the attempt to commit that crime if that person completely and voluntarily gave up the criminal purpose.'[24]

It is submitted that the provision on attempts could apply only to the crime of terrorist financing, and not to the crime of terrorism, since it is related to 'an offence as set forth in paragraph 1 of this Article', and the

[20] Ibid., para. 1622. See also ibid., para. 1613 (by seconding high-level officers to the VRS, Perišić 'created the conditions' for them 'to wage a war that encompassed systematic criminal actions without impediments'). In addition, the Trial Chamber noted that Perišić himself did not believe that the VRS had another significant source of assistance. Ibid., para. 1165: '"They rely *solely on us* and come to us with demands." In an interview conducted after the war, Perišić said, while referring to the FRY, RS and RSK, that there was "one single army" that "was getting its logistics support mostly from the Federal Republic of Yugoslavia".' (Emphasis in original; internal references omitted.)
[21] The judgment was overturned by the Appeals Chamber of the ICTY: *Prosecutor* v. *Perišić*, IT-04-81-A, Judgment, Appeals Chamber, 28 February 2013.
[22] K. Kittichaisaree, *International Criminal Law* (Oxford University Press, 2001), p. 250.
[23] ICC Statute, Article 25(3)(f).
[24] Ibid.

main purpose of the Terrorism Financing Convention is to address collection and provision of funds to terrorist acts, rather than terrorism as such. The person who is accused of an attempted crime must have the same *mens rea* as the provider or collector of the funds.

13.3   Modes of Participation

International criminal law distinguishes between the crime and the mode of participation of the offenders. The latter is seen as a separate category, involving the establishment of a specific 'mode of liability'. The two categories – the crime and the mode of liability – possess both material elements and a mental element.

It is submitted that the Terrorism Financing Convention, together with the Terrorist Bombing Convention and the Rome Statute, has created a new set of modes of liability, different from that of the UN ad hoc tribunals, which have focused on participating as an accomplice, organizing or directing others to commit an offence, and contributing to the commission of an offence perpetrated by a group of persons acting with a common purpose. The modes of participation in the Statutes of the UN ad hoc tribunals, such as planning, ordering, instigation, aiding and abetting, are concrete and the definitions of the *actus reus* and *mens rea* of each mode of liability are concise and clear. By contrast, those in the Terrorism Financing Convention are broad, covering several modes of liability in domestic law but lacking a specific definition. It is expected that the jurisprudence of the ICC will continue to develop interpretations of the modes of liability in the Rome Statute and, where these modes have near-identical wording to the Convention, as in Article 25(3)(d) of the former and Article 2(5)(c)(ii) of the latter, the ICC's textual readings may in future provide a useful source of analogy. Nevertheless, it is helpful to make a comparison between the modes of liability applied by the UN ad hoc tribunals and the definition of the modes of liability in Article 2.5 of the Convention.

13.3.1   *Complicity*

Criminal liability does not attach solely to individuals who physically commit a crime; it may also extend to those who participate in and contribute to the commission of a crime in various ways.[25] One of the

---

[25] *Prosecutor* v. *Simić et al.*, IT-95-9-T, Judgment, Trial Chamber, 17 October 2003, para. 135.

modes of participation is complicity under the principle of accomplice liability. All legal systems punish accomplices. Most of them regard complicity as a form of accessory liability; however, the Convention on the Prevention and Punishment of the Crime of Genocide (Genocide Convention) lists complicity together with inchoate crimes such as conspiracy, attempt and incitement in Article III of the Convention.[26] The Nuremberg Principles formulated by the International Law Commission stated that 'complicity in the commission of a crime against peace, a war crime, or a crime against humanity ... is a crime under international law'.[27] According to the jurisprudence of the ICTY, 'the accomplice has been defined as someone who associates himself or herself in the crime of genocide committed by another'.[28] It has also been noted that, according to the ICTY Appeals Chamber, 'the terms "complicity" and "accomplice" may encompass conduct broader than aiding and abetting'.[29] Complicity may include other modes of participation, such as planning, instigating, counselling, soliciting, encouraging, ordering, and aiding and abetting.

13.3.1.1 Aiding and Abetting

There is no doubt that aiding and abetting are forms of accessory liability. Drawing a comparison with the concept of 'joint criminal enterprise' (JCE), the ICTY Appeals Chamber set out the *actus reus* and *mens rea* of aiding and abetting as follows:

(i) The aider and abettor carries out acts specifically directed to assist, encourage or lend moral support to the perpetration of a certain specific crime (murder, extermination, rape, torture, wanton destruction of civilian property, etc), and this support has a substantial effect upon the perpetration of the crime. ...

(ii) In the case of aiding and abetting, the requisite mental element is knowledge that the acts performed by the aider and abettor assist the commission of the specific crime of the principal. ...[30]

---

[26] Convention on the Prevention and Punishment of the Crime of Genocide, UNGA Res. 260(A)III of 9 December 1948, Article III.

[27] Principles of International Law Recognized in the Charter of the Nürnberg Tribunal and in the Judgment of the Tribunal, *Yearbook of the International Law Commission*, 1950, vol. II, Principle VII.

[28] *Prosecutor v. Blagojević and Jokić*, IT-02-60-T, Judgment, Trial Chamber, 17 January 2005, para. 776.

[29] *Prosecutor v. Brđanin*, IT-99-36-T, Judgment, Trial Chamber, 1 September 2004, para. 729.

[30] *Prosecutor v. Vasiljević*, IT-98-32-A, Judgment, Appeals Chamber, 25 February 2004, para. 102; quoted in *Prosecutor v. Blaškić*, IT-95-14-A, Judgment, Appeals Chamber, 29 July 2004, para. 45.

The *actus reus* of aiding and abetting consists of practical assistance, encouragement or moral support which has a substantial effect on the perpetration of the crime. Assistance may be provided before, during or after the act is committed. For instance, after the crime, if an individual provides safe-haven to the criminals, covers up the evil deeds, receiving and harbouring the proceeds of the crime, he could be convicted as an aider and abettor. In the case of *Blagojević* before the ICTY, the Trial Chamber encountered the issue of whether the reburial of victims of the genocide in Srebrenica could constitute *ex post facto* aiding and abetting. The Trial Chamber found first that *ex post facto* activities could be considered as aiding and abetting. Secondly, the Trial Chamber believed that liability could arise only where there was a prior agreement between the principal and the *ex post facto* aider and abettor.[31] 'If the principal kills a civilian, and another party, with no prior knowledge of the murder, agrees to dispose of the body, no accomplice liability arises.'[32] In national jurisdictions, aiding and abetting after the fact is normally regarded as an obstruction of justice.

According to the jurisprudence of the ICTY, '[a]n omission may, in the particular circumstances of a case, constitute the *actus reus* of aiding and abetting'.[33] For example, in the case of terrorist financing, if a bank manager who has the responsibility to supervise and monitor all the transactions in his bank knew that his subordinate transferred funds to a terrorist group, but he did not take any action to prevent or stop the transaction, he would be held responsible for aiding and abetting the crime of terrorist financing, since his inaction has a substantial effect on the provision and collection of funds to be used for terrorist acts.

Aiding and abetting requires proof of the commission of the principal crime. It is not necessary to establish a cause–effect relationship between the conduct of the aider and abettor and the commission of the crime, nor that such conduct served as a condition sine qua non to the commission of the crime. 'In the case of aiding and abetting, the principal may not even know about the accomplice's contribution.'[34] No proof of a plan or agreement is required for aiding and abetting.

---

[31] *Prosecutor v. Blagojević and Jokić*, IT-02-60-T, Judgment, Trial Chamber, 17 January 2005, paras. 382–3, 730–1.

[32] M. Jackson, *Complicity in International Law* (Oxford University Press, 2015), p. 74.

[33] *Prosecutor v. Limaj et al.*, IT-03-66-T, Judgment, Trial Chamber, 30 November 2005, para. 517.

[34] *Prosecutor v. Tadić*, IT-94-1-A, Judgment, Appeals Chamber, 15 July 1999, para. 229.

Further, '[a] defendant may be convicted for having aided and abetted a crime which requires specific intent even where the principal perpetrators have not been tried or identified'.[35] Although aiding and abetting have consistently been considered together in the jurisprudence of the ICTY, they are not synonymous. '"Aiding" involves the provision of assistance; "abetting" need involve no more than encouraging, or being sympathetic to, the commission of a particular act.'[36]

The *mens rea* of aiding and abetting at the ad hoc tribunals, by providing and collecting funds, is intent and knowledge. First, the aider and abettor must have intended to provide assistance. Second, he or she should have the knowledge that the funds provided and collected are going to be used for terrorist acts. In contrast to aiding and abetting under Article 25(3)(c) of the Rome Statute, which contains the phrase 'for the purpose of facilitating', it is not necessary at the ad hoc tribunals to show that the aider and abettor shared the *mens rea* of the principal. However, it must be shown that the aider and abettor was aware of the relevant *mens rea* on the part of the principal. The same is true for those crimes that require special intent, such as genocide, torture and terrorist acts. It must be shown that the aider and abettor was aware of the essential elements of the crime that was ultimately committed by the principal. However, the aider and abettor need not know the details of the crime, for instance from whom the funds are collected, to whom they are provided and how they were transferred.

13.3.1.2 Instigation

In international criminal law, instigation could also be a form of complicity. The ICTY, following the common law legal tradition, places instigation in the same category as soliciting, inducing, counselling, procuring and encouraging a crime. The ICC, influenced by the civil law legal system, did not list instigation in its Statute. Instead, it includes ordering, soliciting and inducing. The *actus reus* of 'instigation' is to prompt another person to commit an offence. It is not necessary to prove that the crimes would not have been perpetrated without the involvement of the instigator. It is sufficient to demonstrate that the instigation was a factor substantially contributing to the conduct of the person committing the crimes.

---

[35] *Prosecutor* v. *Krstić*, IT-98-33-A, Judgment, Appeals Chamber, 19 April 2004, para. 143.
[36] *Prosecutor* v. *Limaj et al.*, IT-03-66-T, Judgment, Trial Chamber, 30 November 2005, para. 516.

The jurisprudence of the ICTY shows that the nexus between instigation and perpetration must be proved. Van Sliedregt also points out that 'a causal connection between the instigation and the fulfillment of the *actus reus* is required. Causality needs to be established between all acts of instigation and the acts committed by the physical perpetrators. But *conditio sine qua non* or "but for" causation is generally not required.'[37] There is no need to prove that the crime would not have been perpetrated without the accused's involvement.[38] Both positive acts and omissions may constitute instigation, which covers express and implied conduct.[39]

The mental element or *mens rea* of instigation is two-dimensional. First, the person should have the intent to instigate others to commit a crime. Second, although it is not required for the instigator to share the *mens rea* of the principal of the crime, he or she must have the knowledge. The test may be stated as follows: 'A person who instigates another person to commit an act or omission with the awareness of the substantial likelihood that a crime will be committed in the execution of that instigation.'[40]

13.3.1.3   Organizing or Directing Others to Commit an Offence

Organizing or directing others to commit an offence has a very broad spectrum. 'Organizing' may indicate all forms of preparation of the crime of terrorist financing, while directing implies ordering others to commit the crime. Both organizing and directing incorporate two further elements. One is a type of hierarchical structure, similar to a superior–subordinate relationship. Those who could organize or direct others to commit a crime must be in a position of authority, whether *de jure* or de facto. The other is the element of collective criminality, which requires that two or more persons jointly commit the crime. The most relevant modes of participation that come under the umbrella of 'organizing and directing' are planning and ordering.

In accordance with the jurisprudence of the ICTY, '"planning" has been defined to mean that one or more persons designed the commission

---

[37] E. van Sliedregt, *Individual Criminal Responsibility in International Law* (Oxford University Press, 2012), p. 102.

[38] *Prosecutor v. Kordić and Čerkez*, IT-95-14/2-A, Judgment, Appeals Chamber, 17 December 2004, para. 387.

[39] *Prosecutor v. Limaj et al.*, IT-03-66-T, Judgment, Trial Chamber, 30 November 2005, para. 514.

[40] *Prosecutor v. Kordić and Čerkez*, IT-95-14/2-A, Judgment, Appeals Chamber, 17 December 2004, para. 32.

of a crime, at both the preparatory and execution phases, and the crime was actually committed within the framework of that design by others'.[41] The planning was a factor substantially contributing to such criminal conduct. Where an accused is found guilty of having directly committed a crime, he or she cannot at the same time be convicted of having planned the same crime. Involvement in the planning may, however, be considered as an aggravating factor.

The *mens rea* for planning has been defined by the ICTY as follows: 'A person who plans an act or omission with the awareness of the substantial likelihood that a crime will be committed in the execution of that plan, has the requisite *mens rea* for establishing responsibility under Article 7(1) of the Statute pursuant to planning.'[42]

The *actus reus* of 'ordering' is that 'a person in a position of authority instructs another person to commit an offence'[43] and uses his position to convince or direct others to commit the offence. 'A formal superior–subordinate relationship between the accused and the perpetrator is not required.'[44] So long as the offender possesses *de jure* or de facto authority to order, that authority may be implied. The order need not be given 'directly to the individual executing it', or 'in writing, or in any particular form';[45] it can be given explicitly or implicitly.

A causal link between ordering and the perpetration of a crime is needed. In the case of financing terrorism, although the funds need not be proved to have been used for a terrorist attack, the person who received the order must be proved to have provided or collected funds. If a person who gave the order to provide and collect funds goes on to perpetrate the crime, an additional conviction in respect of the act of ordering is not appropriate. This is based on the common law doctrine of the 'lesser included offence' and the civil law 'principle of consumption'. 'Under both doctrines the more serious offence prevails over and absorbs, as it were, the other. Hence, the charge and conviction may be only for the more serious offence.'[46] A standard of *mens rea* that is lower than direct intent may apply in relation to ordering, that is, with an

---

[41] *Prosecutor* v. *Galić*, IT-98-29-T, Judgment, Trial Chamber, 5 December 2003, para. 168.
[42] *Prosecutor* v. *Kordić and Čerkez*, IT-95-14/2-A, Judgment, Appeals Chamber, 17 December 2004, para. 31.
[43] Ibid., para 28.
[44] Ibid.
[45] *Prosecutor* v. *Strugar*, IT-01-42-T, Judgment, Trial Chamber, 31 January 2005, para. 331.
[46] A. Cassese, *International Criminal Law* (2nd ed., Oxford University Press, 2008), p. 180.

awareness of the substantial likelihood that a crime will be committed in the execution of that order.[47]

In order to convict for planning or ordering, the underlying crime must have occurred. However, planning and ordering are subsumed by the commission of the crime by the same perpetrator. That may be one of the reasons why there are few offenders who are convicted for planning and ordering a crime in the judicial practice of the UN ad hoc tribunals. It is still unsettled in international criminal law whether planning and ordering are forms of commission or modes of liability. As Kai Ambos has observed, 'a person who orders a crime is not a mere accomplice but rather a perpetrator by means, using a subordinate to commit the crime'.[48] Both planning and ordering involve the commission of a crime through another person. The person who plans, designs and orders the terrorist financing is the mastermind of the criminal scheme. He or she is the perpetrator behind the perpetrator. It is very difficult to imagine that the mastermind does not possess the criminal intent for the commission of the crime. Maybe that is one of the reasons why the drafters of the Convention did not use the terms planning and ordering. Instead, they used the broader phrase 'organizes or directs others to commit an offence', and regarded organizing or directing as criminal offences, not modes of participation.

13.3.2   Collective Criminality

If organizing and directing are forms of commission, the concept of co-perpetratorship may become relevant. Directing others to commit a crime may include two scenarios. One is to commit a crime jointly with others; the second is to commit a crime through an innocent third party. The distinction mainly depends on the *mens rea* of the 'others'. The ICC Statute gives a good example. Article 25(3)(a) provides for individual criminal responsibility where a person commits a crime within the Statute 'whether as an individual, jointly with another or through another person, regardless of whether that other person is criminally responsible'.

In the situation of financing terrorism, a person knows that the funds provided and collected will be used for terrorist action, and deceives the

[47] *Prosecutor* v. *Kordić and Čerkez*, IT-95-14/2-A, Judgment, Appeals Chamber, 17 December 2004, para. 30.
[48] K. Ambos, 'Article 25: Individual Criminal Responsibility', in O. Triffterer (ed.), *Commentary on the Rome Statute of the International Criminal Court, Observers' Notes, Article by Article* (Nomos Verlagsgesellschaft, 1999), p. 480.

providers and collectors by claiming that the funds will be used for a legitimate purpose, for instance to support a legitimate struggle for national liberation or freedom from foreign occupation. Therefore, the actual providers or collectors do not have the requisite criminal mental state. In this case, it is submitted that the person who prompts others should be treated as the principal perpetrator rather than an instigator.

On most occasions, the act of providing and collecting funds for terrorist use is not conducted by a person acting alone. Instead, those acts involve many participants with a division of labour. In some cases, they even involve a well-organized group or structure. Otherwise, it is impossible to raise the funds necessary to sustain a large-scale terrorist operation. In the situation of the former Yugoslavia:

> [T]he crimes are often carried out by groups of individuals acting in pursuance of a common criminal design. Although only some members of the group may physically perpetrate the criminal act (murder, extermination, wanton destruction of cities, towns or villages, etc.), the participation and contribution of the other members of the group is often vital in facilitating the commission of the offence in question.[49]

The ICTY Appeals Chamber has held that 'to hold criminally liable as a perpetrator only the person who materially performs the criminal act would disregard the role as co-perpetrators of all those who in some way made it possible for the perpetrator physically to carry out that criminal act. At the same time, depending upon the circumstances, to hold the latter liable only as aiders and abettors might understate the degree of their criminal responsibility.'[50]

International criminal law has developed two different approaches to liability for acts committed in a collective context and systematic manner. One is the concept of JCE adopted by the UN ad hoc tribunals; the other is the notion of co-perpetratorship applied by the early jurisprudence of the ICC. These two approaches reflect different degrees of responsibility. According to the jurisprudence of the ICTY, the following elements need to be proved to constitute a JCE:

- a plurality of persons, not necessarily organized;
- a common plan, design or purpose (involving the commission of a crime prescribed in the Statute);

---

[49] *Prosecutor* v. *Tadić*, IT-94-1-A, Judgment, Appeals Chamber, 15 July 1999, para. 191.
[50] Ibid., para. 192.

- the participation of the accused in the common plan or design to perpetrate a crime under the Statute;
- a shared intent between all the participants to further the common plan or design involving the commission of a crime;
- that the accused, even if not personally affecting the crime, intended the result.[51]

Participation in a JCE may take various forms: first, by personally committing the agreed crimes as principal offenders; second, by assisting or encouraging the principal offender in committing the crime; or third, by acting in furtherance of a particular system.[52] 'As joint criminal enterprise is a form of "commission" rather than a form of accomplice liability',[53] so all the participants in the JCE are principals of the crime, rather than accomplices.

As for the theory of co-perpetratorship, the ICC seems to adopt the doctrine of control theory that is based on the German doctrine of functional control over the act (*funktionelle Tatherrschaft*). 'The notion underpinning this third approach is that principals to a crime are not limited to those who physically carry out the objective elements of the offence, but also include those who, in spite of being removed from the scene of the crime, control or mastermind its commission because they decide whether and how the offence will be committed.'[54] This is the theory of indirect perpetration in a civil law system. The director exercises a certain degree of control over the actual perpetrator of the crime or a hierarchical organization for financing terrorism. Perpetration by means requires a sufficiently tight control by the 'perpetrator behind the perpetrators' and also calls for careful assessment of the relationship between the organizer or director and the persons actually carrying out the criminal conduct.

It seems that the theory of co-perpetratorship puts its emphasis on the *actus reus* aspect. Based on the control theory, it implies a kind of hierarchical structure in the relationship between co-perpetrators. In the theory of JCE, it seems that the *mens rea* of all the participants should coincide, based on the requirement that all the participants share the same intent with respect to the common criminal plan.

---

[51] *Prosecutor* v. *Simić et al.*, IT-95-9-T, Judgment, Trial Chamber, 17 October 2003, para. 156.
[52] *Prosecutor* v. *Stakić*, IT-97-24-T, Judgment, Trial Chamber, 31 July 2003, para. 435.
[53] *Prosecutor* v. *Blagojević and Jokić*, IT-02-60-T, Judgment, Trial Chamber, 17 January 2005, para. 696.
[54] *Situation in the Democratic Republic of the Congo, Prosecutor* v. *Thomas Lubanga Dyilo*, ICC-01/04-01/06, Decision on the confirmation of charges, 29 January 2007, para. 330, referring to the 'concept of control over the crime'.

13.3.3 *Contribution to a Criminal Group*

Article 2(5)(c) of the Terrorism Financing Convention copies almost verbatim Article 2(3) of the 1997 Terrorist Bombings Convention and Article 25(3)(d) of the Rome Statute. However, compared to the latter two instruments, the phrase 'in any other way' is missing in Article 2(5) (c). Thus, it is not a residual form of accessory liability and might indicate that the contribution may be constituted by any act or omission, such as complicity, organizing, directing, instigating, aiding and abetting, so long as the provision and collection of funds as well as the attempt are performed by a group of persons acting with a common purpose and the contributor has knowledge of the intention of the group.

The absence of the phrase 'in any other way' raises the possible problem of a double conviction. The ICTY Appeals Chamber has held that 'the established jurisprudence of the Tribunal is that multiple convictions entered under different statutory provisions, but based on the same conduct, are permissible, only if each statutory provision has materially distinct elements not contained within the other'.[55] According to the principle of consumption, if a person contributes to the commission of the crime of financing terrorism by a group of persons acting with a common purpose as an accomplice, organizer or director, he could be convicted only under Article 2(5)(c), and not under Article 2(5)(a) and (b).

13.3.3.1 The Nature of Article 2(5)(c)

When discussing Article 25(3)(d) of the Rome Statute, the ICC Trial Chamber has provided a very detailed interpretation, which might be of some help to understand Article 2(5)(c) of the Convention. According to the Trial Chamber: 'The language of Article 25(3)(d) of the Statute adverts to a species of accessoryship founded on a contribution to the commission of one or more crimes within the jurisdiction of the Court.'[56] The Trial Chamber distinguished this mode of liability from JCE, 'inasmuch as the accused will not be considered responsible for all of the crimes which form part of the common purpose, but only for those to whose commission he or she contributed'.[57] Consequently, 'a person who stands charged pursuant to Article 25(3)(d) will not incur individual criminal responsibility for those crimes which form part of the common

---

[55] *Prosecutor v. Krstić*, IT-98-33-A, Judgment, Appeals Chamber, 19 April 2004, para. 218.
[56] *Situation in the Democratic Republic of the Congo, Prosecutor v. Germain Katanga*, ICC-01/04-01/07, Judgment pursuant to Article 74 of the Statute, 7 March 2014, para. 1619.
[57] Ibid.

purpose but to which he or she did not contribute'.[58] The Trial Chamber listed five elements under Article 25(3)(d) of the Rome Statute:

- a crime within the jurisdiction of the Court was committed;
- the persons who committed the crime belonged to a group acting with a common purpose;
- the accused made a significant contribution to the commission of the crime;
- the contribution was intentional; and
- the accused's contribution was made in the knowledge of the intention of the group to commit the crime.[59]

This interpretation provides useful guidance for the requirement in Article 2(5)(c) of the Terrorism Financing Convention. However, the second element is still disputable, especially on two issues: first, whether the common purpose must be criminal and second, whether the contributor must be a member of the group.

13.3.3.2   Common Purpose

Article 2(5)(c) of the Convention describes a situation in which the crime is committed by a group of persons acting with a common purpose. The question is whether the common purpose (plan, design or scheme) in the chapeau of this paragraph must be criminal as it appears in Article 2(5)(c)(i).

The most relevant cases concerning common purpose as it might apply in the Convention are those before the ICC. In the *Katanga* case, the Prosecution averred that the common purpose must include an element of criminality.[60] The Trial Chamber held that: 'As to the criminality of such purpose, the Chamber considers that the purpose must be to commit the crime or must encompass its execution.'[61] The Trial Chamber continued: 'It need not be specifically directed at the commission of a crime within the jurisdiction of the Court. Nor must the group pursue a purely criminal purpose or must its ultimate purpose be criminal. Hence, a group with a political and strategic goal which also entails criminality or the execution of a crime may constitute a group acting with a common purpose within the meaning of Article 25(3)(d).'[62]

---

[58] Ibid.
[59] Ibid., para. 1620.
[60] Ibid., para. 1600.
[61] Ibid., para. 1627.
[62] Ibid.

The Trial Chamber's finding sheds some light on the meaning of common purpose. In defining the concerted action of the group acting with a common purpose, the Chamber referred to the jurisprudence of the ad hoc tribunals on JCE, which is therefore of the utmost pertinence to the present analysis. The Trial Chamber in *Katanga* considered that it could draw on certain criteria from that jurisprudence, particularly so as to best ascertain the meaning of a statutory phrase or expression, such as 'common purpose', and, in so doing, recourse to the systemic method of interpretation may be had.

The Appeals Chamber of the ICTY has pointed out that: 'The jurisprudence on this issue is clear. Joint criminal enterprise requires the existence of a common purpose which amounts to or involves the commission of a crime.'[63] This implies that a common purpose is not necessarily a criminal common purpose; it could also include a legitimate common purpose, as long as it *involves* the commission of a crime.[64] Judge Afande in his dissenting opinion in the *Stanišić and Simatović* appeals judgment pointed out: 'It is that very *mens rea* which clearly distinguishes JCE liability from another enterprise, such as a "Joint Warfare Enterprise" (JWE). In the JWE, there is a plurality of persons making contributions, whether significant or not, to a common plan, who have the intent to further not a criminal purpose, but rather a legal "warfare purpose", which is common to them.'[65] Heinous crimes may occur even in a so-called 'just war'. The same is true for the common purpose; a legitimate common purpose may also involve criminal activities. During his opening speech at the Tokyo Trial, the Chief Prosecutor, Mr Keenan, started by citing the US case of *Marine v. US*: 'to accomplish a criminal or unlawful purpose, or some purpose not in itself criminal or unlawful, by criminal or unlawful means ... it is the partnership in criminal purposes. The gist of the crime is the confederation or combination of minds.'[66]

---

[63] *Prosecutor v. Kvočka et al.*, IT-98-30/1-A, Judgment, Appeals Chamber, 28 February 2005, para. 117.

[64] *Prosecutor v. Šainović et al.*, IT-05-87-A, Judgment, Appeals Chamber, 23 January 2014, para. 609.

[65] *Prosecutor v. Stanišić and Simatović*, IT-03-69-A, Judgment, Appeals Chamber, 9 December 2015, Dissenting opinion of Judge Koffi Kumelio A. Afande, para. 13.

[66] R. J. Pritchard (ed.), *The Tokyo Major War Crimes Trial: The Records of International Military Tribunal for the Far East with an Authoritative Commentary and Comprehensive Guide*, Vol. 2 (2002). Opening speech by Prosecutor Keenan, Transcript.402. Also see S. Finnin and T. McCormack, 'Tokyo's Continuing Relevance', in Y. Tanaka, T. McCormack and G. Simpson (eds.), *Beyond Victor's Justice? The Tokyo War Crimes Trial Revisited* (Martinus Nihoff, 2011), p. 361.

This is most pertinent to the financing of terrorism. For instance, a national liberation organization's common purpose is to liberate the occupied territories from the control of foreign powers. To implement the common purpose, the organization provides and collects funds to engage in terrorist activities. Thus, it may form a criminal common purpose within the legitimate common purpose and a terrorist group within the group. If a contributor knew the intention of the group to commit a terrorist offence and still made his or her contribution, they may face prosecution and conviction.

13.3.3.3   The *Mens Rea* of the Contributor

The question of whether the contributor has to be a member of the group with a common criminal purpose is controversial. The ICTY Trial Chamber, based on the theory of JCE, seems to believe that the person making the contribution belongs to that group. Regarding the differentiation between Article 25(3)(c) and Article 25(3)(d) of the ICC Statute, the *Furundžija* Trial Chamber held that:

> Article 25 of the Rome Statute distinguishes between, on the one hand, a person who 'contributes to the commission or attempted commission of . . . a crime by a group of persons acting with a common purpose' where the contribution is intentional and done with the purpose of furthering the criminal activity or criminal purpose of the group or in the knowledge of the intention of the group to commit the crime . . ., from, on the other hand, a person who, 'for the purpose of facilitating the commission of such a crime, aids, abets or otherwise assists in its commission or its attempted commission, including providing the means for its commission'. Thus, two separate categories of liability for criminal participation appear to have been crystallised in international law – co-perpetrators who participate in a joint criminal enterprise, on the one hand, and aiders and abettors, on the other.[67]

The starting point of the finding of the ICTY Trial Chamber is that Article 25(3)(d) of the Rome Statute describes a mode of liability consisting of the co-perpetratorship (a joint criminal enterprise) and a contributor to the joint criminal enterprise who is regarded as principal of the crime. Following this logic, the contributor is a member of the group.

According to an alternative view, the contributor should not be regarded as a member of that group. Kai Ambos has pointed out:

---

[67] *Prosecutor v. Furundžija*, IT-95-17/1-T, Judgment, Trial Chamber, 10 December 1998, para. 216.

'[I]ndeed, it is the rationale of the provision to extend punishability to contributions from outside the group since these may otherwise remain exempt from punishment.'[68]

In order to resolve this issue, it is necessary to attain a better understanding of the concept of JCE, which is another way to reflect the concept of co-perpetratorship. The *Tadić* Appeals Chamber described the participation of the accused as 'involving the perpetration of one of the crimes provided for in the Statute'.[69] Rather than involving the commission of those crimes, the participation could 'take the form of assistance in, or contribution to, the execution of the common plan or purpose'.[70] An accused found criminally liable for his participation in a joint criminal enterprise should be regarded as having 'committed' that crime, as opposed to having aided and abetted the crime. In other words, participation in a joint criminal enterprise is a form of co-perpetration.[71] Since JCE constitutes a form of 'commission' in the sense that a participant shares the purpose of the joint criminal enterprise as opposed to merely knowing about it, he or she cannot be regarded as a mere aider and abettor to the crime contemplated.[72] According to the theory of JCE, there is no doubt that a contributor will be regarded as a member of the group.

Since Article 2(5)(c) of the Terrorism Financing Convention is almost identical to Article 25(3)(d) of the ICC Statute, the interpretation of Article 25(3)(d) of the ICC Statute in the jurisprudence of the ICC will assist in understanding Article 2(5)(c) of the Convention. When the Trial Chamber in the *Katanga* case discussed responsibility within the meaning of Article 25(3)(d), it used the term 'accessoryship' and found that Article 25(3)(d) of the Statute provides for individual responsibility as an accessory to a crime.[73]

As for whether a contributor should be a member of the group or not, the ICC Trial Chamber has suggested that it is not an important issue since 'the Chamber does not view an accused's membership of the group of persons acting with a common purpose as a decisive ingredient for ascertaining and establishing that person's individual responsibility for

[68] *Supra*, n. 48, p. 1013.
[69] *Prosecutor* v. *Tadić*, IT-94-1-A, Judgment, Appeals Chamber, 15 July 1999, para. 227 (iii).
[70] Ibid.
[71] *Prosecutor* v. *Simić et al.*, IT-95-9-T, Judgment, Trial Chamber, 17 October 2003, para. 138.
[72] *Prosecutor* v. *Stakić*, IT-97-24-T, Judgment, Trial Chamber, 31 July 2003, para. 432.
[73] *Prosecutor* v. *Germain Katanga* (*supra* n. 56), para. 1628.

the purposes of Article 25.3(d)'.[74] In the view of the Chamber, 'the language of the Article criminalises contribution to the commission of a crime within the jurisdiction of the Court, irrespective of an accused's membership of the group. In this respect, the Chamber recalls that the group does not exclusively consist of those whose criminal responsibility as a principal to the crimes is established or even simply under consideration.'[75]

The Trial Chamber's finding is ambiguous and difficult to understand. If a contributor is a member of the group, he or she must share the *mens rea* of the other members of the group, but the Article requires only intentionally making the contribution with the knowledge of the intention of the group to commit an offence. It does not require a contributor to have the same *mens rea* as the other members of the group to commit an offence. What is more, if the contributor is a member of the group, his or her criminal responsibility is not as an accessory but as one of the principals. As a member of the group, he or she has to share the criminal responsibility with other members who physically committed the crime, while, as an accessory, he or she is mainly liable for his or her participation as a contributor.

13.3.3.4   A New Mode of Participation?

It seems that the Convention created a new form of participation. Its threshold is higher than aiding and abetting, but lower than JCE, which is closely related to the interpretation of the phrase in Article 2(5)(c)(i) of the Convention, 'with the aim of furthering the criminal activity or criminal purpose of the group', and reference may also be made to Article 25(3) (d)(i) of the ICC Statute. However, the ICC Trial Chamber missed an opportunity to elaborate on and discuss the meaning of the phrase.

Some scholars have interpreted this phrase as incorporating the mental state of *dolus specialis*. Albin Eser states: '[W]hereas the "aim" in the first alternative seems to mean some "special intent" to the common purpose, the second alternative merely requires the "knowledge" of group intention to commit the crime.'[76] With respect, it seems that this finding is self-contradictory and difficult to apply in judicial practice where the prosecution may apply the knowledge standard, while the defence could

---

[74] Ibid., para. 1631.
[75] Ibid.
[76] A. Eser, 'Comments on Individual Criminal Responsibility', in A. Cassese et al. (eds.), *The Rome Statute of the International Criminal Count, A Commentary*, Vol. I (Oxford University Press, 2002), p. 803.

use the threshold of *dolus specialis*. The only way out is to interpret the phrase 'with the aim of furthering the criminal activity or criminal purpose of the group' as an ingredient of the *actus reus* of contribution, which raises parallels with the doctrine of 'specific direction'.

The requirement of specific direction as an element of the *actus reus* of aiding and abetting liability was first mentioned in the *Tadić* Appeals Judgment rendered in 1999, which described the *actus reus* of criminal liability for aiding and abetting as follows: 'The aider and abettor carries out acts specifically directed to assist, encourage or lend moral support to the perpetration of a certain specific crime (murder, extermination, rape, torture, wanton destruction of civilian property, etc.), and this support has a substantial effect upon the perpetration of the crime.'[77] It is submitted that the *Tadić* Appeals Judgment did not intend to give a thorough definition of aiding and abetting. The inclusion of the specific direction element in the *actus reus* of aiding and abetting was only for the purpose of distinguishing this mode of liability from joint criminal enterprise. It has no independent meaning and it is a part of the substantial effect requirement. However, in the *Perišić* case, the Appeals Chamber reversed Perišić's convictions for aiding and abetting rendered by the Trial Chamber. This reversal was predicated on the finding that the Trial Chamber erred in holding that specific direction is not a required element of the *actus reus* of aiding and abetting liability.[78] Thus, the *Perišić* case became the most controversial case before the ICTY, with four judges appending declarations and one judge dissenting.[79]

According to the jurisprudence of the UN ad hoc tribunals as well as customary international law, aiding and abetting liability may be established without requiring that the acts of the accused were specifically directed to a crime.[80] On 26 September 2013, the Appeals Chamber judges of the Special Court for Sierra Leone upheld Charles Taylor's conviction together with his fifty-year prison sentence. The Appeals Chamber in *Taylor* dismissed a 'specific direction' requirement and pointed out that it was sufficient that Taylor's conduct had a 'substantial effect' on RUF/

---

[77] *Prosecutor v. Tadić*, IT-94-1-A, Judgment, Appeals Chamber, 15 July 1999, para. 229.
[78] *Prosecutor v. Perišić*, IT-04-81-A, Judgment, Appeals Chamber, 28 February 2013, paras. 73–4.
[79] See ibid. Judges Theodor Meron and Carmel Agius append a joint separate opinion, Judge Arlette Ramaroson appended a separate opinion and Judge Liu Daqun appended a partially dissenting opinion.
[80] See Judge Liu Daqun's partially dissenting opinion in the *Perišić* Appeal Judgment, ibid.

AFRC crimes in Sierra Leone.[81] The judges emphasized that they were not persuaded by the ICTY's finding that 'specific direction' was an element of aiding and abetting.[82]

In the *Šainović* case, a differently constituted Appeals Chamber of the ICTY disagreed with the holding in the *Perišić* Appeal Judgment that specific direction is an element of the *actus reus* of aiding and abetting. The Appeals Chamber recalled that, where it is faced with previous decisions that are conflicting, it is obliged to determine which decision it will follow, or whether to depart from both decisions for cogent reasons in the interests of justice. In view of the divergence between the judgments, the Appeals Chamber carefully examined the jurisprudence of the ICTY and the ICTR as well as customary international law, and concluded that 'specific direction' is not an element of aiding and abetting liability. Consequently, the Appeals Chamber rejected the approach adopted in the *Perišić* Appeal Judgment as it was in direct and material conflict with the prevailing jurisprudence on the *actus reus* of aiding and abetting liability and with customary international law in this regard.[83] If specific direction was an ingredient of the *actus reus* of aiding and abetting, it would raise the threshold for aiding and abetting. However, the issue does not affect other forms of participation, such as contribution to the crime of financing terrorism, especially by a group of persons acting with a common purpose. It is submitted that the phrase 'with the aim of furthering the criminal activity or criminal purpose of the group' is an ingredient of the *actus reus* of the contribution. The contribution should be specifically directed to the furthering of the criminal activity or the criminal purpose of the group.

13.4   State Responsibility

Whether the Terrorism Financing Convention covers state responsibility is an interesting and controversial issue. On 16 January 2017, Ukraine instituted proceedings against the Russian Federation before the International Court of Justice (ICJ) with regard to alleged violations of

---

[81] *Prosecutor* v. *Taylor*, SCSL-03-01-A, Judgment, Appeals Chamber, 26 September 2013, paras. 480–2.

[82] Ibid., paras. 478–9.

[83] *Prosecutor* v. *Šainović et al.*, IT-05-87-A, Judgment, Appeals Chamber, 23 January 2014, paras. 1618–58.

the Terrorism Financing Convention and the International Convention on the Elimination of All Forms of Racial Discrimination.[84] Besides other claims, Ukraine contends that the Russian Federation is in violation of fundamental principles of international law, including those enshrined in the Terrorism Financing Convention. With regard to the latter Convention, Ukraine requested the Court to declare that the Russian Federation had violated its obligations under the Terrorism Financing Convention by:

(a) Supplying funds, including in-kind contributions of weapons and training, to illegal armed groups that engage in acts of terrorism in Ukraine . . . in violation of Article 18;

(b) Failing to take most appropriate measures to detect, freeze, and seize funds used to assist illegal armed groups that engage in acts of terrorism in Ukraine . . . in violation of Articles 8 and 18;

(c) Failing to investigate, prosecute, or extradite perpetrators of the financing of terrorism found within its territory, in violation of Articles 9, 10, 11, and 18;

(d) Failing to provide Ukraine with the greatest measure of assistance in connection with criminal investigations of the financing of terrorism, in violation of Articles 12 and 18; and

(e) Failing to take all practicable measures to prevent and counter acts of financing of terrorism committed by Russian public and private actors, in violation of Article 18.[85]

Further, Ukraine sought a declaration that the Russian Federation bore international responsibility by its sponsorship of terrorism and failure to prevent the financing of terrorism under the Convention in relation to acts including the shooting down of Malaysian Airlines Flight MH17 and the shelling and bombing of civilians in various locations.[86] Finally, Ukraine requested the Court to order the Russian Federation to comply with its obligations under the Terrorism Financing Convention, such as by ceasing and desisting from the provision of money, weapons and training to illegal armed groups engaged in acts of terrorism in Ukraine and to pay reparations.[87]

---

[84] *Application of the International Convention for the Suppression of the Financing of Terrorism and of the International Convention on the Elimination of All Forms of Racial Discrimination (Ukraine v. Russian Federation)*, Press Release, 17 January 2017.

[85] Ibid., Application Instituting Proceedings, 16 January 2017, para. 134.

[86] Ibid., para. 135.

[87] Ibid., para. 136.

It is clear that Ukraine avers that Russia should bear state respon-sibility, not only for failing to prevent the financing of terrorism but also, in terms of international responsibility, for its involvement in and sponsorship of terrorism. Russia argued that state responsibility was not contemplated by the drafters of the Convention. It is true that the Terrorism Financing Convention does not explicitly mention that a state may be a principal perpetrator by directly engaging in the provision and collection of funds for terrorist acts. It speaks only of an obligation to prevent the conduct prohibited in the Convention, as well as an obligation to cooperate in order to investigate and prose-cute those responsible. By comparison, Article 9 of the Genocide Convention stipulates that 'disputes between the Contracting Parties relating to the interpretation, application or fulfilment of the present Convention, including those relating to the responsibility of a State for genocide or for any of the other acts enumerated in Article III, shall be submitted to the International Court of Justice at the request of any of the parties to the dispute'.[88] The Genocide Convention explicitly mentioned the issue of the responsibility of a state for genocide.

Since state sponsors have tended to be a major source of funding, the obligation not to engage in the provision and collection of funds to support terrorist acts on the part of a state, although not explicitly mentioned, appears to be implied in the Convention. The most relevant case is the Bosnian Genocide case before the ICJ. The ICJ found that 'in the view of the Court, taking into account the established purpose of the Convention, the effect of Article I [of the Genocide Convention] is to prohibit States from themselves committing genocide'.[89] The ICJ continues:

> It would be paradoxical if States were thus under an obligation to prevent, so far as within their power, commission of genocide by persons over whom they have a certain influence, but were not forbidden to commit such acts through their own organs, or persons over whom they have such firm control that their conduct is attributable to the State concerned under international law. In short, the obligation to prevent genocide necessarily implies the prohibition of the commission of genocide.[90]

---

[88] Genocide Convention, Article 9.
[89] *Application of the Convention on the Prevention and Punishment of the Crime of Genocide (Bosnia and Herzegovina v. Serbia and Montenegro)*, Judgment, 26 February 2007, I.C.J. Reports 2007, p. 43, para. 166.
[90] Ibid.

The same reasoning and logic are also applicable to the Terrorism Financing Convention. If a state party accepts the obligation to prevent terrorist financing, it should refrain itself from engaging in providing and collecting funds for terrorist acts and be held to account for any breach of this obligation.

Even if the ICJ finds that the Terrorism Financing Convention covers state responsibility, Ukraine has to prove at least two issues. The first is that the receivers of the funds and weaponry were engaging in terrorist acts. The second is that Russia possessed the requisite *mens rea*. Ukraine alleges that specific incidents of shelling civilians, bombings in Kharkiv and shooting down of the Malaysian Airlines Flight 17 constitute acts of terrorism within the meaning of Article 2(1) of the Convention. However, all those incidents occurred during an armed conflict between Ukraine government forces and rebel forces. In any armed conflict, there is a political purpose to compel a government or an organization to do or to abstain from doing any act. In any war, there will inevitably be collateral damage and casualties that have the effect of terrorizing civilians. This presents a significant problem as it concerns the distinction between conventional warfare and terrorist activities. The ICTY Appeals Chamber has established the standard for terrorizing the civilian population as a violation of international humanitarian law by stating that 'while spreading terror must be the primary purpose of the acts or threats of violence, it need not be the only one'.[91] Ukraine has to present evidence that the crimes were committed by the East Ukraine Separatists with the primary purpose of spreading terror among the civilian population.

As for the *mens rea*, Ukraine has to prove two kinds of *mens rea* for two categories of crime. One is the offence of providing and collecting funds; the other is the crime of terrorist activities. As mentioned above, the crime of terrorism not only requires the intent to commit the terrorist act but also the *dolus specialis*, that is, the purpose to intimidate a population or to pursue certain political objectives. Of course, Ukraine could also claim other forms of participation, but it has to present evidence in respect of the specific requirement of each form of liability.

Domestically, it is common practice for a government to abuse the terminology of terrorism and denounce any separatist groups within its territories as terrorist groups. Therefore, it is not straightforward to prove

---

[91] *Prosecutor* v. *Dragomir Milošević*, IT-98-29/1-A, Judgment, Appeals Chamber, 12 November 2009, para. 31, citing the Trial Chamber Judgment, 12 December 2007, para. 875.

that Russia possessed the requisite *mens rea,* especially in the situation that the funds provided could be used both for a legitimate purpose and for illegal activities.

13.5 Conclusion

The Terrorist Bombing Convention and the Terrorism Financing Convention are the most important developments in articulating a general definition of terrorism, and the Terrorism Financing Convention is the first international multilateral treaty to define the financing of terrorism as a *sui generis* crime, rather than a mode of participation. The crime of financing terrorism and the terrorist acts themselves as designated in the Convention are separate but also related. One is the crime of providing and collecting funds for terrorist acts. The second is the terrorist acts themselves. As for the definition of a terrorist act, the definition might be too limited, as it relates only to violent acts but neglects non-violent acts, such as cyber-attacks, which may not cause any death or serious bodily injury to a civilian but could intimidate a population or compel a government or an international organization to do or abstain from doing any act.

As for the mode of participation, it is submitted that the Terrorism Financing Convention, along with the Terrorist Bombing Convention and the Rome Statute, created a new set of modes of liability, different from that of the UN ad hoc tribunals, such as participation as an accomplice, organizing or directing others to commit an offence and contributing to the commission of an offence perpetrated by a group of persons acting with a common purpose. Compared with the modes of participation in the UN ad hoc tribunals, the new set of modes of participation is broader, covering many traditional modes of liability. The ICC Trial Chamber in the *Katanga* case shed light on some of its aspects, but it missed an opportunity to articulate the specifics on each mode of liability.

Although the Terrorism Financing Convention dose not explicitly mention the issue of state responsibility, from the precedents in international law and the case law of the ICJ, the obligation not to engage in providing and collecting funds to support terrorist acts on the part of a state appears to be implied in the Convention. The obligation to prevent the financing of terrorism necessarily indicates the prohibition of the commission of terrorist financing. Since it is the first time for an international court to entertain a case concerning the application of the Terrorism Financing Convention, the ICJ faces a difficult legal task to decide whether the acts performed by separatists in Ukraine are terrorist in nature and whether the *mens rea* on the part of Russia in the providing and collecting of funds to be used for terrorist activities has been established. In the *Bosnian Genocide* case, the ICJ could rely on the finding of the ICTY that the Srebrenica massacre constituted genocide. In the *Ukraine* case, the ICJ has to evaluate the evidence independently. The ICJ's findings are highly anticipated since they will clarify a range of legal issues in the application of the Terrorism Financing Convention.

14

Seeking Accountability of Corporate Actors

JUAN P. CALDERON-MEZA[*]

14.1 Introduction

Added all together, we are a good lawyer.

Judith Chomsky[1]

Movements have (more) power. In seeking accountability of corporate actors, communities, advocates and prosecutors may face the bottomless capital and influence of corporations and executives, who can retain an army of attorneys readily available to litigate at any possible jurisdiction, until 'hell freezes over'.[2] Used wisely, however, inside and outside the courtroom, strategic litigation may (i) 'be a vehicle for achieving accountability – whether at the level of the state or its institutions, corporations or the individual'; (ii) 'help unearth information'; (iii) 'influence attitudes, discourse and behaviour'; (iv) 'energise and empower social movements and civil society'; and (v) 'pursue and strengthen a broad democratic, rule of law agenda'.[3] To show how communities and advocates sparked the life of a movement seeking

---

[*] The views expressed in this chapter are those of the author alone and do not reflect the views of any of the institutions with which he is affiliated. The author would like to thank everyone who inspired this chapter: those who drafted, reviewed and directed the Chiquita communication, those who represent the plaintiffs in the civil litigation, those who reviewed this chapter, those who mentored and introduced him to the movement seeking accountability of corporate actors, and, most importantly, those in the communities who resiliently lead the movement.

[1] Judith Chomsky wrote these words in a Post-it to her co-counsel, Tyler Giannini, during an oral argument. See T. Giannini, co-director of Harvard Law School's International Human Rights Clinic, Address at Harvard Law School (May 2014), 09: 04–09:12.

[2] '"We're going to fight this until hell freezes over. And then we'll fight it out in the ice," a company spokesman once said.' See M. Rosenberg, 'Chevron's US Win in Ecuador Case Looms over Cases Elsewhere', Reuters, May 3, 2009.

[3] H. Duffy, *Strategic Human Rights Litigation: Understanding and Maximising Impact* (Hart Publishing, 2018), pp. 4–5.

accountability of corporate actors under international law, this chapter will provide a chronological account of developments and setbacks that the movement has faced.

In 1980, for the first time, *Filártiga* v. *Peña-Irala* gave victims access to US courts for violations of the law of nations that took place outside the United States, under the Alien Tort Claims Act (ATCA).[4] Such a precedent commenced 'the era of human rights litigation'.[5] While *Filártiga* was a case against a state official, an important part of the movement thus created focused on corporate accountability for violations of the law of nations.

In 1994, a law school student submitted the paper 'Using the Alien Torts Claims Act: Unocal v. Burma' with the idea to use the ATCA against a corporation. With the support of her friends, a fellow law student and an activist from the Karen community, the case *Doe* v. *Unocal* marked a groundbreaking precedent in the history of corporate accountability under international law. In 2003, the Boston Globe reported this student achievement as follows:

> Though the act has been used to sue individuals, it has never been used successfully to sue a corporation for human rights abuses. In her 1994 law school paper, Redford had argued that such violations would include human rights abuses by the Burmese military, which was guarding construction in its country at a pipeline partly owned by Unocal, a California oil company. That is precisely what will be argued by lawyers on Dec. 3, when the case is heard in California Superior Court. As for the federal case, a decision on whether it will proceed to trial is pending. A three-judge appeals panel reversed a lower court's decision and ruled that Unocal may be liable for 'aiding and abetting' the military in forced labor, murder, and rape since the company hired the soldiers and provided maps and information about the pipeline.[6]

Doe v. *Unocal* was the first victory against a transnational corporation under the ATCA for claims of torture, forced labour and summary executions in Myanmar.[7] After *Unocal*, other victories followed in cases such as *Wiwa* v. *Royal Dutch Petroleum*.[8]

Despite these victories, however, the movement faced some backlash. In 2012 and, more recently, in 2017, two decisions, *Kiobel* v. *Royal Dutch*

---

[4] Alien's Action for Tort, 28 U.S.C. § 1350. (Also known as Alien Tort Statute (ATS)).
[5] H. H. Koh, 'Filártiga v. Peña-Irala: Judicial Internalization into Domestic Law of the Customary International Law Norm Against Torture', in J. E. Noyes, L. A. Dickinson and M. W. Janis (eds.), *International Law Stories* (Foundation Press, 2007), p. 45.
[6] B. English, 'Katie Redford's Pipe Dream', *The Boston Globe*, 22 October 2003.
[7] See *Doe* v. *Unocal*, 395 F.3d 932 (9th Cir. 2002).
[8] See *Wiwa* v. *Royal Dutch Petroleum Co.*, 626 F. Supp. 2d 377 (S.D.N.Y. 2009).

Petroleum and *Jesner* v. *Arab Bank*, narrowed the window of corporate liability under the ATCA, by excluding claims that do not sufficiently touch and concern the United States, and cases against non-US corporations.[9]

Fortunately, the reach of the human rights litigation era had already transcended beyond US borders. In the case *In re: Chiquita Brands Int'l*, for example, a litigation that started in the United States, seeking tort liability of Chiquita Brands International (Chiquita) for making contributions to mass crimes in Colombia, has had different ramifications for the individual criminal liability of the executives involved. Although *Kiobel* barred the plaintiffs' claims under the ATCA, the civil complaint proceeded under national tort law. This in turn triggered criminal investigations in Colombia, under the examination of the International Criminal Court (ICC), for the criminal liability of the executives.

Inspired by the Nuremberg trials against industrialists, a group of students and advocates at the Harvard Law School's International Human Rights Clinic, supported by the International Federation for Human Rights (FIDH), Colectivo de Abogados José Alvear Restrepo and the National Security Archives, used the evidence publicly available in the United States to bring a communication on the crimes of fourteen Chiquita executives to the attention of the Office of the Prosecutor (OTP) of the ICC. After the group of students and advocates submitted the communication to the OTP, domestic prosecutors issued an indictment in Colombia, and the OTP made a public announcement that it is following the Colombian investigations on corporate executives of Chiquita and other industries for their links with the paramilitaries.[10] Although there is still a long road ahead, this process would not have started but for the synergies created among survivors and others who unearthed the evidence and used it in different ways to hold the Chiquita executives accountable.

Using Chiquita as a case study, this chapter will distil the recent history of corporate accountability under international law. Despite the setbacks, the pursuit of corporate accountability continues to have momentum because, by 'help[ing] unearth information',[11] the litigation of a movement has been

---

[9]   *Kiobel* v. *Royal Dutch Petroleum Co.*, 569 U.S. 108 (2013); *Jesner* v. *Arab Bank*, PLC, 584 U.S. __, 138 S. Ct. 1386 (2018).

[10]   ICC OTP, *Report on Preliminary Examinations Activities*, 5 December 2018, paras. 151–2. *See also* ICC OTP, *Report on Preliminary Examinations Activities*, 5 December 2019, para. 98.

[11]   See Duffy (*supra* n. 3), p. 5.

strategic in 'contributing to historical clarification',[12] regarding, for instance, the role of the Global (Corporate) North in Colombia, Myanmar, Nigeria and Papua New Guinea, just to name a few examples.[13] This has re-energised, renewed and re-empowered the movement, with a new generation that, having heard and learnt from those who sparked the movement, is now looking into novel ways to seek corporate accountability not only in the North, but also in the South and beyond.

Regarding the movement of communities and advocates that have brought actions against corporate actors, Professor Beth Stephens noted that '[a]ll these actions are part of the expanding international movement toward accountability for violations of international law'.[14] In her view, these actions not only blur the distinction between public and private standing to bring cases under criminal or civil law but, remarkably, in those cases 'the individual plays a key role as an enforcer of international norms'.[15] This role is played in the intersection of civil, criminal and international liability in the pursuit of corporate accountability of corporate actors.

*

Professor Duffy explains that 'done strategically and used properly, both inside and outside the court, [litigation] can have multiple types of impact over extended periods of time'.[16] Strategic litigation gives advocates a combination of different options – civil suit seeking compensation or criminal prosecution seeking punishment, nationally and internationally. Instead of choosing one above the other options, a strategy is to progressively implement them all, through a collaborative network of prosecutors, civil litigators, survivors and witnesses within the community where the abuses happened. In the words of one of the counsel for the plaintiffs in the Chiquita civil litigation: 'There is not one best way to seek liability of corporations that have violated communities' human rights but a number of different ways to hold them accountable.'[17]

---

[12] Ibid.

[13] See generally Harvard Law School International Human Rights Clinic et al., *The contribution of Chiquita corporate officials to crimes against humanity in Colombia. Article 15 Communication to the International Criminal Court*, May 2017; *Doe v. Unocal*, 395 F.3d 932 (9th Cir. 2002); *Wiwa v. Royal Dutch Petroleum Co.*, 626 F. Supp. 2d 377 (S.D.N.Y. 2009); K. McVeigh, 'Canada Mining Firm Compensates Papua New Guinea Women after Alleged Rapes', *The Guardian*, 3 April 2015.

[14] B. Stephens, 'Individuals Enforcing International Law: The Comparative and Historical Context' (2002) 52 *DePaul Law Review* 433.

[15] Ibid.

[16] Duffy (*supra* n. 3), p. 4.

[17] Marissa Vahlsing, 13 April 2018 (notes on file with author).

To that effect, corporate accountability can be understood as the pursuit of accountability in any *fora*, be it under civil or criminal liability of individuals or corporations. This chapter will analyse such different but cooperative efforts.

Something that makes the Chiquita case particularly remarkable from a strategic prosecutorial perspective is that most of the evidence was made publicly available in civil litigation in the United States. Chiquita's confession to the payments to the paramilitary groups known as Autodefensas Unidas de Colombia (AUC), accounting records showing the executives' sophisticated strategies to hide the payments through compensation schemes and third parties linked to AUC, internal memoranda showing the executives' *mens rea* and memoranda from their legal counsel repetitively advising them that a duress defence would not work if they did not stop the payments, which they did not follow, were all made available through civil litigation in the United States. This sets an example for other cases that may have been dismissed in civil litigation under jurisdictional grounds in the United States but that contain allegations falling within the ICC's jurisdiction.

14.2   The Chiquita Case Study

Cincinnati, USA: A group of executives saw no problem in approving payments that the Colombian branch of their banana company would make, from 1997 through 2004, to illegal armed groups operating in Colombia's banana-growing region during the country's conflict. For the executives, it was just another transaction, the '[c]ost of doing business in Colombia,' they said;[18] except that these payments were made to squads of mercenaries who would kill anyone obstructing the banana production. When alerted to the mass crimes to which their money was contributing, one of the executives said, 'Just let them sue us, come after us.'[19]

Thousands of people, including union activists and banana harvesters, were murdered, disappeared, or otherwise forced to either leave or stay

---

[18] The Chiquita Papers, Handwritten notes, 7 May 1997, p. 7 (CBI-V1-001-004809), National Security Archive, https://nsarchive2.gwu.edu/NSAEBB/NSAEBB340/19970507.pdf.

[19] *In re Chiquita Brands International, Inc., Report of the Special Litigation Committee Chiquita Brands International Inc.*, February 2009, p. 89, fn. 132. See also *In re Chiquita Brands International, Inc.*, Order Granting In Part & Denying In Part Defendant's Joint Consolidated Motion to Dismiss (1 June 2016) pp. 11–12 (citing Cyrus Freidheim on the 'just let them sue us sentiment').

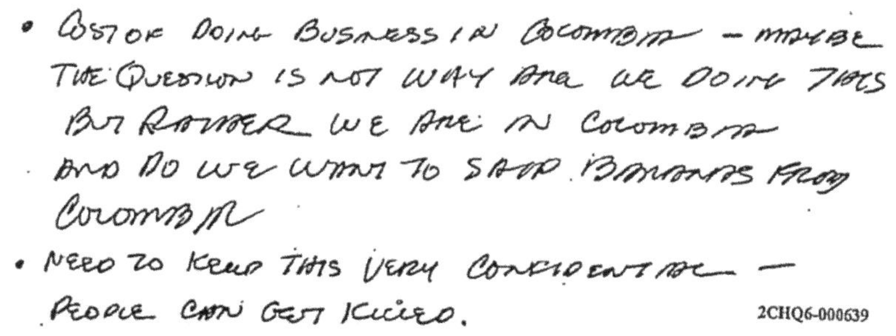

- Cost of Doing Business in Colombia — maybe the question is not why are we doing this but rather we are in Colombia and do we want to stop Bananas from Colombia

- Need to keep this very confidential — people can get killed.

2CHQ6-000639

Figure 14.1 *The Cost of Doing Business in Colombia* ('The Chiquita Papers', National Security Archive)[20]

silent and work in the banana fields. '[P]alm and banana [crops] were fertilized with the blood of our loved ones,'[21] said one of the survivors. Forcibly displaced from their lands, those who survived bear not only the agony of having lost their loved ones but also the impunity stemming from the fact that the executives have faced no justice for the crimes against humanity for which their money paid.

The juridical person of Chiquita managed to pay a fine to the US government, shielding and avoiding any repercussion against its executives, as well as any reparation to the Colombian victims. The US judge who approved this payment said: 'It gives me some pause that no individuals are held accountable, but that's really beyond the matters that this Court can resolve. The Court resolves the question before it, which is the company's culpability for the crime.'[22]

Chiquita admitted that one member of its board of directors, five of its high-ranking officers and two of its employees, as well as one high-ranking officer and one employee of its Colombian subsidiary, Banadex, authorised and made payments to paramilitary groups known as AUC.[23] In its preliminary examination on Colombia, the OTP found that such '[p]aramilitary groups have been attributed responsibility for high profile cases of murder of leaders and activists, such as human rights

---

[20] (*Supra* n. 18). OTP, *Strategic Plan. 2016-2018*, 16 November 2015, para. 104.

[21] Comisión Intereclesial de Justicia y Paz, *Empresas bananeras Vulneración de derechos humanos y narcotráfico en el Bajo Atrato*, October 2016, p. 51.

[22] Transcript of Sentencing Before the Honorable Royce C. Lamberth in *United States v. Chiquita Brands International* Inc., Docket No. 07–55 (17 Sept. 2007) at 30 (lines 23–25) - 31 (lines 1–2).

[23] Factual Proffer in *United States* v. *Chiquita Brands International* Inc, Docket No. 07–55 (Mar. 19, 2007), paras. 9–18. *See also* US Department of Justice, Plea Agreement (March 2007) para. 1.

defenders', and that their strategy included 'mass killings of civilians; selective assassinations of social leaders, trade unionists, human rights defenders, judicial officers, and journalists; acts of torture, harassment, and intimidation; and actions aimed at forcing the displacement of entire communities'.[24] Chiquita thus admitted that its executives paid the perpetrators of these atrocities.

Referring to the contributions the executives made, a former AUC commander confessed to having received support from Chiquita and other companies and to have killed hundreds of unionists to stop strikes in the banana industry:

> [T]he objective was not only fighting the guerrilla but reviving the banana industry to get the banana companies ... back on their feet. What were our orders? To force, to prevent the workers at the banana companies from going on strike. And we did that. Before that, strikes lasted for months, crippling the banana industry. We put a stop to all banana strikes. Close to 100 union members were killed in 1995. Not to mention '96 and '97 ... right up to the 2004 demobilization. So who profited? A few banana industry big shots, as opposed to the people. So the real winners of the Urabá war were banana industry tycoons. All the plantations collaborated – Uniban, Banacol, Chiquita, Dole. They were all in it with us.[25]

Many documents incriminating the Chiquita executives were made publicly available through litigation in the United States. Acting under the Freedom of Information Act, the National Security Archive sought and obtained declassification of internal documents and memoranda that Chiquita turned over to the US Department of Justice's (DOJ) and the Securities Exchange Commission's (SEC) investigations into the payments Chiquita made to the Colombian authorities and the AUC. As for the name of the executives, the Federal Court in the US civil litigation *In re: Chiquita Brands Int'l* issued an order, identifying the names of Chiquita executives who, the plaintiffs allege, were involved in the payments.[26] This was possible thanks to the analysis of the National Security Archive. While the DOJ and the SEC redacted the names of the Chiquita executives, the National Security Archive filed an administrative appeal challenging such redactions. It explains that a process of comparing and cross-referencing the redacted documents with publicly

---

[24] See ICC OTP, *Policy Paper on Case Selection and Prioritization*, 15 September 2016, paras. 25, 42, 59.

[25] Public hearing of Veloza García in *Impunity* (Icarus Films 2010), min. 53:10–55:01.

[26] See *In re Chiquita Brands International, Inc.*, Order Granting In Part & Denying In Part Defendant's Joint Consolidated Motion to Dismiss (1 June 2016) pp. 8–15, fn. 10.

available information made it possible to deduct the names of the executives, rendering the redactions moot.[27]

Based on Article 15(2) of the Rome Statute, which allows the OTP to receive communications from civil society reporting crimes under the ICC's jurisdiction, the Harvard Law School's International Human Rights Clinic submitted a public report with a dossier regarding the payments that the Chiquita executives made to the AUC. The communication asked the OTP to include within its preliminary examination on Colombia and ultimately investigate the accessory liability of fourteen Chiquita executives for knowingly contributing to the crimes that the AUC perpetrated in the banana-growing region.[28]

Nearly four months after the public filing of the communication, and after more than a decade of domestic investigations, the local Colombian prosecutor in charge indicted thirteen executives including some of those listed in the communication.[29] While the charges are still subject to judicial review, the OTP publicly announced in December 2018 that it is following the investigation of the National Attorney General's Office (AGO) into the Chiquita's executives:

> During the reporting period, the AGO initiated proceedings against businessmen allegedly involved in financing the operations of paramilitary groups operating in different regions of Colombia since at least 2002. In August 2018, the AGO issued an indictment ('resolución de acusación') against 13 executives and employees of the company Chiquita brands (Banadex and Banacol branches), for the alleged agreement ('concierto para delinquir') to finance the paramilitary front 'Arlex Hurtado' which operated in the regions of Urabá and Santa Marta from 1996 to 2004.[30]

Moreover, as a spillover effect, the OTP further noted investigations on other industries that supported the AUC, for 'contributions of cattle breeders, flour makers, merchants and some businessmen allegedly linked to the sugar industry operating in Colombia'.[31]

In December 2019, the OTP further noted that the AGO reported that it made some progress in relation to 'cases relating to the promotion and

---

[27] *In re Chiquita Brands International, Inc.*, Declaration of Michael Evans, pp. 2–12.

[28] Harvard Law School's International Human Rights Clinic et al., *The contribution of Chiquita corporate officials to crimes against humanity in Colombia. Article 15 Communication to the International Criminal Court*, May 2017, para. 1.

[29] See A. B. Mora, *Los pagos que Chiquita Brands habría hecho a los paramilitares*, El Espectador, 1 September 2018.

[30] ICC OTP, *Report on Preliminary Examinations Activities*, 5 December 2018, para. 151.

[31] Ibid.

expansion of paramilitary groups "Arlex Hurtado" and "Bloque Calima"'. Specifically, the OTP noted, in relation to such cases on the promotion and expansion of paramilitaries:

> During the reporting period, former executives and employees of the company Chiquita brands (Banadex and Banacol branches), accused by the AGO in August 2018 for the alleged agreement ('concierto para delinquir') to finance the paramilitary front 'Arlex Hurtado', requested the annulment of the accusation. The Deputy Attorney General rejected the request and continued to pursue the accusation against 10 former employees after considering that there was sufficient evidence to call them for trial.[32]

More recently, in January 2020, after its mission to Colombia to assess the progress of national proceedings, the OTP indicated, inter alia, that it 'focused in particular on national proceedings addressing the promotion and expansion of paramilitary groups'.[33] The importance of this statement is that the investigation of the Chiquita executives falls within OTP's focus on the promotion and expansion of such groups.

These public statements come after Colombia had shown itself unwilling or unable to prosecute the executives. In 2008, the Colombian Attorney General had expressed his inability to obtain information to extradite the Chiquita executives.[34] Recently, in July 2018, the Constitutional Court issued its decision noting that corporate executives would not fall within the country's mechanism for transitional justice, the Special Jurisdiction for Peace.[35] Only the future can tell what is next, but one thing is sure: the Chiquita executives who paid AUC are under scrutiny.

14.3   Liability of Corporate Actors in the United States

The Chiquita case shows the spillover effect that strategic litigation can engender: multiple strategies in Colombia and the United States including actions seeking access to classified information and civil litigation

---

[32] See also ICC OTP, *Report on Preliminary Examinations Activities*, 5 December 2019, para. 98.

[33] See also ICC OTP, *The Office of the Prosecutor concludes mission to Colombia*, 23 January 2020.

[34] See *Acuerdo de Confidencialidad impide extradicion de directivos de Chiquita Brands*, El Espectador, 22 April 2008.

[35] See also *Las razones de la Corte Constitucional para sacar los terceros de la JEP*, El Espectador, 13 July 2018.

brought by survivors under the ATCA flourished into additional investigations in Colombia and, eventually, examinations at the ICC.

The ATCA litigation, filed in US federal court in 2007 by family members who had lost their loved ones to paramilitaries funded by Chiquita in its banana-growing region, was one of the first catalysts for this spillover effect. The ATCA grants district courts in the United States 'original jurisdiction of any civil action by an alien for a tort only, committed in violation of the law of nations or a treaty of the United States'.[36] While not granting courts universal jurisdiction to try accused under criminal liability, this statute gave US courts jurisdiction to adjudicate cases seeking civil liability for atrocities and human rights violations committed in violation of the law of nations.[37] An old statute that lay dormant for years, the ATCA gave the human rights movement a basis for a test case that would open a window for the 'ageless dream of justice'.[38] It all began with a few test cases seeking accountability for atrocities committed outside the United States, first against individuals and then against corporations.

In 1980, a court in the Second Circuit of the United States entertained ATCA claims that Paraguayans brought against a former Paraguayan state agent who had relocated to New York, seeking reparations for the crimes of torture and murder in Paraguay.[39] Later, in 1996, the *Kadić* v. *Karadžić* court in the same Circuit entertained claims for atrocities committed during the former Yugoslavia's armed conflict.[40]

Innovatively, during the millennia change, advocates and communities started using the ATCA to enable survivors of atrocity crimes to seek compensation, for the harm that they and their deceased relatives suffered, from corporations and executives that breached the law of nations. This statute has been the basis for US courts to hold, for instance, that avoiding liability merely by incorporating would be inconsistent with the international prohibition against genocide and war crimes.[41] Similarly, US courts have found that 'the prohibition against slavery is universal and may be asserted against ... corporate defendants ...'.[42]

---

[36] Alien's Action for Tort, 28 U.S.C. § 1350.
[37] Ibid.
[38] *Filártiga* v. *Peña-Irala*, 630 F.2d 876 (2d Cir. 1980).
[39] Ibid.
[40] *Kadić* v. *Karadžić*. 70 F.3d 232 (2nd Cir. 1995).
[41] *Sarei* v. *Rio Tinto, PLC*, 671 F.3d 736,760 (9th Cir. 2011).
[42] *Doe* v. *Nestle*, 766 F.3d 1017, 1022 (9th Cir. 2014).

In 2001, a court in the Ninth Circuit of the United States entertained claims in *Doe et al* v. *Unocal*, the first ATCA case against a transnational corporation in the modern era, for claims of torture, forced labour and summary executions to which the civilians in Myanmar were subjected during the construction of a pipeline.[43] After the court denied Unocal's motion to dismiss the lawsuit, the company presented the plaintiffs with a multimillion-dollar proposal to settle the case.[44] This case has been documented as a successful paradigm in corporate accountability.[45] Subsequently, in *Sosa* v. *Alvarez-Machain*, a case about the detention in Mexico and subsequent surrender of a Mexican national to the United States, the US Supreme Court established two important requirements for the ATCA: the rule of international law whose violation is alleged must be (i) generally accepted and (ii) sufficiently specific to create a federal action.[46]

Later in 2012, the Supreme Court settled the law regarding the use of ATCA in the so-called 'foreign-cubed' cases, claims with facts taking place entirely outside the United States. In *Kiobel et al.* v. *Royal Dutch Petroleum*, Nigerian nationals sued Shell's parent company and its subsidiary in Nigeria for assisting the national authorities in a brutal attack against protesters from the Ogoni indigenous community who opposed the construction of an oil field in the surroundings of the Niger River Delta.[47] The Supreme Court recalled that there is a presumption against the extraterritorial application of US law and only when the Congress expresses its intention to the contrary can US law be applied extraterritorially.[48] The Supreme Court held that 'even when the claims touch and concern the territory of the United States, they must do so with sufficient force to displace the presumption against extraterritorial application [of US law]'.[49]

Later, in 2014, the Supreme Court was once again seized with a 'foreign-cubed' case; this time for human rights violations and atrocity crimes perpetrated in Argentina. Plaintiffs who were kidnapped, detained, tortured, and some of them killed in Mercedes-Benz Argentina's plant sought to hold Daimler vicariously liable under the ATCA for the support that the

---

[43] *Doe* v. *Unocal*, (*supra* n. 7).
[44] 'Energy Giant Agrees Settlement with Burmese Villagers', *The Guardian*, 15 December 2004.
[45] See *Total Denial* (Milena Kaneva, 2006).
[46] *Sosa* v. *Alvarez-Machain*, 542 U.S. 692 (2004).
[47] *Kiobel* v. *Royal Dutch Petroleum Co.*, 133 S.Ct. 1659 (2013); 569 U.S. 108 (2013).
[48] Ibid.
[49] Ibid., 133 S.Ct. 1669.

Argentinian subsidiary provided to the country's dictatorship from 1976 through 1983.[50] Since the Court of Appeals had entertained jurisdiction under the ATCA, the corporate defendant asked the Supreme Court to answer the issue of 'whether ... Daimler is amenable to suit in California courts for claims involving only foreign plaintiffs and conduct occurring entirely abroad'.[51]

The Supreme Court explained that a court may have personal jurisdiction on the basis of 'continuous and systematic' in-state activities (general jurisdiction) or 'the commission of some single or occasional acts of the agent in a state' (specific jurisdiction).[52] The Supreme Court expressly rejected the decision to grant personal jurisdiction on the sole basis of agency, because, in the Supreme Court's view, an agent is not always its parent company's alter ego, as it may well represent the latter for some activities but not for other matters.[53] The Supreme Court rejected the Ninth Circuit's approach entertaining general jurisdiction under ATCA, on the basis of its previous decision in *Kiobel*.[54] In short, a foreign corporation doing business in the United States, among many other places, was not sufficient to overcome the *Kiobel* presumption against extraterritoriality.[55] Although *Bauman* was a case about personal jurisdiction, it affected the ability of plaintiffs to bring a case against foreign companies over whom there is no specific jurisdiction whether under ATCA or otherwise.

Unfortunately, after this, it was the turn for the plaintiffs in Chiquita to face this backlash. In *Cardona v. Chiquita*, the Court of Appeals of the Eleventh Circuit entertained the issue of whether *Kiobel* was to bar the

---

[50] *Daimler v. Bauman*, 571 U.S. 117, 120–24 (2014).

[51] Ibid. 125.

[52] Ibid. 126–127.

[53] Ibid. 134. (noting that the importance of services rendered by the agent is not a basis for general jurisdiction either and that while a court may entertain general jurisdiction in the 'home' of a corporation, its place of incorporation or principal place of business, the plaintiffs' request to entertain general jurisdiction on the basis of presence is 'unacceptably grasping', ibid., 138).

[54] Ibid. 141, referring to *Kiobel v. Royal Dutch Petroleum Co.*, 569 U.S. 108 (2013) (restricting the extraterritorial application of ATCA) and *Mohamad v. Palestinian Authority*, 566 U.S. 449 (2012) (restricting TVPA to natural persons).

[55] *Daimler v. Bauman*, 571 U.S. 117, 139 (2014), whereby the Supreme Court found no general jurisdiction in this 'foreign-cubed' case holding that '[i]t was ... error for the Ninth Circuit to conclude that Daimler, even with [Mercedes Benz USA] contacts attributed to it, was at home in California, and hence subject to suit there on claims by foreign plaintiffs having nothing to do with anything that occurred or had its principal impact in California'.

plaintiffs' claims under the ATCA.[56] The court made an overly simplistic application of *Kiobel* to determine its lack of jurisdiction over torts taking place abroad, by noting that *Kiobel* 'did not find any indication of a congressional intent to make the statute apply to extraterritorial torts'.[57] On this basis, it squarely concluded: 'There is no other statute. There is no jurisdiction.'[58] The case, nonetheless, continued under Colombian law and the Torture Victims Protection Act (TVPA).

After this turn of events, the question of whether the ATCA provides for a cause of action against non-US corporations once again occupied the US Supreme Court.[59] In *Jesner* v. *Arab Bank*, plaintiffs brought suit before US courts under the ATCA, arguing that Arab Bank, which has a branch in New York, financed terrorist attacks that injured them or killed their relatives in the Middle East.[60] The Supreme Court decided to exercise its judicial discretion against allowing foreign corporate liability under the ATCA considering other adequate remedies to seek liability of individual corporate actors. The Supreme Court found that absence of 'a clear and well-established international-law rule' of corporate liability under international law was critical in allowing a cause of action against foreign corporations without specific congressional authorisation.[61] It thus made an urgent call for the Congress to 'determine whether victims of human-rights abuses may sue foreign corporations in federal courts in the United States'.[62]

Some observations that the Supreme Court made in passing deserve further analysis. It considered that allowing plaintiffs to bring suit against foreign corporations under the ATCA could discourage investment 'in developing economies where the host government might have a history of alleged human-rights violations, or where judicial systems might lack the safeguards of United States courts',[63] thereby deterring 'active corporate investment that contributes to the economic development that so often is an essential foundation for human rights'.[64] It recognised, nevertheless, that 'natural persons can and do use corporations for sinister purposes, including conduct that violates international law'[65] and that

---

[56] *Cardona* v. *Chiquita*, 760 F.3d 1185 (11th Cir. 2014).
[57] Ibid. 1189.
[58] Ibid.
[59] *Jesner* v. *Arab Bank*, PLC, (*supra* n. 9).
[60] Ibid. p. 3.
[61] Ibid. p. 23.
[62] Ibid. pp. 24–5.
[63] Ibid. p. 24.
[64] Ibid.
[65] Ibid.

'there are strong arguments for permitting the victims to seek relief from corporations themselves'.[66]

This view not only assumes that development is at the forefront of every community within the host countries where transnational corporations operate; it also further portrays host governments as the 'bad guys' and corporations as the 'good guys'. Some governments may share the idea that trade fosters development,[67] but, even if that were the case, this does not mean that all communities within a host country agree with their government's understanding of development. The international community itself recognises the influence that transnational corporations have in host governments.[68] When the 'good guys' are not so good, courts should be open to put the behaviour of their executives and the corporation under scrutiny, regardless of the domicile of the corporation, instead of accommodating the legal system to their investment. Professor David Kennedy warns against the idea that '[b]y changing the rules, the good guys – investors, innovators, entrepreneurs, national champions – would be strengthened and the society transformed'.[69] Limiting the ATCA under the concern that corporations may change their investment behaviour would simply promote forum shopping when corporate actors decide where to set their domicile.

14.4 Corporate Accountability under International Law

To 'determine whether victims of human rights abuses may sue foreign corporations in federal courts in the United States',[70] a better understanding of whether or not there is a rule of corporate liability under international law can be found in history. This section describes that history. To that effect, history accounts for a concept of corporate accountability encompassing any or all of the following modalities: individual criminal liability of executives (World War II industrialists trials), tort liability of corporations and/or executives (US ATCA cases) and criminal liability of corporations (Special Tribunal for Lebanon and African Court of Justice and Human Rights).

---

[66] Ibid.

[67] See E. Zedillo & P. Messerlin, *Trade for Development* (Earthscan, 2005), pp.12–17.

[68] Economic and Social Council, Commission on Human Rights, Sub-Commission on the Promotion and Protection of Human Rights, 55th Sess., U.N. Doc. E/CN.4/Sub.2/2003/12/Rev.2 (Aug. 26, 2003), para. 12.

[69] D. Kennedy, 'Law, Expertise and Global Political Economy' (2018) 23 *Tilburg International Law Review* 119.

[70] *Jesner* v. *Arab Bank, PLC*, (*supra* n. 9), pp. 24–5.

14.4.1   International Criminal Liability of Corporate
Actors after World War II

At the conclusion of World War II, the allies established the International Military Tribunal (IMT) with three judges from the Allied powers and one from the Soviet Union in order 'to try and punish persons who, acting in the interests of the European Axis countries, whether as individuals or as members of organizations, committed any [crimes against peace, war crimes or crimes against humanity]'.[71] Today, the IMT and its counterpart the International Military Tribunal for the Far East (IMTFE) are generally regarded as a major step towards justice for international crimes regardless of opinions labelling them as victors' justice.[72] Both tribunals, nonetheless, are quintessential examples of not only the *justice* of victorious powers but also the *power* of justice.

Justice Robert Jackson, who acted as the Chief Prosecutor at the IMT, referred to the juridical personality of states and corporations as an unacceptable justification for immunity. He maintained that 'it is quite intolerable to let such a legalism become the basis of personal immunity'.[73] The prosecution thus adopted an approach under which '[a]ny person, without regard to nationality or the capacity in which he acted, is deemed to have committed [crimes against peace, war crimes, crimes against humanity], if he ... was an accessory to the commission of any such crime or ordered or abetted the same' or 'if he ... held high position in the financial, industrial or economic life of any such country'.[74]

One could label Justice Jackson's prosecutorial approach under Noam Chomsky's intellectual task to understand very clearly 'the nature of power and oppression, and terror and destruction in our own society', which includes 'the central institutions of any industrial society, namely: the economic, commercial and financial institutions and ... the great multi-national corporations'.[75] Therein lies the importance of understanding the role of corporate actors, both corporations and their individual agents, in the commission of atrocity crimes and how such a role has been addressed under international law.

---

[71] See Nuremberg Charter, Arts. 1–2, 6.
[72] See, e.g., IMTFE, *USA et al.* v. *Araki Sadao et al, Dissenting Opinion of Justice Pal*, 1 November 1948, pp. 1012, 1018.
[73] M. Bazyler and J. Green, 'Nuremberg-Era Jurisprudence Redux: The Supreme Court in Kiobel v. Royal Dutch Petroleum Co. and the Legal Legacy of Nuremberg' (2012–2013) 7 *Charleston Law Review* 41.
[74] Control Council Law No. 10, Art. 2(b).
[75] See N. Chomsky and M. Foucault, *Human Nature: Justice versus Power*, 1971.

It was but for Justice Jackson's prosecutorial approach that the IMT made the frequently quoted, significant finding regarding the role of individuals within juridical persons and, more broadly, the liability of private individuals under international law: 'Crimes against international law are committed by men, not by abstract entities, and only by punishing individuals who commit such crimes can the provisions of international law be enforced.'[76] Subsequently, US and UK military tribunals conducted, under Control Council Law No. 10, trials of industrialists who assisted the Nazi regime. This law had the purpose 'to establish a uniform legal basis in Germany for the prosecution of war criminals and other similar offenders, other than those dealt with by the International Military Tribunal'.[77] It further encompassed measures such as seizure of corporate assets and corporate dissolution, which is comparable to 'corporate death under international law'.[78] The cases of *Zyklon B*, *Flick*, *I.G. Farben* and *Krupp* deserve particular attention as they showed the role of corporations and their agents in the atrocities that took place during World War II.

The accused in the *Zyklon B* case were agents of the company that supplied poison gas to the concentration camps.[79] They held, however, different positions in the company – while Tesch was the owner and Weinbacher was the second in the chain of command, Drosihn was a technician.[80] The court acquitted Drosihn and held both Tesch and Weinbacher liable after hearing the Judge Advocate's reasoning that knowledge of the use given to the gas together with a position to influence or prevent the transfer of gas were the main criteria to assess liability.[81] The Judge Advocate highlighted that Tesch and Weinbacher were 'both competent business men, were sensitive about admitting that they knew at the relevant time of the size of the deliveries of poison gas to Auschwitz'.[82] In the case of Drosihn, however, the Judge Advocate questioned 'whether there was any evidence that he was in a position

---

[76] *The United States of America, the French Republic, the United Kingdom of Great Britain and Northern Ireland, and the Union of Soviet Socialist Republics v. Hermann Wilhelm Göring, et al.*, Judgment, 1 October 1946, p. 466.
[77] Control Council Law No. 10, 20 December 1945.
[78] *Kiobel v. Royal Dutch Petroleum Co.*, Brief of Amici Curiae Nuremberg Scholars Omer Bartov et al., 21 December 2011, p. 3.
[79] British Military Court, Hamburg, *Case No. 9, the Zyklon B, Case trial of Bruno Tesch and two others*, 8 March 1946, p. 93 (www.legal-tools.org/en/doc/297178/).
[80] Ibid.
[81] Ibid., pp. 101–2.
[82] Ibid., p. 102.

either to influence the transfer of gas to Auschwitz or to prevent it'.[83] In the Judge Advocate's view, '[i]f he were not in such a position, no knowledge of the use to which the gas was being put could make him guilty'.[84]

In *United States of America* v. *Friedrich Flick, et al.*, two of the accused, Flick and Steinbrinck, were charged for being members of a circle of influential industrialists known as the Circle of Friends of Himmler.[85] The prosecution successfully argued that they had 'knowledge of the criminal activities of the SS' and further 'contributed funds and influence to its support'.[86] The bench found that each member paid a 'hundred thousand Reichsmarks per year'.[87] The bench observed that '[i]t seems to be immaterial whether it was spent on salaries or for lethal gas'.[88] Referring to the atrocities perpetrated through the SS as an organisation, specifically the mass murders perpetrated in the extermination of the Jews and experiments in concentration camps, the bench observed that '[o]ne who knowingly by his influence and money contributes to the support thereof must, under settled legal principles, be deemed to be, if not a principal, certainly an accessory to such crimes'.[89] Elsewhere in the judgment, the bench entertained the question of individual liability for breaches of international law amounting to crimes. It endorsed the IMT finding that international law applies to individuals.[90] It held that '[i]t cannot longer be successfully maintained that international law is concerned only with the actions of sovereign states and provides no punishment for individuals'.[91] The bench noted that international law 'binds every citizen just as does ordinary municipal law'.[92]

In another case, *I.G. Farben*, the prosecution indicted twenty-three employees of the German pharmaceutical company I.G. Farben for the crimes of slavery, plunder, aggression and mass murder. Five of the directors were found liable for slave labour.[93] While the tribunal did

---

[83] Ibid.
[84] Ibid.
[85] U.S. Military Tribunal, Nuremberg, *United States of America* v. *Friedrich Flick, et al.*, 22 December 1947, p. 1216 (www.legal-tools.org/en/doc/861416/).
[86] Ibid.
[87] Ibid., p. 1220.
[88] Ibid., p. 1221.
[89] Ibid., p. 1217.
[90] Ibid., p. 1192 ('[a]cts adjudged criminal when done by an officer of the government are criminal also when done by a private individual').
[91] Ibid., p. 1191.
[92] Ibid., p. 1192.
[93] U.S. Military Tribunal VI, Nuremberg, *The IG Farben Trial, The United States of America* v. *Carl Krauch et al.*, 30 July 1948 (www.legal-tools.org/en/doc/ce19e9/).

not have personal jurisdiction over the corporation, it made important findings as to its violation of international law and its role in the crimes. The prosecution's theory of the case stated that the accused 'act[ed] through the instrumentality of Farben'.[94] The bench found that 'Auschwitz was financed and owned by Farben' and that '[t]he Auschwitz construction workers furnished by the concentration camp lived and labored under the shadow of extermination'.[95] The tribunal found that the corporation's use of slave labour at concentration camps was a crime against humanity.[96] Furthermore, referring to the corporate activities in Poland, Norway and France, the bench found beyond reasonable doubt that the corporation offended the definition of private property and that such offences 'were connected with, and an inextricable part of the German policy for occupied countries'.[97] It noted that I.G. Farben built its chemical empire through offences against the laws and customs of war such as pillage, plunder and spoliation, in violation of the 1899 Hague Regulations.[98]

In the *Krupp* case, the prosecution charged twelve industrialists with war crimes and crimes against humanity of plunder and spoliation of private property, deportation and forced labour of prisoners of war and inmates of concentration camps, as well as crimes against peace and conspiracy to commit crimes against peace. Six of the accused were convicted for the counts of plunder and spoliation under a policy to exploit occupied territories beyond the army's needs, in disregard of the local economy. The bench found that Krupp benefited from the Nazi anti-Jewish policy, in violation of Article 48 of the Hague Regulations, by acquiring properties taken from the Jews in France and the Netherlands.[99]

Regarding the count of deportation, exploitation and slave labour, the bench referred to Krupp's role in Auschwitz, finding that its employment of concentration camp inmates was a violation of international law.[100] When explaining the process of slavery through which the SS offered inmates from concentration camps to the companies in the armament industry, the bench explained that '[i]t was not a matter of refusing to

---

[94] Ibid., p. 1084.
[95] Ibid., pp. 1140, 1183–4.
[96] Ibid., pp. 1185–7.
[97] Ibid., p. 1139.
[98] Ibid.
[99] U.S. Military Tribunal III, Nuremberg, *United States of America v. Alfried Felix Alwyn Krupp von Bohlen und Halbach et al.*, 31 July 1948, pp. 1338 *et seq* (www.legal-tools.org /doc/ad5c2b/).
[100] Ibid., pp. 1433–4.

accept an allocation' but that '[i]t was up to the enterprises to put in requests' and, while '[m]any armament firms refused', Krupp 'sought concentration camp labor because of the scarcity of manpower then prevailing in Germany'.[101]

As for the charges on crimes against peace, while the evidence did not support liability beyond reasonable doubt, the bench expressly noted that it was 'not hold[ing] that industrialists[,] as such, could not under any circumstances be found guilty upon such charges'.[102] With regard to the crime of aggression, Professor Nerlich considers that, '[i]n line with the *dicta* in *Krupp*, the door is left ajar – albeit in limited circumstances – for principal or accessorial liability of non-state actors, including business leaders and, therefore, business corporations'.[103] In a concurring opinion, one of the Judges explained such limited circumstances where the *actus reus* is 'not merely nominal, but substantial participation in and responsibility for activities vital to building up the power of a country to wage war', while the *mens rea* is 'knowledge that the military power would be used in a manner which, in the words of the Kellogg [Briand] Pact, includes war as an "instrument of policy"'.[104]

14.4.2   Rome Statute

The trials against the industrialists showed that corporate agents are not immune from justice when they facilitate atrocities. Just as the IMT and subsequent proceedings wound down, however, industrialists such as Flick were pardoned and even today still have a vast influential power.[105] On top of this, the view that corporations are not subject to international law continued.[106]

---

[101] Ibid., p. 1412.

[102] U.S. Military Tribunal III, Nuremberg, *United States of America* v. *Alfried Felix Alwyn Krupp von Bohlen und Halbach et al.*, Order of the Tribunal Acquitting the Defendants of the Charges of Crimes Against Peace and Opinion of the Tribunal Concerning its Dismissal of the Charges of Crimes Against Peace, 11 June 1948, p. 393.

[103] V. Nerlich, 'Core Crimes and Transnational Business Corporations' (2010) 8 *Journal of International Criminal Justice* 895, 908.

[104] Order of the Tribunal Acquitting the Defendants of the Charges of Crimes Against Peace (*supra* n. 102), pp. 455–6.

[105] D. de Jong, 'The Nazi Shadow Behind the World's Youngest Billionaires', *Time Magazine*, 7 May 2018.

[106] L. Oppenheim, *International Law: A Treatise* (A. McNair ed., 4th ed. 1928) at 20–1, para. 13 ('the Law of Nations is a law for international conduct of States, and not of their citizens'). See also C. Phillipson, *Wheaton's Elements of International Law* (5th ed., Stevens and Sons/Baker, Voorhis & Co., 1916) at 32 ('Subjects of international law are

This was the context that the UN Diplomatic Conference of Plenipotentiaries on the Establishment of an International Criminal Court (Rome Conference) faced when presented with the issue of accountability of corporate actors under international criminal law. While the personal jurisdiction of the ICC, under Article 25 of the Rome Statute, was ultimately focused on natural persons,[107] the possibility for seeking accountability of corporations was recognised, discussed and ultimately deferred to be addressed again at a later stage before the Assembly of State Parties.

Starting in 1996, the Preparatory Committee on the Establishment of an International Criminal Court (Prep Com) reported that some delegations, simply on the basis of practicalities related to apparent opposition with their domestic law, considered that 'it would be more useful to focus attention on individual responsibility'.[108] While it was not considered as 'useful' as focusing on individual liability, it does not mean that liability of corporations under international criminal law was rejected; nor does it mean that it did not exist. In fact, the Prep Com also reported that 'liability of a corporation could be important in the context of restitution' and that 'the principle had been applied in the Nürnberg Judgement'.[109]

To address the divergence of views on the practicality of allowing the ICC to focus on corporate in addition to individual liability, the Working Group on General Principles of Criminal Law circulated a draft with a draft option including two paragraphs, (5) and (6), in the then-Article 23 – today's Article 25 of the Rome Statute. This option gave the Court personal jurisdiction also over legal persons, other than States, 'when the crimes committed were committed on behalf of such legal persons or by their agencies or representatives'.[110] It was proposed that such 'criminal responsibility of legal persons shall not exclude the criminal responsibility

---

nations, and those political societies called states'); and M. N. Shaw, *International Law* (7th ed., Cambridge University Press, 2014) ('the principal subjects of international law are nation-states, not individual citizens.')

[107] See Rome Statute, Art. 25.

[108] United Nations Diplomatic Conference of Plenipotentiaries on the Establishment of an International Criminal Court (UNDCPICC), 'Report of the Preparatory Committee on the Establishment of an International Criminal Court', Vol. I, A/51/22 (Vol. I), 1996, para. 194.

[109] Ibid.

[110] UNDCPICC, *Report of the Preparatory Committee on the Establishment of an International Criminal Court. Addendum*, 14 April 1998, A/CONF-183/2/Add-1, para. 49.

of natural persons who are perpetrators or accomplices in the same crimes'.[111] Particularly important, regarding the difference but possible conjunction in proceedings seeking both civil and criminal liability, this proposal had a footnote indicating, inter alia, that: 'Some delegations hold the view that providing for only the civil or administrative responsibility/ liability of legal persons could provide a middle ground. This avenue, however, has not been thoroughly discussed. Some delegations, who favour the inclusion of legal persons, hold the view that this expression should be extended to organizations lacking legal status.'[112]

The Chairman of the Working Group, Per Saland from Sweden, noted that France and the Solomon Islands continued discussing the possibility to work on the language of the proposal to make it more amenable to sceptical parties.[113] On 16 June 1998, at the Rome Conference, France tabled a proposal to the group including punishment such as fines and forfeiture for 'criminal organizations', with a view to addressing some delegations' concerns regarding the enforcement of judgments against entities whose personal liberty cannot physically be deprived.[114] On 3 July 1998, the Working Group reached the final text of draft Article 23, paragraphs (5) and (6), placing a necessary condition for corporations to be tried only if the natural person who controls the legal person is convicted and the prosecutor included in the charges against that natural person that he/she was in control of the legal person and acted under 'consent' of the latter.[115]

Conspicuously, draft Article 23, paragraphs (5) and (6), did not appear in the final version of Article 25 of the Statute. Scholars refer to two obstacles for their inclusion. One is the lack of time for delegations to adequately address how to enforce judgments and procedures, such as, in indicting a corporation, who represents the entity, what are the standards of proof and what evidence would meet them at trial.[116] The second obstacle related to complementarity. At the time of the Rome Conference in 1998, more than twenty years ago, some delegations had not yet passed laws on the concept of the liability of legal persons, thereby making them

---

[111] Ibid.
[112] Ibid.
[113] Ibid.
[114] UNDCPICC, *Proposal submitted by France*, A/CONF.183/C.1/L.3, 16 June 1998.
[115] UNDCPICC, *Working Group on General Principles of Criminal Law*, 3 July 1998, A/ CONF.183/C.1/WGGP/L.5/Rev.2.
[116] K. Haigh, 'Extending the International Criminal Court's Jurisdiction to Corporations: Overcoming Complementarity Concerns' (2008) 14 *Australian Journal of Human Rights* 199, 203.

unable to prosecute them domestically before the ICC could do so: 'The fact that negotiators ultimately rejected corporate liability under the Rome Statute had nothing to do with rules of customary international law and everything to do with whether national legal systems already held corporations criminally liable or would be likely to under the principle of complementarity of the Rome Statute.'[117]

As Chairman Per Saland puts it, '[t]ime was running out', during the Rome Conference, to include corporate liability within the Rome Statute.[118] Liability of individual corporate officers, however, has since remained possible at the ICC.

14.4.3   From Soft Law to an Emerging Consensus

In the meantime, the start of the new millennium witnessed an effort to bring about binding regulations for transnational corporations. Notably, in 2002, the UN Commission on Human Rights drafted the Norms on the Responsibilities of Transnational Corporations and Other Business Enterprises with regard to Human Rights.[119] These norms acknowledge that, besides states, 'transnational corporations and other business enterprises, their officers and persons working for them are also obligated to respect generally recognized responsibilities and norms contained in United Nations treaties and other international instruments'[120] and that all of them 'including managers, members of corporate boards or directors and other executives – and persons working for them *have, inter alia, human rights obligations and responsibilities and that these human rights norms will contribute to the making and development of international law as to those responsibilities and obligations*'.[121] Specifically on the point of international crimes, the norms say that corporations 'shall not engage in nor benefit from war crimes, crimes against humanity, genocide, torture, forced disappearance, forced or compulsory labour,

---

[117] D. Scheffer and C. Kaeb, 'The Five Levels of CSR Compliance: The Resiliency of Corporate Liability Under the Alien Tort Statute and the Case for a Counterattack Strategy in Compliance Theory' (2011) 29 *Berkeley Journal of International Law* 368.

[118] P. Saland, 'International Criminal Law Principles', in R. S. Lee (ed.), *The International Criminal Court: The Making of the Rome Statute* (Kluwer Law International, 1999), p. 199.

[119] Economic and Social Council, Commission on Human Rights, Sub-Commission on the Promotion and Protection of Human Rights, 55th Sess., U.N. Doc. E/CN.4/Sub.2/2003/12/Rev.2 (Aug. 26, 2003).

[120] Ibid., p. 2.

[121] Ibid., p. 3. (Emphasis added.)

hostage-taking, extrajudicial, summary or arbitrary executions, other violations of humanitarian law and other international crimes against the human person as defined by international law, in particular human rights and humanitarian law'.[122] The norms, however, are not binding.

Nowadays an advisor for Barrick Gold Corporation,[123] a company reportedly complicit in sexual crimes at its Progera mine in Papua New Guinea and murders at its North Mara mine in Tanzania,[124] former UN Special Representative on Human Rights and Transnational Corporations and other Business Enterprises John Ruggie proposed a 'voluntary framework' under the UN Guiding Principles on Business and Human Rights.[125] Under this framework, states have obligations to protect and to take measures to remedy violations, while corporations simply have the responsibility, rather than obligation, to respect human rights: 'The term "responsibility" rather than "duty" is meant to indicate that respecting rights is not currently an obligation that international human rights law generally imposes directly on companies, although elements of it may be reflected in domestic laws.'[126]

As a result, Principles 29 and 31 of the UN Guiding Principles on Business and Human Rights do not bind corporations to obligations that could be enforceable through a court of law, but simply require them to provide stakeholders with grievance mechanisms. Such mechanisms *should* be legitimate, accessible, predictable, equitable, transparent, rights-compatible, a source of continuous learning, and based on engage-ment and dialogue.[127] It is argued, however, that corporations that have incorporated grievance mechanisms have instead found barriers, due to

---

[122] Ibid.

[123] Barrick Gold Corporation, *CSR Advisory Board.*

[124] See, generally, Columbia Law School Human Rights Clinic and Harvard Law School International Human Rights Clinic, Righting Wrongs? Barrick Gold's Remedy Mechanism for Sexual Violence in Papua New Guinea: Key Concerns and Lessons Learned (November 2015); Business & Human Rights African Barrick Gold lawsuit (re Tanzania).

[125] J. Green, 'Corporate Torts: International Human Rights and Superior Officers' (2016) 17 *Chicago Journal of International Law* 457, referring to the UN Office of the High Commissioner for Human Rights, Guiding Principles on Business and Human Rights. Implementing the United Nations 'Protect, Respect and Remedy' Framework, Annex to Final Report to the Human Rights Council by John Ruggie, Special Representative of the Secretary-General, U.N. Doc. A/HRC/17/31 (Mar. 21, 2011).

[126] The UN 'Protect, Respect and Remedy' Framework for Business and Human Rights, September 2010.

[127] UN Human Rights Council, United Nations Guiding Principles on Business and Human Rights, Resolution 17/4 of June 16, 2011, Principles 29, 31.

'the standards they cover, the eligibility of parties, the scale or gravity of admissible grievances, limits on information and awareness, and questions of trust and confidence'.[128] Instead of promoting remedies for victims, the 'Guiding Principles endorsed private litigation as one appropriate remedy for victims, and rejected attacks on these remedies'.[129]

In practice, soft law has been a distraction from accountability. It 'has been widely criticized and even dismissed as a factor in international affairs'.[130] Despite the clear duty of the Universal Declaration of Human Rights for '*every organ of society* ... to promote respect for these rights and freedoms and ... to secure their universal and effective recognition and observance',[131] it is argued that such recognition 'does not equate to legally binding effect'.[132] Corporate self-regulations rely on the goodwill of corporations to follow a set of good practices, but they do not offer victims a cause of action in case corporations do not follow such good practices. This lack of enforceability before a court of law disenfranchises victims from seeking actual redress. There is a gap in international justice, and soft law simply covers the top of the iceberg.

*

Recent attempts to close this gap, however, have repaved the road for an emerging consensus on corporate accountability under international law. In September 2013, during the twenty-fourth session of the UN Human Rights Council, Ecuador, seconded by countries in the African Union and the Arab League, Pakistan, Sri Lanka, Kyrgyzstan, Cuba, Nicaragua, Bolivia, Venezuela and Peru, presented a proposal for the creation of an international, legally binding instrument on business and human rights.[133] In June 2014, the Human Rights Council created and tasked the Open Ended Intergovernmental Working Group to 'elaborate an

---

[128] C. Rees, Grievance Mechanisms for Business and Human Rights. Strengths, Weaknesses and Gaps, Harv. CSRI Working Papers No. 40, January 2008 at 1.

[129] Green (*supra* n. 125) 457.

[130] See K. Abbott, 'Hard and Soft Law in International Governance' (2000) 54(3) *International Organizations* 422 ('Soft law has been widely criticized and even dismissed as a factor in international affairs. Realists, of course, focus on the absence of an independent judiciary with supporting enforcement powers. [...]').

[131] See Universal Declaration of Human Rights, G.A. res. 217A (III), U.N. Doc A/810 at 71 (1948), Preamble.

[132] Report of the Special Representative of the Secretary-General on the Issue of Human Rights and Transnational Corporations and other Business Enterprises, UN Doc. A/HRC/4/35 (2007), para. 37.

[133] Statement on behalf of a Group of Countries at the 24rd [*sic*] Session of the Human Rights Council, September 2013.

international legally binding instrument to regulate, in international human rights law, the activities of transnational corporations and other business enterprises'.[134] Within this context, the United Nations High Commissioner for Human Rights noted in 2016 'that the "individual liability of corporate officers" is an important aspect of the right to remedy human rights victims'.[135] In 2018, Ecuador presented a 'zero draft legally binding instrument to regulate, in international human rights law, the activities of transnational corporations and other business enterprises'.[136] It was used as a basis for negotiations.[137] A new, revised draft treaty has since been circulated.[138] Notably, Article 7 provides for victims to have a cause of action against executives or corporations at the place where (i) violations were committed, (ii) victims have their domicile, or (iii) corporations or executives are domiciled.[139]

There is some similar progress at a regional level. The African Commission of Human Rights has held that states have the obligation to protect individuals particularly, as in the case of *SERAC* v. *Nigeria*, from the acts of foreign corporations such as those in the oil and gas industry.[140] The Commission found that '[c]ontrary to its Charter obligations and despite such internationally established principles, the Nigerian Government has given the green light to private actors, and the oil companies in particular, to devastatingly affect the well-being of the Ogonis'.[141] It held Nigeria liable for the human rights violations to the Ogoni people.[142]

Meanwhile in the Americas, the Organization of American States (OAS), in June 2014, issued a resolution on the 'Promotion and Protection of Human

---

[134] UN Office of the High Commissioner for Human Rights, Open-ended intergovernmental working group on transnational corporations and other business enterprises with respect to human rights.

[135] Green (*supra* n. 125) 453, referring to UN Office of the High Commissioner for Human Rights, Improving Accountability and Access to Remedy for Victims of Business-Related Human Rights Abuse. U.N. Doc. A/HRC/32/19, at 5, (10 May 2016).

[136] UN Office of the High Commissioner for Human Rights, Fourth session of the open-ended intergovernmental working group on transnational corporations and other business enterprises with respect to human rights.

[137] Ibid.

[138] UN Office of the High Commissioner for Human Rights, Legally Binding Instrument to Regulate, in International Human Rights Law, the Activities of Transnational Corporations and Other Business Enterprises, (16 July 2019).

[139] Ibid., Art. 7.

[140] See *SERAC et al.* v. *Nigeria* (African Commission on Human and Peoples' Rights, Oct. 27, 2001), paras. 46, 58.

[141] Ibid., para. 58.

[142] Ibid., paras. 46, 58.

Rights in Business', urging the member states and the Inter-American Commission on Human Rights to implement the UN Guiding Principles.[143] Later, in 2016, the OAS passed a resolution instructing the IAHCR to conduct a study analysing the conventions and jurisprudence of business and human rights.[144] In response, the Inter-American Commission on Human Rights (IACHR) is preparing a report entitled 'Business and Human Rights: Inter-American Standards'.[145] The IAHCR held more than forty thematic hearings on the threat of corporate activities on human rights.[146] It has further granted precautionary measures in cases related to the impact of corporations on human rights violations.[147] Furthermore, the OAS's Committee on Juridical and Political Affairs of the Permanent Council hosted its first special meetings on business and human rights.[148] Former IACHR Commissioner Professor Jesús Orozco-Henríquez wrote that it is 'highly likely that the Inter-American System will be ever more open and disposed to address claims exposing criminal responsibility of corporate executives, or liability of corporations themselves'.[149]

14.4.4   Emerging Consensus on Criminal Liability of Corporations

Parallel to this process, in 2014, the African Union issued a protocol that, once it enters into force, would expand the jurisdiction of the African Court of Justice and Human Rights over legal persons other than states.[150] Legal persons could be liable for genocide, crimes against humanity, war crimes, aggression and other crimes such as 'mercenarism, corruption,

---

[143] Organization of American States (OAS), General Assembly Res. AG/RES. 2840 (XLIV-O/14), OAS Doc. AG/doc.5452/14 rev. 1 (June 4, 2014) (entitled 'Promotion and Protection of Human Rights in Business').

[144] OAS, Questionnaire – Thematic Report: Business and Human Rights Inter-American Standards.

[145] 'Questionnaire – Thematic Report: Business and Human Rights Inter-American Standards', IACHR and OAS.

[146] OAS, IACHR, Sessions by Topic. Economic, Social, and Cultural Rights.

[147] A. M. Mondrágon, 'Corporate Impunity for Human Rights Violations in the Americas: The Inter-American System of Human Rights as an Opportunity for Victims to Achieve Justice' (2016) 57 *Harvard International Law Journal Online* 53.

[148] OAS, Special Events of 2015 (on Sesión especial sobre promoción y protección de los derechos humanos en el ámbito empresarial); OAS, Special Events of 2018 (on 'Promotion and Protection of Human Rights in Business').

[149] J. Orozco-Henríquez, 'Corporate Accountability and the Inter-American Human Rights System' (2016) 57 *Harvard International Law Journal Online* 48, at p. 50.

[150] Protocol on Amendments to the Protocol on the Statute of the African Court of Justice and Human Rights, 27 June 2014, Art. 22 adding Art. 46C.

money laundering, trafficking in persons, trafficking in drugs, trafficking in hazardous wastes, and illicit exploitation of natural resources'.[151] Interestingly, the jurisdiction of the African Court would not be limited to crimes committed in the territory or by nationals of the states of the African Union that ratify this protocol; it would also encompass crimes victimising nationals of such states and also extraterritorial acts committed by non-nationals if such crimes 'threaten a vital interest' of any state of the African Union that ratifies the protocol.

Article 46C of the Protocol provides that 'the Court shall have jurisdiction over legal persons'.[152] The proposal remarkably deals with the question of how to prove *mens rea* of a juridical person, whose knowledge would come from the information available to its staff.[153] Moreover, the fact that the African Union might at some point have corporate accountability could help tackle, in part, the complementarity concerns that some delegations had at the Rome Conference over twenty years ago.

As part of this background, in October 2014, an international criminal tribunal found jurisdiction over legal persons. In the *Case against New TV S.A.L. Karma Mohamed Tahsin al Khayat*, the Special Tribunal for Lebanon (STL) held, in the context of contempt proceedings, that the word 'person' in its statute included both natural and legal persons, and that there was an emerging international consensus on the role of corporations under international law.[154] It based these conclusions on various international instruments holding that transnational corporations have duties to respect human rights and state practice providing for liability of corporations at a domestic level.[155] The STL noted that 'in a majority of the legal systems in the world corporations are not immune from accountability merely because they are a legal –and not a natural– person'.[156]

---

[151] D. Cassel and A. Ramasastry, White Paper: Options for a Treaty on Business and Human Rights, Legal Studies Research Paper No. 2015-38, 6 *Notre Dame Journal of International and Comparative Law* 37.

[152] Protocol on Amendments to the Protocol on the Statute of the African Court of Justice and Human Rights (*supra* n. 150).

[153] Ibid.

[154] Special Tribunal for Lebanon, Appeals Panel, STL-14-05/PT/AP/AR126.1, *Case against New TV S.A.L. Karma Mohamed Tahsin al Khayat*, Decision on Interlocutory Appeal Concerning Personal Jurisdiction in Contempt Proceedings (2 Oct. 2014), paras. 36–67.

[155] See *Case against New TV S.A.L. Karma Mohamed Tahsin al Khayat*, Decision on Interlocutory Appeal Concerning Personal Jurisdiction in Contempt Proceedings, 2 October 2014, STL-14-05/PT/AP/AR126.1, paras. 33–74.

[156] Ibid., para. 58.

An idea not sufficiently discussed at the Rome Conference, corporate criminal liability was not included in the Rome Statute.[157] However, after more than twenty years, Ambassador David Scheffer, who represented the United States at the Rome Conference, has proposed to amend Article 25 of the Rome Statute as follows:

> Amend Article 25(1) to read: 'The Court shall have jurisdiction over natural *and juridical* persons pursuant to this Statute.'[158]
>
> Amend the second sentence of Article 1 to read: 'It shall be a permanent institution and shall have the power to exercise its jurisdiction over natural *and juridical persons* for the most serious crimes of international concern, as referred to in this Statute, and shall be complementary to national criminal jurisdictions. Any use of "person" or "persons" or the "accused" in this Statute shall mean a natural *or juridical person* unless the text connotes an exclusive usage.'[159]

Today, the international community may be prepared to address this proposal. The concerns over lack of domestic legislation on corporate accountability necessary to fulfil the complementary obligations to investigate and prosecute domestically may have been attenuated. Different jurisdictions currently provide for criminal liability of corporations under domestic law.[160] Considering this change in circumstances, the

---

[157] Saland (*supra* n. 118), p. 199.

[158] D. Scheffer, 'Corporate Liability Under the Rome Statute' (2016) 57 *Harvard International Law Journal Online* 38.

[159] Ibid. 38–9.

[160] See, e.g., Law on the Responsibility of Associations (*Verbandsverantwortlichkeitsgesetz*) of 2005 (Austria); Belgian Criminal Code, Article 5 (Belgium); Law 20.393 (2009) (Chile); Chinese Criminal Code, Article 30 (China); Act No. 151/03 on the Responsibility of Legal Persons for Criminal Offences (Croatia); Criminal Code of Cyprus, Section 4 (Cyprus); Criminal Procedure Law, Sections 46(1)(b), 72, 95 (Cyprus); Act No. 418/2011 Coll., on Corporate Criminal Liability, §§ 2–3 (Czech Republic); French Criminal Code, Article 121-2 (France); Guatemalan Criminal Code, Article 38 (Guatemala); Hungarian Criminal Code, Section 70(1)(8), (3) (Hungary); Act CIV of 2001 on Criminal Measures Applicable to Legal Persons (Hungary); General Criminal Code of Iceland, Article 19(a–c) (Iceland); Law No. 23 of 1997 (Law Concerning Environmental Management), Articles I(24) and 41–8 (Indonesia); Law 31 of 1999 (Eradication of the Criminal Act of Corruption), Article I(3) (Indonesia); Act Preventing Escape of Capital to Foreign Countries (1932) (Japan); Securities and Exchange Act of 2002, Article 207 (Japan); Corporation Tax Act of 2013, Article 163(1) (Japan); Unfair Competition Prevention Act 2005, Article 22(I) (Japan); Lebanese Criminal Code, Article 210 (Lebanon); Lithuanian Criminal Code, Article 20 (Lithuania); Moroccan Criminal Code, Article 127 (Morocco); Dutch Criminal Code, Article 51 (Netherlands); Norwegian Civil Penal Code, Chapter 3(a), Article 48(a–b) (Norway); Portuguese Criminal Code, Article 11(2) (Portugal); Act on Preventing Bribery of Foreign Public Officials in International Business Transactions of 1998,

possibility of corporate liability under the Rome Statute could be revisited.

Inspired by theories of change, Harvard law students have started a process to amend the Rome Statute on topics including accountability of corporate actors, environmental crimes, human trafficking and a special trial chamber with a hybrid composition of judges (the 'Harvard Process').[161] With a view to forming a coalition among state representatives, academics, advocates and communities from civil society, the next stage of the Harvard Process is to hold meetings and public symposia to spread and exchange ideas in writing and also through oral presentations. With this in mind, the following section will show how such momentum emerged to the extent that a new generation of law school advocates are leading this promising process.

14.5   New Approaches Before the ICC

Even if the ICC does not yet have personal jurisdiction over legal persons, individuals who commit atrocities in the interest of profit should be prosecuted. The OTP has previously stated that 'those who direct mining operations, sell diamonds or gold extracted in these conditions, launder the dirty money or provide weapons could also be authors of the crimes'.[162] More recently, in its Policy Paper on Case Selection and Prioritisation, the OTP stated that it would prioritise the investigation and selection of cases whose manner of commission and impact may very likely include crimes where corporate actors participate by putting profit over vulnerable communities, grabbing their land and/or destroying the environment.[163] The policy, however, does not expressly provide any indication that the OTP will focus on the accountability of corporate actors.

The trials against the industrialists under Control Council Law No. 10 showed that corporate agents are not immune from justice when they facilitate atrocities. In the *Flick* case, it was determined that '[o]ne who

---

Article 4 (Republic of Korea); Romanian Criminal Code, Article 45(1) (Romania); Senegalese Penal Code (Senegal), Article 163 bis; Spanish Criminal Code, Article 31 (Spain); Swiss Criminal Code, Article 102 (Switzerland); Syrian Criminal Code (Syria), Article 209(2); United Arab Emirates Penal Code, Article 65 (United Arab Emirates).

[161] See Harvard Law School, Advocates for Human Rights.

[162] See ASP, Report of the Prosecutor of the ICC, 2003, p. 4.

[163] See ICC OTP, Policy Paper on Case Selection and Prioritization, 2016, paras. 40–1.

knowingly by his influence and money contributes to the support [of the extermination of Jews] must, under settled legal principles, be deemed to be, if not a principal, certainly an accessory to such crimes'.[164] In *Zyklon B*, the influential managers who knew about the deliveries of poison gas to Auschwitz were convicted, and only those who had no position of influence were not.[165]

*

In the Chiquita case, the contributions of the executives could be prosecuted under Articles 25(3)(c) or (d) of the Rome Statute. While not the most direct modes of participation, accessories such as the Chiquita executives may have enjoyed more power and responsibility over the crimes committed in the banana-growing regions of Urabá and Magdalena than the paramilitaries that directly perpetrated or commanded them. What makes the accessory role of Chiquita more culpable is the fact that they put profit over people, comfortably sitting outside of the battlefield or the targeted civilians. They had influence and knew what was going on, they were watching as spectators how the paramilitaries increased the homicides, forced displacement and persecution in the region, as well as how the dollars mounted up in Chiquita's accounting balance.

As for complementarity, Colombia is unable to bring the Chiquita executives to justice. In the case of *Prosecutor v. Saif al-Islam Gaddafi et al*, the ICC's Pre-Trial Chamber held that Libya's national judicial system was unavailable to prosecute Gaddafi on the ground, inter alia, that the authorities were unable to obtain him as well as testimony regarding a case against him.[166] In 2008, the Colombian Attorney General expressed his inability to extradite the Chiquita executives: 'Yes, there are some directors of Chiquita Brands, but we cannot request the directors of that multinational in extradition, but we need information that is contained in that agreement that [Chiquita] entered with the North American Court, which is protected by confidentiality.'[167] Furthermore, in July 2018, the Colombian Constitutional Court issued

[164] *United States of America v. Friedrich Flick, et al.*, 22 December 1947, p. 1217.
[165] *Case No. 9, the Zyklon B, Case trial of Bruno Tesch and two others*, British Military Court, 8 March 1946, p. 102.
[166] *Prosecutor v. Saifal-Islam Gaddafi & Abdullah al-Senussi*, 'Public redacted-Decision on the admissibility of the case against Saif Al-Islam Gaddafi', 31 May 2013, paras. 206–11, 215.
[167] See *Acuerdo de Confidencialidad impide extradicion de directivos de Chiquita Brands*, El Espectador, 22 April 2008.

its decision observing that corporate executives would not fall within the country's mechanism for transitional justice, the Special Jurisdiction for Peace.[168]

Colombia is thus admittedly unable to secure extradition and prosecute the Chiquita executives. The current investigation in Colombia mainly focuses only on Colombian nationals who did not hold the highest ranks in the corporation or direct the accounting strategies to hide the payments. In the circumstances, there seems to be material for a case on the criminal liability of the executives of Chiquita who participated in the payments to AUC. The OTP could rely on the information already unearthed by the community of the banana-growing regions and its advocates in the US litigation, in order to bring a case.

**

In analysing the possibility to seek accountability of corporate executives at the ICC, following the examples of the trials against the World War II industrialists, Brown University student organiser Samantha Chomsky asks: 'How can international prosecution collaborate with and strengthen local resistance movements?'[169]

Investigators and prosecutors from the OTP can rely on the networks and information that the corporate accountability movement has achieved through strategic litigation. In the words of Professor Duffy: 'An awareness of how litigation emerges from broader human rights agendas and movements, and how it might feed into them should be an aspect of strategic litigation planning from the outset.'[170]

In seeking accountability of executives within corporations, the investigators and prosecutors from the OTP can, through strategic litigation, rely on the networks and information that the corporate accountability movement has achieved. These networks include not only civil society but also those making the difference at the state and international level, in

---

[168] See also *Las razones de la Corte Constitucional para sacar los terceros de la JEP*, El Espectador, 13 July 2018.

[169] She added: '[I]f international prosecution for a particular crime can ever be more than just an aberration in an otherwise disgustingly successful track record of corporate abuse in a particular place, it will rely on strong connections to the people of that place who can continue to hold corporations accountable after the case is closed. Otherwise, I guess we are just relying on deterring corporations only because they are afraid the ICC will prosecute again, and it is pretty clear that corporations are not easily deterred.' Samantha Chomsky, 22 October 2017 (correspondence on file with the author.)

[170] Duffy (*supra* n. 3), pp. 242–3.

state delegations and other international organisations, through inter-institutional communication between the OTP and regional courts and the UN treaty bodies, fact-finding missions and expert panels, for example. In selecting cases for litigation, the possibility to interact, share information and transfer evidence encompasses domestic courts, as the Chiquita case study demonstrates. This is also the case of entities such as the panels of experts that have publicly reported before the Security Council, 'emphasizing the role played by the private sector in fueling ... resource-related armed conflicts' in state parties, including situation countries under examination or investigation, that have been subject to the Council's sanctions regime as per the public reports of such panels.[171]

In the particular case of the accountability of corporate actors, such proposed synergies between the ICC's OTP and civil society would not only contribute in the sharing of information, as provided for in Article 15(2) of the Rome Statute; they are also in keeping with the OTP's mandate, specifically, its Strategic Goal 'to further strengthen the ability of the Office and its partners to close the impunity gap', through different avenues including 'coordinated investigative efforts' and 'the further development of a global network among investigative and prosecutorial bodies for sharing information and experience relating to genocide, crimes against humanity, war crimes, and related criminal conduct'.[172]

In practice, the OTP could bring about such avenues by establishing a policy on a process of systematisation, akin to a system to lodge applications leading to recommendations on complementarity to the state parties, in order to effectively contribute to the OTP's mandate. Making, at the end of the process, a written recommendation to the concerned state(s), the prosecutor would have a policy through which to apply the independence for which civil society resorts to and trusts them.

---

[171] S. C. Wisner, 'Criminalizing Corporate Actors for Exploitation of Natural Resources in Armed Conflict: UN Natural Resources Sanctions Committees and the International Criminal Court' (2018) 16(5) *Journal of International Criminal Justice* 963–83, fn. 1, referring to UN Security Council, Report of the Panel of Experts on Violations of Security Council Sanctions against UNITA, 2000, UN Doc. S/2000/203, paras. 78–9; UN Security Council, Report of the Panel of Experts Appointed Pursuant to Security Council Resolution 1306, UN Doc. S/2000/1195, 2000, para. 19.

[172] ICC OTP, *Strategic Plan 2019–2021*, 17 July 2019, paras. 48, 52. *See also* ICC OTP, *Strategic Plan 2016–2018*, 16 November 2015, para. 104.

14.6   Conclusion

"'We're going to fight this until hell freezes over. And then we'll fight it out in the ice," a company spokesman once said.'[173] One may wonder when that will happen – When will corporations stop finding ways to escape accountability for human rights violations and atrocity crimes to which their executives contributed?

A corporation can live through generations. The only way to ensure that justice will ever be done is by passing the baton from one generation of advocates and communities to the next one. And that is where the importance of the corporate accountability movement lies. It is not every day that one can change the world. But, some days, '[s]ome cases spawn new ways of looking at the law'.[174] Such cases may transform society. In the best of cases, they create movements, such as the one seeking accountability of corporate actors, by converting victims into resilient survivors and attorneys into courageous advocates who are able to hear: what *actually* happened. Together, they share indignation, a mutual feeling against systemic injustice that moves them to unearth evidence, with a view to strategically preparing to face their perpetrators, look them in the eye and publicly accuse them for what they did; yet hoping – perhaps generously – for an explanation: a symbolic act that cures their pain, be it a judgment giving reasons why their perpetrators are liable, criminally and civilly, to pay damages and, in the best of cases, to make an apology. No matter who wins, together they heal.

Potential synergies among the ICC, civil society and other institutions cannot but empower both the international prosecution of atrocity crimes under the ICC's jurisdiction and the domestic advocacy of communities domestically seeking accountability of a wider, incorporated network of perpetrators. This is particularly crucial at a moment where states have foreseen restrictions to their economic support of different international *fora*, including the ICC.[175] The power of a movement, however, can make budgetary issues just a marginal

---

[173] See Rosenberg (*supra* n. 2).

[174] H. H. Koh, 'Filartiga's Way', in W. J. Aceves, *The Anatomy of Torture: A Documentary History of Filartiga v. Pena Irala* (Martinus Nijhoff, 2007), p. xvii.

[175] See, e.g., ASP, Resolution of the Assembly of States Parties on the proposed programme budget for 2019, the Working Capital Fund for 2019, the scale of assessment for the apportionment of expenses of the International Criminal Court, financing appropriations for 2019 and the Contingency Fund, 12 December 2018, ICC-ASP/17 Res.4, para. 11.

concern. Indignation for injustice works for free. Collaborative, strategic litigation could trigger positive spillover effects at no cost to the ICC. The promotion of communications from civil society, through an OTP policy, for instance, would crucially recognise the power of movements and their essential contribution in the pursuit of justice. This is even more important when the perpetrators have as much power and influence as corporate actors.

Alternatives to Prosecutions

Accountability through Civil Litigation for Human Rights Violations by Private Military Contractors

KATHERINE GALLAGHER[*]

If the court rules in our favour it would be a clear message for any company or officials that torture will not be tolerated. I am not doing this for a grudge, I am doing it to get justice. And not just for me, for everyone.

- Salah Al-Ejaili[1]

15.1 Introduction

Over the last two decades, there has been a dramatic increase in the use of private contractors both in traditional armed conflicts and in counter-terrorism operations, most notably those that have arisen out of the

---

[*] The author has been directly involved as counsel for plaintiffs in the following cases discussed in this chapter: *Saleh v. Titan*; *Al-Quraishi v. Nakhla and L-3 Servcs.*; *Al Shimari v. CACI Premier Tech., Inc.*; and *Abtan v. Prince* (*In re: XE Servcs. Alien Tort Statute Litig.*). She has also served as counsel of record for amici in briefs filed before the United States Supreme Court, including in *Kiobel v. Royal Dutch Petroleum Co.* and *Jesner v. Arab Bank, Plc.* The views expressed herein are made in the author's personal capacity and do not necessarily reflect the views of any organization or party with which the author is, or has been, associated. The author would like to thank Nina Jørgensen for the invitation to contribute to this important and timely collection.

[1] Abu Ghraib torture survivor and plaintiff in *Al Shimari v. CACI Premier Tech., Inc.*, quoted in Richard Hall, "'It Never Really Left Me': Abu Ghraib Torture Survivors Finally Get Their Day in Court," *The Independent*, March 20, 2019. Two weeks after this article was published, the defendant CACI filed an interlocutory appeal, which caused the April 23, 2019 trial date to be suspended. The plaintiffs argued that the appeal was improper and untimely, and the Fourth Circuit Court of Appeals dismissed the appeal for lack of jurisdiction. CACI filed a petition for certiorari to the US Supreme Court in November 2019. As this chapter goes to press, with the case now in its twelfth year, that petition is pending, with the Supreme Court having issued an invitation to the Solicitor General to file a brief expressing the view of the United States in late January 2020.

United States' so-called "war on terror" following the September 11 attacks. Corporations have long been involved in armed conflicts – or "the business of war." Unlike wars of the past, where contractors may have provided ancillary services related to food or transport, in Afghanistan and Iraq for-profit corporations were hired to carry out or assist what have widely been understood as governmental or military functions: providing on-the-ground security for senior government officials or at military bases; identifying targets for drone attacks; developing interrogation techniques and protocols; and serving as interrogators in detention facilities, including, as will be discussed later in the chapter, at the notorious Abu Ghraib detention center.[2] Questions and concerns about such outsourcing have not slowed or stopped the practice.[3] Indeed, currently in the United States, contract employees beholden to shareholders or corporate owners – not to the public in whose names and on whose behalf their work is understood to be performed – constitute

---

[2] See, e.g., Comm'n on Wartime Contracting in Iraq and Afghanistan, "At What Risk? Correcting Over-Reliance on Contractors in Contingency Operations" (2011); A. Fielding-Smith, C. Black, A. Ross and J. Ball, "Revealed: Private Firms at Heart of US Drone Warfare," *The Guardian*, July 30, 2015; S. Ackerman, "Blackwater's Afghan HQ is Really Called 'Camp Integrity,'" *Wired*, March 26, 2012. See also Congressional Research Service, "Department of Defense: Contractor and Troop Levels in Afghanistan and Iraq: 2007–2018," R44116, May 10, 2019 ("CRS, DoD Contractor and Troop Levels").

[3] It has been proposed that there are certain functions that should not be delegated or outsourced to private entities. See, e.g., *Report of the Working Group of the Use of Mercenaries as a Means of Violating Human Rights and Impeding the Exercise of the Right of Self-Determination*, UN Doc A/HRC/15/25 (July 2, 2010), Annex, Draft Convention, Arts. 1(b) and 9, and Art. 2(i) defining "Inherently State Functions" as "functions which are consistent with the principle of the State monopoly on the legitimate use of force and that a State cannot outsource or delegate to PMSCs under any circumstances. Among such functions are direct participation in hostilities, waging war and/or combat operations, taking prisoners, law-making, espionage, intelligence, knowledge transfer with military, security and policing application, use of and other activities related to weapons of mass destruction and police powers, especially the powers of arrest or detention including the interrogation of detainees and other functions that a State Party considers to be inherently State functions"; L. Dickinson, "Public Law Values in a Privatized World" (2006) 31 *Yale Journal of International Law* 384.
 Whether functions such as intelligence gathering or the powers of arrest and detention should be prohibited for contractors or merely regulated is beyond the scope of this chapter – see N. D. White, "Regulatory Initiatives at the International Level," in C. Bakker and M. Sossai (eds.), *Multilevel Regulation of Military and Security Contractors: The Interplay between International, European and Domestic Norms* (Hart Publishing, 2012) – but nothing in this discussion on accountability for breaches of international law in the context of performing such functions should be understood as legitimizing the services that PMSCs provide or the commodification and outsourcing of public functions, particularly in the context of war.

a greater portion of the "government" workforce than either federal employees or active-duty military personnel.[4]

In tandem with the rise of outsourcing of governmental functions to corporate entities, there have been numerous accounts of private contractors committing serious human rights violations in both Afghanistan and Iraq. Two of the most infamous examples are the 2007 shooting of Iraqi civilians by Blackwater employees in Nisoor Square that left fourteen dead and scores injured, and the torture and cruel treatment of Iraqi detainees at Abu Ghraib prison outside Baghdad. This chapter will examine the prospects for accountability of "war profiteers" outside the criminal sphere by assessing civil litigation brought by Iraqi citizens in the United States against private military and security contractors involved in these incidents under the Alien Tort Statute (ATS).[5] As the ongoing case *Al Shimari* v. *CACI Premier Technology* illustrates, there are ever-increasing challenges for holding for-profit corporations working under contract with a government in the context of an armed conflict liable in a federal court in the United States. And, as will be shown, while corporations increasingly operate globally, they consistently resist efforts

---

[4] See, e.g., P. C. Light, "The True Size of Government: Tracking Washington's Blended Workforce, 1984–2015," October 2017, p. 3. For much of this decade, when the United States was to be disengaging from Iraq and Afghanistan, contractors outnumbered military in both those locations. See CRS, DoD Contractor and Troop Levels (*supra* n. 2).

The dramatic increase in outsourcing of governmental functions in the United States is not limited to the sphere of war. Schools, prisons and, notably, immigration detention centers have increasingly been privatized. This trend has faced criticism as well as warnings of corporate capture of the political and policy agenda. See, e.g., V. Strauss, "What and Who Are Fueling the Movement to Privatize Public Education – and Why You Should Care," *Washington Post*, May 30, 2018; L. Luan, "Profiting from Enforcement: The Role of Private Prisons in U.S. Immigration Detention," Migration Policy Institute, May 2, 2018; I. Arnsdorf and J. Greenberg, "The VA's Private Care Program Gave Companies Billions and Vets Longer Waits," ProPublica/PolitiFact, December 18, 2018; E. Warren, "Ending Private Prisons and Exploitation for Profit," *Medium*, June 21, 2019. See also G. Kates, "John Kelly Joins Board of Company Operating Largest Shelter for Unaccompanied Migrant Children," *CBS News*, May 3, 2019.

[5] 28 U.S.C. § 1350. The Alien Tort Statute is also known as the Alien Tort Claims Act (or "ATCA"). Since the United States Supreme Court used "Alien Tort Statute" for 28 U.S. C. § 1350 in *Sosa* v. *Alvarez-Machain*, 542 U.S. 692 (2004), this has been the commonly used title for the statute.

The term "alien" is defined in US law as "any person not a citizen or national of the United States," 8 U.S.C. § 1101(a)(3). Particularly in light of the function that the ATS has played in seeking to advance respect for and compliance with international human rights standards and the derogatory and dehumanizing nature of the term "alien" for non-US citizens, the author will refrain from using the title of "Alien Tort Statute" or the term "alien," unless quoting text.

to be held liable in the foreign jurisdictions where they operate and reap profits, while at the same time challenging efforts to be held to account in their "home" courts for harms that occurred extraterritorially.

This chapter will address the legal framework used by the plaintiffs to seek accountability and the evolving jurisprudence under the ATS; the current status of civil corporate liability for international law violations in US courts; and the particular defenses raised by the contractors to avoid liability, including the government contractor defense, battlefield pre-emption, derivative immunity and the political question doctrine. Notably, the doctrines or principles relied upon by courts to block adjudication are more often grounded in prudential concerns related to domestic enforcement of international law – arguably an expression of a conservative strand of "judicial activism" rather than a normative bar to corporate liability. As part of this assessment, the chapter will bring to the surface some of the issues relevant to negotiations of an international treaty applicable to transnational business entities, including the thresh-old question of corporate liability for international law violations and extraterritorial jurisdiction, and comment on certain "soft law" mechan-isms that have emerged in response to the rising use of private military and security contractors.

It is worth explaining the focus on civil litigation, especially for human rights violations that also qualify as crimes. Abu Ghraib is marked as one of the darkest chapters in modern American history. Multiple military investigations named employees from two contractors working in the prison, Titan Corporation and CACI International Inc., as having parti-cipated in "numerous incidents of sadistic, blatant and wanton criminal abuses" against detainees.[6] The US federal criminal code provides for the prosecution of extraterritorial torture or war crimes committed by US nationals[7] – yet neither company nor any of their employees were prosecuted under those provisions or any other.[8] When the state fails

---

[6] Maj. General Antonio M. Taguba. Article 15-6 Investigation of the 800th Military Police Brigade (May 2004) ("Taguba Report"), p. 16. See LTG Anthony R. Jones AR 15-6 Investigation of the Abu Ghraib Prison and 205th Military Intelligence Brigade; and MG George R. Fay, AR 15-6 Investigation of the Abu Ghraib Detention Facility and 205th Military Intelligence Brigade (August 2004).

[7] See 18 U.S.C. § 2441 (War Crimes); 18 U.S.C. § 2340A (Torture). The concept of corporate criminal liability is well-established in US law. *New York Cent. & Hudson River R.R. Co. v. United States*, 212 U.S. 481 (1909).

[8] A number of low-level soldiers were punished for their involvement in the abuse at Abu Ghraib; only three individuals received prison sentences of more than three years, and none served more than six and a half years. Several officers were demoted or received other

to take action to hold corporations or their employees liable, civil litigation provides victims – survivors – an opportunity to try to achieve some measure of justice and accountability.[9] As this chapter makes clear, the burden that victims/survivors take on is a very heavy one, not only because of the jurisdictional and prudential hurdles or the power imbalances but also as they are called upon again and again to relive some of the most painful moments to advance a case in a foreign court over years of increasingly unpredictable litigation. This burden may indeed be one better borne by the state. But in the absence of action by the state – in the face of the *failure* of the state to fulfill its obligations to prosecute or otherwise redress serious violations of international law – at the very least, states have a duty to provide persons subjected to violations by actors *they* paid and empowered an enforceable and achievable right to a remedy.

15.2   Civil Litigation under the Alien Tort Statute

For the last four decades, the majority of human rights litigation in the United States has been brought under a 230-year-old statute, 28 U.S. C. § 1350, commonly known as the ATS.[10] The ATS allows non-US citizens to bring tort claims for violations of the "law of nations" in US federal courts. The landmark case *Filártiga* v. *Peña-Irala*, involving the torture and murder of a Paraguayan teenager by a Paraguayan police official in Paraguay, established the ATS as a vehicle for vindicating human rights abuses.[11] In assessing the claims of torture, the court in *Filártiga* determined that it "must interpret international law not as it was in 1789 [at the time of the enactment of the ATS], but as it has evolved and exists among the nations of the world today."[12] The court followed

administrative punishments. See S. Brenner, "'I Am a Bit Sickened': Examining Archetypes of Congressional War Crimes Oversight after My Lai and Abu Ghraib" (2010) 205 *Military Law Review* 1, 68–9; "Central Figure of Abu Ghraib Detainee Abuse Freed," *AP*, August 6, 2011.

9   See, e.g., Br. for *Amici Curiae* Abukar Hassan Ahmed et al. in support of Petitioners, *Kiobel* v. *Royal Dutch Petroleum Co.*, 2012 WL 2165343, No. 10–1491 (U.S.), June 13, 2012.

10 The ATS permits non-US citizens to sue for damages in US federal district courts "for a tort only, committed in violation of the law of nations or a treaty of the United States." Due to the determination that many treaties are not self-executing, the treaty prong of the statute has not developed with the same level of success – from the plaintiffs' standpoint – as the "violation of the laws of nations" prong.

11 *Filártiga* v. *Peña-Irala*, 630 F.2d 876 (2d Cir. 1980). See W. J. Aceves, *The Anatomy of Torture: A Documentary History of Filártiga v. Peña-Irala* (Martinus Nijhoff, 2007).

12 *Filartiga*, 630 F.2d at 881.

US precedent to determine what constituted a violation of the "law of nations," essentially identifying the same sources as those dictated by Article 38 of the Statute of the International Court of Justice.[13] In 2004, the US Supreme Court affirmed in *Sosa v. Alvarez-Machain* that customary international law should serve as the guide for determining which norms are actionable under the ATS[14] – the same source of law that informs the decisions of the international criminal tribunals.[15] The Supreme Court held that such norms include violations of human rights or international criminal law that are specific, universal and obligatory, meaning that that the norms must have widespread acceptance and a clear definition.[16]

The door to applying the ATS to corporate actors was opened through the ATS action *Kadić v. Karadžić*.[17] This case was brought against the self-proclaimed president of the Republika Srpska, Radovan Karadžić, by Bosnian Muslim and Croatian victims of rape, torture and other acts alleged to constitute genocide, crimes against humanity and war crimes. As Karadžić was not internationally recognized as a head of state, the

---

[13] *The Paquete Habana*, 175 U.S. 677, 700 (1900), cited in *Filártiga*, 630 F.3d at 880–1, sets out the "law of nations" analysis: "[W]here there is no treaty, and no controlling executive or legislative act or judicial decision, resort must be had to the customs and usages of civilized nations; and, as evidence of these, to the works of jurists and commentators, who [,] by years of labor, research and experience, have made themselves peculiarly well acquainted with the subjects of which they treat."

[14] It is recalled that international law is part of US federal common law. See *The Paquete Habana*, 175 U.S. at 700 ("International law is part of our law, and must be ascertained and administered by the courts of justice of appropriate jurisdiction as often as questions of right depending upon it are duly presented for their determination."). See US Constitution, Art. III, Section 2; Art. VI, Clause 2.

[15] See Report of the Secretary-General Pursuant to Paragraph 2 of Security Council Resolution 808 (1993), UN Doc S/25704, May 3, 1993, para. 34. See also Rome Statute of the International Criminal Court, A/CONF.183/9, Art. 21(1), July 17, 1998, as amended.

[16] *Sosa v. Alvarez-Machin*, 542 U.S. 692 (2004). The Supreme Court found that the ATS was intended to be a jurisdictional statute for a "very limited set" of international law violations. It instructed lower courts to "require any claim based on the present-day law of nations to rest on a norm of international character accepted by the civilized world and defined with a specificity comparable to the features of the 18th-century paradigms we have recognized." *Sosa*, 542 U.S. at 720, 725 and 732.

For discussion on the relationship between international criminal law and ATS civil litigation, see, e.g., K. Gallagher, "Civil Litigation and Transnational Business" (2010) 8 *Journal of International Criminal Justice* 745, 746 and n. 4 (collecting sources); J. G. Stewart, "The Turn to Corporate Criminal Liability for International Crimes: Transcending the Alien Tort Statute" (2014) 47 *New York University Journal of International Law & Politics* 121.

[17] 70 F.3d 232 (2d Cir. 1995).

court assessed whether non-state actors could be held liable for international law violations. The court found that "certain forms of conduct violate the law of nations whether undertaken by those acting under the auspices of a state or only as private individuals."[18] Examining both the text and the purpose of the Genocide Convention and the Geneva Conventions, and reviewing post-World War II precedents,[19] the court found that genocide and war crimes could be committed by non-state actors, and therefore non-state actors could be held liable under the ATS for their participation in at least these offenses.

In the mid-1990s, human rights advocates drew upon the *Filártiga* and *Kadić* precedents and filed the first cases against corporations for their involvement in serious international law violations. Two of these cases become landmarks for corporate accountability, namely *Doe* v. *Unocal*[20] and *Wiwa* v. *Royal Dutch Petroleum/Shell*.[21] In *Unocal*, fifteen Burmese plaintiffs alleged that the US-based corporate defendants jointly participated with Burmese government officials in forced labor, rape, torture and murder in connection with a gas pipeline project. The plaintiffs alleged that Unocal paid the Burmese military to provide security for the Yadana Pipeline, and knew of the serious risk that human rights violations would be committed and that such violations were in fact occurring. The court found that the plaintiffs sufficiently pled that Unocal aided and abetted the commission of forced labor, murder and rape by state actors.[22] The *Wiwa* case was brought by Nigerians who were injured or had family members killed, including the environmental activist Ken Saro-Wiwa, in relation to Shell's activities in the Niger Delta. The plaintiffs brought claims for crimes against humanity, summary execution, torture and cruel, inhuman or degrading treatment. The court found that private actors, such as Shell, could be held liable for

---

[18] *Kadić*, 70 F.3d at 239.

[19] Interestingly, the international sources and precedents cited did not include the Statute of the International Criminal Tribunal for the former Yugoslavia (ICTY) or its case law, as that tribunal had only recently commenced operations; the first indictment at the ICTY of Radovan Karadžić post-dated the commencement of the *Kadić* proceedings.

[20] See *Doe* v. *Unocal Co.*, 963 F. Supp. 880 (C.D. Cal. 1997) (finding that jurisdiction existed over corporation for claims brought under the ATS asserting theories of joint action with a state actor and, for the claim of forced labor, as a direct perpetrator); *Doe I* v. *Unocal Co.*, 395 F.3d 932 (9th Cir. 2002) *vacated by, rehearing en banc granted by*, 395 F.3d 978 (9th Cir. 2003) (following a review of international criminal law sources, adopted a "knowingly providing practical assistance that has a substantial effect" standard for aiding and abetting).

[21] *Wiwa* v. *Royal Dutch Petroleum Co.*, 226 F.3d 88 (2d Cir. 2000).

[22] *Unocal*, 395 F.3d at 946.

these violations.[23] Both *Unocal* and *Wiwa* eventually settled, for an undisclosed amount in the case of Unocal and for 15.5 million USD in the case of Royal Dutch Petroleum/Shell.

In the wake of *Unocal* and *Wiwa*, victims of egregious human rights violations filed ATS cases against transnational corporations operating in a range of sectors, such as extractive industries,[24] and for claims ranging from forced or child labor[25] to nonconsensual medical experimentation[26] to war crimes.[27] The growing focus of ATS litigation on corporate actors brought with it a far more robust defense against such claims, often by counsel from leading global law firms, and, particularly during the administration of George W. Bush, with corporate defendants backed by the Executive Branch of the US government.[28] These challenges generally did not focus on the specific question of whether corporations could be held liable for violations of international law, and, for the next decade, the answer was either explicitly found or presumed to be "yes." In 2010, however, the Court of Appeals for the Second Circuit issued an unprecedented decision in *Kiobel* v. *Royal Dutch Petroleum*, in which the majority found that the ATS could not provide jurisdiction over claims brought against

---

[23] *Wiwa* v. *Royal Dutch Petroleum Co.*, No 96-civ-8386, 2002 WL 319887 (S.D.N.Y. February 28, 2002) at 12–14.

[24] See, e.g., *Mujica* v. *Occidental Petroleum Corp.*, 381 F. Supp. 2d 1164 (C.D. Cal. 2005); *Presbyterian Church of Sudan* v. *Talisman Energy, Inc.*, 582 F.3d 244 (2d Cir. 2009).

[25] See *Doe I* v. *Nestle USA, Inc.*, 766 F.3d 1013 (9th Cir. 2014); *Adhikari* v. *Daoud & Partners*, 697 F. Supp. 2d 674 (S.D. Tex. 2009); *Licea* v. *Curaçao Drydock Co.*, 584 F. Supp. 2d 1355 (S.D. Fla. 2008).

[26] See *Abdullahi* v. *Pfizer, Inc.*, 562 F.3d 163 (2d. Cir. 2009); *Estate of Alvarez* v. *Johns Hopkins Univ.*, 275 F. Supp. 3d 670 (D. Md. 2017).

[27] See, e.g., *Corrie* v. *Caterpillar*, 503 F.3d 974 (9th Cir. 2007).

[28] See B. Stephens, "Corporate Liability for Grave Breaches of International Law: Judicial Deference and the Unreasonable Views of the Bush Administration" (2008) 33 *Brooklyn Journal of International Law* 773.

A number of former Bush administration officials who represented the US Department of State or the US Department of Justice in briefs filed in ATS corporate cases currently work for large law firms, where they regularly advance arguments against corporate liability similar to those they made in briefs filed by the United States during that administration. For example, former State Department Legal Advisor John Bellinger regularly serves as counsel for corporations and foreign government officials defending against ATS claims or amici in support of defendants. See, e.g., Br. of *Amicus Curiae* Chamber of Commerce, *Estate of Alvarez* v. *Johns Hopkins Univ.* No. 19–1530 (4th Cir.) August 5, 2019; see also Petition for a Writ of Certiorari, *Mutond* v. *Lewis*, No. 19–185 (U.S.) August 9, 2019 (seeking Supreme Court review of the application of functional/ conduct-based immunity to foreign officials for claims brought under the Torture Victim Protection Act ("TVPA")).

corporations.[29] The decision was startling and unexpected, first, because it was the judges – not the parties – who raised the question of corporate liability in the context of an interlocutory appeal on another issue, and second, more fundamentally, because the Second Circuit itself had been a central locus of ATS litigation against corporations since *Wiwa*.[30] Writing for the majority, Judge José Cabranes concluded that international criminal law did not recognize corporate liability since none of the post-World War II international criminal tribunals or courts have included corporations within their jurisdiction, and therefore claims against corporations fall outside the jurisdiction provided by the ATS.[31] Soon after *Kiobel*, other courts of appeal affirmed that corporations could indeed be held liable for violations of international law under the ATS.[32]

The Supreme Court agreed to review the decision. Unusually, while the question before the Court in *Kiobel* was whether claims could be brought against corporations under the ATS, after hearing argument on the corporate liability issue, the Court issued a *sua sponte* order for supplemental briefing on the question of whether and under what circumstances claims could be brought for violations occurring within the territory of a foreign state.[33] The question on extraterritoriality, at first blush, appeared to call into question the entire body of ATS jurisprudence – and the developments at the international level that have

---

[29] *Kiobel* v. *Royal Dutch Petroleum Co.*, 621 F.3d 111 (2d Cir. 2010).

[30] E.g., *Wiwa, Talisman, Abdullahi*, as well as *Flores* v. *Southern Peru Copper Corp.*, 414 F.3d 233 (2d Cir. 2003) and *Khulumani* v. *Barclay Nat. Bank, Ltd.*, 504 F.3d 254 (2d Cir. 2007).

[31] *Kiobel*, 621 F.3d at 119–20. Judge Leval wrote a lengthy separate opinion in which he stated that there is simply "no basis" in international law for the majority's conclusion. *Kiobel*, 621 F.3d at 151 (Leval, J., concurring in judgment) (finding that the majority's reasoning is "illogical, misguided, and based on misunderstandings of precedent").

[32] *Flomo* v. *Firestone Natural Rubber Co.*, 643 F.3d 1013 (7th Cir. 2011); *Doe* v. *Exxon*, 654 F.3d 11 (D.C. Cir. 2011). See also *Romero* v. *Drummond Co.*, 552 F.3d 1303, 1315 (11th Cir. 2008).

[33] The Supreme Court ordered that the parties address the question of "whether and under what circumstances courts may recognize a cause of action under the Alien Tort Statute, for violations of the law of nations occurring within the territory of a sovereign other than the United States." *Kiobel* v. *Royal Dutch Petroleum Co.*, 569 U.S. 108, 112–13 (2013).

Both rounds of briefing before the Supreme Court garnered intense interest: more than thirty amicus briefs were filed on behalf of the plaintiffs during each round by legal scholars and historians, former government officials, human rights organizations, current and former United Nations officials, foreign governments, foreign litigators and academics, and former ATS plaintiffs, while numerous corporations, the US Chamber of Commerce and international law scholars filed briefs in support of the defendant.

tracked it.[34] When it rendered its decision on April 17, 2013, the Supreme Court passed over the first question and focused its attention on the extraterritoriality question; that it reached the issue of extra-territoriality has been read as implicit approval of corporate liability.[35] First, examining the plain language of the statute, the Court found that "principles" underlying the "presumption against extraterritoriality" applied to claims brought under the ATS.[36] Reflecting the Court's concern that ATS cases *could* create "international discord" or "diplomatic strife,"[37] it set forth a fact-intensive claim-by-claim test to determine whether the presumption could be displaced, namely whether "the claims touch and concern the territory of the United States . . . with sufficient force."[38]

Four Justices joined the opinion of Chief Justice John Roberts, while three Justices joined Justice Stephen Breyer's opinion, which concurred in the judgment but disagreed with the reasoning.[39] Justice Breyer rejected the application of the presumption against extraterritoriality to the ATS and instead would have been guided by the "principles and practices of foreign relations law." Under such an analysis, Justices Breyer, Ginsburg, Sotomayor and Kagan would find jurisdiction in cases where: (1) the tort occurred on US soil; (2) the defendant is an American national; or (3) "the defendant's conduct substantially and adversely affects an important American national interest, and that includes a distinct interest in preventing the United States from

---

[34] See, e.g., UN Human Rights Council, Human Rights and Transnational Corporations and Other Business Enterprises, U.N. Doc. A/HRC/RES/17/4 (July 6, 2011), Annex, *Guiding Principles on Business and Human Rights: Implementing the United Nations 'Protect*; *Respect and Remedy' Framework*, A/HRC/17/31; Br. for *Amici Curiae* International Human Rights Organizations and International Law Experts in support of Petitioners, *Kiobel* v. *Royal Dutch Petroleum Co.*, 2011 WL 6780140, No. 10–1491 (U.S.) December 21, 2011 (collecting global practice of corporate liability to establish general principle of law).

[35] See *Doe I* v. *Nestle USA, Inc.*, 738 F.3d 1048, 1049 (9th Cir. 2013) citing *Kiobel*, 569 U.S. at 125 (finding that *Kiobel*'s reference to "mere corporate presence" is dicta that suggests that corporations may be liable under the ATS so long as the presumption against extraterritoriality is overcome).

[36] *Kiobel*, 569 U.S. at 116–17. The presumption against extraterritoriality is a canon of statutory interpretation, which courts have found to provide that "when a statute gives no clear indication of an extraterritorial application, it has none." See ibid. at 115 (citations omitted). This presumption "serves to protect against unintended clashes between our laws and those of other nations which could result in international discord." Ibid.

[37] *Kiobel*, 569 U.S. at 116, 124.

[38] Ibid. at 124–5.

[39] *Kiobel*, 569 U.S. at 127 (Breyer, J., concurring in judgment).

becoming a safe harbour (free from civil as well as criminal liability) for a torturer or other common enemy of mankind."[40]

The "touch and concern" test has had varying interpretations and applications in the seven years since the *Kiobel* decision, and assessments of liability for international law violations have continued to vex courts, particularly in the Second Circuit.[41] In 2018, the Supreme Court was again called upon to address the question of corporate liability, in the Second Circuit case *Jesner* v. *Arab Bank*.[42] Once again and despite the question presented in the case being "[w]hether the [ATS] categorically forecloses corporate liability," in a 5–4 ruling, the Court avoided a direct answer and limited its analysis to the propriety of adjudicating liability for *foreign* corporations in US courts. The plurality, concurring and dissenting opinions revealed a Court deeply conflicted on the question of holding corporations liable for international law violations. In an opinion authored by soon-to-be-retired and often swing-vote Justice Anthony Kennedy, the five-Justice majority issued a narrow ruling based on prudential grounds related to the efficacy of enforcing international law in US federal courts, holding that the ATS could not provide a jurisdictional basis for human rights claims against non-US companies.[43] The Court found that litigation involving "foreign corporate defendants create unique problems. And courts are not well suited to make the required policy judgments that are implicated by corporate liability in cases like this one."[44]

Disagreeing "both with the Court's conclusion and [with] its analytic approach," Justice Sonia Sotomayor wrote on behalf of the dissenting Justices that "[n]othing about the corporate form in itself raises foreign-policy concerns that require the Court, as a matter of common-law discretion, to immunize all foreign corporations from liability under the ATS."[45]

---

[40] Ibid.

[41] Compare, for example, *Balintulo* v. *Daimler AG*, 727 F.3d 174 (2d Cir. 2013) (declining to extend ATS jurisdiction to claims involving foreign conduct by South African subsidiaries of American corporations) with *Doe I* v. *Nestle, S.A.*, 906 F.3d 1120, 1125–1126 (9th Cir. 2018) (assessing whether there is any domestic conduct relevant to plaintiffs' claims, even if other conduct occurred abroad). A petition for *certiorari* in the *Nestle* case is now pending before the U.S. Supreme Court, including on the question of liability of U.S. corporations under the ATS.

[42] *Jesner* v. *Arab Bank, Plc*, 584 U.S. ___, 138 S. Ct. 1386 (2018).

[43] The majority in *Jesner* drew upon *Sosa* to conclude that "ATS litigation implicates serious separation-of-powers and foreign relations concerns." *Jesner*, 138 S. Ct. at 1398, citing *Sosa*, 542 U.S. at 727–8. It held that "absent further action from Congress it would be inappropriate for courts to extend ATS liability to foreign corporations." Ibid. at 1403.

[44] Ibid. at 1407. Justice Kennedy also authored a three-Justice plurality, writing on behalf of himself, Chief Justice Roberts and Justice Clarence Thomas.

[45] *Jesner*, 138 S. Ct. at 1419 (Sotomayor, J., dissenting opinion).

Justice Sotomayor also provided a critical assessment of Justice Kennedy's findings on corporate liability (or lack thereof) for international law violations in his plurality opinion. She asserted that the plurality "fundamentally misconceives how international law works" in that it was looking for an international norm of corporate liability; international law sets out "what substantive conduct violates the law of nations" – such as the prohibitions against genocide and torture (the norms) – but generally leaves the mechanism for enforcement to states.[46] The dissent also explains that while international law distinguishes between state actors and non-state actors for determining obligations and breaches in some instances, it does not distinguish between natural persons and corporations.[47]

It is worth pausing to reflect on what the Supreme Court did *not* find in either the *Kiobel* or the *Jesner* case: it did not conclude that international law per se did not apply to or create obligations on corporations. Nor did it find that corporations enjoy immunity from liability for international law violations. The Court instead focused on the narrow question of whether a statutory grant of jurisdiction over violations of the law of nations from 1789 can be read to allow claims to proceed against "artificial entities like corporations" when those entities are *foreign* corporations.[48] The Supreme Court's findings were based largely on doctrines and principles specific to US law and separation of powers, and reflective of the current strain of "originalism" and a disdain for recognizing causes of action that result in monetary judgments.[49]

---

[46]   Ibid. at 1420.

[47]   Ibid. at 1422–3.

[48]   *Jesner*, 138 S. Ct. at 1403.

[49]   In *Jesner*, the majority cited the Supreme Court's "general reluctance to extend judicially created private rights of action" as a guiding principle for its ATS jurisprudence. *Jesner*, 138 S. Ct. at 1402. See also ibid. at 1403 (finding that "the separation-of-powers concerns that counsel against courts creating private rights of action apply with particular force in the context of the ATS").

The decision can also be viewed as just one more in a line of recent pro-business decisions from what can be called a pro-business Court. Indeed, Justice Sotomayor closes the dissent by pointing out the Supreme Court's willingness to bestow *rights* on corporations while shielding them from any legal *responsibility*:

> Immunizing corporations that violate human rights from liability under the ATS undermines the system of accountability for law-of-nations violations that the First Congress endeavored to impose. It allows these entities to take advantage of the significant benefits of the corporate form and enjoy fundamental rights, without having to shoulder attendant fundamental responsibilities.

Jesner, 138 S. Ct. at 1437 (Sotomayor, J., dissenting opinion) (citing *Citizens United v. Federal Election Comm'n*, 558 U.S. 310 (2010); *Burwell* v. *Hobby Lobby Stores, Inc.*, 573 U.S. 682 (2014).

It is submitted, therefore, that because domestic concerns animated their holdings, the effect of *Kiobel* and *Jesner* outside of US courts will necessarily be quite limited – a stark contrast to the considerable impact that litigation brought under the ATS has had on advancing the global human rights accountability movement since *Filártiga*.[50] Accordingly, neither the increased enforcement of international law elsewhere against corporations at the national level[51] nor the efforts underway to further clarify and codify the full scope of corporate liability at the international level including through the development of a binding treaty[52] should be slowed because of recent US Supreme Court jurisprudence.

In the next section, the principles set forth in *Kiobel* and *Jesner* will be examined in detail in the discussion of their application to private military contractors and particularly in the case *Al Shimari* v. *CACI*.

15.3   Civil Litigation against Private Military and Security Contractors

Concomitant with the increase in outsourcing and privatization, the last fifteen years have seen a significant increase in civil litigation against military and security government contractors.[53] While some of these

---

[50] See S. Coliver, J. Green and P. Hoffman, "Holding Human Rights Violators Accountable by Using International Law in U.S. Courts: Advocacy Efforts and Complementary Strategies" (2005) 19 *Emory International Law Review* 169, 175–86.

[51] See, e.g., "France: Opening of a Judicial Investigation Targeting Qosmos for Complicity in Acts of Torture in Syria," FIDH, 11 April 2014; "Submission from Sherpa and ECCHR on an Indictment of Lafarge for Complicity in Crimes Against Humanity," Sherpa/ECCHR Press Release, May 15, 2018; G. Chillier, "Prosecuting Corporate Complicity in Argentina's Dictatorship," Open Democracy, December 19, 2014; S. Taylor, "Court Sets Canada as Jurisdiction for Guatemalan Suit against Tahoe," Reuters, January 26, 2017. See also Z. Booi, "Top Court's Ruling Restores Rights of Landholders Violated by Mining Giants," Business Day, November 13, 2018 (South Africa).

[52] Human Rights Council Res. 26/9, U.N. Doc. A/HRC/RES/26/9, 1 (July 14, 2014) (establishing an open-ended intergovernmental working group on transnational corporations and human rights mandated to "elaborate an international legally binding instrument to regulate, in international human rights law, the activities of transnational corporations and other business enterprises"). The open-ended working group released a revised draft of the legally binding instrument on July 16, 2019. See C. Lopez, "The Revised Draft of a Treaty on Business and Human Rights: A Big Leap Forward," *Opinio Juris*, August 15, 2019.

[53] See, e.g., *Vietnam Ass'n for Victims of Agent Orange* v. *Dow Chemical Co.*, 517 F.3d 104 (2d Cir. 2008) (claims brought by Vietnamese plaintiffs against US manufacturers who provided US military with "Agent Orange" during the Vietnam War); *Jama* v. *Esmor*, 343 F. Supp. 2d 338, 360–61 (D. N.J. 2004) (claims brought against a domestic contractor which ran an immigration detention facility for the Immigration and Naturalization Services). See also *Arias* v. *Dyncorp*, 752 F.3d 1011 (D.C. Cir. 2014).

cases are typical of tort actions arising out of breach of contract or product liability,[54] certain cases arose out of contractors' involvement in activities more closely associated with military or "counter-terrorism" operations post-September 11. For example, *Mohamed v. Jeppessen Dataplan, Inc.* involved claims brought against a wholly-owned Boeing subsidiary for its participation in CIA-operated "extraordinary renditions";[55] that case was dismissed following the government's assertion of the state secrets privilege.[56] More recently, in *Salim v. Mitchell*, ATS claims brought by former detainees held in CIA "blacksites" or their families against two contractor-psychologists who aided and abetted torture by designing, implementing and administering so-called "enhanced interrogation techniques" were permitted to proceed; that case settled on the eve of trial.[57]

15.3.1 Overview of Contractors' Cases in Iraq

15.3.1.1 Blackwater Litigation

One of the more notorious private corporations that contracted with the United States in Iraq was Erik Prince's Blackwater. Survivors and some of the families of those killed in the Nisoor Square shooting in September 2007 filed suit in Washington, DC one month after the mass killing. Over the next year, victims from four more incidents involving Blackwater personnel filed actions against eleven business entities and Erik Prince under the ATS and the cases were consolidated.[58] In a decision that

[54] See. e.g., *In re KBR, Inc., Burn Pit Litig.*, 744 F.3d 326 (4th Cir. 2014); *Carmichael v. Kellogg, Brown & Root Servs., Inc.*, 572 F.3d 1271 (11th Cir. 2009).
  Earlier contractor cases focused on common law tort claims arising out of design or manufacturing defects, with the typical defense to such claims turning on whether the contractor was following government designs or instructions. See, e.g., *Boyle v. United Technologies Corp.*, 487 U.S. 500 (1988); *Koohi v. United States*, 976 F.2d 1328 (9th Cir. 1992).
[55] See Senator Dick Marty (Switzerland), Council of Europe Parliamentary Assembly, "Secret Detentions and Illegal Transfers of Detainees Involving Council of Europe Member States: Second Report," CoE Doc. 11302 rev, June 11, 2007; Committee on International Human Rights of the Association of the Bar of the City of New York and the Center for Human Rights and Global Justice, "Torture by Proxy: International and Domestic Law Applicable to 'Extraordinary Renditions'"(2004).
[56] While the majority acknowledged that the case presents "a painful conflict between human rights and national security," the *en banc* panel upheld dismissal under the judge-made doctrine by a vote of 6–5. *Mohamed v. Jeppessen Dataplan, Inc.*, 614 F.3d 1070, 1093 (9th Cir. 2010) (rehearing en banc).
[57] *Salim v. Mitchell and Jessen*, 268 F. Supp. 3d. 1132 (E.D. Wa. 2017).
[58] *In re: Xe Services Alien Tort Statute Litigation* is the consolidated case against Xe (formerly Blackwater Worldwide) including *Abtan, et al. v. Prince, et al.* (alleging, inter alia, war

predates the Supreme Court's rulings in *Kiobel* and *Jesner*, the district court found that non-state actors can be held liable for war crimes under the ATS.[59] Noting that the Supreme Court in "*Sosa* simply refers to both individuals and entities as 'private actors'" and observing that "all courts to have considered the question have concluded that 'the issue of whether corporations may be held liable under the [ATS is] indistinguishable from the question of whether private individuals may be,'" the court determined that "there is no identifiable principle of civil liability which would distinguish between individual and corporate defendants."[60]

Blackwater also sought to evade liability by filing a motion for the United States to be substituted in its place under the Westfall Act – a statute that allows federal officials to obtain immunity from tort liability when they are carrying out discretionary functions acting within the scope of their employment.[61] Blackwater asked the US government to recognize that the employees of a privately-held corporation hired by the US government to provide security services were, in effect, "employee[s] of the Government ... acting within the scope of [their] ... employment." The United States opposed the motion, based on the history, text and purpose of the statute, making it clear that the for-profit corporation was not entitled to the protections from liability that may exist for government employees.[62] A decision on this motion was never rendered,

crimes for killings and other serious injuries sustained by Iraqi civilians following the shooting in Nisoor Square) and *Albazzaz et al* v. *Prince et al* (alleging, inter alia, war crimes for killing of Iraqi civilians following a shooting in al Watahba Square). The case was transferred from Washington, DC to the Eastern District of Virginia, before Judge T. S. Ellis.

[59] The district court reviewed both international law sources and domestic statutes implementing treaty obligations, including those under the Geneva Conventions, to reach this conclusion. *In re: Xe Services Alien Tort Statute Litig.*, 665 F. Supp. 2d 569 (E.D. Va. 2009).

[60] Ibid. at 588, quoting *Sosa*, 542 U.S. at 732, n. 20. The fact that the district court cited numerous decisions from the Second Circuit for its conclusion makes it all the more notable – and bewildering – that a panel in that Circuit concluded that corporations could not be held liable under the ATS in *Kiobel* in 2010, thereby setting in motion the restrictions on using the ATS to hold corporations accountable that the Supreme Court instituted in *Kiobel* and *Jesner*.

[61] See *Westfall* v. *Erwin*, 484 U.S. 292 (1988), *superseded by* 28 U.S.C. § 2679.

[62] *In re: Xe Services Alien Tort Litig.*, 1:09-cv-615 (E.D. Va.), Docket No. 76, United States of America Consolidated Brief in Opposition to Defendants' Motion to Substitute Party the United States in Place of all Defendants pursuant to the Westfall Act, October 16, 2009. The United States also took the position that neither any of the legal entities nor Blackwater's founder, Erik Prince, could enjoy immunity in this case because "[g]iven the nature of the Plaintiffs' claims, [the] Defendants have not come even close to carrying [the] burden" that "they in fact were acting within the scope of their supposed Federal employment." Ibid. at 5.

as the parties reached a confidential settlement covering all of the cases in January 2010, thereby terminating the litigation.[63]

15.3.1.2 Abu Ghraib Litigation and the Application of *Kiobel* and *Jesner* to Contractors

Multiple cases have been brought in federal courts by former Iraqi detainees against two private military contractors, under contract with various components of the US government, for torture and other serious mistreatment suffered in US-run detention facilities in Iraq, including Abu Ghraib. Through *Saleh* v. *Titan, Al Shimari* v. *CACI Premier Technology, Inc.* and *Al-Quraishi* v. *Nakhla and L-3 Services, Inc.*, more than 330 Iraqi civilians – all of whom were released without charge – brought claims under the ATS of war crimes, torture and cruel and inhuman and degrading treatment, as well as common law claims of assault and battery, sexual assault and negligent hiring and supervision, for the contractors' alleged role in a conspiracy to torture. CACI provided interrogation services, and Titan, which has changed its name twice (to L-3 Services and then to Engility Corporation), provided translation services and, later, also interrogation services. As determined in US military investigations into the abuse of detainees at Abu Ghraib, CACI and Titan employees were involved in the torture and other serious mistreatment of detainees.[64]

US federal regulations require that all private military contractors abide by US laws, including the War Crimes Statute (18 U.S.C. § 2441) and the Torture Statute (18 U.S.C. § 2340) and that contractors retain the responsibility of supervising and disciplining their employees. US regulations made clear that contractors were non-combatants and, as such, fell outside the military chain of command and the military system of discipline.[65] Defendants have argued, however, that they were essentially

---

[63] After many procedural difficulties and delays, the US Department of Justice prosecuted four Blackwater employees who directly participated in the Nisoor Square massacre; all were convicted of crimes ranging from attempted manslaughter to first-degree murder. See "Former Blackwater Contractor Sentenced to Life Over Iraq Shootings," AP, August 14, 2019. Neither the company nor any of the senior management including founder Erik Prince – defendants in the civil ATS case – were prosecuted.

[64] See, e.g., Taguba Report (*supra* n. 6). Plaintiffs also rely on the court martial testimony of military co-conspirators and statements of other detainees.

[65] Retired military members have filed amicus briefs explaining the fundamental principles of international humanitarian law applicable to contractors, the military structure and military disciplinary system, and the distinction between corporate contractors and members of the armed services. See, e.g., Br. of Amici Curiae Retired Military Officers

soldiers in all but name, and should enjoy the same legal protections that they argue are bestowed on members of US military. Plaintiffs have strongly challenged this characterization, citing US and international humanitarian law provisions that place these for-profit employees-at-will outside the military structure.

Decisions rendered in the litigation of these three cases exemplify the possibilities and challenges of seeking to hold private military contractors accountable through civil proceedings in US courts. It is a mixed outcome. *Saleh* v. *Titan*, filed in June 2004, including ATS and state law claims brought on behalf of 252 Iraqis, was lost when the Court of Appeals for the District of Columbia rendered a 2–1 decision on September 11, 2009 dismissing the case,[66] and the Obama administration urged the Supreme Court to decline review.[67] The second case, *Al-Quraishi* v. *Nakhla and L-3 Services, Inc.*, brought in June 2008 against both the corporation and an individual contractor who resided in Maryland, was settled in October 2012 on behalf of seventy-one former detainees for an undisclosed amount, following a decision in favor of the plaintiffs by the Fourth Circuit Court of Appeals sitting *en banc*.[68] *Al Shimari* v. *CACI Premier Technology,* also filed in 2008, continues to be litigated in Virginia on behalf of Suhail Al Shimari, Asa'ad Al-Zuba'e and Salah Al-Ejaili, who were detained in the "hard site" of Abu Ghraib in 2003–2004.[69]

15.3.2   Threshold Legal Issues

15.3.2.1   Corporate Liability

Corporate defendants have challenged claims brought under the ATS for violations of international law on numerous grounds. First, defendants have argued that non-state actors, including corporations, cannot be held liable for violations of international law including torture and war crimes. Defendants have also argued both sides of the state-action requirement: on the one hand, they argue that the challenged conduct constitutes private acts that fall outside the scope of international law; and, on the

in Support of Petitioners, *Al Shimari* v. *CACI Int'l, Inc.*, Nos. 09–1335; 10–1891; 10–1921 (4th Cir.) December 20, 2011.
[66] *Saleh* v. *Titan*, 580 F.3d 1 (D.C. Cir. 2009), *cert. denied*, 131 S. Ct. 3055 (2011).
[67] Br. Amicus Curiae of the United States, *Saleh* v. *Titan*, No. 09–1313 (U.S.), May 27, 2011.
[68] *Al-Quraishi* v. *L-3 Servs. and Nakhla*, 679 F.3d 205 (4th Cir. 2012) (en banc).
[69] For a detailed account of the factual allegations and the harms suffered by the plaintiffs, see *Al Shimari* v. *CACI Premier Tech., Inc.*, 324 F. Supp. 2d 668, 673–82 (E.D. Va. 2018).

other, they argue that the alleged acts involve state action, in which case the conduct should be immunized under theories of sovereign immunity.

Judges have differed in their responses to the contractors' arguments. In *Saleh v. Titan*, the district court dismissed the ATS claims against Titan, finding merit in defendants' argument that non-state actors could not be held liable for torture, and that if the plaintiffs were alleging that defendants acted under color of law, then the claims would be non-justiciable because of the political question doctrine.[70] In *Al Shimari*, in the first decision, the district court initially applied the *Sosa* test of "specific, obligatory and universal" *not* to the norms of war crimes, torture and cruel, inhuman and degrading treatment but rather to claims against "government contractors" which it deemed "fairly modern and therefore not sufficiently definite among the community of nations."[71] Upon the plaintiffs' urging, it reviewed its decision and reinstated the ATS claims after agreeing that there was consistent precedent for finding corporate liability under the ATS, most notably in other private contractor cases. In addition to the Blackwater decision, the court relied upon *Al-Quraishi*, in which the district court judge surveyed cases brought under the ATS including in the first decades after the enactment of the ATS and found that private parties could be held liable for international law violations and specifically for war crimes and torture when private actors are acting under color of law.[72] The court in *Al Quraishi* further found that there was "no basis for differentiating between private individuals and corporations in this respect since '[a] private corporation is a juridical person and has no *per se* immunity under US domestic or international law.'"[73] The district court in *Al Shimari* recently reaffirmed its holding.[74]

15.3.2.2   *Kiobel* and Extraterritoriality

Al Shimari v. CACI was one of the first cases to apply the Supreme Court's "touch and concern" *Kiobel* test. The plaintiffs argued that the constellation

---

[70] *Saleh v. Titan*, 436 F. Supp. 2d 55 (D.D.C. 2006) (finding "there is no middle ground between private action and government action" and "the more plaintiffs assert official complicity in the acts of which they complain, the closer they sail to the jurisdictional limitation of the political question doctrine"). The district court allowed the plaintiffs' common law claims to proceed against CACI.

[71] *Al Shimari v. CACI*, 657 F. Supp. 2d 700, 726 (E.D. Va. 2009).

[72] *Al-Quraishi v. L-3 Services and Nakhla*, 728 F. Supp. 2d 702, 742–51(D. Md. 2010).

[73] Ibid. at 753–6 (citations omitted).

[74] *Al Shimari v. CACI Premier Tech., Inc.*, 263 F. Supp. 3d 595, n. 4 (E.D. Va. 2017). See also *Al Shimari v. CACI Premier Tech., Inc.*, 324 F. Supp. 3d 668 (E.D. Va. 2018). Judge Leonie Brinkema replaced Judge Gerald Bruce Lee as district court judge in October 2016.

of facts in this case "touched and concerned" the United States with sufficient force to displace the presumption against extraterritoriality: it was brought against a US corporation that entered into a contract with the US government to provide services in a US-run detention center in US-occupied Iraq with oversight provided by US-based corporate officers who traveled back and forth to Iraq, and that CACI's co-conspirators included US servicemembers whose actions had been condemned by the President and Congress and who were court-martialed in US military courts. In June 2013, the district court rejected the plaintiffs' argument that the presumption against extraterritoriality could be displaced, and instead found that the presumption could be rebutted only by an act of Congress.[75]

The Fourth Circuit reversed the decision. First, it agreed with the plaintiffs that it is the "claims," as opposed to "the alleged tortious conduct," that must "touch and concern" US territory with sufficient force and, accordingly, that "courts must consider all the facts that give rise to ATS claims, including the parties' identities and their relationship to the causes of action."[76] The court instructed that "it is not sufficient merely to say that because the actual injuries were inflicted abroad, the *claims* do not touch and concern United States territory."[77] In so finding, the court recalled the object and purpose of the ATS, namely to enforce customary international law.[78]

The Fourth Circuit then conducted a "fact-based analysis" of the Abu Ghraib torture survivors' claims and found "substantial ties to United States territory" such that the claims "'touch and concern' the territory of the United States with sufficient force" to displace the presumption.[79] The court found the following factors relevant:

---

[75] *Al Shimari* v. *CACI*, 951 F. Supp. 2d 857, 866–7 (E.D. Va. 2013).

[76] *Al Shimari* v. *CACI Premier Tech., Inc.*, 758 F.3d 516, 527 (4th Cir. 2014). In dismissing CACI's argument that the tortious conduct must occur on the territory of the United States to be actionable under the ATS, the court observed that this argument represented the view of Justice Alito's concurring opinion in *Kiobel*, which was joined by only Justice Thomas, and that the analysis advanced in this concurrence was "far more circumscribed than the majority opinion's requirement that the claims touch and concern the territory of the United States." Ibid.

[77] Ibid. at 528 (emphasis in original).

[78] See ibid. at 530. See also *WesternGeco LLC* v. *ION Geophysical Corp.*, 138 S. Ct. 2129, 2137 (2018) ("The focus of a statute is the object of its solicitude, which can include the conduct it seeks to regulate, as well as the parties and interests it seeks to protect or vindicate." (quotation marks and brackets omitted)).

[79] *Al Shimari*, 758 F.3d at 527–8.

(1) CACI's status as a United States corporation; (2) the United States citizenship of CACI's employees, upon whose conduct the ATS claims are based; (3) the facts in the record showing that CACI's contract to perform interrogation services in Iraq was issued in the United States by the United States Department of the Interior, and that the contract required CACI's employees to obtain security clearances from the United States Department of Defense; (4) the allegations that CACI's managers in the United States gave tacit approval to the acts of torture committed by CACI employees at the Abu Ghraib prison, attempted to "cover up" the misconduct, and "implicitly, if not expressly, encouraged" it; and (5) the expressed intent of Congress, through enactment of the TVPA and 18 U.S.C. § 2340A, to provide aliens access to United States courts and to hold citizens of the United States accountable for acts of torture committed abroad.[80]

The court further observed, that "litigation of these ATS claims will not require unwarranted judicial interference in the conduct of foreign policy" in part because the "political branches already have indicated that the United States will not tolerate acts of torture, whether committed by United States citizens or by foreign nationals."[81] Notably, that the claims were brought against a corporation as opposed to a natural person was of no moment to the court.

15.3.2.3   *Jesner* and Corporate Liability Redux

CACI next argued that the Supreme Court's 2018 decision in *Jesner* v. *Arab Bank* compelled dismissal of the plaintiffs' claims. Because

---

[80] Ibid. at 530–1.

[81] Ibid. at 530.

Despite multiple decisions affirming jurisdiction over the ATS claims – and after a trial date had been set for April 2019 – CACI again called into question whether the court has subject-matter over the ATS claims. CACI argued that a 2016 decision in the *RJR Nabisco, Inc.* v. *European Community*, 136 S. Ct. 2090 (2016) case warranted review of the "touch and concern" test. In *RJR Nabisco*, the Supreme Court found that another civil statute (Racketeer Influenced and Corrupt Organizations Act, or "RICO") did not have extra-territorial effect. The plaintiffs argued the Court's analysis of RICO claims in *RJR Nabisco* did not alter the analysis of claims brought under the ATS, with its distinct object and purpose of providing redress for international law violations and its "touch and concern" test that was tailored to assess "relevant conduct" underlying claims in order avoid international discord. The plaintiffs submitted that the absence of any citation to *RJR Nabisco* in the Supreme Court's 2018 ATS decision, *Jesner* v. *Arab Bank*, provided strong support for their argument. The district court agreed with the plaintiffs and dismissed CACI's motion. *Al Shimari* v. *CACI*, 1:08-cv-827, Dkt. No. 1143 (E.D. Va. Feb. 27, 2019).

CACI is a Virginia-based corporation and *Jesner*'s holding barred adjudication of claims against *foreign* corporations only, CACI advanced an argument that was more animated by the principles underlying the holding in *Jesner* than by the holding itself. CACI argued that allowing the case to proceed implicated separation-of-powers concerns and could cause friction with foreign states. It argued that the court must conduct an "independent analysis akin to a *Bivens* [v. *Six Unknown Fed. Narcotics Agents*, 403 U.S. 388 (1971)] 'special-factor analysis,'" where the burden is on the plaintiffs to establish that the case advanced the goal of the ATS to "prevent foreign entanglements and international friction" while avoiding separation of powers concerns.[82] Notably, neither Iraq nor the United States had ever argued for the case to be dismissed. The district court rejected CACI's argument, noting that "the ATS was originally intended to apply to situations where a foreign citizen was the victim of an international law violation committed by an American national" – the very circumstance facing the court in the long-running Abu Ghraib litigation against a US contractor.[83] It found that the Supreme Court's "careful analysis and holding suggests . . . that the *Jesner* Court did not intend to disturb this *status quo* with respect to domestic corporations."[84]

15.3.3 Defenses Raised by Private Military Contractors

In addition to routinely challenging subject-matter jurisdiction and the application of the ATS, private military contractors regularly raise certain defenses that they argue serve as a bar to liability or a bar to suit. In essence, the contractors argue that their actions were ordered, if not sanctioned, by the government, and that it would be inappropriate to hold private actors liable for carrying out government instructions and policies. The for-profit corporations also argue that they are the equivalent to the government or its officials when they are acting under contract, and thus should enjoy all the immunities of the government. These defenses, invoked primarily in relation to the state law claims, include the "government contractor defense," "battlefield preemption," "derivative sovereign immunity" and the political question doctrine. All of these defenses have been ruled upon in the Abu Ghraib cases.

---

[82] *Al Shimari* v. *CACI Premier Tech., Inc.*, 320 F. Supp. 3d 781, 784–5 (2018).
[83] Ibid. at 787.
[84] Ibid. at 788, n. 6.

15.3.3.1 Government Contractor Defense

The government contractor defense is a judge-made defense that originally developed in the products-liability context.[85] Under this defense, a government contractor cannot be held liable for state law claims when, first, there is a conflict between state law and federal law such that the contractor cannot comply with both, and second, the contractor acted in compliance with the instructions and specifications ordered by the federal government. The preemption of state law in such cases is grounded in the Supremacy Clause of the US Constitution. In the context of providing interrogation and interpretation services, rather than a product, CACI and Titan/L-3 have both argued that the common law tort claims such as assault and battery should be "preempted" under the "combatant activities" exception of the Federal Tort Claims Act ("FTCA").[86] In response, the plaintiffs have argued that, first, there is no conflict between state and federal law since both seek to prevent and punish acts of torture and, second, the contractors are required to comply with the legal prohibitions on torture, and thus any act of torture by them or their employees contravened the instructions of the government. In *Al Quraishi*, the district court judge rejected the application of the government contractor claims on the grounds that the plaintiffs' claims, including sexual assault and battery, violate federal law and policy and that there was therefore no conflict between the application of state law and federal policy if the claims proceeded.[87] The United States echoed the plaintiffs' argument at the appellate stage in *Al Shimari* v. *CACI* arguing in an amicus brief that "the strong federal interest" in remediating violations of the federal torture statute trumps any countervailing interest in preempting the application of state law to contractors under the combatant activities exception.[88] Thus, this defense is not available for acts of torture.

---

[85] The lead case for the government contractor defense is *Boyle* v. *United Technologies Corp.*, 487 U.S. 500 (1988). The Supreme Court drew inspiration for the defense in the "discretionary function" exception to the FTCA. 28 U.S.C. § 2680(a).

[86] 28 U.S.C. § 1346; 28 U.S.C. §§ 2671–80, and specifically 28 U.S.C. § 2680(j). The FTCA explicitly states that it does not apply to contractors. 28 U.S.C. § 2671 provides that an "employee of the government" includes persons acting on behalf of any "federal agency," which includes "corporations primarily acting as instrumentalities or agencies of the US, but does not include any contractor with the United States." See also *Saleh* v. *Titan*, 580 F.3d 1, 17 (Garland, J., dissenting) ("the only statute to which the defendants point expressly excludes private contractors from the immunity it preserves for the government"); *c.f., Koohi* v. *United States*, 976 F.2d 1328 (9th Cir. 1992).

[87] *Al-Quraishi*, 728 F. Supp. 2d 702 at 738–41.

[88] Br. of United States as Amicus Curiae, *Al Shimari* v. *CACI Int'l, Inc.*, No. 09–1335 at 22 (4th Cir.) January 14, 2012. The application of the government contractor defense was

15.3.3.2   Battlefield Preemption

"Battlefield preemption" originated as a defense in the *Saleh* v. *Titan* litigation. On appeal, a two-judge majority of the Court of Appeals of the District
of Columbia found, in essence, that the application of tort law in the context
of war must be preempted so as not to hamper the battlefield
commanders.[89] This novel and far-reaching defense to liability evolved
out of another theory of preemption, namely field preemption under
which it is recognized that federal law can "occupy the field" (such as in
immigration matters or recognition of a foreign state), leaving no room for
the application of state law.[90] The plaintiffs petitioned the Supreme Court
for review. The Obama Administration submitted an amicus brief in which
it argued that the legal issues related to private military contractor liability
should be allowed to "percolate" in the lower courts and were not yet ripe for
Supreme Court review. Thereafter, the plaintiffs' petition was denied and
the case was closed in June 2011.

No court has followed the *Saleh* precedent in applying this sweeping
defense to liability, which effectively serves as a block to the enforcement
of international humanitarian law through civil actions – a particularly
dangerous occurrence when corporate actors are so deeply intertwined
with the business of war.

15.3.3.3   Derivate Immunity

Government contractors have sought to avoid suit by claiming that they
are entitled to immunity "derivative" of the sovereign or government
officials. Plaintiffs have argued that the various reasons underlying sovereign immunity, whether under either international law or domestic law,
are inapplicable to for-profit corporations and that the public interest is
not served by allowing corporate actors to enjoy impunity for serious

---

effectively rendered inapposite in *Al Shimari* when the plaintiffs voluntarily dismissed
their common law claims in late 2016. In *Saleh* v. *Titan*, following limited discovery, the
district court found that CACI did not enjoy the protections of the government contractor defense because it retained some supervisory capacity over its employees working at
Abu Ghraib. The court found that the defense was applicable in the case of Titan/L-3,
which provided interpreters, because these contractors were integrated into the military
chain of command. 556 F. Supp. 2d 1 (D.D.C. 2007). The Court of Appeals ultimately
dismissed all claims against both defendants under "battlefield pre-emption."

[89] *Saleh*, 580 F.3d at 7. The majority included now Supreme Court Justice Brett Kavanaugh.
Notably, the dissenting judge in *Saleh* v. *Titan* was Merrick Garland—President Barack
Obama's nominee for the US Supreme Court whose nomination was blocked from
proceeding to a vote by the Republican-controlled Senate.

[90] See, e.g., *American Ins. Ass'n* v. *Garamendi*, 539 U.S. 396 (2003).

breaches of law. To the extent that contractors have argued that they should receive the same immunities as US officials, plaintiffs have argued that US officials are not given automatic immunity but must show that they were acting within the scope of their employment.

To date, the argument for derivative immunity has not been successful in the torture contractor cases. It has, however, resulted in a notable decision in the *Al Shimari* case. In February 2019, two months before trial was set, CACI filed a motion to dismiss based on derivative sovereign immunity; it argued that it should enjoy the same immunity to liability as the United States.[91] The plaintiffs argued that CACI is not entitled to derivative sovereign immunity based on *Campbell-Ewald Co. v. Gomez*, which held that a contractor will not receive derivative immunity if it is found to have "violated both federal law and the Government's explicit instructions."[92] In a lengthy and scholarly opinion, the district court found that the United States was not entitled to immunity for *jus cogens* violations, leaving no immunity for CACI to "derive."[93] CACI filed an immediate appeal, which caused the district court to suspend the trial date. That interlocutory appeal was dismissed as procedurally defective, leaving intact the district court's decision that the US government could be sued for *jus cogens* violations – a precedent that might prompt a new wave of lawsuits against the government for its many breaches of international law in its foreign operations. In November 2019, CACI filed a petition for certiorari at the US Supreme Court. In January 2020, the Supreme Court invited the US Solicitor General to file a brief expressing the views of the United States. As this book goes to press, briefing is ongoing – and the Abu Ghraib torture survivors are yet to have their long-awaited day in court.

15.3.3.4   Political Question Doctrine

The political question doctrine is a judicially-created doctrine that keeps courts from adjudicating matters that raise so-called "political

---

[91] CACI had filed a third-party complaint against the United States in 2018, in which it sought to hold the United States liable if a judgment was rendered against it. The plaintiffs have pointed out the double-standard of CACI trying to benefit from the US immunity on the one hand, while seeking to hold it liable on the other.

[92] 136 S. Ct. 663, 672 (2016).

[93] *Al Shimari* v. *CACI Premier Tech., Inc.*, 368 F. Supp. 3d 935 (E.D. Va. 2019). After concluding that CACI cannot avail itself of a sovereign immunity that the United States does not possess, the district court further observed that, alternatively, it is not clear that CACI would be granted derivative immunity under *Campbell-Ewald*, because of the factual allegations that the contractor violated federal law and international regulations in conspiring with military personnel in committing acts of torture. Ibid. at 970.

questions"[94] – a category without a clear definition. Under this separation-of-powers doctrine, cases may be deemed non-justiciable because adjudication would require the judicial branch to overstep its role and intrude on matters constitutionally committed to the executive or legislative branches. CACI and Titan/L-3 Services both moved for dismissal under the political question doctrine, arguing that to allow the cases to proceed would require the courts to review military decision-making, including in the sensitive area of detainee interrogations. Notably, the United States has not sought to have any of the ATS contractor law cases dismissed under the political question doctrine.[95]

Both the district courts in *Saleh* v. *Titan* and *Al-Quraishi* rejected the defendants' political question arguments. The district court in *Al Shimari*, however, accepted that adjudication could require review of sensitive military judgments and dismissed the case in 2015. The Fourth Circuit Court of Appeals reversed, finding that intentional acts that are prohibited either by domestic criminal law or by international law, such as war crimes and torture, cannot fall within the purview of the political question doctrine.[96] The court held:

> [T]he military cannot lawfully exercise its authority by directing a contractor to engage in unlawful activity. Thus, when a contractor has engaged in unlawful conduct, irrespective of the nature of control exercised by the military, the contractor cannot claim protection under the political question doctrine . . . . [W]e conclude that a contractor's acts may be shielded from judicial review . . . only to the extent that those acts (1) were committed under actual control of the military; and (2) were not unlawful.[97]

In a separate opinion that is particularly powerful in the current political moment in the United States, Judge Henry Floyd further

---

[94] See *Baker* v. *Carr*, 369 U.S. 186 (1962).
[95] The political question doctrine has barred adjudication of cases against contractors involving negligent tort claims. See, e.g., *Carmichael* v. *Kellogg, Brown & Root Servs., Inc.*, 572 F.3d 1271 (11th Cir. 2009); *Taylor* v. *Kellogg Brown & Root Services, Inc.*, 658 F.3d 402 (4th Cir. 2011).
[96] See *Al Shimari* v. *CACI Premier Tech., Inc.*, 840 F.3d 147 (4th Cir. 2016).
[97] *Al Shimari*, 840 F.3d at 157. The court continued: "[A]ny acts of the CACI employees that were unlawful when committed, irrespective whether they occurred under actual control of the military, are subject to judicial review. Thus, the plaintiffs' claims are justiciable to the extent that the challenged conduct violated settled international law or the criminal law to which the CACI employees were subject at the time the conduct occurred." Ibid. at 159.

elaborated on the appropriate role of courts vis-à-vis the political branches in adjudicating torture claims:

> The precise contours of "what the law is" may be uncertain until a court evaluates the lawfulness of specific conduct. For example, despite repeated judicial application of torture laws, the precise legal scope of the prohibition on torture is not perfectly defined. There is, in other words, conduct for which the judiciary has yet to determine the lawfulness: loosely, a grey area.
>
> But this greyness does not render close torture cases nonjusticiable merely because the alleged torturer was part of the executive branch. While executive officers can declare the military reasonableness of conduct amounting to torture, it is beyond the power of even the President to declare such conduct lawful. The same is true for any other applicable legal prohibition. The fact that the President—let alone a significantly inferior executive officer—opines that certain conduct is lawful does not determine the actual lawfulness of that conduct. The determination of specific violations of law is constitutionally committed to the courts, even if that law touches military affairs.[98]

On remand, the new district court judge determined that the plaintiffs had sufficiently pled acts recognized as unlawful under both domestic criminal and international law and provided a sufficient evidentiary basis to support those claims, rendering the political question doctrine inapplicable.[99] Private military and security contractors are thus on notice that they can neither invoke their status to break the law nor hide behind government contracts to avoid liability if they do so.

15.4 Conclusion

Corporations are for-profit entities that have been created for the express purpose of limiting liability. As this discussion demonstrates, the goal of limiting – or avoiding – liability is often achievable for powerful and politically connected corporations through prolonged, well-resourced litigation. The question of whether private, for-profit, limited liability legal entities are the appropriate vehicle through which to carry out some of the most sensitive and impactful government functions – from incarceration to waging war – merits serious and continued scrutiny. Such scrutiny is even more pressing when governments have thus far been largely unwilling to hold government contractors accountable for even

---

[98] Ibid. at 162 (Floyd, J, concurring opinion) (internal citations omitted).
[99] *Al Shimari* v. *CACI*, 324 F. Sup. 3d 668 (E.D. Va. 2018).

the most serious breaches of international law, while too many judges have been willing to endorse theories that allow contractors to violate the law without consequence and leave victims without a remedy.

As US courts move closer to shutting their doors to accountability of contractors for some of the most egregious acts, it is even more important that other jurisdictions continue to explore and expand avenues to hold such corporations accountable, and work continues at the international level to both codify and enforce principles of corporate liability, particularly for those companies taking on state functions.

PART VI

Discovering and Recovering the Profits of War

Fines, Forfeiture and Reparations

Catching War's Funders and Profiteers

The Disjointed Web of Corporate Criminal Liability in England and Wales

RUSSELL HOPKINS[*]

16.1 Introduction

'The laws', wrote the French novelist Honoré de Balzac, 'are spiders' webs, laid out to catch little insects, which the great insects pass through unscathed.'

So began Lord Sumption's 2012 lecture on 'Foreign Affairs in the English Courts', and he quickly followed up with the observation that, in the law's bestiary, there are few greater insects than the state.[1] His Lordship did not address corporate liability for atrocity crimes,[2] but the metaphor resonates when contemplating powerful corporate actors and their involvement in wars in general and international crimes in particular. Lord Sumption concluded that the law's 'web is spun more finely, and the State may escape it less often than before'.[3] Similar assessments have been offered, possibly optimistically, in relation to catching corporate involvement in atrocities. The official commentary to the UN Guiding Principles on Business and

---

[*] Thanks are owed to Nina Jørgensen, Anita Clifford, Tomas Hamilton, Olivia English and Felicity Gerry QC for their comments on earlier drafts. Any errors are the author's alone.
[1] Lord Sumption, 'Foreign Affairs in the English Courts since 9/11' (2012), p. 1, www .supremecourt.uk/docs/speecu_120514.pdf. The quote which Lord Sumption attributed to Honoré de Balzac (1799–1850) has also been attributed to the Scythian philosopher Anacharsis (sixth century BC): 'Laws are like spiders' webs. They catch the little flies, but cannot hold the big ones.' See N. Shaxson, *The Finance Curse: How Global Finance Is Making Us All Poorer* (2018, Kindle version), chapter 3, footnote 20.
[2] See D. Scheffer, *All the Missing Souls: A Personal History of the War Crimes Tribunals* (Princeton University Press, 2012) pp. 424–8, proposing the unifying terms 'atrocity law' and 'atrocity crimes' to refer to the laws governing a wide range of violations.
[3] Lord Sumption (2012), p. 20.

Human Rights[4] and prominent experts[5] describe, using similar arachno-logical imagery, corporate actors facing an expanding 'web' of liability.

This chapter tests the accuracy of that image from the perspective of England and Wales, to evaluate the web of international criminal respon-sibility as seen from one jurisdiction. Liability may also be civil or admin-istrative, and catch individuals as well as corporates, but this chapter focuses on the use of criminal law against legal persons because this has received significant focus at the international level in recent years. Impressive scholarship has examined the notable, but tentative, develop-ments towards corporate liability for international crimes, such as the provision for corporate criminal liability in the Malabo Protocol,[6] deci-sions on corporate criminal liability for contempt at the Special Tribunal for Lebanon,[7] and the inclusion of corporate liability in the proposed draft Convention on the Prevention and Punishment of Crimes Against Humanity.[8] Partly based on these developments, Professor Stahn suggests that '[i]nternational criminal law is at a tipping point', while stressing the

---

[4] *Guiding Principles on Business and Human Rights: Implementing the United Nations 'Protect, Respect and Remedy' Framework*, A/HRC/17/31, Commentary to Guiding Principle 23. The Human Rights Council endorsed the Guiding Principles in its Resolution 17/4, 16 June 2011.

[5] See, e.g., *Corporate Complicity & Legal Accountability*, Report of the International Commission of Jurists Expert Legal Panel on Corporate Complicity in International Crimes (Geneva, 2008), Vol. 2, Criminal Law and International Crimes, p. 52: 'The Panel notes that there is an ever-growing web of laws which make it increasingly difficult for those involved in gross human rights abuses amounting to crimes under international law, includ-ing company officials, to find jurisdictional sanctuaries'; A. Ramasastry and R. C. Thompson, *Commerce, Crime and Conflict: Legal Remedies for Private Sector Liability for Grave Breaches of International Law*, A Survey of Sixteen Countries (2006), FAFO Report 536, p. 27. See also, C. Stahn, 'Liberals vs. Romantics: Challenges of an Emerging Corporate International Criminal Law' (2018) 50(1) *Case Western Reserve Journal of International Law* 91, 115, referring to 'a rich compliance web for human rights violations that includes not only hard law, but soft law and voluntary compliance mechanisms'.

[6] J. Kyriakakis, 'Article 46C: Corporate Criminal Liability at the African Criminal Court', in C. Jalloh, K. Clarke and V. Nmehielle (eds.), *African Court of Justice and People's Rights in Context*, forthcoming.

[7] *Prosecutor* v. *New TV S.A.L. and Al Khayat*, STL-14–05/PT/AP/ARI26.1, Decision on Interlocutory Appeal concerning personal jurisdiction in contempt proceedings, 2 October 2014, para. 67 (suggesting that '[c]orporate criminal liability is on the verge of attaining, at the very least, the status of a general principle of law applicable under international law'. For a discussion, see N. Bernaz, 'Corporate Criminal Liability under International Law' (2015) 13 *Journal of International Criminal Justice* 313.

[8] The International Law Commission adopted draft articles in 2019, including the following proposed article 6(8): 'Subject to the provisions of its national law, each State shall take measures, where appropriate, to establish the liability of legal persons for the offences referred to in this draft article. Subject to the legal principles of the State, such liability of legal persons may be criminal, civil or administrative.'

need for realism.[9] Professor Kyriakakis suggests that, although corporate liability for international crimes is 'no panacea', greater engagement with the relationship between commerce and atrocity offers great potential whereby 'international institutions may invite a re-investment of faith in the international criminal justice project'.[10] Looking towards national jurisdictions, Professor Stewart contends that coupling corporate criminal liability with international crimes is the next obvious 'discovery' in corporate responsibility.[11] Indeed, national *criminal* laws may seem to be a preferable form of reckoning following the US Supreme Court's decision in *Jesner* v. *Arab Bank* that foreign corporations cannot be subject to *civil* liability under the Alien Tort Statute.[12] If international criminal law is at a tipping point, and corporate liability could tilt the scales in the right direction, what does this look like in a national jurisdiction such as the UK?

One aspect of the tantalising threads said to be capable of catching corporates is the incorporation of the Rome Statute of the International Criminal Court (ICC) into domestic law – specifically in jurisdictions that, like the UK, recognise corporate liability as part of their general criminal law.[13] The first half of this chapter questions the viability of that theory. The second half explores alternative ways to catch the corporates involved in atrocities. The chapter identifies blind spots in the UK's tangled legislative framework, but it concludes that realism need not mean pessimism: powerful remedies do exist, poised to be pursued.

16.2 UK Liability of Legal Persons for International Crimes: A Web Poorly Spun?

The theory that legal persons can face criminal liability in the UK for international crimes is usually put in the following way. The legislation

---

[9] Stahn (*supra* n. 5), p. 9.

[10] J. Kyriakakis, 'Corporations before International Criminal Courts: Implications for the International Criminal Justice Project' (2017) 30 *Leiden Journal of International Law* 221–41 at 241.

[11] J. G. Stewart, 'The Turn to Corporate Criminal Liability for International Crimes: Transcending the Alien Tort Statute' (2014–2015) 47 *New York University Journal of International Law and Politics* 121.

[12] *Jesner et al* v. *Arab Bank plc*, No. 16–499, 584 U. S.___(2018).

[13] The official commentary to UN Guiding Principle 23 refers to 'the incorporation of the provisions of the Rome Statute of the International Criminal Court in jurisdictions that provide for corporate criminal responsibility'. See generally J. Kyriakakis, 'Corporate Criminal Liability and the ICC Statute: The Comparative Law Challenge' (2009) 56(3) *Netherlands International Law Review* 333.

incorporating the Rome Statute into domestic law refers to 'person', and other legislation mandates that references to 'person' include legal persons.[14] In other words, even though corporate criminal liability did not get through the front door at Rome, it comes in through a side door, perhaps even inadvertently, via incorporation into domestic law.[15]

Part 5 of the UK's incorporating legislation, the ICC Act 2001, sets out the offences of genocide, crimes against humanity and war crimes in domestic law. Section 51(1) provides that it is an offence for 'a person to commit' those crimes. Section 51(2)(2) provides for jurisdiction over acts committed 'outside the United Kingdom by a United Kingdom national, a United Kingdom resident or a person subject to UK service jurisdiction'. The meaning of United Kingdom national is defined in section 67(1) to mean 'an individual' (who meets specified criteria). The meaning of United Kingdom resident was left undefined in 2001: section 67(2) rather unhelpfully just repeated that residence means 'a person who is resident in the United Kingdom'. It took until 2010 for the meaning of residence to be clarified.[16] Even allowing for the complexities inherent in the concepts of corporate nationality and/or residence, it is difficult to see how these sections envisage jurisdiction over legal persons for international

---

[14] See J. G. Stewart, *Corporate War Crimes: Prosecuting the Pillage of Natural Resources* (Open Society Foundations, 2011), para. 133, referring to s. 51(2)(b) and 67(2) of the ICC Act 2001 and s. 5 of the Interpretation Act 1978. The FAFO Report (2006), p. 15 makes the same point: 'Since most of the countries that have incorporated ICL into their domestic statutes also do not make a distinction between natural and legal persons ... these jurisdictions include corporations and other legal persons in their web of liability.' See also, J. Kyriakakis, 'Prosecuting Corporations for International Crimes: The Role for Domestic Criminal Law', in L. May and Z. Hoskins (eds.), *International Criminal Law and Philosophy*, ASIL Studies in International Legal Theory, (Cambridge University Press, 2010), pp. 108–37; and ICJ Expert Panel Report (2010), p. 57 ('in countries that have incorporated the ICC crimes into their national legislation, companies may be exposed to criminal responsibility in domestic courts for the crimes enshrined in the ICC Statute').

[15] On the failure to accept a French proposal to include a provision on the liability of legal persons in the Rome Statute, see N. Bernaz, *Business and Human Rights: History, Law and Policy – Bridging the Accountability Gap* (Routledge: 2017), pp. 107–9; Supplemental Brief of Ambassador David J. Scheffer, Northwestern University School of Law, as Amicus Curiae in Support of the Petitioners, *Kiobel* v. *Royal Dutch Petroleum Co.*, 133 S. Ct. 1659 (2013) (No. 10–1491); and A. Clapham, 'The Question of Jurisdiction Under International Criminal Law Over Legal Persons: Lessons from the Rome Conference on an International Criminal Court', in M. Kamminga and S. Zia-Zarifi (eds.), *Liability of Multinational Corporations Under International Law* (Kluwer, 2000), pp. 139–95.

[16] The Coroners and Justice Act 2009, s. 70 provides a definition of residence based on immigration status.

crimes.[17] Other legislation in related areas contains much clearer provisions for corporate liability.[18]

Further difficulties emerge with the theory that the ICC Act 2001 provides for corporate criminal liability, and it is telling that the theory has not been tested in any cases. The preamble to the 2001 Act explains its purpose as being to 'give effect to the Statute of the International Criminal Court' and to 'provide for offences under the law of England and Wales and Northern Ireland corresponding to offences within the jurisdiction of that Court'.[19] Although a preamble is just an aid to construction, and cannot itself override clear provisions of a statute,[20] the Interpretation Act 1978 provides that 'person' includes bodies corporate 'unless contrary intention appears'.[21] Such a contrary intention appears in the preamble to the 2001 Act. Can it sensibly be maintained that Parliament, through its use of the word 'person'. intended to supplement the Rome Statute with corporate liability for international crimes in the UK's legal system, when such liability would not correspond to the offences triable in The Hague? One response might be to insist on a distinction between the 'offences' on the one hand, and personal

---

[17] See I. Brownlie, *Principles of Public International Law* (Oxford University Press, 2008), pp. 419–21, 482–90 on nationality.

[18] See, e.g., (1) the Biological Weapons Act 1974 provides in s. 1A(4) for extraterritorial application for acts done outside the UK by UK corporates; (2) the Landmines Act 1998 provides in s. 6(1)–(4) for extraterritorial obligations on corporates incorporated in the UK prohibiting the development, acquisition or transfer of anti-personnel mines or other prohibited objects, subject to a defence of not having either knowledge or any 'reason to suspect'; (3) the Chemical Weapons Act 1996 provides in s. 3(2) for extraterritorial offences involving 'United Kingdom nationals, Scottish partnerships, and bodies incorporated under the law of any part of the United Kingdom'; (4) the Cluster Munitions (Prohibitions) Act 2010 specifically applies by way of s. 4(3) to 'bodies incorporated under the law of any part of the United Kingdom'; and (5) the offences created by the Cultural Property (Armed Conflicts) Act 2017 define UK nationals at s. 3(5)(d) to include 'a body incorporated under the law of any part of the United Kingdom'.

[19] An Act of the Scottish Parliament makes provision for corresponding offences in Scots law: see International Criminal Court (Scotland) Act 2001 asp 13. It is also worth noting, in light of the role of offshore jurisdictions in international financing arrangements, that statutory instruments have been adopted for certain Crown Dependencies and Overseas Territories. See ICC Act 2001 (Overseas Territories) Order 2009/178; ICC Act 2001 (Jersey) Order 2014/2706; and ICC Act 2001 (Isle of Man) Order 2004/714. For the Bailiwick of Guernsey, the provisions appear to be limited to war crimes; see Geneva Conventions Act (Guernsey) Order 2010/2965.

[20] *Bennion on Statutory Interpretation* (LexisNexis, 2017), s. 16.4.

[21] The position is the same in relation to devolved legislation in Scotland pursuant to Schedule 1 to the Interpretation and Legislative Reform (Scotland) Act 2010. For a discussion of the historical development of corporate personality, see C. Wells, *Corporations and Criminal Responsibility* (Oxford University Press, 2001), pp. 84–105.

jurisdiction on the other. It is far from clear, however, whether a court would be persuaded to draw such a distinction in this context, given the express intention in the preamble to the 2001 Act to mirror the 'jurisdiction' of the ICC and the persons identified in section 51.[22]

A further difficulty emerges when analysing the available penalties. Offences involving murder are dealt with as the existing offence of murder in domestic law – that is, they carry a mandatory sentence of life imprisonment.[23] Part 5 continues that '[i]n any other case a person convicted of an offence is liable to imprisonment for a term not exceeding 30 years'.[24] Part 5 does not contain any express provision for fines or other penalties relevant to legal persons. There are provisions for fines or financial orders in Part 4 of the 2001 Act, but these (for example in section 49) merely empower the Secretary of State to make regulations to enforce orders issued by ICC itself. In English law, the position generally accepted is that a legal person cannot commit murder. One leading textbook explains the rationale: when 'the only punishment the court can impose is corporal', the court 'will not stultify itself by embarking on a trial in which, if a verdict of guilty is returned, no effective order by way of sentence can be made'.[25] This is the position reflected in the guidance issued to prosecutors in England and Wales.[26]

There may be a counterargument. Courts retain a general power to impose fines unless the punishment is fixed by law. The Crown Court

---

[22] The preamble to the 2001 Act states as follows: 'An Act to give effect to the Statute of the International Criminal Court; to provide for offences under the law of England and Wales and Northern Ireland corresponding to offences within the jurisdiction of that Court; and for connected purposes.'

[23] Murder carries a mandatory sentence of life imprisonment under the Murder (Abolition of Death Penalty) Act 1965. There are other serious offences that carry a maximum sentence of life imprisonment, including rape and manslaughter, but life sentences for these offences are discretionary rather than mandatory.

[24] ICC Act 2001, s. 53(5)–(6) in relation to England and Wales; s. 60(5)–(6) in relation to Northern Ireland.

[25] *Archbold Criminal Pleading, Evidence and Practice* (Thompson Reuters, 2018), s. 1–136. For the principle that a company cannot be indicted for a crime where the only punishment is imprisonment, see *R v. ICR Haulage Ltd* [1944] KB 551, CCA at 554, 557, per Stable J (a case involving the common law offence of conspiracy to defraud, the Court of Appeal concluding that where 'the only punishment the court can impose is corporal [,] ... the court will not stultify itself by embarking on a trial in which, if a verdict of Guilty is returned, no effective order by way of sentence can be made').

[26] Crown Prosecution Service, *Legal Guidance on Corporate Prosecutions*, available at www .cps.gov.uk/legal-guidance/corporate-prosecutions. In a section headed 'Limitation Governing Corporate Liability', however, is the following guidance: 'The offence must be punishable with a fine (this excludes murder, treason, piracy).'

retains a statutory power to pass an unlimited fine except in murder cases, where a life sentence is mandatory, or where another minimum sentence of imprisonment applies.[27] On this basis, *Halsbury's Laws* surmises that the 'limitation on a corporation's criminal liability by reference to punitive sanctions is of little practical importance'.[28] As to the 2001 Act, the argument would be that a sentencing discretion survives, at least for offences other than murder or other crimes with minimum custodial sentences. In other words, the reference to 'liable to imprisonment for a term not exceeding 30 years' imposes a maximum liability rather than any minimum custodial penalty. The viability of such an argument is, however, doubtful given that the 2001 Act stipulates imprisonment rather than a fine.

It is somewhat curious that the reference to 'person' in the 2001 Act has generated such hopeful attention. The thrusts of the points made are not unique to the 2001 Act. Indeed, the points may be better made in relation to earlier UK legislation. Both section 134 of the Criminal Justice Act 1988 (in relation to torture) and section 1 of the Geneva Conventions Act 1957 (in relation to grave breaches) provide UK courts with universal criminal jurisdiction over persons, without reference to nationality or residence (although the points in relation to crimes involving murder arise here too). Section 1 of the Criminal Law Act 1977 further provides for universal jurisdiction over conspiracies to commit such offences.[29] Although a person who commits torture 'shall be liable on conviction on indictment to imprisonment for life', this is not a mandatory sentence; and, as to conspiracy, section 3 of the Criminal Law Act 1977 expressly preserves the court's general power to fine and states that this extends to

---

[27] Criminal Justice Act 2003, s. 163, provides that where a person is convicted on indictment of any offence, other than an offence for which the sentence is fixed by law or fails to be imposed under certain specified statutory provisions, then the court may impose a fine instead, subject to any enactment requiring the offender to be dealt with in a particular way.

[28] *Halsbury's Laws of England*, 1 Principles of Criminal Liability, 40 Corporations, at footnote 6.

[29] See s. 134(6) of the Criminal Justice Act 1988; and s. 1A(5)–(6) of the Geneva Conventions Act 1957, both of which provide that a convicted person is liable to imprisonment. On the existence of accessorial liability for torture under English law, see K. Grady, 'International Crimes in the Courts of England and Wales' (2014) 10 *Criminal Law Review* 693 at 712. It is notable that the Geneva Conventions Act 1957, s. 6(5) as amended, contains a specific provision for corporate liability in the case of abuse of the Red Cross and other emblems contrary to the Third Protocol to the Geneva Conventions of 1949. The penalties available in s. 6(3) include fines and the forfeiture of any goods or other article on which the emblem was used.

underlying offences – including murder.[30] The theory therefore seems to be more persuasive in relation to these pieces of legislation that are older than the ICC Act 2001.

The more realistic conclusion is that, when it comes to corporate criminal liability for atrocity crimes under the ICC Act 2001, there is not much of a web of liability after all. This explains why, in his 2015 survey of remedies against business enterprises in the UK, Professor McCorquodale stated that, although legislation such as the ICC Act 2001 provides the UK with jurisdiction over international crimes, 'these do not apply to business enterprises'.[31] A recent Report of the UN High Commissioner for Human Rights to the Human Rights Council does not even refer to the Rome Statute or its incorporation into domestic systems.[32] On analysis, it is unlikely that the UK's criminal law supplements the Rome Statute so as to provide for corporate liability for ICC crimes.[33]

16.3   The 'Directing Mind and Will' of the Company: A Mental Block to Liability

Even if the above analysis is wrong, and corporate liability for international crimes is theoretically possible, it would be challenging to establish in practice. The attribution of criminal liability to legal persons is

---

[30] On 19 July 2005 in *R v. Faryadi Sarwar Zardad*, Treacy J imposed a sentence of twenty years' imprisonment for conspiracy to torture and conspiracy to take hostages in Afghanistan between 1992 and 1996. These convictions and sentence were upheld on appeal: see also *R v. Zardad* [2007] EWCA Crim 279. The offence of conspiracy is found in s. 1 of the Criminal Law Act 1977, with the penalties set out in s. 3, which retains the general power to fine under s. 163 of the Criminal Justice Act 2003, including in relation to murder.

[31] R. McCorquodale, 'Survey of the Provision in the United Kingdom of Access to Remedies for Victims of Human Rights Harms Involving Business Enterprises', 17 July 2015, available at: corporate-responsibility.org/wp-content/uploads/2015/12/BIICL-McQuordale_-uk_access_to_remedies.pdf. See also R. Chambers and K. Tyler, 'The UK Context for Business and Human Rights', in L. Blecher, N. K. Stafford and G. C. Bellamy, *Corporate Responsibility for Human Rights: New Expectations and Paradigms*' (American Bar Association, 2014), p. 309.

[32] Report of the United Nations High Commissioner for Human Rights, 'Improving Accountability and Access to Remedy for Victims of Business-Related Human Rights Abuse', A/HRC/32/19, 10 May 2016.

[33] This raises a potential inconsistency within the ICC Act 2001: s. 37 (Investigation of proceeds of ICC crime) and s. 38 (Freezing orders in respect of property liable to forfeiture) could, if used, be directed towards legal persons, such as banks. This would entail 'person' having divergent meanings in the same Act.

difficult. Whereas vicarious liability for wrongdoing by agents and employees is accepted in many civil cases in the UK, this is not generally accepted as a basis for corporate criminal liability.[34] For offences requiring proof of *mens rea*, attribution to the legal person depends on proof of the 'directing mind and will of the corporation'. It is a curious aspect of the development of English law in this area that this 'identification principle' was first described in a civil case.[35] The leading criminal case is *Tesco Supermarkets Ltd* v. *Nattrass*, in which Lord Reid held that 'directing mind and will' means the 'board of directors, the managing director and perhaps other superior officers of the company' who speak and act as the company, whereas 'subordinates' do not.[36] This is a restrictive basis for attribution. In December 2015, the then Director of Public Prosecutions expressed her regret that the present state of the law unduly inhibits the criminal prosecution of corporates: 'Unlike other countries, the principles of vicarious liability or poor corporate governance, which are matters that are easier to prove, play no part in establishing corporate criminal liability. The present state of the law means it is especially difficult to establish criminal liability against companies with complex or diffuse management structures.'[37] A previous director of the Serious Fraud Office has also criticised the identification principle: 'In a world of increasingly complex corporate structures, the identification

[34] For a comparative discussion of models of corporate attribution, see Dr J. Zerk, 'Corporate Liability for Gross Human Rights Abuses: Towards a Fairer and More Effective System of Domestic Law Remedies', Report prepared for the Office of the UN High Commissioner for Human Rights, February 2014, pp. 31–43, www.ohchr.org /Documents/Issues/Business/DomesticLawRemedies/StudyDomesticLawRemedies.pdf.
[35] *Lennard's Carrying Company Limited* v. *Asiatic Petroleum Company* [1915] AC 705.
[36] *Tesco Supermarkets Ltd* v. *Nattrass* [1972] AC 152, per Lord Reid at 171. The identification principle also applies in Scots law: see *Transco* v. *HM Advocate* 2005 SLT 211. An argument could be developed that cases since *Tesco Supermarkets* give undue prominence to the idea of a company's directing mind and will. In *Meridian Global Funds Management Asia Ltd* v. *Securities Commission* [1995] 2 AC 500 PC, an appeal to the Judicial Committee of the Privy Council from New Zealand, Lord Hoffmann held that the *only* relevant question is one of statutory construction rather than corporate metaphysics. He regretted the 'anthropomorphism' which has seeped into the case law. Lord Hoffmann suggested greater flexibility, but English cases since *Meridian* have defaulted to the seductive anthropomorphic metaphor: *R* v. *Regis Paper Co Ltd* [2011] EWCA Crim 2527, [2012] 1 Cr App Rep 177; [2012] EWCA Crim 1847 (refusing leave to appeal to the Supreme Court); *Attorney-General's Reference (No 2 of 1999)* [2000] QB 796; [2000] 3 All ER 182, per Rose LJ.
[37] A. Saunders, Director of Public Prosecutions, Press Statement explaining that no further action would be taken against News Group Newspapers following a phone-hacking scandal, 11 December 2015, blog.cps.gov.uk/2015/12/no-further-action-to-be-taken-in-operations-weeting-or-golding.html.

principle can hobble the prosecutor in those cases where it is right to prosecute the company.'[38]

Such expressions of frustration illustrate that the circumstances in which the identification principle can be satisfied are limited, especially when larger companies are involved with more disparate corporate structures. Prosecutions of corporates for complex offences involving a mental element seem likely to remain vanishingly rare, until legislative changes are made to the basis on which corporate criminal liability is established.

16.4   A Corporate 'Duty to Prevent' Atrocity Crimes: An Alternative Basis for Criminal Liability?

The limitations imposed by the identification principle have prompted significant legislative changes to specific areas of corporate criminal liability in the last decade. Three examples are commonly given. Each change resulted from specific scandals or campaigns, and involves their own intricacies beyond the scope of this chapter. They are highlighted here because they offer a possible model that might be replicated in the context of corporate involvement in atrocity crimes. First, the Corporate Manslaughter and Corporate Homicide Act 2007 provides in section 1 that a company may be guilty of corporate manslaughter if the way in which its activities are managed or organised causes a person's death, and amounts to a gross breach of a duty of care. A major and possibly unjustified limitation is that the offence applies only to deaths occurring in the UK.[39] Second, the Bribery Act 2010 introduced an offence in section 7 of commercial organisations failing to prevent bribery committed by their employees, agents or associated persons, subject to a defence of 'adequate procedures designed to prevent' bribery. This offence has extraterritorial effect and there is no requirement for the prohibited conduct to have been committed in the UK or have a close connection to the UK, provided that the company is

---

[38] D. Green, Remarks at the Cambridge Symposium, 5 September 2016, www.sfo.gov.uk /2016/09/05/cambridge-symposium-2016/. As has the Law Commission, as long ago as August 2010, when it described the identification principle as 'an inappropriate and ineffective method of establishing criminal liability of corporations': The Law Commission, *Consultation Papers No. 195,* Criminal Liability in Regulatory Contexts, paragraph 5.84.

[39] Corporate Manslaughter and Corporate Homicide Act 2007, s. 28 (Extent and territorial application) provides that the Act extends to England and Wales, Scotland and Northern Ireland, with some limited extension to British registered or controlled ships and aircraft, etc).

incorporated in or otherwise carries on business in the UK.[40] Bribery offences include bribing foreign public officials, and intending to induce or reward the improper performance of a person's (including private persons) usual functions. A commercial organisation may be found guilty of an offence if a person associated with it bribes another, intending to obtain or retain business or a business advantage for that organisation. Penalties for failure to comply include unlimited fines. Third, the Criminal Finances Act 2017 recently introduced offences in sections 45–6 of failing to prevent domestic or overseas tax evasion.

Each of these examples can loosely be described as an organisational failure to prevent model. When the proscribed conduct has occurred, be it a death, bribery or tax evasion, the onus is on the company to show that it had in place adequate procedures designed to prevent the crime.[41] Otherwise it will bear some criminal liability and be penalised. While the analogy is far from perfect, there are similarities with the theoretical underpinnings of superior responsibility in international criminal law. It will also be observed that, in the cases of bribery and tax evasion, extraterritorial effect is specifically envisaged.

The UK government is consulting on extending the failure to prevent model to additional economic crimes. At the Anti-Corruption Summit in May 2016, the government launched a consultation on the introduction of a broader offence of failure to prevent economic crimes. The proposed offence would cover a range of economic crimes such as money laundering, false accounting and fraud. Addressing the Cambridge Symposium on Economic Crime in September 2016, the Attorney General emphasised that the purpose of this consultation was to 'secure a change in corporate culture by ensuring boards set an appropriate tone from the top' and commented that 'both corporations and individuals are responsible' when it comes to financial crime.[42] In January 2017, the UK government issued a call for evidence on the proposal to extend corporate criminal liability to

[40] Ministry of Justice, *The Bribery Act 2010*, Circular 2011/05 (Ministry of Justice, 2011), para. 22.
[41] For a comprehensive discussion of recent developments in the UK, see C. Wells, 'Corporate Criminal Liability: A Ten-Year Review' (2014) 12 *Criminal Law Review* 849–78; and C. Wells, 'Corporate Failure to Prevent Economic Crime: A Proposal' (2017) 6 *Criminal Law Review* 426–39.
[42] Attorney General Jeremy Wright, *Speech to the Cambridge Symposium on Economic Crime*, 5 September 2016, www.gov.uk/government/speeches/attorney-general-jeremy-wright-speech-to-the-cambridge-symposium-on-economic-crime.

wider economic crimes.[43] The consultation closed on 24 March 2017. It remains to be seen whether any concrete proposals emerge.[44]

In the meantime, there have been calls to extend the corporate failure to prevent model beyond economic crimes. In April 2017, the Parliamentary Joint Committee on Human Rights published a report on 'Human Rights and Business', which criticised the UK's current legal framework, including the identification principle. The Committee, which included the former Lord Chief Justice of England and Wales Lord Woolf, recommended that 'the Government should bring forward legislation to impose a duty on all companies to prevent human rights abuses, as well as an offence of failure to prevent human rights abuses for all companies, including parent companies, along the lines of the relevant provisions of the Bribery Act 2010'.[45]

In January 2018, however, the UK government provided a terse response to this proposal, stating simply: 'The Government has no immediate plans to legislate in this area.'[46] Alison MacDonald QC observed that this response is 'baffling – if companies can be placed under an obligation to prevent bribery and the facilitation of tax evasion, why not gross human rights abuses?'[47] There appears to be considerable force in her view. It is difficult to identify any principled basis on which the criminal law should obligate corporates to take reasonable measures to prevent their involvement in bribery or tax evasion but not atrocities.[48]

---

[43] Corporate liability for economic crime: call for evidence, 13 January 2017, consult .justice.gov.uk/digital-communications/corporate-liability-for-economic-crime/suppor ting_documents/corporateliabilityforeconomiccrimeconsultationdocument.pdf.

[44] A prior director of the SFO described himself as an 'enthusiastic supporter of a new "failing to prevent economic crime" offence since 2012'. See footnote 38.

[45] Joint Committee on Human Rights, 'Human Rights and Business 2017: Promoting Responsibility and Ensuring Accountability', Sixth Report of Session 2016–2017, 5 April 2017, para. 193, publications.parliament.uk/pa/jt201617/jtselect/jtrights/443/443.pdf.

[46] Joint Committee on Human Rights, 'Human Rights and Business 2017: Promoting Responsibility and Ensuring Accountability: Government's Response to the Committee's Sixth Report of Session 2016–2017', First Special Report of Session 2017–2019, 12 January 2018, p. 15, publications.parliament.uk/pa/jt201719/jtselect/ jtrights/686/686.pdf.

[47] A. MacDonald QC, 'Should Companies Have a Duty to Prevent Human Rights Abuses?', 19 February 2018, lawofnationsblog.com/2018/02/20/companies-duty-prevent-human-rights-abuses/.

[48] It is worth noting, in this context, that in regulated sectors such as financial services, other possibilities include administrative enforcement for failure to maintain effective controls under the Financial Services and Markets Act 2000, s. 206; or, depending on the issues involved, legal persons could face related penalties for false accounting under the Companies Act 2006 or the Theft Act 1968. One example is that in January 2017, the

That being said, the duty to prevent model is not without critics, and there is a lack of cogent empirical evidence on its impact, even in the bribery context.[49]

16.5   Other Ways to Catch Corporate Wrongdoing

Given the difficulties with establishing corporate liability for atrocity crimes, the remainder of this chapter examines alternative ways to catch funders and profiteers. Atrocity crimes often accompany a range of other crimes. Professor Stahn notes that '[c]ertain forms of economic crime have become part of atrocity crime'.[50] This might even understate the grubby reality of human history. US Marine Corps Major General Smedley Butler famously argued, for example, that war itself is a racket, turning blood into gold.[51] Whether or not this is true in the case of all wars, it is uncontentious that corporate actors are sometimes fallible and greedy, especially those involved in atrocities. Other criminal laws may provide a firmer peg on which to hang corporate liability, including economic crimes such as money laundering, breaches of sanctions, tax evasion, smuggling or perhaps human trafficking offences involving victims fleeing from conflicts. Even if it is difficult to establish corporate criminal liability for the underlying atrocities, this does not mean that corporate actors can bypass the legal system entirely.

The UK government's anti-corruption strategy for 2017–2022 recognises the link between economic crimes and overseas atrocities. It notes the prevalence of corruption in 'conflict affected states' and calls for a 'stronger focus on the role of corruption in driving conflict and fragility'. It gives well-worn examples of the link between egregious international crimes and economic crimes, including Islamic State's use of oil fields to fund terrorism, with corruption and bribery enabling the movement of oil onto international markets, or the illicit trade in natural resources in the Democratic Republic of Congo, which generates up to 1.25 billion USD per annum and finances some eight thousand armed

---

FCA fined Deutsche Bank £163 million for failing to maintain an adequate anti-money laundering framework.

[49] See, e.g., A. Clifford and N. Reurts, 'Corporate Criminal Liability in the Supply Chain: A Coherent Divergence' (2014) 8 *Criminal Law Review* 633–45.

[50] Stahn (*supra* n. 5 above) 10.

[51] S. Butler, *War Is a Racket* (New York Round Table Press, 1935), archive.org/details/WarIsARacket: 'WAR is a racket. It always has been. It is possibly the oldest, easily the most profitable, surely the most vicious . . .. It is the only one in which the profits are reckoned in dollars and the losses in lives.'

fighters destabilising that country.[52] The rest of this chapter looks beyond the theoretical attempts to establish corporate liability for the underlying atrocities, to highlight some practical alternatives capable of catching the corporate aspects of international criminality, including ways to 'follow the money', block funding, or seize ill-gotten gains.

Before delving into these alternatives, a dose of caution and humility is in order. The UK is one of the most attractive destinations for laundering the proceeds of international corruption, some of which is undoubtedly linked to atrocity crimes. The government recognises that professional enablers and intermediaries such as lawyers, accountants and financiers play a significant role by creating complex and sophisticated structures that distance individuals from money while retaining control of illicit funds.[53] Although it is difficult to estimate precisely the sums involved, up to 90 billion GDP and possibly even more of illicit funds are believed to be laundered through the UK every single year.[54] It is not much use giving examples such as Islamic State and/or DRC without pausing to reflect on the global financial system more broadly. Nicholas Shaxson's 2011 classic *Treasure Islands* even reverses the arachnological metaphor, arguing that the UK itself sits 'spider-like, at the centre of a vast international web of tax havens, hoovering up trillions of dollars' worth of business and capital from around the globe and funneling it up to the City of London'.[55]

The massive data leaks of our times such as that of Panama Papers highlight the role that offshore jurisdictions, including those linked to the UK, can play in facilitating international crimes. Obermayer and Obermaier contend that Mossack Fonseca ran a 'web of shell companies' associated with the Syrian regime of Bashar al-Assad, including a BVI company for his cousin Rami Makhlouf – even though he had been on US sanctions lists since 2008 and the EU lists since 2011. They argue that

---

[52] United Kingdom Anti-Corruption Strategy 2017–2022, December 2017, www.gov.uk/govern ment/uploads/system/uploads/attachment_data/file/667221/6_3323_Anti-Corruption_Strate gy_WEB.pdf.

[53] National Strategic Assessment of Serious and Organised Crime, National Crime Agency, 9 September 2016, p. 5, www.nationalcrimeagency.gov.uk/publications/731-national-strategic-assessment-of-serious-and-organised-crime-2016/file.

[54] National Strategic Assessment (2016), para. 91.

[55] N. Shaxson, *Treasure Islands: Tax Havens and the Men Who Stole the World* (2011, Kindle version). See also *The Spider's Web: Britain's Second Empire* (2017), a documentary written, directed and produced by M. Oswald, vimeo.com/ondemand/spiderswebfilm. For a discussion of some of the role of offshore in 'accountability avoidance', see P. Beckett, *Tax Havens and International Human Rights* (Routledge, 2017).

the Makhlouf case demonstrates why 'the existence of anonymous shell companies poses an existential threat to millions of people'.[56] Further examples can be offered. In 2008, British arms broker John Knight was convicted and sentenced to four years' imprisonment. He had shipped machine guns from Iran to Kuwait using a BVI company, despite having been refused a UK export licence.[57]

It should also be acknowledged that, although private companies, brokers, professional enablers and offshore all play a broader role, the UK is a major arms exporter itself.[58] The Defence and Security Organisation (DSO) provides substantial support to exporters. The DSO's website boasts that the UK is one of the world's most successful defence exporters, averaging second place in the global rankings on a rolling ten-year basis. In 2016, the UK's share of the 89 billion USD global defence market was approximately 9 per cent. In addition, UK security exports that year were estimated to be a further 4.29 billion GDP.[59] In April 2018, the UK's defence minister indicated in Parliament that UK defence exports amounted to some 70 billion GDP over the last ten years.[60] These figures are underestimates because they

---

[56] See B. Obermayer and F Obermaier, *The Panama Papers: Breaking the Story of How the Rich and Powerful Hide Their Money* (2017, Kindle version), chapter 5, 'Mossack Fonseca's Role in the Syrian War'.

[57] *R v. Knight (John)* [2008] EWCA Crim 478, para. 9, noting that Knight operated primarily through a BVI-registered company which he controlled. Another example is the conviction in Jersey in 2010 of Raj Bhojwani for money laundering on behalf of General Sani Abacha of Nigeria. Further, in *R v. Gary Hyde* [2014] EWCA Crim 713, an individual was convicted for brokering an arms deal between China and Nigeria without obtaining the relevant UK licence. The Court of Appeal held that the trial judge was wrong to order the forfeiture of firearms on the basis that they had been in the possession of a company director who had been convicted of unlawfully trading in firearms. They had been in the possession of the company, not the director, and there was no justification for piercing the corporate veil.

[58] See A. Feinstein, *The Shadow World: Inside the Global Arms Trade* (Penguin Books, 2011), chapters 7 and 9 for a discussion of the UK, BAE Systems and the Al Yamama (the dove) deal with Saudi Arabia and South Africa. See also *R (on the application of Campaign Against Arms Trade) v. Secretary of State for International Trade* [2019] EWCA Civ 1020 for a successful challenge to the grant of export licences for the sale or transfer of arms or military equipment to Saudi Arabia, for possible use in the conflict in Yemen.

[59] DSO publishes figures annually (typically around July) for the previous calendar year. According to DSO, it is 'not advisable to combine the defence and security export figures as they are recorded via a different methodology and report on a different metric', www.gov.uk/government/publications/uk-defence-and-security-export-figures-2016/uk-defence-and-security-export-statistics-for-2016.

[60] Hansard, 23 April 2018, Vol. 639, Col. 582, hansard.parliament.uk/commons/2018-04-23/debates/345457B5-2B0A-4D65-9523-58D8C277CB9E/DefenceIndustry.

are based on voluntary surveys with no internationally agreed definition of defence exports. Notwithstanding the uncertainty, these figures are official UK national statistics and provide a useful baseline.[61]

The possibility of vested interests and/or allegations of British hypocrisy must therefore be acknowledged.[62] Also, there is little use pointing to laws or powers that appear to have teeth if, in the real world, they rarely bite. The challenge of the identification doctrine pervades the field of economic crime as well. No company or bank has been prosecuted for money laundering, despite the vast sums involved.[63] Therefore, although alternatives exist, to which we now turn, the UK's track record is not without difficulty.

16.6   Sanctions, Serious Crimes, Asset-Freezes and Anti-Money Laundering Legislation

Sanctions take many forms, including arms embargoes, trade restrictions, travel bans and various financial remedies. This is a complex area of law in a state of Brexit-induced flux: the Sanctions and Anti-Money Laundering Act 2018 creates a new legislative framework for the imposition and enforcement of sanctions after the UK leaves the European Union. When introducing the Bill for its second reading in the House of Commons, then Foreign Secretary Boris Johnson summarised that some '2,000 individuals and entities are listed for sanctions, varying from asset freezes and travel bans to trade restrictions and arms embargoes. At this moment, assets worth £12.5 billion are frozen in the UK.'[64] The UK currently implements some thirty-four sanctions regimes,

---

[61] Other useful sources of defence export data are the Stockholm International Peace Research Institute (SIPRI) and the USA's Congressional Research Service.

[62] One example of how insidious such vested interests can be is the 1992 trial involving allegations that a company Matrix Churchill supplied bomb-making equipment to Saddam Hussein which was then used against British soldiers in the first Gulf War. The trial exposed government-approved 'arms to Iraq' during the 1980s with a minister famously admitting under cross-examination that he had been 'economical with the actualité'. See G. Robertson QC, *The Justice Game* (Vintage, 1999), p. 313.

[63] In March 2018, the House of Commons Treasury Select Committee announced an inquiry into the UK's approach to money laundering, terrorist financing and sanctions. The Law Commission is also conducting a review as part of its programme on law reform.

[64] Hansard, 20 February 2018, Vol. 636, Col. 77. It appears, however, that the vast majority of assets currently frozen relate to Libya. At the close of business on 29 September 2017 the total value of Libyan assets frozen in the UK was 12.061 billion GDP: Written Answer, 27 March 2018, Freezing Assets: Libya: www.parliament.uk/business/publications/written-questions-answers-statements/written-question/Lords/2018-03-13/HL6295/.

around half of which result from UN Security Council resolutions and half from the 'autonomous' measures agreed with EU partners.[65] In relation to asset freezes and confiscation more broadly, however, a July 2016 Home Affairs Select Committee found significant problems in the UK's capacity to freeze assets and confiscate the proceeds of crime, pointing to insufficient capacity and resources for law enforcement, and the poor use of existing tools.[66] Official figures on the implementation of confiscation orders indicate a lax approach, with somewhere in the region of 1.9 billion GDP outstanding in spite of court orders.[67]

Together with sanctions and the power to freeze assets come risks of injustice and unintended consequences. The UK Supreme Court held in *Ahmed & others* v. *HM Treasury* that the government's imposition of asset freezes, using powers under the United Nations Act 1946 to implement UN Security Council decisions, was ultra vires and risked infringing human rights.[68] This led to the Terrorist Asset Freezing Act 2010, which gives clearer powers to the government.[69] Then, in *Bank Mellat* v. *HM Treasury*, the Supreme Court held that measures taken under the Counter-Terrorism Act 2008 to restrict the access of an Iranian bank and its subsidiaries to the UK's financial markets (on the ground that it posed a significant risk to national security by providing services to those involved in the development of nuclear weapons) were arbitrary, disproportionate and entirely unlawful.[70] Concerns have also been raised that banks' efforts to de-risk in the context of money laundering, terrorist financing and/or sanctions breaches have the regrettable and unintended consequence of denying entirely legitimate customers access to the UK's financial system. There is a danger that, if sanctions regimes are drawn too broadly, they end up doing more harm than good. The FCA's 2016/

---

[65] HC Deb, 19 July 2017, c925; B. Smith, *The Sanctions and Anti-Money Laundering* Bill, HC Briefing Paper, 15 February 2018, pp. 4, 13.

[66] Home Affairs Select Committee, *Proceeds of Crime Report*, 11 July 2016, publications .parliament.uk/pa/cm201617/cmselect/cmhaff/25/2502.htm.

[67] See 'An Ocean of Fish But Where's the Rod? Exploring the £ on UK Confiscation Orders', Research Briefing by White Collar Crime Centre, 27 September 2017, www .brightlinelaw.co.uk/images/2017.09.27_Confiscation_Research_Briefing.pdf.

[68] [2010] UKSC 2, [2010] 2 AC 534 (Holding that fundamental rights could be overridden only by express language or necessary implication, the general language of the 1946 Act was insufficient and the relevant UN Resolution was not phrased in terms of 'reasonable grounds for suspecting' being the basis to freeze assets).

[69] For the UK Government's assessment of the first five years of this Act's operation, see www.gov.uk/government/uploads/system/uploads/attachment_data/file/561408/tafa_ web_final.pdf.

[70] [2013] UKSC 39.

2017 report noted, for example, that '[c]ustomers such as overseas correspondent banks and charities operating in war-torn regions are said to be particularly affected'.[71]

It remains to be seen how the law in this area will function post-Brexit, but some other concrete developments should be highlighted. One prominent recent example is section 146 of the Policing and Crime Act 2017. This gives the Treasury significant new powers to impose monetary penalties on persons, including corporates, for breaches of sanctions: up to 50 per cent of the value of the breach or 1 million GDP (whichever is greater). These penalties offer a tempting alternative to criminal prosecution. They can be imposed by reference to the civil standard of proof.[72] The newly created Office of Financial Sanctions Implementation (OFSI)[73] has published official guidance stating that companies that voluntarily disclose breaches will be eligible for reductions in fines of up to 50 per cent in 'serious' cases and 30 per cent in the 'most serious' cases.[74] Information on any penalties imposed will be made publicly available. Only two (relatively small) penalties have been published at the time of writing, but this is an area to monitor. For instance, the government has released metrics for 2017: a total of 133 suspected sanctions breaches were reported to OFSI, the total value of which was 1.4 billion GDP.[75] It is reasonable to expect that some of those breaches will lead to monetary penalties as an alternative to criminal prosecution.

Money laundering is another area to emphasise, in relation to which various UK offences are found in Part 7 of the Proceeds of Crime Act 2002 (POCA). Perhaps the most important point to note for present

---

[71] See www.fca.org.uk/publication/annual-reports/annual-anti-money-laundering-report -2016-17.pdf.

[72] Under s. 147(3)-(6) of the Policing and Crime Act 2017, a decision to impose a penalty can be reviewed by a government minister and there is a right of appeal to the Upper Tribunal.

[73] This new unit was announced in the summer budget of 2015, and it is intended to work closely with law enforcement to ensure that financial sanctions are 'properly understood, implemented and enforced'. See the UK's Summer Budget Report (2015), www.gov.uk /government/publications/summer-budget-2015/summer-budget-2015.

[74] Monetary Penalties for Breaches of Financial Sanctions: Guidance, Office of Financial Sanctions Implementation, HM Treasury, April 2017, www.gov.uk/government/uploads/ system/uploads/attachment_data/file/637102/Monetary_penalties_for_breaches_of_financial _sanctions.pdf.

[75] UK Parliament, Sanctions: Written Question for Helen Goodman MP, answered on 8 February 2018, then corrected on 21 February 2018, www.parliament.uk/business/ publications/written-questions-answers-statements/written-question/Commons/2018- 02-05/126717/.

purposes is that the UK takes an 'all crimes' approach to predicate offences that generate proceeds to be laundered. Conduct committed abroad is caught provided it would constitute an offence in the UK had it occurred there.[76] Criminal property is defined broadly in section 340(3) to constitute a 'benefit from criminal conduct', which means that the benefit can be direct or indirect or in whole or in part.[77] Prosecutors are not required to prove that the property in question is the benefit of a particular or a specific act of criminal conduct, as such an interpretation would restrict the operation of the legislation.

The Court of Appeal held in *R v. Rogers (Bradley)* [2014] EWCA Crim 1680 that UK courts have jurisdiction over money laundering offences even where the relevant conduct took place outside the UK, provided a significant part of the underlying scheme took place in the UK and it had harmful consequences in the UK. The court accepted the prosecution's submissions that, notwithstanding the historical presumption against the extraterritorial effect of legislation, 'more modern views on jurisdiction' hold that absent express geographic limitations in a statute, international comity permits the court to look to where a 'substantial measure of the activities constituting a crime' took place, and if that was in England or Wales, then these courts have jurisdiction. The court held that money laundering is 'par excellence an offence which is no respector of national boundaries' so it would be surprising if Parliament had not intended the provisions in POCA to have extraterritorial effect, despite the absence of any express language to say so.[78]

---

[76] POCA, s. 340(2)(b), s. 340(11)(d). See Archbold, s. 33-29. It is sometimes a defence if the alleged conduct was legal in the overseas country or territory. However, this defence was narrowed by the POCA (Money Laundering: Exceptions to Overseas Conduct Defence) Order 2006.

[77] See E. Rees, R. Fisher and R. Thomas, *Blackstone's Guide to the Proceeds of Crime Act* 2002 (Oxford University Press, 2015), paras. 5.14–5.24.

[78] *R v. Rogers (Bradley)* [2014] EWCA Crim 1680; [2015] 1 WLR 2017. The Court of Appeal's approach has been criticised on the basis that it conflated the internationalisation of predicate offences for money laundering with the question of UK jurisdiction. It remains unclear the extent to which this particular decision turned on the close connection on the facts between the predicate offending and the UK. This point was specifically noted by the Law Commission in its (2019) review of money laundering reporting requirements. For the otherwise well-established presumption against the extraterritorial effect of legislation creating criminal offences, see *Air India* v. *Wiggins* [1980] 71 Cr App R 213, HL (per Lord Diplock, at 217). However, in *R v. Smith (Wallace Duncan) (No. 4)* [2004] 2 Cr App R 17 (CA), the Court of Appeal held that the courts of England and Wales have jurisdiction where a substantial measure of the activities constituting a crime takes place within the jurisdiction; it is not necessary that the 'final act' or 'gist' of the offence occurs in England or Wales.

The Serious Crime Act 2007 is an even clearer example of the increasingly extraterritorial effect of the UK's criminal laws. It criminalises conduct occurring in England and Wales if that conduct is capable of encouraging or assisting an offence overseas.[79] A bizarre feature of this legislation is that the list of offences specified as 'serious' in Schedule 1 to the Act (e.g. drug trafficking, modern slavery, firearms, money laundering, fraud, etc.) does not include express reference to genocide, crimes against humanity or war crimes, some of the most serious offences of all. Although there is a residual judicial discretion in section 2(5)(b)(ii) to treat conduct not specifically enumerated in Schedule 1 as being 'serious', this is another example of the UK's legislative framework failing to mesh.

The potential reach of bribery offences is another important area, aptly demonstrated by a 2009 case (i.e. pre-Bribery Act 2010).[80] Mabey and Johnson, a British construction and bridge-building company, was found to be liable for bribing foreign officials in order to win contracts and for breaching UN–Iraq sanctions relating to the 'Oil for Food Programme'. The company entered a plea agreement, including a financial penalty of 3.5 million GDP, further compensation and costs. This was the UK's first conviction of a company for such offences.[81] In September 2009, the company pleaded guilty to charges of corruption, which resulted in fines, reparations to the affected countries and the confiscation of contract proceeds of some 6.6 million GDP. Some former directors of the firm were later sentenced for providing kickbacks to the Iraqi government by inflating contract prices for the supply of bridges and disguising illegal payments through Jordanian banks. Of further interest, in 2012 the holding company Mabey Engineering (Holdings) Limited agreed to pay back dividends that it had received, as a shareholder, as a result of the corruption, paying a further penalty of some 130,000 GDP. After this development, the SFO issued a press release stating that it 'intends to use the civil recovery process to pursue investors who have benefited from illegal activity. Where issues arise, we will be much less sympathetic to institutional investors whose due diligence has clearly been lax in this respect.' This suggests that, in certain circumstances, the web of liability could even stretch to shareholders.

[79] Serious Crime Act 2007, ss. 44–6, 52 and Schedule 4.

[80] Prior to the Bribery Act 2010, the criminal offence of bribery was found in the Public Bodies Corrupt Practices Act 1889, the Prevention of Corruption Act 1906 and the Prevention of Corruption Act 1916.

[81] K. Harrison and N. Ryder, *The Law Relating to Financial Crime in the United Kingdom* (Routledge, 2016), p. 153.

16.7   Civil Recovery Orders

Part 5 of POCA created a new regime whereby enforcement authorities, that is, a specified group of public bodies (primarily the National Crime Agency, but also the Serious Fraud Office, the Financial Conduct Authority, the Crown Prosecution Service and Her Majesty's Revenue and Customs), may seek a 'civil recovery order' or 'CRO' from the High Court to recover assets that are, or represent, 'property obtained through unlawful conduct'.[82] This is a non-conviction-based asset recovery tool, to be distinguished from remedies such as confiscation orders that are available only following a criminal conviction.[83] Interim freezing orders can be obtained until the CRO application is determined. Notwithstanding the underlying basis for a CRO being alleged criminal conduct, the standard of proof is the balance of probabilities and the Civil Procedure Rules apply, including more flexible rules of evidence. The targeted property can be located anywhere in the world.[84] The requirement that the property has been obtained through 'unlawful conduct' generally means contrary to the criminal law of the country where it took place, and it must also be unlawful had the conduct occurred in the UK – that is, it must pass a dual criminality test.[85] It is not necessary to prove a specific offence, provided 'it is shown that the property was obtained through conduct of one of a number of kinds, each of which would have been unlawful conduct'. This is a tool directed towards assets rather than the person. It offers significant potential in circumstances where a criminal prosecution would be unrealistic or evidentially impossible.[86]

---

[82] POCA, ss. 240–2.

[83] See *R v. Innospec Ltd* [2010] Lloyd's Rep. F.C. 462, a pre-2010 case which involved bribes in relation to the UN's Oil for Food Programme in Iraq. The company and the SFO reached a settlement for confiscation and civil recovery rather than a fine, but Thomas LJ held that the court could not endorse such an agreement. He observed that it will 'rarely be appropriate for criminal conduct by a company to be dealt with by means of a civil recovery order'. The court imposed a fine instead, but stuck to the agreed level of penalty.

[84] In *Perry v. SOCA* [2012] UKSC 35, the Supreme Court held that the powers of civil recovery under POCA did not have extraterritorial reach to property or persons located outside the jurisdiction. Parliament quickly legislated to reverse this result. The CCA 2013 introduced POCA, ss. 282A–282F to extend the potential reach of civil recover orders to property 'wherever situated' and a person 'wherever domiciled, resident or present' as long as there is some connection with the UK.

[85] POCA, s. 241.

[86] Although, according to the SFO's website, it has not obtained a single CRO since 2014/2015: see www.sfo.gov.uk/about-us/. In *Gale v. SOCA* [2011] UKSC 49, the Supreme Court rejected a challenge to a civil recovery order that was based on evidence used in a Portuguese criminal trial that had ended in an acquittal. This decision resolved to some

Section 13 of the Criminal Finances Act 2017 amended the civil recovery provisions in Part 5 of POCA, inserting what was referred to during the Parliamentary debates as the UK's 'Magnitsky Amendment'.[87] This was a more limited provision than the sweeping sanctions powers available in countries such as the United States. New section 241A POCA amends the definition of 'unlawful conduct' to include 'gross human rights abuses or violations' and expands potential liability to include conduct 'connected with' those violations. Such violations are defined based on three carefully crafted conditions. First, the conduct must involve the torture or cruel, inhuman or degrading treatment or punishment of a person who sought to either expose illegal activities involving public officials or 'obtain, exercise, defend or promote human rights and fundamental freedoms'. Second, the conduct must have been carried out in consequence of the person having sought to either expose such illegality or obtain, exercise, defend or promote human rights. Third, the conduct must have been carried out by a public official or person acting in, or purported performance of, an official capacity.

These three conditions impose some limitations upon the extended civil recovery powers: they proscribe particular conduct, against particular persons, by particular persons. Notwithstanding these limitations, there is potential for stretch so as to catch conduct only tangentially related to the underlying abuses. The mere exercise or promotion of human rights is a very broad basis indeed. The inclusion of conduct 'connected with' human rights violations has significant reach. Further, section 241A(5) includes acting as an agent, directing, sponsoring, profiting from or materially assisting the human rights violation(s). Material assistance is defined in section 241A(8) to include the provision of goods, services, financial or technological support. Although the definition of unlawful conduct in section 242 POCA remains untouched (i.e., the property must have been obtained 'by or in return' for the unlawful conduct), the expanded provisions in section 241A are significant. There is retrospective effect in relation to property connected with torture, subject to a twenty-year limitation period, because this is an offence over which the UK applies universal jurisdiction (under section

extent the tension that exists when civil recovery is premised upon an inference of criminality without a predicate criminal conviction. It is possible, however, that future cases will revisit the issues that arise.

[87] See B. Browder, *Red Notice: A True Story of High Finance, Murder, and One Man's Fight for Justice* (Penguin Random House, 2015) for details of the death of Sergei Magnitsky in Russia following the discovery of a 230 million USD tax fraud.

134 of the Criminal Justice Act 1988). As a result, it is conceivable that CROs can now be sought against any property tangentially linked to torture that took place from 31 January 1998 onwards.

Lastly but relatedly, during the third reading of the Sanctions and Anti-Money Laundering Bill's passage through Parliament, after much toing and froing, the UK government changed its position by agreeing to include much more sweeping 'Magnitsky' sanctions. These are much broader powers than those in the Criminal Finances Act 2017. The SAMLA 2018 includes powers to enable a government minister to impose financial and other sanctions in order to 'provide accountability for or be a deterrent to gross violations of human rights, or otherwise promote – (i) compliance with international human rights law, or (ii) respect for human rights'. Other relevant purposes include to 'promote the resolution of armed conflicts or the protection of civilians in conflict zones'; to 'promote compliance with international humanitarian law'; and even to 'promote respect for democracy, the rule of law and good governance'. A minister will be able to designate and sanction persons if he or she has 'reasonable grounds to suspect that that person' is involved or associated with activities.[88] This is an extensive power, in relation to which legal challenges seem to be inevitable despite the presence of certain due process provisions, such as a requirement to notify designated people and entities, the possibility of review, and the requirement for measures to be 'appropriate' (a new standard) having regard to the purpose of any implementing regulations.[89] These are loosely defined concepts which, assuming the power is used, are destined to be interpreted by the courts.

16.8   Transparency Measures

Further developments may lift the lid on opaque financial structures in order to identify beneficial owners and, in some circumstances, the source of their wealth. The potential exists for these to catch corporate involvement in atrocity crimes. Four developments are worth highlighting.

---

[88] In *Youssef* v. *Secretary of State for Foreign and Commonwealth Affairs* [2016] UKSC 3, the Supreme Court unanimously rejected a challenge to such a standard of proof in the context of freezing assets said to be linked to terrorist activity; although Lord Carnwath, in the only judgment, stated (at para. 48) that he found the issue 'more troubling than (seemingly) did the courts below'.

[89] For example, large-scale and difficult litigation is ongoing in the *Bank Mellat* case following a decision by the UK Supreme Court and the European Court of Justice that freezing measures against the bank should not have been taken in relation to the bank's listing under the Iran nuclear sanctions arrangements.

First, since 6 April 2016, UK companies are required to maintain a register of persons with significant control over them (a 'PSC register').[90] A PSC is a person who holds, directly or indirectly, more than 25 per cent of a company's shares or voting rights; or can appoint/remove directors holding majority voting rights and has the right to service or actually exercises significant influence or control over it. The statutory guidance seeks to explain what is meant by 'significant influence or control'. It is an expansive concept and broadly amounts to a person who can direct the company's activities. It is now possible to search a company on the Companies House website or, alternatively, download the entire PSC register, to find out who exerts significant control over a company. Before the advent of this register, researchers were restricted to reviewing a company's annual return and its list of shareholders, but often these are other companies – thereby obfuscating ownership and those who really benefit from corporate structures. Although significant challenges remain, including the verification of the data and the format in which it is presented, the new PSC register is a major change.[91]

Second, in June 2017 the UK introduced a register of beneficial ownership for trusts. As required by the EU's Fourth Anti-Money Laundering Directive, Part 5 of the Money Laundering, Terrorist Financing and Transfer of Funds (Information on the Payer) Regulations 2017 requires trustees of express trusts to report all trusts with tax consequences in the UK, even when those consequences are only occasional. Under the 2017 Regulations, HMRC will create a beneficial ownership register of trusts. There are limitations: it will not be publicly available, it will not apply to statutory, constructive or resulting trusts, and it will be contingent upon the trust incurring UK tax consequences (which some might say is the very thing many trust structures seek to avoid). Notwithstanding these limitations, this new register will be a significant source of centralised information for UK enforcement authorities. Moreover, the EU's Fifth Anti-Money Laundering Directive goes further still, with provisions to increase access to information on beneficial ownership and improve the transparency of information on the ownership of companies as well as

---

[90] The relevant legislation was inserted into Part 21A of the Companies Act 2006 by the Small Enterprise, Business and Employment Act 2015, supplemented by secondary legislation.

[91] For a recent discussion, see Briefing Paper No. 8259, Registers of Beneficial Ownership, House of Commons Library, 15 March 2018, researchbriefings.parliament.uk/ResearchBriefing/Summary/CBP-8259.

trusts.[92] At the time of writing, it is understood that the UK will transpose these requirements into domestic law notwithstanding the UK's exit from the European Union.

Third, the Criminal Finances Act 2017 further amended POCA (via a new section 362A-I) by providing enforcement authorities with a new civil investigatory tool to obtain a High Court order to compel a person to explain the source of their assets. These 'Unexplained Wealth Orders' or UWOs (the temptation to name them Unexplained Finances Orders having been resisted) are directed towards either: (1) persons reasonably suspected of involvement in serious crimes (whether in the UK or overseas); or (2) 'Politically Exposed Persons' from outside the European Economic Area. A respondent can be ordered to explain assets that appear to be disproportionate to their known income. Section 326H POCA further clarifies that the person who holds the targeted property can include UK or foreign corporates. If the respondent fails to comply with a UWO without reasonable excuse, the legislation provides for a rebuttable presumption that the property is recoverable via the civil recovery route discussed above. Making false or misleading disclosures in response to a UWO is a criminal offence. UWOs are therefore transparency measures with a sting. These are intricate provisions destined for litigation, for instance on whether purported explanations comply with the UWO; and how the presumption in favour of civil recovery may be rebutted in practice.[93] UWOs are a further area to monitor for the link between economic crimes and atrocities. It is a major change to English law to provide for a presumption that property is recoverable based solely, in the first instance at least, on a reasonable suspicion of involvement in wrongdoing.

Fourth, the government is working on proposals to create a new register of the beneficial owners of UK property, in particular properties owned by overseas entities. A draft bill was published in mid-2018, with the register to be operational in 2021.[94]

As promising as these changes seem, another dose of caution is needed. Paul Beckett argues that the 'global drive' on beneficial ownership is 'not

---

[92] Directive (EU) 2018/843 of 30 May 2018.

[93] POCA, s. 362D appears to provide that, if the respondent complies or purports to comply, the enforcement authority must simply determine whether or not to take further 'enforcement or regulatory proceedings' in relation to the property.

[94] A Register of Beneficial Owners of Overseas Companies and Other Legal Entities: The Government Response to the Call or Evidence, 22 March 2018, assets.publishing.service. gov.uk/government/uploads/system/uploads/attachment_daxta/file/681844/ ROEBO_Gov_Response_to_Call_for_Evidence.pdf.

correctly targeted and appears half-hearted'.[95] Such measures remain susceptible to 'beneficial ownership avoidance' structures, including statutory purpose trusts in offshore jurisdictions (at common law, non-charitable purpose trusts would be void for want of identifiable beneficiaries and for breach of the rule against perpetuities). Indeed, Beckett concludes that offshore structures are the 'global engines of human right abuse'.[96] These 'orphan structures' have no beneficial owners and various jurisdictions have introduced them in the form of legal persons – that is, the corporate equivalent of a trust. There is therefore a risk that registers of beneficial ownership are 'fighting the wrong war' (or at least the last war).[97] There is significant force in these points, but it remains the case that registers (including the trusts register), so-called Magnitsky powers and UWOs are major changes to the UK's legal landscape. They offer further means to catch war's funders and profiteers and seize their illegitimate gains.

16.9   The Reach of Terrorist Financing Legislation

Numerous pieces of UK legislation, some with controversial reach, target terrorist financing and related matters. Examples include the Terrorism Act 2000, the Anti-terrorism Crime and Security Act 2001, the Prevention of Terrorism Act 2005, the Terrorism Act 2006, the Counter-Terrorism Act 2008 and the Terrorist Asset-Freezing etc. Act 2010.[98] These create extensive obligations on the financial sector which merit much lengthier analysis than is possible here. This section focuses on points that result from recent cases on the definition of terrorism and the relevant *mens rea*.

International lawyers prefer to avoid confusion between the legal regime applicable to terrorism compared to other areas, such as international humanitarian law. The ICRC explains that '[w]hen a situation of

---

[95] Beckett (*supra* n. 55), p. 78.

[96] Ibid., p. 68.

[97] P. Beckett, Orphan Structures: Transparency Initiatives and Counter-Initiatives, 16 April 2018, www.brightlinelaw.co.uk/news/orphan-structures-transparency-initiatives-and-counter-initiatives.html.

[98] The Terrorist Asset Freezing etc. Act 2010 implemented UN Security Resolution 1373, and gives HM Treasury the power to freeze the assets of individuals and groups believed to have been involved in terrorism, and deprive them of access to financial resources. SAMLA 2018 (Schedule 3, Part 2) repeals the Terrorist Asset Freezing Act 2010 (the previous regime for terrorist asset freezing in the UK), such that terrorist asset freezing and other forms of sanctions are now consolidated in one piece of legislation.

violence amounts to an armed conflict, there is little added value in calling such acts "terrorism" because they already constitute war crimes under international humanitarian law'.[99] This may be so at the international level (although even there, terrorism charges have occasionally been pursued). Complex issues arise in UK domestic law, however, as a result of the Supreme Court's judgment in *R v. Gul (Mohammed)* [2013] UKSC 64.

Mr Gul was convicted of disseminating terrorist publications contrary to section 2 of the Terrorism Act 2006. He uploaded videos to the Internet showing attacks against coalition forces in Afghanistan and Iraq, accompanied by inciting commentary. He argued this did not encourage 'terrorism' because the footage showed legitimate self-defence by persons resisting the UK's armed forces. The Supreme Court unanimously dismissed his appeal, holding that the definition of terrorism in section 1 of the Terrorism Act 2000 is far-reaching and intentionally so. The Court held that, although there is support for the idea that, as a matter of international law, terrorism does not extend to acts of insurgents or 'freedom fighters' in non-international armed conflicts, such support falls short of amounting to a general understanding that could be invoked to construe narrowly the domestic provisions on terrorism.

This expansive interpretation has far-reaching implications.[100] One example is that the offences in the Terrorism Act 2000 have a broad *mens rea* test based on whether a person either 'knows' or, notably, 'has reasonable cause to suspect'. In another recent terrorist financing case, the Supreme Court confirmed that the latter test is purely objective and satisfied even if the person did not actually hold any such suspicion.[101] Even with the identification principle discussed above, this standard is more easily attributable to corporate entities. The specific money laundering offence in the Terrorism Act 2000 criminalises dealing with assets, and tilts the burden to the accused person to show that he or she did not *actually* know that the financial arrangements related to terrorist property, and there was *no reasonable cause* for suspicion. A further example is the Terrorism Act 2006, which contains provisions on corporate liability for the offences in that Act, including incitement, attempts and

---

[99] See *Challenges for IHL – terrorism: overview*, ICRC, October 2010, www.icrc.org/en/document/challenges-ihl-terrorism.

[100] See S. Larkin, 'Court Ruling Points MLROs to Wider Terrorism Definition', *Money Laundering Bulletin* (2013) 208.

[101] *R v. AB and CD* [2018] UKSC 36.

aiding and abetting. The broad (domestic law) definition in *R* v. *Gul* together with such objective *mens rea* tests provide greater scope for corporate liability in relation to terrorism offences – acts which international criminal lawyers might otherwise have viewed through a very different lens. Whether UK enforcement authorities would be prepared to pursue corporates implicated in overseas atrocities by using this extended definition of terrorism is another matter.

16.10   Other Legislative Provisions

The recurring theme in this chapter has been that legislation other than the ICC Act 2001 offers better prospects for catching corporates involved in atrocities. Take, for instance, the Cluster Munitions (Prohibitions) Act 2010, which implements the Convention on Cluster Munitions 2008 and creates domestic offences including the use, development, production, acquisition, facilitation of acquisition, possession, transfer and facilitation of transfer of prohibited munitions. It prohibits any person from assisting, encouraging or inducing any person to engage in any such activities.[102] This legislation specifically applies to bodies incorporated in the UK and to conduct in the UK 'or elsewhere'.[103] It provides a defence in section 7 if a charged person neither knew nor suspected, nor had reason to suspect, that the object in question was a prohibited munition. Placing the burden on the corporate in this way means that the offence would be easier to prove, even with the identification principle. Nor is this formulation unique to this particular Act. To some, such offences might seem like an insufficiently robust response: they do not attribute direct responsibility for any underlying atrocity committed using such weapons. Such legislation, if enforced rigorously, could have far-reaching effects.

A further development is the Cultural Property (Armed Conflicts) Act 2017, which enabled the UK to (finally) ratify the 1954 Hague Convention for the Protection of Cultural Property in the Event of Armed Conflict and accede to its two Protocols of 1954 and 1999. The Act creates a criminal offence of dealing in unlawfully exported cultural property.[104] The legislation provides for penalties of confiscation and unlimited fines.[105] A serious limitation, however, is that the offence is

---

[102] Cluster Munitions (Prohibitions) Act 2010; see s. 2 for the full list of prohibited conduct.
[103] Cluster Munitions (Prohibitions) Act 2010, s. 4(3)(c).
[104] Cultural Property (Armed Conflicts) Act 2017, s. 17 specifying that dealing includes acquiring and disposing of cultural property.
[105] Cultural Property (Armed Conflicts) Act 2017, s. 17(6).

limited to property exported from a territory occupied by a state party to the Protocols, or which was the territory of such a state occupied by another state.[106] This appears to exclude territory occupied by ISIS in Syria and Iraq, for example.[107] The UK government's impact assessment published before the legislation was put before Parliament suggested that there might be one case every thirty years. On the other hand, aspects of the dealing offence are broadly framed: section 17(1) provides that the offence is committed if the perpetrator knew or had 'reason to suspect' that the cultural property concerned had been unlawfully exported. Here, too, the broader *mens rea* test would be easier to prove against corporates. It is broader than the corresponding test in the Dealing in Cultural Object (Offences) Act 2003, which requires dishonest dealing 'knowing or believing that the object is tainted', where tainted refers to objects removed from buildings or monuments of historical, architectural or archaeological interest.[108] As long as the identification principle remains the primary basis for corporate criminal liability in the UK, catching corporate funders and profiteers may depend on identifying such tangential offences with broader *mens rea* tests.

16.11   Conclusion

Returning to our arachnological theme, in the Hollywood movie *Spiderman*, Uncle Ben says to Peter Parker: 'Remember, with great power comes great responsibility.'[109] The original 1962 comic differed in a small but significant respect. The line was unattributed, hanging in a text box as follows: 'In this world, with great power there must also

---

[106] Cultural Property (Armed Conflicts) Act 2017, s. 16(1). Further, s. 16(5) provides that the test for 'occupied territory' is drawn from Article 42 of the Regulations respecting the Laws and Customs of War on Land annex to the Convention respecting the Laws and Customs of War on Land (Hague IV) 1907.

[107] However, other legislation may catch such conduct: see Dealing in Cultural Objects (Offences) Act 2003; Export Control (Syria Sanctions) Order 2014; Iraq (United Nations Sanctions) Order 2003.

[108] So far as the author has been able to determine, there has been only one conviction of an individual in the UK under the 2003 Act, and it related to the theft of items from UK churches. Christopher Cooper was sentenced to three years and eight months' imprisonment on 10 May 2016.

[109] Felicity Gerry QC highlighted this line in her keynote address to the 2017 International Bar Association Conference: 'Towards a Global Corporate Criminal Law Act', December 2017, www.felicitygerry.com/felicity-gerry-qc-gives-keynote-address-international-bar-association-conference-2017/. The sentiment has also been attributed to humans including Voltaire and Churchill.

come – great responsibility.'[110] It was an imperative *must*, which Peter's on-screen version retrospectively attributed to his late Uncle Ben. One theme running through *Spiderman* is that Peter decides to use his fantastical powers responsibly. Unfortunately, corporations do not have Spiderman's capacity for self-reflection. The law is therefore humanity's best hope: it is the primary means by which the sentiment from a 1962 comic must be made to stick to war's corporate funders and profiteers.

Yet the web of UK corporate liability to catch war's funders and profiteers is not tightly spun. The UK's incorporation of the Rome Statute into domestic law may not provide for corporate criminal liability after all. There is unnecessary uncertainty over whether UK criminal law can catch corporate involvement atrocities. Even if legislation could be clarified, the identification principle presents significant challenges. And the UK's recent track record of prosecuting corporate wrongdoing is weak.

For now, the most effective webs must shoot from alternative sources. Corporate liability for atrocity crimes may not yet stick in the United Kingdom, but other webs are capable of catching corporate funders and profiteers. Enforcement authorities have significant powers up their sleeves which, if used robustly, could have a major impact on addressing corporate involvement in atrocity crimes. These powers have developed in a reactive and haphazard way. Notwithstanding their disjointed nature, the responsibility to use them, and to do so with some of Uncle Ben's wisdom, is great.

---

[110] S. Lee and S. Ditko, Amazing Fantasy No. 15: 'Spider-Man' (1962), p.13, quoted by Justice Kagan in her majority opinion in Kimble v. Marvel Entertainment LL, 578 U.S. (2015), p. 18.

Asset Recovery at International(ised) Criminal Tribunals

Fines, Forfeiture, and Orders for Reparations

DALEY J. BIRKETT[*]

17.1 Introduction

International(ised) criminal tribunals (ICTs) have traditionally had two tools at their disposal with which to recover assets, whether ill-gotten or otherwise, belonging to persons convicted of international crimes: fines and orders for forfeiture as penalties additional to imprisonment. However, following the establishment of the permanent International Criminal Court (ICC), increasingly victim-oriented ICTs have been equipped with a third tool for asset recovery in international crimes cases: orders for reparations. This tool provides a vehicle through which victims of international crimes might be awarded compensation, among other forms of reparation.

This chapter critically analyses the availability and use of these three asset recovery mechanisms at ICTs from Nuremberg until the post-ICC era. It will be shown that, while the majority of ICTs have been empowered to order fines and forfeiture measures, such procedures have been scarcely utilised in practice. An additional aim of the chapter is to show that the Rome Statute system has influenced the approach toward fines, forfeiture (including protective measures), and orders for reparations taken by a number of ICTs established following its adoption in 1998.

[*] The author would like to thank Nina Jørgensen, Gregory Gordon, Göran Sluiter, Denis Abels, and the two anonymous external reviewers for their comments on earlier drafts of this chapter [d.j.birkett@uva.nl].

17.2   The Post-World War II Military Tribunals

The International Military Tribunal (IMT) was explicitly empowered to order asset forfeiture measures. However, although Article 28 of the IMT Charter afforded the Tribunal 'the right to deprive the convicted person of any stolen property and order its delivery to the Control Council for Germany',[1] this provision was never utilised by the Judges sitting in Nuremberg.[2] The Tribunal found the accused Alfred Rosenberg guilty of war crimes and crimes against humanity based in part upon his 'responsib[ility] for a system of organized plunder of both public and private property throughout the invaded countries of Europe',[3] but it made no orders for restitution against him or other convicted persons under Article 28 of the IMT Charter.[4]

Conversely, the International Military Tribunal for the Far East (IMTFE) had no such explicit power. The IMTFE Charter contains no comparable provision to Article 28 of the IMT Charter, despite the fact that these two ICTs' constituent instruments share several common elements, including with regard to punishment.

As for fines, although neither ICT was explicitly granted the power by its constituent instrument to order fines, it has been suggested that Article 27 of the IMT Charter and Article 16 of the IMTFE Charter did not exclude the possibility of the imposition of financial penalties.[5] These near-verbatim provisions conferred upon the IMT and the IMTFE the power to impose upon a convicted person 'death or such other punishment as shall be determined by it to be just'.[6] Although perhaps more likely to refer to 'the most serious forms of punishment, such as imprisonment',[7] Article 27 of the IMT Charter could arguably have allowed for the imposition of fines by the IMT. Further, Article 16 of

---

[1]   Charter of the International Military Tribunal (adopted 8 August 1945, entered into force 8 August 1945) 82 UNTS 279 (IMT Charter) Art 28.

[2]   For an argument in support of postponing restitution claims, see S. Weil, 'The American Legal Response to the Problem of Holocaust Art' (1999) 4 *Art, Antiquity & Law* 285, 287.

[3]   IMT, 'Judgment of the Nuremberg International Military Tribunal 1946' (1947) 41 *American Journal of International Law* 172(IMT Judgment) 287.

[4]   Ibid. 332. Rosenberg was sentenced to death by hanging.

[5]   R. Young, 'Fines and Forfeiture in International Criminal Justice' in R. Mulgew and D. Abels (eds.), *Research Handbook on the International Penal System* (Edward Elgar, 2016), pp. 102, 103.

[6]   IMT Charter (*supra* n. 1), Art 27; Charter of the International Military Tribunal for the Far East (adopted 19 January 1946, entered into force 19 January 1946) TIAS No 1589 (IMTFE Charter) Art. 16.

[7]   Young (*supra* n. 5), p. 104.

the IMTFE Charter could have enabled the IMTFE to order fines as well as asset forfeiture measures akin to those provided for in Article 28 of the IMT Charter. In other words, the main focus was on the death penalty or imprisonment, and if fines had ever been in question, the two military tribunals could have asserted the power to impose them even though no such power was explicitly conferred by their constituent instruments. Despite this possibility, no such measures were imposed by either ICT.

Control Council Law No. 10, which was promulgated by the victorious Allied powers after World War II to enable the prosecution of those who were not in the category of major war criminals tried in the main proceedings at Nuremberg, contains more extensive fine and asset forfeiture procedures than those contained in the IMT Charter and the IMTFE Charter.[8] Under Article II(3) of Control Council Law No. 10, the tribunals established thereby were able to order the following punishments:

(c) Fine . . . .
(d) Forfeiture of property.
(e) Restitution of property wrongfully acquired.
(f) . . .

> Any property declared to be forfeited or the restitution of which is ordered by the Tribunal shall be delivered to the Control Council for Germany, which shall decide on its disposal.[9]

Notably, fine and forfeiture procedures are not listed in Control Council Law No. 10 as available 'in addition to imprisonment'.[10] Rather, these measures are listed as forms of punishment in their own right. Control Council Law No. 10 also provides for the first *pre-conviction* asset forfeiture procedures in the history of international criminal justice. At this time, however, there was no express provision that the forfeited assets were ultimately to be put to use for the benefit of victims. Article III(1) of Control Council Law No. 10 provides as follows:

> Each occupying authority, within its Zone of Occupation,
>
> (a) shall have the right to cause persons within such Zone suspected of having committed a crime . . . to be arrested and shall take under

---

[8] Control Council Law No. 10 (adopted 20 December 1945, entered into force 20 December 1945) 3 Official Gazette Control Council for Germany 50–55 (Control Council Law No. 10).
[9] Control Council Law No. 10 (*supra* n. 8), Art. II(3).
[10] Cf. IMT Charter (*supra* n. 1), Art. 28.

control the property, real and personal, owned or controlled by the said persons, pending decisions as to its eventual disposition.[11]

Turning to the case law, of the 142 convicted persons in the 12 trials carried out in the American zone of occupation, only the industrialist Alfred Krupp was ordered to forfeit property under Control Council Law No. 10.[12] Moreover, the United States High Commissioner for Germany, John McCloy, later rescinded this forfeiture order,[13] as recommended by the Advisory Board on Clemency for War Criminals.[14] McCloy reasoned as follows:

> This is the sole case of confiscation decreed against any defendant by the Nuremberg courts. Even those guilty of personal participation in the most heinous crimes have not suffered confiscation of their property and I am disposed to feel that confiscation in this single case constitutes discrimination against this defendant unjustified by any considerations attaching peculiarly to him. General confiscation of property is not a usual element in our judicial system and is generally repugnant to American concepts of justice[.][15]

The reasons given by McCloy in support of his decision to rescind the forfeiture order against Krupp are unconvincing. As to his first ground, that is, the discrimination between Krupp and other convicts, although 'literally correct, . . . it conveniently overlooked the difference between confiscating the property of an industrialist and confiscating the property of a soldier or government official'.[16] As to the second ground provided by McCloy, Article II(3) of Control Council Law No. 10 explicitly allowed the tribunals to order the penalty of forfeiture. In addition, American law did not apply to the trials conducted under Control Council Law No. 10. As a result, according to Kevin Heller, McCloy's invocation of American law 'to trump a specific provision of Law No. 10 was . . . *ultra vires*'.[17]

---

[11] Control Council Law No. 10 (*supra* n. 8), Art. III.
[12] US Military Tribunal Nuremberg, Judgment of 31 July 1948, in Trials of War Criminals before the Nuremberg Military Tribunals under Control Council Law No. 10, Vol. IX, 1449–50. See also K. J. Heller, *The Nuremberg Military Tribunals and the Origins of International Criminal Law* (Oxford University Press, 2011), p. 313.
[13] McCloy had the power to do so having created the Advisory Board on Clemency for War Criminals, with the support of then Secretary of State Dean Acheson. See Heller (*supra* n. 12), p. 344 describing Acheson's support as 'reluctant'.
[14] See *Landsberg: A Documentary Report* (Office of the US High Commissioner for Germany 1951) 10. See also Heller (*supra* n. 12), p. 355.
[15] Ibid.
[16] Heller (*supra* n. 12), p. 355.
[17] Ibid.

The post-World War II military tribunals consequently did not lack the power under their constituent instruments to order fines and forfeiture measures. Nor, as Conor McCarthy has maintained, did those convicted under Control Council Law No. 10 want for wealth;[18] indeed, several affluent industrialists and financiers were convicted of international crimes by the Control Council Law No. 10 tribunals.[19] Instead, these tribunals either focused on sentencing convicted persons with the death penalty and periods of imprisonment or other interests prevailed, as in the case of the decision by John McCloy to revoke the forfeiture order issued against Alfred Krupp. Nonetheless, the inclusion of reasonably broad fine and asset forfeiture measures at this nascent stage of development of the project of international criminal justice is notable.

17.3 The Ad Hoc International Criminal Tribunals

After the Cold War, the UN Security Council (UNSC) established the International Criminal Tribunal for the Former Yugoslavia (ICTY) and the International Criminal Tribunal for Rwanda (ICTR) in response to the commission of mass atrocities in the former Yugoslavia[20] and Rwanda,[21] respectively. As for asset forfeiture procedures, Article 24(3) of the ICTY Statute permits the Trial Chamber, at the sentencing phase of proceedings, to order forfeiture of assets as follows: 'In addition to imprisonment, the Trial Chambers may order the return of any property and proceeds acquired by criminal conduct, including by means of duress, to their rightful owners.'[22] Article 23(3) of the ICTR Statute is identical to Article 24(3) of the ICTY Statute.[23] The ad hoc tribunals were therefore empowered by their constituent instruments to order post-conviction forfeiture measures – but not fines – as a penalty additional to imprisonment, similar to the powers afforded to the IMT.[24] However, Rule 61 of the Rules of Procedure and Evidence of the ICTY and the

---

[18] C. McCarthy, *Reparations and Victim Support in the International Criminal Court* (Cambridge University Press, 2012), pp. 44–5.

[19] Ibid.

[20] See UNSC Res 827 (18 May 1993) UN Doc S/RES/827.

[21] See UNSC Res 955 (8 November 1994) UN Doc S/RES/955.

[22] Statute of the International Tribunal, UN Doc S/25704, Annex (ICTY Statute) Art. 24(3).

[23] See Statute of the International Tribunal for Rwanda, UNSC Res 955 (8 November 1994) UN Doc S/RES/1995, Annex (ICTR Statute) Art. 23(3) ('In addition to imprisonment, the Trial Chambers may order the return of any property and proceeds acquired by criminal conduct, including by means of duress, to their rightful owners.').

[24] Cf. IMT Charter (*supra* n. 1), Art. 28.

ICTR extends the power of Trial Chambers to order pre-conviction asset freezing measures more akin to those granted to the military tribunals established under Control Council Law No. 10:

> (D) ... Upon request by the Prosecutor or *proprio motu*, after having heard the Prosecutor, the Trial Chamber may order a State or States to adopt provisional measures to freeze the assets of the accused, without prejudice to the rights of third parties.[25]

This Rule was implicated in 1999 in respect of former Serbian President Slobodan Milošević and his four co-accused – Milan Milutinović, Nikola Šainovic, Dragoljub Ojdanić, and Vlajko Stojiljković.[26] In response to the application for the freezing of assets by the ICTY Prosecutor, Judge David Hunt ordered 'all States Members of the United Nations [to] make inquiries to discover whether the accused (or any of them) have assets located in their territory and, if so, adopt provisional measures to freeze such assets, without prejudice to the rights of third parties, until the accused are taken into custody'.[27] Shortly after Judge Hunt's Decision, Switzerland took steps to freeze assets in the possession of Milošević and his co-accused located on its territory.[28]

Ruling on two applications by African NGOs to appear as *amicus curiae*, ICTR trial chambers have confirmed that orders for restitution could have been made only if the accused person(s) had been charged with the unlawful taking of property.[29] No forfeiture order was granted by the ICTR. As for pre-conviction measures, in 1999, the ICTR Prosecutor requested the French Ministry of Justice to freeze bank accounts in the name of Félicien Kabuga,[30] who is accused of genocide

---

[25] ICTY, Rules of Procedure and Evidence, as amended on 8 July 2015 (adopted 11 February 1994, entered into force 14 March 1994) UN Doc IT/32/Rev. 50 (ICTY RPE) Rule 61; ICTR, Rules of Procedure and Evidence, as amended on 13 May 2015 (adopted 29 June 1995, entered into force 29 June 1995) UN Doc ITR/3/Rev.23 (ICTR RPE) Rule 61.

[26] ICTY, *Prosecutor v. Slobodan Milošević and others* (Decision on Review of Indictment and Application for Consequential Orders) IT-02-54 (24 May 1999).

[27] Ibid., para 38.

[28] See Décision de l'Office fédéral de la police dans l'affaire *Milosevic Slobodan* et autres (23 June 1999), www.admin.ch/opc/fr/federal-gazette/1999/4796.pdf. The freezing measures against Milošević's assets were lifted following his death in March 2006. See McCarthy (*supra* n. 18), p. 47.

[29] See ICTR, *Prosecutor v. Alfred Musema* (Decision on an Application by African Concern for Leave to Appear as Amicus Curiae) ICTR-96-13-T (17 March 1999) paras. 12–14; ICTR, *Prosecutor v. Théoneste Bagosora and others* (Decision on Amicus Curiae Request by African Concern) ICTR-98-41-T (23 March 2004) paras. 5–11.

[30] See ICTR, *Miscellaneous–Kabuga Family* (Appeal of the Family of Felicien Kabuga against Decisions of the Prosecutor and President of the Tribunal) 01-A (22 November 2002).

and crimes against humanity and remained at large until 2020. The French authorities complied with the request,[31] while the Prosecutor has also sought the cooperation of Kenya in adopting such measures against Kabuga.[32]

The Statute of the International Residual Mechanism for Criminal Tribunals (MICT) largely reverts to the approach of the ICTY and the ICTR toward the forfeiture of assets (including protective measures).[33] However, as the MICT was established to conduct some of the remaining tasks of the ICTY and the ICTR at the time of their closure,[34] its approach to forfeiture is arguably best regarded as a continuation of that adopted by its predecessors rather than a departure from the post-Rome Statute approach.

The inclusion of asset forfeiture powers, including pre-conviction measures, in the legal frameworks of the two ad hoc tribunals created by the UNSC in the mid-1990s represents continuity in the approach adopted in the establishment of the post-World War II military tribunals. These powers were used more extensively by the ICTY and the ICTR than their predecessors. At the same time, however, the ICTY and the ICTR lacked the power to order fines and neglected to utilise the asset forfeiture measures at their disposal, despite clear indications that certain accused persons possessed property and proceeds susceptible to such measures. This underuse can be imputed, at least in part, to the absence of a holding related to the unlawful taking of property, as indicated in the decisions by ICTR trial chambers in *Musema* and *Bagasora and others*.

17.4   The Rome Statute System

17.4.1   Fine and Forfeiture Measures

The Rome Statute provides for the imposition of fines and forfeiture as penalties in addition to imprisonment. Under Article 77(2) of the Rome Statute:

[31] Ibid.
[32] See 'Statement by Justice Hassan B. Jallow Prosecutor of the ICTR, to the UN Security Council' (4 June 2009), http://ictr-archive09.library.cornell.edu/ENGLISH/speeches/jallow090604.html.
[33] Statute of the International Residual Mechanism for Criminal Tribunals, UNSC Res 1966 (22 December 2010) UN Doc S/RES/1966, Annex 1 (MICT Statute) Art. 22(4); MICT, Rules of Procedure and Evidence, as amended on 26 September 2016 (adopted 8 June 2012, entered into force 8 June 2012) UN Doc MICT/1/Rev/2 (MICT RPE) Rule 63(D).
[34] UNSC Res 1966 (22 December 2010) UN Doc S/RES/1966, preamble ('*reaffirming* the need to establish an *ad hoc* mechanism to carry out a number of essential functions of the Tribunals ... after the closure of the Tribunals') (emphasis in original).

In addition to imprisonment, the Court may order:

(a) A fine under the criteria provided for in the [RPE];
(b) A forfeiture of proceeds, property and assets derived directly or indirectly from that crime, without prejudice to the rights of bona fide third parties.[35]

The Rome Statute definition of proceeds, property, and assets prone to forfeiture is noteworthy when compared with that employed at the ad hoc ICTs. In contrast to the terminology adopted in the Statutes of the ICTY and the ICTR, 'property and proceeds acquired by criminal conduct',[36] the ICC is also able to order forfeiture of proceeds, property, and assets derived *indirectly* from the Rome Statute crime(s) of which the convicted person is found guilty.[37] According to Conor McCarthy: 'In sum, Article 77(2)(b) permits the Court to order the forfeiture of property obtained as part of the *actus reus* of the offence; property for the acquisition of which the crime was committed; property purchased with or pursuant to the sale of property directly deriving from the offence in one of the two foregoing ways; and profits from property obtained in any of these ways.'[38] Moreover, the Court's asset-freezing powers are much wider than those afforded to earlier international criminal justice mechanisms. Pursuant to Article 93(1)(k) of the Rome Statute, the ICC can request states parties to identify, trace, freeze, and seize assets, proceeds, property, and/or instrumentalities of crimes 'in relation to investigations or prosecutions'.[39] The Pre-Trial Chamber can request such measures, under Article 57(3)(e) of the Rome Statute, 'after a warrant of arrest or a summons has been issued'.[40] In other words, the ICC can request an asset freeze at the pre-trial phase of proceedings, before an accused person has been arrested.

The first fines to be ordered by the Court were those against Jean-Pierre Bemba Gombo, a former Vice President of the Democratic Republic of the Congo, and his co-accused, Aimé Kilolo Musamba. Having been convicted by Trial Chamber VII of offences against the

---

[35] Rome Statute of the International Criminal Court (adopted 17 July 1998, entered into force 1 July 2002) 2187 UNTS 90 (Rome Statute) Art. 77(2).
[36] ICTY Statute (*supra* n. 22), Art. 24; ICTR Statute (*supra* n. 23), Art. 23.
[37] Rome Statute (*supra* n. 35), Art. 77(2)(b).
[38] McCarthy (*supra* n. 18), p. 202.
[39] Rome Statute (*supra* n. 35), Art. 93(1)(k).
[40] Rome Statute (*supra* n. 35), Art. 57(3)(e).

administration of justice, Bemba and Kilolo were fined 300,000 EUR and 30,000 EUR, respectively.[41]

Given the relatively few cases to have reached the sentencing phase at the ICC,[42] it is perhaps unsurprising that the Court had issued only two fines by late 2018 – and, moreover, in the context of proceedings concerning offences against the administration of justice, not international crimes. In the *Bemba and others* Sentencing Decision, Trial Chamber VII took into consideration not only 'Bemba's culpability' but also his 'solvency'.[43] On the other hand, Trial Chamber III, in sentencing Bemba for crimes against humanity and war crimes, offences of which he was acquitted on appeal,[44] did not order fine or forfeiture measures, 'noting that the parties and Legal Representative do not request the imposition of a fine or order of forfeiture'.[45] The lack of enthusiasm for the imposition of fines and asset forfeiture measures for international crimes seen in the practice of the ICTY, the ICTR, and the post-World War II military tribunals appears to have resurfaced in the sentencing practice of the ICC, despite Bemba's wealth.

In the *Bemba and others* Sentencing Decision, the Trial Chamber observed that the contents of Bemba's bank account had been transferred to the Court in order to meet his defence expenses.[46] In addition, in the

---

[41] See ICC, *Prosecutor v. Jean-Pierre Bemba Gombo and others* (Decision on Sentence pursuant to Article 76 of the Statute) ICC-01/05-01/13-2123-Corr (22 March 2017) (*Bemba and others* Sentencing Decision) Disposition. The fines were confirmed in ICC, *Prosecutor v. Jean-Pierre Bemba Gombo and others* (Decision Re-sentencing Mr Jean-Pierre Bemba Gombo, Mr Aimé Kilolo Musamba, and Mr Jean-Jacques Mangenda Kabongo) ICC-01/05-01/13-2312 (17 September 2018) (*Bemba and others* Re-sentencing Decision) Disposition.

[42] As of June 2020, the cases against Thomas Lubanga Dyilo, Germain Katanga, and Ahmad Al Faqi Al Mahdi are at the reparations phase.

[43] *Bemba and others* Sentencing Decision (*supra* n. 41), para. 261.

[44] The ICC Appeals Chamber acquitted Bemba of war crimes and crimes against humanity on 8 June 2018, thereby vacating his sentence of imprisonment for these crimes. See ICC, *Prosecutor v. Jean-Pierre Bemba Gombo* (Judgment on the appeal of Mr Jean-Pierre Bemba Gombo against Trial Chamber III's 'Judgment pursuant to Article 74 of the Statute') ICC-01/05-01/08-3636-Red (8 June 2018); ICC, *Prosecutor v. Jean-Pierre Bemba Gombo* (Decision on the appeals of the Prosecutor and Mr Jean-Pierre Bemba Gombo against the decision of Trial Chamber III of 21 June 2016 entitled 'Decision on Sentence pursuant to Article 76 of the Statute') ICC-01/05-01/08-3637 (8 June 2018) para. 8 ('As a result of the Appeal Judgment on Conviction, there is no basis for any sentence to be imposed on Mr Bemba in the present case and the Sentencing Decision therefore ceases to have effect.').

[45] ICC, *Prosecutor v. Jean-Pierre Bemba Gombo* (Decision on Sentence pursuant to Article 76 of the Statute) ICC-01/05-01/08-3399 (21 June 2016) para. 95.

[46] *Bemba and others* Sentencing Decision (*supra* n. 41), para. 241.

Bemba and others Re-sentencing Decision, issued following a partially successful appeal by the prosecutor against the original decision on sentencing handed down by Trial Chamber VII,[47] the same Trial Chamber held that 'Mr Bemba may use his frozen assets to pay his fine, and once it is paid the asset freezing order issued in this case ceases to have effect with respect to him'.[48] Trial Chamber VII held similarly with respect to Kilolo's frozen bank account.[49]

Seized assets can thus be used to pay legal fees,[50] but also, if a convicted person is not considered to be indigent, to provide reparations to victims, even if the conviction is for an offence against the administration of justice rather than an international crime. Indeed, one of the principal functions of the fines and forfeiture system in the Rome Statute is to serve as a mechanism facilitating the enforcement of reparation awards. This purpose is confirmed by Article 57(3)(e) of the Rome Statute, which provides that pre-trial protective measures requested by the Court for the purpose of eventual forfeiture are intended 'in particular for the ultimate benefit of victims'.[51] This is also evidenced by the Court's case law. In its 2012 'Decision establishing the principles and procedures to be applied to reparations',[52] the first decision on reparations issued by a Chamber of the ICC,[53] Trial Chamber I expressed the following view: 'The Statute and [RPE] introduce a system of reparations that reflects a growing recognition in international criminal law that there is a need to go beyond the notion of punitive justice, towards a solution which is more inclusive, encourages participation and recognises the need to

---

[47] ICC, *Prosecutor v. Jean-Pierre Bemba Gombo and others* (Judgment on the appeals of the Prosecutor, Mr Jean-Pierre Bemba Gombo, Mr Fidèle Babala Wandu, and Mr Narcisse Arido against the decision of Trial Chamber VII entitled 'Decision on Sentence pursuant to Article 76 of the Statute') ICC-01/05-01/13-2276-Red (8 March 2018) paras. 359, 361. See also *Bemba and others Re-sentencing Decision (supra* n. 41), para. 3.

[48] *Bemba and others* Re-sentencing Decision *(supra* n. 41), para. 128.

[49] Ibid, para. 109.

[50] See *Bemba and others* Sentencing Decision *(supra* n. 41), para. 241. See also, generally, ICC, *Prosecutor v. Jean-Pierre Bemba Gombo* (Decision on the Defence's Application for Lifting the Seizure of Assets and Request for Cooperation to the Competent Authorities of Portugal) ICC-01/05-01/08-251-Anx (10 October 2008); ICC, *Prosecutor v. Jean-Pierre Bemba Gombo* (Decision on the Second Defence's Application for Lifting the Seizure of Assets and Request for Cooperation to the Competent Authorities of the Republic of Portugal) ICC-01/05-01/08-249 (14 November 2008).

[51] Rome Statute *(supra* n. 35), Art. 57(3)(e).

[52] ICC, *Prosecutor v. Thomas Lubanga Dyilo* (Decision Establishing the Principles and Procedures to be Applied to Reparations) ICC-01/04-01/06-2904 (7 August 2012) (*Lubanga* Reparations Decision).

[53] Ibid., para 20.

provide effective remedies for victims.'[54] Further, in the *Bemba and others* Sentencing Decision, Trial Chamber VII ordered that the proceeds of the fines were to be transferred to the Court's Trust Fund for Victims (TFV),[55] which underscores the reparative nature of the Rome Statute.[56]

17.4.2   Orders for Reparations

If ultimately forfeited after conviction, Article 79 of the Rome Statute provides that assets collected through fines and forfeiture can be transferred to the TFV.[57] Article 75(2) of the Rome Statute further provides as follows: 'The Court may make an order directly against a convicted person specifying appropriate reparations to, or in respect of, victims, including restitution, compensation and rehabilitation. Where appropriate, the Court may order that the award for reparations be made through the Trust Fund provided for in article 79.'[58] Again, as relatively few cases before the ICC have reached the reparations phase of proceedings,[59] the Court has issued orders for reparations[60] directly against convicted persons under Article 75(2) on only three occasions at the time of writing, in the cases against Thomas Lubanga Dyilo, Germain Katanga, and Ahmad Al Faqi Al Mahdi. The first order for reparations issued by the ICC was directed against Thomas Lubanga on 3 March 2015,[61] without specifying his individual financial liability,

---

[54] Ibid., para 177 referring to UNGA 'Basic Principles and Guidelines on the Right to a Remedy and Reparation for Victims of Gross Violations of International Human Rights Law and Serious Violations of International Humanitarian Law', UN Doc A/ RES/60/147 (21 March 2006).

[55] *Bemba and others* Sentencing Decision (*supra* n. 41), paras. 199, 262. See also *Bemba and others* Re-sentencing Decision (*supra* n. 41), paras. 109, 128.

[56] On reparative justice, see C. McCarthy, 'Reparations Under the Rome Statute of the International Criminal Court and Reparative Justice Theory' (2009) 3 *International Journal of Transitional Justice* 250.

[57] Rome Statute (*supra* n. 35), Art. 79(2).

[58] Ibid., Art. 75.

[59] See *supra* n. 42.

[60] ICC Trial Chamber I established that '[r]eparations fulfil two main purposes that are enshrined in the Statute: they oblige those responsible for serious crimes to repair the harm they caused to the victims and they enable the Chamber to ensure that offenders account for their acts'. *Lubanga* Reparations Decision (*supra* n. 52), para. 179. An 'order for reparations' gives effect to this procedure.

[61] ICC, *Prosecutor v. Thomas Lubanga Dyilo* (Order for Reparations) ICC-01/04-01/06-3129-AnxA (3 March 2015).

which was later set at 10 million USD.[62] On 24 March 2017, Trial Chamber II issued an order for reparations against Germain Katanga, finding that, despite his indigence, he was liable for the sum of 1 million USD.[63] Because of Katanga's inability to pay, the Trial Chamber directed the TFV to consider using the resources at its disposal to implement the order.[64] As for Ahmad Al Faqi Al Mahdi, Trial Chamber VIII issued a reparations order against him on 24 March 2017, setting his total individual financial liability at 2.7 million EUR.[65] Although the reparations order was partially amended by the Appeals Chamber in March 2018,[66] the total amount remained undisturbed.

The evident turn toward reparative justice in the Rome Statute has been attributed to a 'growing attention to victims within national criminal justice systems and . . . a reaction to criticism of the manner in which

[62] ICC, *Prosecutor* v. *Thomas Lubanga Dyilo* (Corrected version of the 'Decision Setting the Size of the Reparations Award for which Thomas Lubanga Dyilo is Liable') ICC-01/04-01/06-3379-Red-Corr-tENG (21 December 2017).

[63] ICC, *Prosecutor* v. *Germain Katanga* (Order for Reparations pursuant to Article 75 of the Statute) ICC-01/04-01/07-3728-tENG (24 March 2017) para. 264. Although Katanga was found to be indigent, Trial Chamber II observed that, because of the potential future identification and freezing of his property and assets and the continued monitoring of his financial situation, 'Katanga's current financial situation cannot be regarded as material to the determination of the size of the reparations award for which he is liable'. Ibid., para. 246. See also ICC, *Prosecutor* v. *Thomas Lubanga Dyilo* (Judgment on the appeals against the 'Decision establishing the principles and procedures to be applied to reparations' of 7 August 2012 with AMENDED order for reparations (Annex A) and public annexes 1 and 2, ICC-01/04-01/06-3129 (3 March 2015) paras. 102–5.

[64] Ibid., para. 342. The TFV is funded from four sources: '(a) Voluntary contributions from governments, international organizations, individuals, corporations and other entities, in accordance with relevant criteria adopted by the Assembly of States Parties; (b) Money and other property collected through fines or forfeiture transferred to the Trust Fund if ordered by the Court pursuant to article 79, paragraph 2, of the Rome Statute . . .; (c) Resources collected through awards for reparations if ordered by the Court pursuant to rule 98 of the Rules of Procedure and Evidence; [and] (d) Such resources, other than assessed contributions, as the Assembly of States Parties may decide to allocate to the Trust Fund.' Regulations of the Trust Fund for Victims, ICC-ASP/4/Res.3 (3 December 2005) Regulation 21. According to Sara Kendall, compared with the Court's four organs, the 'material resources [of the TFV] are arguably the most tenuous given their voluntary nature, as the Fund relies heavily on annual pledges from interested states'. S. Kendall, 'Commodifying Global Justice: Economies of Accountability at the International Criminal Court' (2015) 13 *Journal of International Criminal Justice* 113, 124.

[65] ICC, *Prosecutor* v. *Ahmad Al Faqi Al Mahdi* (Reparations Order) ICC-01/12-01/15-236 (17 August 2017) para. 134.

[66] ICC, *Prosecutor* v. *Ahmad Al Faqi Al Mahdi* (Public redacted Judgment on the appeal of the victims against the 'Reparations Order') ICC-01/12-01/15-259-Red2 (8 March 2018).

victims' concerns were considered by the ICTY and the ICTR'.[67] Further, Shuichi Furuya points to the attention to victims in 'universal and regional human rights systems'.[68] But this turn can also arguably be ascribed to a shift toward more inquisitorial proceedings – which generally provide for more extensive victim reparation (and participation) rights – on the international plane. Several ICTs, discussed in the following section, are based, at least partly, in national jurisdictions with civil law legal traditions. Such a development is likely to lead to a more prominent role for victims in proceedings in view of the more active participation of victims (or their legal representatives) in a number of civil law systems.[69]

17.5   ICTs Established after the Adoption of the Rome Statute

It is not the aim of this chapter to demonstrate uniformity in the approach of ICTs to the issue of fines and forfeiture; rather, it seeks to demonstrate that while most ICTs have been able to order such measures, they have been barely utilised in practice. This said, after the adoption of the Rome Statute, a more victim-oriented approach to asset forfeiture was followed in the legal instruments of number of ICTs.

17.5.1   The Special Court for Sierra Leone

There is no provision for fines in the governing documents of the Special Court for Sierra Leone (SCSL), which was established in 2002. However, Article 19(3) of the SCSL Statute provides for the forfeiture of assets as

[67] C. Evans, *The Right to Reparation in International Law for Victims of Armed Conflict* (Cambridge University Press, 2012), pp. 87–8. See also A.-M. de Brouwer and M. Heikkilä, 'Victim Issues: Participation, Protection, Reparation, and Assistance', in G. Sluiter and others (eds.), *International Criminal Procedure: Principles and Rules* (Oxford University Press, 2013), pp. 1299, 1300.
[68] F. Shuichi, 'Victim Participation, Reparations and Reintegration as Historical Building Blocks of International Criminal Law', in M. Bergsmo and others (eds.), *Historical Origins of International Criminal Law: Volume 4* (Torkel Opsahl Academic EPublisher, 2015), pp. 837, 839.
[69] See, e.g., C. P. Trumbull IV, 'The Victims of Victim Participation in International Criminal Proceedings' (2008) 29 *Michigan Journal of International Law* 777, 778 ('In these countries, the victim (or often the victim's legal representative) can request investigatory measures, review the evidence against the accused, submit declarations, present evidence, cross-examine witnesses, and make closing arguments.'); S. Zappalà, 'Comparative Models and the Enduring Relevance of the Accusatorial–Inquisitorial Dichotomy', in Sluiter and others, *International Criminal Procedure: Principles and Rules* (*supra* n. 67), pp. 44, 51.

follows: 'In addition to imprisonment, the Trial Chamber may order the forfeiture of the property, proceeds and any assets acquired unlawfully or by criminal conduct, and their return to their rightful owner or to the State of Sierra Leone.'[70] Rule 104 of the SCSL RPE also allowed the tribunal to order provisional measures as follows:

(A) After a judgement of conviction ... the Trial Chamber, at the request of the Prosecutor or at its own initiative, may hold a special hearing to determine the matter of property forfeiture, including the proceeds thereof, and may in the meantime order such provisional measures for the preservation and protection of the property or proceeds as it considers appropriate.

(B) The determination may extend to such property or proceeds, even in the hands of third parties not otherwise connected with the crime, for which the convicted person has been found guilty. [71]

The limited SCSL case law on this issue, limited to one decision on a request for the freezing of bank accounts,[72] demonstrates an approach akin to that at the ICTY and the ICTR, requiring 'clear and convincing evidence that the targeted assets have a nexus with criminal conduct or were otherwise illegally acquired'.[73] The prosecutor having failed, in the opinion of the Trial Chamber, to adduce sufficient evidence to establish this nexus,[74] the motion to freeze the accounts of Sam Hinga Norman was rejected.[75]

The SCSL did not impose asset forfeiture as a penalty against any convicted person, despite making several findings of guilt in respect of the war crime of pillage,[76] a conspicuously profitable offence,[77] and

---

[70] Statute of the Special Court for Sierra Leone (adopted 16 January 2002, entered into force on 12 April 2002) 2178 UNTS 138 (SCSL Statute) Art. 19.

[71] SCSL, Rules of Procedure and Evidence, as amended on 31 May 2012 (adopted 16 January 2002, entered into force 12 April 2002) (SCSL RPE) Rule 104.

[72] See SCSL, *Prosecutor v. Sam Hinga Norman and others* (Norman – Decision on *Inter Partes* Motion by Prosecution to Freeze the Account of the Accused Sam Hinga Norman at Union Trust Bank (Sl) Limited or at Any Other Bank in Sierra Leone) SCSL-04-14-PT (19 April 2004).

[73] Ibid., para. 13.

[74] Ibid., para. 16.

[75] Ibid., para. 18.

[76] See SCSL, *Prosecutor v. Issa Hassan Sesay and others* (Judgment) SCSL-04-15-T (2 March 2009) (*Sesay and others* Judgment) paras. 679 (in respect of Issa Hassan Sesay), 683 (in respect of Morris Kallon), 686 (in respect of Augustine Gbao).

[77] See M. G. Martínez, 'Forfeiture of Assets at the International Criminal Court: The Short Arm of International Criminal Justice' (2014) 12 *Journal of International Criminal Justice* 193, 199–201.

also hearing evidence that civilians were forced to mine diamonds.[78] But bank accounts belonging to persons accused of crimes under the jurisdiction of the tribunal were frozen at the request of the SCSL. In 2003, Switzerland froze assets amounting to approximately 2 million CHF in the name of former Liberian President Charles Taylor, his relatives, members of his regime, and his company.[79] However, in 2006, the SCSL Principal Defender determined Taylor to be 'partially indigent'[80] and no order for forfeiture was ultimately made against him.[81]

Similar to the ad hoc ICTs, the SCSL does not allow for orders for reparations to be made directly against convicted persons. However, Rule 105 of the SCSL RPE does provide that victims of crimes for which persons were found guilty at the SCSL may attempt to seek compensation in a national court 'or other competent body'.[82] Rather than establishing reparation mechanisms similar to those in the Rome Statute, as will be further discussed in Section 17.5.5, the drafters of the constituent instruments of several ICTs preferred victims to claim reparations under the relevant provisions of national law. This might be indicative of another trend, namely that reparations procedures at ICTs have developed based on individual experience and that there is no single model.

17.5.2   The Special Panels for Serious Crimes

The Special Panels for Serious Crimes (SPSC) in East Timor were empowered by their constituent instrument to impose fines and asset forfeiture measures against persons convicted of international and serious domestic offences falling under their jurisdiction. Section 10.1 of Regulation No. 2000/15 on the Establishment of Panels with Exclusive Jurisdiction over Serious Criminal Offences empowered the SPSC to impose the following penalties:

[78] See, e.g., *Sesay and others* Judgment (*supra* n. 76), paras. 945, 1415, 1433.
[79] See Swiss Confederation, Federal Office of Justice, 'Taylor's Accounts Blocked as Provisional Measure: Legal Assistance Requested by Special Court for Sierra Leone' (Press Release, Bern, Switzerland, 23 June 2013), www.bj.admin.ch/bj/en/home/aktuell/news/2003/2003-06-230.html.
[80] SCSL, *Prosecutor v. Charles Ghankay Taylor* (Principal Defender's Determination of Mr Charles Ghankay Taylor's Indigence) SCSL-03-01-I-85 (3 April 2006). This was a provisional finding.
[81] See SCSL, *Prosecutor v. Charles Ghankay Taylor* (Sentencing Judgment) SCSL-03-01-T (30 May 2012).
[82] SCSL RPE (*supra* n. 71), Rule 105.

(b) A fine up to a maximum of US\$ 500,000.

(c) A forfeiture of proceeds, property and assets derived directly or indirectly from the crime, without prejudice to the rights of *bona fide* third parties.[83]

The UN Transitional Administration in East Timor (UNTAET), which promulgated the constituent instrument of the SPSC, also legislated for the possible formation of a Trust Fund. Section 25 of Regulation No. 2000/15 provides as follows:

25.1 A Trust Fund may be established ... for the benefit of victims of crimes within the jurisdiction of the panels, and of the families of such victims.

25.2 The panels may order money and other property collected through fines, forfeiture, foreign donors or other means to be transferred to the Trust Fund.

25.3 The Trust Fund shall be managed according to criteria to be determined by an UNTAET directive.[84]

This provision reflects Article 79 of the Rome Statute, which establishes the TFV.[85] In practice, such a Trust Fund was never established by UNTAET.

17.5.3   The Iraqi High Tribunal

The influence of the Rome Statute can also be seen in Article 24(f) of the Statute of the Iraqi High Tribunal (IHT), which was established under Iraqi law in 2005 to try Iraqi nationals and residents for international crimes and other violations of Iraqi law. Article 24(f) of the IHT Statute provides as follows with regard to forfeiture: 'The Trial Chambers may order the forfeiture of proceeds, property or assets derived directly or indirectly from that crime, without prejudice to the rights of the bona fide

---

[83] Regulation No. 2000/15 on the Establishment of Panels with Exclusive Jurisdiction over Serious Criminal Offences (6 June 2008) UN Doc UNTAET/REG/2000/15 (Regulation 2000/15) Section 10.

[84] Ibid., Section 25.

[85] Rome Statute (*supra* n. 35), Art. 79 ('1. A Trust Fund shall be established by decision of the Assembly of States Parties for the benefit of victims of crimes within the jurisdiction of the Court, and of the families of such victims. 2. The Court may order money and other property collected through fines or forfeiture to be transferred, by order of the Court, to the Trust Fund. 3. The Trust Fund shall be managed according to criteria to be determined by the Assembly of States Parties.').

third parties.'[86] The IHT was not empowered by its constituent instrument or Rules of Procedure and Evidence to impose fines as a penalty or to order protective, pre-conviction measures. Additionally, similar to the approach at the ICTY, the ICTR, and the SCSL, the governing documents of the IHT do not allow orders for reparations to be made directly against convicted persons. Of course, each ICT does not, and is not expected to, replicate the institutional design of its predecessors. Where there are discrepancies, these can be attributed to various factors, including but not limited to the tribunal's applicable law.

17.5.4 The Extraordinary Chambers in the Courts of Cambodia

The Extraordinary Chambers in the Courts of Cambodia (ECCC), established jointly by the UN and the government of Cambodia, is also able to order forfeiture of assets as a penalty in addition to imprisonment, but it cannot order fines. According to Article 39 of the ECCC Law, one of the tribunal's constituent instruments:[87] 'In addition to imprisonment, the Extraordinary Chamber of the trial court may order the confiscation of personal property, money, and real property acquired unlawfully or by criminal conduct. The confiscated property shall be returned to the State.'[88] This resembles the approach in the constituent instruments of the ICTY, the ICTR, and the SCSL. At the time of writing, the ECCC has yet to order forfeiture as a penalty, although inquiries were made into the assets of KAING Guek Eav

---

[86] Law of the Supreme Iraqi Criminal Tribunal (adopted 18 October 2005, entered into force 18 October 2005) Official Gazette of the Republic of Iraq, No. 4006, 18 October 2005 (IHT Statute) Art. 24(f).

[87] The ECCC were established jointly by the Law on the Establishment of Extraordinary Chambers in the Courts of Cambodia for the Prosecution of Crimes Committed during the Period of Democratic Kampuchea, with inclusion of amendments as promulgated on 27 October 2004, NS/RKM/1004/006 (ECCC Law) and the Agreement Between the United Nations and the Royal Government of Cambodia Concerning the Prosecution under Cambodian Law of Crimes Committed During the Period of Democratic Kampuchea (adopted 6 June 2003, entered into force 29 April 2005) 2329 UNTS 117. The tribunal is governed by these documents and the ECCC, Internal Rules as amended on 16 January 2015 (adopted 12 June 2007, entered into force 19 June 2007) (ECCC Internal Rules). See D. Scheffer, 'The Extraordinary Chambers in the Courts of Cambodia' in M. Cherif Bassiouni (ed.), *International Criminal Law Volume III: International Enforcement* (3rd ed., Martinus Nijhoff, 2008), pp. 219, 239.

[88] ECCC Law (*supra* n. 87), Art. 39.

alias Duch,[89] with the Trial Chamber ruling that no assets susceptible to forfeiture were identified.[90]

In addition to allowing for the forfeiture of illicitly gained assets in this manner, the ECCC Internal Rules also provide for an extensive civil party participation – and, of particular note for purposes of the present chapter – reparations regime.[91] According to this schema, civil parties can apply for 'collective and moral reparations', which may not consist of 'monetary payments'.[92] The ECCC, in part as a result of its civil law foundations,[93] perhaps reflects more than any other tribunal the turn towards a more victim-centred internationalised criminal justice after the adoption of the Rome Statute.

17.5.5   The Special Tribunal for Lebanon

The Special Tribunal for Lebanon (STL) is also rooted in the civil law tradition. Rule 82 of the STL RPE provides as follows:

(C) Upon request of the Prosecutor or the Registrar, or *proprio motu* after having heard the Defence, the Pre-Trial Judge or the Trial Chamber may request a State or States to adopt provisional measures to freeze the assets of the accused, without prejudice to the rights of third parties.[94]

Although the STL is not permitted to order fines and forfeiture of assets as penalties additional to imprisonment, unlike the majority of ICTs, victims are able to apply to national courts or 'other competent bod[ies]' for compensation pursuant to Article 25 STL Statute.[95] This measure is similar to that in the SCSL RPE, according to which victims may, after a decision by the tribunal confirming the guilt of the accused, seek compensation in accordance with the relevant national procedures. The STL and the SCSL

---

[89] ECCC, *Co-Prosecutors* v. *KAING Guek Eav alias Duch* (Inquiry into income and assets of the Accused) E175 (15 October 2009).

[90] ECCC, *Co-Prosecutors* v. *KAING Guek Eav alias Duch* (Judgment) E188 (26 July 2010).

[91] ECCC Internal Rules (*supra* n. 87), Rule 23.

[92] ECCC Internal Rules (*supra* n. 87), Rule 23 *quinquies*.

[93] The ECCC is housed in the Cambodian court structure and legal system. See Scheffer (*supra* n. 87), p. 239.

[94] STL, Rules of Procedure and Evidence as amended on 3 April 2017 (adopted 20 March 2009, entered into force 20 March 2009) STL-BD-2009-01-Rev.8 (STL RPE) Rule 82.

[95] Statute of the Special Tribunal for Lebanon, UNSC Res 1757 (30 May 2007) UN Doc S/RES/1757, Annex (STL Statute) Art. 25.

therefore provide an avenue at the national level, at least in principle, through which victims might seek redress for international crimes.

17.5.6   The Extraordinary African Chambers

The Extraordinary African Chambers (EAC) was established by the African Union and the Republic of Senegal to try international crimes committed in Chad between 7 June 1982 and 1 December 1990. The EAC is housed within the Senegalese court system, which, like the ECCC and the STL, has its basis in the civil law legal tradition.

The EAC is authorised to order fines in accordance with Senegalese law.[96] Under Article 24(2) EAC Statute, the EAC is also able to order, as a penalty in addition to imprisonment, forfeiture of proceeds, property, and assets derived directly or indirectly from crime(s) for which a person is convicted.[97] Moreover, according to Article 87 *bis* of the Senegalese Code of Criminal Procedure, the EAC may request protective, pre-conviction measures in respect of the assets of an accused person.[98]

As it concerns reparations measures, the EAC is able to order restitution, compensation, and rehabilitation under Article 27 of the EAC Statute.[99] In regard to compensation, the EAC can request that such measures be implemented by a trust fund,[100] which is established by Article 28 of the EAC Statute for the benefit of victims of the crimes within the tribunal's jurisdiction as well as their beneficiaries.[101]

Notably, however, the EAC Statute does not include provisions akin to Article 79(2) of the Rome Statute, which permits the ICC to order the transfer of the proceeds of fines and orders for forfeiture to the TFV,[102] or

---

[96] *Statut des Chambres africaines extraordinaires au sein des juridictions sénégalaises pour la poursuite des crimes internationaux commis au Tchad durant la période du 7 juin 1982 au 1er décembre 1990* (Statute of the Extraordinary African Chambers within the courts of Senegal created to prosecute international crimes committed in Chad between 7 June 1982 and 1 December 1990) (adopted 30 January 2013, entered into force 8 February 2013) (2013) 52 ILM 1028 (EAC Statute) Art. 24(1).

[97] EAC Statute, Art. 24(2).

[98] *Code de Procédure Pénale Sénégalais* (Senegalese Code of Criminal Procedure) Art. 87 *bis* ('*Lorsqu'il est saisi d'un dossier d'information, le juge d'instruction peut d'office ou sur demande de la partie civile ou du ministère public, ordonner des mesures conservatoires sur les biens de l'inculpé.*').

[99] EAC Statute (*supra* n. 96), Art. 27(1).

[100] EAC Statute (*supra* n. 96), Art. 27(2).

[101] EAC Statute (*supra* n. 96), Art. 28(1).

[102] See Rome Statute (*supra* n. 35), Art. 79(2).

Article 44 of the KSC Law,[103] which allows the KSC to request the sale of forfeited assets to fund reparation awards.[104]

In the case against former President of Chad Hissène Habré, the EAC did not order the forfeiture of assets or a fine as a penalty. A fine was not requested by the EAC's prosecutor and the EAC Trial Chamber rejected the prosecutor's request to impose asset forfeiture,[105] despite assets belonging to Habré having been frozen earlier in the proceedings. The Trial Chamber held that the prosecutor had failed to show that the assets resulted, directly or indirectly, from the commission of Habré's crimes.[106] The failure to charge Habré with the war crime of pillage – a potentially profitable offence – may have caused difficulties for the prosecutor in meeting this forfeiture threshold, which closely resembles the Rome Statute.[107]

The EAC also ordered significant reparations to Habré's victims. The EAC Appeals Chamber set the total amount of reparations due at more than 82 billion XAF, equivalent to over 140 million USD, and ordered Habré to pay this sum.[108] At the same time, the Appeals Chamber held that, at the time it issued its judgment, Habré's assets were not sufficient to meet the totality of the reparations awarded.[109] Although financing orders for reparations is – and will continue to be – undoubtedly challenging for ICTs in view of their limited resources and reliance on voluntary donations from states,[110] the finding that Habré is individually liable for this amount of compensation, as with Germain Katanga at the ICC, is vital in recognising the harm suffered by the victims of the serious crimes for which these two men were convicted.

---

[103] Law on Specialist Chambers and Specialist Prosecutor's Office (adopted 3 August 2015, entered into force 15 September 2015) Official Gazette of the Republic of Kosova, No. 27, 31 August 2015 (KSC Law).

[104] Ibid., Art. 44(6).

[105] *Ministère Public c. Hissein Habré* (Jugement) (30 May 2016) para. 2329.

[106] Ibid., para. 2330.

[107] Rome Statute (*supra* n. 35), Art. 77(2)(b). On the failure of the EAC Prosecutor to charge Habré with pillage, see also D. J. Birkett, 'Victims' Justice? Reparations and Asset Forfeiture at the Extraordinary African Chambers' (2019) 63(2) *Journal of African Law* 151–61, 158–9.

[108] *Le Procureur Général c. Hissein Habré* (Arrêt) (27 April 2017) 226. The exact figure was 82 billion and 290 million XAF.

[109] Ibid. 226.

[110] On which, see N. I. Diab 'Challenges in the Implementation of the Reparation Award against Hissein Habré: Can the Spell of Unenforceable Awards across the Globe be Broken?' (2018) 16 *Journal of International Criminal Justice* 141.

17.5.7   *The Kosovo Specialist Chambers*

The most recently established ICT, the Kosovo Specialist Chambers (KSC), adopts an approach to fines, asset forfeiture, and orders for reparations similar to that in the Rome Statute. The KSC is permitted to order forfeiture of assets as a penalty and orders for reparations under Article 44 of the KSC Law, as follows:

6. In addition to imprisonment, the Specialist Chambers may order only the convicted person to make restitution or pay compensation to a Victim or to Victims collectively, or may order the forfeiture of property, proceeds and any assets used for or deriving from the commission of the crime and their return to their rightful owner or sale and share between Victims under Article 22 ('a Reparation Order').[111]

Turning to fines, the KSC Law does not allow for their imposition for international crimes.[112] However, the KSC can order such measures for the failure to comply with witness summonses. Under Article 42 of the KSC Law, failure to appear and refusal to testify as a witness, respectively, are punishable by a fine of up to 250 EUR.[113]

As for protective measures, Article 39 of the KSC Law provides as follows:

11. The Pre-Trial Judge may, where necessary, provide for the protec-tion and privacy of victims and witnesses, the preservation of evi-dence, the protection of persons and national security information or the preservation of assets which may be subject to a forfeiture under this Law and the Rules of Procedure and Evidence, including temporary freezing orders, temporary confiscation orders or other temporary measures.[114]

This victim-oriented provision provides the Pre-Trial Judge of the KSC with similar powers to those available to Pre-Trial Chambers at the ICC under the Rome Statute. Likewise, Article 53(1)(l) of the KSC Law, which concerns cooperation and judicial assistance, is similar to Article 93(1)(k) of the Rome Statute:

---

[111] KSC Law (*supra* n. 103), Art. 44.
[112] This approach is similar to that adopted at the MICT. See MICT Statute (*supra* n. 33), Art. 22(1).
[113] KSC Law (*supra* n. 103), Art. 42.
[114] KSC Law (*supra* n. 103), Art. 39.

1. Subject to the rights of the accused provided for in Article 21, all
   entities and persons in Kosovo shall co-operate with the Specialist
   Chambers and Specialist Prosecutor's Office and shall comply without
   undue delay with any request for assistance or an order or decision
   issued by Specialist Chambers or Specialist Prosecutor's Office,
   including, but not limited to, those concerning: . . .
   1. the identification, tracing and freezing or seizure of proceeds,
      property and assets or instrumentalities of crimes for the purpose
      of eventual forfeiture, without prejudice to the rights of *bona fide*
      third parties[.][115]

Matthew Cross identifies a subtle difference between the Rome Statute
asset-freezing regime and that embraced by the drafters of the KSC
Law.[116] Cross contends that the wording of the latter, 'proceeds, property
and assets *or* instrumentalities of crimes',[117] instead of 'assets *and* instrumentalities of crimes' found in the Rome Statute,[118] 'may broaden the
scope of the assets which may be frozen prior to trial'.[119]

In sum, therefore, the KSC has at its disposal a victim-oriented asset-
freezing and forfeiture regime akin to the Rome Statute system. The KSC
is empowered to order both pre- and post-conviction measures to freeze
the assets of accused and convicted persons, respectively. Such assets may
subsequently be used to provide reparations to victims. That the drafters
of the KSC Law included such a regime demonstrates that reparation is
viewed as a vital component of the institution's restorative mandate.

17.6 Some Suggested Reasons behind ICTs' Failure to Order Asset Recovery Measures

It has thus far been demonstrated that, although a number of ICTs have
been invested with the power to order fines, forfeiture of property,
proceeds of crimes and/or assets, and, more recently, to order reparations
against convicted persons, these powers have barely been invoked in
practice. A key question is therefore why ICTs have appeared to be

---

[115] KSC Law (*supra* n. 103), Art. 53(1)(l).
[116] M. E. Cross, 'Equipping the Specialist Chambers of Kosovo to Try Transnational Crimes: Remarks on Independence and Cooperation' (2016) 14 *Journal of International Criminal Justice* 73, 92.
[117] KSC Law (*supra* n. 103), Art. 53(1)(l) (emphasis added).
[118] Rome Statute (*supra* n. 35), Art. 93(1)(k).
[119] Cross (*supra* n. 116) 92.

reluctant to employ the asset recovery tools at their disposal. Three options will be presented in turn.

17.6.1   Theoretical Basis

First, the caution on the part of those ICTs empowered to do so to order fines or asset forfeiture measures could arguably be attributable, at least in part, to the grave nature of international crimes. In other words, penalties of a financial corrective nature could seem ill-fitting when imposed for the commission of, in the words of the preamble to the Rome Statute, 'the most serious crimes of concern to the international community as a whole'.[120] This can be contrasted with orders for reparations, which appear to be more readily used by ICTs than fines and forfeiture measures. It is suggested that the former, which find their basis in the law of civil responsibility, do not suffer from this perception. It therefore seems reasonable to assume that the ICC, and other ICTs with the capacity to order reparations directly against convicted persons, will employ such powers more readily than fines and forfeiture measures for this reason. Indeed, such a willingness to issue reparations orders is already borne out in the early practice of the ICC, which has found that all three individuals guilty of crimes under its jurisdiction are also liable to make reparations pursuant to Article 75 of the Rome Statute.

17.6.2   Dearth of Assets

A second possible reason behind ICTs' reluctance to make use of fines and forfeiture measures is practical: despite certain persons convicted of international crimes having (had) access to substantial assets, ICTs have struggled to have them traced and frozen. For example, although Charles Taylor and Hissène Habré were reported to have held vast sums of money and other assets accumulated during their presidencies of Liberia and Chad, respectively, investigators have not been able to identify, trace, seize, or freeze them. This could be because the assets have been located beyond the reach of financial investigators by the suspect (or, depending on the phase of the proceedings, accused person or convicted person) or because their ownership has been disguised.

---

[120] Rome Statute (*supra* n. 35), preambular para. 4.

At the other end of the financial spectrum, it must be acknowledged that many of the persons convicted of international crimes are indigent, meaning that they do not have sufficient assets to fund their defence. When faced with this reality, coupled with the frequently high number of victims potentially eligible for reparations in international crimes cases, the limited use by ICTs of fines and forfeiture measures, with a view to using their proceeds to fund reparation awards, appears rather more justifiable.

17.6.3   Other Reparations Paradigms

Although not necessarily a reason behind the lack of enthusiasm shown by a series of ICTs for the imposition of fines and forfeiture measures for the commission of crimes under their jurisdiction, the availability and use of other reparations paradigms ought to be taken into account. For example, it was noted above that only one order for forfeiture of assets, against industrialist Alfred Krupp, was made by the post-World War II military tribunals. It was also observed that the constituent instrument of the IMT, as well as Control Council Law No. 10, failed to provide for the imposition of measures akin to orders for reparations. However, although reparations were not awarded in the course of the *criminal proceedings* before ICTs, this does not mean that victims received no reparations whatsoever for harm suffered. Indeed, post-World War II West Germany developed a reparations programme as a political-administrative tool complementing the criminal process. The measures sought, inter alia, to address the responsibility of the German state to individual victims, as opposed to intra-state reparations, although the latter were also paid.[121] Through a series of federal reparations laws,[122] Germany aimed to indemnify victims of persecution suffered under the Nazi regime.[123]

---

[121] See A. Colonomos and A. Armstrong, 'German Reparations to Jews after World War II: A Turning Point in the History of Reparations', in P. de Greiff (ed.), *The Handbook of Reparations* (Oxford University Press, 2006), pp. 390, 391.

[122] This series of laws began with the Federal Supplementary Law for the Compensation of Victims of National Socialist Persecution of 18 September 1953 (*Bundesergänzungsgesetz zur Entschädigung für Opfer der nationalsozialistischen Verfolgung (BEG) vom 18. September 1953*), which was subsequently modified, most pertinently for the purposes of the present chapter, on 29 June 1956 (amending, inter alia, residency and deadline requirements) and 14 September 1965 (amending, inter alia, requirements relating to the burden of proof and eligibility). See Colonomos and Armstrong (*supra* n. 121), pp. 402–8.

[123] See Colonomos and Armstrong (*supra* n. 121), pp. 402–8.

It is beyond the scope of this chapter to discuss the advantages of different reparations models, within and beyond the criminal process, in respect of the extent to which they meet the need to make restitution to (groups of) victims of war. Nonetheless, it is worth noting that paradigms akin to the foregoing German national reparations scheme, as a political-administrative mechanism designed to complement the criminal process, could function alongside reparations under the ICC system, but only where there is state involvement in the commission of offences, as was the case with Nazi Germany. These mechanisms are therefore limited and operate to meet the responsibility of the state, as opposed to that of individuals, that is, convicted persons in the ICC system, to make reparations to individual (or groups of) victims. Fines, asset forfeiture, and particularly orders for reparations consequently retain an important role in funding reparations made to the victims of international crimes.

17.7 Conclusion

This chapter has sought to demonstrate, first, that most ICTs have been permitted by their constituent instruments to order fines, forfeiture of assets (including protective measures for the purpose of eventual forfeiture), and/or reparations directly against convicted persons. However, despite possessing these powers, and despite evidence that a number of persons found guilty of international crimes had significant wealth, ICTs have seldom invoked such measures in proceedings other than those involving offences against the administration of justice. In addition, the chapter has also aimed to show that the inclusion in the Rome Statute of more victim-centred procedures in respect of fines and forfeiture, targeted at the provision of reparations, has led to the adoption of similar measures in the law (if not the practice) of certain subsequently-established ICTs.

In order to recover the proceeds of international crimes, and to finance reparations to the victims of such atrocities, ICTs' prosecutors could more readily utilise fines and forfeiture measures. This approach could be especially advantageous in cases where convicted persons (or, in respect of protective, pre-conviction measures with a view to forfeiture, accused persons) have access to substantial assets. The adoption of an extensive reparations system in the Rome Statute demonstrates a turn toward a more reparative international criminal justice, which is also reflected in the law governing a number of ICTs established after 1998.

Most ICTs have at their disposal at least some tools with which they are able to locate and recover assets belonging to those (accused or) convicted of international crimes. Not least to secure the funds required to finance awards for reparations, prosecutors at ICTs could devote greater attention to these tools, for which procedural structures are largely already in place.

Reparation Mechanisms for Victims of Armed Conflict

Common and Basic Principles

SHUICHI FURUYA

Introduction

In the past few decades, there has been a clear trend in international law to admit a right to reparation for victims of armed conflict. This does not mean, however, that victims have successfully obtained reparation before domestic courts by relying on the relevant rules of international law. Looking at the cases in which victims claimed reparation for their harms allegedly caused by Germany and Japan during World War II, the domestic courts of Germany, Japan and the United States have denied their claims in most cases, if not all. Rather, those domestic practices clearly indicate that the courts of responsible states were unwilling to admit the existence of an individual right to reparation at least at the time of World War II.[1] In addition, they also reveal that victims may face

---

[1] See Italian Military Internees Case, A (an Italian citizen) and 942 other claimants, Joint constitutional complaint, 2 BvR 1379/01, NJW 2004, 2357, ILDC 438 (DE 2004), 28 June 2004, Germany, Constitutional Court [BVerfG], para. 38, in Oxford Public International Law, Oxford Reports on International Law (opil.ouplaw.com/home/oril); Distomo Case, S and ors, Joint constitutional complaint, BVerfG, 2 BvR 1476/03, ILDC 390 (DE 2006),15 February 2006, Germany, Constitutional Court, paras. 20–1, in Oxford Public International Law, Oxford Reports on International Law (opil.ouplaw.com/home/ oril). See also M. Rau, 'State Liability for Violations of International Humanitarian Law: The Distomo Case Before the German Federal Constitutional Court' (2005) 7 *German Law Journal* 707–10. For Japanese cases, see 'X et al. v. State of Japan, Tokyo District Court, Judgment, 30 November 1998' (1999) 42 *Japanese Annual of International Law* 143–51; 'X et al. v. State of Japan, Tokyo High Court, Judgment, 7 August 1996' (1997) 40 *Japanese Annual of International Law* 116–18; 'X et al. v. State, Tokyo High Court, Judgment, 6 December 2000' (2001) 44 *Japanese Annual of International Law* 173–5; 'X et al. v. the Government of Japan, Tokyo High Court, Judgment, 8 February 2001' (2002) 45 *Japanese*

significant legal and procedural hurdles at the domestic proceedings, such as immunities, statutes of limitations and evidential thresholds.

On the other hand, it is to be noted that various ad hoc reparation mechanisms, such as the United Nations Compensation Commission and the Housing and Property Claims Commission in Kosovo, have been established at the domestic or international level since the 1990s. They include programmes that were set up to resolve disputes over post-conflict land and property rights, and claims processes that paid compensation to victims of gross violations of human rights and serious violations of international humanitarian law. More significant is that the Rome Statute of the International Criminal Court (ICC), adopted in 1998, brought in the innovative procedure in which victims may claim reparations for the harms that convicted persons caused to them.[2] The emergence of these mechanisms suggests that decision-makers who were involved in peace-building and reconciliation in war-torn states became conscious of the importance of taking appropriate measures for individual victims. This attitude contrasts sharply with the traditional inter-state resolution of reparation payments, such as the conclusion of lump sum agreements, which had been dominant until the 1980s.[3] The practice

---

Annual of International Law 142–4; 'X et al. v. State of Japan, Tokyo High Court, Judgment, 18 March 2005' (2006) 49 *Japanese Annual of International Law* 149–55; 'State of Japan v. Y, Tokyo High Court, Judgment, 23 June 2005' (2007) 50 *Japanese Annual of International Law* 194–209; 'X v. State of Japan and Y, Nagoya High Court (Kanazawa Branch), Judgment, 8 March 2010' (2011) 54 *Japanese Yearbook of International Law* 514–22. See also S. H. Bong, 'Compensation for Victims of Wartime Atrocities: Recent Developments in Japan's Case Law' (2005) 3 *Journal of International Criminal Justice* 187–206.

[2] Article 75 of the Rome Statute. See also Rules 94–99 of the Rules of Procedure and Evidence. For the reparations in the ICC, see E. Dwertmann, *The Reparation System of the International Criminal Court: Its Implementation, Possibilities and Limitations* (Brill-Nijhoff, 2010); P. Lewis and H. Friman, 'Reparations to Victims', in R. S. Lee (ed.), *The International Criminal Court: Elements of Crimes and Rules of Procedure and Evidence* (Transnational Publishers, 2001), pp. 474–91; D. L. Shelton, 'Reparations for Victims of International Crimes', in D. L. Shelton (ed.), *International Crimes, Peace, and Human Rights: The Role of the International Criminal Court* (Brill-Nijhoff, 2000), pp. 137–47; T. Ingadottir, 'The Trust Fund of the ICC', in Shelton, ibid., pp. 149–61.

[3] Approximately 95 per cent of all claims for reparation in the aftermath of World War II were regulated by lump sum agreements, under which the responsible state paid a fixed amount of money or provided reparations in kind to the home state of individual victims. However, the distribution of assets received under these agreements was within the discretion of the home state. R. Hofmann, 'Compensation for Personal Damages Suffered during World War II' (Article last updated: February 2013), para. 7, in *Max Planck Encyclopaedia of Public International Law*, (opil.ouplaw.com/home/EPIL). See, for instance, Agreement on reparation from Germany, on the establishment of an Inter-Allied

of setting up those mechanisms shows the clear shift from state-centred reparation to victim-oriented reparation, and constitute the strong trend in international law affirming the existence of a right to reparation.

There is a crucial difference between the reparation mechanisms established to date and the ICC. The former have been established on an ad hoc basis only for dealing with the issue of reparation in a particular situation of a targeted state. On the other hand, the ICC is a permanent organization that is designed to handle the situation of any states if falling within its jurisdiction. However, processing reparations is just ancillary to the findings of individual criminal responsibility for the most serious crimes of international concern.[4] Thus, the former in most cases relates to the responsibility of states or other organized armed group to make reparation, while the latter confines itself to the reparation to be made by convicted persons. Even among the ad hoc reparation mechanisms, there are considerable varieties, depending on the political and social circumstances of each armed conflict, the needs of victims and the political and financial situations of responsible parties.

Nevertheless, it is also true that most mechanisms have faced common fundamental dilemmas. Some have had to resolve a very large number of

Reparation Agency and on the restitution of monetary gold, done at Paris on 14 January 1946, Article 2, U.N.T.S. 555 (1966), No. 8105, pp. 69–110; Convention (with annex) on the Settlement of Matters Arising out of the War and the Occupation, signed at Bonn on 26 May 1952 (as amended by Schedule IV to the Protocol on the Termination of the Occupation Regime in the Federal Republic of Germany, signed at Paris on 23 October 1954), U.N.T.S. 332 (1959), No. 4762, pp. 219–386; Treaty of Peace with Japan, signed at San Francisco on 8 September 1951, Article 14(a), U.N.T.S. 136 (1952), No. 1832, pp. 45–164. Even in armed conflicts taking place during the Cold War, the states concerned preferred to mutually renounce their reparation claims including those of victims in peace treaties or simply disregard the issue of reparations. For instance, Suez Crisis in 1956, General Agreement, signed at Zurich on 22 August 1958, Article 7, U.N.T.S. 732 (1974), No. 10511, pp. 86–9; Armed conflict between El Salvador and Honduras, General Peace Treaty between the Republics of El Salvador and Honduras, signed at Lima on 30 October 1980, Article 42, U.N.T.S. 1310 (1983), No. 21856, pp. 213–50; Falkland Islands War, Joint statement issued at Madrid on 19 October 1989 by the delegations of the Republic of Argentina and the United Kingdom of Great Britain and Northern Ireland, Section 3 (1990) 29 *International Legal Materials* 1293–5.

[4] In the *Lubanga* case, the Appeals Chamber found that 'the obligation to repair harm arises from the individual criminal responsibility for the crimes which caused the harm and, accordingly, the person found to be criminally responsible for those crimes is the person to be held liable for reparations'. Situation in the Democratic Republic of the Congo in the Case of the *Prosecutor* v. *Thomas Lubanga Dyilo*, Appeals Chamber, Judgment on the appeals against the 'Decision establishing the principles and procedures to be applied to reparations' of 7 August 2012 with AMENDED order for reparations (Annex A) and public annexes 1 and 2, 3 March 2015, ICC-01/04–01/06, para. 99.

claims within a restricted time, and with limited financial and human resources available to fund compensation and administer the mechanism.[5] At the same time, potentially eligible victims usually have high expectations that their claims will be processed in a fair and effective manner. Fast processing may reduce administrative costs and, thereby, both maximise the funds available to victims and provide reparations sooner; however, the risk is that processing accuracy may be sacrificed, and victims may feel dissatisfied with the automated and impersonal treatment of their claims.[6] Thus, although reparation mechanisms may take many different forms, most have needed to address such common issues as how to expeditiously process a huge number of claims and what is the fairest and most efficient method to evaluate the claims received. On surveying the special procedures and methods created by the reparation mechanisms to meet these challenges, it is apparent that certain common principles have been evolving, which would direct decision-makers involved in reparation mechanisms to create more victim-oriented systems. To this extent, these common principles constitute rules of international law applicable to reparation for victims in a broad sense.

The aim of the present chapter is to examine the common characteristics and basic principles that can be extracted by the comparative analysis of past and ongoing various mechanisms including the ICC.

Cross-Fertilization of Reparation Mechanisms

The development of reparation mechanisms to date is a product of cross-fertilization deriving from three main historical developments: the United Nations' focus on victims' rights since the mid-1980s, increasing awareness of reparation for victims in international criminal justice and the successive establishment of ad hoc mechanisms after the end of the Cold War.

---

[5] V. Heiskanen, 'Virtue Out of Necessity: International Mass Claims and New Uses of Information Technology', in International Bureau of the Permanent Court of Arbitration (IBPCA) (ed.), *Redressing Injustices through Mass Claims Process: Innovative Responses to Unique Challenges* (Oxford University Press, 2006), p. 28; H. Das, 'The Concept of Mass Claims and the Specificity of Mass Claims Resolution', in IBPCA, ibid., p. 9.

[6] E. Kristjánsdóttir, 'International Mass Claims Process and the ICC Trust Fund for Victims', in C. Ferstman, M. Goetz and A. Stephens (eds.), *Reparations for Victims of Genocide, War Crimes and Crimes against Humanity: Systems in Place and Systems in the Making* (Martinus Nijhoff, 2009), p. 178.

In 1985, the UN General Assembly (UNGA) adopted the Declaration of the Basic Principles of Justice for Victims of Crime and Abuse of Power (Victim Declaration).[7] This is the first international instrument to refer explicitly to the right of victims to access justice and present their views and concerns at the appropriate stage of proceedings. While the main concern of this instrument was the victims of ordinary domestic crimes, it also dealt with those who suffered harm 'through acts or omissions that do not yet constitute violations of national criminal law but of internationally recognized norms relating to human rights'.[8] Following the adoption of the Victim Declaration, the Sub-Commission on the Prevention of Discrimination and Protection of Minorities began, in 1988, its work on reparation for victims with Resolution 1988/11.[9] The work driven by a Special Rapporteur, Theo van Boven, and then an Independent Expert, M. Cherif Bassiouni, led to the adoption by the UNGA in 2005 of the Basic Principles and Guidelines on the Right to a Remedy and Reparation for Victims of Gross Violations of International Human Rights Law and Serious Violations of International Humanitarian Law (Basic Principles).[10] This instrument, unlike the Victim Declaration, focused on the victims of gross violations of international human rights law or serious violations of international humanitarian law,[11] and provided for the victims' rights to equal and effective access to justice; adequate, effective and prompt reparation for harm suffered; and access to relevant information concerning violations and reparation mechanisms.[12]

Almost at the same time as the adoption of the Basic Principles, the United Nations issued two important documents, namely the Secretary-General's report on the Rule of Law and Transitional Justice in Conflict and Post-Conflict Societies[13] in 2004, and the Updated Set of Principles for the Protection and Promotion of Human Rights through Action to

---

[7] Declaration of the Basic Principles of Justice for Victims of Crime and Abuse of Power, UN Doc. A/Res/40/34/Annex (29 November 1985).

[8] Ibid., para. 18.

[9] Resolution 1988/11: Compensation for victims of gross violations of human rights (1 September 1988), Paragraph 1, in Report of the Sub-Commission on Prevention of Discrimination and Protection of Minorities on its Fortieth Session, UN Doc. E/CN.4/1989/3, E/CN.4/Sub.2/1988/45 (25 October 1988), 35–6 (36).

[10] Basic Principles and Guidelines on the Right to a Remedy and Reparation for Victims of Gross Violations of International Human Rights Law and Serious Violations of International Humanitarian Law, UN Doc. A/RES/60/147, Annex (16 December 2005).

[11] Ibid., para. 8.

[12] Ibid., para. 11.

[13] Report of the Secretary-General, The rule of law and transitional justice in conflict and post-conflict societies (23 August 2004), UN Doc. S/2004/616.

Combat Impunity (Updated Set of Principles)[14] in 2005. These documents not only addressed the issue of reparations for victims of armed conflict but also framed reparations as a part of transitional justice in post-conflict states and local communities that may also include a criminal tribunal, a non-judicial fact-finding body (such as a truth commission) and the promotion of democracy and the rule of law.[15]

In relation to the movement above in the United Nations, it should be noted that it took seventeen years to complete the Basic Principles. The period from 1988 to 2005 witnessed dramatic changes in the field of international criminal justice, with the establishment of the International Criminal Tribunal for the Former Yugoslavia (ICTY), the International Criminal Tribunal for Rwanda (ICTR), other hybrid courts in Sierra Leone, Kosovo, Timor-Leste and Cambodia, and finally the ICC. Furthermore, this period also overlapped with the period when ad hoc reparation mechanisms were established one after another.

When the ICTY and the ICTR were established in 1993 and 1994, respectively, the drafters of their Statutes had less interest in reparation for victims than the fair and effective operation of criminal proceedings.[16] Actually, there was no provision concerning reparations in their Statutes. Only the Rules of Procedure and Evidence provided for a system of compensation under which victims were required to bring an action in national courts to obtain compensation,[17] but eventually it did not work at all.[18] A sign of change came in 2000 when Carla Del Ponte, then Chief Prosecutor, proposed to the Security Council the incorporation of victims' compensation and participation in proceedings.[19] Almost simultaneously,

---

[14] Updated Set of Principles for the Protection and Promotion of Human Rights through Action to Combat Impunity, 8 February 2005, UN Doc. E/CN.4/2005/102/Add.1.

[15] The Secretary-General explained: 'No single form of reparation is likely to be satisfactory to victims. Instead, appropriately conceived combinations of reparation measures will usually be required, as a complement to the proceedings of criminal tribunals and truth commissions. Whatever mode of transitional justice is adopted and however reparations programmes are conceived to accompany them, both the demands of justice and the dictates of peace require that something be done to compensate victims.' Report of the Secretary-General (*supra* n. 13), para. 55.

[16] V. Morris and M. P. Scharf, *An Insider's Guide to the International Criminal Tribunal for the Former Yugoslavia*, Vol. I (1995), p. 286.

[17] Rule 106.

[18] M. Cherif Bassiouni, 'International Recognition of Victims' Rights' (2006) 6 *Human Rights Law Review* 242–3.

[19] Address to the UN Security Council by Carla Del Ponte, Prosecutor of the International Criminal Tribunals for the Former Yugoslavia and Rwanda, Press Release, The Hague, 24 November 2000, JL/P.I.S./542-e, www.icty.org/sid/7803.

the judges of the ICTY made a report examining the possibility of amending the Statute to create a more effective reparation system, which pointed out as follows:

> [T]here is a clear trend in international law to recognize a right of compensation in the victim to recover from the individual who caused his or her injury. This right is recognized in the Victims Declaration, the Basic Principles, other international human rights instruments and, most specifically, in the ICC Statute, which is indicative of the state of the law at present. . . . Thus, in view of these developments, there does appear to be a right to compensation for victims under international law.[20]

Although the report rejected the amendment of the Statute, it is significant that it affirmed the existence of a victim's right to reparation with reference to UN instruments including the Victims Declaration and the Basic Principles as well as the Rome Statute.

The Rome Statute, on the other hand, as a result of hard and long negotiations,[21] introduced an innovative and more victim-oriented system for reparation, under which the ICC directly orders convicted persons to make reparation to victims having suffered harms caused by the crimes for which they are found guilty. Nevertheless, this system did not arise out of a vacuum and does not stand alone. Rather, it shares the progress that had been made in the United Nations until 1998, and also includes the possibility of further development by incorporating principles provided for in other instruments adopted after the Rome Statute was adopted. The following finding of Trial Chamber I of the ICC in the *Lubanga* case indicates this explicitly:

> The Chamber accepts that the right to reparations is a well-established and basic human right, that is enshrined in universal and regional human rights treaties, and in other international instruments, including the UN Basic Principles; the Declaration of Basic Principles of Justice for Victims of Crime and Abuse of Power; the Guidelines on Justice in Matters involving Child Victims and Witnesses of Crime; the Nairobi Declaration; the Cape Town Principles and Best Practices on the Recruitment of Children into the Armed Forces and on Demobilization

---

[20] Letter dated 12 October 2000 from the President of the International Criminal Tribunal for the Former Yugoslavia addressed to the Secretary-General, *annexed to* the Letter dated 2 November 2000 from the Secretary-General addressed to the President of the Security Council, UN Doc. S/2000/1063 (3 November 2000), paras. 20–1.
[21] As to the negotiation on reparation, see S. Furuya, 'Victim Participation, Reparations and Reintegration as Historical Building Blocks of International Criminal Law', in M. Bergsmo and others (eds.), *Historical Origins of International Criminal Law*, Vol. IV (Torkel Opsahl Academic EPublisher, 2015), pp. 857–61.

and Social Reintegration of Child Soldiers in Africa; and the Paris Principles. These international instruments, as well as certain significant human rights reports, have provided guidance to the Chamber in establishing the present principles.[22]

Among the six instruments enumerated above, four were adopted after 1998: the Basic Principles (2005), the Guidelines on Justice in Matters involving Child Victims and Witnesses of Crime (2005),[23] the Nairobi Declaration on Women's and Girls' Right to a Remedy (2007)[24] and the Paris Principles and Guidelines on Children Associated with Armed Forces (2007).[25] These instruments were drafted under the strong influence of the ICC system on victim reparation. Conversely, as the Trial Chamber mentioned in its decision, it relied on these instruments for the concrete reparation principles applied to the victims of Lubanga's crimes. This suggests, quite symbolically, that the victim-oriented rules and mechanisms have been developed through cross-referencing.[26]

At the same time, it is important to note that, in tandem with the drafting process of the Basic Principles during the period of 1988–2005, various ad hoc reparation mechanisms were established or proposed to resolve reparation issues in post-conflict situations, which are as follows in chronological order:

1991: United Nations Compensation Commission (UNCC) for claims resulting from the Gulf War (1990–1991)[27]
1995: Commission for Real Property Claims of Displaced Persons and Refugees (CRPC) in Bosnia and Herzegovina[28]

---

[22] Situation in the Democratic Republic of the Congo in the Case of the *Prosecutor v. Thomas Lubanga Dyilo*, Trial Chamber I, Decision establishing the principles and procedures to be applied to reparations, 7 August 2012, ICC-01/04-01/06, para. 185.
[23] Guidelines on Justice in Matters involving Child Victims and Witnesses of Crime, ECOSOC Resolution 2005/20 (22 July 2005); see paras. 35–7.
[24] The Nairobi Declaration was issued by women's rights advocates and activists, as well as survivors of sexual violence in situations of conflict at the International Meeting on Women's and Girls' Right to a Remedy and Reparation, held in Nairobi from 19 to 21 March 2007, www.fidh.org/IMG/pdf/NAIROBI_DECLARATIONeng.pdf.
[25] The Paris Principles were adopted at the international Free Children from War conference, Paris, February 2007, www.unicef.org/emerg/files/ParisPrinciples310107English.pdf.
[26] Furuya (*supra* n. 21), p. 862.
[27] UNCC was established and guided by SC Res. 687 (3 April 1991).
[28] CRPC was established by the Agreement on Refugees and Displaced Persons annexed to the Dayton Peace Agreement. However, the parties to this agreement included non-state entities involved in the internal armed conflicts in Bosnia and Herzegovina. Agreement

1997: Claims Resolution Tribunal for Dormant Accounts in Switzerland (CRT-I)[29] for Holocaust victims

1998: International Commission on Holocaust Era Insurance Claims (ICHEIC)[30]

1999: CRT-II, a successor to the CRT-I, and the Holocaust Victim Assets Programme (HVAP)[31]

1999: Housing and Property Claims Commission (HPCC) in Kosovo[32]

2000: German Forced Labour Compensation Programme (GFLCP)[33]

2000: Eritrea-Ethiopia Claims Commission (EECC)[34]

on Refugees and Displaced Persons, Annex 7 to the General Framework Agreement for Peace in Bosnia and Herzegovina, www.nato.int/ifor/gfa/gfa-an7.htm.

[29] CRT-I was based on a Memorandum of Understanding between the World Jewish Restitution Organization and the World Jewish Congress on the one hand, and the Swiss Bankers Association on the other. The CRT-I was established as an independent international arbitral tribunal under Swiss law. Memorandum of Understanding between the World Jewish Restitution Organization and the World Jewish Congress, representing also the Jewish Agency and Allied Organizations, and the Swiss Bankers Association (2 May 1996), Appendix A to the Final Report of the Independent Committee of Eminent Persons (1999), p.A-1, www.crt-ii.org/ICEP/ICEP_Report_Appendices_A-W.pdf.

[30] ICHEIC was constituted by a Memorandum of Understanding concluded between several European insurance companies, US insurance regulatory authorities, and Jewish and survivor organizations. Memorandum of Understanding (25 August 1998), www .insurance.ca.gov/01-consumers/150-other-prog/05-hei/hei-mou.cfm.

[31] CRT-II and HVAP were created by a US federal district court to implement part of a settlement agreement reached in class action lawsuits, known as the Holocaust Victim Assets Litigation. Class Action Settlement Agreement (26 January 1999), www.crt-ii.org /court_docs/Settleme.pdf. Their functions were based on the settlement agreement and the Plan of Allocation and Distribution proposed by a Special Master. See Summary of Special Master's Proposed Plan of Allocation and Distribution, www.swissbankclaims.com /DistributionPlan.htm.

[32] HPCC was established by regulations promulgated by the Special Representative of the UN Secretary-General within the mandate of the UN Interim Administration Mission in Kosovo (UNMIK). Regulation No. 1999/23 on the Establishment of the Housing and Property Directorate and the Housing and Property Claims Commission, UNMIK/REG/ 1999/23 (15 November 1999).

[33] GFLCP was launched by an agreement between the United States and Germany concerning the Foundation 'Remembrance, Responsibility and Future'. Agreement between the Government of the Federal Republic of Germany and the Government of the United States of America concerning the Foundation 'Remembrance, Responsibility and Future' (17 July 2000), U.N.T.S. 2130 (2003), No. 37134, 249–322. Subsequently, the German parliament passed the federal law creating the Foundation and its organizational framework. Law on the Creation of a Foundation 'Remembrance, Responsibility and Future' of 2 August 2000, entered into force on 12 August 2000 (BGBl 2000 I 1263), last amended by the Law of 1 September 2008, entered into force on 9 September 2008 (BGBl 2008 I 1797), www.stiftung-evz.de/eng/the-foundation/law.html.

[34] EECC was established pursuant to an agreement between Eritrea and Ethiopia. Its proceedings were administered by the Permanent Court of Arbitration in The Hague.

2004: Proposed Cyprus Property Board (CPB)[35]
2004: Iraq Property Claims Commission (IPCC)[36]
2005: Proposed Compensation Commission for international crimes perpetrated in Darfur, Sudan (CCDS)[37]
2006: Kosovo Property Claims Commission (KPCC).[38]

The structure and procedures of these reparation mechanisms varied considerably, depending on the political and social circumstances of each conflict and the victims' needs.[39] These mechanisms also differed according to the legal framework under which each was (or was proposed to be) established. However, they basically shared the same philosophy that individual victims possess a right to reparation, and worked in accordance with the principles that were fostered in the drafting process of the Basic Principles and the relevant instruments of the ICC reparation system.

To take the three courses of development as a whole, they have become closely intertwined, to create one solid trend of international law that acknowledges a right to reparation for victims.

Agreement between the Government of the Federal Democratic Republic of Ethiopia and the Government of the State of Eritrea (12 December 2000), pca-cpa.org/en/cases/71/.

[35] CPB was envisaged to be based on a Foundation Agreement to be concluded as part of the 'Comprehensive Settlement of the Cyprus Problem', submitted by the then UN Secretary-General Kofi Annan. Treatment of Property affected by Events since 1963, Annex VII to the Foundation Agreement, the Comprehensive Settlement of the Cyprus Problem (31 March 2004), www.peacemaker.un.org/sites/peacemaker.un.org/files/Annan_Plan_MARCH_30_2004.pdf.

[36] IPCC was based on a regulation promulgated by the Coalition Provisional Authority. Coalition Provisional Authority Regulation Number 12, Iraq Property Claims Commission, Annex A: the Statute Establishing of the Iraq Property Claims Commission (24 June 2004), https://govinfo.library.unt.edu/cpa-iraq/regulations/. An Iraqi law later superseded the regulation and replaced the IPCC with the Commission for the Resolution of Real Property Disputes, which was an entirely domestic organ.

[37] CCDS was proposed by the International Commission of Inquiry on Darfur which had been established by the Security Council. Report of the International Commission of Inquiry on Darfur to the Secretary-General, UN Doc. S/2005/60 (1 February 2005), paras. 590–603.

[38] KPCC was established by regulations promulgated by the Special Representative of the UN Secretary-General, within the mandate of the UN Interim Administration Mission in Kosovo (UNMIK). Regulation No. 2006/50 on the Resolution of Claims Relating to Private Immovable Property, Including Agricultural and Commercial Property, UNMIK Regulation 2006/50, www.unmikonline.org/regulations/unmikgazette/index.htm.

[39] P. A. Karrer, 'Mass Claims Proceedings in Practice: A Few Lessons Learned' (2005) 23 *Berkeley Journal of International Law* 463.

The Victim's Right to Access an Effective Mechanism to Claim Reparation

Irrespective of the legal framework in which the reparation mechanisms listed in the previous section were established, they share the principle that victims have not only a substantive right to reparation but also a procedural right to access an effective mechanism to claim reparation. In fact, the right to access a reparation mechanism has been emphasized in various international instruments. The Updated Set of Principles, for instance, provides as follows:

> All victims shall have access to a readily available, prompt and effective remedy in the form of criminal, civil, administrative or disciplinary proceedings subject to the restrictions on prescription set forth in principle 23. . . . Reparations may also be provided through programmes, based upon legislative or administrative measures, funded by national or international sources, addressed to individuals and communities. . . . Exercise of the right to reparation includes access to applicable international and regional procedures.[40]

The Victims Declaration,[41] the Basic Principles[42] and the Nairobi Declaration on Women's and Girl's Right to a Remedy and Reparation[43] also provide for a right to access a reparation mechanism. The emergence of the right to access an effective reparation mechanism inevitably leads to an obligation of responsible states to provide such a mechanism to victims,[44] while it would depend on the circumstances of the armed conflict in question as well as the situations of the states concerned whether a new reparation mechanism should be created or an existing mechanism made use of. Whatever the mechanism available to victims, it needs to be a fair and impartial mechanism that would be able to contribute to the realization of transitional justice in a post-conflict state and its communities. The Secretary-General emphasized in his report that '[p]rogrammes to provide reparations to victims for harm suffered can be effective and expeditious complements to the contributions of tribunals and truth commissions, by providing concrete remedies, promoting reconciliation and restoring victims' confidence in the State'.[45]

[40] Updated Set of Principles (*supra* n. 14), Principle 32.
[41] Victims Declaration (*supra* n. 7), para. 4.
[42] Basic Principles (*supra* n. 10), paras. 12 and 14.
[43] Nairobi Declaration (*supra* n. 24), 2-Access to Reparation.
[44] Bassiouni (*supra* n. 18), p. 232.
[45] Report of the Secretary-General (*supra* n. 13), para. 54.

The right to access a reparation mechanism includes effective access to appropriate information concerning that mechanism.[46] A reparation mechanism has little practical value if potentially eligible victims are unaware of the opportunity to claim or not given information on how to do so in a language they understand.[47] For this, the Victims Declaration, the Basic Principles and the Updated Set of Principles provide for the obligation of responsible parties to conduct outreach activities to inform eligible victims of their right to reparation and the procedures they may invoke.[48] In fact, the mechanisms established to date have emphasized the importance of such outreach activities and actually invoked them. In the *Lubanga* case, for instance, Trial Chamber I pointed out as follows: 'Outreach activities, which include, firstly, gender- and ethnic-inclusive programmes and, secondly, communication between the Court and the affected individuals and their communities are essential to ensure that reparations have broad and real significance.'[49] In the *Katanga* case, the United Nations submitted its observation on reparation and stressed the significance of outreach:

> Outreach and awareness-raising on the right to reparation are essential to ensure that victims are aware of their rights and of the processes dealing with their harm. Outreach should take place in a language and through means that victims, whether literate or not, can understand and relate to in a culturally appropriate way. It is also important that this awareness-raising is conducted in a way that manages victims' expectations.[50]

In the orders for reparations, the Chambers have directed the Registrar to take all the necessary measures, including outreach activities aimed at the national authorities, the local communities and the affected populations, in order to publicize the principles and any reparation proceedings before the ICC for affording the victims detailed and timely notice and

---

[46] S. Furuya, 'Draft Procedural Principles for Reparation Mechanisms', in International Law Association, *Report of the Seventy-Sixth Conference held in Washington D.C.* (2014), p. 794.

[47] H. M. Holtzmann and E. Kristjánsdóttir (eds.), *International Mass Claims Processes: Legal and Practical Perspectives* (Oxford University Press, 2007), p. 141.

[48] Victims Declaration (*supra* n. 7), para. 5; Basic Principles (*supra* n. 10), para. 24; Updated Set of Principles, Principle 33 (*supra* n. 14), p. 17.

[49] *Prosecutor* v. *Thomas Lubanga Dyilo*, Trial Chamber (*supra* n. 22), para. 205.

[50] Situation in the Democratic Republic of the Congo in the Case of the *Prosecutor* v. *Germain Katanga*, United Nations Joint Submission on Reparations, 14 May 2015, ICC-01/04-01/07-3550, para. 25.

access to any awards.[51]Furthermore, the ad hoc mechanisms have also carried out such outreach activities. The Regulations of the CRPC, for instance, instructed its staff members to disseminate relevant information as follows: 'Before claims registration takes place, an authorized staff member is obliged to inform the potential claimant as to how to submit a claim, about evidence and other information relevant for submitting a claim. The authorized staff member is also obliged to ensure that the potential claimant has expressed his free will regarding the disposal of the claimed real property.'[52] The mechanisms for the Holocaust victims, including ICHEIC, CRT-I and CRT-II, have conducted outreach activities using various techniques, such as public service announcements, posters, brochures, press releases, newspapers advertisements, radio spots, websites and press conferences to reach particularly disadvantaged victim communities.[53]

In addition to providing an effective reparation mechanism to victims, it is significant to listen to the voices of victims and to consult with them in each reparation proceeding. In the ICC, the voices of victims are taken into account in determining the types of reparation and the scope of beneficiaries. In the *Katanga* case, Trial Chamber II stressed that '[i]n determination of the reparations most appropriate to the case, it is paramount, in the Chamber's view, to heed the expectations and needs voiced by the victims in the various consultation exercises'.[54] Furthermore, the Appeals Chamber in the *Lubanga* case emphasized accessibility and consultation with victims and found that '[t]he Court should consult with victims on issues relating, *inter alia*, to the identity of the beneficiaries and their priorities'.[55]In the case of ad hoc reparation mechanisms, it seems necessary to hear the voices of victims in advance and reflect them in planning and designing a mechanism most suitable

---

[51] Situation in the Democratic Republic of the Congo in the Case of the *Prosecutor* v. *Thomas Lubanga Dyilo*, Appeals Chamber, Amended order for reparations (Annex A), 3 March 2015, ICC-01/04-01/06-3129-AnxA, paras. 51–2; Situation in the Democratic Republic of the Congo in the Case of the *Prosecutor* v. *Germain Katanga*, Trial Chamber II, Order for Reparations pursuant to Article 75 of the Statute, 24 March 2017, ICC-01/04-01/07, para. 345.

[52] Article 25, CRPC Book of Regulations on the Conditions and Decision Making Procedure for Claims for Return of Real Property of Displaced Persons and Refugees (4 March 1999), www.refworld.org/docid/3ae6b57c4.html.

[53] Holtzmann and Kristjánsdóttir (*supra* n. 47), pp. 144–7.

[54] *Prosecutor* v. *Germain Katanga*, Trial Chamber II (*supra* n. 51), para. 266.

[55] *Prosecutor* v. *Thomas Lubanga Dyilo*, Appeals Chamber, Amended order for reparations (*supra* n. 51), para. 32.

for their expectations and needs. Particularly the voices of relatively vulnerable victims should be heard and respected. The Updated Set of Principles therefore emphasizes this as one of the principles to be followed: 'Victims and other sectors of civil society should play a meaningful role in the design and implementation of [reparation] programmes. Concerted efforts should be made to ensure that women and minority groups participate in public consultations aimed at developing, implementing, and assessing reparations programmes.'[56] However, this principle has not necessarily been applied to all the reparation mechanisms established to date. In some mechanisms concerning the Holocaust, such as CRT-I, CRT-II and ICHEIC, victims or their representatives were involved in their design and became parties to the instruments for establishing them.[57] However, there was no involvement or participation of victims or victim representatives in the planning of the UNCC, the EECC or the CRPC.

Equal Treatment and Particular Support to Specific Groups of Victims

Victims are to be treated equally in every phase of the reparation mechanism. Several human rights treaties provide for a right to equal treatment without discrimination,[58] which is also applicable to the reparation mechanism. The Victims Declaration and the Basic Principles likewise stipulate a right to equal access to justice and emphasize that their application and interpretation have to occur without any discrimination of any kind or on any ground.[59] The need to provide reparations on a non-discriminatory basis has also been acknowledged in the jurisprudence of the ICC. Relying on the Basic Principles, the Appeals Chamber in the *Lubanga* case found, as echoed by Trial Chamber VIII in the *Al Mahdi* case, as follows: 'Reparation shall be granted to victims without adverse distinction on the grounds of gender, age, race, colour,

---

[56] Updated Set of Principles (*supra* n. 14), Principle 32.
[57] Holtzmann and Kristjánsdóttir (*supra* n. 47), p. 92. For the details of the instruments establishing these mechanisms, see *supra* notes 29, 30 and 31.
[58] See Article 26, International Covenant on Civil and Political Rights; Articles 2 and 3, African Charter on Human and Peoples' Rights; Article 24, American Convention on Human Rights; Article 14, Convention for the Protection of Human Rights and Fundamental Freedoms; Article 1, Protocol No. 12 to the Convention for the Protection of Human Rights and Fundamental Freedom.
[59] Victims Declaration (*supra* n. 7), para. 3; Basic Principles (*supra* n. 10), paras. 12 and 25.

language, religion or belief, political or other opinion, sexual orientation, national, ethnic or social origin, wealth, birth or other status.'[60]

However, it may not be incompatible with the prohibition of discrimination to provide particular support to specific groups of victims. Rather, during the implementation phase, it may be appropriate to prioritize reparations to those victims who were the most harmed by the violations of international law.[61] This consideration is reflected in the Report of the UN Secretary-General on the rule of law and transitional justice in conflict and post-conflict societies, which highlights the necessity to recognize 'the differential impact of conflict and rule of law deficits on women and children and the need to ensure gender sensitivity in restoration of rule of law and transitional justice, as well as the need to ensure the full participation of women'.[62] Furthermore, various human rights instruments stress that a reparation mechanism should take gender-sensitive measures to address the obstacles faced by women and girls in seeking access to it, particularly if they are claiming reparation for harm caused by sexual and gender-based violence,[63] and also the measures sensitive to the rights of children.[64] Taking these instruments into consideration, the Appeals Chamber found:

> A gender-inclusive approach should guide the design of the principles and procedures to be applied to reparations, ensuring that they are accessible to all victims in their implementation. . . . Priority may need to be given to certain victims, who are in a particularly vulnerable situation or who require urgent assistance. The Court may adopt, therefore, measures that constitute affirmative action in order to guarantee equal, effective and safe access to reparations for particularly vulnerable victims.[65]

---

[60] *Prosecutor v. Thomas Lubanga Dyilo*, Appeals Chamber, Amended order for reparations (*supra* n. 51), para. 16; Situation in the Republic of Mali in the Case of the *Prosecutor v. Ahmad Al Faqi Al Mahdi*, Trial Chamber VIII, Reparations Order, 17 August 2017, ICC-01/12-01/15, para. 31.

[61] Ibid., para. 29.

[62] Report of the Secretary-General (*supra* n. 13), para. 64(g).

[63] Nairobi Declaration (*supra* n. 24), General Principle 2; Beijing Declaration and Platform for Action (15 September 1995), Annex II: Platform for Action, para. 141.

[64] Guidelines on Justice in Matters involving Child Victims and Witnesses of Crime, Economic and Social Council, Resolution 2005/20 (22 July 2005), para. 35. See also Article 39 of the Convention on the Rights of the Child.

[65] *Prosecutor v. Thomas Lubanga Dyilo*, Appeals Chamber, Amended order for reparations (*supra* n. 51), paras. 18–19. It also held: 'In reparation decisions concerning children, the Court should be guided, *inter alia*, by the Convention on the Rights of the Child and the fundamental principle of the "best interests of the child" that is enshrined therein.' Ibid., para. 24.

Common Aspects of Claims Processing

A reparation mechanism must process large numbers of claims within a limited period of time, while guaranteeing a minimum degree of due process. Striking a suitable balance between these requirements has generated similar procedural features in the mechanisms established to date.

Collection and Processing of Claims

In terms of the methods used in the collection of claims, the past mechanisms have basically adopted two kinds of system. In the CRPC, the HPCC, the GFLCP and the IPCC, victims had the capacity to submit their claims directly to the mechanism. The ICC also follows this system. The UNCC and the EECC, on the contrary, adopted the system of consolidated claims under which only states were entitled to submit the claims of their nationals and corporations.[66] If prospective claims are limited in number, the direct submission system would be more convenient for victims. If it is expected, however, that a very large number of claims will be submitted, the indirect system would be eventually beneficial to victims in that it can lead to prompt reparation by reducing the time taken to process the claims.

The processing and resolution of large numbers of claims inevitably require a lot of time and resources, and as a consequence are very costly. A reparation mechanism can be expected to accomplish its task in a more efficient manner than would otherwise be possible through case-by-case decisions in domestic courts. Since judicial individualized proceedings that examine alleged facts and legal issues case-by-case are often not feasible in reparation mechanisms dealing with large numbers of claims, such mechanisms have to employ methods of processing the claims en masse. At the same time, however, a reparation mechanism must ensure

---

[66] Criteria for Expedited Processing of Urgent Claims, UN Doc. S/AC.26/1991/1, para. 19; Article 5(1), Provisional Rules for Claims Procedure, annexed to the Decision taken by the Governing Council of the United Nations Compensation Commission at the 27th meeting, Sixth session held on 26 June 1992, S/AC.26/1992/10 (26 June 1992); Article 5(8), Agreement between Ethiopia and Eritrea (*supra* n. 34). It is to be noted that, even in this system, the submission by states for their nationals is not based on the traditional rule of diplomatic protection; rather, those states merely assume a role of collection and transmission of individual claims for the purpose of processing a huge number of individual claims in an efficient and prompt way. See Report of the Secretary-General Pursuant to Paragraph 19 of Security Council resolution 687 (1991), S/22559 (2 May 1991), para. 21.

the fairness and due process of proceedings as much as possible. Striking a balance between the demands of speed and efficiency on the one hand and of fairness on the other is the central challenge in all efforts to design and implement a reparation mechanism.[67] This consideration led the past mechanisms to adopt special methodologies that facilitate the processing of large numbers of claims as expeditiously as circumstances permit.

One of the efficient methodologies in this respect was to divide the claims into different groups and give priority to some of them. The Governing Council of the UNCC, for instance, adopted a policy of classifying the claims into six categories on the basis of the type of claimants, the nature of their loss and the claimed amount of loss.[68] The UNCC appeared to give priority mainly to two considerations: the first was that the claims of individual victims were prioritized over those of legal persons, and the second was that the claims for smaller amounts were put before those of larger ones.

However, there might be other criteria for the grouping and priority of claims. Interestingly, Trial Chamber I of the ICC in the *Lubanga* case held as follows:

> The Chamber recognises that priority may need to be given to certain victims who are in a particularly vulnerable situation or who require urgent assistance. These may include, *inter alia*, the victims of sexual or gender-based violence, individuals who require immediate medical care (especially when plastic surgery or treatment for HIV is necessary), as well as severely traumatized children, for instance following the loss of family members. The Court may adopt, therefore, measures that constitute affirmative action in order to guarantee equal, effective and safe access to reparations for particularly vulnerable victims.[69]

The Trial Chamber's decision suggests that more carefully defined groups or sub-groups should be given priority.[70] In light of the distinct characteristics of victims in current armed conflicts (for example, violations or crimes against women and children), the gender and age of

---

[67] H. Das and H. van Houtte, *Post-War Restoration of Property Rights under International Law*, Vol. 2: Procedural Aspects (Cambridge University Press, 2008), p. 2.

[68] Criteria for Expedited Processing of Urgent Claims (*supra* n. 36), para. 66.

[69] *Prosecutor* v. *Thomas Lubanga Dyilo* (*supra* n. 22), para. 200.

[70] Rule 65 of the Regulations of the Trust Fund for Victims provides that: 'Taking into account the urgent situation of the beneficiaries, the Board of Directors may decide to institute phased or priority verification and disbursement procedures. In such cases, the Board of Directors may prioritize a certain sub-group of victims for verification and disbursement.' Resolution ICC-ASP/4/Res.3 (3 December 2005).

victims are important factors that should be taken into consideration in grouping claimants.[71]

While often very large numbers of claims are submitted to a reparation mechanism, most of the claims, if not all, typically arise out of incidents occurring in the same geographical area, having been committed by the same entities and having caused the same or similar harms. This means that practically most of the claims are quite similar in terms of the factual and legal issues that they raise. This similarity allowed past mechanisms to use, in addition to grouping, various methods that enabled them to process numerous claims in an expeditious manner and at a minimal transaction cost, including sampling, the use of information technology (such as computerized data matching and database facilities), statistical tools (such as regression analysis), making precedent-setting decisions and applying them to similar claims, standardized verification and valuation of claims, and awarding fixed amounts.[72]

Valuation of Claims

When a reparation mechanism is established in the wake of an armed conflict, it is quite likely that victims do not have any documentary evidence available to demonstrate their losses and, if they do, the quality of the evidence may be poor.[73] For the mechanism, on the other hand, it is important to avoid spending disproportionate amounts of time and resources verifying and valuating all the claims.[74] These factors have led many mechanisms to adopt a lower standard of proof as compared with strict evidentiary requirements to be fulfilled in arbitration and court litigation.[75]

---

[71] See Nairobi Declaration (*supra* n. 24), para. 7.

[72] See Heiskanen (*supra* n. 5), pp. 27–9; Das and van Houtte (*supra* n. 67), pp. 147–257; Holtzmann and Kristjánsdóttir (*supra* n. 47), pp. 244–7.

[73] Das and van Houtte (*supra* n. 67), pp. 59–61; The Trial Chamber I of the ICC also pointed out: 'Several factors are of significance in determining the appropriate standard of proof at this stage, including the difficulty victims may face in obtaining evidence in support of their claims due to the destruction or unavailability of evidence.' *Prosecutor* v. *Thomas Lubanga Dyilo* (*supra* n. 22), para. 252.

[74] Holtzmann and Kristjánsdóttir (*supra* n. 47), p. 246.

[75] 'The circumstances in which the claimants' losses occurred, specifically those in Iraq or Kuwait, may have had a significant impact on claimants' abilities to provide evidence in support of their claims. Thus, for example, consideration was given to the general emergency conditions prevailing in Kuwait and Iraq under which many thousands of individuals were forced to flee or hide or were held captive, without safely securing their possessions or retaining documents that later could be used to substantiate their losses.'

The UNCC applied more simplified verification procedures for urgent individual claims than for the larger claims of categories, and also applied different standards of proof for the claims of different amounts within a category. The HPCC also adopted rather flexible rules of evidence and proof, because the cadastral records had been removed from Kosovo to Serbia and claimants in many cases had difficulty demonstrating their rights by official records. The HPCC Rules of Procedure and Evidence provided that '[t]he Commission may be guided but is not bound by the rules of evidence applied in local courts in Kosovo. The Commission may consider any reliable evidence, which it considers relevant to the claim . . . .'[76]

Simplified verification is also needed for mechanisms dealing with claims arising from events long past. In the case of the mechanisms concerning reparation for Holocaust victims, the lapse of time from the events causing their harms brought about various delicate evidentiary problems. Evidence that might easily have been obtained at that time was lost or quite difficult to obtain when the mechanisms were established. Thus, most of them adopted an innovative concept of 'relaxed standard of proof' for finding facts, based on the test of what is 'plausible' in place of the traditional judicial standards according to which facts are determined by a 'preponderance of the evidence'.[77] The CRT-I Rules of Procedure, for example, stated as follows:

> The claimant must show that it is plausible in light of all the circumstances that he or she is entitled, in whole or in part, to the dormant account. The Sole Arbitrators or the Claims Panels shall assess all information submitted by the parties or otherwise available to them. They shall at all times bear in mind the difficulties of proving a claim after the destruction of the Second World War and the Holocaust and the long time that has lapsed since the opening of these dormant accounts.[78]

In line with a lower standard of proof, presumptions and inferences have often been used in the past mechanisms. In the CRPC, it was

---

Report and Recommendations Made by the Panel of Commissioners Concerning the First Instalment of Individual Claims for Damages up to $100,000, UN Doc. S/AC.26/1994/3 (21 December 1994), p. 27.

[76] Section 21.1, Regulation No. 2000/60 on Residential Property Claims and the Rules of Procedure and Evidence of the Housing and Property Directorate and the Housing and Property Claims Commission, UNMIK/REG/2000/60 (31 October 2000), www.unmikonline.org/regulations/unmikgazette/02english/E2000regs/RE2000_60.htm.

[77] Holtzmann and Kristjánsdóttir (*supra* n. 47), p. 211.

[78] Article 22(1), CRT-I Rules of Procedure for the Claims Resolution Process, www.crt-ii.org/_crt-i/frame.html. See also Article 17(2), CRT-II Rules Governing the Claims Resolution Process (as amended), www.crt-ii.org/_pdf/governing_rules_en.pdf.

presumed that claimants were refugees or displaced persons at the time of registering their claims. Besides, the claimants were not required to prove that they had not been in possession of the real property they claimed.[79] The CRT-II also invoked several presumptions including in relation to claims to certain closed accounts, and the value of accounts with unknown or low values.[80] Moreover, in order to establish a claim for slave labour before the GFLCP, it was sufficient for a claimant to show that he or she had been held in a concentration camp, ghetto or comparable place of confinement. As these examples indicate, the victims benefiting from presumptions are exempt from having to prove the presumed fact, and it is incumbent upon the responsible party to present counter-evidence rebutting the presumptions.[81]

The presumptions and the lower standards of proof are also used at the ICC. For instance, Trial Chamber II in the *Katanga* case, citing the examples of the Inter-American Court of Human Rights, the GFLCP and the UNCC, found that 'having regard to the practice of the Inter-American Court and certain transitional justice mechanisms, the Chamber sees fit to proceed on presumptions and to act on circumstantial evidence to satisfy itself of certain facts in the case'.[82]

In addition to the lower standards of proof, simplified proceedings will often be necessary for the efficient operation of the mechanism. In judicial proceedings, the holding of hearings and the opportunity to examine witnesses are essential elements of due process. However, one can find a clear tendency from relatively old mechanisms to new ones, and certainly from smaller to larger ones, to reduce or even abandon the possibility of a hearing. According to the UNCC Provisional Rules, 'each panel will normally make its recommendations without holding an oral proceeding, though the panel may determine that special circumstances warrant holding an oral proceeding concerning a particular claim or claims'.[83] In practice, however, oral hearings were not held at all in the urgent claims categories, and only a few were held in the larger categories.

---

[79] Articles 11 and 12, CRPC Book of Regulations on the Conditions and Decision Making Procedure for Claims for Return of Real Property of Displaced Persons and Refugees (8 October 2002), www.law.kuleuven.be.

[80] Articles 28 and 29, CRT-II Rules Governing the Claims Resolution Process (as amended) (*supra* n. 78). See also Article 25 on joint accounts.

[81] Das and van Houtte (*supra* n. 67), pp. 142.

[82] *Prosecutor* v. *Germain Katanga*, Trial Chamber II (*supra* n. 51), para. 61.

[83] Article 37(c), Provisional Rules for Claims Procedure, annexed to the Decision taken by the Governing Council of the United Nations Compensation Commission at the 27th meeting, Sixth session held on 26 June 1992, S/AC.26/1992/10 (26 June 1992).

The CRT-I Rules of Procedure provided that the Sole Arbitrators and Claims Panels should, to the extent possible, conduct the proceedings as a documents-only arbitration, but if necessary they could examine the parties, interview witnesses and hear oral arguments.[84] In practice, all claims were decided without hearings. This is also true for the HPCC, which had the discretion to consider oral submissions,[85] but had no hearing in practice. In contrast, the CRT-II, the GFLCP and the ICHEIC were conducted on the basis of documents only, and their constituent instruments and rules did not provide for hearings at all. In this respect, an exception is the ICC in which oral hearings are held with the participation of legal representatives of victims.[86] While holding hearings would be desirable from the standpoint of due process, it is clear that hearings are costly and time-consuming, and would therefore in many situations impair the interests of victims. Therefore, where a mechanism has to deal with large numbers of claims, hearings are generally not feasible.

Funding for Reparations

A reparation mechanism needs a secure financial foundation so that it can be carried through after its launch.[87] Depending on the political and social context in which a reparation mechanism becomes necessary, as well as the expectations and needs that victims have, there may be various potential sources of funding.[88] Nevertheless, the basis of funding may be divided into two types: responsibility-based funding and solidarity-based funding.

Responsibility-based funding means that the parties, whether state, organized armed group or individual, responsible for the harms suffered by victims fund a reparation mechanism. At least theoretically, it is well-accepted that a responsible party is obliged to make effective reparation to victims and, therefore, to fund the mechanism under which those victims' reparation claims are processed. In essence, responsibility-based

---

[84] Article 17(iv), CRT-I Rules of Procedure for the Claims Resolution Process (*supra* n. 78).
[85] Section 19.2, UNMIK Regulation No. 2000/60 (*supra* n. 76).
[86] See Rome Statute, Article 75(3) and the Rules of Procedure and Evidence, Rule 91(2).
[87] J. R. Crook, 'Mass Claims Processes: Lessons Learned over Twenty-Five Years', in IBPCA (*supra* n. 5), p. 57.
[88] H. van Houtte, B. Delmartino and I. Yi, *Post-War Restoration of Property Rights under International Law*, Vol. I: Institutional Features and Substantive Law (Cambridge University Press, 2008), p. 131.

funding rests on the traditional model of 'right-holder' and 'duty-bearer' relations.

However, in the wake of armed conflict, this model does not necessarily work well. First, it may be difficult to identify the responsible parties, as states are usually reluctant to admit their responsibility in the aftermath of armed conflict. Second, certain political needs sometimes obscure violators' responsibility and frustrate identifying the responsible parties. This arises particularly in cases where finger-pointing at a responsible party in a ceasefire agreement or peace treaty can be counterproductive and detrimental to ending an armed conflict. Finally, the responsibility-based model relies on the responsible parties' solvency, but, sometimes, they lack sufficient assets to fund the mechanism.[89] This particularly applies to individuals or organized armed groups with limited assets available for reparation. From a legal perspective, indigence does not obstruct the imposition of responsibility for reparations on a responsible party.[90] From a practical and financial standpoint, however, it is a serious problem that may jeopardize the entire scheme of compensating victims.

In some mechanisms concerning the Holocaust, such as the GFLCP, the certain amount of funding for reparations was provided by companies which had been criticized for their involvement in the forced labour and for gaining considerable benefits during the armed conflict. However, the funding by these companies was not based on their *legal* responsibility for the human rights abuses that they had allegedly committed; rather, it took the form of *voluntary* contribution with a view to cooperating with the redress project for victims, while substantially being based on moral responsibility. To materialize the responsibility-based funding, whether legal or moral, it is crucial for decision-makers to examine who actually profited from an armed conflict and thereon to construct a suitable mechanism for funding. It is also important to mobilize international public opinion to drive those substantially responsible for armed conflict to contribute to the funding of a reparation mechanism. The mechanisms for Holocaust victims are successful examples. However, apart from those Holocaust cases, past experience indicates that it is not necessarily easy to effectuate responsibility-based funding and, even if it is successfully brought into a mechanism for

---

[89] Ibid., pp. 132–3.
[90] *Prosecutor* v. *Thomas Lubanga Dyilo*, Appeals Chamber, Judgment (*supra* n. 4), paras. 102–5.

reparation, that funding is not sufficient for providing victims with effective reparation.

To overcome these difficulties, solidarity-based funding has been introduced. The solidarity-based model involves raising funds in the public interest, irrespective of the legal or moral responsibility of the perpetrators of harm.[91] There may be various types of funding in this model, such as voluntary contributions from third states, international organizations, corporates, NGOs and individual donors. However, these contributions are commonly made to indicate solidarity with the victims, at least to a certain extent. In fact, several past reparation mechanisms were designed and operated on the basis of such voluntary contributions.

In terms of the CRPC, for instance, the Agreement on Refugees and Displaced Persons annexed to the Dayton Peace Agreement provided that the parties to the agreement should bear its expenses equally;[92] in fact, however, the CRPC did not receive any funding from them.[93] Instead, the CRPC operated through voluntary contributions from several European states, Canada and the United States, as well as from international organizations, including the European Union and the World Bank.[94] Similarly, the HPCC, though partly funded by the Kosovo Consolidated Budget of the UNMIK, largely relied on voluntary contributions from international donors, including various states and the European Union.[95] The Trust Fund for Victims of the ICC is, likewise, funded by voluntary contributions from governments, international organizations, individuals, corporations and other entities.[96]

---

[91] The concept of the solidarity-based model is inspired by the analysis of van Houtte, Delmartino and Yi, but its meaning here is somewhat different from the original. See van Houtte, Delmartino and Yi (*supra* n. 88), p. 136.

[92] Article X(2), Agreement on Refugees and Displaced Persons (*supra* n. 28).

[93] End of Mandate Report (1996–2003), Executive Summary, 13, www.pict-pcti.org/publica tions/Bibliographies/EMR-Part1-CoverExec1-Summary-EMR.pdf.

[94] See Chart: History of Funding of CRPC (US Dollars) Sorted by Largest Donor, ibid., 14; See also H. van Houtte, 'The Property Claims Commission in Bosnia-Herzegovina: A New Path to Restore Real Estate Rights in Post-War Societies', in K. C. Wellens (ed.), *International Law: Theory and Practice: Essays in Honour of Eric Suy* (Brill, 1998), pp. 553–4.

[95] According to the Kosovo Property Agency, direct funding from individual governments constituted 60 per cent of total contributions. UNMIK and the Kosovo Consolidated Budget covered 12 per cent and 28 per cent of the annual budget of 2006, respectively. The Housing and Property Directorate and the Kosovo Property Agency, Joint Annual Report 2006, 45, www.kpaonline.org/PDFs/AR2006.pdf.

[96] Establishment of a fund for the benefit of victims of crimes within the jurisdiction of the Court, and of the families of such victims, Resolution ICC-ASP/1/Res.6 (9 September 2002), para. 2(a).

Inevitably, the motives underlying such contributions, given the absence of a legal obligation, vary between donors. Some may consider it in their own long-term interest, while others may feel certain moral obligations to contribute or be guided by a spirit of dedication as a *neighbour* of the victims. Regardless, it is undeniable that donations are often unpredictable and related to external factors.[97] Private donors are easily influenced by changes in media coverage from one armed conflict to another. There may also be a risk of donor fatigue. While states, corporates and other organizations are often willing to pledge money during the early stages of a mechanism, this commitment normally wanes over time. To this extent, the reality of voluntary contributions to the reparation mechanisms cannot be regarded as perfectly following the solidarity-based model.

Nevertheless, the practice of the ad hoc reparation mechanisms and the ICC indicates a tendency in the international community to support victim reparation mechanisms through voluntary donations, particularly in cases of non-international armed conflict. In this respect, the right of victims to receive reparations is given substance by the commitment of the international community, not only to the initiatives taken to establish suitable mechanisms but also to drawing potential donors' attention to post-conflict states and communities.

Conclusion

The structure and procedure of reparation mechanisms vary depending on the political and social circumstances of conflict and the needs of victims. In this respect, there is no ready-made model for a future reparation mechanism, and it must be concluded that the success of any model lies in the individual approach adopted by the policy-makers involved in blueprinting the mechanism. However, the comparative analysis of past mechanisms clarifies that there are some common and basic principles, or at least similar considerations, to be taken into account when a new reparation mechanism is established.

Such common principles provide future policy-makers with necessary information on the core points that need to be examined, and thereby assist them in establishing an effective mechanism as promptly as possible after an armed conflict ends. At the same time, these principles are in fact sending a strong signal to the international community that victims

---

[97] Van Houtte, Delmartino and Yi (*supra* n. 88), p. 135.

should enjoy a right to a fair and effective mechanism for reparation. Only sufficient support by the international community can ensure the realization of a truly effective mechanism before which victims are able to exercise their substantive right to reparation granted under international law. In particular, political and social pressure exerted by the international community is an important element to establish more effective funding mechanisms to which private entities such as companies and banks, who have gained considerable benefits illegally from armed conflict, are also obliged to make contributions. In this respect as well, we need to learn more from the experiences of past mechanisms and elaborate common and basic principles for establishing a more effective reparation mechanism for the future.

Conclusion

The Relationship between Economic and Atrocity Crimes

Challenges and Opportunities

STEPHEN J. RAPP

During my work at the International Criminal Tribunal for Rwanda (ICTR) and the Special Court for Sierra Leone (SCSL) prosecuting the alleged perpetrators of atrocities – genocide, crimes against humanity and war crimes – I saw how these crimes were often motivated by a desire to gain or hold power over a state or territory in order to plunder public resources.

In the case of Rwanda, evidence pointed to a narrow group that controlled the state and used the state's power to place its leading members at the head of parastatal enterprises or governmental offices, where they could collect corrupt rewards. When these leaders were threatened with the loss of access to this wealth during a civil war, and then by implementation of a peace agreement that would have required them to share power, they sought to divert attention from their corruption through propaganda that blamed an ethnic minority for all of the nation's problems. They communicated messages through the mass media that awakened old ethnic animosities, and they then deployed the resources and the workers under their control to finance and fill the ranks of militias that would commit genocide against the ethnic minority. The result was the murder of 800,000 men, women and children in only 100 days.

In Liberia and Sierra Leone, armed groups conducted campaigns of terror against civilian populations in order to gain control of territory or state institutions for no apparent reason other than to control and exploit national resources. In Liberia, Charles Taylor and his NPFL were not content with the control of abundant upcountry natural resources but sought to take formal power in Monrovia in order to access the government treasury and to be able to legally license the continued exploitation. In Sierra Leone, the RUF, led by Foday Sankoh and actively supported by Taylor, initiated the conflict and was responsible for the majority of atrocities, but it did not have a program to further the interests of any aggrieved religious or ethnic group. The absence of political objectives beyond empowerment (and enrichment) of the leadership made it difficult for the RUF to recruit adults to fight, and the warriors of choice became children – kidnapped, doped and trained to blindly commit acts of brutality in order to bludgeon communities into submission.

Elsewhere in a large part of the world, there has existed the perception that political power carries with it the right to plunder public resources or control state institutions in order to provide employment, land or projects to specific ethnic or regional groups. This has led to political contests, even democratic elections, having "all or nothing" consequences. Thus, electoral fraud has become a means to retain control of economic resources, and these contests create flashpoints for violence, even the commission of atrocities, for those aggrieved by electoral loss, whether they were defeated by means fair or foul.

From a prosecutor's point of view, this relationship between economic crime and atrocity crime may open opportunities to achieve accountability where the economic crime route is open while other routes are effectively blocked. There is the Al Capone approach – the pursuit of the infamous mobster not for murder, extortion, or robbery, but for tax evasion. At the international level, it should be observed that Slobodan Milošević was originally charged and detained by national authorities for corruption, and that Omar al-Bashir now sits in jail in Khartoum not for international crimes but because of the unexplained wealth that he gained during his long years in power. One could only wish that the international community was as unified in 2019 to negotiate the "win-win" solution to bring Bashir to The Hague as it was to bring Milošević there in 2001.

Indeed, sometimes economic crimes prosecution has been followed to a conclusion not available with atrocity prosecution. In Guatemala, the CICIG-assisted investigation of President Perez-Molina led in 2015 to his prosecution for a massive customs fraud and also to a popular mobilization that brought more than a hundred thousand citizens into the streets of Guatemala City to demand that he face justice and for an end to political corruption. Because the theft was from the whole public, the mobilization was broadly based, and protected the judicial process from political interference, all of which led to Perez-Molina's resignation, arrest and immediate detention. At the same time, the prosecution of former President Efraim Rios-Montt, which had resulted in his historic conviction of genocide after trial in 2013, was not as broadly supported or protected, allowing it to be aborted by a politically-inspired appellate court decision that set aside the conviction and ordered a re-trial that could never be completed. Nonetheless, the survivors of Rios-Montt's crimes were in the street in 2015 cheering for justice in the corruption case of Perez-Molina and reminding everyone that he had been known as "Major Tito," a lieutenant of Rios-Montt in the genocidal campaign against the Maya in the 1980s – an involvement that came to light during testimony in the Rios-Montt trial.

Can a Focus on the Economic Aspects of Atrocity Crimes Lead to Greater Justice for Victims?

The survivors of the genocide and other atrocities committed in Guatemala would certainly have preferred that alleged perpetrators, like Perez-Molina, faced justice on charges of responsibility for atrocity crimes. And the pursuit of accountability for the atrocity crimes, combined with a focus on economic resources that the responsible persons had sought to gain or protect, might have opened the way for the survivors to see not just punishment of the perpetrators but also payment by these perpetrators or their enablers for the benefit of those who suffered.

As Shuichi Furuya shows us in Chapter 18, the international community has come to recognize reparations as an essential entitlement of the victims of these serious crimes. Yet, as Daley Birkett informs us in Chapter 17, the limitations in the statutes and the lack of will or capacity at international courts and tribunals has meant that there have almost never been direct recoveries of ill-gotten gains for the benefit of victims. As Birkett notes, the only realistic present prospect of such recoveries arises from the reparations award pronounced by the Extraordinary African Chambers against Hissène Habré for about 140 million USD and the availability of assets equal to a fraction of this amount in Senegal. Otherwise, even when courts, or non-judicial mechanisms, have had the power to award reparations, they have had to rely on "solidarity-based" funding, generally from international donors, which method is woefully insufficient to remedy the human harm caused by atrocity crimes.

I saw it in Sierra Leone, where a separate victim reparations program was established by the government and received contributions from the United Nations (UN) Peacebuilding Commission and a few foreign states to a total of about 8.5 million USD. After extensive consultations led by the Sierra Leone National Commission for Social Action (NaCSA), a plan was developed to share these contributions with the tens of thousands of victims of sexual violence and amputations, as well as the survivors of murdered noncombatants. In the end, cash payments averaging about 100 USD were made to individual victims, and skills training and start-up kits were provided to members of specific groups. I know from speaking with amputees that the awards and services were so limited that the program had no real impact on their lives. Indeed, the more than 1,200 registered victims in Sierra Leone who survive without hands and other limbs have rarely received the simplest prostheses, let alone what is available to accident victims in richer countries.

The ICC has the best statutory framework for victim reparations, but it still must rely on the solidarity-based donations from a handful of generous countries for all of the funds in its Trust Fund for Victims (TFV). So far, with final convictions only in the *Lubanga*, *Katanga* and *al-Mahdi* cases on evidence that focused on narrow crime bases, the number of court-recognized victims has been very low. When the first conviction founded on a wide crime base is finalized, unless there is some monetary recovery from those who committed or benefited from the crimes, the victims will almost certainly be deeply disappointed.

In fact, none of the post-Cold War tribunals, courts and other mechanisms has been as successful in pursuing economic actors and obtaining reparations as those employed after World War II, two approaches of which are described by Kirsten Sellars and Hans Otto Frøland in Chapters 1 and 2.

The Use of Financial Recoveries from US Prosecutions of Banks and Other Corporations to Fund Victims' Reparations and Assistance

My own earlier experience as a US Attorney has given me some hope that victim reparations need not be always underfunded. My office and those of other federal prosecutors were provided with the resources to locate and recover assets from those who had violated federal law, not only for the benefit of defrauded government agencies but also for individual victims of federal crimes. Statutory tools were enacted by Congress to enable the reversal of conveyances made to hide assets and the pursuit of compensation from third parties who had failed in their protective duties. Even in cases of "Ponzi schemes," where assets are generally dissipated by fraudsters who pay outsize returns to investors in order to attract new ones, there have been substantial recoveries. For instance, in the case of Bernard Madoff, who was charged in 2008 for stealing and dissipating 19 billion USD from his clients, recoveries by 2018 totaled 13.3 billion USD and more were in sight.

The US statutory framework has benefited not only the victims of federal crimes but also the victims of violent crimes prosecuted at the local level, where the vast majority of such cases are charged. The Victims of Crimes Act of 1984 (VOCA) established a Crime Victims Fund (CVF) into which fines and financial forfeitures of federal crimes were to be deposited and then made available to assist local violent crime victims. The assistance included financial support for state programs to reimburse victims' out-of-pocket expenses incurred for medical care and rehabilitation services, which awards were initially capped at 2,500 USD but are now allowed up to 50,000 USD. The CVF also has provided funding for victim/witness support units in local prosecutors' offices across America and has made grants to community organizations to provide aid and advocacy for crime victims. The amount allocated to reparations and assistance rose from 68 million USD in 1985 to 3.6 billion USD in 2015. At the same time, the fines and forfeitures deposited in the CVF rose during the same years from 100 million USD to 4.5 billion USD, with Congress sometimes sending the excess to the general federal budget.

Financial recoveries by US prosecutors exploded after the "Great Recession" of 2008 that was brought on by predatory mortgage lending and the reckless repackaging of mortgage debt. Prosecutors were criticized for not jailing individuals; for allowing bank executives to "buy" their freedom from prosecution with their shareholders' value. Nevertheless, the recoveries were enormous. In the period between 2008 and 2018, US fines and financial settlements with banks totaled a whopping 243 billion USD, with recoveries ranging from 6.5 billion USD from UBS to 76.1 billion USD from Bank of America. Increasingly, large shares of these recoveries were not denominated as criminal fines (that would have gone into the CVF) but instead were sent to settlement-created mechanisms to provide relief for aggrieved consumers.

But not all the recoveries were for crimes like mortgage fraud, as the 8.9 billion USD settlement with BNP-Paribas announced by US Attorney General Eric Holder in 2014 arose from the bank's violations of US sanctions against Sudan, Iran and Cuba. There also have been large recoveries for violations of the Federal Corrupt Practices Act (FCPA) from nonbanking corporations, many of them domiciled abroad but transacting business through the New York financial hub. During 2008 to 2018, there were twenty-six companies that paid settlements of more than 100 million USD, ranging from 105 million USD paid by Singapore's Keppel Offshore & Marine to 800 million USD paid by Germany's Siemens AG. While there are critics of the US approach, it does show that legal enforcement tools can be used effectively to achieve enormous financial recoveries from organizations that are implicated in violating criminal law. "There's gold in them thar hills."

Overcoming the Corporate Impunity Gap at International Courts and in Many Domestic Systems

As we are reminded by Juan Calderon-Meza in Chapter 14, the statutes of the ad hoc and hybrid tribunals and of the International Criminal Court (ICC) do not provide for jurisdiction over corporations, and so it is impossible for international prosecutors to seek recoveries from corporations in the same way that US prosecutors have pursued banks and other companies. This could be corrected in the statutes of future tribunals, and ideally by amendment to the ICC Statute, though it would require a vote of seven-eighths of the state parties under Article 121(4). It is significant that the proposed Crimes Against Humanity treaty includes corporate criminal liability, and one can hope that it will be ratified and implemented in domestic statutes.[1]

But even before international courts are granted jurisdiction, the increased reliance on third-countries to prosecute international crimes in domestic systems and the criminal liability of corporations in many of these systems have opened the way to pursue companies for complicity in international crimes, as shown in the French prosecution of LaFarge Holcim Ltd. for making payments to the Islamic State (IS) during 2011–2014. In Sweden, it has been possible to attribute corporate acts to senior corporate executives as shown by the government's authorization in 2018 of the investigation and prosecution of Ian Lundin and Alex Schneiter for war crimes committed during 1998–2003 near Bentiu, in

[1] International Law Commission, A/CN.4/L.935, Texts and titles of the draft preamble, the draft articles and the draft annex provisionally adopted by the Drafting Committee on second reading, "Prevention and punishment of crimes against humanity," May 15, 2019, Article 6(8).

what is now South Sudan. It has been alleged that in their management of Lundin Petroleum, there was criminal complicity with armed groups that cleared territory of civilians in order to facilitate oil exploration and drilling – exactly the kind of "landgrabbing" that is described by James Stewart in Chapter 8.

Of course, for many atrocity crimes, there is presently no international criminal tribunal with jurisdiction even over natural persons, and national systems are the only route to justice. But even where there is an international tribunal pursuing individuals, there is nothing to prevent them from cooperating with national prosecutors who are using domestic remedies to pursue related cases against other defendants. At the SCSL, where we prosecuted Liberian President Charles Taylor for atrocity crimes committed in Sierra Leone, we cooperated with US authorities who were prosecuting his son "Chucky" Taylor (Charles Taylor Jr.), aka Roy Belfast, for acts of torture and murder committed in Liberia while serving as head of his father's Anti-Terrorism Unit (ATU). That cooperation was particularly important at the investigatory stage but continued through trial where a common victim-witness testified in both The Hague and Miami. In the end, the father received a fifty-year sentence, and the son one of ninety-seven years.

The same thing could happen where national prosecutors in third states are pursuing corporate actors while, or even before, national prosecutors are investigating individuals in the territorial state. And the action against the corporations in the third state may be possible on a civil rather than a criminal basis. In the grand corruption case of 1MBD arising out of Malaysia (though it is without a clear atrocity crime connection), US federal authorities filed a civil forfeiture action in July 2016 seeking to recover against companies and individuals that had received investments and gifts from the stolen loot. The case was part of the US Justice Department's "Kleptocracy Initiative" that had earlier made recoveries of assets stolen by political leaders in Nigeria, Kazakhstan and Equatorial Guinea, and that had then negotiated arrangements to return the assets to the rightful owners in the affected countries. In the 1MBD case, US prosecutors were able to recover 60 million USD that had been siphoned by 1MBD to Red Granite, the production company of the Hollywood film *The Wolf of Wall Street*, and the voluntary return of a Picasso worth 3.2 million USD that had been given to its star, Leonardo DiCaprio. In May 2018, Malaysian Prime Minister Najib Razak was unexpectedly defeated for re-election, and was thereafter prosecuted in Malaysia, together with his wife and entourage, for their role in the pilferage of 1MBD. With this change in national leadership, the way was opened for the US-seized assets to be returned directly to the public treasury of Malaysia.

The Pursuit of "Flying Money" at the Special Court for Sierra Leone

In Chapter 10, Nina Jørgensen has provided a comprehensive overview of the prosecution of Charles Taylor, which resulted in his conviction and fifty-year sentence on eleven counts of war crimes and crimes against humanity but not any recovery of his "flying money" for the benefit of victims.

Whether Taylor had continued access to significant assets was very much a matter of dispute and the SCSL provided him with a court-funded defense team on the grounds of indigency, as it had all the other defendants. However, there were numerous public reports alleging that Taylor had seized millions of dollars in public resources and had run Liberia as "Charles Taylor Inc." While the SCSL Statute did not provide for awards of reparations, Article 19(3) allowed for restitution of stolen property or its proceeds to the rightful owner or to the government of Sierra Leone, and Rule 104 provided a procedure for post-judgment determination as to property or proceeds to be forfeited, even when held by third parties. The SCSL had also entered into an agreement which provided that awards of forfeited property that were transferred to the Sierra Leone government would go into the national fund for victim reparations managed by NaCSA. If Taylor's assets were found and seized and some part attributed to diamonds pillaged in Sierra Leone, then there could have been some recovery for the victims of the crimes for which he was convicted.[2]

---

[2] It was only in the Prosecutor's Case Summary filed in August 2007 that it was explicitly asserted that Taylor had "participated in a common plan ... in order to pillage the resources of Sierra Leone, in particular the diamonds." This document was filed because Trial Chamber II, which was to try Taylor, had decided in its previous judgment in June 2007 concerning former members of the Armed Forces Revolutionary Council (AFRC) that the "common plan [or joint criminal enterprise]" required a "criminal purpose," and that the originally-pleaded purpose of taking control of the territory of Sierra Leone was not criminal under the SCSL Statute. While it would be asserted in the Prosecutor's appeal of the AFRC trial judgment that the law only required a showing that the common plan be accomplished by "criminal means," the Case Summary was filed defensively to assert a criminal purpose (the commission of the war crime of pillage) to protect the JCE theory of criminal liability in the event the Prosecutor's appeal was not

However, proving that Taylor's funds included the proceeds of diamonds and then following those funds downstream required active cooperation of Liberian authorities, particularly for access to bank records. The prosecution's efforts to pursue Charles Taylor's assets were hampered by the absence of government capacity and political will in Liberia. As Nina Jørgensen notes in Chapter 10, the UN Security Council ordered sanctions against Taylor and the members of his entourage who were believed to be holding his largesse. These were implemented across the globe, even by Gaddafi's Libya, but not in Liberia. When I pursued the matter with the Liberian government, I was told by the Minister of Justice that President Sirleaf did not wish to use an executive order that could have only a year's duration, and would instead seek passage of a legislative bill to implement the UN Security Council (UNSC)-ordered asset freeze. But the Liberian peace accord negotiated in Accra in 2003 had been a power-sharing agreement. After the election of November 2005 brought Sirleaf to power, the Liberian Legislature included former war criminals and several other members who benefited from the patronage of the rich individuals on the UN sanctions list. The Sirleaf government provided no effective support for the legislation to implement UN sanctions, and when her bill was put to a legislative roll call, it received exactly zero votes.

Moreover, the SCSL had not been provided with the budget to hire experienced financial investigators, and the prosecution needed to devote its in-house investigative personnel to efforts to find witnesses who could tie the high-level actors like Charles Taylor to the commission of atrocities by fighters on the ground. This meant seeking expert assistance from supportive states. In 2007, the UK Department for International Development (DFID) awarded a "scoping grant" to a London firm of solicitors that had been successful in recovering assets stolen from Nigeria by its late President Sani Abacha. The scoping report concluded that there were likely to be hidden Taylor assets, and suggested several possible avenues for recovery. In 2008, I was able to convince the Swiss government to deploy an experienced former Geneva prosecutor, Laurent Kasper-Ansermet, to assist in tracing Taylor's assets. Laurent

successful. The Prosecutor won the issue in the AFRC Appeals Judgment decided in February 2008. This reduced the need to focus on diamond pillage to obtain a JCE-based conviction, but led to the confusion about the JCE case theory as noted by Nina Jørgensen in Chapter 10, and resulted in there not being a clear precedent on pillage of natural resources as a war crime that would have been so useful to Eve La Haye in her analysis in Chapter 7.

prepared detailed *commissions rogatoires internationales* (CRIs) which were served on the Liberian Ministry of Justice. He was intensely frustrated that none of his requests received a response from the Liberians and he departed after the end of his six-month deployment (and was later nominated by the UN to be co-investigative judge at the Khmer Rouge tribunal (Extraordinary Chambers in the Courts of Cambodia)). In the end, the SCSL obtained no bank records from Liberian authorities, and received only the Liberian bank records that were taken during a separate US-supported investigation of corrupt timber concessions that was completed in 2005.

At the SCSL, there was the alternative of seeking judicial assistance from other third states, and authorities of several were willing to assist even in the absence of formal powers under Chapter 7 of the UN Charter that had been provided to the ad hoc tribunals by the UNSC. But given the lack of evidence from Liberia as to the criminal origin of assets, this was challenging. In 2003, Swiss authorities froze about 2 million CHF of Taylor-related assets. But the freezing order was later lifted because it was not possible to tie the assets to his alleged criminal activity. Cooperation was potentially available in the United States because 28 U.S.C. § 1782 allowed prosecutors of international tribunals to access judicial process, usually through the office of International Affairs in the Justice Department. Early in the SCSL's investigations, a prosecution request to US authorities yielded bank records of the correspondent account at Citibank in New York where the Liberian Bank of Development and Industry (LBDI) held funds for transactions on behalf of the Liberian government. That this was an LBDI account was relevant because the "timber concessions" investigation had revealed that Taylor had used an account at LBDI for large cash transactions and had often been permitted to be deeply overdrawn.

The DFID-funded scoping report identified multiple transactions from the records of the LBDI correspondent account at Citibank that suggested that Taylor had used the government funds in the account for personal purposes. But when the prosecution sought assistance from US authorities to subpoena the records of banks other than Citibank to follow suspicious outflows from the correspondent account, the US response was a demand for more specificity. This was difficult to provide in the absence of information from Liberia and at a time when almost all investigative positions had been eliminated under the SCSL's completion strategy. Even if additional bank records had been obtained from the United States, it is likely that the trail would have led to banks in third countries where cooperation would be even more difficult and where one would still have been years behind fast-moving "flying money."

At the SCSL, we also had to keep in mind that victims of Taylor's crimes in Sierra Leone for which he was eventually convicted represented only part of the universe of his victims. The largest part was represented by the public of Liberia whose wealth he allegedly pilfered as he placed Liberia's territory and government under the control of "Charles Taylor Inc." If the SCSL prosecution had been successful in finding funds that Taylor had taken from the Liberian government's LBDI account, the Liberian authorities would have had a strong argument that the funds should go to the public treasury of Liberia. Attributing the fund to diamonds taken in Sierra Leone would have been impossible without documentary or insider evidence obtainable, if at all, only with Liberian assistance. This suggested that the effective approach would have been a cooperative effort between Sierra Leone and Liberia under which recovered assets could have been shared out under an equitable formula. But there has not to date been the political will on the Liberian side to undertake such an effort.

Seeking Compensation from the Profits of Enablers

The absence of Liberian cooperation was particularly significant because of the way Taylor used his power to control and exploit economic assets. When Taylor sent his NPFL into Liberia in 1989 and when he provided essential support to the RUF in Sierra Leone beginning in 1991, he gave the fighters the right to "pay themselves" by pillage of the population or the territory that they had taken. Taylor was then able to recover whatever part of the loot that he demanded, as shown in a report recovered from the RUF leader's house in Freetown that documented one transfer to Taylor of more than a thousand rough-cut diamonds. From the time he ruled most of Liberia from Gbagna as his self-styled "Greater Liberia" beginning in the early 1990s through his official Presidency of Liberia between 1997 and 2003, Taylor was able to provide concessions to exploit upcountry resources in return for weapons and other rewards. This was the basis for the successful Dutch prosecution of Guus Kouwenhouven of the Oriental Timber Company for obtaining corrupt lumber concessions by providing Taylor with military arms and other material – the kind of crime that Tomas Hamilton describes in Chapter 6 and Göran Sluiter details in Chapter 12. When he was President of Liberia, Taylor could hand out lucrative cell phone licenses to persons who would then be deeply in his debt, which was the basis upon which the sanctions ordered by the UNSC were applied to the owners of Liberian cell phone companies.

There have been warlords who become long-term dictators with such a firm grip on power that they can hide substantial stolen funds in foreign accounts, while relative short-termers like Taylor may be less able to do so because they remain insecure in power or are engaging in ongoing conflicts. With the latter, the wealth may be represented more by their capacity to demand payments from those to whom they have granted concessions. Of course, once such warlords lose power, it is very hard for them to enforce demands for "rents" from their concessionaires. If the warlord's loss of power is not accompanied by transitional justice, then the concessionaires are likely to become patrons of new leaders to protect themselves from efforts to investigate the source of their wealth. Eventually, the blood source of their assets can be bleached away by the passage of time, or hidden behind the argument that, like all wealth, it originated from those who took risks at the right place and time.

New Mechanisms to Link Crimes to Perpetrators and Proceeds

If it is challenging to investigate in countries where there have been power-sharing transitions, it is even more difficult where there have been no transitions from regimes that are implicated in atrocities. This is the present situation in Syria and Myanmar, where there are no genuine domestic investigations of those who committed or benefited from atrocity crimes and no state cooperation with investigations launched by international bodies or third countries. As shown by William Wiley and Nina Jørgensen in Chapter 4, it can nonetheless be possible for NGOs that operate in zones of shifting control like Syria to employ local actors to recover physical documentation. This is what the Commission for International Justice and Accountability (CIJA) did to gain possession of almost 800,000 pages of Syrian regime paperwork that were abandoned in the offices of the security services at times when the regime lost control of various population centers. These papers included signed and sealed orders and government reports regarding atrocities, to which CIJA was able to add the digitized records of over twenty-seven thousand photos taken by the defector known as "Caesar" of the victims of torture and murder committed in the regime's detention centers. The Syrian regime documents recovered by CIJA also cast light on economic transactions between the regime and individuals who enabled the crimes and stood to gain from the regime's remaining in power.

The CIJA approach may also be effective in gaining documentation originating from non-state actors, such as the Islamic State (IS), who have exercised state-like control over territory, populations and resources, as Marina Lostal describes in Chapter 5. The involvement of NGOs like CIJA may also be necessary even when the government in the national capital opposes the armed group and wishes to see the group's fighters brought to justice and its enablers required to pay reparations. In the context of an ongoing armed conflict and its aftermath, national justice system officials may simply not have access to the battlefield or to the papers, smartphones or laptops found in ruined buildings or seized from captured fighters by the security services. The officers of these security services may see the captured material as being primarily of intelligence value in defeating the armed groups and in identifying continuing threats, and may place a lower priority on sending the material to justice officials. Meanwhile, justice officials in the capital may have the "easy out" of prosecuting captured fighters on the basis of group membership in a terrorist organization for which, in the case of Iraq, they can achieve a life or death sentence after only the briefest of trials.

However, a group like CIJA may be able to manage greater risks than justice officials and deploy local personnel who can develop "win-win" relationships with the security services that have access to evidentiary material. They can conduct forensic analyses which can then be provided to the originating services and to other national authorities who have the jurisdiction and capacity to investigate and prosecute consistent with international standards. As reported by a *New York Times* journalist who arrived in Mosul not long after it was taken from IS, there were abandoned documents available in abundance from which she gathered 15,000 pages showing how IS had financed and administered public services.

The digital data on smartphone and laptops seized from IS combatants in Iraq and Syria, and now held by Iraqi authorities in Baghdad, by regional officials in the Kurdestan region of Iraq and Syrian-Kurdish forces (SDF/SDC) in northeast Syria, would be of immense value to criminal investigators. It could provide evidence not only of command, control and communication of vital importance to conduct-related prosecutions of IS members but also of transactions in which foreign actors may have provided economic resources to IS of the kind that are already the subject of the French investigation and prosecution of LaFarge

Holcim Ltd. This digital documentation could provide evidence against funders for "aiding and abetting" the violent acts carried out as IS policy if it satisfied the legal requirements described by Jan Wouters and Hendrik Vandekerckhove in Chapter 11. Given the notoriety of IS actions in enslaving and selling Yazidi women and girls, it could be used in prosecutions of such funders for complicity in human trafficking constituting the crime against humanity of enslavement, similar to what is discussed by Michael Ramsden in Chapter 9. This evidence would also be great value in prosecutions of the kind outlined by Liu Daqun in Chapter 13 for violations of statutes enacted to implement the Convention to Suppress Terrorist Financing.

Of course, it can be argued that groups like CIJA are funded by governments that have particular interests in a conflict or its outcome and thus cannot be expected to be objective when it comes to collecting evidence against actors whose cooperation they need in the conflict zones. These challenges can be mitigated by adherence to high standards, and by practices under which material can be verified by independent analysis of metadata or by the presence of recognized indicia of reliability. Additionally, the creation of new UN-mandated entities such as IIIM for Syria or UNITAD for Iraq provide neutral bodies that can collate and corroborate the documentation obtained by groups like CIJA together with material from other sources. These entities are valuable additions to the international community's response to atrocity situations where there is not an international court with jurisdiction. However, these new mechanisms need to be able to rely on groups such as CIJA to do the primary collection given the legal and practical impediments that constrain their actions as UN-created bodies.

Monetary Recoveries through Enforcement of Sanctions

The use of targeted sanctions to freeze the assets of or prohibit transactions with implicated individuals or entities may open a very useful avenue for economic recoveries for the benefit of the victims of mass atrocities. Of course, sanctions in the past may have only tangentially related to atrocity crimes or to serious human rights violations. The UNSC has authority under Chapter 7 of the UN Charter to impose sanctions in order to maintain or restore international peace and security. Thus, the UNSC sanctioned actors in Iran in order to prevent or hinder the development of nuclear weapons that could threaten international security. But these UNSC sanctions were removed when Iran signed and implemented the Joint Comprehensive Plan of Action (JCPOA).

The UNSC established sanctions against Taylor-related individuals and entities in February 2004. This was six months after Taylor had surrendered power in Liberia and gone into exile in Nigeria but when there existed the threat that Taylor could tap funds held by these sources to disturb the peaceful transition in Liberia. After Taylor was arrested and transferred to the SCSL in March 2006, and as Liberia progressed through its transition with peaceful presidential elections in 2005 and 2011 and with the UN Peacekeeping Force (UNMIL) reducing in size and then finally withdrawing from the country, a succession of individuals were removed from the list, and all of the sanctions were terminated in 2015.

But there have also been sanctions implemented because of atrocities or human rights violations. While the UNSC ordered sanctions on Sudan because of the conflict in Darfur, the United States and the European Union (EU) added sanctions that were directly related to human rights violations. In the case of Syria, only the United States and the EU have applied sanctions, because Russia's actual or threatened use of the veto in the UNSC blocked any sanctions whatsoever against the Syrian regime. Beginning with the passage of the Global Magnitsky Act by the US Congress in December 2016, the US Treasury has been able to sanction notorious human rights violators around the world without the need for an Executive Order focused on actions or threats in a specific state. On March 14, 2019, the European Parliament directed the European Council to establish a Global Magnitsky-like sanctions authority in the EU.

Of course, care must be taken to ensure that the rights of innocent persons are protected in the imposition of sanctions. The UNSC generally relies on Panels of Experts to establish the grounds for sanctions against individuals or entities. But these determinations are made without the kind of extensive investigation that would be required by a judicial proceeding. In reaction to concerns about overreach, the UNSC established the office of an ombudsman to review and recommend relief from sanctions that have been implemented under counterterrorism resolutions. EU sanctions have been the subject of successful challenges by sanctioned entities in the European Court of Justice. These legal challenges present a significant obstacle to those who would expand the use of sanctions against serious human rights violators. The evidence used for listing in the United States, and to some extent in Europe, is often based on intelligence information that has been determined to be highly reliable. However, if challenged in court, it may not be possible for it to be declassified. The use of information from organizations like CIJA, especially when vetted and verified by neutral bodies like IIIM or UNITAD, may be one way to make the sanctions process fairer and more transparent.

However, this does not yet provide the route for the victims of the human rights violators to be compensated for their injuries. In the case of Charles Taylor Jr. aka Roy Belfast, the victims of the torture for which Taylor Jr. was convicted sought to recover from the assets frozen by the UNSC under the Liberia sanctions. Taylor Jr. was subject to UNSC sanctions, and in fact had been arrested in Miami because he was using a false passport to avoid the travel ban. But the legal bases for his liability to the victims and for the sanctions were entirely different, so in the end the money went back to the former associates of Taylor Sr.

But with sanctions imposed by the United States under the Global Magnitsky Act, there should be the possibility of victims of human rights violators being eligible to recover from the frozen assets of persons responsible, as perpetrators or enablers, for their victimization. This was already promised in the case of violations of Sudan sanctions at the time of the announcement of the US settlement with BNP-Paribas in 2014. The victims of the bank's hidden transactions with Khartoum included the survivors of the crimes that Khartoum's officers and agents committed in Darfur and that the US government determined in 2004 constituted genocide. However, the promised mechanism has not yet been opened to claims arising in Darfur. Nonetheless, the US criminal prosecution and settlement with BNP-Paribas opened the door for a civil suit in the US federal court of the kind described by Katherine Gallagher in Chapter 15. In May 2019, the US Court of Appeals for the 2nd Circuit ruled that victims and survivors could use state causes of action and federal diversity jurisdiction to sue BNP-Paribas for injuries inflicted in Darfur. This decision and state laws like the California 2015 statute allowing private claims for ICL violations are providing a route around the US Supreme Court's *Kiobel* decision that limited federal Alien Tort Claims actions.[3]

The route to recovery may be much easier with violations of Global Magnitsky sanctions which are specifically tied to human rights violations. It is important to note that such actions need not be based on complicity in the crimes as the French prosecutors must show to succeed

[3] *Kashef* v. *BNP-Paribas SA*, No. 18–1304 (2nd Cir. 2019), www.courthousenews.com/wp-content/uploads/2019/05/bnp-sudan.pdf.

against LaFarge Holcim Ltd. as to its payments to IS, or that Swedish prosecutors must show as to the Lundin Petroleum executives who engaged with the armed groups that cleared land where the company would drill for oil. It would be necessary to show only that the defendants knowingly dealt with sanctioned individuals or companies, whatever the purpose.

The non-implementation of a mechanism for Darfur victims in the BNP-Paribas settlement and the temptation for US officials to use recovered assets to reduce the federal budget deficit suggest that consistent action will require specific Congressional direction. This might be difficult, given what Mark Kielsgard has described in Chapter 3 of the exercise of "economic protectionism" by national governments as well as the UN in deciding where and from whom to seek accountability. Indeed, the US government has opposed expanding criminal liability for atrocity crimes to corporations. Where US law has permitted actions against corporations for conduct abroad, US prosecutors have been criticized by European governments for focusing too much on foreign corporations, particularly in enforcement of the FCPA. But where the conduct has resulted in the death or suffering of individuals, particularly young children, it is harder for members of Congress to support corporations over innocent fellow human beings. In the past, the US Congress has provided avenues for relief for the survivors of the Holocaust and for the victims of terrorist acts, and it has opened the door with Global Magnitsky, for which the initiation of enforcement actions is only a matter of time. Why would it not make some fraction of recovered fines and forfeitures available to victims to help support and protect them where they are living rather than leaving them often with little choice but to seek refuge and security elsewhere?

Of course, it is not only under US law where such recoveries could be achieved. Russell Hopkins in Chapter 16 has described the range of options under the law of England and Wales. Now, with the EU moving to establish Global Magnitsky-like sanctions, and EU authorities having begun to levy substantial fines against companies for anti-trust and data protection violations, one could anticipate remunerative enforcement actions on the eastern side of the Atlantic as well.

Increasing Joint Efforts to Prosecute and Prevent Economic and Atrocity Crimes

The strengthening of the tools for pursuing recoveries from those who have committed and benefited from atrocity crimes can also aid those whose focus is the fight against economic crimes, particularly public corruption. The investigators of economic crimes already have the use of the provisions of international agreements such as Article V of the Convention Against Corruption that opens the way for them to achieve multi-state cooperation in building their cases for prosecution and for recovery of stolen public resources. But, as shown by the leak of the Panama Papers, there is a multiplicity of methods and means to hide corruptly gained assets. Indeed, banking havens appear to owe their existence to evaders of accountability for economic crimes. If pressed to answer for their conduct, the authorities in these havens may admit that they serve persons who wish to avoid the hassle of compliance with confusing and inconsistent national rules that are merely *malum prohibitum* (like national taxation), not *malum in se* (like violent crimes).

That is where those engaged in prosecution of atrocity crimes can strengthen the hand of their colleagues who are pursuing the perpetrators and proceeds of economic crime. Particularly, in cases where individuals and entities have benefited from their relationships with the violators of human rights, there is the potential for much more visibility, embarrassment and opprobrium for those who refuse to assist the enforcement of the law. When one can show proof, obtained from the scene of the crime, of the relationship between an accountholder and the perpetrators of murder, torture and rape of innocent human beings, it is harder to say no, and easier to apply the available tools with maximum effectiveness.

This volume should awaken a desire in all of its readers to develop new tools to prosecute and recover assets from the economic beneficiaries of atrocities, and then to deploy and use the tools in actual practice to achieve accountability and relief for the victims of past crimes and to deter the repetition of selfish and heinous acts that harm so many. This is what is needed to protect all of us from mass violence and also from extortion and theft of the resources necessary for our future survival and security.

For EU product safety concerns, contact us at Calle de José Abascal, 56–1°,
28003 Madrid, Spain or eugpsr@cambridge.org.

www.ingramcontent.com/pod-product-compliance
Ingram Content Group UK Ltd.
Pitfield, Milton Keynes, MK11 3LW, UK
UKHW020404140625
459647UK00020B/2642